The Devil
Knows How
to Ride

The Devil Knows How to Ride

The True Story of
William Clarke Quantrill and His
Confederate Raiders

Edward E. Leslie

Random House
New York

Library of Congress Cataloging-in-Publication Data
Leslie, Edward E.
The devil knows how to ride: the true story of William Clarke
Quantrill and his Confederate raiders/Edward E. Leslie.
p.   cm.
Includes bibliographical references and index.
ISBN 0-679-42455-5 (hardcover)
1. Quantrill, William Clarke, 1837–1865.   2. Guerrillas—Missouri—
Biography.   3. Soldiers—Missouri—Biography.   4. United States—
History—Civil War, 1861–1865—Underground movements.   5. West
(U.S.)—History—Civil War, 1861–1865—Underground movements.
I. Title.
E470.45.Q3L47   1996   973.7'48—dc20   96-7321

Random House website address: http://www.randomhouse.com/
Printed in the United States of America on acid-free paper
2 4 6 8 9 7 5 3

Book design by J. K. Lambert
First Edition

This book is dedicated with love and gratitude to my parents:

MARY FREBURGER LESLIE

and

JAMES FREDERICK LESLIE

"You are a man of marvels," said the king. "Always you move in mystery like a dream. As a prophecy, tell me—is it true that I must die in battle?"

"It is God's will that you be punished for your sins," said Merlin. "But you should be glad that you will have a clean and honorable death. I am the one who should be sad, for my death is to be shameful and ugly and ridiculous."

A heavy cloud blotted out the sky and a quick wind rattled in the tops of the forest trees.

The king asked, "If you know the manner of your death, perhaps you can avoid it."

"No," said Merlin. "It is there as surely as if it had already happened."

Arthur looked upward and he said, "It's a black day, a troubled day."

"It is a day, simply a day. You have a black and troubled mind, my lord."

And as they talked, retainers brought up fresh horses, and the king and Merlin mounted and made their way to Caerleon, and the dark sky fringed and steely rain fell sullenly.

JOHN STEINBECK,
*The Acts of King Arthur
and His Noble Knights*

Acknowledgments

I would like to express my gratitude to my agent, Robert Gottlieb, vice president of the William Morris Agency, New York, New York.

Robert D. Loomis became my editor about halfway through the writing of this book. His insights and his talents as an editor were enormously beneficial to me. I am especially appreciative of his kindness, considerateness, and his unfailing enthusiasm for this project. I would also like to express my appreciation to his assistant, Barbé Hammer.

Tom Conwell, a resident of Dover, Ohio, and a lifelong Quantrill aficionado, brought me into his house on many occasions and shared documents from his files and his ideas with me. I know that the Dover Historical Society and the J. E. Reeves Home and Museum have benefited enormously from Tom's dedication. My thanks also to Tom's wife, Doris.

Donald R. Hale—who is a descendant of one of Quantrill's Raiders and has written two valuable books related to the Quantrill story—read and criticized my manuscript, shared research, and was always willing to help despite his unfortunate conviction that I am from Ohio and therefore the very worst sort of Yankee. He is a true gentleman.

Albert Castel generously shared material from his files, patiently answered innumerable questions, and read and criticized an early draft of this book. Thanks for everything, Albert.

I first met Robert L. Hawkins III at the conclusion of the funeral for Quantrill's remains, October 24, 1992. He allowed me to interview him at length, shared his thoughts on many occasions, and he, too, carefully read and criticized my manuscript. He has assisted me many times and in many ways. Thanks, Bob.

Jim O'Connor guided me through the haunts and hollows of Jackson County, Missouri, and together we explored Baxter Springs, Kansas. He has researched a number of issues for me, and I am grateful for his friendship.

Randy Thies shared information on Quantrill's bones in the Kansas State Historical Society and kindly allowed himself to be put to work on a number of occasions as a researcher and fact checker. He has also become a valued friend.

A writer who works on a book for more than five years becomes indebted to a lot of people. I regret that space limitations preclude my being more specific in acknowledging the assistance I have been given by the individuals listed below.

I would like to express my appreciation to Cris Nixon, director of the J. E. Reeves Home and Museum, and Jim Nixon, president of the Dover Historical Society. My thanks also to the trustees and volunteers of the Historical Society and Museum.

I would like to thank the following staff members of the Kansas State Historical Society: Virgil Dean, director of publications; Leslie Cade, director of the reference section; John Mark Lambertson, reference archivist; Dale E. Watts, research manager, Historic Sites Division; Tom Witty, state archaeologist; Bob Knecht, acting curator of manuscripts; Nancy Sherbert, still photographs collections; Sarah J. Wood-Clark, museum registrar; Ramon S. Powers, executive director, Kansas Museum of History; Christie Stanley, photographs registrar; Marion Bond, newspaper room.

I am grateful to the following staff at the Kansas Collection, the University of Kansas Libraries, Lawrence: David Benjamin; Nicolette Bromberg, photographs librarian; and Sheryl Williams, curator.

I would like to thank the staff of the Ohio Historical Society, especially Clift Eckle and John Barsotti.

I would like to express my appreciation to the staff and volunteers of: the Nelson County, Kentucky, Historical Society; the Spencer County, Kentucky, Historical Society; the Baxter Springs, Kansas, Museum; and the Kentucky State Library and Archives.

I am grateful to David L. Boutrous, associate director, Western Historical Manuscript Collection, University of Missouri at Kansas City; William R. Erwin, Jr., senior reference librarian, special collections department, William R. Perkins Library, Duke University; Don Shaw, manager, Oak Hill Cemetery, Lawrence, Kansas; Theresa A. McGill, archives and manuscripts, Chicago Historical Society, Chicago, Illinois; Amy Barnum, librarian, New York State Historical Association, Cooperstown, New York; Christina Southwell, University Libraries, Western

Historical Collections, University of Oklahoma at Norman; Theodore H. Fossieck, chairman, genealogy committee, Albany County Historical Society, Slingerlands, New York; Gieselle A. B. Fest, historic sites director, Clay County Department of Historic Sites; Kathleen Halcro, director, Jackson County Historical Society; Kathee Howard, librarian, South Carolina Historical Society; Cathy Barton and Dave Para; Robert L. Parkinson, chief librarian, Circus World Museum Library; Penni Lynn Porter, administrative services, city of Lawrence, Kansas; James M. Prichard, archivist, Kentucky Department for Libraries and Archives; James Rush, assistant branch chief, civil reference branch, National Archives, Washington, D.C.; Lewis N. Wynne, executive director, Florida Historical Society, Tampa.

My thanks to the following staff of the Kentucky Historical Society: Ron Bryant, director of the library reading rooms; Mary Winter, curator of photographs and maps.

I would like to express my appreciation to the following employees of the Elizabeth Watkins Community Museum: Judy M. Sweets, registrar; Steven Jansen, Ph.D., director.

I would like to thank the following staff members of the Filson Club, Louisville, Kentucky: Kathryn A. Bratcher, reference archivist; Mary Jean Kinsman, curator of photography; James Holmberg, manuscript department.

I am grateful to the following staff of the State Historical Society of Missouri, Columbia: Sue McCubbin, secretary; Fae Sotham; Kay Pettit and Ara Kaye, newspaper library.

I would also like to express my gratitude to Sharon L. Hall, manuscript specialist, and the rest of the staff of the Western Historical Manuscript Collection, University of Missouri at Columbia.

I extend my thanks to the following staff members of the Denver Public Library, Denver, Colorado: Lisa Backman, manuscript specialist, western history department; Pat Hodapp, marketing director.

I am indebted to the staff and volunteers of the following institutions: Franklin County, Kansas, Historical Society; the Ray County, Missouri, Historical Society; the Cass County, Missouri, Historical Society; the Clay County, Missouri, Historical Society; the Bates County, Missouri, Historical Society; the James Family Farm Museum, Kearney, Missouri; the James Bank Museum, Liberty, Missouri; Kansas Supreme Court Law Library, Topeka, Kansas; newspaper room, Margaret I. King Library,

University of Kentucky, Lexington; reference department, Texas Historical Commission Library, Austin; reference department, Oklahoma Historical Society, Oklahoma City; microfilm publications division, National Archives, Washington, D.C.

I would like to thank the following individuals: N. B. "Yank" Albers; Portia Allbert; Robert Barnes, Jr.; Louise Bedichek; Mary Beck, Missouri State Archives; Vicki Beck; Father Hugh Behan; Jonathan F. Buchter, attorney-at-law; Hattie Clements; Kimberley Colwell, president, the William Clarke Quantrill Society; Peter J. D'Onofrio, president, Society of Civil War Surgeons; Dr. Alan S. DeShazo, O.D.; Chris Edwards; John Marcus Ellis, attorney-at-law; Chris Galloway; Dr. Carson Gibb, Ph.D.; Tom Goodrich; Linda Harper; Jerry Hopkins; Denise Kelley, registrar, City of Albany, New York; Jim Keown; Betty Kyrias; Ralph Lawson; Dr. Franklin Leslie, M.D.; Leon McCorkle, descendant of John McCorkle; Earl Olmstead, trustee, Tuscarawas County, Ohio, Historical Society; Robert L. Parkinson; Professor Richard D. Poll; Robert C. Stevens; Professor Richard B. Sheridan; Joan Sherman; Dr. Thomas Sweeny, M.D.; Betty Tarr; Barbara Treasure; Richard Turner; Nathan Ward, associate editor, *American Heritage* magazine; John Britton Wells; Edward F. Murphy, Medal of Honor Historical Society.

I would like to express my appreciation to the always patient and indefatigable Rosemary Hayes and her assistant Ruth Pedrotty, interlibrary loan department, and all the staff of the Massillon, Ohio, Public Library, especially the following: Sherie Brown, Doris Dean, Richard Gercken, Cheryl Jackson, Chris Perry, Leslie Picot, Tom Casey, and Marlene Derrick.

Without the constant encouragement and the unfailing support of my wife, Camille, this book would never have been written.

Contents

List of Maps

Introduction

At approximately 2:30 P.M. on October 30, 1992, two maintenance men lowered a white, fiberglass infant's coffin into a shallow grave in the Fourth Street Cemetery, Dover, Ohio. The coffin contained the skull of William Clarke Quantrill. As a drizzling, cold rain fell, they filled in the grave, tamped down the dirt, and covered it with sod, then threw their shovels into the back of their truck and drove away. Their departure signaled an end to one hundred years of shenanigans with regard to Quantrill's bones, which have been stolen, bartered, put up for sale, used in fraternity rituals, and displayed in glass museum cases and which have come to be buried in three graves in three different states.

I knew little about Quantrill before I moved to Massillon, thirty miles north of Dover, his hometown, in 1982. Then one day James Huberty, a former neighbor of mine, committed a monstrous crime, which led me to become curious about Quantrill, who has been called "the bloodiest man in the annals of America." The first thing I learned about Quantrill was the bizarre history of his bones, and I was so intrigued that I set out on what proved to be a six-year course visiting archives and battlefield sites in seven states and the District of Columbia to research and write his biography.

All because of Jim Huberty.

The neighbors warned me about Huberty when I moved to Fifth Street. He was crazy, they said. A gun nut with a short fuse. He had bought a big house next to his own, then torched it for the insurance money. When the firemen showed up, he had warned them away, saying that there was a large quantity of ammunition stored in the basement. He had two huge dogs that he let run loose; if one of his dogs got after you and you called Huberty to complain, he would threaten to kill you. If you called the cops, he would threaten them.

There were other, wilder stories, but by the time I heard them I had become acquainted with Huberty, and I tended to discount them. I should have known better: Twenty years earlier I had been a classification counselor in a Maryland prison with a caseload of 150 adult male felons; I had handled my fair share of psychopaths, including, most memorably, a man who had killed several people under the delusion that the CIA was broadcasting orders to him through a filling in one of his molars. Still, I must confess that Huberty did not seem any loonier than a lot of other working men I had encountered in Massillon or one of the other rust belt mill towns I have lived in over the past nineteen years.

I used to stop to talk to him as he sat on his side stoop, petting his dog. He had a sociology degree from a Quaker college and had been an apprentice embalmer—a job he loved—but he had been fired because he couldn't get along with living human beings. More recently he had worked as a welder; however, he had been laid off. Mostly we spoke of the weather, the troubles at the mill, or the losses of the area sports teams. One day he abruptly asked me to buy his house—he had decided to make a new life for himself and his family in Mexico.

He got as far as San Ysidro, California.

On July 17, 1984, after hearing voices for several days, he called a mental health clinic and asked for an appointment. He was put on the waiting list. The following afternoon, at approximately 4:00 P.M., he walked into a one-story, redbrick McDonald's wearing a black T-shirt and camouflage pants with a nine-millimeter Browning automatic pistol stuck in the waist; an Uzi submachine gun was slung over his shoulder, and he carried a twelve-gauge pump shotgun in one hand. "Everybody get down on the floor or I'll kill somebody!" he cried, then opened fire on the crowd. Over the next hour and seventeen minutes, until a SWAT team sniper put a single bullet into his chest, he walked back and forth in the restaurant, coolly shooting people at point-blank range and methodically reloading his weapons. Just before he died, he shouted, "I've killed a thousand, and I'll kill a thousand more!" In fact, he shot forty and killed twenty-one, thus becoming for a time the "largest one-day mass murderer in American history."

And I used to talk to him while he petted his dog.

Near midnight a few years later on the anniversary of the massacre, I sat in a bar down the block from his house drinking from a frosted mug, thinking about him, and half listening to some locals play a mocking, can-you-top-this game of naming monsters and murderers native to Ohio. William Clarke Quantrill's name came up along with the stale, old epithets attached to his name by Northern historians—"the bloodiest man in American history," "the most hated man in the Civil War."

The next day, my mind still on Huberty, I drove to Dover. The historical society is housed in a lovely old Victorian mansion, and a young woman volunteer took me on a guided tour. On display in a glass case in a second-floor room were a powder horn that had belonged to Quantrill and a couple of nineteenth-century dime novels about him. At the end of the tour I allowed as how I was interested in Quantrill and asked if they had anything else of his.

"Well, we have his head," the guide answered. "Would you like to see it?" For an instant I tried to imagine what a cadaver's face would look like 125 years after death. I came up with a fantastically grotesque mental image, something that would make even Stephen King throw up in his wastebasket.

"Absolutely," I said. "Love to."

As she led me back down through the mansion, then out through the gardens and into the carriage house, she told me this story:

In 1887, William Walter Scott, a boyhood friend of Quantrill, had traveled to Kentucky, opened Quantrill's grave, and taken the remains back to Dover for reburial. Not all the bones went into the ground, however: Scott secretly retained the skull and at least five bones. After his death the skull "disappeared," only to resurface in 1972, when it was donated to the Dover Historical Society. The director sent it to the Kent State University anthropology department, where a wax head and face were constructed using the skull as a model, adding glass eyes and a wig.

The historical society put both the skull and the head on display side by side in a glass case, but summers can be hot in Ohio, and it was feared that the wax would soften. Until funds for an atmospherically controlled case could be raised, a cool storage place was needed.

By now we had arrived in the society's kitchen display area and were standing in front of an ancient, wheezing refrigerator, in which the staff and volunteers kept their lunches. The guide swung open the door, and there behind the deviled eggs in waxed paper and the tuna fish sandwiches in ziplock Baggies, peering out at me from between the necks of sixteen-ounce Coke bottles was a dead-eyed, unwrinkled, young face. Cold or static electricity had caused the hair of the cheap toupee to rise slightly, giving its owner a startled look, as if he had been caught in the middle of some nefarious deed.

From the moment I glimpsed that head through the forest of sculptured glass, I knew Quantrill was in my line of work.

———◆•◆———

What follows is not a psychoanalytic biography. Psychoanalyzing the dead seems to me to be a dubious enterprise at best, and it would be particularly difficult in Quantrill's case because there is so little material that reveals the inner workings of his mind: He never kept a diary or wrote a memoir; before the war began he sent perhaps two dozen letters to family and friends; during the war he penned a short military report and a brief appeal to the Confederate governor of Missouri. Even the most imaginative armchair Freudian would be pressed to make a diagnosis on such scant information. If we know little about his thinking processes, however, we know a great deal about his deeds. What follows, then, is an anecdotal history of William Clarke Quantrill, the guerrilla band he led, the enemies he fought, and the war they waged on the Kansas-Missouri border.

———◆•◆———

Some of the writers of the letters, diaries, and unpublished memoirs that are essential sources for me were poor grammarians and worse spellers. In quoting from their work, I have occasionally removed superfluous commas, but I have not corrected their spelling or grammatical mistakes and have usually dispensed with the term *sic,* meaning "error in the original," because I would have to use it so repetitively that it would become as annoying as the sound of a jackhammer. For the sake of clarity I have occasionally found it necessary to slightly edit a quotation, most often by deleting a word or two.

Finally, there is the problem of the spelling of personal names. Quantrill's contemporaries constantly misspelled his name, most often as "Quantrell." There is still debate today over whether his middle name (and his mother's maiden name) should be rendered "Clarke" or "Clark." Quantrill's parents disagreed over how to spell the name of their youngest son—"Thompson" or "Thomson"; he always signed his name "Thomas." And so on. The annotations begin with an examination of the sources for the correct spelling of personal names.

The Devil
Knows How
to Ride

CHAPTER 1

"War to the Knife!": The War over Kansas Territory, 1854-1861

When Quantrill first became involved in the ongoing strife on the Kansas-Missouri border in 1860, he was only twenty-two years old. Many of the Missourians who joined his guerrilla band in later years were teenagers and so were even younger and more immature than he was. They had grown up in what we would call a subculture, characterized by extreme rhetoric, callousness, and violence, and in which figures of authority—such as sheriffs and judges—acted not from fairness but undisguised bias, and the forces of order, the federal militia, sometimes murdered, stole, and burned property. In the eyes of these Missourians the state and federal governments had failed to perform their most elemental function: the protection of individuals' lives and homes. It is not surprising that what became Quantrill's Raiders began as a Jackson County home-guard band formed by some Blue Springs boys to defend their neighborhood and families from the incursions of Kansas guerrillas.

The subculture of violence shaped the attitudes of these impressionable young men, and some of them, caught in the downward spiral of a four-year guerrilla war, became increasingly hardened and brutal, so that Quantrill gradually lost control of them, and in 1864 they actually usurped him.

Even the Quantrill biographers who have judged him and his followers most harshly have acknowledged the singular circumstances that molded them.

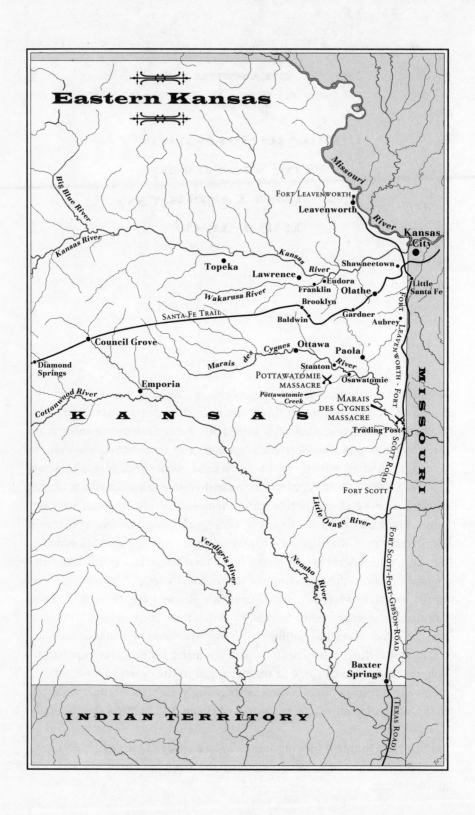

Eastern Kansas

Big Blue River

Missouri River

FORT LEAVENWORTH
Leavenworth

Kansas City

Kansas River

Kansas River

Topeka

Lawrence

Shawneetown

Eudora

Little Santa Fe

Wakarusa River

Franklin

Olathe

Brooklyn

SANTA FE TRAIL

Baldwin

Gardner

Aubrey

FORT LEAVENWORTH - FORT

Council Grove

Marais des Cygnes

Ottawa

Paola

Diamond Springs

Stanton

River

POTTAWATOMIE MASSACRE

Osawatomie

Emporia

Cottonwood River

Pottawatomie Creek

MARAIS DES CYGNES MASSACRE

K A N S A S

Trading Post

Scott Road

M I S S O U R I

FORT SCOTT

Little Osage River

Verdigris River

Neosho River

FORT SCOTT - FORT GIBSON ROAD

Baxter Springs

(TEXAS ROAD)

I N D I A N   T E R R I T O R Y

The story of William Clarke Quantrill and his band begins, then, with the prewar struggle over the Kansas Territory and the ferocious men who waged it.

———•◆•———

It is usually said that the Civil War started with the firing on Fort Sumter on April 12, 1861. But when the cannons boomed in that predawn darkness, people living on the Kansas-Missouri border had already been fighting for six years over the issues of slavery and "Southern rights." Their conflict had been followed avidly in the North and the South, and events along the border had defined the debate over slavery and states' rights for many Americans, affected the policies of administrations and political parties, influenced political conventions and choices of presidential nominees, and contributed significantly to bringing about the Civil War.

In describing the border conflict as it evolved during the period 1854–61, it would be incorrect to leave the impression that all Kansas settlers were abolitionists and all Missourians "slaveocrats," as slave owners were sometimes mockingly called. The available evidence suggests that in the early days the majority of the Kansas territorial population actually favored slavery. Even after the tide of immigration altered the equation, there remained in Kansas entire towns and villages whose residents were overwhelmingly proslavery—notably, Franklin, New Georgia, Hickory Point, Paola, and Kickapoo. In addition, most of the new arrivals who settled in the territory were motivated by economics far more than ideology. Given a chance, they might vote to make Kansas a free state but were far more interested in planting crops and starting businesses than fighting over slavery. Indeed, many of them wanted to keep all blacks—slave or free—out of Kansas due to prejudice or a desire to reduce the competition for work.

Furthermore, there were wide and diverse opinions on the issues of the day among Missourians. In the 1860 election, the majority of voters voted against secessionist candidates and in favor of more moderate ones. This majority was made up of individuals loyal to the Federal government and "conditional Unionists," who approved of slavery yet wanted some compromise to be found that would keep the Southern states in the Union. Perhaps typical of this latter group was the father of Cole Younger, Colonel Henry Younger, a slave owner and businessman who had contracts with the Federal government and supported the Union right up until he was robbed and murdered by thieving Federal militia.

The prewar conflict, then, was between a relatively small number of radicals on either side. Just as in Northern Ireland and the Middle East in recent decades, it was a tit-for-tat war, a war of retribution and retaliation. It was characterized by fiery rhetoric, with talented and unscrupulous propagandists on both sides. "War to the knife, and knife to the hilt!" one newspaper editor cried. It does not matter which side he was on; such sentiments were echoed by both sides. Caught in the middle was the great mass of people who, while they might have had strong opinions on the issues of slavery and states' rights, did not endorse either set of extremists and yet were potential victims of both, who on any given day might lose their money, possessions, homes, or even their lives.

The trouble began with the Kansas-Nebraska Bill of 1854. This federal legislation, brainchild of the politically ambitious Stephen A. Douglas, allowed for the opening of the two territories to settlers, leaving it to the voters in each territory to decide whether slavery was to be legal or prohibited.

The bill had worrisome implications for the minority of white Missourians who owned slaves: If Kansas entered the Union as a free state, then Missouri would be bounded on the east, north, and west by states that prohibited slavery; abolitionists would have an enhanced opportunity to liberate slaves, and slaves would have an easier time escaping.

While the number of slave owners in Missouri was small—in 1860 there were fewer than twenty-five thousand in a population of 1.2 million—the state was largely populated by Southerners or those with a Southern cultural perspective: "In the 1850s," observed Canadian historian Michael Fellman, "approximately 75 percent of Missourians were of southern ancestry, and many of the remainder came from regions in Ohio, Indiana, and Illinois, which were settled earlier in the nineteenth century by Southerners."

Yet if Missouri had a Southern outlook, it was not a typical Deep South slave state. Cotton was not king; farmers prospered growing corn and raising hogs. The average Missouri slave owner had just a couple of slaves, and it was only in the counties bounding the Missouri River, running east and west across the state, that tobacco and hemp were important crops, ones that required backbreaking labor and the consequent use of large numbers of slaves.

Missouri was a rural state, and most of its residents worked small farms. There were only a few towns of any size, and the one large city—St. Louis—was at the extreme eastern end of the state and something of an anomaly, with an economy based on manufacturing and a 60 percent foreign population. (At the onset of the war, many St. Louis Germans would rush to join the Union forces, and their units would play a crucial role in seizing the state for the Federal government, earning them the lasting enmity of some Confederate sympathizers.)

Southern senators, voting in favor of Douglas's legislation, had assumed that while Nebraska would be admitted to the Union as a free state, Kansas would be a slave state, neatly balancing the equation. Eastern abolitionists had other ideas. Their emigration societies, especially Eli Thayer's New England Emigrant Aide Company, raised money to assist those who wished to settle in the Kansas Territory. Thayer was determined to destroy slavery and believed, as he explained in 1889,

> the way to do this was to go to the prairies of Kansas and show the superiority of the free labor civilization; to go with all our free labor trophies: churches and schools, printing-presses, steam-engines, and mills; and in a peaceful contest convince every poor [white] man from the South of the superiority of free labor.

During the summer of 1854, six of Thayer's Emigrant Aide Company–sponsored parties, totaling some seven hundred people, embarked from Boston. As these pilgrims made their way west they sang "The Kansas Emigrants," a poem written by Quaker John Greenleaf Whittier and set to the tune of "Auld Lang Syne":

> *We cross the prairie as of old*
> *The pilgrims crossed the sea,*
> *To make the West, as they the East,*
> *The homestead of the free!*

Other emigrants were drawn to the Kansas Territory, too. A large number of Missourians crossed the borderline and staked out claims; some then returned to their own farms, but others built cabins and settled. People embarked from other parts of the country, some desiring to participate in the upcoming struggle over slavery; however, many others—including teenage William Clarke Quantrill—were motivated by economic opportunity, especially the availability of land.

The first of Thayer's parties disembarked at the Kansas City landing on July 28 and set off down the Santa Fe Trail, hauling a printing press with which to publish *The Herald of Freedom*. The party numbered only twenty-nine, but among them were two men who will be mentioned later in these pages: Dr. John Doy and Daniel Anthony. Doy, a physician, was determined to establish and run a station on the Underground Railroad, carrying slaves to freedom; while the radical Anthony, whose sister, Susan B., would attain national prominence in the cause of women's suffrage, would become the mayor of Leavenworth and publisher of the town's leading if badly misnamed newspaper, the *Daily Conservative*. A contemporary described Anthony as being "a hot-headed, impracticable, energetic, smart, money-making ambitious abolitionist."

The pilgrims founded a town on a stretch of flat land south of the Kansas River and just north of a high hill at a point some forty miles west of the border. The location had actually been chosen for them by an advance agent of Thayer's company, Dr. Charles Robinson, a physician and future first governor of the state. They named the town Lawrence after Amos A. Lawrence, the Boston financier who was the benefactor of the New England Emigrant Aide Company. The hill was christened Mount Oread, after Oread Castle, the stone structure complete with serrated towers that on an earlier day Thayer had built in Massachusetts to house a women's college. Later an actual fort would be built on Mount Oread.

Lawrence, dubbed the "Boston Colony" and "Yankee Town" by Southern sympathizers, quickly became the center of the Free State Movement in Kansas and an abolitionist stronghold. Citizens formed gangs and raided nearby proslavery settlements, and Lawrence became a headquarters for jayhawkers—bands of disreputable guerrillas who proclaimed their loyalty to the Union while pillaging and murdering.

On November 29, 1854, several thousand proslavery Missourians crossed the borderline to vote in the Kansas territorial election for a delegate to Congress. (These men felt they had as much right to vote as the newly arrived New Englanders and other Northern emigrants, who, they believed, had been hired to emigrate for the sole purpose of voting; anyway, ballot stuffing was far from unknown in America. Indeed, on an earlier day Iowans had crossed the line to vote in the Nebraska election, and the results were accepted by authorities.) Ironically, such shenanigans were probably not necessary in Kansas: Census records show that at the time, a majority of voters were from slaveholding states. One man was killed at the polls—he was proslavery, his murderer "free soil."

In the spring of 1855 emigrants poured into Kansas, coming from the Mid-Atlantic and newer Midwestern states, as well as the South and New England. Alarmed Missourians traded rumors that many of the new arrivals from the North were not accompanied by womenfolk and brought the latest-model rifles instead of plows and other farm implements. It was said that tens of thousands of New Englanders were on their way, their votes in the upcoming territorial legislature election having already been bought by abolitionists for $100 apiece. Worse, it was rumored that the New England Emigrant Aide Company was sending convicts, paupers, diseased slum dwellers, "vicious" European immigrants, and other undesirables.

In western Missouri firebrands railed, and newspapers urged their readers to cross the line again and vote or pay someone else to do it for them. On Election Day, March 30, 1855, thousands did, led by some of the state's most prominent men, including wealthy slave owner Joseph O. "Jo" Shelby, who, when the war began, would decorate his hat with a black plume and make a name for himself as a cavalry officer.

The appeasing territorial governor, Andrew H. Reeder, chose to disregard most of the reports of massive vote fraud. He certified returns in twelve of eighteen districts and ordered a new election in only six.

"It looks very much like war," wrote Charles Robinson to Eli Thayer, "and I am ready for it and so are our people. Wouldn't it be rich to march an army through the slave-holding States and roll up a *black cloud* that should spread dismay and terror to the ranks of the oppressors?" He appended a request for "200 Sharps rifles" and "a couple of field-pieces," promising that they "will be *well used*." The company duly sent a shipment of rifles. Other emigrant aid companies and benefactors also shipped firearms to free-soil men in the territory, often in boxes marked "books." A cannon arrived in Lawrence in a crate labeled "machinery."

The newly elected proslavery legislators initially met at Pawnee, then Shawnee Mission, before choosing, in 1857, Lecompton as their capital. Among the first pieces of legislation they passed was an "Act to punish offenses against slave property." Under the act every person convicted of "raising a rebellion of slaves, free negroes, or mulattoes, in this Territory shall suffer death." The death penalty was also prescribed for anyone aiding, assisting, or furnishing arms "in furtherance of such a rebellion or insurrection," as well as for advocating that slaves rebel in a speech or "any book, paper, magazine, pamphlet, or circular." Those who led slaves out of the territory "with the intent to deprive the owner thereof of the services of such slave or with the intent to effect . . . the freedom of such slave . . . shall be adjudged guilty of grand larceny, and . . . shall suffer death or be imprisoned at hard labor for not less than ten years." Lesser penalties were to be exacted for lesser crimes, such as harboring or assisting an escaped slave (a sentence of not less than five years), and the act forbade "those opposed to the holding of slaves" from being jurors in a case involving slavery, while also ensuring that only proslavery men could hold office. All this for a territory that had only a handful of slaves: Few slave owners were willing to risk their property in such a turbulent situation in such close proximity to abolitionist settlers.

———•◦•———

The growing town of Lawrence spread south from the Kansas River toward Mount Oread. On Massachusetts Street, Lawrencians set about building a three-story stone building called the Free State Hotel, which was also known as the Eldridge House after its lessee, Shalor Eldridge. The hotel was meant to provide comfortable shelter for emigrants until they could build their own homes—part of Thayer's plan to make emigration more attractive—but portholes were built in the walls of the top story. From the outside the building looked ominously like a fortress.

Along with the new immigrants came newspaper correspondents, many of them from the North, biased against the South, often quite young and inexperienced but possessed of a great determination to make news as well as report it. One coined the term "border ruffian" to describe the low class of white riffraff inclined to drunkenness, violence, and ballot stuffing. The brand became unfairly synonymous with all "Southern men," as those in sympathy with the South called themselves, regardless of where they originally hailed from.

William Phillips, who traveled to Kansas as a special correspondent for the *New York Tribune*, observed that many border ruffians were veterans of the Mexican war or had seen a "great deal of trouble" in Texas. "Among these worthies," he told the readers of his 1856 book, *The Conquest of Kansas by Missouri and Her Allies,*

> a man is estimated by the amount of whiskey he can drink; and if he is so indiscreet as to admit he "drinks no liquor," he is set down as a dangerous character, and shunned accordingly. Imagine a fellow, tall, slim, but athletic, with yellow complexion, hairy faced, with a dirty flannel shirt, or red, or blue, or green, a pair of common-place but dark-colored pants, tucked into an uncertain altitude by a leather belt, in which a dirty-handled bowie-knife is stuck rather ostentatiously, an eye slightly whiskey-red, and teeth the color of a walnut. Such is your border ruffian of the lowest type.

By summer of 1855, the Kansas population had doubled, to fifteen thousand. Among the recent arrivals were John Brown and five of his sons. Brown, a stubborn, arrogant failed businessman, had consecrated his life to the destruction of slavery. For years he had dreamed of fighting a guerrilla war against slave owners, hoping to induce "the most reckless and daring" of the field slaves to join the fight.

Another of those who emigrated to the territory in 1855 was a tall, gaunt, hollow-cheeked, thin-lipped philanderer with a mass of unruly black hair and what have been described as the "sad dim eyes of a harlot"—James Henry Lane. "The Grim Chieftain of Kansas," as he came to be called, was a Democrat and a former lieutenant governor of Indiana who had served with distinction as a colonel in the Mexican war. As a U.S. congressman he had voted in favor of the Kansas-Nebraska Act, earning the disapproval of many of his Indiana constituents. So he came to the territory looking for new political opportunities, but he had no moral qualms about slavery. "I would as leave sell a negro as a mule," he commented shortly after arriving.

Lane had an enormous gift for intrigue, devilment, and fiery rhetoric. "He talked like none of the others," one Kansan would later recall. "None of the rest had his husky rasping, blood-curdling whisper or that menacing forefinger, or could shriek 'Great God!' on the same day with him." Being a voracious ladies' man, Lane would be the subject of not a few rumors of sexual impropriety. Despite his attitude toward slavery, he would opportunistically switch sides, joining the new Free State party and becoming an important free-soil advocate. Beginning in 1856, he led a series of brutal pillage-and-burn raids in eastern Kansas and western Missouri. He freed numerous slaves, believing that this was the quickest way to destroy the South, but, ironically, he advocated the passage of "Black laws" that would deny Kansas residency to all Negroes.

In late June 1861, Lincoln appointed Lane a brigadier general of volunteers. This may seem surprising given Lane's character, but Lincoln was in Lane's debt. Washington had been thrown into chaos during the month of April 1861. On April 17, five days after the bombardment of Fort Sumter, Virginia adopted an ordinance of secession, and the governor signed a proclamation announcing the dissolution of the Union. The next day several companies of Old Dominion militia captured Harpers Ferry and shipped the gun-manufacturing machinery to Richmond. If Maryland seceded, as seemed likely, the nation's capital would be trapped between two rebellious states. At the same time, the United States Army was being seriously weakened by the resignations of talented Southern officers. Only a small number of troops was stationed in Washington, and wild rumors spread that regiments of Virginia and Maryland secessionists were converging on the city to seize government buildings and capture the president. Other rumors told of plots to assassinate him.

Lane, who had been an ardent Lincoln supporter in 1860 and was in Washington, having been elected to the U.S. Senate, went to the White House with his handpicked company of Kansans, the "Frontier Guard." On an earlier day, following Lincoln's election, Lane had offered to provide a bodyguard of Kansans to escort him from Illinois to Washington for his inauguration, but Lincoln had declined; now he gratefully accepted the offer of protection.

Years later two of Lincoln's wartime secretaries, John G. Nicolay and John Hay, set down a striking description of the Frontier Guard in the White House:

> At dusk they filed into the famous East Room, clad in citizens' dress, but carrying very new, untarnished muskets, and following Lane, brandishing a sword of irreproachable brightness. Here ammunition boxes were opened and cartridges were dealt out; and after spending the evening in an exceedingly rudimentary squad drill, under the light of

the gorgeous gas chandeliers, they disposed themselves in picturesque bivouac on the brilliant-patterned velvet carpet—perhaps the most luxurious cantonment which American soldiers have ever enjoyed. Their motley composition, their anomalous surroundings, the extraordinary emergency, their mingled awkwardness and earnestness, rendered the scene a medley of bizarre contradictions—a blending of masquerade and tragedy, of grim humor and realistic seriousness—a combination of Don Quixote and Daniel Boone altogether impossible to describe. However, their special guardianship of the East Room lasted only for a night or two, until more suitable quarters could be extemporized; and for many days they lent an important moral influence in repressing and overawing the lurking treason still present in a considerable fraction among the Washington inhabitants.

At the end of the month, more troops having arrived in the city, the Frontier Guard was disbanded. It is sometimes said that the president and Lane became "intimate friends." Whether or not Lincoln was taken in by the senator, he certainly accepted Lane as an ally and often acquiesced to his patronage demands, though in 1864 he complained to Kansas governor Thomas Carney that Lane "knocks at my door every morning. You know he is a very persistent fellow and hard to put off. I don't see you very often and have to pay attention to him." Motivated either by admiration or cynical political opportunism, Lane remained a steadfast supporter of the president, working tirelessly for his reelection in 1864.

———————

On November 21, 1855, Charles Dow was murdered by Franklin Coleman at Hickory Point, some ten miles south of Lawrence. Although Dow was a free-stater and Coleman proslavery, their dispute was over the boundary separating their land claims, not politics. However, subsequent events seemed to give the crime a political cast, which provided an opportunity for propagandists on both sides.

Having blasted Dow with a shotgun, Coleman hurriedly turned himself in to the Douglas County sheriff, Samuel J. Jones, a proslavery Missourian; Coleman was taken before a proslavery judge and promptly released on bail.

A few nights after Dow's burial, a mob gathered at the place where his body had been found. They vowed to bring the murderer to justice and burned the cabins of Coleman and several other proslavery men.

Sheriff Jones formed a posse and arrested Dow's friend, Jacob Branson. Sources disagree about the charge: Some say that Branson had threatened Coleman and in self-protection Coleman had sworn out a peace warrant against him, while others have Sheriff Jones accusing Branson of leading the vengeance-seeking mob. In any case, as Jones was carrying his prisoner to Lecompton, a gang of free-staters blocked the road and rescued him.

Sheriff Jones retreated to Franklin, a proslavery stronghold. Since Branson's rescuers were believed to be from Lawrence, hotheads organized a twelve-hundred-man "posse" of Missouri border ruffians and marched on the town, determined to wipe it out. The posse had two wagonloads of guns as well as seven cannons, brought from the Federal arsenal at Liberty, Missouri. Five hundred volunteer defenders (among them John Brown and some of his sons) poured into Lawrence from outlying settlements. Jim Lane supervised the construction of four circular earthwork forts seventy-five feet in diameter with five-foot-high walls; these were connected with earthwork entrenchments and rifle pits. Women made cartridges, and Lane drilled the Lawrence Free State Militia daily.

On December 3, most of the border ruffians were camped on the Wakarusa River, six miles southeast of Lawrence, consuming large quantities of whiskey. Their leader, ex-Senator David R. Atchison, demanded that Branson's rescuers be surrendered along with the shipment of Sharps rifles, but Charles Robinson, who had been elected "major general" of the militia, lied: He swore that none of the men were in Lawrence and that the rifles were private property.

Many in the posse doubted Robinson's word and wanted to fight; however, then territorial governor Wilson Shannon—one of six who would be appointed by Washington between 1854 and 1860 in an attempt to bring peace and stability to the region—arrived on the scene and negotiated a face-saving compromise with Robinson, in which Lawrencians promised not to interfere further with the execution of the law and disavowed Branson's rescue. Posse firebrands were not satisfied and still wanted to do battle, but a heavy snowstorm struck, making the border ruffians, who were living in tents, hurry home. The "Wakarusa War," as it came rather grandly to be known, was over.

In January 1856, free-soil advocates held their own election. Charles Robinson was elected "governor." Territorial Kansas now had two delegates to Congress and two opposing legislatures and chief executives.

There were few disturbances at the polls; however, an election-night fracas resulted in the death of a proslavery man. In retaliation, the next day a free-stater was "arrested" for the crime by some Kickapoo "rangers," who mortally wounded him. This was an indication of the ongoing violence in the territory: During the thirteen-month period from November 1, 1855, to December 1, 1856, an estimated two hundred people lost their lives, and the amount of property destroyed was valued at $2 million.

In April, Sheriff Jones went to Lawrence, still looking for Branson's rescuers. Despite the Shannon-Robinson agreement, Jones was roughed up and relieved of his pistols. He returned to Lecompton, then came back to "Yankee Town" with ten Federal dragoons. He arrested six men but was shot at three times by one or more skulking, would-be assassins; the last shot gave him a "nasty" wound in the back.

A Lecompton grand jury indicted Robinson, Jim Lane (who was second-in-command of the Lawrence militia and given to increasingly incendiary pronouncements), and other well-known free-soil proponents for treason. Furthermore, the grand jury indicted Lawrence's two newspapers, the *Kansas Free State* and the *Herald*, for using "inflammatory and seditious" language and the Eldridge Hotel for being "designed as a stronghold for resistance to law" since its walls were "regularly parapeted and port-holed for the use of cannon and small arms."

Once again a large posse of border ruffians—complete with a battery of cannon—threatened Lawrence, but this time there was no resistance offered because the militant free-soil leaders had fled. Several men were arrested, and the Lawrencians' cannon was surrendered—though not their Sharps carbines. The posse's artillery was trained on the Free State Hotel, and Shalor Eldridge was given two hours to remove the furnishings from the building. Meanwhile, in accordance with the grand jury's indictment of the *Free State* and the *Herald*, their presses were destroyed, and the type was hauled down to the river in a wagon and thrown in.

When the Eldridge House's walls withstood the barrage, and when kegs of powder placed inside the building and ignited failed to destroy it, newspaper stock was used to set the fire that finally gutted it. This was a signal for the looting to begin. "Nearly every house was entered, and many of them robbed," wrote the Reverend Richard Cordley in *A History of Lawrence.* "Trunks were broken open, clothing stolen, and everything taken off to which they took a fancy. In the evening Governor Robinson's house was set on fire and burned to the ground."

The posse then disbanded, and many of its members rode east to spend their newfound wealth. "I had just arrived in Kansas City," reported a prim English newspaper correspondent, Thomas H. Gladstone,

and shall never forget the appearance of the lawless mob that poured into the place, inflamed with drink, glutted with the indulgence of the vilest passions, displaying with loud boasts the "plunder" they had taken from the inhabitants, and thirsting for the opportunity of repeating the sack of Lawrence [or] some other offending place. Men, for the most part of large frame, with red flannel shirts and immense boots worn outside their trousers, their faces unwashed and unshaven, still reeking with the dust and smoke of Lawrence, wearing the most savage looks, and giving utterance to the most horrible imprecations and blasphemies; armed, moreover, to the teeth with rifles and revolvers, cutlasses and bowie-knives. . . . Some displayed a grotesque intermixture in their dress, having crossed their native red rough shirt with the satin vest or narrow dress-coat pillaged from the wardrobe of some Lawrence Yankee, or having girded themselves with the cords and tassels which the day before had ornamented the curtains of the Free State Hotel.

Gangs of free-staters fanned out to revenge Lawrence. One ambushed some of the raiding party, killing three. Another looted a Missourian's store, taking $4,000 worth of goods, while a third burned the cabins of some proslavery settlers, warning them to leave the territory. On the night of May 24, some seventy-two hours after the raid on Lawrence had ended, John Brown and several of his sons and disciples used double-edged artillery cutlasses to hack to death five men. They were accused of being proslavery ruffians, but there was something pathetic about the atrocity: Among the dead were a father and two sons. Nearly all the victims had been dragged from their cabins, despite the pleas of their wives and children. The next morning their bodies were found by kinfolk and friends in varying degrees of disfigurement—throats cut; ears sliced off; skulls split open; bodies with multiple stab wounds; fingers, hands, or arms chopped off.

John Brown's son Jason had not taken part in the butchery, and when he heard of it, he was sickened. "Did you have a hand in the killing?" he asked his father.

John Brown had not wielded a cutlass himself; however, he had supervised the murders. His only act of violence was to shoot one man in the head, just to make certain he was dead. Now challenged by an appalled son, he quibbled. "I did not do it," he answered, "but I approved it."

"I told him that who ever did it," Jason remembered later, "I thought it was an uncalled for, wicked act."

"God is my judge," John Brown replied, "we were justified under the circumstances."

Jason next sought out his brother Frederick. "Did you kill any of them with your own hands?" he asked.

"No," Frederick replied, weeping, "when I came to see what manner of work it was, I *could not* do it."

Missourians crossed the line looking for Brown. Two of his sons were caught: Jason and John, Jr. As it happened, John, Jr., like Jason, had not participated in the atrocity; their captors thought otherwise but surprisingly did not lynch them, instead turning them over to the authorities. Federal soldiers were less benign: Certain that John, Jr., had had a hand in the "Pottawatomie Massacre," as it came to be called, they chained him to a tent pole and beat him with rifle butts and fists until, according to William Phillips, "[he] startled his remorseless captors by the wild ravings of a maniac, while he lashed his chains in fury till the dull iron shone like polished steel."

Henry Clay Pate, a deputy U.S. marshal and a militia captain, left Franklin with his twenty-nine-man company, determined to capture Brown and the others. Instead, Brown, leading twenty-six volunteers, launched a predawn surprise attack against Pate's camp, killing four and wounding several others. Pate approached Brown under a flag of truce to negotiate; however, Brown demanded his company's unconditional surrender. When Pate asked for fifteen minutes, presumably to talk it over with his men, Brown drew his revolver, and his followers drew a bead on Pate with their rifles.

"You can't do this!" Pate cried. "I'm under a white flag. You're violating the articles of war!"

"You are my prisoner," Brown simply replied, the barrel of his pistol speaking volumes about his intent.

"I had no alternative, but to submit or be shot," Pate commented subsequently, adding, "Had I known who I was fighting, I would not have trusted to a white flag."

The "Missouri attack on Lawrence and John Brown's gruesome reprisal were the beginning of a period of lawlessness worse than anything that had preceded it," observed historian Stephen Z. Starr. There was an upsurge in shootings, lynchings, thievery, and arson.

Southerners boarded incoming steamboats that docked at Lexington, Kansas City, and Leavenworth, questioning passengers about their politics and relieving free-soil men of their weapons before turning them away from the border. "Border Ruffians infested the Santa Fe Trail, stopping all travelers and asking them across leveled guns whether they were 'Free State or Pro-Slave,' " Kansas historian Dr. Albert Castel has written.

> Those giving the wrong answer were liable to "short shrift and long rope." Similar gangs of Free-Soil militants raided proslavery settlements and forced their inhabitants to leave the territory. Each side accused the other of horrible outrages, always with exaggeration but rarely without foundation. In the words of a contemporary, "Murder and assassination were the program of the day."

In August Jim Lane initiated a campaign to "sweep all proslavery forces from the Kaw Valley." Lane's men captured three forts and raided the town of Franklin. Once more Governor Shannon appeared in Lawrence and negotiated a peace treaty, but when he tried to speak to a large crowd of free-staters, he was shouted down.

Near the end of August, George Washington Clarke led an army of Missouri border ruffians into Kansas, going through Linn and Miami counties, intending to raid Osawatomie. Since many "Northern" people had taken refuge in the area, Clarke, according to nineteenth-century historian Leverett Wilson Spring, "threw down fences, destroyed crops, seized horses and cattle, burnt a few cabins, and occasionally drove an obnoxious settler out of the country."

At noon on August 25, during a halt at Middle Creek, nine miles from Osawatomie, Clarke's force was attacked by a band of jayhawkers led by James Montgomery, a small, black-bearded Campbellite preacher from Ohio. The border ruffians were routed. In their pell-mell flight they abandoned their boots, coats, vests, hats, most of their horses, two wounded men, a dinner they had just finished cooking, and a black flag bearing the inscription, in red letters, "Victory or Death."

The jayhawkers returned home loaded with the abandoned plunder, but that was not revenge enough for Montgomery. Leverett Spring, a professor of rhetoric at Williams College, who while writing a book in the mid-1880s was in touch with many of those involved in the prewar border conflict, wrote that

> To obtain a list of the men concerned in [Clarke's raid, Montgomery] visited Missouri in the disguise of a teacher searching for a school, which he succeeded in obtaining and actually taught for two weeks— long enough to get the information he wished. That secured, the school suddenly closed, and the schoolmaster soon reappeared transformed into a guerrilla chief. Twenty of the ex-raiders were captured and pretty thoroughly spoiled of money, weapons, and horses.

While Clarke's men were still running through the brush, another army of border ruffians struck Osawatomie, pillaging stores and burning cabins. Frederick Brown, who suffered from a brain disorder and was considered "half-witted," was recognized and shot down—by a minister and chaplain of the Lecompton legislature, the Reverend Martin White, who had formerly resided in Osawatomie but had been driven out because of his proslavery beliefs. Four other free-staters and several of the proslavery raiders were also killed.

Lane's army clashed briefly with the force that raided Osawatomie, then marched on Lecompton, invested it, and demanded the proslavery inhabitants release some free-soil prisoners.

Newspapers from as far away as Chicago and Mobile, Alabama, appealed to readers to arm themselves and head for Kansas.

Wagon trains of free-soil emigrants crossed into the territory with weapons hidden under spinning wheels, sacks of grain, and plows.

Newly appointed Governor John W. Geary, who arrived in the territory in September 1856, managed to restore a level of peace by dispensing evenhanded justice and arresting troublemakers on both sides. Geary lasted only six months, but his successor, Robert J. Walker, continued his policies.

In 1857, an estimated 100,000 emigrants arrived in the territory, the largest number from Ohio. The population was now decidedly free soil. On October 5 voters elected a free-state man as a delegate to Congress and gave like-minded individuals thirty-three of fifty-two seats in the territorial legislature. Then, on August 2, 1858, in a fair election guaranteed by Federal troops guarding the polling places, voters rejected by a six-to-one margin the Lecompton Constitution, which upheld slavery. Ironically, emigration, not violence, had decided the issue.

In the spring of 1858, James Montgomery and his band of jayhawkers drove a collection of proslavery partisans out of the Fort Scott area, in southeastern Kansas, and across the border into Missouri. These men rallied around one of their own, a slave owner from Georgia named Charles A. Hamilton, and on May 19, he led them back into Kansas. They rode into Trading Post and, working from a list compiled by Hamilton, seized eleven men and herded them to a gulch near the Marais des Cygnes River. Hamilton ordered that the men be lined up and had his followers, still on horseback, form an opposing line on the rim of the gulch. One of Hamilton's followers, whose name was Brockett, suddenly realized what was about to take place. He wheeled his horse and, despite Hamilton's wild curses and furious commands to the contrary, rode away, crying, "I'll be damned if I'll have anything to do with any such goddamned piece of business as this."

The impromptu firing squad aimed their revolvers, and a victim shouted, "If you are going to shoot, take good aim!" As it happened his wish was not granted: Only two died in the volley that Hamilton himself initiated; eight others were wounded, and one had not even been hit, though fortunately for his sake he was covered with the blood of others. Hamilton and some of his boys dismounted, climbed down into the gulch, and repeatedly kicked the men to be sure they were dead. The survivors tried to play possum, but three of the wounded were found out. One was shot in the mouth, another was shot twice, and, it would later be alleged, Hamilton himself dispatched the third, putting a pistol's barrel against his ear and pulling the trigger. The pockets of all the "dead" were rifled, and then their assailants rode away.

The cold, premeditated savagery of the deed made a profound impression on many people in the North. In the September issue of *The Atlantic Monthly,* John Greenleaf Whittier published a poem, "Le Marais du Cygne," which began:

> A blush as of roses
> Where rose never grew!

> Great drops on the bunch-grass,
>> But not of the dew!
> A taint in the sweet air
>> For wild bees to shun!
> A stain that shall never
>> Bleach out in the sun!

Bands of jayhawkers and abolitionists fanned out, looking for Hamilton and his gang, but none was located.

Although Lane might have wanted to join the hunt, he was preoccupied by problems of his own: In an argument over a claim boundary he killed Gaius Jenkins and was shot in the leg by one of Jenkins's friends. Despite being acquitted in court, the murder hurt him politically, and he found it expedient to retire temporarily to private life and to be converted to the Methodist Church.

As winter settled in, many Kansans were distracted from the border troubles by tales of riches in the Pikes Peak gold rush. Only in southeast Kansas did border ruffians and jayhawkers continue their depredations.

On December 19, John Brown raided into Missouri, liberating ten slaves and stealing eight horses, one yoke of oxen, and a wagon, as well as some "bed clothing," wearing apparel, and provisions. Meanwhile, a splinter party of Brown's followers went to the home of wealthy sixty-year-old David Cruise and took his female slave, two horses, two yoke of oxen, and a wagon laden with clothing and provisions. When Cruise tried to resist, he was murdered. (Brown himself had less than a year to live: In October 1859, he and his disciples made the famous raid against Harpers Ferry, in what was then still Virginia. He was hanged on December 2. "I John Brown am now quite *certain* that the crimes of this guilty land will never be purged *away;* but with Blood," he wrote in a last prophetic message. "I had *as I now think vainly* flattered myself that without *very much* bloodshed it might be done.")

Ten days after the Brown foray into Missouri, jayhawker Eli Snyder led a band into Bates County, Missouri, robbing merchant Jeremiah Jackson of four horses and $6,000 worth of goods and burning his store and house to the ground. Jackson, his wife, and children escaped the flames with only the clothes on their backs.

Authorities on both sides of the line attempted to stamp out jayhawking. The southeast portion of the Kansas Territory was placed under martial law, and on February 24, 1859, the Missouri legislature passed a bill that authorized the raising of a military force to suppress the "banditti" on the border and offering a reward of $3,000 for the capture of any criminal who committed "outrages" on Missouri citizens.

In 1860, James Montgomery and Dr. Charles R. Jennison organized vigilante committees throughout southeast Kansas and stole prime horseflesh. On the border jayhawkers and border ruffians continued to ply their piratical trade. In August, Missourians elected Claiborne Jackson governor and Thomas C. Reynolds lieutenant governor, on the Douglas ticket. Both men were proslavery but muted their views, and a vote for them was perceived as a vote for moderation, a choice for the middle ground between the extremes.

In St. Louis, German gymnastic societies were converted into military companies; native-born staunch Unionists and Southern sympathizers formed companies, too. All drilled in secret.

In November, Montgomery announced he would drive every man in favor of slavery out of the territory, then invade Missouri to free the slaves, kill their masters, and destroy their masters' property.

On November 11, Charles Jennison "tried" in an impromptu "vigilance court" Russell Hinds, a Missouri resident who had made the mistake of crossing the line to visit his mother. Hinds was accused of having caught a fugitive slave and hauling him back to Missouri for the reward. After the sham of a trial Hinds was hanged, and a note was stuck in his pocket identifying his crime—no doubt as a warning to others.

A week after Hinds's hanging, Jennison took Samuel Scott from his home in Linn County, Kansas, and tried him. The terrified old man promised to convey to Jennison all his "considerable" property and leave Kansas if he were spared. The offer did no good: He, too, was hanged. Jennison visited the cabin of Lester D. Moore after dark a short time later. Moore was alleged to have participated in the lynching of two free-state men. Jennison offered Moore a trial if he surrendered, but Moore, perhaps recalling the fate of Hinds and Scott, chose to die fighting.

Territorial Governor Samuel Medary offered a $1,000 reward for Jennison's arrest, and soldiers sought both Jennison and Montgomery, but they had disappeared.

Meetings were held in Missouri border towns and appeals were sent to the governor for protection. Volunteer militia companies were organized.

Many residents of Bates and Vernon counties abandoned their homes for the interior of Missouri. The refugees included not only slave owners and their slaves but also many other individuals who were frightened by Jennison and Montgomery.

Throughout the war the Lincoln administration regularly reorganized the command structure in the West and played musical chairs with commanding officers. Thus, for example, in early November 1861, Major General John C. Fremont, who had been the commander of the Department of the West, was replaced by Major General David M. Hunter, who was put in charge of the newly created Department of Kansas, which also included Colorado, Nebraska, and the Indian Nations or Indian Territory (what is now Oklahoma). Hunter did not last long: Less than five months later Kansas became part of the Department of the Mississippi, under the command of General Henry H. Halleck. Just two months later, on May 2, 1862, the War Department restored Kansas as a separate department and placed Brigadier General James G. Blunt in charge. By fall Kansas had been made part of the Department of the Missouri, under Major General Samuel Ryan Curtis. And so on. No sooner had a new commander gotten his bearings, begun to focus on combatting the partisans, and gained some valuable experience and insight than he was replaced. Clearly the frequent changes in command did not foster a continuity of leadership and policy. Rather, they would seem almost designed to promote an insecurity in commanding officers, as well as to encourage among high-ranking subordinate officers unfortunate tendencies toward jealousy, squabbling, martial hesitancy, and bureaucratic infighting and maneuvering for position. Thus Washington's meddling caused a constant, monumental distraction from what should have been the tasks at hand: the suppression of the Northern and Southern guerrillas and the restoration of order in Kansas and Missouri.

Jayhawkers would remain a constant problem on the border for much of the war. One of the worst was the aforementioned physician and sometime lieutenant of Lane and protégé of Montgomery, "Doc" Jennison. His commitment to abolitionism caused him to free as many blacks as he could, but beyond that he was after loot and was not too discriminating about from whom he took it. He was so corrupt that in 1862, Montgomery, who had a deep allegiance to the Union cause, would brand him "an unmitigated *liar*[,] black-leg and Robber." Jennison himself liked to brag that Missouri mothers quieted naughty children by invoking his name. Captain Henry E. Palmer called Jennison "a coward and a murderer," adding that his regiment, the 7th Kansas Volunteer Cavalry, "was little [more] than an armed mob."

On one raid into Bates County, Missouri, recalled Mrs. N. M. Harris in 1913,

> Jennison's command carried off all the silverware in sight in the neighborhood of the Masons, the Stonestreets, Cowards, Fields, Thorntons and others of the well-to-do residents of that section. They tore up the hearths to seek hidden treasures; they took the family carriages and drove away towards Kansas with negro women as their occupants; they packed in wagons all wearing apparel, household articles, harness, plows or whatever they wanted and could make room for. They left not a horse, mule or any cattle they could manage to drive away; they robbed hen roosts, took children's toys, even compelling one gentleman to take off his coat, pants and shoes and give them; they broke dishes they could not carry away; handsome party finery that did not appeal to their pilfering proclivities they wiped their muddy boots on. All this, and the half has not been told.
>
> One Sunday afternoon I counted in the Sni Hills seven dwellings burning at once, two the homes of poor widows. . . .

In mid-July 1861, Jennison attacked Morristown, southwest of Harrisonville in Cass County, and drove off a company of cavalry, capturing seven, and then plundered the village. Among the loot were seven wagons loaded with flour and bacon. Once more, the property of Unionists was stolen along with that of Southerners. The booty taken was valued at $2,000. The seven unlucky prisoners were given a drumhead court-martial and sentenced to death. Their graves were dug, and they were forced to kneel down beside them. They were blindfolded and shot. The graves were then filled in, and the jayhawkers rode away.

One man who had enlisted only a few days earlier could not help being shocked. This was "my first lesson of the horrors of what was then called the 'border war,' " he remarked many years later. "It was a sickening evidence that we were fighting under the black flag. This execution was in retaliation for the murder, only a few days previous, of seven men of our command."

Less than a week later Jennison struck Harrisonville, where the stores were emptied of goods, men were roughed up—Unionists as well as Southerners—and a great deal of property was "confiscated," supposedly to keep it out of rebel hands. The town was burned. Among the Harrisonville victims was the previously mentioned conditional Unionist, Colonel Younger, who lost some $20,000 worth of property, including livery wagons and forty head of horses.

In September—the exact date is disputed—Jennison raided Independence, a few miles east of Kansas City, at the head of a 450-man column, which included a number of armed blacks. (Because a slave insurrection posed a threat to every white in a slaveholding community, the sight of armed blacks was frightening even to those whites who did not approve of the "peculiar institution.")

The male residents were herded into the public square—the decrepit elderly and others who did not step lively enough were prodded with the points of sabers and bayonets—and surrounded by jayhawkers on horseback, who threatened to kill them. Meanwhile other jayhawkers and blacks pillaged stores, stables, and houses. Fifty slaves chose to leave their owners, and an escort was provided to carry them to Kansas. A dozen houses and stores were burned, and two citizens were murdered.

Famed Missouri artist George Caleb Bingham, an uncompromising Unionist who saw action as a captain in the Battle of Lexington and who would spend most of the war as the treasurer of the loyal Missouri state government, was appalled at the way Jennison and his men had conducted themselves in Independence. "Without hesitation or compunction, [Jennison's men] confiscated for their own benefit whatever tickled their fancy or tempted their cupidity," Bingham wrote in a letter to his friend James S. Rollins.

Watches, jewelry, shawls, scarfs, and other articles of female ornament and apparel, rarely escaped their lynx-eyed vigilance. Indeed, they seemed to pounce at once, by a kind of rogues instinct, upon the most carefully concealed depositories, bringing forth each coveted and glittering prize in triumph before the eyes of the discomfited owners. They were not wanting either in a proper regard for the substantially useful. Many of them, doubtless, had wives and daughters who could appreciate, in their bleak prairie homesteads, the advantages of a full supply of comforts, blankets, counterpanes, quilts &c. during the prevalence of those cutting Northwesters, with which we are so frequently favored during the winter season . . . and our Jackson county matrons may console themselves in their losses with the benevolent reflection, that many a Kansas spouse and lass lies as cosily as the silk worm in its cocoon, during these long winter nights, as the result of their involuntary contributions, through their self appointed, but, nevertheless, very efficient agents.

Jennison's troops behaved no better on the return march:

[the] entire route from Independence to West Point may be traced by the ruins of the dwellings of our citizens, which were first pillaged and then burned without discrimination or mercy. As they were generally constructed of wood, they are now but heaps of ashes, above which the tall chimneys remain in their mute solitude—sad and mournful monuments of the ever to be remembered march of a desolating fiend.

If Jennison were hung, Bingham disgustedly told Rollins, Confederate General Sterling Price would lose the best recruiting agent he ever had. Indeed, Bingham added on another occasion, Jennison's "execution upon a scaffold would do more for the Union Cause in Missouri than the defeat of a Rebel army."

Captain Palmer claimed that Jennison's men returned from the raid with a large quantity of women's dresses and bonnets, "spinning-wheels and even gravestones lashed to their saddles; their pathway through the country strewn with (to them) worthless household goods, their route lighted by burning homes."

When Major General Hunter ordered Jennison to march from Leavenworth southeast to West Point, in Bates County, Missouri, he detoured through Kansas City and Independence. "Again property was taken by force," noted historian Hildegarde Rose Herklotz,

and the ruins of dwellings marked the route he had taken. It has been said that after a ten day campaign, Jennison's soldiers carried off a train of stock and richly loaded wagons four to five miles long and valued at two hundred and fifty thousand dollars. Very little, if any, of this property was ever turned over to the Government. Much of it was subsequently sold by Jennison at his residence near Squiresville.

Federal authorities came to understand how counterproductive the activities of Jennison and the other jayhawkers were. In a letter to Major General George B. McClellan, dated December 19, 1861, Halleck stated that the "conduct of the forces under Lane and Jennison has done more for the enemy in this State than could have been accomplished by 20,000 of his own army. I receive almost daily complaints of outrages committed by these men in the name of the United States, and the evidence is so conclusive as to leave no doubt of their correctness." A month later Halleck ordered General John Pope to drive Jennison's men out of Missouri, and if they resisted, Pope was to "disarm them and hold them prisoners." Writing to Brigadier General Lorenzo Thomas, Adjutant-General of the Army, in Washington, DC, Halleck commented that Jennison's men "are no better than a band of robbers; they cross the line, rob, steal, plunder, and burn whatever they can lay their hands upon. They disgrace the name and uniform of American soldiers and are driving good Union men into the ranks of the secession army. Their conduct within the last six months has caused a change of 20,000 votes in this State."

Eventually the military bureaucracy bestirred itself, and Montgomery was dispatched east, where he was placed in charge of a regiment of black volunteers. In late March 1862, Jennison's 7th Volunteer Regiment was ordered to New Mexico—nearly one thousand miles from the Missouri border. Jennison resigned his commission on April 10, and three days later he gave an emotional speech to the regiment, accusing various generals by name of being drunkards, "pro-slavery-ites," and traitors. The speech was clearly calculated to incite desertion, and approximately one hundred men went over the hill.

Jennison was arrested and jailed; however, powerful abolitionists went to work in Kansas and Washington, DC, securing his release. (The expedition to New Mexico, of which the 7th Volunteer Regiment was to have been a part, was canceled, so the regiment was sent to Kentucky instead.)

Despite efforts by the Federal military authorities to suppress the jayhawker bands, they remained active and cruel, inspiring fear and outrage among their victims and potential victims, and a source of irritation and frustration to Yankee generals.

Union commanders had even less luck in suppressing Confederate guerrillas, who were more commonly known as "bushwhackers." This failure is attributable in part to the poor quality of troops available in the region. Most of those serving in western Missouri were local militia—badly trained and often badly led, poorly armed and issued uniforms ill-suited for winter. Some units were composed largely of Southerners forced into service and therefore unreliable. Too many others, however, were made up of loyalists whose families had suffered under the threats and raids of the border ruffians and bushwhackers and who therefore harbored a desire for revenge against all those they deemed Southern sympathizers. While in the field these units generally lived off the "disloyal," which afforded them ample opportunity for thievery. "About my first recollection of the war was seeing whole companies of soldiers marching through the country," wrote Jackson County resident Mrs. J.A.B. Adcock many years later.

> The Federal soldiers were stationed at Independence, consequently they lived on the people. They would go out with those large government wagons, and were particular to go to the homes of southern men and fill them with corn from the barn, then kill hogs and chickens and put [their carcasses] on top of the corn. Then they would drive all [the] cattle and horses and take all [the] household goods that they could use, and some things they had no use for, such things as fancy articles and as large and heavy a book as an unabridged dictionary.

High-ranking Federal officers were also hampered in their efforts to defeat the guerrillas by their own attitudes. In the early stages of the war, many wrongly assumed that all Missourians were disloyal, and those who claimed to be neutral simply were not believed or tolerated. As General Halleck put it, "Those who are not for us will be regarded as against us. . . . There can be no individual neutrality in the rear in Missouri." Forced to choose sides, many Missourians of Southern ancestry chose to join or support the bushwhackers. Policies and regulations established by various Federal commanders only increased this tendency.

Persons thought to have secessionist views were forbidden from possessing a gun, caps, or powder; searching for such contraband provided further golden opportunity for theft and the "accidental" destruction of household property. In addition, Union cavalry, authorized to burn the property of those giving aid to partisans, were, in the opinion of historian Richard S. Brownlee, "extremely careless with fire" and were "frequently guilty of plain arson." He added that "many citizens were simply murdered by Union troops. Men were called to their doors at night by the militia and shot dead, or were taken from their homes and families and hung. A favorite trick of the Union cavalry was to trap civil-

ians into admitting friendship for the Confederacy, or aiding and harboring guerrillas, and then executing them on the spot."

In early 1862, in an attempt to prevent bushwhacker raids into
Kansas or at least give warning of them, Generals James G. Blunt and
Thomas Ewing, Jr., organized a company of scouts to patrol the border.
The scouts came to be known as "redlegs" because of the red leather leggings they wore. At various times the company was led by Jennison or
his disciple, Lieutenant George H. Hoyt. Since some of Jennison's 7th
Volunteers had become redlegs, the band soon earned an unsavory reputation that was further sullied as gangs of outlaws adopted the red leggings as a cover for their own misdeeds. Thus what began as a
well-meaning effort to stem violence and robbery succeeded only in
making matters worse. Things had gotten so bad by the summer of 1863
that many border residents saw little distinction among bushwhackers,
jayhawkers, and redlegs.

In the latter part of the summer, newspaper editor C. M. Chase passed
through the border region while writing a series of dispatches to the
Sycamore, Illinois, *True Republican and Sentinel.* On August 10,
undoubtedly reflecting the attitude of many with whom he had spoken,
he informed his readers that

> A Jayhawker is a Unionist who professes to rob, burn out, and mur-
> der only rebels in arms against the government. A Redleg is a Jay-
> hawker originally distinguished by the uniform of red leggings. A
> Redleg, however, is regarded as more purely an indiscriminate thief
> and murderer than the Jayhawker or Bushwhacker. A Bushwhacker is
> a rebel Jayhawker, or a rebel who bands with others for the purpose of
> preying upon the lives and property of Union citizens. They are all
> lawless and indiscriminate in their iniquities. Their occupation, unless
> crushed out speedily, will lead into a system of highway robbery
> exceeding anything that has existed in any country. It excites the mind,
> destroys the moral sensibilities, creates a thirst for wild life and adven-
> ture which will, on the restoration of peace, find gratification in
> nothing but highway robbery.

General Fremont's August 30, 1861, martial-law decree, which successive departmental commanders continued and expanded until the spring
of 1865, caused untold hardship and suffering to the civilian population.

Under martial law massive numbers of citizens—including voters, officeholders, and those in public service—were forced to swear loyalty to the United States and to the provisional Missouri government and provide performance bonds. Those who refused could be arrested and imprisoned. The same prospect faced those *suspected* of holding disloyal sentiments: Thousands of men and a lesser number of women were arrested and charged with "believing in rebellion, expressing disloyal sentiments, communicating with and aiding the enemy, or violating the numerous Union orders issued under martial law." They were held in jails that were enormously overcrowded, poorly ventilated, unsanitary, and disease-ridden. Fines were levied, property confiscated, and individuals were imprisoned, banished, or executed.

Various commanders also tried to stem guerrilla activity by putting in place systems that forced civilians to pay for the cost of maintaining the militia and compensating the families of soldiers and loyalists who were killed. In some cases entire counties were assessed, but the money was always paid by the "secesh"—those thought to favor secession. Individuals who did not have the money to pay the assessments had their property seized. Unfortunately, the civilian provost marshals given the assignment of identifying the secesh tended to be the most radical in their sympathies, and their judgments were sometimes suspect.

Some commanders forbade "disloyal" men from raising crops or operating a business or, more subtly, instituted permit systems for persons engaged in trade or business.

During the summer of 1862 Brigadier General John M. Schofield, Union commander in Missouri, took perhaps the boldest step yet, ordering that every able-bodied man in the state enlist in the militia "for the purpose of exterminating the guerrillas."

Newspapers were the one means of mass communication, offering the opportunity to express diverse ideas as well as keep readers informed of events in neighboring communities and throughout the region. It is hardly surprising that in the early years of the war, newspapers came in for special attention by the Federal military as well as by jayhawkers. In the summer of 1861, wrote Brownlee,

the *St. Louis Morning Herald* was suspended because of its secessionist expressions, the Lexington *Expositor* was raided by Kansas Jayhawkers and its press stolen, and the *Express* of the same town closed by military order. The *Platte City Sentinel* was burned by Jennison, and when troops were sent to destroy the *Argus* in the same community, its editor loaded his type and press into a wagon, skipped town, and joined Price's army where he became the official printer of the Missouri Confederate government. The St. Louis *Missouri State Journal,* the Cape Girardeau *Eagle,* and the *Hannibal Evening News* were shut down by Union troops, and when the editors of the Fayette *Banner* joined the Confederate forces their paper was seized, sold, and opened under a new name. The *California News* was ransacked by Union soldiers, and the Independence *Border Star* demolished by Kansans. During 1862 the *Carrollton Democrat,* the *Franklin County Weekly Advertiser,* the *Shelby County Weekly,* and the *Columbia Standard* were all suppressed. The editor of the *Standard,* Edmund J. Ellis, was banished and his press sold. Other papers, their names now lost, were "smashed" by Union troops at Boonville, Warrensburg, Troy, Osceola, Oregon, and Washington. The *Macon Register* was seized, its editor run off, and the paper published by soldiers.

These various harsh and repressive measures did not end guerrilla activity. To the contrary, an incalculable number of partisan bands were formed, and bushwhackers remained fierce and active to the end of the war. As noted earlier, what the measures did do was force many civilians who would have preferred to remain unaligned to choose between sides—and many of them either joined guerrilla bands themselves or secretly supported them, providing intelligence, food, clothing, weapons, and horses.

Quantrill first arrived in Kansas Territory in the latter part of March 1857, seeking to make his fortune. He was nineteen years old. Those who knew him during the prewar period described him as being "about five feet nine inches in height," "weight about 150 or 160 pounds," with a "Roman nose" and "sandy" or "yellowish-brown" hair. He typically wore a "drab slouch hat," a "woolen shirt," a "drab corduroy suit," and "high-heeled boots." He walked with an "easy gait." In the years that followed, Quantrill farmed, drove cattle, and taught school; his students and their parents considered him an excellent teacher. He forayed out to Utah and returned to Kansas by way of Colorado, working as a teamster and mining for gold. He was extremely bright, always hungry for knowledge. In his spare time he read and studied and memorized English poetry, so that his letters show a gradual improvement in spelling and grammar.

He was "rather reticent," recalled Sidney S. Herd in 1901. "He did not strike me as having any braggadocio or desire to make any display. If he had any money, to amount to anything, no one knew it but himself. I don't think he had any very positive convictions on [the] questions that were agitating the territory at that time; if he did he certainly kept them to himself."

In fact, he did have strong opinions on the events of the day. At first he maintained something of his father's perspective, admiring the free-soil proponents. Eventually, however, he changed his mind and sided with the Southerners. Still, he kept his opinions to himself and maintained his distance from the violence and political struggle.

In the spring of 1860, with all his various schemes to make his fortune having come to naught, he set off for Ohio. Quite by accident he encountered a gang of border ruffians near Lawrence, fell in with them, and altered the course of his life. Over the next five years he became the most famous and hunted guerrilla in the West, a clever tactician and fearsome fighter, loathed and feared by many, admired and adored by others.

"One-half the country believes Quantrell to have been a highway robber crossed upon [a] tiger; the other half that he was a gallant defender of his native South," wrote John N. Edwards, a nineteenth-century Missouri newspaperman with an unbridled fondness for strong drink and purple prose, who was Quantrill's first biographer.

> One-half believes him to have been an avenging Nemesis of the right; the other a forbidding monster of assassination. History cannot hesitate over him, however, nor abandon him to the imagination of romancers. . . . He was a living, breathing, aggressive, all-powerful reality—riding through the midnight, laying ambuscades by lonesome roadsides, catching marching columns by the throat, breaking in upon the flanks and tearing a suddenly surprised rear to pieces; vigilant, merciless, a terror by day and a superhuman if not supernatural thing when there was upon the earth blackness and darkness.

During the war Major Edwards had served as adjutant to General Jo Shelby, who was lionized by Missouri Southerners, and had followed the general to Mexico at war's end in the hopes of founding a new Confederate colony. Later Edwards would become a personal friend and chief public champion of Frank and Jesse James. Thus Edwards earned the trust of Quantrill's veterans and friends and with such sources might have written a masterpiece of American biography and an invaluable resource to generations of Civil War historians and aficionados. However, Edwards was writing in 1875, in the midst of a protracted postwar period of severe persecution of Missouri Southerners by Radical Republicans and Unionists, and he seems to have chosen to create a mythology to give heart to his downtrodden comrades. Steeped in classical mythology and the novels of Alexandre Dumas and Sir Walter Scott, mixing fact with considerable fancy, he depicted Quantrill and his men as blood-drenched heroes, gallant as musketeers and as implacably violent as Ulysses and Achilles.

Thirty-five years after Major Edwards wrote *Noted Guerrillas*, historian William Elsey Connelley published *Quantrill and the Border Wars*. Connelley had been born and raised in Kentucky, and he never claimed that either he or any member of his family had suffered at Quantrill's hands. However, in adulthood Connelley fervently embraced his adopted state of Kansas, becoming what might be called a Kansan's Kansan, and he developed a hatred for his long-dead subject that was as deep and abiding, perhaps, as that of any Lawrence massacre survivor. Connelley had the trust of many Kansans and even some Missouri Southerners who had known Quantrill and were part of his story; Connelley was also an indefatigable researcher and wrote valuable histories of other subjects, so he, too, might have produced a masterpiece of American biography. Instead he wrote a book that is sometimes quite accurate but that all too often is badly flawed by his prejudice against his subject: Given a choice between an obviously reliable source that cast Quantrill in a moderate or favorable light and an obviously disreputable source that vilified him, Connelley invariably chose the latter.

Consciously disputing Edwards at every turn and occasionally lapsing into as purple a prose, Connelley depicted Quantrill as being something nearly inhuman:

> In cruelty and a thirst for blood he towered above the men of his time. Somewhere of old his ancestors ate sour grapes which set his teeth on edge. In him was exemplified the terrible and immutable law of hered-

ity. He grew into the gory monster whose baleful shadow falls upon all who share the kindred blood. He made his name a Cain's mark and a curse to those condemned to bear it. The blight of it must fall upon remote generations, those yet unborn and innocent, so inexorable are the decrees of fate and nature. Because of him widows wailed, orphans cried, maidens wept, as they lifted the lifeless forms of loved ones from bloody fields and bore them reeking to untimely graves.

Those who have written about Quantrill since Edwards and Connelley have tended to follow their extremes, presenting him either as a heroic Confederate knight-errant or a brilliant but brutal psychopath.

William H. Gregg knew better. Gregg had been Quantrill's lieutenant and friend, although he was not blind to his faults. "One thing I do know," wrote Gregg after the turn of the century,

and that is, he was a soldier, and not afraid to die, that he was equitable and just to friend and foe up to a certain period in the war. . . . Quantrill and his men have been unjustly slandered by the people of the North, a people who even to this day know nothing of [that time], except what they have read in irresponsible books and newspapers. The time has come when their minds should be disabused.

Gregg added, "The greatest fault in the people who write of us is that they only tell one side of the story, just as though [the redlegs, jayhawkers, and Yankee troops] had the right to murder, burn, rob and steal and those whom they murdered, robbed and plundered had no right to resist."

CHAPTER 2

"The Blight That Falls on Remote Generations": Quantrill's Family Background and Early Years

Frank James was certain that Quantrill had been born and raised in Kentucky. Quantrill himself told other members of his band that he was from Hagerstown, Maryland, and that his family was in sympathy with the South. In 1856, he said, his older brother, who was living in Kentucky, invited him to go on a trip to California. Traveling along the Santa Fe Trail with two heavy-laden mule-drawn wagons, the brothers camped one night beside the Little Cottonwood River, deep in Kansas Territory. Thirty-two of James Montgomery's jayhawkers rode out of the darkness and without a word opened fire at point-blank range. Quantrill was struck in the right breast and left leg; his brother died instantly. The murderers rifled the pockets of both men and took all their money, relieved the corpse of a watch, and twisted a ring off Quantrill's finger. As they were harnessing the mules, the free black man who had accompanied the brothers as a cook and hostler pleaded that food and a tent be left for Quantrill.

"Of what use?" the jayhawker's leader sneered. "He will die at best, and if we did not think that he would die, we would be sure to finish him."

They rode off with the wagons and the black man. Quantrill dragged himself over to his brother's body and for two nights and two days, feverish and crazed, he guarded it against the buzzards and prairie wolves.

"He heard the clangor of ominous pinions and the flapping of mysterious wings," wrote John N. Edwards.

And in the darkness came other sounds than the rising of the night wind. A long, low howl at first that had the subdued defiance of hunger in it, and then the shuffling of creeping feet and the mingling of gray and darkness in the nearest cover. The wolves were abroad—coming ever closer and closer, and crouching there in the prairie grass, knowing scarcely aught of any difference between the living and the dead. He did not cry out, neither did he moan. All night long by the corpse he watched and defended—seeing on the morrow the sun rise red out of a sea of verdure. . . .

When his thirst became unbearable, he rolled twenty yards down a steep, rocky slope to the river's edge, then pulled himself hand over hand back up it again. He stanched his "swollen and inflamed wounds" with the "rankest grass," and on the third day he was found by an old Shawnee Indian, known to whites as Golightly Spiebuck. The Indian buried the festering corpse while Quantrill watched, dry-eyed and ghastly pale. When the last handful of dirt was thrown onto the mound, Quantrill hauled himself to his feet and swore vengeance before God.

Spiebuck carried him in a wagon by slow stages to his cabin, where Quantrill was painstakingly nursed back to health by the Indian's wife.

Two years later Quantrill located the company of jayhawkers who had murdered his brother and, calling himself Charley Hart, enlisted as a private. He managed to rise to the rank of lieutenant, despite the fact that men who went out with him on scouts had a disturbing tendency not to return; their bodies, when they were found at all, each bore a single bullet hole between the eyes. Quantrill claimed to have eventually killed all but two of his brother's slayers, and he solemnly assured his followers that revenge was the motive for all the fury he visited on the border throughout the war.

The truth, as usual, is something else entirely.

———

William Clarke Quantrill was born in Dover, Ohio, on July 31, 1837. He was the eldest of eight children, four of whom died in infancy. The father, Thomas Henry Quantrill, was a native of Hagerstown, born there on February 19, 1813, and was a tinker by trade. One day while visiting Chambersburg, Pennsylvania, he met an orphaned girl six years his junior named Caroline Cornelia Clarke. The courtship was a brief one, and they were married on October 11, 1836. They soon left for Dover, where Thomas Henry had a promise of work, taking seven days to make the trip overland by horse and buggy.

Rascality would seem to be William Quantrill's heritage. An uncle was a pirate in the Gulf of Mexico, and his grandfather, Captain Thomas Quantrill, was a libertine, professional gambler, and horse trader. Captain Quantrill's reputation for sharp horse trading was such that many were wary of dealing with him.

Quantrill's father, while a trustee of the Dover school, misappropriated funds to pay for the printing of an instructional manual on tinsmithing he had written. A man named Harmon V. Beeson discovered and exposed the theft, a fact that so annoyed Thomas Henry that he was determined to kill him. His timing was as unfortunate as his embezzlement was clumsy: He arrived at Beeson's house just as the fellow, seated before his hearth, was preparing to plunge a red-hot poker into a cup of cider, to heat it. When Thomas Henry burst into the room and produced a derringer, Beeson jumped to his feet and brought the poker down on his assailant's skull, knocking him unconscious to the floor with a long gash in his scalp. Neighbors carried the would-be assassin to his own house, where he made a slow recovery.

The blow did not knock any sense into Thomas Henry. Not long thereafter he began to defame a Mrs. Roscoe, whom he found to be deeply suspicious because she was married to a Frenchman and—even worse—was an artist who gave lessons in painting. He gossiped far and wide that she was a loose woman. The talk eventually reached the lady, who was vivacious, impulsive, and possessed of a low tolerance for foolishness. She armed herself with a bullwhip and went looking for her slanderer. She found him standing on a street corner making jokes with a bunch of idle men and proceeded to give him a sound "cowhiding."

Quantrill males were often blessed with manipulative, charming personalities, and Thomas Henry was no exception. These several scandals did no permanent damage to his reputation: In the fall of 1850 he was appointed assistant principal of the Canal Dover Union School; the following term he became the principal, a post that he held until he died.

The greatest scalawag of the Quantrill clan was Thomas Henry's eldest brother, Jesse Duncan, whose felonies and misdemeanors are sometimes mistakenly attributed to his famous nephew. Since Jesse was the eldest son, observed William E. Connelley, "he was his father's favorite, was indulged, and grew up in idleness and mischief." Connelley added that he was a "deadbeat and confidence man," and "a sort of fop or dandy with criminal instincts and tendencies, a dashing, handsome man, wholly devoid of moral character." Returning home to Hagerstown after being educated in an exclusive New York City school, Jesse met Mary Lane, the lovely, impressionable daughter of Seth Lane, one of Hagerstown's foremost citizens. She unfortunately became infatuated with the young rogue, and they married secretly. Mary, who was twenty years old, was due to inherit a considerable sum on her twenty-first birthday, but Jesse was too impatient and greedy to wait. Connelley wrote that "by making a very full and sweeping relinquishment [Jesse] secured this money from the bank in which it had been deposited, and which, it was affirmed, belonged in part to Seth Lane and his son. When his wife had attained her majority he endeavored to collect the money again, alleging that the bank had no legal right to pay the money at the time it had been paid."

He invested Mary's entire fortune in a grocery business in Williamsport, Maryland. It quickly failed, and the money was lost. Jesse, undefeated and unembarrassed, traveled to New York, where he posed as the son of a wealthy, highly reputable Virginia merchant. He purchased a large quantity of goods on credit and was in the process of having them shipped to himself at a Baltimore address when his creditors discovered that they were being swindled. They managed to stop one shipment and retrieve some of their goods, but Jesse had already disposed of the remainder "in a way which baffled all attempts to trace it." He tried to avoid the legal consequences by declaring bankruptcy; however, he was thrown into a Maryland jail on fraud charges. For reasons that are no longer clear, his innocent wife was incarcerated with him. He put his time behind bars to good use: He read law under the supervision of a leading western Maryland attorney named William Price, and after only six months was able to win an acquittal for himself and freedom for Mary.

The couple traveled to St. Louis, Missouri, where Jesse was again jailed. Mary, who was still devoted to him, worked frantically to secure his release. They boarded a boat for Cincinnati, but before they could reach the city, Jesse had perpetrated a fraud on some fellow passengers.

However, the misdeed was uncovered so quickly that Jesse had not had time to squander or hide his ill-gotten gains; since no harm had been done, he was allowed to go free.

He seems to have made his way from Cincinnati to New Orleans without committing a crime—or perhaps just this once he managed to avoid detection—but as soon as he was settled in the Crescent City he gave himself over to riotous living and dissipation. He first neglected and then abused his wife. This was too much even for her: She became disheartened and fell ill.

Her sudden decline scared him, and for a brief time he played the doting husband, booking passage for both of them on a Mississippi steamboat with the intention of taking her back to Hagerstown. Hardly had the vessel gotten under way, however, than he was up to his old tricks, this time committing a forgery against a bank in Cincinnati. He was held behind bars in that city for seven months before Mary, rallying to deal with the crisis, was finally able to raise the substantial bail. He expressed his gratitude for her herculean efforts and her long-suffering devotion by disappearing, in the process deserting her and causing her to forfeit the bail money.

While she wrung her hands in Cincinnati, he made his way back home, where, in that tiresome way of his, he committed another forgery and somehow escaped conviction. He slipped across the Mason-Dixon line, which was a mistake because Pennsylvania judges turned out to take a dim view of scoundrels: He served three years in the penitentiary for forgery.

Mary returned to Maryland, no doubt by pleading with wary relatives for the fare. Scalded and wise at last, she arranged for a divorce. (Apparently because state laws were severe and her husband absent, she found it necessary to get a bill passed in the Maryland legislature that granted her her freedom.) When Jesse learned of the action, he paced his cell, raging and savagely threatening her life. Yet upon his release he was at least temporarily distracted from thoughts of revenge by the cheering discovery of another trusting, domestic victim—a Pennsylvania woman, whom he quickly made his bride. In short order she was visiting her new husband in the hoosegow, where he was slated to spend seven years.

Mary found another spouse, too. The proprietor of the United States Hotel in Cumberland, Maryland, he is identified only as A. Cowton. Years rolled by, and one hopes that Mary found in her second marriage some joy and peace. On March 5, 1849, a servant led a stranger to Mary's apartments. Entering the room where she stood, the stranger, keeping his face averted, dismissed the servant and then suddenly slammed and bolted the door. When he turned, Mary was horrified to see it was Jesse and that "there was murder in his looks." She shrieked frantically as he announced that her hour had come and then stalked across the room and seized her by the throat. He threw her to the floor, placed a knee on her breast, and shoved a pistol in her face. It misfired, and he was just drawing out a long dagger when neighbors, alerted by her screams, broke down the door and dragged him off her. He was sentenced to a long prison term.

"He must have possessed a fascinating personality," Connelley suggested, "for he soon obtained an unaccountable influence over the prison officials and was allowed considerable freedom, even acting as a guard over other prisoners." After just three years Maryland authorities granted him a pardon—but only on the condition that he leave the state forever.

He went to Dover, where his brother had become an important man in the community, and found that his father, the sharp horse trader, was also ensconced there. For a time Jesse made money as a jockey, and he and the old man worked a confidence game. According to Connelley, they bought horses and scored their tails

> on the under side and then tied [them] up in an elevated position to heal, usually suspended for a time from an over-head beam. This was a cruel process, resorted to for the purpose of causing the horse's tail when healed to stand away from the body, giving it a graceful carriage, greatly improving the general appearance of the animal.

The value of the horses having thus been artificially inflated, they were shipped to unsuspecting buyers in the East.

Eventually, Jesse slipped away to look for fresh victims. Sometimes he said his last name was Elliott; at other times he introduced himself as Dr. Hayne. It is known that over the course of his confidence career he married and abandoned six women. "He traveled through the Southern States," wrote John W. Harmon, a traveling salesman from Dover who kept coming across his tracks, "locating in some city where he could engage himself to the Belle of the place and buy all the jewelry, watches, carriages, etc., he could get credit for and just about the time the bills would come due, would skip to some other place and go through the same performance." For many years after, rumors would drift back to Dover telling of Jesse's latest swindle, his latest imprisonment. (Once an exasperated judge gave him twenty years.) "He [has] been in about every Penitentiary in Penn., Maryland, Virginia & Kentucky and Perhaps Ohio," wrote Harmon V. Beeson to a putative Quantrill biographer. No doubt the list is conservative and incomplete.*

———•◆•———

Dover was a bustling little town, which had been established by tavern owners and the operators of a salt mine only thirty years before William Quantrill's birth. It had recently become prosperous as the result of the building of the Ohio & Erie Canal, which greatly raised the prices farmers could get for their crops and livestock and reduced the cost of shipping locally made goods.

William, whose boyhood nickname was "Will," had a round face, a high forehead, and a slender build. He was a sturdy youngster, although he suffered from a number of maladies, including a rupture and chronic throat problems. (His family feared that he would develop consumption, from which his father suffered and which eventually killed him.)

* Not everyone in Quantrill's family was of dubious character. Some historians argue that it was an aunt by marriage, Mary A. (née Sands) Quantrill, whose insistence upon displaying Old Glory despite the threats of Confederate General Stonewall Jackson's men, inspired the creation of John Greenleaf Whittier's famous poem, "Barbara Frietchie." According to this version of events, Fritchie—Whittier altered the spelling of her name—"a decrepit and bed-ridden lady of Frederick [was] given the honor for something she did not do." No one doubts Fritchie's loyalty to the North—she certainly "would have waved her flag in the face of General Jackson himself if she had been given the opportunity"—merely her locale. Her house on the banks of Carroll Creek was well outside the rebel troops' line of march. Mary Quantrill and her daughter, Virginia, stood at their gate waving Union flags. Twice a lieutenant used his sword to cut flags from Virginia's hands, which made her mother wave a larger flag all the more vigorously, winning the applause of the boys in gray and the grudging respect of their officers.

In his introduction to his poem, Whittier describes Fritchie's supposed deed but explains that he had heard about it secondhand, adding that "May [sic] Quantrill, a brave and loyal lady in another part of the city, did wave her flag in the sight of the Confederates. It is possible that there has been a blending of the two incidents."

During the last decades of the nineteenth century a number of correspondents from newspapers all across the country made their way to Dover, attempting to shed light on Quantrill's life, and they interviewed neighbors and other townsfolk. The resulting articles described Quantrill as a "light-hearted," "remarkably bright boy," "fond of books and quick to learn," and although shy, "he had a ready smile and a warm heart and was never known to be quarrelsome." It was further reported that Quantrill was an honest child, even tempered and modest. He had a strong "inclination to avoid a conflict, but when forced to do battle he fought desperately with anything he could lay his hands upon." His shyness caused him to prefer to walk alone in the woods rather than play with other boys. He loved to hunt and became an expert marksman early in life. He also learned to "throw stones with much force and velocity and with unerring accuracy."

Connelley had all of these articles in his files when he wrote *Quantrill and the Border Wars,* but he chose to ignore their uniform depiction of Quantrill as a decent, normal boy and instead presented a very different, very dark picture. Connelley claimed that Quantrill loved to bring small snakes to school in his pockets and then throw them on his sister and the other girls, laughing "heartily at their terror." He once painted a cow red, and the animal succumbed before the paint could be removed. He "would often nail a snake to a tree and let it remain there in torture until it died." He entertained himself by catching hapless cats, tying the tails of two of them together, and then slinging them over a fence rail so that, suspended and panicked, they would bite and claw each other until both bled to death. Finally, Connelley alleged that Quantrill was inclined, while strolling down a country lane, to pull out a knife and casually stab a cow or a horse (a particularly vicious bit of vandalism to people living in a rural area with an agricultural economy).

Connelley's sole source for these disturbing accusations was Harmon V. Beeson, whom Thomas Henry Quantrill had tried to kill. Furthermore, as will be seen shortly, Beeson also came into conflict with young William Clarke Quantrill—this time Beeson was at fault—resulting in lasting bitterness between the two men. Thus, rather than believe a variety of reliable sources with a uniformly positive view of Quantrill, Connelley chose a single, highly biased source who confirmed his own severe prejudice.

There is only one allegation to which one must give any credence, and this because of the identity of the source: William Walter Scott, a Dover newspaperman who had been Quantrill's boyhood friend and a lifelong benefactor of his mother. Over the course of twenty-five years Scott devoted much time, money, and energy to researching Quantrill's life. Scott had served in the Union army, and his association with the family did not blind him to the violence and mayhem of Quantrill's wartime exploits; indeed, he came to have a very dark view of his old friend. "There was nothing about him to indicate his subsequent career," wrote Scott in an article for the Joplin, Missouri, *Morning Herald,* "except that he would occasionally shoot a pig through the tip of the ear to make it run and squeal, and then would laugh immoderately at its antics. Such things in illiterate persons might be attributed to thoughtlessness; but in a young man of his intelligence it looked like a vein of cruelty."

Mr. Scott, a nineteenth-century, cultivated gentleman, may have been a bit harsh in his judgment. Many an intelligent, normal farm boy has taken mean delight in making pigs run frantically. Scott himself asserted that "in no other way did [Quantrill] ever exhibit an evil disposition. He was strictly temperate and honest."

At the age of sixteen Quantrill graduated from high school and secured a position teaching lower grades at the Dover school. Midway through the following term, on December 7, 1854, Quantrill's father died of consumption. The two did not get along, at least in part because William, even as a teenager, had often been beaten by his father, sometimes, most humiliatingly, in public. So the elder Quantrill's demise may not have been a terrible blow for his son. It did have the effect, however, of drawing William and his mother still closer together. Since he was the eldest son, he had always been her favorite, and now she came positively to dote on him.

Caroline Quantrill had brown hair and a strong jaw, and in her youth she was exceptionally pretty. She was short, slim, and quite graceful. She has been described as being a very good housewife and mother, and she was fiercely devoted to her children. Beyond these traits, little is known about her personality in her youth, except the idle remark of an acquaintance that "she was of a solitary turn, of a brooding disposition, never going to visit her neighbors, but sometimes attending the Presbyterian church." Such nonconformity was noticed in nineteenth-century rural America.

Mrs. Quantrill had little education, and with her husband dead, she had no means of supporting herself and her children except to turn her home into a boardinghouse and have her daughter, Mary, take in sewing. Quantrill was deeply embarrassed that his mother and sister, who suffered from curvature of the spine, should be forced into such demeaning straits. At the end of the term he took another teaching position in a nearby country school. However, the vocation was not lucrative no matter where practiced, and the following summer he accompanied a Dover family on their move out West, seeking to make his fortune and rescue his family from their distress.

The plains of Illinois—immense, flat, and covered with tall grass—astonished him. Wherever the train stopped, hawkers sold ripe peaches to the passengers; since he dreamed of buying a farm and bringing his family out to be with him, he was dismayed that the soil did not seem to support other kinds of fruit. Still, corn, potatoes, and cabbages grew in abundance. As soon as he arrived in Mendota, on August 8, 1855, he hurried a letter off to his mother. "I have $6 of my money left," he told her, "& maybe the next time I write I will send a little along. I am about 600 miles from home." Until he could raise the money to buy a farm, he would have to return to his former occupation: "There are two schools here [and] probably I can get one of them."

Before long he wrote to her with the first of his money schemes. He had heard that men who had fought for Texas's independence from Mexico were entitled to land grants, and he wondered if any of his father's brothers were veterans of the conflict. If so, he could sell the land and use the money to buy a farm. Could his mother find papers proving that a Quantrill had served in the Texas army? She could not.

On September 18, he wrote again, this time asking for copies of his father's tract, the "Tinman's Guide."

you must be sure to send me those tinner books all of them as soon as you can for those six that I brought with me I sold in one town & could have sold more if I had them for $2.00 a piece which just paid my board. be sure & send them for I can sell 50 in Chicago there are so many tin shops there. If you send them I can send you some money in a week I have only $8 dollars now. As soon as you send them books in a week I will send you $20 certain. be sure [to] send them by express You had better try to borrow a little money of Dr. Brashear or Dr. Winnul until I can get those books. for you know I wont get my pay for teaching only every three months. I get $25 a month & boarded.

He still could not give up the idea that his family might have a right to land in Texas—he already had a buyer lined up. He asked his mother to contact his grandfather, who had moved away from Dover, to see if he knew anything about relatives who might have fought against Mexico. Poverty and desperation were bringing the manipulative side of Quantrill's nature to the fore: "I would like to have those texas papers very much. You had better write to Grandfather & ask him if he has got them & tell him I can do well with them. And I would ask him to help me a little. I think I shall write to him for I guess he dont know I am out here."

At the beginning of October, he was still able to muster excitement at the prospects of owning Illinois land. He wrote to a friend of his, Edward T. Kellam, that "this is the country for farming, it beats Ohio all to pieces. A man can raise a crop of corn & wheat in one year that will pay for the farm & all the expenses of fencing & ploughing. You had better come out here & buy a farm you cant do better I know." At the same time, struggling against spirit-sapping poverty, he admitted—though he tried to put the best face on it—that he had been forced to become a "pot-hunter," feeding himself on what he could shoot and supplementing his meager wages besides. "This too is the country for hunting & it pays well," he told Kellam.

> Here a man that understands the business can shoot from 50 to 60 prairie chickens every day & get $1.50 per dozen [for] all he can shoot. There is a place 16 miles from here called inlet pond, where there are thousands of ducks and geese. I was up last Saturday & I killed 2 geese and 11 ducks, but the fellow that was with me killed 9 geese and 32 ducks. we got 50 cts apiece for the geese & 25 cts for the ducks. If you was here we could go every day.

Six weeks later, with winter closing in and the prospects for filling his belly with game declining, Quantrill was forced to face up to his failure. "I am tired of the west already," he admitted to his mother in a letter dated November 17, "and I do not think I shall stay in it very much longer than I can help; I must stay as long as my school lasts & that is all." He was still hoping to make some money, which he promised to send her express.

> You may expect me home early in the spring, for I was a dunce to go away for I could have done just as well at home as out here & the[n] I would have been at home. I have learned one good lesson that I would never have learned at home & when I get there again (which will not be long) I will turn over a new leaf entirely You said the children had the ague [fever]; you must try [and] cure them if possible & this is the last winter you will ever have to keep boarders if I keep my health. I feel that I have done wrong in going from home & hope you will forgive me for it.

Not long after this letter was written, rumors reached Dover that Quantrill, while at work as a bookkeeper for a lumberyard to earn extra money, had killed a man. One version had it that he was attacked while dozing in the office by a man who intended to rob him; another version said simply that Quantrill had been discovered in the yard behind a woodpile, standing over a dead man, a smoking pistol in his hand. Either way, the authorities held him for a time. Since no evidence was found contradicting his claim of self-defense, he was released.

Although the school year was far from over, Quantrill quickly left Mendota. He surfaced three months later in Fort Wayne, Indiana, where he wrote his mother another chagrined letter on February 21, 1856.

> I suppose you thought I was dead but not so, for I had and still continue to have, better health than I ever had at home. I suppose that you think that something has happened to me, and you think right; for if it had not been so you would have heard from me before this. I think I will not tell you in this letter what it was as this is the first one I have wrote you since it happened. The last letter I wrote you was then. You will not think so hard of me when you know it all. I hope you will forgive me then for not writing.
>
>   I am now in Indiana near Fort Wayne teaching a school, and a very good one I have. I have from 35 to 40 schollars every day. I have got in a good neighborhood, and they say I am the best teacher they ever had. I get 20 dollars a month and boarded. I took up school for three months and my time is half out now.
>
>   Well Mother I have concluded to come home in the spring when school is out if you are willing, not that I have not fared so well since I

left, because I have good clothes, and I have not had to miss one meals victuals. But this is the reason why I think of coming home, it is because I can make just as much money there as any place else, and save a great deal more, and also I think I done wrong in going from home and leaving you by yourself, and let you earn your own living. I have earned enough if I had been at home to keep us all comfortably So in the spring I will come home not to seek an asylum, but rather to make one. I suppose if Grandfather is there he has scolded me completely but when he knows all he will think different.

One thing I will tell you this trip I have had has done me more good and I have learned more than I would in three years steady schooling. What I have learned will be of more benefit to me than any thing I now know of I would be willing to stay away another year, if it was not for you and the children, if I thought I could be benefited as much as I have been the few months I have been gone. I have been studying book keeping this winter and I think I will try that in the spring if I am spared that long. I think I can make more money at it, and it will be better for my health.

It has been very cold here. two weeks ago the snow in the woods is about 30 inches deep and it bids fair to be still deeper. Two weeks ago last Tuesday the thermometer stood at 30 degrees below zero at day break and at noon was 19 degrees below. both Tuesday and Wednesday it was the same and for five days it did not go above zero. I suppose it has not been so cold there. There was one man here had 160 head of sheep froze in one night and most every body had their pigs and calves froze, and people have had their toes froze so bad that they think they will drop off. among the rest I had my toes and ears froze but not very bad. Every body here most has got the ague, and a great many have died with the typhoid fever. This country is a low flat swampy unhealthy place, and covered with very heavy timber, more than in Ohio. Almost every body lives in log houses and to take it all around I would not advise any one to buy a farm in the state, for really I would hardly live here one year for a good farm. almost every body here wants to sell out and leave the country.

I would just as soon be at home as any place else for a while. I suppose the furnace has been going all winter and Dover is a little more lively than it was. I suppose some of the boys have got situations in it by this time. Well mother I am tedious I suppose with such a long letter. Give my respects to all my friends & especially the boys & tell them I will write soon. Tell them I am well and doing well. The next time I will tell you all about what has happened. But I want you to never tell any body else whoever it may be for my sake.

I still remain yours Respectfully

Your Son
William Quantrill

Despite his homesickness, Quantrill lingered in Fort Wayne into July, going to summer school and studying chemistry, physiology, Latin, and plane trigonometry. He wrote his mother that he would probably remain in the area for another year and teach, but shortly after she received that letter, he turned up in Dover.

He secured a teaching post in the Blicktown district, south of Dover. "The venture into the world in quest of wealth and success had failed," observed Dr. Castel. "His mother still took [in] boarders, his sister continued to sew other people's clothes, [and] they all remained poor. As bleak winter days passed, he sat in his little backwoods schoolhouse bored and restless, and filled with a spirit of longing."

He fled before the term was over, leaving behind family, friends, and unpaid bills. He headed for Kansas. The situation on the border was still simmering, and Quantrill, accidentally stumbling into the conflict rather than drawn to it, would nevertheless eventually take his place at its very center.

He would never see home again.

CHAPTER 3

"Hard & Scaly Times": Quantrill's Western Travels

Quantrill's mother had arranged his escape by asking Harmon Beeson and another Dover man, Henry Torrey, to take him with them to Kansas. (The fourth member of the party was Beeson's son, Richard.) Beeson and Torrey agreed to pay Quantrill's way to the territory, buy a claim on his behalf, and hold it until he was twenty-one; he would pay off his debt by working for them.

On February 26, 1857, Quantrill and the Beesons boarded an Ohio River steamboat and embarked for St. Louis, while Torrey, who was deeply in debt, detoured to New York first in order to collect some money that was owed him. The boat was so overcrowded with Kansas-bound settlers—and the troops assigned to protect them from Southern sympathizers—that many men were forced to sleep on the deck, and Quantrill was not able to find the privacy even to change his clothes. His poverty so oppressed him that every time the boat docked, he rushed ashore to hawk copies of his father's tinsmithing book. Sales were slow: He still had a number left when he reached the territory.

By prior arrangement Torrey joined the other Dover emigrants in St. Louis, and together they proceeded across the state by Missouri River steamboat to Independence, where they disembarked on March 15. They purchased two teams of oxen and supplies, including bacon, flour, beans, and salt, then set off on a southwesterly course. After a week of rough travel they arrived on the banks of the Marais des Cygnes River in Franklin County, Kansas. The country was very promising for farming: The land was flat and the soil rich; timber was plentiful, and sweet grass grew long for the grazing animals. Torrey and Beeson each spent $500 to purchase a claim from a resident squatter, and each put up $250 to buy a claim for Quantrill.

The four men lived in a cabin on Torrey's farm, hanging their boots, guns, skillets, side meat, and surveying chains on the walls. They built crude tables and chairs and worked hard clearing land and rolling logs, plowing and planting potatoes and corn. Quantrill frequently went hunting in the woods to put squirrel meat into the communal pot. "The only job that we have to do that we all dislike," he informed his mother, "is dishwashing. . . . We have to take turn[s] at it; no one will do it more than twice in succession."

In this letter, dated May 16, 1857, Quantrill urged his mother to sell the Dover house and send him part of the money so he could buy a farm and

> then we will all be square with the world & able to say our soul is our own without being contradicted. Is this not worth sacrificing something for? I think it is and so will you, I know. If we cannot do this I will not stay here longer than fall, for I can make more money in the States at teaching than by hard work here. I am here now as an agent to get a home for us all, which I can do if there is not too much opposition. I have thought over the matter. . . . Do not let anybody persuade you out of this until they produce better grounds for not doing as I have said than I have for doing so. It is the best we can do, and everybody will say so who reasons the case well.

The fact that Quantrill was still determined to buy a farm despite knowing that Torrey and Beeson had bought a claim on his behalf suggests that he may have already begun to harbor suspicions that he would never get the land. Sometime after he wrote this letter Quantrill had a falling out with the two men. (He later charged that they had "euchred" him.) A. T. Andreas, in his 1883 *History of the State of Kansas,* wrote that Quantrill decided to sell the claim, but "as he and Mr. Torrey could not agree as to what was rightly due Quantrell, the matter was submitted to a 'squatter's court' for arbitration." This court, composed of respectable settlers, ruled in Quantrill's favor and decreed that he should receive $63.00 in two installments of $33.00 and $30.00.

Torrey may have owed Beeson money, because they mutually agreed that Torrey would make both payments. However, $63 was no small sum of money in Kansas Territory, and Torrey was in debt to various creditors. When he failed to make the first payment, Quantrill, egged on by John Bennings, a secret Southern-sympathizer with whom he was now staying, stole a yoke of oxen from Beeson and a brace of revolvers and several blankets from Torrey.

A few days later, Beeson encountered Quantrill, put a gun to his head, and forced him to show where the oxen were hidden.

Quantrill returned Torrey's pistols but not the blankets, which were eventually found rotten in a hollow log. So far as is known, he was paid only half what the squatter's court had awarded. The breech between Quantrill and Beeson never healed; however, Quantrill remained on good terms with Torrey, who allowed him to stay in his cabin whenever he wished. Long after Quantrill died, Beeson and his family would continue to disparage him, while Torrey and his family remained among the staunchest defenders of his reputation.

Beeson returned to Ohio late in the summer of 1857 in order to move his family out to his claim, and he painted for friends and neighbors such a rosy picture of life in the territory that a number of ambitious or discontented young men were soon on their way there. Some of them bought adjoining claims in Johnson County and built a communal cabin on one of them. They called their little settlement Tuscarora Lake.

Quantrill moved in with them, and on January 22, 1858, he wrote a letter to a Dover friend in which he showed he still had a very Northern point of view: He called the proposed Lecompton Constitution that would make Kansas a slave state a "swindle" and said Jim Lane was "as good a man as we have here." He reported that free-staters had recently killed two Missouri Southerners "in self defense" and regretted that they had not killed many more: "The democrats here are the worst men we have for they are all rascals, for no one can be a democrat here without being one; but the day of their death is fast approaching & they will be like the jews scattered to the four winds of the earth. . . ."

After this rare political outburst, he turned to more mundane subjects, talking of farms and weather and his hunting prowess, before he closed with the sort of crass ruminations all too typical of immature twenty-year-old males.

About the girls I cannot say much but . . . this is certain a man can have his choice for we have all kinds & colors here Black White & Red But to tell you which I like the best is a mixture of the two latter colors if properly brought up for they are both rich and good looking & I think go ahead of your Dover gals far enough. Em Walton would pass very well for a squaw if she was better looking but I think from present appearances John Diehl will squaw her about next fall or winter & that will bleach her a little probably. When you write tell me all about the girls & especially yours & my fair one that used to be in years past, if she is still around yet. You and the rest of the boys there must attend to the girls well while we are here in Kansas & tell them we are all going to marry squaws & when they die we are coming to old Dover for our second wives so that they must not despair.

Connelley alleged that Quantrill stole from the boys at Tuscarora Lake and sold the goods—blankets, provisions, and firearms—to some nearby settlers. After his friends caught him red-handed, they "were so disgusted with him that they forced him to leave the camp," but they did not otherwise punish him "because of his mother and his having grown up with them."

According to Connelley, Quantrill disappeared for several weeks and then showed up at Bennings's cabin. However, word of his petty crimes had gotten around, and he found that everyone distrusted him and watched him closely. He soon left the area and made his way to Fort Leavenworth.

Connelley's book is heavily footnoted, but he did not identify the source for these allegations. He was in contact with the Beesons and other people who knew Quantrill during the prewar period and pre-sumably heard the story from one of them. But, given his lapses of judg-ment in evaluating the reliability of sources, it is hard to know how seriously to take this story without being able to evaluate its origins.

It is true, however, that Quantrill showed up at Fort Leavenworth, where he was hired by an army contractor to be a cattle driver on a drive to Fort Laramie. Quantrill sported a bright red woolen shirt, which was the subject of considerable jocularity for his fellow cowboys.

After he returned to Fort Leavenworth, he hired on as a teamster on a Utah-bound expedition to resupply the command of Brigadier General Albert Sidney Johnston. (For some reason Quantrill used an alias—Charley Hart.) Government agents had been forced by the press of time to recruit teamsters rather hurriedly and had done so by posting notices in the saloons of Leavenworth. Consequently, the group of men who signed up soon came to be notorious for their gambling, drunkenness, violence, and riotous behavior. Many of these men were recently transplanted hot-headed Southerners who had come to Kansas to fight the abolitionists, and Quantrill spent a great deal of time in their company. Several would become lifelong friends and would be members of his band. In one of the first letters he wrote to his mother after he returned to Kansas from Utah, he railed against abolitionists and free-soil proponents. Thus in the space of less than two years—including the many months he spent among Southern teamsters—Quantrill underwent a radical conversion, doing a 180-degree turn on the crucial issues of his day. It seems likely that the Southern teamsters converted him to their point of view, or at least had a profound impact on his thinking. Therefore, although Quantrill's part in the "Mormon War" was small, it is appropriate to digress briefly on this obscure but fascinating moment in U.S. history.

The Mormon War, sometimes called America's first Civil War, was an extremely expensive exercise that resulted in much misery on both sides but few casualties. It was the culmination of a long-standing mutual animosity between Americans and members of what they perceived as a peculiar sect. The Saints had been driven continually westward by violence and government persecution, from their original home in New York State to Ohio and then to Missouri and Illinois, where Joseph Smith was besieged in his Carthage jail cell by a mob and, after he leaped out of a twenty-five-foot-high window in an effort to escape, was riddled with bullets.

The new prophet, Brigham Young, led his flock to Utah Territory, but distance did not end the mutual suspicion and hostility. Americans, suffering a feverish nativism that caused them to suspect Irish Catholics of wanting to hand the country over to the pope, were just as certain that Mormons were conspiring to seize control of the federal government and install Young as the head of a "despotic theocracy." The Saints were said to have formed a secret society of assassins to undermine social order by murdering judges and elected officials, as well as the church's critics and other nonbelievers. The Saints were perceived as arrogant and stupid; xenophobics noted that many new converts were arriving from Europe as penniless immigrants. The Mormons' sympathetic treatment of Indians, who their theology taught were their brothers and the "fallen people of the Book of Mormons," infuriated many Westerners, who charged them with inciting Indian attacks against whites. Southerners felt threatened by Saints' abolitionism, while Northerners saw in the issue of their disregard of federal authority a precedent that was exceedingly dangerous if applied to the South.

Perhaps the greatest cause of friction was the Mormon doctrine of polygamy, which deeply offended many Americans, who thought of it as "barbaric," a kind of white slavery "forced upon defenseless women by debauched priests." Male "Gentiles," as Mormons referred to nonbelievers, who returned from a visit to Utah indulged in the popular pastime of estimating how many wives Brigham Young had (those with the most overactive libidos put the number at sixty or more), while female Gentiles reported with alarm that Mormon women universally had chalky, tearstained faces and sunken eyes, the result of the marital torments they endured. Polygamy produced not sensuality but "bestial behavior, with men marrying women and their daughters at the same time, sleeping with several wives in the same bed," and indulging in "dark acts" of "oriental" degeneracy. "We are unquestionably in the midst of fanatics, who are controlled by a gang of licentious villains," an envoy's wife wrote from Salt Lake City.

Americans could not imagine that women would be contented with polygamy and were equally certain that many sensible men chafed under the tyrannical Brigham Young, that "inspired prophet of Hell" with his many "harlots around him, polluting the very atmosphere in which he lives." When the troops finally crossed into Utah to reestablish the federal government's authority over the territory, it was thought that they would be greeted as liberators by tens of thousands of wildly cheering Saints. (In fact, only 5 percent of Mormon marriages were polygamous, and when the army finally gained control of the valley of the Great Salt Lake, fewer than two hundred people asked to be sent East—and their motivation for leaving was chiefly economic.)

In May 1857, President James Buchanan declared the Utah Territory to be "in a state of rebellion against the laws and authority of the United States," but indecision and ineptitude on the part of government bureaucrats delayed the dispatching of troops from Fort Leavenworth until July 18, which was dangerously late for an expedition that would be crossing the Rockies. The soldiers endured long marches, snowstorms, and bitter cold. They wintered within the charred stone walls of Fort Bridger, in what is now southwestern Wyoming, the fort itself having been burned by Mormon cavalry to deny them fortifications. They patched their clothes as best they could and chopped firewood. Those who had money bought dog meat from the Indians, who claimed it was mountain sheep, while those who were broke subsisted largely on turnips and thin broth.

Teamsters opened gambling dens, where soldiers were often cheated and those who complained savagely beaten. A more wholesome entertainment was provided by some artistic types who built a theater and staged plays; others sewed five tents together to make a ballroom and held dances on special occasions such as Christmas and New Year's Eve. Everyone harbored a murderous resentment of the Saints.

In Salt Lake City, Brigham Young gave heart to his followers by blustering and threatening the extermination of Federal troops, but behind the scenes he maneuvered, seeking a face-saving compromise. When he was slow to find one and warm weather arrived, he ordered the evacuation of the city's populace—thirty thousand men, women, and children—to a treeless expanse west of Provo, where they suffered the heat in makeshift huts, tents, or even burrows they dug in the ground.

The first resupply train reached Fort Bridger in early June 1858. The Washington bureaucrats, finally having overcome their inertia, sent more reinforcements and supplies, so that by midsummer Johnston had four thousand men and enough supplies to carry on a large-scale war, but he never got to unsheath his saber. Reports of the suffering of the ragged Mormons in their hovels elicited sympathy from the American public, and the staggering cost of the campaign (more than $15 million) sobered editorial writers and Buchanan administration officials, who found themselves distracted by the effects of the financial panic of 1857 and the insoluble problems in Kansas. They dispatched a civilian peace commission, and Brigham Young, after a great deal of posturing, surrendered. "The whole story of the war is crowded by as much ignorance, stupidity and dishonesty, as any Government ever managed to get into the annals of a single year," wrote the disgusted editor of *The New York Times*.

Johnston marched a contingent of his troops through the deserted streets of Salt Lake City on June 26. The only sounds they heard were the eerie echo of their own footfalls and the ribald tune the band played when they passed Brigham Young's house. Thirty thousand ragged, filthy, and disheartened Saints returned home soon afterward. By then Johnston, knowing his soldiers' unforgiving attitude toward the populace, had established a camp strategically located forty-five miles to the south, which was far enough away to prevent reprisals or clashes.

While amateur thespians were organizing the "Military Dramatic Association" and performing plays with female leads imported from Salt Lake City, the ever rowdy and enterprising teamsters threw together "Frogtown," a collection of shanty saloons and gambling tents convenient to the camp.

It is usually said that Quantrill was among the original teamsters who accompanied the forward elements of the expedition to Utah and wintered at Fort Bridger, but in the summer of 1857, he was still in Kansas. In fact, he came out a year later. Although exactly when the supply train he signed on with left Kansas is not known, it was caught in a sudden blizzard in western Wyoming's South Pass on September 3, 1858. "It snowed hard all day," he subsequently told his mother in a letter, "and froze ice from an inch to two inches thick in our buckets for a week afterwards." Quantrill would have probably arrived at Fort Bridger in middle or late September.

An ex-cavalryman named R. M. Peck saw him there, and Quantrill made a lasting impression on him. One day, Peck, who had just arrived as part of a cavalry escort for a supply train, walked into a huge tent that had been set up near the sutler store and was being used as a casino. The soldiers had just been paid, and a few "sharpers" were proceeding to relieve them of their money. Peck heard someone call out the name of Charley Hart and turned to get a good look at the man who was already the talk of the camp because of his "reckless betting and phenomenal winnings." Peck was not impressed. "I could see nothing heroic in his appearance, but considerable of the rowdy, as I now recall the impression I then got of him," he wrote in 1907. "He was apparently about twenty-two or twenty-three years of age; about five feet ten inches in height; with an ungraceful, slouchy walk; and by no means prepossessing in features."

He advertised his status as a "wild plunger in gambling" by sporting fancy duds: He wore a decorative blue flannel shirt and had tucked his trouser cuffs into a pair of high-heeled calfskin boots; a brightly colored silk handkerchief was tied around his neck and a Navy pistol banged against his hip; his long hair hung to his shoulders General Custer–style, and perched on his head was the "inevitable cow-boy hat."

When Peck first glimpsed him, Hart was working his way through the crowded tent carrying a large, knotted, colorful silk handkerchief in his left hand. He stopped at a table where a "banker" was dealing monte and put the handkerchief down and opened it, showing the contents to be gold coins, and seeming in bulk about equal to the stacks of gold coins tiered up on the table in front of the banker.

Hart then asked, "Take a tap, pard?" meaning would the banker accept a bet of Hart's pile against the dealer's, on a turn of a card. The banker accepted the challenge, shuffled the cards, passed the deck to Hart to cut, then threw out the "lay-out" of six cards, in a "column-of-twos" style. Hart then set his handkerchief of gold on a card, at the same time drawing his pistol, "Just to insure fair play," he remarked, seeing that the banker had his gun lying on the table convenient to his right hand. Keeping his eye on the banker's hands, to make sure that the deal was done "on the square," Hart said, "Now deal."

Turning the deck face up the banker drew the cards off successively. Hart's card won. As the dealer looked up with a muttered oath he found himself looking into the muzzle of Hart's pistol.

"Back out," said Hart quietly. "Don't even touch your pistol. I'll give it back to you when I rake in the pot."

The banker did as directed, while Hart, without showing any nervousness, still holding his pistol in one hand, reached across the table and with the other arm swept the banker's money and pistol over to him[self]. Picking out the twenties, tens, fives and two-and-a-half pieces, he tossed them into his handkerchief. There still remained on the table about a double handfull of small silver and a handfull of gold dollars. . . . Hart said, "I don't carry such chicken feed as that," as he tossed the small coins up in the air and let the crowd scramble for them.

Then handing the dejected looking banker his pistol and a twenty-dollar gold piece, he said: "There, pard, is a stake for you," and gathering up his plethoric handkerchief, he meandered on seeking new banks to "bust."

The next day Hart's "marvelous luck" deserted him, and he lost everything. For a time he hung around Fort Bridger, waiting for his luck to return, but after a few weeks, "discouraged and disgusted with gambling," he struck out for Salt Lake City.

There is definitely a dime-novel quality to the scene in the tent as Peck related it, and since he was recalling the incident a half-century later at the height of Quantrill's fame, Peck may have been guilty of some exaggeration. Still, the core of the anecdote seems believable enough. After all, Quantrill had been a crack shot since boyhood, and within a few years of that day in the tent he would be killing men with a Navy Colt. It is also true that Quantrill's grandfather, a professional gambler, lived in Dover for a time, so he might have whiled away more than a few winter evenings teaching his grandson the tricks of the trade.

The passing years undoubtedly also affected the accuracy of Peck's memory as to the date he saw Quantrill: Peck thought the incident had occurred in June 1858, although we know that Quantrill's confrontation with the dealer must have occurred in middle or late September.

Quantrill arrived in Salt Lake City on or about October 1, intending to winter there and in the spring work his way as a teamster to the Colville gold mines in western Canada.

He was at first greatly impressed with the Mormons. They were not the lazy libertines that their enemies and critics depicted them as being; in fact, he told his mother, "they are an industrious people and all hold to their religion in a manner which shows no hypocrisy, and I think their morals are as good as any people I have met in my travels."

His good cheer and optimism extended to his own prospects. His failure to realize his dreams was not at this moment daunting to him. He sought to reassure his mother that he was not a ne'er-do-well and would yet make a success of himself.

You need not expect me home till you see me there, but bear in mind that I will do what is right, take care of myself, try to make a fortune honestly, which I think I can do in a year or two. I will always let you know where I am & how I am doing & by the next mail I will send you my picture as I appeared in camp coming out here, and also a letter. I have given up long ago thinking my Grandfather will help me, & that is why I am here to make my fortune for the poorest laborer can command $40 per month & I think I can do more. I have not [missed] a meals victuals since I left Kansas, and I weighed when I came to the city 171 lbs., so you may not be afraid of my losing my health. I have got rid of that trouble in my throat. I am not thinking of getting married yet, although every man here has from 5 to 8 wives, & the rich have from 12 to 20 & Brigham has at present 43.

He sought temporary employment as a schoolteacher but came down with a severe case of "mountain fever." Kindly Saints nursed him, and, as he lay sweating and weary with the illness, he found himself once more intensely longing for home. But as he recovered he again resolved not to go back defeated, tail between his legs. If he could not make a vast fortune in the West, he would at least stay out there until he had a roll of cash, something to show for his travels.

He secured a position as an army quartermaster's clerk for $50 a month. Although the salary was inadequate in the inflated frontier economy, where everything cost twice what it did in Ohio, he was thrilled to have the job; however, it did not last long. He never explained what happened, only commented elliptically that his being fired "was all my own fault."

Penniless and hungry in the dead of winter, when work was scarce, he fretted and floundered before he eventually managed to hire on as a mess cook for twenty-five men. His letter to his mother dated January 9, 1859, shows that hard work and constant disappointment had considerably dampened his enthusiasm. He no longer trusted the Saints—or anybody else—and even his usual jokes about their polygamy had gone stale:

> I have a notion to marry 4 or 5 women here if I can for here is the only place I will ever have a chance I expect, the Mormons have from 3 to 8 on an average. They are a very ignorant set of people generally & generally great rogues & rascals thinking nothing to be to[o] bad to do a gentile as they call us & I must say that the gentiles are generally the same way.

Still, he did not want her to despair, and he rallied to make another one of his predictions of a bright future, although this one seemed a bit shopworn after his four-month sojourn in Utah: He was sure he would soon be able to put aside his pots and pans and get a government job; she should "not greeve any more than possible about me for I will surprise you some of these days which will be worth something dont fear."

Instead he surprised her by disappearing for seven months. He resurfaced in Lawrence, Kansas, on July 30, 1859. On that day he sent her a letter in which he explained that he had just been through "some pretty hard & scaly times."

Before he had been able to secure employment with Uncle Sam in Salt Lake City, word arrived of the Pikes Peak gold strike, and he set off for Colorado in a party of nineteen. Crossing the mountains they ran into bitterly cold weather and were soon out of supplies. Starving, they struggled on and were repeatedly attacked by Indians. Quantrill became snow-blind, and many men suffered from frostbite. Only seven of the original nineteen reached the diggings.

Pikes Peak turned out to be "undoubtedly *the* Humbug of all Humbugs," as far as he was concerned: The gold deposits were spread out over what seemed to be eight thousand square miles, and he broke his back digging for forty-seven days just to find $54.34 worth. The money hardly paid his living expenses.

Quantrill joined up with another, equally disgusted man, and they headed east toward Kansas. One day Quantrill was hunting a mile and a half from where they had camped on the Kansas plains, when he heard gunfire. He raced back and arrived in time to see Indians driving off their horses and

> my friend lying on the ground apparently dead but still breathing with difficulty having been shot three times, his leg broke below the knee [and] shot in the thigh with 7 slugs & last shot through the body with an arrow which I first thought would kill him but he lives yet & if taken care of properly will be as well as ever in 6 or 8 weeks.

Quantrill showed up in Lawrence so weather-beaten that he appeared much older than his years. He somehow made the acquaintance of some Indians who lived outside of town, and, on July 30, 1859, he wrote his mother that he was bound for Osawatomie, some thirty-five miles southeast of Lawrence, and pleaded with her not to lose faith in him: "I expect every body thinks and talks hard about [me] but I cannot help it now it will be all straight before another winter passes."

Quantrill's exact whereabouts and activities during the next two months are not certain, but in October he resumed his old occupation, teaching in a "rude log school-house" in Stanton Township, Lykins County (today Miami County), Kansas. It was a private school that charged $2.50 per student for a three-month term. He wrote letters to his family filled with reflection and longing.

Whenever he looked out his window at the vast fields of snow and heard the cold wind whistle through the trees, he thought of the disastrous trip to Pikes Peak. "One year ago," he told his sister Mary,

> I was amid snow and desolation in the Rocky Mountains, where nothing was to be seen but snow & sky; no signs of life except in our lit-

tle company. Some of us strove to be merry & occasionally would start some song, which would be broken off by someone calling for help to get some poor animal out of the snow. Or by the time one verse would be sung then [the singer's] merriment would be ended. But when night came and we were about to lie down to rest, and nothing but the snow to make a bed upon, it was enough to make any one have cool thoughts.

There was one night in particular when they had lost their way in the mountains, and a German, who had been acting as forward scout and had spent the day futilely looking for the trail, despaired. "Well, boys," he cried out, "my heart is almost broke . . . I think that we may all die here tonight." The others had laughed at him, but the laughter was hollow. After all, twelve men had died amid the craggy peaks.

When I have thought of it afterwards & could see what danger we had been exposed to [he wrote to his mother], I feel thankful for having got off as well as I did. But I have slipped through it all comparatively easy and I now begin to realize my situation, and see how much easier I have been dealt with than most of my traveling companions were, and I often think that there must have been something else for me to do, that I was spared; for my companions were all strong [and] healthy men & endured no more hardship than myself, still the greater part of them have seen their friends for the last time on this earth; all this has had a tendency to rouse me & let me see what I have been doing.

But what had he been doing? Nearly five years had gone by since he first left Dover for Illinois, and, although he had "seen a great many people and countries" and had enough adventures "to make a novel," he had nothing substantive to show for the passage of time. He was as poor as ever, still giving mulish youngsters the most rudimentary of educations. He realized what a terrible mistake it was for him to have left home and was determined to do "something noble" to make up for his wasted life. "I am done roving around seeking a fortune," he assured his mother, "for I found [that] it may be obtained being steady and industrious. And now that I have sown wild oats so long, I think it is time to begin harvesting; which will only be accomplished by putting in a different crop in a different soil."

In a letter to his mother dated January 26, 1860, Quantrill revealed the radical shift in his thinking that had taken place. Two years earlier he had been an admirer of Jim Lane and applauded the murder of Southerners, but no longer:

> You have undoubtedly heard of the wrongs committed in this territory by the southern people, or proslavery party, but when one once knows the facts they can easily see that it has been the opposite party that have been the main movers in the troubles & by far the most lawless set of people in the country. They all sympathize for old J. Brown, who should have been hung years ago, indeed hanging was too good for him. May I never see a more contemptible people than those who sympathize [with] him. A murderer and a robber, made a martyr of; just think of it.

Yet his newfound allegiance did not make him feel obligated to involve himself in the struggle. When he wrote to his mother on February 8, he informed her that

> There is no news here but hard times, and harder still coming, for I see their shadows; and "coming events cast their shadows before" is an old proverb. But I do not fear that my destiny is fixed in this country, nor do I wish to be compelled to stay in it any longer than possible, for the devil has got unlimited sway over this territory, and will hold it until we have a better set of men and society generally. The only cry is, "What is best for ourselves and our dear friends?"

Seven weeks later school was over, but instead of starting east for Ohio, he made his way again to Lawrence, some forty miles northwest of his school in Stanton Township. He stopped off at the Delaware reservation four miles west of town and renewed his friendship with several Indians with whom he had become acquainted after coming to Lawrence from Pikes Peak. He moved into the Mud Creek cabin of John Sarcoxie, the son of a chief.

Quantrill made frequent forays into Lawrence, and one day while headed for town on an Indian pony, he came upon a disreputable gang of loafers lounging at the north landing for the rope ferry across the Kansas River. They were border ruffians—much like the teamsters with whom he had traveled to Utah.

This casual encounter would change the course of his life. So often he had tried to make his fortune and had failed. Now he had made the acquaintance of men who shared at least superficially his recently acquired political convictions, and they knew how to make money from them.

Once years before, when he had still been living in the cabin on the Marais des Cygnes River—it must have seemed to him an eternity ago—Quantrill had gotten into a tussle with Harmon Beeson and been whipped. "You'll hear a-plenty about me one of these days!" he had sworn to the older man with teary defiance. Now he had accidentally happened on the means to make the prophecy come to pass.

———•◆•———

On June 23, he wrote to his mother for the last time. The letter itself is unremarkable—he mentions that he has sent money home twice recently and is worried because he has not heard that she received it; he talks about the weather and crops and his recent bout with fever; he promises to send more cash as soon as someone to whom he has loaned money pays him back; he writes of missing home and family and promises to return before the beginning of September—"by that time I will have done with Kansas." But there is a distance in his prose, a coolness and distinct lack of passion that is singular among his letters home, as if he is writing by rote now and no longer believes at all in what he has to say.

Hereafter he will fall into complete silence, and no one in Dover will ever hear from him again. Thus he will mysteriously and completely cut himself off from his former life, making himself in fact the orphan he sometimes pretended to be. Even as he lies paralyzed and dying in a military prison infirmary an easy ride by rail from Dover, he will maintain his cover, like some modern double agent, and long after his death, his mother will insist that she does not know what has become of him and will have to visit his grave and see his skull before acknowledging that the deceased, infamous guerrilla and her beloved, devoted son are one and the same.

CHAPTER 4

"Abolitionist and Extreme Pro-slavery Man": The Morgan Walker Raid

Quantrill continued to live in John Sarcoxie's cabin for a time, and he made visits to Lawrence, where he rented a room at the Whitney House and usually introduced himself as Charley Hart. (He gave his true name to only one or two respectable men whom he decided for reasons of his own to trust.) He said that he was a detective for the Delaware Nation.

Most often he could be found loitering with the rabble at the north ferry landing. As with other gangs of border ruffians, some of these men may have had a sincere allegiance to the causes of Southern rights and the preservation of slavery, but others used the border strife as a cover for criminal activity. To entertain themselves through the idle days, they wrestled and ran footraces, gambled, and passed the bottle around. They rustled stock, and occasionally they stole a slave and ransomed him back to his owner or kidnapped a free black in Kansas and sold him into slavery in Missouri.

Prominent among these men were the members of a recently transplanted Pennsylvania family, the McGees. There was Old Man McGee and his two sons, Tom and Jake, and their cousin, "a very hard character," said Connelley, "who, because of the marital calamity which befell him very frequently, was called 'Cuckold Tom' McGee." The other miscreants, who on any given day might be squatting in the dirt on the riverbank, dealing cards and bubbling the bottle, included Esau Sager, Jack Elliott, John Stropp, Jay Vince, Frank Baldwin, and Sidney S. Herd. The most notorious of the group was Jacob Herd. Connelley seemed almost to have a sneaking admiration for him: "He was known in every town on the border as being . . . a holy terror, violent, quick and deadly with a revolver, fearless and daring, and a man who would risk his life to capture a negro, either free or a runaway slave. . . . Herd was open, bold, loud of tongue, drunken, relying alone upon his force and courage for success. . . ."

In 1859 Jake Herd became locally famous when he intercepted a party of abolitionists and blacks who were making their way north on the Underground Railroad and delivered them to the jail in Platte City, Missouri. After the botched abductions of several free black residents of Lawrence, a town meeting had been called and sympathetic white citizens, realistically seeing no way to protect the black population, passed the hat to raise funds to resettle those willing to go to Iowa. Eight men, three women, and two children set out in two covered wagons escorted by a party of armed whites led by Dr. John Doy. After they had gone only twelve miles, they stumbled into an ambush set by Herd. He and the McGees wanted to kill all the whites and sell the blacks, but others in the band, fearing equally violent retribution, convinced Herd that everyone should be carried to Platte City.

——— •◦• ———

One day not long after Quantrill began associating with these border ruffians, a black man came out of the woods near the north ferry landing. Although young and strong, he was exhausted and terrified and obviously a fugitive. He asked Sidney Herd, who was working the ferry, for directions to James Lane's house, and Herd took him across the river, turning him over to Quantrill and Frank Baldwin. They led him to Jake McGee's cabin under the pretense of taking him to Lane; on the way they pointedly questioned him and found out that he was Ike Gaines, the property of the widow Joanna Gaines of Platte City. At the cabin he was tied up and, after dark, thrown across the back of a horse. Quantrill and Baldwin waited with him in the woods outside Platte City while McGee rode on to Mrs. Gaines's place to negotiate. The statutory reward for the return of a runaway was $200, but

McGee charged the widow $500. Sidney Herd got $100, and the other three men divided the rest.*

Quantrill pocketed his share of the loot and disappeared, riding into Lawrence three weeks later astride a brown racehorse with white legs. He had bought the sorrel, inevitably named White Stockings, near Paola, which was just west of the border, and rode him north to Westport (now part of Kansas City). He proposed to race him against Mulky Colt, a local runner renowned throughout the region. The owner, William Mulky, was a shrewd man and, reputedly, an excellent judge of horseflesh; Quantrill, employing a simple trick that would have made his grandfather proud, put a heavy, high-horned saddle on White Stockings and left him muddy and unbrushed. Mulky was so unimpressed with the animal, he wagered $150. Frank Baldwin rode White Stockings and easily defeated Mulky's horse.

Baldwin and Quantrill hung around Westport for several weeks, hoping to scare up more races. When other horsemen proved timid, Quantrill took White Stockings to southern Kansas and sold him to some Cherokee Indians.

Soon after Quantrill returned to Lawrence he began to associate with Captain John E. Stewart, "the Fighting Preacher," a notorious jayhawker second in reputation only to "Doc" Jennison and James Montgomery. Stewart had been a highly respected Methodist minister who, it was said, had preached "to good acceptance" for many years in Salem, New Hampshire. In the summer of 1860 he was living in a fort he had built in a stand of timber on the Wakarusa Creek, four miles south of

---

*All sources are biased, and it is a gross understatement to say that this is true of the sources for the Quantrill story. Throughout most of the book it is possible to balance sources against one another, compensating for their prejudice either in favor of or against Quantrill and his raiders. However, for the eight-month period spanning April through November 1860, the only available information about Quantrill comes from the recollections of Kansans, most of them Lawrencians. These include Samuel A. Riggs, the Douglas County prosecutor who had Quantrill indicted on several charges in the summer or fall of 1860 and who indicted him again after the Lawrence raid; Colonel Samuel Walker, the Douglas County sheriff, who tried to arrest Quantrill; Henry S. Clarke, whose furniture store was destroyed in the Lawrence raid, although he escaped harm; John Dean, an abolitionist whose relations with Quantrill will be set forth in the following pages; and Sidney Herd, who, though he consorted with border ruffians before the war and believed that only white people should be allowed to reside in Kansas, would later serve in the Union army. As biased as these men were, most were highly respected, and no one disputes that they knew Quantrill well. Their testimony cannot be ignored.

Lawrence. A friend and confederate of John Brown, he was a fierce abolitionist and was busily engaged in rescuing slaves and hiding them in his fort until he could transport them to safety.

His commitment to what he saw as a holy cause did not require that he take a vow of poverty, however, and in addition to liberating blacks, he was stealing horses and cattle in Missouri. However, his Kansas neighbors chose to ignore this venality: A nineteenth-century Lawrence newspaper editor remarked that Stewart's "burning zeal in behalf of the Free State cause and the freedom of the colored race caused his irregularities to be winked at . . . by those who became aware of them and his excesses to be excused."

The Missouri legislature was less tolerant and put a price on his head, which is what drew Quantrill to Stewart's fort. He hoped to accompany the preacher across the line on a raid or somehow lure him across and then turn him over to the authorities for the reward. Stewart trusted no one, including Quantrill, and would not go with him, but Quantrill learned a thing or two from the preacher: He stole horses and cattle in northeastern Kansas, drove them to Stewart's fort, and then sold them to people who did not ask too many questions. Quantrill, who had struggled for years to make his fortune through honest labor, had found that thievery paid much better. "One thing [is] certain," remarked Sidney Herd of Quantrill during this period in his life, "he was always willing to go into anything that had a dollar in it for Charley Hart."

On one occasion Quantrill and Walt Sinclair stole eighty head of cattle from some residents of Kickapoo, Kansas. These men trailed the rustled stock to the banks of the Kansas River just north of Lawrence. They enlisted the aid of Sam Walker, who had earlier that day seen Quantrill and Sinclair driving a herd across the river and heading them in the direction of Stewart's fort. When Walker and the others arrived at the fort, they found a corral holding seventy-eight of the animals; the other two had already been butchered and were being skinned. Covering for Quantrill, Stewart solemnly swore that some strangers had left the herd for temporary safekeeping and that he had paid for the two slaughtered cattle. The lie was transparent, but perhaps because the camp was well armed, Walker contented himself with seeing to it that the remaining animals were surrendered to their rightful owners.

Quantrill repaid Stewart's kindness in covering up for him by participating in a raid against the fort. Stewart was concealing a large number of slaves until "passage" could be arranged on the Underground Railroad, but some of the slaves' owners, hunting their lost property, arrived and enlisted the help of the north-ferry border ruffians, including Jake Herd and Quantrill. They approached the fort after dark and, with Quantrill hanging back so he would not be recognized, demanded the slaves be turned over to them. Stewart refused and passed out firearms to the blacks. The gunfight lasted throughout the night. At one point the attackers breached the defenses and managed to seize one slave before being driven back. They told themselves as they retreated in the morning that the remaining slaves must have all been so badly wounded as to now be worthless. This was comforting, but it was not true: Most or all of the other blacks took the next "train" to freedom.

------◆-◆------

At about the same time, Stewart and John M. Dean—whom Connelley characterized as "an earnest anti-slavery man of the impracticable and visionary type"—asked Quantrill and a man named Bob Wilson to assassinate Allen Pinks, a twenty-year-old free black from Pittsburgh.

Pinks, whose grandmother was German, had worked as a waiter and a cook on Mississippi and Missouri river steamboats and had been paid off for his last job in St. Joseph, Missouri, in 1859. He set out on foot for Leavenworth, but he should have stayed on a steamboat: The ferry-man on the Rialto ferry stopped him, suspecting he was a fugitive slave, and Pinks was incarcerated in the Weston jail until he could be trans-ferred to the one in Platte City. He sent to Pittsburgh for the papers that would prove he was a free man, but after three months they still had not arrived and he knew that in another month, as was the custom in Mis-souri, he would be sold on the auction block. He escaped from custody barefoot, limping into Lawrence sometime later with his clothes badly torn and his feet and legs swollen and severely lacerated by the thorns and briars of the undergrowth through which he had run.

He established a barbershop in town, and his affidavits finally arrived from Pittsburgh, but by then he was bitterly aware of how useless they were to him. "What good will they do me?" he asked John Doy, who had befriended him while incarcerated himself in the very same cala-boose. "Haven't we seen plenty of free papers torn up and burnt in the Platte City jail?"

Doy, having led the Underground Railroad party that Jake Herd had ambushed and carried to Platte City, understood Pinks's predicament:

"A colored man's free papers are not worth one red cent to him in the border towns of Missouri, even if he carries them with him and has them registered in every town on the river in which he works. . . . Free-born men are kidnapped and sold into hopeless slavery."

Pinks, perhaps to avoid such a fate, turned against his own people and went to work as a Judas goat: He led free Negroes into traps and slaves away from their masters and into the hands of border ruffians. Stewart and Dean learned of Pinks's villainy and told Quantrill and Bob Wilson to kill him. Wilson was in effect a double agent: He pretended to be an abolitionist while he kidnapped blacks and sold them. Wilson, who along with Jake Herd had occasionally used Pinks as a Judas goat, saw no reason to murder him when he could be sold at a Missouri slave market.

Wilson, claiming that his wife was too incapacitated by illness to care for herself, asked Pinks to come to his house and "attend to her hair." Pinks was wary, but he was at last persuaded and was just beginning to work on Mrs. Wilson's coiffure when he glanced out the window and saw two men alight from a closed carriage. They separated, and he heard them enter the house through the only two entrances, moving toward him from opposite directions, trapping him. Pinks understood immediately what was happening and plunged through a window and into a thicket of hazel bush. The would-be kidnappers searched for him but could not find him.

Dean was furious when told that the "assassination" had been botched. Holding Pinks to be a vile "traitor to the negro people and the holy cause," he decided to bypass Quantrill and Wilson and kill Pinks himself. He hid near the public well in Lawrence with a small-caliber rifle and waited for Pinks. When the mulatto came by and bent over the bucket for a drink, Dean drew a bead on the back of Pinks's head and fired. The ball pierced the skin but not the skull, wounding Pinks only superficially.

Dean, completely unnerved, fled to Stewart's fort, where the preacher gave him an alibi, claiming he had been there the entire day. Pinks's luck eventually ran out: Word of his treachery got around, and one day a mob of enraged Leavenworth blacks chased him down and shot him to death.

———◆—◆—◆———

In the fall, Quantrill formed a small band to make a raid into Cass County, Missouri, to steal horses, mules, and cattle. He planned the crime carefully—scouted the targeted area and noted which farms had good stock. Things went well for Quantrill and the other rustlers until, heading home with the stolen animals, they neared the state line and were attacked by a posse of thirty Missourians. Outnumbered five or six to one, Quantrill and his boys fought fiercely, drove most of the stock forward, and escaped into the night. They traded the animals to farmers along the road to Lawrence. Quantrill brazenly contracted with the victims to locate and return their stock at so much per head.

An abolitionist had hidden a runaway slave in a partially completed barn until passage could be arranged on the Underground Railroad; however, some children spotted the black man and reported his whereabouts to Jake Herd, who went with Quantrill and a few other men to capture him. In the process they set the barn ablaze, and the flames attracted abolitionists, who fought a pitched battle to save him. However, Herd, Quantrill, and the others managed to make off with him and sold him in Missouri.

Douglas County attorney Samuel A. Riggs indicted Quantrill on charges of arson—the burning of the barn—and kidnapping. For good measure Riggs threw in burglary and larceny, accusing Quantrill of having pried up a corner of the roof of the Ridenour & Baker warehouse in Lawrence, snaked inside, and pilfered a keg of gunpowder.

The indictment was supposed to be kept secret until Quantrill could be arrested, but one of the grand jurors was Nathan Stone, a friend of Quantrill and the proprietor of the Whitney House. Stone quietly passed the word to Quantrill. One day Sheriff Walker spotted him strolling down Massachusetts Street in Lawrence and immediately deputized George Earle to help him with the capture. When Quantrill saw the two armed men bearing down on him, he began to run down the street, bullets whizzing past him, and bolted into John Dean's place. He barred the door, and by the time Walker and Earle broke it down, Dean and Quantrill were gone. Walker searched Quantrill's known haunts that night, but the two men were safely hidden in a friend's house. The next night Dean borrowed a wagon from Stone to spirit Quantrill, concealed in the back, out of town. Walker hunted Quantrill through the rest of the year, forcing him to keep on the move, dodging and running.

Late in November or early December a party of seven men arrived in Lawrence. There were four white abolitionists and three former slaves—John Martin and two brothers, William and John Thompson. The black men had previously made their way to Canada on the Underground Railroad but had returned to the States to liberate members of their families who were still in bondage in the Cherokee Nation, which was in the northeast corner of the Indian Territory. They had stopped off in Pardee, Kansas, and enlisted the aid of four abolitionists: Charles Ball, Chalkley T. Lipsey, Edwin S. Morrison, and Albert Southwick. They were all in their early twenties and were of Quaker backgrounds; most of them had grown up in Springdale, Iowa. John Brown had visited Springdale in the winter of 1857–58 and set up a mock Congress or debating society in which many passionate speeches were delivered denouncing slavery and the "outrages" perpetrated on the free-soil men in Kansas. Ball and the others, already members of the Underground Railroad, had been inspired to go to Kansas to fight for "freedom." They settled in Pardee and formed a secret lodge to arrange for transportation of escaped or rescued slaves. During the day they worked communally on a farm, and at night they planned invasions of Missouri and raged against "the peculiar institution," keeping their indignation white hot. It is known that they participated in at least one raid led by Dean and Stewart in which twelve slaves were liberated and taken to Springdale. (Some of the blacks had gone on to Canada, and one wonders if Martin and the Thompson brothers were among them.)

When the seven contacted Dean, saying they wanted to slip into the Cherokee Nation and rescue the slave families, he readily agreed to help; Quantrill and a jayhawker named John S. Jones signed on as well. No one else in Lawrence was willing to make the long trip and then fight on unfamiliar terrain, so the would-be rescuers decided that they would go by way of Osawatomie, where they would try to find additional recruits.

Quantrill arrived in Osawatomie first. He registered at an old hotel and then hung around the post office because the postmaster was a Southern sympathizer. The others, in order to throw off any suspicion of their real intention, announced they were going on a buffalo hunt and took a circuitous route in a rented wagon from Lawrence to Osawatomie. Dean sent the wagon back to Lawrence, then met with Captain Eli Snyder and some other jayhawkers. After Dean revealed the plan, he offered Snyder command of the expedition if he would furnish some men for it. Snyder said it was impractical because of the imminent onset of cold weather and the lack of money with which to buy weapons, ammunition, and horses. Dean took Quantrill with him to a second meeting to bolster his arguments, but Snyder was suspicious of Quantrill and warned Dean that he strongly suspected Quantrill was a traitor.

It is not clear whether the other would-be rescuers met with Snyder and heard directly from him his objections to the plan and his suspicions about Quantrill or whether Dean relayed them. Either way, Jones and all three of the black men reluctantly decided to abandon the rescue mission. They would have nothing more to do with Quantrill.

However, Dean and the other whites still trusted Quantrill, and since the liberation raid into the Cherokee Nation had been canceled, they listened enthusiastically as he proposed an alternate plan. He wanted to attack the Jackson County, Missouri, farm of James Morgan Walker. A native Kentuckian, Walker was a wealthy man with a mansion, a two-thousand-acre spread, thirty slaves, and a hundred horses and mules. He was also rumored to keep a large quantity of gold hidden on the premises. Quantrill, of course, stressed the impressive number of slaves who could be liberated. He pointed out that there would be no need for additional recruits on the Walker raid, and they could steal some of Walker's horses to make good their escape.

William Connelley was certain that Quantrill had been contemplating the Walker raid for some time. Quantrill had hoped to use the rather enticing bait—slaves, horses, and gold—to lure an important jayhawker with a price on his head into a trap, but he had not succeeded: Dean, a self-important braggart, had been fancifully claiming that $5,000 in gold was being offered for him in Missouri—Quantrill could only hope it was true.

Quantrill set out on foot, heading east for Missouri, accompanied by Ball, Lipsey, and Morrison. They carried blankets and cooking utensils and camped in the woods at night. To avert suspicion they left their rifles behind in Kansas, arming themselves only with concealable weapons—knives and pistols. If anyone asked, they said they were on their way to Lafayette County to work grading the Missouri Pacific Railroad. Dean and Southwick returned to Lawrence, borrowed Nathan Stone's wagon, and took it to a prearranged rendezvous near the Walker place.

Quantrill and his men remained in Jackson County for a day or two while they gathered intelligence by surreptitiously questioning slaves.

Early on the morning of December 10, they set out on the road to the farm. As it happened they soon ran into Morgan Walker himself, who was on his way to Independence. Quantrill did not recognize his intended victim—or pretended not to—and asked him directions to the Walker plantation.

"I am the man," Walker told him.

Quantrill coolly claimed to have business with his sons and asked if they were at home.

On being told that they probably were, he and the others proceeded on. He hid them in a thicket on the edge of the farm and slipped away under the pretense of reconnoitering the house. Instead he went to the home of one of Walker's sons, Andrew J. Walker, which was a quarter mile from his father's place, arriving there at about 11:00 A.M.

Quantrill quickly told Andrew about the plan to rob his father later that night. He promised to lead his men into an ambush after dark in return for a guarantee that he would not be killed—and that Andrew would give him a temporary haven, a hiding place from Kansans who might want to punish him for his duplicity.

Quantrill returned to his men, while Andrew sent messages asking for assistance to four neighbors: John Tatum, Lee Coger, D. C. Williams, and Clark Smith. They met at the elder Walker's house before nightfall and loaded their double-barreled shotguns with buckshot. Ten minutes before Quantrill and his men appeared, Morgan Walker returned home. When Andrew explained what was about to take place, Morgan was stunned, then furious, and was determined to kill Quantrill along with the rest. His wife and his son managed to change his mind.

It was raining and cold, and clouds hid the moon, so candles were put in the front windows to illuminate the porch, where the ambush would take place. Adjoining the house was a harness room, and Andrew hid three of his neighbors there because it had a clear line of fire on the porch. He and Tatum crouched down behind a loom on the porch itself just as the raiders arrived. Dean and Southwick waited in the yard beside the wagon, ready to cart off the slaves and the gold. Morrison stayed on the porch to act as a lookout, while Quantrill, Ball, and Lipsey barged into the house with drawn revolvers.

"We have come to take your niggers to Kansas," Quantrill told Morgan Walker. "We also want your horses and mules and what money you have in the house."

Walker asked Ball if he had talked to the slaves to be sure that they all wanted to go. He demanded Ball's promise that any who wanted to stay would be left alone. Ball lied and said he had talked to them, that they all wanted to go.

Walker added huffily that since he was losing his slaves, he did not know why he should have to give up his stock and money, too. The raiders' drawn weapons spared them the necessity of tiresome debate.

Quantrill told the others he would stand guard on the "old folks," while they rounded up the slaves.

Just as Ball and Lipsey stepped out onto the porch where Morrison was standing sentinel, the overeager John Tatum rose from behind the loom and fired. Morrison fell dead with 19 buckshot in his hide. Ball and Lipsey leaped off the porch into the darkness as Andrew Walker and the men in the harness room cut loose. Lipsey was struck in the thigh and groin. Ball, unharmed, raced across the yard for the wagon, but Lipsey was crying out pitifully for help. Ball came back and half carried Lipsey to where the wagon was to be waiting—but it was gone. Dean's heel had been struck by stray buckshot, and he hobbled to the wagon, pulled himself in, and, without waiting for Southwick to climb on board, lashed the horses in the direction of Lawrence. Southwick ran after the wagon so as not to be left behind.

Abandoned and frantic, Ball lugged Lipsey into the woods.

The ambushers dragged Morrison's body into the harness room and stretched it out on the floor. Quantrill stood over the corpse and regaled his hosts with accounts of the dead man's many ferocious and despicable crimes against Missourians.

In the morning, as word of the attack spread, neighbors gathered to view the body. The menfolk were well armed and outraged. Many of them sought to add luster to their own reputations by claiming to have had run-ins with Morrison in the past or to have met him on lonesome roads and discerningly marked him for an abolitionist or a jayhawker.

Quantrill was repeatedly questioned about his role in the affair, and many of his interrogators were inclined to hang him on the spot. To save himself he spun out his invented tale of having been ambushed with his brother on the Santa Fe Trail and how he had joined the band of men who were responsible for his brother's murder and killed them one by one. Those he had brought to the Walker farm were the last of the culprits, he said, and leading them into ambush was an efficient way of completing his revenge.

Not everyone who heard the bloody recitation was convinced, and there was still much angry talk of putting a rope around his neck. Andrew Walker had to intervene repeatedly, insisting that he had given his word and would not allow anyone to harm Quantrill.

It was late in the afternoon before Mrs. Walker and the other women could get the men to bury the corpse. There was a cemetery on the farm, but that was for family, not slave-stealing rogues. Morrison was thrown into a crude coffin that had been hastily hammered together by a slave, and the coffin was dropped into a grave dug beside the road. Then everyone went home.

———◆◆◆———

Ball had managed to get Lipsey off the Walker place before dawn. He hid him in a thicket on George Rider's farm and washed his wounds and applied a poultice of leaves and bark. Sometime during the next twenty-four hours, Ball stole one of Rider's horses and killed a wild hog. The following morning a slave belonging to Rider stumbled on the thicket. It is variously reported that he was looking for the missing horse or that he was hunting in the woods or that he was cutting timber. Whatever the case, he found the two men beside a small fire with a spit of meat over it; the horse was tied to a nearby sapling.

Ball had hoped to use the horse to carry Lipsey to Kansas, but Lipsey was in terrible pain and unable to stay on the animal. Ball begged the slave not to reveal their whereabouts and promised him his freedom if he would steal a wagon and team. Together they would carry Lipsey to Lawrence, and then Ball would arrange for the black man to go to Canada. The slave promised to help and returned to his master—and promptly betrayed the two abolitionists.

Rider sent word to the Walkers, and they assembled a posse of neighbors. All were armed with shotguns, except Quantrill with his Navy Colt and Morgan Walker, who hefted an ancient Hawken rifle.

Rider's slave guided them to the thicket; they fanned out in a semicircle as they got close.

In later years, some people would claim that when Ball heard the posse coming, he turned on his heel and started to run. He was out of range of the shotguns, but Morgan Walker took aim with his buffalo gun and sent a bullet into the back of his head. This is certainly possible—Lipsey was too badly wounded to get away, and Ball, who was no coward, would have been justified in trying to make good his own escape. But on the night of the raid he had gone back for the wounded Lipsey at the risk of his own life and had stayed with him from then on, even though doing so kept him in constant peril, which gives credence to those who said that instead of running he drew his revolver and stood over Lipsey as if to protect him. The bullet from Morgan Walker's Hawken rifle blew a sizable hole in Ball's forehead. Quantrill, so the story goes, then rushed up to Lipsey. The wounded man was flat on his back, delirious with pain, but Quantrill could not take the chance that he might recover enough to tell what he knew. He thrust his pistol barrel into Lipsey's mouth and pulled the trigger.

There is no disagreement about what happened to the corpses. They were dumped into a hole and covered over with dirt. A day or two later a couple of grave-robbing physicians located the spot, exhumed the cadavers, and hauled them away for dissection.

———◦•◦———

There is a curious footnote to the death of the two abolitionists. During the war, Quantrill told members of his band the story, including his callous execution of Lipsey, whom he swore was one of those who murdered his brother on the Santa Fe Trail. At this time Quantrill was leading some very hard men, and he surely found it in his interest to depict himself as being cold and utterly ruthless. After the war Dean came to hear Quantrill's version secondhand and seized on it for use in his ongoing campaign to ruin entirely his former comrade's reputation. Dean added a strategic embellishment: that Ball, standing over Lipsey, had pointed a pistol at Quantrill and invited him to come within range and fight fair, and that the cowardly Quantrill had declined to duel.

Despite Dean's enmity for Quantrill and despite the fact that Connelley had a low opinion of Dean—labeling him "bombastic, theoretical, bigoted, self-important" and "shallow," as well as "a boaster" and "an arrant coward"—Connelley nevertheless accepted Dean's version of events and perpetuated it, so it has come down to the present day. A very different tale was told, however, by Andrew Walker. Whereas Dean was a braggart and, like so many other people who came in contact with Quantrill, inclined to claim a larger role in events for himself than he actually had had, Walker seems to have been a modest man who in later years tried only to set the record straight. In letters to W. W. Scott and in interviews with newspapers, he swore that as the posse approached, Ball

jumped to his feet and drew his pistol, and Lipsey, who was not delirious, propped himself up on one elbow and also pulled out a revolver.
Shotguns and the Hawken rifle spoke, and the two men died instantly.
Quantrill—and Walker was emphatic on this point—never unholstered
his pistol.*

———•◆•———

The Jackson County sheriff went to Walker's farm to investigate the raid
and its aftermath. He took Quantrill to Independence and had him make
a written statement (in which he claimed he was born in Hagerstown,
Maryland). Then, since there was much outrage in town that Quantrill
had not been killed along with the abolitionists, the sheriff put him in a jail
cell for safekeeping. Andrew Walker went to Independence and managed
to convince the sheriff to release Quantrill into his custody. "I took him to
the Hotel and we slept in the same room," Walker recalled in 1883.

> A great many people were in town the next day and the excitement ran
> very high. In the afternoon I thought it time to start home and went to
> the stable to get my horse. When I arrived on the public square, I found
> a great crowd gathered about. I rode up to them to see what it meant
> and learned that they were going to hang Quantrill.

Once again Walker stood up for Quantrill: "I told them they must not
do it; but some of them seemed inclined to be stubborn about it. I told
them if they did, they would do it over my dead body and they gave it up."
Walker must have been supremely confident of the impression he had
made on the mob because instead of hurrying Quantrill away, he took
the time to buy him a "suit of clothes of which he was badly in need."

---

*After escaping from the Walker farm and making his way back to Lawrence, Dean,
afraid that Quantrill would kill him if he could, decided that the only safe place for him
would be in Sheriff Walker's custody. He turned himself in and confessed to the attempted
assassination of Allen Pinks. He remained incarcerated until the war began and a failed
attempt on the life of a long-since-lynched race traitor lost whatever importance it may
have once had. The sheriff formed a company of men, and Dean joined up along with the
rest of the other prisoners, who must have longed for the outdoors and a little excitement
after dull confinement and forced, mundane drudgery.

Albert Southwick enlisted in Company C, 10th Kansas Regiment, on October 28,
1861, and served almost three years before being mustered out on August 20, 1864.

Once Quantrill was safely back at the farm, Morgan Walker began to fear that abolitionists would come looking for him and would burn the house and barn in retribution for Walker's sheltering him. He asked Quantrill to leave temporarily and gave him fifty dollars, a bridle, a saddle, and a coal black mare named Black Bess. The horse had only one eye, but she was from Kentucky racing stock, a Thoroughbred, and a swift runner.

Quantrill was restless and constantly on the move over the next few months. He went to Paola, a Southern stronghold where Henry Torrey now had a tavern, and was treated like royalty by the family. He visited other Kansas haunts, though he stayed clear of Lawrence and Sheriff Walker. When it was safe to return to Jackson County, Quantrill moved in with Mark Gill, who lived in the Blue Springs area and was a neighbor of Morgan Walker.

——— • • • ———

A number of people who had known Quantrill in Kansas before the war remarked on his "pronounced but not abnormal interest in women." It is alleged that during the period he lived in Lawrence he had an affair with a local woman and was often seen riding in her carriage. Cast adrift following the Morgan Walker episode, he is thought to have taken up with another Kansas woman, though nothing else is known about her. Living with Gill, Quantrill also began a passionate affair with Morgan Walker's daughter, Anna.

Anna Walker had a good figure and a beautiful face, marred only by her nose, which was large and crooked. She had been previously married to a merchant. When he caught her in bed with a boarder, he tried unsuccessfully to kill him and then divorced her, sending her back to her father. For a time Quantrill was madly in love with her, and after their liaison ended, she had a number of other lovers, notably George Todd, a Quantrill lieutenant. In April 1862, she married another member of the band, Joe Vaughan. They moved to Clay County, Missouri, where they remained until the end of the war. When her father died, she inherited a large tract of land, which she sold for a hefty price. She then sent Vaughn packing and used her fortune to open a bawdy house in Baxter Springs, Kansas.

——— • • • ———

Claiborne Jackson was inaugurated as Missouri's governor on January 4, 1861, and in his inaugural speech he advocated that Missouri "stand by her sister slave-holding States . . . with whose institutions and people she sympathizes." His fellow citizens disagreed: The results of elections held in November 1860 and in February 1861 clearly showed that the majority of voters wanted Missouri to remain in the Union.

On January 29, 1861, after several years of stalling by Southern senators, Kansas was admitted to the Union as a free state. Charles Robinson was elected governor and Jim Lane, U.S. senator.

Now that the issue of slavery in Kansas was settled, proponents on both sides were much less inclined to violent adventures and more interested in the peaceful pursuit of their livelihoods.

Quantrill continued to slip across the border on occasion, staying with his friend John Bennings in a cabin a mile south of Stanton. This proved a mistake, because Eli Snyder, who had sworn vengeance for Quantrill's treachery, still lived only a short distance away in Osawatomie and eventually heard of these visits. On March 25, Quantrill rode to Stanton for the third time in as many months, sporting a handsome denim suit Andrew Walker had bought him, and one of Snyder's confederates hurriedly carried the word to him. He and twelve of his gang rode to Stanton the next day, where he swore out a warrant against Quantrill for horse stealing before Justice of the Peace Samuel H. Houser. Snyder wanted to make the arrest himself and thereby have a legally sanctioned cover for killing Quantrill, but Houser was suspicious of his intentions and ordered E. B. Jurd, the local constable, to serve the warrant. Facing the unhappy prospect of arresting an armed and dangerous man, however, Jurd deputized Snyder and his men to act as a posse.

Shortly before dawn the posse surrounded Bennings's cabin, and Jurd shouted for Quantrill to surrender. Quantrill, awakened by the shouting, peered outside and saw Snyder. He yelled back that he would rather die fighting than let Snyder gun him down. Jurd convinced Quantrill to let him into the cabin to negotiate and then promised no harm would come to him if he gave himself up. To show his good faith he deputized a couple of Quantrill's friends. Eventually Jurd emerged from the cabin holding Quantrill's heavy Colt high for all to see; Quantrill followed behind.

As the posse rode away, Bennings's son, Adolphus, saddled a horse and rode hard in a northeasterly direction for Paola.

During the ride to Stanton, Snyder tried continually to goad Quantrill into a fight; when he would not be baited, the exasperated captain took aim, but someone knocked his gun away as he fired. "This courageous and creditable action," observed Albert Castel, "saved a man whose life was to mean death for hundreds."

The office of the justice of the peace was above Wilkerson's store, and either there was no proper jail in Stanton Township, or Houser was convinced that Quantrill would be lynched if confined in it, because he proposed sending him on to Lawrence. Quantrill protested that an assassin would surely get him on the way. While Quantrill and the magistrate debated the move, Snyder and his men glowered and jeered. Quantrill's argument was given a certain validity when one bystander tried to shoot him, but the gun misfired. Another man, standing outside the office, thrust a rifle barrel through the door, trying to get a shot at Quantrill; however, the barrel was pushed back out and the door slammed shut. Snyder tried several times to shoot him himself but was always restrained.

Sometime during all this excitement W. L. Potter arrived leading sixteen border ruffians from Paola. They flew into town in hacks and buggies and on horseback, brandishing revolvers, rifles, and shotguns. They brazenly cursed and swaggered and strutted. They had a brief Mexican standoff with Snyder and his posse, but the captain backed down and withdrew.

Quantrill's passionate arguments and the threatening presence of the border ruffians (who had been pointedly buying sizable quantities of ammunition from Wilkerson's store) convinced Houser to reverse his decision and send the prisoner to the Paola jail instead. Quantrill arrived in Paola in a three-seated hack as a conquering Roman hero in a chariot with a personal bodyguard of unwashed barbarians. There was a feast waiting for him at Torrey's tavern, and then he was escorted by a large crowd to the jail. Once he was comfortably ensconced in the cell, Potter slipped him a Navy Colt and some ammunition and told him that if the jail were attacked he should "make every shot tell." As soon as Potter heard the shooting, he would come running with "thirty or more armed men" and would "commence firing on any mob."

Such bold derring-do did not prove necessary. On April 2, Quantrill, assisted by several Paola lawyers, applied to the Honorable Thomas Roberts, the probate judge of Lykins County, for a writ of habeas corpus. Arguing that his "arrest was malicious, false and illegal," Quantrill's petition pointed out that the crimes which he was alleged to have committed did not take place in Lykins County, and therefore Justice of the Peace Houser had no authority to issue a warrant against him. The following day, Roberts, though he was a Republican, ordered Quantrill's release.

Quantrill was again escorted to Torrey's place, where another banquet had been hastily arranged by Torrey's wife and daughters. Afterward Potter and some of the others, who were aware that Snyder had picketed a large force of men west of town, pleaded with Quantrill to leave Paola as quickly as possible. "Come here no more," Potter urged, "until you can come without danger to yourself and [your] friends." Quantrill, stuffing his pockets with extra sandwiches and cake, readily agreed.

Black Bess was outside, saddled and waiting. Just as Quantrill mounted, Snyder and some of his followers clattered into town bearing a warrant for his arrest signed by a Lawrence magistrate. Quantrill paused to thumb his nose at his enemies—first with one hand and then the other—and then leaned forward in the saddle and patted his buttocks in another universally understood vulgar and insulting gesture. He dug his spurs into his horse's flanks and galloped away, heading east toward the border, waving his revolver over his head.

CHAPTER 5

"Desperate Leader of the Most Desperate Demons": Quantrill Becomes a Guerrilla

One day after the surrender of Fort Sumter, on April 15, 1861, Lincoln issued a call for 75,000 volunteers to suppress the Southern rebellion. Governor Jackson replied publicly that Missouri would not furnish a single man "to subjugate her sister states of the South" and appealed to Missourians to "rise . . . and drive out ignominiously the invaders who have dared desecrate the soil which your labors have made fruitful, and which is consecrated by your homes."

Now that the war had begun, Mark Gill carried his slaves to Texas, where they would be out of the reach of Yankees. Quantrill went along but was soon bored. He wandered north into the Cherokee Nation and made friends with Joel Mayes, a half-breed, who later became chief of his tribe. Mayes, a Confederate sympathizer, formed a company of Cherokees and was elected captain. Quantrill rode with the Cherokees and undoubtedly learned some tactics from them that would serve him well after he became a guerrilla chieftain. Mayes put his men under the command of Confederate General Benjamin McCulloch, fifty, who was famous in the West for his exploits as the leader of a company of scouts during the Mexican war.

On May 3, the proslavery militia mustered at Lindell Grove, on the western edge of St. Louis; their commander named the encampment Camp

Jackson in honor of the governor. The militia posed an ominous threat to the St. Louis arsenal, which was considered to be, as historian Jay Monaghan phrased it, "the only safeguard to Federal authority in Missouri." It also happened to contain a million rounds of small-arms ammunition.

The arsenal's commandant, Captain Nathan Lyon, a West Point graduate and fiercely antislavery Unionist, recognized the danger. He reconnoitered Camp Jackson (allegedly dressed in women's attire) and then, on May 10, he surrounded it with four regiments of volunteers—many of them Germans—forcing its immediate surrender. While marching the seven hundred disarmed prisoners to the arsenal, Lyon's soldiers were pelted with stones and dirt clods by a mob shouting, "Damn the Dutch!" and "Hurrah for Jeff Davis!" A man fired a pistol, wounding a German officer, and another officer gave the order to open fire. The soldiers cut loose and killed twenty-eight civilians, including two women and an infant. Southern sympathizers rioted throughout the night.

Lyon had drawn a line in the sand, forcing many Missouri conditional Unionists to take sides for the first time. They reacted with fury upon learning of the seizure of the arsenal and the murder of helpless civilians. Of course, the fact that so many of the troops involved were Germans—antislavery foreigners—only made matters worse.

Reacting to Lyon's bold move the state legislature, sitting in special session in Jefferson City, approved a military bill that authorized the recruitment of a state guard, gave the governor almost dictatorial powers to repel invasion and put down rebellion, and appropriated the entire state treasury—$8.2 million—for the purchase of war materials. Governor Jackson commissioned Sterling Price a major general, and Price set about organizing the state guard.

Jackson traveled to St. Louis by rail with his secretary, Thomas Snead, and Price. They met with Lyon, whom Lincoln had commissioned a brigadier general. Jackson and Price tried to work out a compromise with Lyon that would prevent the Federal military's domination of Missouri and preserve its sovereignty. Jackson and Price pledged to disband the fledgling state guard and offered other concessions in return for Lyon's promise that no additional U.S. troops would be brought into the state, no new garrisons would be established, and no troops would be transported through the state. Jackson and Price even went so far as to promise to resist any invasion of the state by Confederate forces and guaranteed that Missouri would maintain "a strict neutrality in the present unhappy contest."

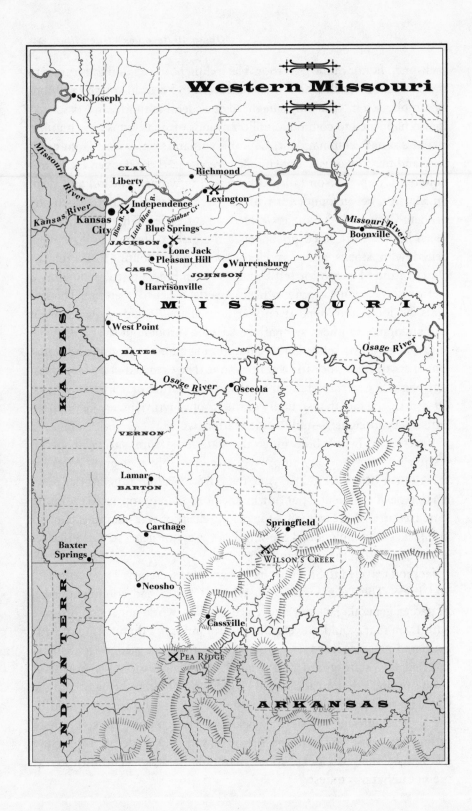

Rising out of his chair and speaking slowly and deliberately, Lyon said, "Rather than concede to the State of Missouri for one single instant the right to dictate to my Government in any manner however unimportant, I would see"—here he jabbed a finger at each of the distinguished delegates—"you and you and you and every man, woman, and child in the State dead and buried." Then turning to the governor, he cried, "This means war!" Twenty-five years later, Snead would still recall vividly how Lyon dramatically "turned on his heel and strode out of the room, rattling his spurs and clanking his sabre."

Jackson, Snead, and Price returned to Jefferson City, and certain Lyon would attack the capital, they stopped along the route to burn several railroad bridges and cut telegraph wires. Young men in counties all across the state formed companies to defend their homes against the "Dutch."*

Lyon brought his army to Jefferson City via steamboats on the Missouri River, but by June 15, the day he and his men disembarked, the governor and the legislators had fled to Boonville, fifty miles upstream. Lyon

---

*While slavery was an issue for the small number of radicals on either side who were engaged in the struggle over the Kansas Territory during the prewar period, the preservation of the peculiar institution does not appear to have motivated most Missouri Southerners to fight in the Civil War. These Southerners, like their cousins in the South, had a variety of reasons for fighting against the Union—and it is obvious that an individual might have more than one, including such personal motives as parental expectation, what we would call peer pressure, friendship, a desire for adventure, notions of masculinity, and concepts of duty and honor.

The relatively small number of Missourians who were slaveowners or the sons of slave-owning families, of course, desired to protect a profitable institution and a way of life. But most Missouri Southerners who fought did not own slaves and had no hope of owning slaves, and many would have opposed the institution of slavery. Many Missourians, viewing the federal government in far-off Washington, DC, as ominously tyrannous, fought for what one lieutenant, wounded in the Battle of Pea Ridge, called "the undying principles of Constitutional liberty and self-government." They believed they were acting in the tradition and protecting the legacy of their great grandfathers, who fought in the American Revolution of 1776. The Federal troops—so many of them German or other foreigners or from faraway northern states—seemed a hired army of occupation that threatened hearth, home, and family and so must be driven out. Further, some Missouri Southerners embraced the Confederacy as their new country and, patriotically, sought to prevent its subjugation.

Southerners from the western border counties—particularly those who joined partisan ranger bands like Quantrill's—had an additional and overriding motivation: a powerful

followed and routed five hundred untrained troops under the command of Colonel John Sappington Marmaduke, Price having been temporarily felled by an attack of cholera.

Jackson and the legislators fled south with Marmaduke and the state troops, pursued by Lyon's columns. They eventually took refuge at Cowskin Prairie, below Carthage in the southwestern corner of the state, where the recovered Price established a camp. Lyon camped at Springfield, about fifty miles east of Carthage, and plotted strategy, while Price proceeded to whip the seven thousand volunteers and troops who made their way to Cowskin Prairie into a fighting force known officially as the Missouri State Guard. In late July 1861, he marched southeast to Cassville, where he linked up with an army under Brigadier General Ben McCulloch. Then Price led the combined force some forty miles in a northeasterly direction. The Confederates spent the night of August 9 camped along the banks of Wilson's Creek, ten miles southwest of Springfield.

Quantrill's first experience with legitimate warfare came the next day. Another young man who received his blood christening was eighteen-year-old Private Alexander Franklin James, whose Clay County home-guard unit had been mustered into Price's army. "I was at Wilson's Creek," Frank James told a newspaper correspondent for the Columbia

---

desire to take revenge for the plunder and murder raids committed by the likes of Lane, Jennison, and Montgomery, and by the various jayhawking bands both before and during the war. "From the first six to sixty men who went to Quantrill [after he formed the band]," ex-bushwhacker Morgan T. Mattox said in 1909, "all were of the best families in Jackson, Cass and Lafayette counties. The Federals had committed depredation[s] on all their families, and the men went to Quantrill with vengeance in their hearts. No other motive than revenge prompted them. Of course, all were Southern sympathizers." Indeed, Mattox claimed that Quantrill would accept no one into the band who was not "moved by injury to selves or family, imbued with malice and bent on revenge." Mattox added that as the war dragged on "men of bad principle, thieves and robbers got into the band to rob, murder, and plunder."

Some men who rode with Quantrill came from slave-owning families—notably the Jameses and Cole Younger—but others did not. I can document the fact that two abject racists were members of the band and undoubtedly there were more, but at least three free black men belonged. Little is known about one of these men, John Lobb, but the other two, Henry Wilson and John Noland, were in later years extremely proud of having served with Quantrill and made a point of attending the band reunions. Noland was especially well liked by his white fellow veterans and was described by them as "a man among men."

Missouri Herald in 1897. "That was a slow fight. The idea of that many thousand men fighting for hours and killing so few. I want results when I fight." At the time of the interview, Frank was fifty-four years old and had become a much fawned-over celebrity, which may explain this lapse into preposterousness. The Battle of Wilson's Creek was one of the bloodiest and most memorable of the early western battles of the war, one which would make the victorious general famous and be compared by some modern historians with Bull Run.

At dawn on August 10, Brigadier General Lyon struck the Confederate camp just as many of the surprised rebels were drawing water from the creek. Lyon's troops were outnumbered by more than two to one, but nearly a third of Price's army was unarmed, and many of the rest had only shotguns and squirrel rifles brought from home. Their ammunition was so low that they had recently been manufacturing cartridges in the field and using timber to make buckshot. Faced with a superior force, Lyon chose to violate a hoary rule of military strategy, splitting his force in two. He advanced on Price from the north while his second-in-command, Colonel Franz Sigel, struck from the southeast. Sigel's German troops were initially successful, putting a cavalry detachment and a large number of unarmed infantry to flight, but then the "hired Hessians," who believed they had already won the day, stopped to take plunder. McCulloch's counterattack routed and scattered them. Sigel, who was a veteran of the German Revolutionary War of 1848, fled to Springfield accompanied by just one private, without even taking the time to notify Lyon of the debacle.

McCulloch next went to the assistance of Price, but the state guard bore the brunt of the fighting, which took place on Oak Hill, quickly and aptly renamed by both sides "Bloody Hill." Bodies piled up, and the ground literally became slippery with blood as first one side and then the other charged and was repulsed. Price rode wherever the fighting was hottest and shouted encouragement to his men. They, in turn, pleaded with him to be careful. "Don't lead us, General! Don't come with us! Take care of yourself for the sake of us all! We will go without you!" But Price would not heed; his clothes were ripped by bullets, and he was wounded in the side. "That isn't fair," Price, who weighed 250 pounds, joked to an aide. "If I were as slim as Lyon, that fellow would have missed me entirely." He rode forward again, keeping the wound hidden from his troops.

Lyon, too, kept himself in the thick of battle, exhorting his infantry from the back of his iron gray horse, until a bullet struck him in the breast just beside his heart. He died almost instantly. A brilliant tactician and an aggressive soldier, his death disheartened his junior officers, and the new commander, Major Samuel D. Sturgis, ordered a retreat. In their haste, the Yankees abandoned Lyon's body. An hour and a half later they sent back a party under a flag of truce to ask for the corpse, but in their continuing pell-mell flight they abandoned it a second time in Springfield.

Colonel Thomas Snead, who had been Governor Jackson's secretary and would subsequently serve as chief of staff of the Army of the West and who was McCulloch's adjutant at Wilson's Creek, said it was "one of the stubbornest and bloodiest battles" of the Civil War. In a few hours of fighting, the Confederates suffered 279 killed and 951 wounded. The Union army lost a quarter of its strength—258 killed, 873 wounded, and 186 captured or missing. The victors were too exhausted and disorganized to pursue the vanquished and thus perhaps secure Missouri for the Confederacy.

Cold statistics do not reflect the human suffering that resulted from the fight. Many men lost arms or legs; others received painful wounds that caused them to linger for many months or even years before dying. Still others, their resistance lowered by loss of blood, contracted diseases and died in heightened misery. Mrs. Julia L. Lovejoy glimpsed some of these often glossed-over consequences of war when she, along with three other ladies, visited several Leavenworth hospitals on March 17, 1862. In a letter to her brother written the following day, Mrs. Lovejoy, a Kansan whose son was in Lane's Kansas Brigade, reported that many of the Wilson's Creek convalescent wounded were

> sick with typhoid fever, pneumonia, measles, [etc.,] and we found three who will soon breathe their last, far from home and kindred dear. There was the empty pallet from which one had just been lifted to his rude grave; there another soldier speechless, and grappling with the grim monster; there another emaciated to a skeleton, sobbing as though his heart would break, and trying to tell us of his poor mother away up in Wisconsin. Our own emotions at times quite overcame us as we grasped the skeleton fingers of one after another of these poor creatures, who had come hundreds of miles to fight for their country, and now must find a grave unmarked, and be buried by a stranger's hand.

Price took Springfield on August 12. After a thirteen-day occupation of the town, he marched west: He intended to cross the Kansas border and capture Fort Scott, where Jim Lane was headquartered. Lane and his followers had been making plunder and murder raids into the Missouri counties east of the state line, and Price meant to put a stop to them. After he dealt with Lane, Price planned to head north toward the Missouri River.

A few days later McCulloch departed for Arkansas, informing Price that his troops were dangerously low on ammunition, and his orders from the Confederate war department were to above all protect Arkansas and the Indian Territory from Federal invasion. Privately, he had little respect for the untrained, undisciplined Missourians and even less for their commander—although Price had fought in the Mexican war, McCulloch thought him "nothing but an old militia general."

Mayes and his Cherokee cavalry followed McCulloch, but Quantrill stayed with Price, enlisting as a private. Connelley suggested without elaboration that Quantrill was motivated to forsake his Indian friends by his passion for Anna Walker. Presumably he meant Quantrill wanted to stay in Missouri so that he could be near his mistress. An equally likely explanation is that Price's ultimate goal was to drive the Federal troops from the state—Quantrill's adopted home—and his march on the Missouri River offered the prospect of action, while McCulloch would be at least temporarily quiescent.

On August 30, Union Major General John C. Fremont, commander of the Department of the West, which included Missouri, put the state under martial law. He decreed that slaves belonging to masters disloyal to the United States would be set free and that any man found bearing arms without authority would be court-martialed and, if convicted, shot. Lincoln, anxious to hold the loyalty of other border slave states, forced Fremont to cancel the emancipation provision.

Price skirmished with a detachment of Lane's Kansas Brigade on the evening of September 2 at Drywood Creek, near the border. After the Kansans fled, Price turned north because he had learned that Lane had withdrawn from the fort.

Fremont ordered Lane to overtake Price's army, but the Kansas Brigade, which Lane had recruited with promises of plunder, had only fifteen hundred men, so Lane cautiously chose merely to trail in Price's wake. He was far more interested in plunder than engaging Price: "Everything disloyal, from a Durham cow to a Shanghai chicken, must be cleaned out," he instructed his men. They obeyed with enthusiasm, "cleaning out" Butler and Parkville. They also looted and burned other towns that had welcomed the Confederates. Even one of the Kansas Brigade's chaplains got into the act: He plundered Missouri churches to supply his own unfinished church in Lawrence.

Price arrived at Lexington on September 13. While waiting for his ammunition wagons to catch up, he drilled his troops and reconnoitered the situation. The enemy commander, Colonel James A. Mulligan, had only two regiments of militia and his own Irish brigade available—a total of 3,500 men—and so was badly outnumbered. (Price's early success had electrified the border region and the West, and recruits flocked to him every day, swelling his army so dramatically that by mid-September he is estimated to have had eighteen thousand men with him.) Mulligan, with two steamboats at his disposal, might have evacuated his troops on the Missouri River, but, since he expected that a relief column would arrive in time, he chose to dig in on a bluff north of town, the site of the Masonic College. He buried a large quantity of confiscated property, which included the Great Seal of Missouri and $900,000 from the Lexington Bank, beneath the college building and constructed an earthen rampart twelve feet thick by twelve feet high. In front of the rampart was, in the words of Albert Castel, "an irregular line of earthworks and rifle pits, protected by traverses, ditches, sharpened stakes, and trip wires."

Price waited five days before he invested the fort. "They came as one dark moving mass," Mulligan later remembered, "their guns beaming in the sun, their banners waving, and their drums beating—everywhere, as far as we could see, were men, men, men, approaching grandly." Mulligan pounded them with heavy artillery fire, which forced prudent officers to dismount, but Price remained in the saddle, galloping along the front line. "Perfectly self-possessed, he seemed not to heed the storm of grape and canister," wrote Ephraim M. Anderson in his memoir.

Many officers urged him to retire or dismount, but he refused. A grape shot struck his field glass, breaking it in pieces, but without the slightest apparent emotion, he continued giving his orders. After twenty minutes he retired, leaving a lasting impression upon his men, who have ever loved him as their chief, and admired him as their "beau ideal" of honor and chivalry.

The Confederates encircled the fort, and their attack forced the Irish to withdraw inside the ramparts; in the process they abandoned the spring that was their only source of water. The Missourians, believing they had been shot at by sharpshooters posted in the Oliver Anderson house, despite the flag flying over it that signaled it was being used as a hospital, not only took the place but captured the Federals' only surgeon. The Irish knew nothing of the snipers and were furious at the apparent breach in battlefield etiquette. They retook the hospital and killed without mercy all the enemy they found inside. Every attempt to make an exchange for the surgeon was rebuffed, and consequently many wounded died for want of his skills. Mulligan never forgot their suffering. "It was terrible to see those brave fellows mangled and wounded, without skillful hands to bind their ghastly wounds," he told a newspaper correspondent.

> Captain Moriarty of the Irish Brigade, who had been in civilian life a physician, was ordered to lay aside his sword and go into the hospital. He went, and through all the siege worked among the wounded with no instrument other than a razor. The suffering in the hospital was horrible—the wounded and mangled men dying of thirst, frenziedly wrestling for water in which the bleeding stumps of mangled limbs had been washed, and drinking it with horrible avidity.

Finally a nurse volunteered to risk a gauntlet of enemy fire and carry a bucket to the spring. The Missourians lowered their weapons and waved their hats and cheered her courage until she was safe back behind the ramparts; then they resumed their deadly fire.

During the three-day siege, Quantrill is said to have distinguished himself by his "conspicuous daring" in combat. In *Noted Guerrillas,* John N. Edwards painted a dashing picture of him: "Mounted on a splendid horse, armed with a Sharpe's carbine and four navy revolvers, for uniform a red shirt, and for oriflamme a sweeping black plume, he advanced with the farthest, fell back with the last, and was always cool [and] deadly. . . . General Price—himself notorious for being superbly indifferent under fire—remarked his bearing and caused mention to be made of it most favorably." No report mentioning Quantrill's bravery in this battle has ever been found, so either it was lost or it was the product of Edwards's vivid imagination.

On the morning of September 20, Price had 132 hemp bales, which had been found in a warehouse by the river, carried to the top of a hill overlooking the Yankee fortress. Dirty water was poured over the bales, and then they were moved forward in a snaking line, a three-man team propelling each bale: The men crawled on their hands and knees and butted it with their heads. The bales absorbed the bullets fired by the alarmed defenders, and the impact of cannonballs simply caused them to rock slightly and then be still. In desperation the Federals tried heated shot, but the dampened straw would not ignite. As the bales neared the ramparts, the Irish ran out of shells and very nearly out of ammunition. A panicked junior officer, disobeying Mulligan's explicit orders, hoisted a white flag. Both sides stopped firing, and Price halted his advance. He sent Mulligan a note under a flag of truce in which he asked, "Why has the firing ceased?" Mulligan had not lost his sense of humor. "General, I hardly know," he replied, "unless you have surrendered."

The mobile breastworks resumed their ponderous progress, but the Yankees could not hold out much longer. Mulligan's officers voted overwhelmingly to surrender. When they offered their swords to Price, he declined them, explaining, "You gentlemen have fought so bravely that it would be wrong to deprive you of your swords. Keep them. Orders to parole you and your men will be issued, Colonel Mulligan, without unnecessary delay."

Two days after Price's victory, Jim Lane approached the outskirts of Osceola. When his advance was fired on by twenty-five or thirty Confederate soldiers who had concealed themselves in the brush, the fire was returned, killing one and wounding eight. No further resistance was offered, and Lane's troops quickly secured the town. Lane had all the records taken from the courthouse—for some reason he sent them back to Lawrence—then set the building on fire. Since Osceola was an important port on the Osage River, there were many wealthy merchants in residence, and its warehouses were filled with salt, coffee, and a large quantity of other goods. Several appropriated wagons were loaded with loot. The bank was robbed, the take said to have been $8,000. One hundred and fifty barrels of liquor were found in a cellar dug into a hillside, and because, as Captain Henry E. Palmer put it, "our men were dangerously thirsty," he and some other officers and men were detailed to break in the heads of the barrels and spill this stock of "wet goods," to prevent the men from indulging too freely. The "mixed drinks" . . . ran out of a rear door down a ravine, where the boys filled their canteens and "tanks" with the stuff, more deadly for a while than rebel bullets, and nearly 300 of our men had to be hauled from town in wagons and carriages impressed into the service for that purpose. Had the rebels then rallied and renewed the fight we would have been captured and shot. The town was fired and was burning as we left.

Palmer was right about the deadliness of the "wet goods": The river of liquor, which was still flowing out of the cellar, caught fire, too. Among the "dwelling houses" that were torched was the home of one of Lane's senatorial colleagues, Democrat Waldo P. Johnson. More than one hundred houses were burned, along with every store, shop, and warehouse. Only a few houses and one livery stable were spared. At least ten citizens were murdered.

About one third of Osceola's population was loyal, and many of the men were serving in the Federal army; however, when Lane and his men stole property there, they made no distinction between Unionists and secessionists, destroying or stealing almost everything that they could lay their hands on. His personal share of the plunder included a piano, $1,000 in gold, a quantity of silk dresses, and a handsome carriage. He would brag of having done a million dollars' damage in Osceola. (Two years later, during the raid on Lawrence, some of Quantrill's followers would repeatedly shout "Osceola!" as they plundered, burned, and murdered in retaliation for what Lane had done.)

As Lane continued to march north, dozens of blacks made their way to his column, some on fine horses or mules, while others rode in wagons appropriated from their former masters. White riffraff also joined, eager to enrich themselves. When Lane camped outside Kansas City, the area suffered an upsurge in highway robbery. One appalled Union officer described Lane's brigade as "a ragged, half-armed, diseased, mutinous rabble, taking votes whether any troublesome or distasteful order should be obeyed or defied." Although Lane could not maintain any military discipline over his men, he loudly called for the creation of more regiments of jayhawkers and advocated unleashing Indians on the Confederate states to lay waste with "fire and tomahawk."

On September 27, Fremont left Jefferson City, heading northwest, in command of 38,000 troops arranged in five divisions. He intended to destroy Price's army; however, two days later Price, who had learned of Fremont's approach, withdrew from Lexington, and, trailed by Fremont, retreated south to Neosho, in the southwest corner of the state.

The Federal military now effectively controlled almost all of Missouri. It was left to the growing number of guerrilla bands to resist the Yankees.

Lane, who had followed Fremont to Springfield, returned to Kansas City. Along the way he burned the homes of Southerners, and so many blacks flocked to him that he formed a "Black Brigade," which he sent into Kansas to help harvest the fall crops. At the Kansas line, the Reverend H. D. Fisher, one of the brigade's white chaplains, halted the mile-long column and, standing in his stirrups, cried, "In the name of the Constitution of the United States, the Declaration of Independence and the authority of General James H. Lane, I proclaim you forever free!"

Emancipation was against military orders, to "protect private property," and Lane, censured for disobeying regulations, repeatedly promised to stop his troops' plundering and the freeing of slaves, but nothing changed.

Quantrill left Price's army sometime during the retreat to Neosho and made his way back to the Blue Springs area of Jackson County. As usual his detractors cast him in the worst possible light, sneering that he was a coward and deserter who had no stomach for regular army discipline and organized combat. In fact, Quantrill was a brave man, and there is no evidence that he deserted; indeed, Price actively encouraged men to go home. Although his victories had brought him an embarrassment of riches as far as new recruits were concerned, his supply problems had not been much alleviated by the capturing of arms and matériel at Wilson's Creek and Lexington: Many of the recent arrivals were unarmed, and others still carried only farmers' weapons. Furthermore, he was desperately low on percussion caps, and few in his army had warm clothing suitable for the cold months ahead. The imminent winter's hiatus left him no choice but to reduce the size of his army.

Many were only too happy to oblige: Propelled by their own romantic notions of war and the belief that it would be won before the fall was over, they had rushed to volunteer, only ruefully to discover that war was not glory but tedium, illness, and long marches interspersed with brief, chaotic clashes punctuated by the pleas of the wounded and the shrieks of the dying. Understanding at last that the conflict might drag on for a very long time, thousands penitently scurried back to their families.

———— • ◆ • ————

One day not long after Quantrill arrived back in Blue Springs, word reached him that a band of Kansas jayhawkers had crossed the border and was raiding nearby settlements. He hurried with the news to Andrew Walker, and together they quickly raised a posse of ten men. Walker led them north until they came to the house of a man named De Witt, whom the marauders had robbed a short time before. The trail led to the farm of Strawder Stone, whose house had been plundered and was still burning when Walker and the others rode up. Mrs. Stone was in the yard, nursing a head wound; she had scolded the jayhawkers for their villainy and been struck by a pistol. The indignant Missourians galloped a quarter mile to the Billy Thompson place. The house was ablaze, and the culprits were just mounting up. The Missourians spurred their horses and opened fire, killing the man who had pistol-whipped Mrs. Stone. Several others were hit, but all managed to get away; they fled to Independence, where two of them subsequently died of their wounds.

Given the presence of Union troops in Independence, officials thought it prudent to take some action in the matter. They had the marshal arrest Strawder Stone and Billy Thompson on a murder charge. Quantrill went to Independence and wrote an affidavit in the presence of a justice of the peace in which he set forth the facts of the case and swore that he had killed the man and that Stone and Thompson had not even participated in the gunfight. The authorities released the prisoners and for some reason chose not to arrest Quantrill. Federal militiamen in the area wanted to murder him, however, so he was forced to go into hiding for a time.

———— • ◆ • ————

In late October the Missouri legislature convened for two weeks in Neosho. Scholars still debate today whether there was a quorum and thus whether the session was legal, but the legislators passed an ordinance of secession and elected senators and representatives to the Confederate Congress. Whether or not these actions were at odds with the sentiments of a majority of Missourians, the Confederate Congress declared Missouri to be the twelfth member of the Confederate States of America on November 28, 1861.*

———— ◆•◆ ————

Throughout the rest of the fall and winter, bands of jayhawkers and cattle thieves forayed into Jackson County, so the Walker band patrolled the countryside. Morgan Walker finally prevailed upon his son to give up being a home guard and stay on the farm, and some of the other men dropped out as well. Those who remained formed the nucleus of Quantrill's Raiders. His "becoming the leader was only natural," argued Albert Castel.

> To begin with he was an accomplished horseman and a good shot—the two skills most prized along the frontier—and in addition he was, so to speak, an expert in irregular warfare by virtue of his experience in Kansas. Furthermore, he had participated in Johnston's Utah expedition and had served in Price's army, and so had a certain knowledge of military organization and tactics. Finally, although an outsider, he had gained the confidence, sympathy, and perhaps even the admiration of the people around Blue Springs by the false story he had told in order to explain his part in the Morgan Walker affair, and by his action in exonerating Thompson and Stone. All these factors, plus his superior education, obvious intelligence, and winning personality, made him a logical choice for the commander and, as time was to show, an excellent one as well.

New recruits made their way singly or in small groups to whatever farmhouse or camp was his temporary headquarters, and as his fame grew in later years he sometimes had hundreds of men riding with him. As 1861 drew to a close, however, there were just fifteen: William Haller, Joseph Gilchrist, Perry Hoy, John and James Little, Joe Vaughan, James

---

*In January 1862, General Halleck, who was then still in charge of the Department of the Mississippi, dispatched General Curtis to drive Price from southwestern Missouri. Price retreated into Arkansas and linked up once again with General McCulloch, but their combined force—christened the Army of the West and under the command of Major General Earl Van Dorn—was defeated in the two-day Battle of Pea Ridge, March 7–8, 1862. Among those who were killed in the fight was General McCulloch.

Price resigned as commander of the state guard, accepted an appointment as major general in the Confederate army, and embarked for Memphis. Most of the men who made up the state guard were mustered into the Confederate service and fought in Mississippi, Tennessee, Alabama, Georgia, and the Carolinas.

A. Hendricks, Ed and John Koger, Harrison Trace, Oliver "Ol" Shepherd, George W. Maddox, Fletch Taylor, William H. Gregg, and George Todd. These seem all to have been Jackson County farm boys, with the exception of Todd, who was Canadian and had apparently migrated to Kansas before the war to work as a stone mason; he was twenty years old and strikingly handsome, with blond hair and blue eyes. He has been described as being "illiterate, hot-tempered, callously brutal, a deadly shot, and absolutely fearless."

A Confederate deserter named George Searcy arrived in Blue Springs at Christmastime. He had served honorably under Price, but now he made a nuisance of himself by stealing horses and mules from Union families. He also made the mistake of trying to assassinate Quantrill. Quantrill and his men tracked him down and gave him a perfunctory trial beside the Little Blue River. As there were seventy-five head of horses marked with various brands in his herd, and as he had a large number of deeds, notes, mortgages, and private accounts that bore other people's names, the proceedings were quickly drawn to a close. A rope was thrown over a tree limb, and the noose slipped over his head. "Not so fast, gentlemen!" he protested. "It's awful to die until red hands have a chance to wash themselves. . . ." His speech promised to be a long and moving one, but unfortunately, his listeners were anxious to get back to Blue Springs, so they hauled him into the air. Quantrill returned the animals and other property to their rightful owners—despite their Unionist sympathies.

A few days later Quantrill struck a Federal patrol at Manasseth Gap on the road to Independence. Several Yankees were wounded, and the rest surrendered. After their arms and ammunition were taken from them, Quantrill paroled them.

(The point should be made that, however unscrupulously he may have behaved in the summer and fall of 1860, once the war began he thought of himself as a Confederate soldier fighting for the Cause, and he adhered strictly and consistently to a personal code of honor: He kept promises he made to the enemy, accepted surrender, granted paroles, tried to exchange prisoners, and made certain that none of his men ever raped or assaulted a woman. True, the code might not be one which Virginia gentleman Robert E. Lee could endorse without amendments—civilian or military foe who resisted him, tried to escape, or refused to provide information were summarily dealt with—but how many other bushwhacker, jayhawker, or redleg leaders adhered to even his spare principles? It was only *after* the Federal authorities issued orders outlawing all partisans and began executing Quantrill's captured followers without benefit of trial that he adopted a merciless policy of no quarter.)

Quantrill temporarily disbanded his men on Christmas Day because of inclement weather. Jayhawkers continued to ride despite the cold, however, and hunted the guerrillas, visiting their homes and seeking their camps in the bush.

Riley Alley, an east Blue Springs farmer, attempted to set a trap by giving a ball; he invited all the young people of the area, specifically requesting the presence of Quantrill and his men. While the dance was in progress a squadron of Federal cavalrymen burst through the door with drawn revolvers. No guerrillas were found—they had seen through the ruse—but the Yankees confined the male celebrants upstairs and the females downstairs and waited twenty-four hours in the hope that some of their quarry might show up. When none did, the ladies were released, but the men were put into wagons and taken to Independence. Many of the cavalrymen were hardly able to stay in the saddle, having gotten roaring drunk on peach brandy. Riley Alley was carried to Independence with the rest to cover his treachery, but he was quickly released. He returned to his farm to find Quantrill and Todd waiting for him. In the darkness of the night he managed to get away unharmed and fled in terror to Kansas City. He never again went back to Blue Springs.

The other prisoners were examined by Federal authorities, who decided, for unknown reasons, to send one, Sol Basham, to the Rock Island Penitentiary in Illinois; he languished there until the end of the war. All the rest were released after having been roughed up or at least threatened. The Union garrison commander himself tried to intimidate young Frank Smith, who was only fifteen: "You damn little rebel, I'm going to let you go, but if I hear of you getting into anything down there at Blue Springs, or taking any part in assisting the rebel cause, I'll send down and have you brought in here and will cut your damn head off." Frank promptly joined Quantrill.

Ed Koger, who played the banjo, attempted to immortalize the incident in words and music.

> *Old Rile Alley gave a ball,*
> *The Feds came down and took us all*
> *Over the ice and over the snow—*
> *Sing-Song Kitty, won't you kiss-me-o!*

Old Rile Alley gave a ball,
Planned to catch Quantrill and bushwhack all,
But Quant was smart and didn't go—
Sing-Song Kitty, won't you kiss-me-o!

Quantrill called the band together before the end of January. Several new recruits showed up, among them a man named John Jarrett and his brother-in-law, Thomas Coleman Younger.

Cole was almost six feet tall and had an erect carriage. "He was an exceedingly handsome fellow, stalwart, alert, and intelligent and every inch a soldier," remembered Major Warren C. Bronaugh of Company K, 16th Missouri Infantry, C.S.A. The major had first encountered Cole in the late summer of 1862, while riding on a lonely Jackson County road just after the Battle of Lone Jack. Cole was on picket duty. "He wore a black slouch hat, dove-colored trousers and a colored shirt. Around his waist, suspended from a glossy black belt, was a brace of fine revolvers. He had tied his horse a little way off, and was afoot while conversing with us." It was a fortunate meeting for both men: Bronaugh was inadvertently riding straight for enemy lines and certain capture when Cole stopped and warned him; later they became friends, and, after the Northfield robbery, the major would devote twenty years to the herculean effort of getting Cole and his brothers pardoned.

Bronaugh was not alone in describing Cole as handsome—some other contemporaries thought him so, too—but photographs show him to have had thin lips, large ears, and a bulbous nose. These are hardly prepossessing features by modern standards, and in middle age he would go bald and become wattle-necked and paunchy. However, his eyes remained magnetic, and one suspects that his friends were heavily influenced by their affection for him when they characterized him as being good-looking.

His family was perhaps the closest thing to Southern aristocracy in Missouri. His mother Bursheba (née Fristoe) was a descendant of a wealthy Tennessee family. Her father, Richard Marshall Fristoe, had fought in the Battle of New Orleans under General Andrew Jackson and, according to a family tradition, lobbied successfully to have Jackson County named after the general. According to another family tradition, Richard was a nephew of Chief Justice John Marshall. Richard himself was one of the first judges of Jackson County, was twice elected to the Missouri state legislature, and was postmaster of Independence.

Cole's paternal great-grandfather had served with George Washington's army at Valley Forge, and his paternal great-grandmother was related to the Revolutionary War general "Light-Horse Harry" Lee, father of Robert E. Lee. Cole's paternal grandfather, Charles Lee Younger, a native Virginian, emigrated first to Kentucky and then Missouri, where he became one of the wealthiest landowners in the western part of the state. (Charles sired nineteen children, including eleven who were illegitimate; one of the latter was Adeline Wilson, whose sons—Grat, Bob, and Emmett Dalton—were the Younger brothers' cousins and would become notorious as the Dalton Gang.)

Cole's father, Henry Washington Younger, was a native of Kentucky. He was elected mayor of Harrisonville, Cass County, and was also a prosperous businessman. He had acquired a fine house in Harrisonville and large farms in Cass and Jackson counties. He owned several slaves and was a Southern sympathizer, but he was adamantly opposed to secession.

Cole was born on January 15, 1844, the seventh of fourteen children. "We were given the best education the limited facilities of that part of the West then afforded," Cole wrote in his 1903 autobiography, *The Story of Cole Younger By Himself.* "[We] were reared in ease, though the border did not then abound in what would be called luxury." Cole, or "Bud," as he was sometimes called, became an excellent marksman while still a boy, hunting wild game. "I cannot remember when I did not know how to shoot," he told his readers. "I hunted wild geese when I could not have dragged a pair of them home unaided." The practice stood him in good stead in later years.

Cole claimed that early in the summer of 1861, at the age of seventeen, he joined Price's army in time to participate in the Battle of Carthage on July 5. But it was not until the onset of winter that the war finally closed in on him irrevocably and changed the course of his life forever.

Colonel Cuthbert Mockbee, who lived outside of Harrisonville, held a dance in honor of his daughter. The gentleman was a native Southerner, and his guests were also partial to the Cause. As a result, some members of the 5th Missouri Federal Militia decided to make mischief by crashing the party. "Among them," wrote Cole, "was Captain Irvin Walley, who, even though a married man, was particularly obnoxious in forcing his attention on the young women." When Cole's sister refused to dance with him, Walley picked a fight with Cole.

"Where is Quantrell?" he demanded with a sneer.

"I don't know," Cole answered.

Walley, who believed that Younger was passing intelligence to the guerrillas, shouted, "You are a liar!"

Cole knocked him down. As the captain drew his pistol, some of Cole's friends stepped between them. Cole and his sister were hurried to their horses.

Back at the house, Cole told his father what had happened, and the old man bade him to go to the Jackson County farm and hide out in the woods to avoid further trouble with Walley. Cole left in the morning, and that night Walley and some of his scouts came to the house. The captain demanded that Cole's father hand him over, charging that he was Quantrill's spy. Henry Younger called Walley a liar. Walley and his men searched the premises, then sullenly rode away.

Cole's parents decided that the only safe course was to send him off to college, but before they could make arrangements, Walley had Cole formally charged with spying. Cole, who had wanted to stay and fight and had only very reluctantly acceded to his parents' wishes to continue his education, now knew there was no choice. "Watch was being kept for me at every railroad station, and the only school I could reach was the school of war close at home." He took his shotgun and revolver and set himself adrift on the border.

Among his various business enterprises, Henry Younger had won a contract to deliver mail to a five-hundred-mile stretch of western Missouri. As a "mail agent" he was required to appear periodically in Washington, DC, to sign papers and confer with the authorities. While he was away on his first trip after Cole's disappearance, jayhawkers struck his stage line and livery stable, stealing horses and wagons; they also looted his store and burned some of his property. Upon his return, Henry rode in a buggy to the headquarters of the state militia at Kansas City, Missouri, to lodge a complaint. As he returned home he was waylaid by Walley and his men. Shot three times, he fell out of the buggy and died in the road. His assailants tied his horse to a tree and hastily searched his body before riding off.

Later in the day Mrs. Washington Wells and her son, Samuel, happened by. The lady recognized the corpse and stayed with it while her son rode back to Kansas City to report the murder to Colonel Peabody, the Federal commander.

Henry Younger's assassination was not the last bit of villainy visited on the Younger family by Yankees. They so harassed Mrs. Younger that she left Harrisonville and moved to the farm in Cass County. A year after her husband's murder, militia came in the middle of the night and tried to force her at gunpoint to set fire to her own house. As it had been snowing and was bitterly cold, she begged her tormentors to allow her to wait until morning. They agreed but at dawn required her to put a torch to the place. As the flames engulfed the walls, she set out on foot, leading her four youngest children and her house slave, Suse, on an eight-and-a-half-mile trek through the drifts back to Harrisonville.

Life was made so difficult for her there that she moved to Waverly, where, Cole said, "she was hounded continually." Among the more petty vexations, she was required to report weekly to the authorities in Lexington, as if she were a criminal on parole.

During the spring and summer of 1863, various Federal commanders instituted a policy of arresting women and teenage girls who were sus-pected of aiding guerrillas. Among those taken into custody were three of Cole's sisters and two of his cousins—Mrs. Charity Kerr and Mrs. Nannie (née Harris) McCorkle, who were, respectively, the sister and sister-in-law of John McCorkle, another member of Quantrill's band. All the females were confined on the second floor of a three-story brick building on Grand Avenue, between Fourteenth and Fifteenth streets, in Kansas City, Missouri. They had been held for nearly six months under miserable conditions while they awaited transportation to Arkansas in the hope that their bushwhacking menfolk would follow them. Then, on August 13, the building suddenly collapsed. Mrs. McCorkle managed to escape by jumping out a window, but five other women died, one of them being Charity Kerr, who, Cole wrote, "was helpless in bed with the fever, and she went down with the wreck and her body, frightfully man-gled, was afterwards taken from the ruins."

The guerrillas believed that the Yankees had intentionally engineered the collapse by undermining the foundations of the building. To the end of his days Cole never wavered in his conviction that there had been a plot. He accepted without question the rumor that the grocery store owner on the first floor "had moved his stock of groceries from the building in time to save it from ruin, showing that the wrecking of the house was planned in cold blood, with the murder of my sisters and cousins and the other unfortunate women in mind."

In September soldiers ransacked the home of Reuben Harris, Mrs. McCorkle's father. They stole everything that was valuable and set the house ablaze. A daughter, Kate, was in bed upstairs but was rescued from the flames by her sister.

Many bushwhackers took savage reprisals against Yankees for the collapse of the Grand Avenue building. Bill Anderson, for instance, who was already extremely violent, seems to have been driven into psychopathy by the death of one sister and the crippling of another on that dreadful day. Thereafter he rode into battle sobbing his sisters' names. His revenge was so terrible that he was posthumously given the nickname "Bloody Bill," and legend has it that after his death, a silken cord was found on his body with fifty-three knots in it—one for each man he had killed for his sisters' sake, Bloody Bill's way of keeping score. He and his followers even festooned their horses' bridles and saddles with Yankee scalps.

The painful memories of the Younger family's persecution would continue to enrage Cole even after he had slipped into paunchy, sad old age. The mistreatment "planted a bitterness in my young heart which cried out for revenge and this feeling was only accentuated by the cruelties of war. . . . I refer in particular to the shameful and cowardly murder of my father . . . and the cruel treatment of my mother at the hands of the Missouri Militia." Having described the death of his cousin and the other women in the Grand Avenue disaster, he added, "This was cruelty . . . enough to harden and embitter the softest of hearts, but it was mild compared with the continuous suffering and torture imposed upon my mother during the years from 1862 to 1870."

Given his attitude, it is hardly surprising that he might become vicious and take terrible revenge. Yet while there is no doubt that he was a fierce combatant, so far from being cruel was he that after his incarceration in a Minnesota prison, several of his wartime foes voluntarily stepped forward to testify to his humane treatment of them and to plead for his release. One of these was Senator Stephen B. Elkins of West Virginia, who had been captured by Quantrill's men in the spring or summer of 1862 and carried to their camp. Cole was there, and Elkins, who as a boy had known Cole and his parents, was certain he would be killed and pleaded with Cole to save him. Although Elkins was a dedicated loyalist and had enlisted just before he was taken, Cole lied to Quantrill, solemnly insisting that he was a noncombatant who had stayed home to care for his mother. He added that Elkins's father and brother were in the Confederate army and were "good fighters." Quantrill ordered Elkins released, and Cole made sure he got safely away.

Major Emory S. Foster, U.S.A., had a similar experience. He and his brother had both been severely wounded and captured at the Battle of Lone Jack. They were being held in a cabin, and a guerrilla stood over them in a rage. He pointed a pistol at them and swore to shoot them forthwith. Cole walked in, heard the threats, grabbed the man, and shoved him out of the room. Major Foster then recognized Cole as the young man who had acted with conspicuous bravery during the fight, riding up and down in front of the Confederate lines, distributing ammunition despite withering enemy fire. He told Cole that he and his brother had a lot of money on them—a thousand dollars between them—and asked him to carry the cash and their revolvers to their mother in Warrensburg, Missouri. Cole said that he would and kept his promise.

———————

After Walley's accusations that he was a spy forced him into hiding, Cole made his way to Quantrill's camp. A few days after he joined the band, which now had about forty members, they hit the camp of a Federal detachment near Independence. Using the element of surprise against a vastly more numerous foe, they killed five in the fight's first moments. The rest broke and fled pell-mell back to the safety of town, where their regiment was billeted.

While Quantrill and his followers were chiefly occupied during the winter with protecting Jackson County from marauding jayhawkers, they also staged a few hit-and-run raids and committed other depredations. Federal authorities quickly became frustrated with Quantrill's tactics and elusiveness. On February 3, 1862, Captain William S. Oliver, 7th Missouri Infantry, sent to his superior, Brigadier General John Pope, a dispatch that, as it happens, contains the first mention of Quantrill in official U.S. government records.

> General:
>   I have just returned from an expedition which I was compelled to undertake in search of the notorious Quantrell and his gang of robbers in the vicinity of Blue Springs. Without mounted men at my disposal,

despite numerous applications to various points, I have seen this infamous scoundrel rob mails, steal coaches and horses, and commit other similar outrages upon society even within sight of this city [Independence]. Mounted on the best horses of the country, he had defied pursuit, making his camp in the bottoms of the——and Blue, and roving over a circuit of 30 miles. I mounted a company of my command and went to Blue Springs. The first night there myself, with 5 men, were ambushed by him and fired upon. We killed two of his men (of which he had 18 or 20) and wounded a third. The next day we killed four more of the worst of the gang, and before we left succeeded in dispersing them. . . .

Quantrell will not leave this section unless he is chastised and driven from it. I hear of him tonight 15 miles from here, with new recruits, committing outrages on Union men, a large body of whom have come in tonight, driven out by him. Families of Union men are coming into the city tonight asking of me escorts to bring in their goods and chattels, which I duly furnished. I had 1 man killed and 2 wounded, during the expedition.

On February 22, Quantrill and fifteen followers charged down the streets of Independence. They had expected to meet with little resistance, but a regiment of Ohio cavalry had just passed through town, and stragglers galloped hard to alert their colonel to the enemy's arrival. The guerrillas were in the northeast corner of the town square when the cavalry entered it from the southwest. There was a dense fog, so the Yankees were almost on the bushwhackers before they were aware of them. The guerrillas fired a quick fusillade, wheeled their horses, and beat a hasty retreat down Spring Branch Road. The Ohioans, in close pursuit, fired their pistols and then drew out their sabers. A cavalryman rode up beside William Gregg, but in the fog and confusion mistook him for a comrade. Gregg put his pistol barrel inches from the fellow's ear and pulled the trigger three times in quick succession, but each time the gun misfired. The undeceived trooper, Gregg remarked many years later, "proceeded to belabor me with his sabre, the only harm he did was to blacken my arm from elbow to wrist."

Quantrill was wounded in the leg, and Black Bess was shot out from under him. He scrambled up a steep bank and disappeared behind some boulders.

The bushwhackers' superior mounts soon pulled away from the army plugs, ending the engagement.

Quantrill had lost two men: Gabriel George and Hop Wood. He showed up at Gabriel George's funeral a day or two later, limping and leaning on a cane. After the service he temporarily dispersed the outfit, as was his custom when things got hot: "Captain Quantrell believed that it was harder to trail one man than a company, and every little while the company would break up, to rally again at a moment's notice," Cole Younger explained. The tactic ensured that the entire band would not be wiped out.

The men regrouped less than two weeks later for a raid on Aubry, Kansas, which was close to the border. The raid was in retaliation for Daniel Anthony's burning of Columbus and Dayton, Missouri. Forty bushwhackers rode into Aubry at dawn on March 7, yelling and cursing and shooting in all directions.

Two men asleep in a second-floor room of the tavern were awakened by the innkeeper's pounding on guest room doors and shouting, "Cutthroats are coming!" The first man out of bed, Lieutenant Reuben A. Randlett, grumbled that this was just an outrageous ruse by a greedy landlord to get his guests to vacate their beds early so that he could rent them again, but he dressed anyway. By the time he had finished, the innkeeper was back wailing through the door that the place was being surrounded. Having discharged his responsibility to sluggish guests, he raced down the stairs and fled with two hired hands into a cornfield, where they were pursued and shot down.

Randlett knew nothing of the murders and was still skeptical of the attack. The windowpanes were covered with frost, and he wandered from room to room, trying to get a look outside. He heard shots and shouting in the street and finally saw a mob of bushwhackers through a thin strip of clear glass along a sash. Another guest, furious and half naked, wanted to put up a fight, but as there were only three pistols in the building and a large number of enemy outside, Randlett dryly advised against that course of action. He went downstairs into the innkeeper's office, where he handed his revolver to a guerrilla and said that he was a Union officer. He demanded "the treatment due a soldier" who surrendered. He was led outside and turned over to two men, who cursed him menacingly; one of them stuck the muzzle of his pistol into Randlett's mouth, the other put his revolver against the lieutenant's ear. At this moment Quantrill rode by and ordered the men not to kill Randlett but to take him back into the office.

After the town was secured Quantrill returned to interrogate Randlett. He was the second lieutenant of A Company, 5th Kansas, and he had been on sick leave since contracting a fever earlier in the winter. Although still not well, he was on his way to rejoin his unit at Barnesville, Kansas. As Quantrill talked with him, it came out that they both had been present at the "battle" of Drywood, while Quantrill was still serving under Price. On September 2, 1861, Colonel Thomas Moonlight and a company of Federal soldiers were pursuing Confederate pickets through a ravine when they suddenly came out onto a wide prairie and sighted Price's army. Moonlight had a small cannon hurried forward, and the gunner fired twice, both times ineffectively. Moonlight, who had been an artillery officer himself, was disgusted at the ineptitude and jumped from his horse, wheeled the gun about, aimed it, and fired. As Connelley put it, "The shot struck a Confederate gun which was pouring out grape, dismounting it and sending it turning end over end several yards into the ranks marshaled behind." Faced with an overwhelmingly superior force, Moonlight then quick-marched his men away in triumph. As it happened, Randlett was standing beside the cannon when Moonlight aimed it, and Quantrill had been quite near the wrecked gun.

While the two men were exclaiming over this coincidence, an even odder coincidence presented itself in the form of a civilian who staggered into the office, literally covered in his own blood. Despite his ghastly appearance, Quantrill recognized him.

"Why, Ellis, is that you?" he cried.

Abraham Ellis was a native of Greene County, Ohio. An abolitionist, he had moved his family to Lykins County, Kansas, in 1857, and become a friend and comrade of John Brown. He was elected to the territorial legislature in 1859 and the first Kansas state legislature in 1861. He also served as a Lykins County commissioner and superintendent of public instruction. In that capacity he had interviewed Quantrill in 1859 and awarded him a certificate to teach in Stanton. Despite Ellis's ardent abolitionism, Quantrill remained grateful to him for the job.

Ellis, a quartermaster in Lane's Kansas Brigade, had shared the tavern room with Randlett and been slower to dress. Despite hearing the raiders screaming and the thud of bullets against the building's walls, Ellis had ventured a look out a second-story window. Quantrill was riding by and took aim at the figure above him. The bullet went through the window sash and embedded itself in the center of Ellis's forehead. He fell on the floor and passed out. Guerrillas searching the second floor initially thought him dead, but when he came to, they pointed their revolvers at his head. One of them shouted, "If you have any money, God damn you, give it to me . . . or I'll blow you to Hell." "As I had no hankering after that place," Ellis commented later, "I handed him $250."

The raiders went back to searching the rooms and found "a damned fat" wallet, then ordered Ellis downstairs.

Although Quantrill could not help being proud of "the damn'd good shot" he had made, he was genuinely regretful that Ellis turned out to have been the target. He sat him in a chair and called for a washcloth and water and personally washed his face, apologizing profusely all the while. He told Ellis that he was "damned sorry I shot you—you are one of the Kansas men I do *not* want to hurt."

He asked if Ellis had had any property in the house and was told that he had $50 worth of groceries stored in the tavern and a team and wagon in the stables. (Groggy from loss of blood, Ellis momentarily forgot the $250, much to his later regret.) Quantrill sent for the horse and wagon and learned that the animal had already been appropriated by one of his men. He ordered that the horse be brought to Ellis immediately—or it would be the last time the offender disobeyed orders. He saw to it that Ellis's other possessions were returned to him and apologized one more time.

Quantrill had Randlett's mare saddled and brought from the stables; he intended to swap the officer for one of his own captured men, whose last name was Brady.

Out in the street, Randlett wiped the fresh blood from Ellis's face, then mounted and sat beside Quantrill as the other bushwhackers gathered round. They had pillaged every store and house, robbed every male inhabitant, and had murdered at least five. One building was set ablaze. As they rode away with Randlett, Ellis was fastening the wagon lines to the bits. Randlett looked over his shoulder once and saw Ellis fall backward into the road and was certain there was one more fatality to be added to the casualty list.

But "Bullet Hole" Ellis, as he came to be known, did not die. He lay on the frozen ground for four hours before reviving. Three days later a U.S. army surgeon extracted the ball and some skull fragments, then sewed the skin flap closed over the hole. Ellis donated the ball and pieces of bone to the Army and Navy Medical Museum in Washington, DC.

He recuperated for six months, then rejoined the Kansas Brigade and was later commissioned first lieutenant of Company D, 15th Kansas; he resigned on February 22, 1865. After the war he did not go back into politics, but instead moved to Chautauqua County, Kansas, and devoted himself to horticulture. He died on March 14, 1885. To the very end there was a large indentation in his forehead as well as an enormous scar, clearly evident in photographs, as ugly and unchanging as his opinion of Quantrill and his band. The callow young teacher he hired had showed great promise, but a few short years of border strife had hardened his features into those of a true "desperado" with a bushy mustache and long sideburns. The kindness he had shown Ellis on that day in Aubry was his only redeeming personality trait. It showed, posited Ellis,

> that he was not entirely a Demon—But history will record him a desperately bad man—a highway robber of the darkest shade and a desperate leader of a set of the most desperate Demons that ever disgraced the name of man—infinitely worse than he was. None of them with bravery enough to meet an enemy—But they took every advantage of the surroundings—by treachery to drench the earth with blood and carnage. . . .

Randlett was kept with the band for eleven days and was treated very well. "He was a splendid fellow," remembered William Gregg, "and we all became much attached to him. We allowed him the liberty of the camp and lines, and his uniform alone distinguished him from one of our men." On one occasion Quantrill received a report that redlegs were in Cass County, robbing people and burning houses. He ordered his men to saddle up, and, with Randlett riding along, they located the enemy. When the redlegs saw the guerrillas, they fled for Kansas, were hotly pursued, and run down near the state line. Quantrill had Randlett escorted to a hilltop where he could observe the engagement in safety. Several of the enemy were wounded in the brief fight that followed, but they all fought well and managed to escape.

On another occasion two Yankee deserters stumbled on Quantrill's temporary camp. Although they announced they wanted to join the Confederate army, Quantrill had them put under guard in a farmhouse and interrogated them. They had heard that Randlett was his hostage and advised Quantrill to string him up without delay. Amused, Quantrill invited the lieutenant to dress in a guerrilla's borrowed outfit, question them himself, and hear what fate they advocated for him. Afterward Quantrill asked him his opinion of them. They were either thieves or spies, Randlett said. Shortly after leaving the house, he heard a volley of shots. . . .

Quantrill wrote several letters to the commandant of Fort Leavenworth, in which he requested an exchange of Randlett for Brady, but he received no reply. Since, like all guerrillas, he was considered an outlaw rather than a soldier, the officer refused to communicate with him. Quantrill then had Randlett write letters requesting the exchange, and these were passed up the chain of command to Colonel John McNeil, commander of the Kansas City post. McNeil was not inclined to negotiate. He knew that Colonel Robert H. Graham's 8th Kansas Infantry was at this very moment scouring the countryside, and he was so confident that Graham would find and destroy Quantrill that on March 17, 1862, he sent Randlett a note in which he said, "I can assure you that you will soon be liberated and if the party who holds you dares harm a hair of your head they will one and all be hung when taken which is now only a matter of time and that time short."

Whether this would have been comforting to Randlett will never be known because on the very next day, long before the missive could have made its way to him, an impatient Quantrill carried him to a hotel in Independence. Quantrill wrote a safe-passage pass on hotel stationery, gave Randlett a ten-day parole so that he might negotiate an exchange in person, and rode away.

Randlett, who had been thoroughly soaked by a rainstorm on the ride to Independence, sat by a stove trying to warm himself while a crowd of men gathered in the hotel bar to drink whiskey and glare at him. In no time at all they were drunk and boisterous. Out in the street a larger but no more sober mob had gathered, whooping and yelling and threatening his life. Randlett, knowing Quantrill's pass would not be honored by these murderous drunks, roamed through the hotel's public rooms looking for a means of escape. He encountered an old man named Perry who was an avowed Union supporter, though he was not averse to working both sides of the street: He often carried messages for Quantrill and made himself otherwise useful. "I am a friend of any soldier," Perry assured him and led him out a side door, through a maze of alleys to his own stable, where he hid him in a manger and covered him with straw.

Perry brought him supper and, at 3:00 A.M., breakfast, and then his saddled mare. He escorted him to Kansas City.

When Randlett reported to McNeil, the colonel cursed Quantrill's name and ordered Randlett to return at 8:00 P.M. When Randlett entered the office at the appointed hour, he found McNeil with a captain whom he did not recognize. They were studying a huge wall map. "Here he is now," the colonel said to the captain and remarked to Randlett that Quantrill's turning him loose was opportune. The 8th Infantry had indeed encountered the bushwhackers and killed two of them, wounded several more, and shot two of their horses. The guerrillas had beat a hasty retreat, though they managed to drive an abolitionist family from their home and set it ablaze. They had disappeared into the bush. McNeil now proposed to send Randlett out as a scout to guide the captain and a company of men to Quantrill's haunts, ambush him, and destroy him. Randlett refused the assignment. He told McNeil that he had given his word to the guerrilla chieftain and had no choice but to live up to the terms of his parole: He would try to negotiate a prisoner exchange but, failing that, would go back to Quantrill and tell him what had happened. McNeil was furious and engaged in a shouting match with Randlett that only ended when Randlett roared, "I will not go, and, damn you, you can't make me go!" He stormed out of the office in such high dudgeon that he blundered into another officer on the sidewalk and knocked him down.

As it happened McNeil was about to be replaced, and the new commander allowed Randlett to proceed on his mission, but Brigadier General Samuel D. Sturgis, Leavenworth's commanding officer, continued to refuse to strike any bargain with "Bandit Quantrell." He told Randlett he could do as he pleased but advised him not to return to his captor. Randlett, still clinging to the nineteenth-century code of gentlemanly conduct, felt "honor bound to go back to him" and tell him there would be no exchange.

Twelve hundred Union troops were quartered in Independence when Randlett returned, and he had a hard time getting any civilian to admit even knowing Quantrill, much less where he was. However, he eventually found one of Quantrill's spies and gave him a message for his leader, telling him that no exchange would be made. Satisfied at last that he had discharged his duty as an officer and a gentleman, Lieutenant Randlett rode for Kansas City.

He never saw Quantrill again.

CHAPTER 6

"The Bullets Were Whizing Thick and Fast Around Me": Ambushes and Reprisals

Quantrill's hit-and-run tactics had already become more than annoying to Federal authorities. The Aubry raid had been particularly shocking because of the cold-blooded murder of civilians, and Unionists on the border were not only outraged but frightened.

On March 13, 1862, in response to the depredations of Quantrill's band and of the many other guerrilla bands operating in Missouri, Major General Henry W. Halleck, commander of the Department of the Missouri, issued a proclamation that outlawed guerrillas and promised that "they will not, if captured, be treated as ordinary prisoners of war, but will be hung as robbers and murderers."

Five days after Halleck's proclamation was issued, Quantrill and forty followers crossed the Missouri River on skiffs, landing on the north bank, with the intention of attacking the small Federal garrison at Liberty, fourteen miles northeast of Kansas City. They encountered a Union soldier as they entered the town and demanded the location of the troops; when he refused to disclose it, he was killed. His death was for nothing: The bushwhackers soon located the eight Yankees, who barricaded themselves in a brick building and held out for three hours before surrendering. Quantrill paroled them all, and then, since many of the residents of Liberty were Southern in sympathy, he and his men enjoyed the hospitality of the town. When the feted raiders recrossed the Missouri, they made camp at the Little Blue Baptist Church, twelve miles southeast of Independence.

Either no one in Liberty had known of Halleck's order or no one who knew informed Quantrill or his men, because Quantrill did not learn of it until the evening of March 19, when he came across the March 14 issue of the St. Louis *Missouri Republican*. What Quantrill read radically changed his attitude toward the war—and thus his conduct. Heretofore he had accepted the surrenders of Yankees and then paroled them. He believed himself to be a Confederate officer, and he had expected to be treated as a soldier if taken. However, Halleck disabused him of the notion of honorable treatment. Quantrill understood that he would be summarily executed if captured and reacted accordingly. "One thing I do know," William Gregg said of him, "and that is he was a soldier and not afraid to die, that he was equitable and just to friend and foe alike up to a certain period in the war. . . ." Quantrill himself told Thomas C. Reynolds, the Confederate governor of Missouri, that he felt he had been "forced" into a no-quarter manner of fighting.

On the morning of March 20, Quantrill called his men together and read Halleck's proclamation to them. Then he melodramatically drew a line in the dirt and spurred his horse across it. "Now, boys," he said, "I accept the challenge. All of you who wish to remain and fight with me ride over on this side of the line. All of you who wish to leave the outfit go ahead and nothing will be held against you. Every man now will make his own choice."

Forty-five men immediately crossed the line, and only fifteen held back. These were new recruits from Cass County, and they went home but returned to the band within a month: The brutality of the Federal militia and the persecution of their loyalist neighbors made it impossible for them to live peacefully on their farms.

Despite Halleck's edict other young men continued to make their way to Quantrill's camp, so that on March 22 he had more than a hundred followers. On this date he struck back at Halleck. He had intended to attack the seventy-five-man Federal garrison at Independence, but last-minute intelligence warned him of the arrival of three hundred reinforcements, so he headed in the direction of Kansas City instead. On the bridge over the Little Blue, south of town, his men captured a Yankee sergeant—one of the hated Dutch. The man had been disarmed and had dismounted when Quantrill rode up, drew his revolver, and shot him down. For Quantrill, this was measure for measure: The Yankees would do exactly the same to him if they caught him.

"Boys," Quantrill shouted, flourishing his smoking pistol over his head, "Halleck issued the order, but we draw the first blood!"

The bridge's toll keeper and young son had also been captured, and some guerrillas accused the father of being a Union spy. He was tried on the spot, convicted, and shot—while his child looked on.

The raiders burned the bridge, remounted, and rode away, leaving in their wake two dead men and an orphaned boy. Eighteen miles southeast of Kansas City, the bushwhackers stopped at the Majors farm and ate lunch and rested from their exertions. As evening fell they broke up into four groups and dispersed. Quantrill led twenty-one men to the David Tate farm, three miles south of Little Santa Fe. After a leisurely supper, they bedded down in the house, falling asleep around 8:00 P.M.

A few hours later the Federals struck.

Colonel Robert B. Mitchell, 2nd Kansas Volunteers, had learned of the burning of the bridge and set out from Kansas City at 6:30 P.M. in pursuit of Quantrill's band. Mitchell arrived at Little Santa Fe sometime after 10:00 P.M. and dispatched a cavalry squadron under the command of Major James M. Pomeroy to arrest David Tate. The old man was a known confidant of Quantrill's, and Mitchell wanted to question him as to the whereabouts of the guerrilla chieftain.

Quantrill had put out two pickets, but they had fallen asleep and did not awaken until the Yankees were nearly on top of them. They slipped into the woods without firing so much as a single warning shot. The unsuspecting Pomeroy pounded on the farmhouse door, demanding that a lamp be lighted, and to be let in. Quantrill fired a shot through the door and shouted for his men to barricade the doors and windows with bedding and furniture. His bullet had missed Pomeroy, who raced back to his troops and ordered them to open fire. The first volley struck the house and was answered by Navy Colts. Pomeroy heard the terrified shrieks of the Tate women and children above the sounds of the weaponry and ordered a cease-fire so that they could come out. When they were clear, the gun battle resumed, Yankee single-shot rifles against rebel revolvers and shotguns.

Two guerrillas slipped out through a window and surrendered. They told Pomeroy that he had cornered none other than Quantrill himself and, they estimated, more than two dozen of his followers. Pomeroy shouted, "Come out, Quantrell! I have the house surrounded by five hundred men!" The reply was another fusillade of pistol shots. Pomeroy and Private William Wills tried to set fire to the log house. They made excellent targets: Pomeroy went down with a minié ball in his right thigh, and Wills was wounded in the right arm near the shoulder and took a load of buckshot in the groin.

Captain Amaziah Moore assumed command of the siege and sent a message to Colonel Mitchell, asking for reinforcements. He shouted another warning to Quantrill and, when the only response was more gunfire, managed to set the house ablaze.

As the flames roared higher Moore again shouted a demand that the rebels surrender, promising to kill all who did not. Cole Younger and some others taunted and cursed him, but as the fire spread and began to envelop the structure, a number of the guerrillas became unnerved. Quantrill calmly went from room to room, steadying his men and looking for a means of escape. He found a section of wall made up only of weatherboarding and called everyone together. He told Cole and the other men with shotguns to exit the building first; those with only revolvers were to follow. Then he broke through the weatherboard with a chair. "Steady, boys, follow me!" he cried, and the guerrillas plunged through the hole and sprinted for the timber behind the house, firing in all directions as they went. The startled Yankees in their path scrambled to get out of the way, but others came running and fired at the fleeing forms. Two brothers named Rollen were shot down; one was killed instantly, the other, mortally wounded, lingered until the next afternoon.

When Colonel Mitchell arrived, the house was still burning. He peered through various windows and saw five bodies of bushwhackers who had been wounded or killed during the battle. The deaths of the Rollen brothers brought the total enemy dead to seven; three others had been captured and two surrendered. "We took 25 horses," Mitchell reported, "some of which have already been identified as belonging to parties in this State, from whom they were stolen, and about 20 sets of horse equipments [saddles and bridles]." On the Union side, Major Pomeroy recovered, but Private Wills died of loss of blood from his groin wound. Two horses had been killed.

Mitchell decided to press his advantage and marched at dawn on the Wyatt farm, where, as it happened, George Todd and eleven men had spent the night. They fled on foot into the brush at the approach of the cavalry. The undergrowth was too dense to permit pursuit on horseback, so some of Mitchell's men leaped from their saddles and raced after the bushwhackers, capturing three.

Despite the order that guerrillas were to be treated as outlaws and summarily executed, those captured were taken back to the garrison, incarcerated, and interrogated. Afterward most of them were hung.

Quantrill arrived on foot and exhausted at David Wilson's house in lower Jackson County. He sent word to the scattered members of his band to meet near the headwaters of the Little Blue. In the meantime he moved from farm to farm to keep the Federals from finding him. Many of the band came to the rendezvous on foot because they had not yet been able to replace their abandoned horses, and Quantrill dispersed them until they could all procure mounts. He set another rendezvous on the Sni for some days hence.

The units of 1st Missouri Cavalry, under Captain Albert P. Peabody, had been scouring the countryside, and on March 30 informers reported rumors to him that Quantrill and sixty men were camped in the Pink Hill area. Peabody took sixty-five troopers from C and D Companies and galloped nineteen miles, then divided his forces into two search parties. Peabody and thirty men came upon a two-story log house and saw three men in the front yard: One, John Koger, was just tying his horse to a rail fence, having returned from visiting a neighbor; the second man, William Gregg, was cutting the third man's hair. As the Yankees rode up, gunfire erupted from the house, and they returned it as the men in the yard dove for cover. Koger was wounded.

Peabody ordered his men to dismount, had the horses taken out of range, and directed fire against the house's windows and doors.

Some guerrillas managed to shoot from the windows and doorways, while others knocked out chunks of plaster from between the logs to make loopholes. Quantrill was downstairs with half the men; the rest were upstairs with Todd and old Sam Clark, a locally renowned hunter, who blasted away at the attackers with a shotgun. Gregg, the wounded Koger, and the third man who had been in the yard had managed to reach a cluster of slave cabins behind the house and take refuge in them. All the bushwhackers' horses were in a barn seventy yards from the house.

The Federal spies had greatly overestimated Quantrill's force: He had only thirty men, so that in the beginning the sides were evenly matched. Peabody sent a messenger to Pink Hill for reinforcements and another to locate a lieutenant named White, who was in command of the other search party, telling him to come posthaste; as the fight progressed, farmers, drawn by the sound of gunfire, gathered on the hills above the house and sniped at the Yankees with Sharps rifles.

After an hour and a half of sporadic fighting, Lieutenant White and thirty-five troopers arrived, and Peabody on horseback launched a charge against the house. His mount was wounded three times and the charge repulsed, but Quantrill was afraid that the Federals would eventually bring in an overwhelmingly superior number of reinforcements. With Todd and the others covering from the second floor, he led the men from the first floor on a dash toward the barn. Just as the run began, however, Peabody launched a second attack, forcing a retreat back into the house.

With the added firepower of Lieutenant White's reinforcements it was clear that few bushwhackers would survive a seventy-yard sprint across open ground to the barn. In order to save his band Quantrill would have to abandon the horses once again. He gathered everyone together and then feigned another try for the animals. Six men leaped out of the side door and just as quickly leaped back inside; the Yankees on that side of the house had opened fire with their single-shot carbines. Before they could reload, however, all the guerrillas burst out of the house and raced into the timber to the rear.

Prior to putting a torch to the farm buildings, the Federals searched them and found six bodies. Spies subsequently relayed rumors that two of the wounded who had made it into the brush died as well. The guerrillas had lost another twenty horses, saddles, and bridles.

They made their way to the Little Sni Creek and concealed themselves in the undergrowth on the top of a high bluff overlooking the Ball Ford. When a Captain Murphy and fifty-one men who had been dispatched from Pink Hill to reinforce Peabody rode into the ford, the bushwhackers opened fire. A number of troopers and horses dropped into the water, and the other men fled in panic. Captain Murphy rallied them and attempted to scale the cliff, but it was too steep. He was pinned down until Peabody, following the enemy's trail, came up behind them.

The guerrillas scattered, and each man looked for a new horse. The search was not difficult: "The region abounded in splendid horseflesh," explained Dr. Castel, "and most of the inhabitants were more than willing to help out Quantrill's boys. Even those who opposed the guerrillas dared not refuse them if they 'requested' a mount. Otherwise, it might mean losing more than a favorite mare."

The next rendezvous was at the house of Reuben Harris, ten miles south of Independence. Quantrill decided to capture Harrisonville, the county seat of Cass County, and so moved the band to Job Crabtree's house, eight miles east of Independence. But the Federals were still on his trail, and he had to give up the raid and hide out on an abandoned farm known as the Jordan Lowe place, twelve miles southwest of Independence. He and his men slept in the woods to forestall another house siege. On the night of April 15, a particularly fearsome thunderstorm struck the area. The soaked guerrillas took refuge in the Lowe house. No guards were posted because it was assumed that no troops would be out on such a night.

The assumption was wrong. Lieutenant Colonel Egbert B. Brown, 7th Missouri Infantry, had been tracking Quantrill for five days and, believing his quarry was close, would not be denied by bad weather. Shortly before midnight a spy located the bushwhackers, and Brown dispatched Lieutenant G. W. Nash and thirty men to capture them. Nash galloped through the storm, which finally broke at 4:00 A.M., arriving just at dawn.

He had his men quietly surround the house and secure the enemy horses, which had been hitched to a fence behind it. He then opened fire. The guerrillas awoke to the sound of bullets thudding against the walls.

For the third time in four weeks, Quantrill had been trapped, and for the third time he led a break-out charge. As Cole Younger raced away from the house, he heard gunfire coming from over his shoulder and realized someone had been left behind. He turned and ran back. Actually, three men—George Todd, Andy Blunt, and Joe Gilchrist—had been sleeping in the loft, and, after their rude awakening, had been taking pot shots from the second-story windows. They had not heard Quantrill's order to charge above the sounds of their own gunfire. Cole managed to save Todd, but in the belated dash to the timber, Gilchrist was killed and Blunt captured.

Two other bushwhackers were also killed: William Carr and a newly arrived teenage recruit whose name no one could recall and who was known thereafter simply as "the Irish boy." The Federals shot Blunt and left him for dead. He came to and crawled to a farmhouse, where he was nursed back to health. The brush with death did not reform him: As soon as he was sufficiently recovered, he rejoined Quantrill.

The Yankees were jubilant as they rode away from the Lowe place. They were certain they had killed four rebels (although they mistakenly included Blunt in that number) and wounded at least four more; in addition, they captured—as Colonel Brown noted in his report—"five prisoners, all the horses, accoutrements, most of their arms and clothing." Above all, they had the inexpressible pleasure of seeing the notorious guerrillas "running off barefooted and coatless."

William Gregg remarked in his unpublished memoir that from the end of March to the middle of April, "it was a series of surprises for [us], in each case losing our horses, which was a great drawback, however we soon got onto the enemies tactics, and never afterwards did we lose horses in any considerable number, but often beat the enemy out of theirs."

William Quantrill may have been a natural guerrilla tactician, but lacking any formal military instruction, he was forced to learn solely by experience. The ambushes at the Tate, Clark, and Lowe farms taught him the absolute necessity of always putting out pickets and of using for the detail only the most stalwart and reliable men. He also began to choose his camping sites with an eye to defense against ambush. The lessons were valuable beyond eliminating the tiresome and frequent necessity of replacing all the horses: Never again—at least not until the last fight of his life—would Quantrill be taken completely by surprise and threatened with the instant annihilation of his band.

On April 21, the Congress of the Confederate States of America, meeting in Richmond, Virginia, approved "An Act to organize bands of Partisan Rangers." The "Partisan Ranger Act of 1862," as it became known, authorized President Jefferson Davis to commission officers "with authority to form bands of Partisan Rangers, in companies, battalions or regiments. . . . Such Partisan Rangers, after being regularly received into service, shall be entitled to the same pay, rations and quarters during their term of service, and are subject to the same regulations as other soldiers."

Despite the cloak of legitimacy that the act cast over the incalculable number of guerrilla bands operating in the South and West throughout much of the war, Federal military authorities steadfastly refused to recognize guerrillas as soldiers. Nowhere was this more true than in the

Transmississippi. Indeed, on the very day the act was passed, Brigadier General James Totten, commander of the District of Central Missouri and headquartered at Jefferson City, issued Order No. 47:

> It is represented on reliable authority at these headquarters that bands of . . . guerillas, marauders, murderers and every species of outlaw are infesting to an alarming extent all the southwest portion of Jackson County and that persons of influence and wealth in these vicinities are knowingly harboring and thus encouraging (if not more culpably connected with) these bands of desperadoes. Farmers generally in these neighborhoods are said to be knowing[ly] encouraging the lawless acts of these guerillas. . . . Murders and robberies have been committed; Union men threatened and driven from their homes; the U.S. mails have been stopped; farmers have been prohibited planting by the proclamation of a well-known and desperate leader of these outlaws by the name of Quantrell, and the whole country reduced to a state of anarchy. This state of things must be terminated and the guilty punished. All those found in arms and open opposition to the laws and legitimate authorities, who are known familiarly as guerillas . . . murderers, marauders, and horse-thieves, will be shot down by the military upon the spot when found perpetrating their foul acts. All who have knowingly harbored or encouraged these outlaws in their lawless deeds will be arrested and tried by a military commission for their offenses, and those who have harbored and fed such miscreants as guerillas, but against whom clear proof cannot be obtained and who profess ignorance of having done these wrongs will be put under heavy bonds and security for their future good conduct or confined until they give such bonds. . . .

Quantrill did not call his men to a quick rendezvous after the escape from the Lowe farm. He had business in Hannibal, in northeast Missouri, and left the others to find new mounts at their leisure. This does not mean that they were idle: They formed themselves into small groups and robbed mail carriers and stagecoaches and committed other malefactions. "The Union people here [in western Missouri] are suffering greatly from the hands of these ruffians," reported Captain John B. Kaiser to his superior. "They are driven daily from their homes and many of them are either caught or shot. No Union man is safe 1 mile from camp unless a force is with him."

Quantrill, accompanied by Todd, went to Hannibal to buy pistol caps. Heretofore some Jackson County women had gotten caps, lead, and powder for Quantrill and his followers in Kansas City, and they had supplemented this supply by stripping the bodies of dead soldiers and relieving those captured of their weapons. Federal authorities in the city had recently become more watchful, however, and the guerrillas' ammunition was running low.

In his autobiography, Cole claimed to have gone along on the trip disguised as a Yankee captain, while Todd and Quantrill were majors. They stayed in a fine hotel, related Cole, and had a conversation with the regimental commander, who "talked very freely with us about Quantrell, Todd, Haller, Younger, Blunt, Pool and other guerrillas of whom he had heard. While in Hannibal we bought 50,000 revolver caps and such other ammunition as we needed." Cole wrote that a merchant told him, "I hope you may kill a guerrilla with every bullet I have sold you. I think if ever there was a set of devils let loose, it is Quantrell, Todd, Cole Younger and Dave Pool."

From Hannibal the three men took a train west to St. Joseph. Here, according to Cole, they were entertained by the garrison commander, Colonel Harrison B. Branch, at his headquarters, and "our disguise was undiscovered." They rode to Kansas City in a hack before making their way back to rural Jackson County.

Many of the men who fought on the border before and during the war displayed a marked tendency in their later years to exaggerate their own importance. We know from other sources that Quantrill and Todd did go to Hannibal to buy ammunition, but we have only Cole's word that he accompanied the other two and twice hoodwinked Federal officers. Cole's autobiography, written in 1903 to promote his Wild West show, is an odd mixture of fact, exaggeration, and outrageous tall tales. Much of what he wrote about his childhood and youth can be independently verified or at least is credible, but beginning with his descriptions of his experiences in 1862, his veracity becomes increasingly dubious. Immediately following his account of the ammunition-buying trip, for instance, he spun out a tale of how he once scouted Independence dressed as an "old apple-woman," complete with a gray wig, spectacles, faded sunbonnet, ragged skirt, and a basket laden with "beets, beans, and apples." Describing himself in the third-person female, he said he struck a picket line, where a sergeant sought to banter with "grandmother."

"Were you younger and prettier, I might kiss you."

"Were I younger and prettier, I might box your ears for your impudence."

"Oh, ho! you old she-wolf, what claws you have for scratching!" he retorted, and reached for her hand.

The quick move she made started the horse suddenly or he might have been surprised to feel that hand.

Intercepted by a mounted sentry as he fled the scene, Cole claimed to have produced a cocked revolver from the apple basket and shot the man dead.

Cole lived an extraordinary life—guerrilla fighter, outlaw, prisoner of twenty-five years—and it is too bad he did not set down a more factual account of it. In his later years, he told reporters and even friends preposterous stories. Cole may have fallen into the habit of lying during his outlaw days and years of confinement to protect himself and his comrades, or he may just have become, with the passage of time, one of those old men who love to fib and yarn to no purpose and entertain themselves with their own faintly humorous inventions. He could have written a fascinating autobiography that would have proven enormously valuable to generations of historians and aficionados of the West, but the fabrications he set down are not even all that interesting.

———— ·•·• ————

After returning to Jackson County, Quantrill called the band together. In the month he had been gone, his men had acquired excellent horses, and a number of new recruits had joined up.

During the early summer months of 1862, the bushwhackers ambushed Yankee detachments and waylaid the mails. Exasperated local commanders, ordered to keep the mail routes open at whatever cost, sent out rebel-hunting patrols and beefed up escorts for the mail carriers. They succeeded only in providing Quantrill with ever more enticing targets. On June 11, for instance, his guerrillas struck a mail carrier riding between Independence and Pleasant Hill, in Cass County, although he was escorted by twenty-five Missouri State Militia. Ten miles from the post the escort commander, Captain J. F. Cochran, learned

that some of Quantrell's men had been seen in the vicinity. I proceeded very slowly and cautiously, with 6 men riding by file as an advance.

They had proceeded only a short distance when they were fired upon, 2 of them being killed on the spot and 3 dangerously wounded. I was about 50 yards in the rear with 18 men. We charged in the brush after them and routed them and then dismounted and searched the brush, and fired at them a number of times. I do not know what their loss was, as I had to leave to take care of the mail. The mail is safe.

Upon hearing of the attack, Lieutenant Colonel James T. Buel, the garrison commander at Independence, sent out a patrol of 7th Missouri Cavalry, which was ambushed by thirty bushwhackers. The infuriated Buel put half his command in the field, futilely hunting Quantrill. "I am unwilling that any more of my men shall be murdered escorting this mail," Buel informed his superiors.

I have therefore ordered it to be carried for the present by secessionists. I shall hold them accountable for its safe transmittal. Have also cautioned the postmaster not to send any more valuables or important dispatches in this mail, but by the way of St. Louis. I am keeping my troops constantly on the move, leaving the post at times so much exposed that it gives me some uneasiness.

Late in June Confederate Colonel Upton Hays came to Jackson County from Arkansas to raise a cavalry regiment. He sought out Quantrill and asked his help. Together they decided that Quantrill should draw the Federal troops away from the area so that Hays would be unhampered in his recruiting. With Hays riding along as an observer, Quantrill took a hundred men eighty miles south into Henry County, Yankees trailing close behind, and camped on Walnut Creek. The next morning the Federals struck and were driven off. One wounded man was left behind, to be taken prisoner.

Quantrill ranged northwest into Cass County and back again, terrorizing Union men wherever he went. His worst crime was the capturing and plundering of a river steamboat, the *Little Blue*. Federal officers alleged that his guerrillas committed "outrages on 40 sick soldiers on board"; at most they were threatened and shoved around.

On June 23, Major Eliphalet Bredett, furious at the mistreatment of the convalescents, took a 110-man detachment of 7th Cavalry from Lexington southeast into Lafayette County to find Quantrill's band. At Wellington, he arrested fifty-four men and charged them "with aiding and abetting the rebellion." He roared on to Napoleon, where he had his men thoroughly search the town—even cellars, haystacks, and outhouses; when they turned up contraband articles, he took another twenty-five prisoners on suspicion of being implicated "in the affair of capturing and plundering the steamer Little Blue." He formed his men into skirmish lines and swept them through several wooded areas below Sibley, arresting anyone who seemed remotely suspicious and firing at anyone who ran. He heard rumors that Quantrill was at St. Clair or Pink Hill or the Mapa Settlement, and raced from one place to the next in the intense, midsummer heat. He traveled one hundred miles in nine days. Like many other regular army officers, Bredett, frustrated because he could not engage an elusive enemy, lashed out at the civilian population. He appropriated precious livestock, seized or destroyed property, and made indiscriminate arrests: "I have caused to be delivered to the provost-marshal in all 107 prisoners, any of whom, except two or three, could be proven guilty of treason or misprision of treason," he reported to his superior.

Other angry or anxious commanders sent out patrols—sometimes the troopers even masqueraded as bushwhackers—and reported back to headquarters rumors that made it seem Quantrill was everywhere at once, leading eight hundred men who rode like lightning and shot like fiends. Most often the guerrillas seemed to have left a camp or town two hours before their pursuers arrived, but when the Yankees did encounter them and gave chase, they alternately fought and ran for a time, then faded into the woods and scattered. More than a few disheartened officers were forced to conclude their reports with the same sad litany: "The manner of their dispersion and the condition of our men and horses rendered further pursuit impossible."

Upton Hays, restless and anxious to get on with his mission, asked Quantrill for an escort back to Jackson County and was assigned Todd and thirty men. Quantrill continued the diversion with the remaining sixty-five bushwhackers.

On July 8, Major James O. Gower, the garrison commander at Clinton, Henry County, received intelligence "that a band of guerrillas, numbering some 200 men, commanded by Quantrell, was in camp on Sugar Creek, near Wadesburg, Cass County." So anxious was Gower to destroy the raiders that, although it was nearly midnight and the exact location of the camp unknown, he quickly dispatched Lieutenant R. M. Reynolds and ninety-three officers and troopers from the 1st Iowa Cavalry. The advance guard found the band just at dawn and immediately charged. They were repulsed, by which time Reynolds had arrived with the main column; he launched another attack and was also driven back. That was enough for the cautious lieutenant: He returned to Clinton. In his report he further exaggerated the number of the enemy and claimed that they held strategically superior ground and could not be dislodged.

Major Gower, furious at his subordinate's timidity, took personal charge of the operation. He sent dispatches to Warrensburg and Butler, ordering that details of men meet him at the Lotspeich farm in Cass County, about one mile west of the enemy camp. He himself set off at 5:00 A.M. with four commissioned officers and seventy-five enlisted men. He arrived at the rendezvous at 11:00 A.M. and then proceeded on to Sugar Creek. By now his force had grown to 293. The ashes of the guerrillas' campfires were cold, and Gower sent out patrols. One of them, led by Captain Martin Kehoe, picked up the trail and hurried in pursuit, after sending a message back to Gower. The major pressed on, following Kehoe northeast into Johnson County, and finally overtook him around 7:00 P.M. at the Hornsby farm, where the bushwhackers had eaten supper just a few hours before. Many of Gower's men had ridden more than fifty miles that day and had been in the saddle for fourteen hours. They had not stopped to eat, and their horses were played out. The major called a halt for the night. He would resume his pursuit of the rebels at daybreak.

Captain Kehoe was as aggressive and ambitious as Lieutenant Reynolds had been timid: He had his men in the saddle before the rest of the company was fully awake. Disobeying orders, he rode off in the direction the raiders had taken and, three miles west of Pleasant Hill, saw their pickets just ahead of him. Believing that Quantrill had three hundred men and that he had found just a small portion of the band, Kehoe sent a message back to Gower, saying he was about to engage their advance guard and requesting reinforcements. He then gave orders to draw sabers and charge.

The guerrillas had spent the previous night in the woods, and in the morning made their way to the Sears farm, whose owner was a Union man. They had planned to torch the house, but it had rained during the night, and they lingered to dry their blankets and coats in the sun. When the pickets sounded the alarm, the blankets and coats were snatched from the fence rails, and Quantrill ordered that the horses be saddled and taken to a nearby ravine. He had his men lie down behind the lot fence facing the lane down which the Federals would be coming.

When pickets raced down the road an instant later with Kehoe's column in pursuit, the only man visible was Gregg, caught out in the open in the middle of the lot. The Yankees took aim at him as they galloped into the ambush. "The bullets were whizing thick and fast around me," Gregg remembered, and it seemed like an hour before Quantrill, standing behind a gatepost, shouted, "Let 'em have it, boys!" Six troopers toppled to the ground dead; nine more reeled in their saddles wounded. Kehoe's horse was shot from under him, and he went down with a bullet in the shoulder. The surviving cavalrymen desperately reined in their horses, wheeled them around, and thundered back down the road. Kehoe was forced to retreat ignominiously on foot.

The panicked, riderless horses ran on toward the gate at full speed, and Gregg shouted to Quantrill to open it. Once the gate swung shut behind them, they were quickly secured. The bodies of the slain cavalrymen were stripped of carbines and revolvers—and canteens of whiskey, which many of the guerrillas were, no doubt, delighted to commandeer.

Once his men were out of pistol range, Kehoe shouted for them to dismount, and they commenced firing with rifles. Bushwhacker John Hampton was killed, and George Maddox and William Tucker were wounded. Quantrill led a charge against the enemy, killing two, and driving the rest back. He placed pickets to keep watch and sent away Tucker, who was ambulatory, in the care of his brother. Maddox was shot through both lungs, so Quantrill appropriated Sears's yoke of oxen, two featherbeds, and a wagon. The wounded man was put on one mattress in the back of the wagon, Hampton's corpse on the other, and the wagon was driven away.

Kehoe had withdrawn to a farmhouse visible in the distance, and through his powerful spyglass Quantrill could see the surgeons caring for the wounded. He did not need a spyglass, however, to note the cloud of dust moving toward the farmhouse. Kehoe was receiving massive reinforcements—Major Gower and his command.

Quantrill ordered a withdrawal into the ravine, where the horses had been hidden. It was surrounded by thick brush, and its banks were five to seven feet high and forty to sixty feet apart.

The Gower's advance guard, Company G, 1st Iowa Cavalry, charged the defile, but was driven back by the guerrillas' fusillades. Captain

William A. Martin, of Company G, 7th Missouri Cavalry, reported that
he came in sight with his command

> and, observing the position of the enemy, advanced at once upon their
> lines. But on riding up within 15 paces of the precipice from behind
> which they were pouring a galling fire upon us, I dismounted my men,
> and, being under so strong a fire, did not wait to form more than 29 of
> my men until I charged upon their lines, not firing a shot until I reached
> the brink of the precipice, when I opened a volley of fire upon their
> lines . . . which produced a most dreadful effect.

Martin leaped into the ravine, calling for his men to follow him.
"Then ensued a hand-to-hand and bloody struggle for the mastery of the
defile; but my gallant men drove them from their strong position with
not more than half the number of men they had on their side. [We]
scaled the opposite bank after them and drove them back near 100 yards
to the edge of the brush, they disputing every inch of ground."

Major Gower had sent a detachment to that side of the brush, and
these men fired a volley, driving the guerrillas back to and through
Martin's weaker line and again into the ravine. Martin and his men followed them, and the hand-to-hand fight resumed. This was Missourian
against Missourian, and the Federals fought so courageously and with
such ferocity that the bushwhackers, remembering the canteens of
whiskey they had taken from Kehoe's slain soldiers, would always insist
they must have been drunk. As men on both sides ran out of ammunition, firearms were used as clubs, and it was pistol butt against saber,
knife against rifle stock. The undergrowth was thick in the ravine, and
men blundered about, trampling the wounded and stumbling into one
another.

Quantrill, badly wounded in the thigh, realized his men would all be
killed or captured unless they escaped soon. He ordered those with
horses to try to break out. The men heaved rocks at the enemy to beat
them back and give themselves time to mount. Even so, Ezra Moore was
shot out of his saddle, and Jerre Doors was shot through the knee as he
tried to pull himself up on his horse. Twenty-one guerrillas, led by
William Gregg, broke through and got away; others scattered on foot in
small groups in the opposite direction, lugging some of their wounded
with them as they went. "In the jaded condition of the men and horses,"

Martin wrote, "Major Gower thought it inexpedient to attempt to follow them any farther."

The bushwhackers had left thirty horses behind, along with, Martin noted proudly, "a vast number of saddles, blankets, coats, guns, and one mail bag and lock and also their company roll." One of the rebel wounded identified Quantrill's own horse, saddle, overcoat, and the precious, powerful spyglass.

William Gregg said it was the greatest battle he had ever witnessed, and other guerrillas remembered it with awe and wonder. The engagement lasted an hour, and Major Gower admitted to casualties of eleven killed, twenty-one wounded; he estimated the enemy lost eighteen and had thirty wounded, although the exact numbers could never be determined because some of the wounded who were carried off may have died later. (It is known today that Jerre Doors, shot in the knee, subsequently bled to death.)

"With good reason Quantrill's followers always spoke of the fight with Gower's troopers as the hardest one the band ever had," observed Albert Castel.

In it they proved themselves capable of holding their own in an open, stand-up battle against trained and disciplined soldiers, even though heavily out-numbered. But while their performance might be termed magnificent, it was not bushwhacking. By remaining to fight it out with Gower's command they violated one of the cardinal rules of guerrilla warfare: Never do battle against a superior force on its own terms unless absolutely necessary. Quantrill and the other bushwhacker leaders realized their mistake and, as in the case of the surprises at the Tate, Clark, and Lowe houses, profited from it. Henceforth, they always carefully reconnoitered the enemy, fought only under the most favorable possible circumstances, and constantly endeavored to make surprise attacks. By the same token, they avoided battle in open country, attempted to keep personal risks to a minimum, and scattered into the bush whenever hotly pursued by large Union forces. Such tactics were not a matter of courage or cowardice, but rather of necessity and common sense. The guerrilla's purpose is to kill, not be killed. And by the summer of 1862, Quantrill's bushwhackers had become accomplished killers.

CHAPTER 7

"Boys, We Had Better Surrender!": The Raid on Independence

After his escape from Sears's farm, Quantrill hid out on the Little Blue. While he nursed his leg wound and a high fever, the men who had abandoned their horses and equipment once again fanned out through the region searching for replacements.

Before Quantrill recovered, three of his men were ambushed. Jim Knowles, the city marshal of Independence, had heard it whispered that members of Quantrill's band often crossed the Little Blue at a certain ford. Knowles carried the intelligence to Lieutenant Colonel Buel at Independence. Buel dispatched a detachment under Lieutenant Aaron Thomas to the ford. Thomas hid his men in the undergrowth beside the river and waited. Three guerrillas eventually appeared: Ed Koger, John Little, and George Todd. They rode into the water and then stopped to let their horses drink. The Yankees opened fire, and Koger and Little toppled out of their saddles dead. Todd, who was not even wounded, wheeled his mount and galloped away.

Koger and Little had been Todd's close friends, and their deaths were a bitter blow. From that day on he was filled with a murderous rage against all Federal soldiers, and he was determined to kill as many of them as he could. His wild recklessness in battle became legendary. "I have seen him," observed Frank Smith, "in more tight places than any other man in the outfit, where it looked impossible for him to escape, but he always came through unscathed."

As with Bloody Bill Anderson and Cole Younger, the war had become a personal matter for George Todd, and he waged it mercilessly until his death. But unlike the other two men, he got a chance to settle the score directly—during the raid on Independence, Missouri, just a week or two after the ambush.

———— ·•·•· ————

Confederate Colonel Upton Hays had received unintended assistance from the Federal authorities for his recruiting drive in Jackson County. On May 29, the nervous, young Federal commander of the Missouri State Militia, Brigadier General John M. Schofield, fearing a general insurrection, had reinforced Halleck's directive, branding the partisans simply as "robbers and assassins" and ordering that when captured they be "shot down upon the spot." Fifty-four days later, on July 22, he went a step further, issuing General Order No. 19, which required all able-bodied male Missourians to enlist in the state militia "for the purpose of exterminating the guerrillas that infest our state." Some indignant Southern sympathizers, faced with the prospect of fighting against friends and relatives, had gone over to Quantrill's Raiders or one of the other bands of partisans; others had joined Hays, so that by the end of July, he had three hundred men.

On August 1, Confederate Colonel John T. Hughes entered Jackson County, having come from Arkansas with seventy-five men. Hughes, a hero of the Mexican war, was a talented officer and had been assigned the task of recruiting a brigade for the Confederate army. He intended to get most of his men from the northwestern counties, but he realized that the presence of a large Federal garrison at Independence might hamper enlistments. Some of his potential recruits would be casting uneasy glances over their shoulders. Hughes also understood that after Southern setbacks in the region during the spring and summer—particularly at the demoralizing, three-day Battle of Pea Ridge, Arkansas, in which two Confederate generals died, well over a thousand men were killed or wounded, and hundreds more captured—an audacious victory would go far toward arousing the patriotic fervor of young Missourians. Nothing excites the uncritical faculties of youth like sudden, easy success.

Hughes decided to attack and temporarily occupy Independence. Since the garrison was variously estimated to have three hundred to five hundred troops, he would need more men. He established a camp and recruiting station at Strother (now Lee's Summit), raising a large Confederate flag on a tall pole so that it could be seen from the courthouse at Independence. This brazen challenge was ignored by Colonel Buel; however, it was also largely ignored by the young men of the area, only twenty-five of whom signed up. Hughes was forced to appeal to Hays and Quantrill for help.

On Sunday, August 10, Quantrill sent one of his band, Morgan T. Mattox, into Independence, disguised as a farmer selling onions and pies. While Mattox was busy surreptitiously studying the layout of the town and the disposition of the troops, Quantrill took twenty-five men to Strother, joined there by Hays and his three hundred fresh recruits.

Mattox appeared at Strother with cheering news: Buel, an arrogant fool, could hardly have made Independence a more inviting target: He had billeted his troops in tents in a low-lying, unfortified cow pasture a full half-mile outside town. His headquarters was located in the first story of the Southern Bank building on Lexington Street, just off the southwest corner of the public square. However, the headquarters guard company, composed of twenty-one men, was billeted in buildings on the opposite side of the street. To make matters even worse, the provost marshal's twenty-four-man detachment was occupying the jailhouse a block north of the square. In order to capture the town, it would simply be necessary to isolate these pockets of troops, prevent communication between them and their commander, and subdue them one by one.

Hughes drew up the battle plan. The combined forces would strike before dawn, seizing the town, hopefully without even firing a shot. Quantrill's men were to surround Buel's headquarters. "You will be well supported," Hughes told the guerrilla chieftain. "In fact, I shall be right behind you when you enter the public square." After the town was taken, Quantrill's men were to act as pickets. The troops in the pasture would be the victims of a surprise attack.

While Hughes was drawing up his plans, an ardent Unionist named Mrs. Wilson was trying to thwart him. She had seen Hays's troops march by her Blue Springs–area house and heard rumors from neighbors that a second body of men was also converging on Independence for an attack that very night. (So many rumors had been prevalent during the previous week that numerous prudent townsfolk had left for Kansas City.) Mrs. Wilson hurried to Buel with a warning; in her alarm, she exaggerated the number of men she had seen, telling the colonel that he was about to be hit by a thousand rebels.

"Madam, we have heard such reports several times lately, and don't you see we are here yet!" Buel mocked. He then cavalierly dismissed her, advising her to go home, or, if she was afraid of the dark, to stay with some friend overnight and return to her house in the morning.

Mrs. Wilson had a low tolerance for condescending morons. She went looking for an acquaintance, Colonel Samuel D. Lucas, and told him what she had seen.

Lucas went to Buel and vouched for the lady's honesty, but Buel remained unimpressed. Why, he had had Captain Breckinridge and a scouting party out for eleven days, and Breckinridge had just gotten back two days ago to report that there was no large concentration of enemy troops to be found anywhere. "I wish people would stop bringing me these rumors," Buel added. "We always know how to take care of ourselves."

Lucas turned abruptly on his heel and stormed out of the office.

Not only did Buel fail to issue orders to the headquarters' guard and to the detachment in the pasture to be on the alert for attack and to take extra precautions accordingly, he gave permission to his chief subordinate officers to spend the night at their lodgings in town as was their custom when things were quiet. However, one of these officers, Captain William H. Rodewald, was impressed by Mrs. Wilson's warning. He had been in the office when she talked to Buel, and she had buttonholed him in the street afterward. Rodewald was in charge of the headquarters guard. He stayed in his quarters that night and told his men of the possible attack and ordered them to load their carbines and keep them by their beds.

At 3:40 A.M. the following morning Quantrill's Raiders approached the outskirts of town on Spring Branch Road. They encountered pickets, whom they killed. They entered the public square, Hughes's detachment following a moment later. One of Rodewald's pickets shouted "Halt!" three times, then fired his rifle at them and ducked into the building where his unit was billeted, slamming the door behind him. He shouted a warning into the bunk room on the first floor, then raced upstairs to awaken those sleeping on the second floor. The sound of his shot had gotten most of the soldiers moving. They peered out the windows and dimly saw through the darkness the forms of many men in the street.

Quantrill had ordered most of his men to dismount and to picket the town, sending George Todd with the rest to capture the jail. Hughes was quick-marching his troops through the public square and west on Lexington Street. Rodewald's militia fired a half-dozen shots from the second-story windows, but the guerrillas did not shoot back. One of them shouted, "For God's sake, don't fire, it's your own men!"

The ruse worked until Rodewald led his company out of the building. Hughes's troops were still marching through the square, and the first Confederate soldier Rodewald saw happened to be a man he knew, a longtime resident of Independence. Rodewald grabbed the man by the arm and took him prisoner; he yelled that the men in the streets were rebs and ordered his company to fall in line. The line cut off the last of the Confederates from their main column. Rodewald gave the order to fire a volley at the backs of the men in the main column, killing several.

Bushwhackers and Confederate soldiers attacked Rodewald, but he managed to hold the crossing of Lexington and Liberty streets for the next two hours, beating back three fierce charges. In the last of these a Confederate major named Hart was mortally wounded and a lieutenant and eleven privates were captured.

Federal Lieutenant Charles W. Meryhew, who was in charge of the detachment guarding the jail, fired a single volley at the approach of George Todd and his small contingent and then fled. Keeping to the woods and wild country, Meryhew made his way to Kansas City, accompanied by thirteen or fourteen of his men.

Quantrill had sent George Todd to the jail to free a farmer named Frank Harbaugh and Bill Bassham, a stage driver, who had been wrongly charged with being bushwhackers. Todd used a sledgehammer to break down the jail cell doors. Having released the two prisoners, he discovered a pleasant surprise in a neighboring cell: Marshal Knowles had recently killed a drunken Irishman who was "cutting up a little" and had been incarcerated in his very own hoosegow. Todd shot Knowles to death.

Some other guerrillas subsequently found Lieutenant Thomas, who had ambushed Todd and the others, in a hotel room. They killed him and kicked his body down a flight of stairs.

There were no pickets around the Federal camp. The Confederate force formed skirmish lines on the north and east borders of the pasture and opened fire on the tents below them. The firing in town had not been heard in the pasture, so the militia were still sleeping. A dozen or more died in the first volley; the rest rushed to arms.

Captain James Breckinridge, the senior officer in camp, was entirely unnerved by the sudden assault. "Boys," he cried, "we are completely surrounded, and we had better surrender."

Captain Jacob Axline heard Breckinridge yelling. Axline had arrived just the night before with sixty-four officers and troopers from the 2nd Battalion, Missouri Cavalry. Since it was already dark, they had hitched their horses to a fence rail and slept behind them on the open ground at the south end of camp. When the shooting began, Axline led his men forward, then heard Breckinridge start shouting to surrender. "Boys," Axline bellowed above the din, "get your guns and ammunition and rally behind the rock-fence!" The farmer's stone wall was on the south side of the field and ran east and west. Axline kept the men firing at the enemy as they fell back to it. (Having fired their first volley, many of Hays's new recruits were distracted from the battle by the opportunity to plunder the tents.)

Some of the retreating Federals went over the rock fence—and continued running all the way to Kansas City. The rest hunkered down, shared their ammunition, and kept shooting.

Axline spread some men along the wall and sent the rest into a four-foot-deep gully that ran perpendicular to it. The Confederates charged the rock fence and were driven back. Someone reported that a white flag was being waved farther down the wall, and Axline went to investigate, leaving a sergeant named Blake in command of the firing line. After proceeding some four hundred yards Axline found Captain Breckinridge with a piece of his own white shirt tied to a ramrod. Breckinridge had been trying to wave it over his head, but every time he lifted his arm, other men pulled it down. Now he appealed to Axline for support. "He asked me if he should hoist it," Axline recalled later. "I told him certainly not; that if he did it would be at his peril."

Axline spied fifty or sixty Federal troops in the yard of the McCoy house, a half-mile west of the camp. He sent a Lieutenant Herington to collect them and use them to clear the street north of the pasture, which he did. Meanwhile Axline corralled some stragglers, assigned them places along the rock fence, and went back to his former position on the firing line. In his absence Sergeant Blake had been severely wounded.

Lieutenant Herington attempted to march to the town square and make contact with Buel, but he encountered a squad of rebels and was driven back to the McCoy house. (He held the house until the battle was over and he learned Buel had ordered a surrender. Then, unwilling to stack his arms, he quietly slipped away with his men to Kansas City.)

The Confederates charged the wall five times and were driven back. Colonel Hughes was shot in the forehead while leading an attempted flanking maneuver and died instantly. Colonel Gideon W. Thompson took command and tried to turn the Federal right. His force was repulsed, and he was wounded in the knee. Colonel Hays then took charge of the battle, and Thompson returned to town, perhaps seeking medical treatment. Hays prudently gave up trying to overrun the enemy position. He had sharpshooters firing at any Yankee who stuck his head above the rock fence. Hays himself was wounded in the foot but continued to direct the fighting.

Axline ordered two thousand rounds of ammunition passed out to his troops and divided them into three detachments. He was just preparing to charge the rebel position in the hope of breaking out and marching on the town to rescue Buel when three men appeared at the end of the pasture with a piece of bed sheet tied to a ramrod. Axline ordered a cease-fire and sent a messenger to bring the delegation to him. There were two Confederates and a Union officer named Preble, who was Buel's adjutant. The tiresome Captain Breckinridge joined them. Adjutant Preble informed Axline that Buel had surrendered and had ordered him to surrender, too. Axline replied that Buel was no longer in command and that he would not surrender, but Breckinridge shouted to the men of his unit to lay down their arms, which they did. Preble told Axline that he had no chance—the enemy numbered seven hundred—and Axline, who was no fool, looked around. "I was left with less than 75 men, who were fatigued with near four hours' hard fighting, and our strength and position fully known to the enemy. I saw that we were thus completely placed in their power, without a hope of further success. I reluctantly consented to surrender and ordered my men to do so, under promise that the private property of the officers and men should be respected."

The fight in town had gone well for the Federals at first, considering how badly Buel had botched things. Rodewald continued to defend one corner of the square until approximately 6:00 A.M., when Buel ordered him to bring his men into the Southern Bank building and post them so that they could shoot from windows on the first and second floors. This was a foolish mistake: The bushwhackers immediately surrounded the building, and Quantrill broke into the large brick store across Liberty Street; from the second-story windows he and his men poured tremendous fire into the bank.

At 7:30 A.M. Colonel Buel asked Rodewald where his flag was—he wanted to hoist a flag over the headquarters to show the soldiers in the pasture that he was still holding out. Rodewald had not brought his flag from his unit's quarters when the fight began. William O. Buhoe, a sixteen-year-old bugler, volunteered to retrieve the flag. He ran barefoot across the street and back again, bullets whistling past him.

Since there was no flagpole on the building, two of Rodewald's men got on the roof and tried to fasten the flag to a chimney. Guerrillas shot them down. Two Confederate prisoners were forced to fasten the flag to the chimney. They were not fired on, having been recognized by their comrades.

A battle in which opposing forces fired at one another from behind walls was hardly bushwhacker fare, and Quantrill grew tired of it after awhile. He called for volunteers to set fire to the building abutting the Southern Bank. Cole Younger and Jabez McCorkle spoke up. They piled wood shavings from a nearby carpenter's shop against two doors and lighted them. In a few minutes the flames were roaring high and rapidly spreading.

Buel waved a flag of truce and insisted on talking to Colonel Thompson, who, he learned from a prisoner, had succeeded to command after Hughes was killed. Buel agreed to surrender only if "the officers and men of my command were to be considered prisoners of war," and, he added pointedly, no one was turned over to Quantrill.

Twenty-six Federal troops were killed outright in the battle and seventy-four were wounded, eleven of whom subsequently died. More than 150 were captured—the rest had run away. It was not possible for Colonel Buel to make an accurate count of enemy casualties because, as he complained, "early in the action they commenced carrying off their dead into the country." They did leave twenty-three corpses behind, and the losses in the officer corps were particularly heavy. In addition to Hughes, two other colonels had been killed, along with three captains and two lieutenants.

Thompson paroled all the Yankee soldiers. He had his men burn a considerable amount of property and then led them away from the town at five o'clock in the afternoon with twenty wagons loaded full of arms and ammunition and quartermaster and commissary stores, going southeast in the general direction of Blue Springs. Now that Hughes was dead there was no thought of going north to raise a battalion. The captured muskets and sabers would be used to arm Hays's regiment, and most of the remaining plunder was given to Quantrill. He broke away from the column and hid some of it; the rest he and his men took with them to the Morgan Walker farm.

Buel had Breckinridge arrested as soon as Axline made his report. Another Union officer had acted in a cowardly fashion—a militia captain named Cochran had hid himself in a cellar when the fighting began and stayed there until it was over. Buel wanted to arrest him too, but he was nowhere to be found: Once the firing had stopped, Cochran had slipped out of the basement, run for Kansas City, and lost himself in its population, which had been greatly swollen by terrified refugees.

The paroled Federal soldiers stayed in Independence for several days, taking care of the wounded of both sides and burying the dead. On the morning of the third day, Colonel Buel, with officers and enlisted men totaling just over 150, started on foot for Kansas City and Leavenworth to be exchanged. Two weeks later they were transferred to Benton Barracks in St. Louis to be mustered out.

— ◆ —

Quantrill returned to Anna Walker with his reputation greatly enhanced. Border folk assigned much of the credit for the victory to him. After all, he had held the town and forced Buel to surrender.

On the evening of August 12, Quantrill led his band to the Ingraham farm, six miles west of Lone Jack. Three days later Colonel Thompson, acting under the authority of General Thomas C. Hindman, officially mustered them into Southern service as Partisan Rangers. One hundred and twenty bushwhackers then elected their officers: Quantrill was named captain; William Haller, first lieutenant; George Todd, second lieutenant; and William Gregg, third lieutenant. (Todd was furious that Haller had been chosen over himself, and the two men quarreled. Haller soon left the band and was killed shortly thereafter.)

"Actually," observed Albert Castel,

the organization set up at the Ingraham farm meant little. Lacking true military discipline, serving with boyhood friends in their own neigh-

borhoods, ever-varying in numbers, frequently operating in small parties, and constantly scattering and regrouping, the bushwhackers found
it impossible to maintain a regular, rigid military organization. In practice, therefore, the real leaders were whoever became so by virtue of personality, daring, and ability—men such as Todd, Cole Younger, Andy
Blunt, Gregg, Dave Pool, Fletch Taylor, and Dick Yeager, to name only
the more prominent of Quantrill's followers. Quantrill relied on these
subchieftains to carry out his orders and they in turn exercised considerable operational independence except when Quantrill was in direct
personal charge.

The capture of Independence was, in the estimation of Richard S.
Brownlee, a "fearful blow to all western Missouri." Rumors flew that Lexington and Kansas City would be next. Spies reported that Confederate
forces were massing in the Lone Jack area and would total four thousand
men when the commands of Quantrill, Hays, and Thompson combined
with fifteen hundred Confederates coming from Arkansas under Colonel
John T. Coffee. Although the total number of troops was a wild exaggeration, it was Coffee's ambition to capture Lexington, and he was marching
north from southern Missouri in order to link up with Quantrill and the
others.

Not content with wringing their hands over real dangers, Union sympathizers and some Yankee soldiers went a step further, indulging in
paranoid delusions of a conspiracy to subjugate the state. It was charged
that Colonel Buel and Captain Breckinridge had made a secret pact with
the Confederates to surrender the Federal forces "without offering any
resistance." Much was made over the fact that despite rumors of an
impending attack that put residents to flight, Buel had not taken even
the most elemental precautions; Buel and Breckinridge had compelled
Axline to surrender, although he held a supposedly impregnable position
and, left alone for a brief time longer, might have turned the tide.

Union generals were at pains to calm the populace. Buel and Breckinridge were court-martialed on charges of conspiracy and cowardice, but
since they were being mustered out momentarily, the military took care
of its own: The prosecution was not vigorous, and they were not convicted. Interestingly, Captain Rodewald, whose loyalty, courage, and
competence were never in doubt, came to his former commander's
defense. "I believe that Colonel Buel acted in good faith, and did not

betray his command into the hands of the enemy," he asserted. "He did not display any lukewarmness during the fight, but even seized a musket and fired several shots into the rebel attacking force."

Judicial proceedings alone would not quiet nervous civilians nor restore order in the border region. Military action was needed. On August 13, General Schofield ordered Brigadier General James G. Blunt, commanding the Department of Kansas, to lead a column of cavalry and infantry in support of Colonel Clark Wright, 6th Missouri Cavalry, who was pursuing Colonel John T. Coffee and Colonel Vard Cockrell north from Springfield. Schofield expected that Wright's and Blunt's combined force of 3,200 men would be able to prevent Coffee and Cockrell from joining up with Quantrill, Hays, and Thompson.

General Totten sent orders to Major Emory S. Foster to take a column to Lone Jack and rendezvous the next day with General Fitz Henry Warren and fifteen hundred of the 1st Iowa Cavalry from Clinton. Together they were to locate and attack the Confederates.

Major Foster received the orders at 1:00 A.M. on August 15, fourteen hours after arriving in Lexington following a two-day march northwest from Sedalia. His men and horses were worn out, having gone forty-eight hours without food or rest. Foster was a good soldier, however, and at daybreak he left Lexington at the head of an eight-hundred-man column of Missouri cavalry and infantry. His spies found Coffee's camp after nightfall, and Foster, though he was outnumbered two to one, apparently judged the element of surprise to be worth more than sixteen hundred Confederates, because he launched an attack. The enemy was routed.

Many of Foster's troops were asleep in their saddles, and some of the officers, having resorted to the comfort of liquor, had acted badly during the fight and had been placed under arrest. Foster withdrew to Lone Jack, expecting to meet Warren in the morning.

Colonel Warren had taken the wrong road and gotten lost, so he was twenty-four hours behind schedule. The only men who arrived in Lone Jack in the morning were fourteen hundred howling Confederates led by Hays and Thompson.

Major Foster was not caught napping. He had put out pickets the night before, required his men to sleep in line, and had sent out two thirty-man scouting parties before daybreak. When his pickets told him excitedly that three thousand Johnny Rebs were closing in, he drew into a sound defensive position, with thick hedges in front and on either flank and a deep stream at his back.

The fight lasted five hours. The Confederate cavalry were at first greatly hampered by the hedges and the sharpshooters positioned behind them. The troopers retreated, dismounted, and launched frontal assaults on foot using cornfields and rock fences for cover. The Federals' two cannons wreaked havoc.

After four hours, the rebels began to pull back.

Union Lieutenant J. S. Develin, who had been in charge of the battery the night before, until arrested for drunkenness, rushed out onto the field and ordered his men to fall back. They obeyed, abandoning the guns. "Seeing this, the enemy rallied and made an attempt to capture the artillery, but were repulsed with terrible slaughter," Foster later recalled. He then led a charge to retrieve the cannon; of the sixty men who followed him, "only 11 reached the guns, and they were all wounded. In the act of dragging the cannon out of the enemy's reach I was shot down." Foster was, in fact, so badly wounded that he would be nearly a year recuperating before being able to return to active duty.

Captain Milton H. Brawner took command. The fighting was hand to hand. Twice the Confederates managed to seize the battery, and twice it was retaken. By the end of the fifth hour, many of the Union officers had been killed, all the rest wounded; ammunition was running low. Still, the Yankees fought on, desperation adding to their ferocity: Certain that Quantrill was in front of them, they believed they dare not surrender and fall into his hands. Finally they drove the enemy from the field—just as Colonel Coffee, who had been long in rallying his routed men, arrived on the left flank with fifteen hundred fresh Confederate troops and plenty of ammunition.

Brawner watched as Coffee began to maneuver to surround his position and bleakly assessed the situation. "The men being utterly exhausted, and our ammunition almost gone, I deemed it unadvisable to hold the ground longer, and accordingly got the command together and marched off in good order toward [Lexington], unmolested by the enemy."

Forty-five Union soldiers had been killed in what was dubbed the Battle of Lone Jack, 156 wounded, and forty-four were missing. One hundred and eighteen Confederates were known to have been killed, though the actual total may have been higher, and it was not possible to estimate the total of their wounded.

One small irony of the battle was that the Federals had had nothing to fear from Quantrill's presence. Very early on the morning of the fight he had gone to Independence with ninety men to retrieve the plunder he had been given by Thompson but had been unable to carry away. (The plunder consisted chiefly of barrels of gunpowder, and the Yankees had not as yet reoccupied the town, so it was an opportune moment to retrieve them.) He left Haller in charge with strict instructions not to move until he returned.

Major Foster was not even known to be in the area until he struck Coffee's camp, so Quantrill could not have anticipated a battle would be waged when he left for Independence.

At 8:00 A.M., a messenger from Hays arrived at the camp with a request for aid. Following Quantrill's instructions, Haller refused. Hours later Hays sent a much more urgent message. This time Gregg convinced Haller to disobey orders. Haller shouted for the men to saddle up, and they galloped hard but soon encountered Union deserters, who told them the battle was over. Haller contented himself with capturing as many of the fleeing "blue coats" as he could.

It will be recalled that Cole Younger participated in the fight. The circumstances under which he came to be at Lone Jack remain a mystery. In his autobiography, he stated that "in August, 1862 . . . I was formerly enrolled in the army of the Confederate States of America by Col. Gideon W. Thompson. I was eighteen, and for some little time had been assisting Col. Hays in recruiting a regiment around my old home." He added that "a day or two" after the Battle of Independence, "I was elected as first lieutenant in Capt. Jarrette's [sic] company in Col. Upton Hays' regiment, which was a part of the brigade of Gen. Joseph O. Shelby." Cole said that since his enlistment he had been acting as Hays's courier and had arrived at Lone Jack on the evening of August 15, accompanying the colonel. As will be seen, however, no Confederate service record exists for Cole, nor is there any other reliable substantiation of his claim to having been mustered into Hays's regiment, although, of course, his name does appear on a roster of Quantrill's men—as does that of John Jarrett.

Even though he was not in the regular Confederate army, it is possible that because of his intimate familiarity with the area, Cole had been carrying messages between Hays and Quantrill, which is what brought him to Lone Jack. Whatever the case, as we know, Union Major Bronaugh encountered Cole there, and Major Foster witnessed Cole's courage and got a chance to find out just how gallant a fellow he could be:

> During the progress of the fight my attention was called to a young Confederate riding in front of the Confederate line, distributing ammunition to the men from a "splint basket." He rode along under a most galling fire from our side the entire length of the Confederate lines, and when he had at last disappeared, our boys recognized his gallantry in ringing cheers. I was told by some of our men from the western border of the state that they recognized the daring young rider as Cole Younger. . . .
>
> My brother and I were severely wounded in the fight, and we were taken prisoners. After we were put in a cabin a Confederate guerrilla came in and threatened to shoot us both. As he stood over us, pistol in hand, the young man we had seen distributing ammunition to the Confederate line rushed in, seized the guerrilla and shoved him out of the room. Other men entered and addressed the newcomer as Cole Younger. My brother had $300; I had $700. This money and our revolvers Cole took from us at our request and delivered safely to my mother at Warrensburg, Missouri.

Massive numbers of Federal troops began converging on Lone Jack from the east, south, and southeast in the days following the battle. Coffee, Thompson, and Cockrell decided to retreat to the south, eluding their pursuers and joining Colonel Jo Shelby. Hays and Quantrill remained behind to continue the struggle against the Yankees.

Union Lieutenant Colonel John T. Burris arrived at Independence on August 21 from Kansas City. Although he had a large contingent of fresh troops, he was apparently not anxious to tangle with the rebels. He paused to burn the house and outbuildings of Benjamin Rice, whom one of Burris's junior officers characterized as a "notorious rebel and infamous scoundrel" and to arrest the editor of the treasonous *Border Star,* "a lying, dirty sheet." Since he could not easily destroy the type, Burris had it scattered on the ground.

He then began a leisurely pursuit of the enemy. After two or three days he encountered a black man who guided him to Quantrill's camp near the headwaters of the east branch of the Little Blue. Since the camp was in what Burris considered to be "an almost impenetrable forest of timber and bush," and he was unwilling to engage the enemy in such a lair, he tried to lure the bushwhackers onto open ground or alternatively maneuver his light artillery close enough to effectively shell the camp. His troops managed to capture several pickets and get the partisans to form a battle line in a field one thousand yards away from their position. Rather than do battle, however, Burris broke their line and threw them "into confusion" with "a few well-directed shots from [Lieutenant Charles S.] Bowman's battery."

The guerrillas retreated south in the direction of Pleasant Hill. Burris did not follow: "Theirs being entirely a cavalry force, and wholly unencumbered by camp equipage or transportation of any description, their flight was much more rapid than it was possible for our pursuit to be." Instead he located a farm and burned the house, outbuildings, "and the immense ricks of grain and hay found on the premises." This was because the "contrabands and prisoners" alleged and "the ladies of the house" unwisely confirmed that rebel officers had stayed there and obtained forage supplies.

Some 280 "loyal colored persons" followed Burris's command back to Kansas City.

Near the end of August Upton Hays decided to return to Arkansas. As a parting gesture he turned over to Quantrill Levi Copeland, a lieutenant of the Missouri State Militia who had been captured at Lone Jack. Copeland was, in Gregg's estimation, "a man who was very obnoxious to the Southern soldier and citizen, a man who had in cold blood, murdered numerous old men, among them, two of the Longacres of Johnson Co." He was no kindlier to the elderly of Jackson County: On one occasion, for instance, he had gone to the house of a man who had two sons with Quantrill's band and demanded the surrender of the boys. When the old man claimed not to know their whereabouts, Copeland had him hanged from a tree in his own front yard while his wife and daughters wailed and begged for his life. As Copeland rode away, he remarked, "This is what I do to all damned rebel sympathizers."

Quantrill meant to exchange Copeland for Perry Hoy, one of the earliest members of his band, who had been captured and was confined at Fort Leavenworth, awaiting execution. Immediately after Hays turned Copeland over, Quantrill sent a message to the fort in which he asked for a prisoner exchange.

Quantrill then established a new camp four miles northeast of Strother. A short time later, two men turned up, and one of them handed him a copy of a recent issue of the St. Louis *Missouri Republican*. Quantrill read the paper while Gregg sat beside him waiting his turn. Gregg saw Quantrill's expression suddenly change, and he dropped the newspaper. Without a word he took a "blank book" from his pocket, wrote something on a page, folded it, and handed it to Gregg. "Give this to [Andy] Blunt!" he said, then told him that the newspaper had given an account of Perry Hoy's execution by firing squad.

Before delivering the note, Gregg sneaked a look at it. "Take Lieut. Copeland out and shoot him," Quantrill had written. "Go to Wood-small's camp, get two prisoners and shoot them."

As soon as shots were heard coming from the woods, Quantrill ordered his men to saddle up. When Gregg asked where they were going, Quantrill replied, "We are going to Kansas to kill ten men in revenge for poor Perry!"

They reached Red Bridge, near the border, before nightfall and camped there. On the morning of September 6 they set out for Olathe; they stopped along the way at various farms and homesteads where they knew Union sympathizers lived and shot them down. Before they reached the outskirts of town late in the afternoon, they had already killed ten, but it did not matter: There were horses and jewelry in Olathe.

Quantrill halted and divided his force: He sent Gregg with sixty men to form a cordon around the town; he took the remaining eighty and rode for the public square. On the way they encountered three recently enlisted soldiers and killed them. One hundred and twenty-five militia had formed a line on the sidewalk at the south end of the square. Quantrill ordered his men to dismount and hitch their horses to the courtyard fence. He had them stand behind their animals and, using them for shields, draw their weapons and take aim at the soldiers. Quantrill shouted an invitation for them to surrender and hand over their guns, promising no harm would come to them. Only one man fool-ishly and fatally declined to accept the offer.

The guerrillas fanned out in all directions. They went into houses and shops, drove men into the street, and loaded up with all the plunder they could carry. They stole horses and wagons and threw the loot into the beds. Hiram Blanchard, a visitor from Spring Hill, kicked up a fuss about losing his horse—and was immediately murdered. Two other civilians also voiced objections to being victimized and paid with their lives.

Dr. Thomas Hamill lost all his clothes, a good horse, and a gold watch but had the sense to keep silent—for the moment. Two months later, still seething, he wrote a furious and partly inaccurate letter to Major General Samuel R. Curtis, who was at the time the commander of the Department of the Missouri, headquartered in St. Louis. "We did not care for being robbed," Hamill stated, then with perhaps understandable exaggeration he added that Quantrill had "killed our citizens in cold blood, taking our best citizens from the bosom of their families and shooting them down like so many hogs. It is horrible to relate."

The raiders put all the militia and the male civilians into a corral. Quantrill, surveying the crowd, spotted a face he recognized—Judge E. W. Robinson. He invited the jurist out of the corral, and the two men sat on a bench on the public square. "We talked for more than an hour," Robinson recalled in a letter in 1881. "During the conversation I addressed him once as 'Bill'—he very politely requested me to address him as 'Captain Quantrill,' and took from his pocket and showed me what he claimed was a commission from the Confederate government, but I did not read it—being an old acquaintance, and having no grudge against me, he treated me kindly."

The bushwhackers stayed overnight, and in the morning Quantrill kept his word to his prisoners: He marched them to a prairie two miles east of town and paroled them. He and his men then continued east back to Missouri, managing to avoid the various militia units dispatched to intercept them.

The sack of Olathe, coming on top of the Aubry and Independence raids, drove Union sympathizers to new heights of rage and fear. Some wrote indignant letters or personally called on politicians or military commanders demanding that more troops be stationed along the border and that an expedition be sent into Jackson County to destroy Quantrill once and for all. Others, particularly those who lived between Olathe and the line, prudently packed up their goods and left their homes.

If Olathe was a cause of alarm to Unionists and an annoyance to politicians, it was a positive embarrassment to Colonel John Burris. He had had the guerrillas literally within his sights and let them get away. On the morning of September 10, Burris, leading a mixed force of militia and cavalry, found the bushwhackers camped on a bank of the north branch of the Grand River, in Cass County. They immediately took flight, and the chase was on. It lasted ten days. "We pursued [the enemy] from day to day through Jackson, Cass, Johnson, and La Fayette Counties," Burris reported,

> being sometimes twenty-four hours in his rear, at other times in sight of him, but without being able to bring on an engagement, or to effect anything further than an occasional firing on their rear by our advance guard and the capture . . . of three wagons loaded with arms, dry goods, groceries, &c., previously captured by the enemy at Olathe, Kans., until the 19th instant, when, after a chase of 15 miles at almost full speed, I overtook him at Smithfield, 5 miles north of Pleasant Hill, with my advance, being . . . less than 50 in all.

The guerrillas halted, dismounted, and formed a line, and the Federals charged. After ten minutes of "brisk firing," the bushwhackers remounted and galloped away, scattering and taking their wounded with them. They left the corpses of two comrades behind; they had killed one soldier and wounded three more.

For two days Burris stumbled through the brush, looking for "the detached fragments" of the band, and then he returned to Kansas, leaving behind one cavalry squad under Captain Daniel H. David to continue the exhausting, seemingly futile hunt.

The bone-weary, saddle-sore colonel arrived safely back at Fort Leavenworth late on the evening of September 23. The following day he assessed his accomplishments.

> We captured during the expedition over 100 stand of arms, 10,000 rounds of ammunition, nearly 100 head of horses, 4 yoke of oxen, 5 or 6 wagons, a number of tents and other camp equipage, also a considerable quantity of dry goods, groceries, &c., of which the guerrillas had previously robbed the people of Olathe, Kans. We burned the houses, out-buildings, grain, hay, &c., of about a dozen noted marauders whose premises had been favorite haunts for guerrillas.

Furthermore, his troops had lived off the land while in Missouri, which was a polite way of saying that they had taken food from the kitchens, smokehouses, and cellars of Southerners and animal fodder from their barns. They had slaughtered their cows and pigs, wrung the necks of their chickens. There would be some empty bellies across the line this winter because of John Burris's ride.

There would be some empty slave quarters, too. "Upward of 60 loyal colored persons, tired of the rule of rebel masters, furnished their own transportation and subsistence"—meaning they took horses, mules, oxen, and food belonging to their former owners—"and accompanied my command to Kansas."

Quantrill let his men rest for a week following the fight with Burris, then sent word for them to meet him at a mill near Sibley, which was northeast of Independence. Captain David was a diligent bloodhound, however, and, nosing around Blue Springs, picked up the band's scent. On the night of October 5, he bivouacked on the Morgan Walker farm and the next day marched north, continuing to scour the countryside, arrest suspicious men, and question ladies and blacks.

David routed Quantrill's pickets on the Independence-Lexington road, about two miles from Sibley. Continuing on he spied still more pickets on Big Hill and realized the enemy camp must be close by. Since he had heard Quantrill had anywhere from 150 to three hundred men, he sent a dispatch to Colonel William Penick at Independence requesting reinforcements and then, proceeding with extreme caution, approached Sibley.

Quantrill had only one hundred men with him, but he decided to ambush the Yankees. He withdrew his band down the road to the farm of a Mrs. Garrison and then laid out his plan for his lieutenants: Seventy-five men would stay with him at the farm and conceal themselves beside the road; the other twenty-five would hit David and then retreat, drawing him into the trap.

Now, as to who should lead the hit-and-run party—Dick Chiles interrupted. He had just arrived in camp that morning, bragging of his many daring exploits. He asserted he was entitled to be given command of the advance.

Quantrill demurred. "No, I don't know you," he said. "I don't know if you'll carry out my instructions." He gestured in the direction of Todd and Gregg. "I know that either of them will do just as I tell them."

But Gregg wanted to see what this noisy braggart was made of. "Let him have it," he said, and Todd seconded the motion.

Chiles took the advance forward, but before he encountered the Federals he came to a log cabin with a high rail fence around it sitting beside a sharp bend in the road. He must have thought it was the perfect place for an ambush because he ordered his men to dismount, placing them behind the fence and the back wall of the cabin. He had the horses concealed in some nearby woods.

When the lead elements of the Federals' column came in view, the overeager Chiles screamed an order to open fire. Two cavalrymen dropped from their saddles. A half-dozen horses fell down, some dead, some kicking and shrieking. Many other horses reared, their riders toppled, and they bolted. A sergeant and a private kept control of their mounts but decided to declare a separate peace, wheeled their horses, and dug their spurs into them.

Chiles had been disastrously premature: He should have waited until the whole column was much closer. David rallied his troops and had them dismount, draw their sabers, and charge the cabin on foot. As the guerrillas turned and ran for their horses, Chiles went down, shot through the lungs. The Yankees ran past him, pursuing the others into the trees. Some of them were fleet enough to overtake them, and hand-to-hand fighting ensued.

Eventually all the bushwhackers got on their horses and took off through the trees. David double-quick marched his troops back to their mounts, but, fearing another ambush, he then led them cautiously through the woods. When he came out onto an open prairie with no enemy in sight, he gave up the chase and returned to the log cabin to ascertain his losses.

One of the two men shot in the first moment of battle was dead, the other clearly dying. A number of men had been wounded, and there were, noted David, "many others with holes shot through their clothes and hats, which shows that they were standing close up to their work."

As was so often the case, David had no way of knowing how many of the guerrillas had been killed or wounded, but he later swore that the ground around the cabin and across the field into the trees was liberally sprinkled with blood, indicating that "they must have suffered severely."

In the coming days Dick Chiles told his captors everything he knew about Quantrill's Raiders—and invented a great deal more besides. He survived the war but, never having fully recovered from his wound, died soon after.

David pressed horses, harnesses, and buggies from area residents to carry the dead and wounded to Independence. (He was comforted to learn from other disgruntled local ladies that Quantrill had been forced to do the same.) David had marched only five miles before meeting reinforcements from the garrison. He sent the buggies on with a guard and countermarched, scouring the country around Big Hill and Pink Hill long after dark, determined to find the enemy.

> Early the following morning we struck their trail, and followed in pursuit until about 8 a.m., when we came upon their pickets, giving them a round of musketry, and Captain Johnson, ever ready with his battery, turned his little gun upon them and gave them a few canister, which sent them off on a double-quick. We captured 3 horses and Government horse equipments, 1 Savage revolver, cartridge box and belt. We kept in hot pursuit over hills and through the worst brush thicket that I ever saw, they scattering and concentrating alternately during the day, until we came within six miles of [Independence], where they changed direction, again pointing for another thicket. I then called a halt and assembled the officers for consultation, upon which we almost unanimously agreed to return to camp for rest, as myself and men had been under a heavy march for three days and only eaten three meals, and our horses almost exhausted from fatigue and light forage.

Concluding his report to Colonel Penick, David added wearily that "We do not believe guerrillas can ever be taken by pursuit; we must take them by strategy."

Nine days after Captain David gave up the chase, Quantrill led his raiders to Shawneetown to steal warm clothes for the coming winter. Along the way they came on a wagon train camped beside the Santa Fe Trail for the night. The commander of the infantry escort had foolishly neglected to put out pickets or post a camp guard. Most of the soldiers were asleep when the bushwhackers opened fire. Panicked men leaped to their feet and ran in every direction, trying to get away. Fifteen did manage to escape, but an equal number died. The guerrillas plundered the wagons and then rode into town.

The Shawneetown stores had only small stocks of clothing, so the raiders stripped male residents. Several men objected to losing their pants and were shot. William Laurie had better sense and was soon shivering in his underwear. He was put to work loading plunder onto a wagon by lamplight. When the wind blew it out, Laurie ran into a field and escaped. Two or three other men tried the same tactic but were killed.

The raiders set fire to every house and building in the village and then rode away. As the flames spread, Laurie decided to move on. A photographer by trade, he had come to Shawneetown from Kansas City after his life was threatened because he refused to assist some rebels in hoisting Confederate flags. His business partner had been wounded in the Shawneetown raid, and Laurie was afraid again. His next choice of locale was not a lucky one: He settled on a farm near Lawrence.

———•–•———

On Saturday, October 18, 1862, the Federal military executed ten Southern prisoners at Palmyra, in northeast Missouri. Some weeks earlier Confederate Colonel Joseph C. Porter had raided the town. After Porter and his guerrilla band rode away, an elderly loyalist and Union army veteran named Andrew Allsman could not be found. Since Allsman had recently been appointed a "special Provost Marshall's guard" and had been using the position to persecute Southerners, Porter was thought to have kidnapped him. (Long after the war ended, Porter veterans would reveal that the colonel had indeed captured Allsman and carried him along during the withdrawal from town but, heeding the terrified old man's pleas, had released him and sent him home with an escort. Disobeying orders, the escort secretly murdered Allsman and hid his corpse.)

Colonel W. R. Strachan, the region's notoriously cruel provost marshal general, had local newspapers publish a letter addressed to Porter that promised the execution of ten of Porter's captured followers unless Allsman was immediately "returned unharmed to his family." When nothing was heard from Porter, ten prisoners were taken from the Palmyra jail to the fairgrounds. Three of these men had served under Porter, but the others apparently had no connection to him (among their number were an elderly man and a retarded boy). The prisoners were made to sit on coffins that had been lined up in a row on the ground. Opposite them stood a firing squad of thirty militia. "A few minutes after one o'clock," reported the Palmyra *Courier,*

Colonel Strachan and the Rev. Mr. [R. M.] Rhodes, shook hands with the prisoners. Two of them accepted bandages for their eyes—all the rest refused. A hundred spectators had gathered around the amphitheater to witness the impressive scene. The stillness of death pervaded the place.

The officer in command now stepped forward and gave the word of command: "Ready; aim; fire!" The discharges, however, were not made simultaneously—probably through want of a perfect previous understanding of the orders and of the time at which to fire. Two of the rebels fell backward upon their coffins and died instantly. Captain [Thomas A.] Snider sprang forward and fell with his head toward the soldiers, his face upward, his hands clasped upon his breast, and the left leg drawn half way up. He had requested the soldiers to aim at his heart, and they obeyed but too implicitly. The other seven were not killed outright; so the reserves were called in, who dispatched them with their revolvers.

As word of the "Palmyra Massacre" spread across the state, many Unionists were aghast, and Southerners were horrified. Although any number of large- or small-scale atrocities were committed in Missouri and Kansas during the years 1854 to 1865, "the horrible butchery at Palmyra," as one staunch Unionist dubbed it, made a profound and lasting impression on many people—perhaps due in part to the clumsiness of the execution itself and the fact that it was premeditated and officially sanctioned. Half a century after the ten corpses were put into coffins and the lids screwed down, some of Quantrill's men still spoke of the massacre with bitterness.

———◆———

Four days after the massacre, on October 22, Quantrill and twenty-five men visited the Lafayette County home of Luther Green, a Union sympathizer. They demanded he fix them breakfast. While they were eating, the mail coach came by and Quantrill hailed it. His men ransacked the mail bags, casually finished their meal, and rode away.

Captain Joseph H. Little took a squad of cavalry and set out from Lexington in pursuit. Informants told him the band was in Chapel Hill, which was twenty-six miles southwest of Lexington. The Yankees crept through the woods on the outskirts of town, then charged down the main street, expecting to surprise Quantrill. The raiders were nowhere to be seen. Little conducted a house-to-house search, but the enemy had left the night before.

The Federals then raced for Hopewell, having heard that Quantrill was there. On the road they encountered a man on horseback who fled from them. They gave chase, firing rapidly, until he plunged into a thicket. They fired volleys into the thicket, and several men burst out the other side and took off across the prairie at full speed.

Little pursued the fugitives until night began to fall, then billeted his men in a church. In the morning he went to Wellington, seven miles southwest of Lexington, again sneaking up on the town and charging down its streets, but Quantrill was not there either. Little followed a rumor west to Napoleon, and actually captured five men; however, they were suspected of being Confederate recruits, not guerrillas. Totally frustrated, Little gave up and returned to Lexington, arresting along the way, as he put it, "all suspicious and disloyal persons whom I could find."

A few days later Quantrill decided to take the band to Arkansas. It was the changing of the seasons, not ineffectual annoyances like Joe Little, that prompted the decision. Winter arrived on the border more troublesome than a bluecoat regiment. It was a great enemy of partisans because it deprived them of cover. Once the cold and wind had stripped the leaves from trees and bushes, it was much more difficult to find a secluded hiding place for a camp or to set an ambush.

Quantrill started for Arkansas on November 3 with 150 men. Late in the afternoon his advance reported a wagon train up ahead. The wagons, which were on their way to pick up supplies from the Pacific railhead at Sedalia, were empty, but the train was just too tempting a target: Quantrill told Gregg to take forty men and capture it. The wagons were pulled by oxen and guarded by twenty-three cavalry troopers. When the guerrillas struck, the teamsters circled the wagons, but the tactic hardly prolonged the fight. Four teamsters and six soldiers were killed; two soldiers and one teamster were wounded. The escort commander, Lieutenant W. M. Newby, and four privates were taken prisoner. The rest of the soldiers ran for the hills. The bushwhackers turned the oxen loose and burned all the wagons.

They rode south for ten more miles and camped for the night. As they were finishing their supper, their pickets raced into camp, shouting that Yankees were right behind them.

Shortly after 4:00 P.M. that afternoon, Colonel Edwin C. Catherwood had learned a large band of guerrillas was moving through Cass County. Since he had dispatched the wagon train from his headquarters at Harrisonville that morning, he immediately became, as he put it in his report, "apprehensive for [its] safety." He took 150 men and started for Rose Hill, "hoping to overtake the train and also to intercept the enemy." When his advance reported finding the burned wagons, Catherwood swung his column south. Sighting Quantrill's pickets, he charged with such ferocity that the pickets could only run for their lives. The other guerrillas fled, too, abandoning their spare mounts but dragging their prisoners along.

The Federals closed on the bushwhackers, and a running battle ensued, until the guerrillas at last began to pull away. "The flight of the enemy was so precipitate," reported Catherwood, "and my men and horses so exhausted that I found it impracticable to proceed farther without rest." Six bushwhackers had been killed, and Catherwood estimated their wounded at twenty-five. Lieutenant Newby and one private were rescued.

In the morning Catherwood resumed the chase, joined by Captain David and seventy-five militiamen, but the enemy rode hard and got away.

———— ◆ ————

On November 5, Quantrill ran into Confederate Colonel Warner Lewis and three hundred cavalrymen just north of Lamar, in southwest Missouri. Lewis wanted a reluctant Quantrill to join him in an attack on the town garrison. The Yankees were quartered in a formidable brick courthouse, but Lewis managed to overcome Quantrill's objections. They agreed upon a coordinated, simultaneous attack at 10:00 P.M., with Quantrill entering Lamar from the south and Lewis from the north. Quantrill actually approached the town limits a little ahead of schedule and had to call a halt to wait for the precise moment, then slammed into the pickets and clattered up to the courthouse.

The Federals, who had been informed that guerrillas were in the area and had barricaded themselves inside, opened fire, killing two, Peter Burton and James Donohoe. The rest of the band took cover, and a desultory firefight began.

For some reason Lewis never showed up, and after two hours Quantrill disgustedly broke off the fight. The town was set ablaze, and the bodies of Burton and Donohoe were tied to their horses and taken to a pasture a few miles south of town. Since the bushwhackers were not pursued, they had the luxury of properly burying their dead. They even took down a section of rail fence and put it up around the graves.

They continued riding south, then swung west around Carthage and crossed into the southeast corner of Kansas. They followed the Texas Road into the Cherokee Nation and turned east into Arkansas. Since their already fearsome reputation had proceeded them, their entry into the Confederate camp at Cross Hollows caused quite a stir.

———————————•◦•———————————

Quantrill's absence from the border region may have significantly lowered the level of violence, but it did nothing to lessen the climate of hysteria. Some civilians packed their belongings into carriages and wagons and fled the area; many others seriously considered that disheartening option. Letters were written to politicians and military commanders demanding better protection from bushwhackers, jayhawkers, redlegs, and Federal militia. Town meetings were held during which Union officers tried to calm audiences by reassuring them that steps would be taken to restore order.

Privately, however, more than a few high-ranking Federal officers were deeply worried. They wrote reports warning that their troops were poorly trained and armed and that they lacked even basic necessities. "The Enrolled Missouri Militia, you are probably aware, has not been furnished clothing suitable for service in the field at this season of the year," General Egbert Brown informed General Schofield as winter closed in. "Requisitions made for clothing four months since remain unfilled. Trains that left Rolla the last week partially loaded with clothing have been turned off the road at Lebanon and sent to the Army of the Frontier. The troops under my command are suffering for want of this clothing, being shoeless, coatless, and hatless in many cases."

Even officers who were more concerned with the progress of the war in the region than the problems of particular units were deeply pessimistic. The report to the headquarters of the Central District of Missouri written by Brigadier General Benjamin Loan is a case in point. Although Loan sought to summarize conditions in the eastern part of the state as well as those in the west, his attitudes are representative of many men stationed along the border. "I design leaving here [St. Louis] for Independence tomorrow," he informed Major General Curtis on November 19.

The inhabitants [here] are generally disloyal, and a large majority of them are actively so. They are fierce, overbearing, defiant, and insulting; whilst the Union spirit is cowed and disposed to be submissive. There is no earthly hope for peace in this portion of the State until a separation can be effected. With a view to this end I have caused the disloyal to be arrested and held in close custody. The milder prisoners I have allowed to give their parole to leave the State in ten days, not to return; many are availing themselves of this privilege. The others must be sent out of the State and held in custody until the close of the war, or at least until society is so far reconstructed here as to allow the courts to be held and civil rights to be enforced. Another reason that has induced me to have these disloyal persons arrested is to break up the social relations here.

General Loan complained that "Good society here, as it is termed, is exclusively rebel." He added that the traders, merchants, and bankers "who transact the business of the country, are all traitors and . . . are making large fortunes as the reward for their disloyalty, and . . . have the bad taste to laugh at honest patriots for serving so faithfully a Government that discriminates against [the patriots] so fearfully." He asserted that the

business of the country must be conducted by loyal men only, and loyal men only must be left here to do it. Regulations of trade which have no stronger guard than oaths and bonds will not exclude a rebel from embarking in the trade of the country that promises a profit. Nineteen out of every twenty traders in stock who supply the Government from this part of the country are disloyal, and it is through these channels that such bands as Quantrell's find a market for their stolen property.

He reported that he had been sending out patrols "almost daily in every direction for the last ten days" and had driven the bushwhackers out of the county,

but they will return immediately. It is much easier to catch a rat with your hands in a warehouse filled with a thousand flour barrels than it is to catch a band of guerrillas where every, or almost every man, woman, and child are their spies, pickets, or couriers. There are some 200 here held as prisoners on the general charge of disloyalty. They are generally actively disloyal. The remainder of the disloyal inhabitants I propose to have brought in as rapidly as possible. In Jackson, Cass, Johnson, and Saline the same course will be pursued, until none but loyal men will be allowed to remain at large in the country. Among the prisoners captured are some notoriously bad men; others of like character have fled the country precipitately. If you would direct the transfer of these prisoners (or the worst of them) to some depot for prisoners the effect would be most beneficial.

Within a few months a similar policy of arrest and forced deportation would indeed be applied to western Missouri. Women accused of being wives or kin of bushwhackers would be transported to Kansas City. One of the "depots" chosen to house them would be a brick building on Grand Avenue.

CHAPTER 8

"Meet Slaughter with Slaughter": Prelude to the Lawrence Massacre

In Arkansas during the winter of 1862–63, Quantrill's Raiders acted as scouts for Jo Shelby's Missouri Brigade, which was part of a cavalry division under the command of General John S. Marmaduke. A West Point graduate and the son of wealthy parents (his father had been a governor of Virginia), Marmaduke had served in Albert Sidney Johnston's Utah expedition and had resigned from the Union army to follow Johnston into the Confederate service. He fought at Shiloh, where Johnston was killed.

In the coming months Marmaduke's division saw considerable action and was much bloodied; Shelby's brigade earned the nickname the "Iron Brigade," but Quantrill would miss all the fighting. In the middle of November he left Todd in charge of the band and, accompanied by Andy Blunt and a man named Higbee, went to Richmond. There he obtained an interview with Confederate Secretary of War James A. Seddon. John N. Edwards indicated that Quantrill was motivated in part by his concern about his fate if captured by Yankees: He asked to be commissioned a colonel under the Partisan Ranger Act, expecting that the rank might afford him some measure of protection, and offered to recruit a regiment, saying it would be no trouble for him. He also advocated an escalation of the fighting in Missouri and in the East.

According to Edwards, Quantrill told Seddon that the war was going badly and predicted that the Southern states would fall one after another:

Missouri would be subjugated first, then Kentucky, Tennessee, Mississippi, and Arkansas.

"This secession, or revolution, or whatever you call it cannot conquer without violence, nor can those who hate it and hope to stifle it, resist without vindictiveness. . . . Your young Confederacy wants victory, and champions who are not judges. Men must be killed. To impell the people to passion there must be some slight illusion mingled with the truth; to arouse them to enthusiasm something out of nature must occur. That illusion should be a crusade in the name of conquest, and that something out of nature should be the black flag. . . ."

"What would you do, Captain Quantrell, were yours the power and the opportunity?" Seddon is supposed to have asked.

"Do, Mr. Secretary? Why, I would wage such a war and have such a war waged by land and sea as to make surrender forever impossible. I would cover the armies of the Confederacy all over with blood. I would invade. I would reward audacity. I would exterminate. I would break up foreign enlistments by indiscriminate massacre. I would win the independence of my people or I would find them graves."

"And our prisoners, what of them?"

"Nothing of them; there would be no prisoners. Surrounded, I do not surrender; surprised, I do not give way to panic; outnumbered, I rely upon common sense and stubborn fighting; outlawed, I feel through it my power; hunted, I hunt my hunters in turn; hated and made blacker than a dozen devils, I add to my hoofs the swiftness of a horse, and to my horns the terrors of a savage following. Kansas should be laid waste at once. Meet the torch with the torch, pillage with pillage, slaughter with slaughter, subjugation with extermination. . . ."

Quantrill knew that after such an outburst Seddon would never give him a colonel's commission, so he bowed his way out of the room. He dallied in Richmond for the rest of the winter. "Before the last of the snows had melted," wrote Edwards, "and ere yet the trees had begun to awaken to an idea of verdure and the spring, Quantrill was back again in Jackson County, marshalling his Guerrillas and closing up his ranks."

Edwards's sole source for this exchange was Senator Louis T. Wigfall of Texas, who claimed to have been present. Obviously the dialogue is a product of Edwards's imagination, perhaps with some assistance from the politician. Whether or not Quantrill harbored the sentiments expressed in such gaudy and soaring rhetoric is unclear.

We know from other, more reliable sources, however, that Quantrill did at least go to Richmond in the winter of 1862–63. In later years some of his veterans would assert that he was indeed given a colonelcy there, but his Confederate service records contain documents dated after this period in which he is addressed as a captain or signs his name giving that rank.

———— ·—·—· ————

Not long after Quantrill departed for Richmond, George Todd found himself discontented with regular army life. Although Quantrill had left him in charge of the band, he decided to go back to Jackson County with seven or eight equally unhappy cohorts. They slipped away without telling anyone they were going just hours before the onset of the Battle of Cane Hill. Gregg, suddenly realizing that Todd was absent, took charge.

On the morning of November 28, Union General James G. Blunt approached Cane Hill with five thousand men and thirty pieces of artillery. Marmaduke's forces were spread out, outnumbered almost three to one, and had only six pieces of artillery. Still, they made a hard fight of it for an hour, with Shelby's brigade taking the brunt of the cannon barrages, and repelled three infantry charges before retreating through the Boston Mountain chain. Those of Shelby's men who covered the retreat were repeatedly subjected to heavy volleys of grape, canister, and minié balls. Shelby's horse was shot out from under him, and a bushwhacker named Dick Turpin went to his assistance. Three more of Shelby's mounts were killed—and they all happened to be sorrels. "During the rest of the war Shelby would ride only a sorrel, believing that he bore a charmed life as long as he rode one," observed the general's biographer, Daniel O'Flaherty.

At Prairie Grove the Confederates formed themselves into a horse-shoe-shaped battle line on a hill. Shelby's men were dismounted and placed at the center. The bluecoats came in wave after wave, supported by tremendous artillery fire. The Missourians repulsed the charges with shotguns and rifles and counterattacked.

The fighting lasted throughout the afternoon, and the Yankee batteries continued to fire after darkness fell. The heavy casualties on both sides were remarkably balanced: 167 Union soldiers died, 798 were wounded, and 183 were missing; 164 Confederates were killed, 817 wounded, and

336 missing. These figures do not convey the special horror of the day. There were five gigantic ricks of straw in an apple orchard near the battlefield, and two hundred Federal wounded crawled under the hay to escape the cold. Errant shells from their own artillery pieces ignited the straw, and they were burned alive. The odor and the sight of the blackened bodies was sickening enough, but a large herd of swine, accustomed to feeding on the fallen apples, were drawn by the scent of the roasting flesh and gorged themselves.

"Intestines, heads, arms, feet, and even hearts were dragged over the ground and devoured at leisure," Major Edwards wrote in *Shelby and His Men.* In this book, he was reporting his own experiences and observations rather than manufacturing a mythology drawn from events and personalities heard about only secondhand. He was also writing in 1866, when the full magnitude of the postwar persecution may not have been evident and its protracted duration unimaginable. Thus, *Shelby and His Men* is much more reliable than *Noted Guerrillas,* although its prose style is hardly more restrained.

Few of Shelby's soldiers will forget the horrors of their night bivouac upon the gory field of Prairie Grove. Around them in every direction lay the dead and dying, the full glare of a cold battle moon shining white on their upturned faces, and the chilling wind singing freezing dirges among the naked and melancholy trees. Soon upon the night air rose great heart-sobs wrung from strong men in their agony, while the white hoar frost hardened the fever drops into ice that oozed from clammy brows. Death stalked in silently amid the sufferers and plied his busy sickle. . . . Through all the long, long watches, the burial parties from both armies flitted over the field with lights that gleamed like phantoms, and mingled friendly in a common work of mercy. Daylight came slowly and solemnly, yet the dead were not buried, and many wounded were dying slowly and lingeringly in the dark and lonesome places. Fires were strictly forbidden . . . and sleep was necessarily an utter impossibility.

A few days later, after the retreat to Van Buren, Arkansas, one of the bushwhackers approached McCorkle.

"John, let's go back to Missouri," he said simply.

"All right," McCorkle replied.

Six slipped away together. They forded creeks and slept in the woods, hiding from Federal units or, if encountered on the road, running. They stopped once at a farmhouse, which turned out to belong to a Union militiaman. From their plundered blue uniforms he judged they were on the same side and was only too happy to feed them and their horses. They left the house with him under the guise of accompanying him to his company's camp, then pulled their revolvers and forced him to guide them out of the area. He must have expected they would kill him after reaching familiar territory, but perhaps they had seen enough blood to last them a while, because they gave him his parole.

After a joyful reunion with his mother, McCorkle went looking for Cole Younger. Cole had remained behind in Jackson County, nursing members of the band who had been seriously wounded in recent engagements. He had built a lean-to in the woods and threw dirt over the roof to camouflage it. When the Yankees came nosing around, he was forced to move his field hospital from one hollow to another.

McCorkle soon found his current camp, seven miles south of Independence. Cole's ministrations had restored all his patients back to health, and Cole's mind was now focused entirely on avoiding military patrols and waiting for the arrival of spring and Quantrill. George Todd was with him, as were McCorkle's brother, Jabez, and a half-dozen others.

As the ranks were swelled by other bushwhackers drifting back from the south one or two at a time and by the arrival of new recruits, they divided themselves into small squads and scattered their camps around the countryside. They dug caves in the sides of hills and covered the entrances with logs and brush or constructed lean-tos, making chimneys out of mud and sticks. They built cooking fires only at night so the smoke would not be seen. When money and supplies ran low, a squad would cautiously slip over the border and commit a quick robbery.

One evening John McCorkle and George Wigginton set out to visit their families. They reached the edge of a prairie and saw fires in the distance—militia were burning the homes of Southerners. McCorkle and Wigginton sat on their horses and tried to count the fires and decided that seventeen more families were now destitute in the winter snow. From the location of one blaze, Wigginton knew that his parents were among the victims.

Vastly outnumbered and unable to intervene, the two men watched until the fires slowly burned themselves out. They cursed the Federals impotently and rode back to Cole's camp.

A few days later a man named John McDowell showed up. He had ridden with Cole on a Kansas raid earlier that year, which had been interrupted by a large party of jayhawkers. Outnumbered four or five to one, the guerrillas fought briefly, took heavy casualties, and fled. McDowell's horse was shot out from under him, and he had been wounded. He had called to Cole for help, and Cole went back for him, put him on his own horse, and carried him to safety.

Back in Jackson County after the raid, McDowell had turned himself in to Colonel Penick at Independence. McDowell claimed that the hated Federal officer had then paroled him, but John McCorkle for one did not believe him: He accused McDowell of having made a deal with Penick to act as a spy and urged that he immediately be put to death.

Cole shrugged off the suggestion. A few days later McDowell asked Cole's permission to leave camp in order to visit his wife, and McCorkle objected, telling Cole right in front of him, "Don't let him go. He is a traitor, and if I was in command of this squad, I would either hang him or shoot him."

"John, you are too hard on him," Cole replied. "He's all right."

McCorkle shook his head. "As soon as he gets out of our sight, he will run his horse to Independence and tell Penick where we are."

McDowell soon returned to camp—leading sixty militiamen. Some of the outfit were hunting hogs in the woods, a few others were scattered around the entrance to the cave, and the rest were inside. The militia advance had tried to disguise themselves as bushwhackers, and several of the band, seeing them at a distance, did indeed mistake them for Todd's men.

They got within fifty yards of the cave before someone realized the truth and called out, "Break for your guns, boys!" Cole Younger drew a pistol and blasted away, and the Federals started shooting. John McCorkle jumped into the cave, yanked his pistol off a nail protruding from a rafter, and burst back outside. He leveled the pistol and pulled the trigger, but it only snapped.

Ike Bassham stepped out of the cave, was hit, and fell dead beside the entrance. Doc Hale fared a little better: He ran a hundred yards before being cut down. Cole, Joe Hardin, Otho Hinton, and Tom Talley all raced for the woods together. Hardin was struck in the back and collapsed in the snow. Talley, hampered by heavy boots, managed to pull one off as he ran, but he could not get the other one off. He stopped, sat down, and Cole pulled off the boot. Then they ran side by side until they reached the timber, where they made a brief stand with three or four others, firing at their pursuers. Tom Talley's brother, George, was killed when the fire was returned.

The rest retreated into the woods. They threw away their heavy over-coats and boots and ran through the snow in their socks.

John McCorkle tripped over a log and sprawled across the ground, with bullets kicking up the snow all around him. He rolled to his feet and sprinted through a shallow stream.

"John, wait!" he heard someone call. It was George Wigginton. McCorkle stood, trying to catch his breath as Wigginton neared him, then saw Wigginton spin around suddenly and shoot a militiaman who was closing on him.

"John, let's turn and fight them," Wigginton said.

McCorkle did not need to calculate the odds. "We better save our loads until the last and get away if we can," he replied.

They ran on. McCorkle heard another shout, saw a man coming toward him in a Federal cap, and leveled his pistol. The man cried out again, and McCorkle recognized him—Jim Morris. He wanted to fight, too, not withstanding the fact that he had lost his pistols.

"You get in front of us and do some of your best running," McCorkle told him.

They crossed a clearing with the Yankees close behind, then plunged into the woods again. There was blood on the snow in their wake: Morris had been shot in the hand. McCorkle tied a handkerchief over the wound so the pursuers would not be able to follow a trail of blood. He and the others splashed through a creek and kept running until they found a cattle path, followed it for awhile, then crashed through the undergrowth until they came to Carroll Johnson's house. They borrowed two horses and, with Wigginton and Morris sharing one of them, went looking for Todd's camp.

Other bushwhackers took similar tacks, going single file down hog trails, crossing rock bridges, and climbing down bluffs until they came to the homes of sympathizers and could ask in hoarse whispers for mounts and spare footwear, stamping their frozen feet and shuddering and shivering with the cold.

•—◆—•

Small numbers of Quantrill's Raiders may have continued to defect from Shelby's brigade and return home as the winter progressed, but others stuck it out to the end of the campaign. They endured long marches, fought hand to hand, and chased jayhawkers. They were with Shelby during the invasion of Springfield, fighting from house to house on foot before darkness and the imminent arrival of bluecoat reinforcements precipitated a withdrawal. They were with him at the capture of Hartville, where they put the enemy to flight and then once again had to retreat. They suffered on the bitterly cold January march to Batesville, Arkansas, as hundreds of horses fell by the wayside because of the weather and lack of forage. By the time the column reached the White River Valley, Shelby's own men were so desperately hungry that they took whatever food was to be had at farms, regardless of where the owners' sympathies lay and the colonel's own stern orders against looting.

The supply train sent to Batesville from Lewisburg was marooned by snowstorms, and Shelby's troops were forced to bivouac in an open field without tents or cooking utensils; most did not even have a change of clothing. The townspeople came to their rescue, however, with food and clothing and took the sick into their homes.

In the spring Marmaduke and Shelby laid plans to invade eastern Missouri and do battle with Federal troops. In the spring Quantrill's men went back to Jackson County.

———◆———

Early in May, as soon as the grass was long enough for grazing horses, a Quantrill follower named Dick Yeager led a raid into Kansas. Rather than assemble a large body of men and boldly cross the line as Quantrill might have done, Yeager and his boys slipped over in groups of twos and threes to avoid detection. They rendezvoused on the afternoon of May 4, 1863, in some heavy woods outside Council Grove, more than two hundred miles west of the border. Yeager had intended to burn the town, but he had developed a toothache, so instead of the whole gang roaring into Council Grove, yelling and shooting and applying torches, he rode in accompanied by only one man. They dismounted in the early evening outside the office of a dentist, Dr. J. H. Bradford.

"Doctor, I expect you know me," Yeager told Bradford. "I have a tooth that aches like hell, and if you will give me relief I will be good."

Bradford was a transplanted Missourian and knew Yeager's reputation well. He accepted the deal, yanked the offending cuspid, and gave him a bottle of potent medicine so that Yeager left the office in a good mood.

Yeager and his men remained camped in the woods that night, drinking from their ample supply of liquor and talking over old times with fellow Missourians who lived in Council Grove and dared visit them only under the cover of darkness. Yeager had been a teamster before the war, working in his father's freight business until, returning from leading a wagon train across the plains, he found that Jennison's redlegs had stripped the family farm of everything they could carry away. He immediately joined the guerrillas. He felt he had good cause, therefore, to reduce Council Grove to ashes, but he kept his part of the bargain with the dentist, contenting himself in the morning with allowing his men to curse and threaten loyalist citizens before setting off on the Santa Fe Trail, still heading west.

The band struck the Diamond Springs stage station and store at 10:00 P.M., killing the proprietor, Augustus Howell, and wounding his wife in the arm when she tried to protect him. They took all the horses and looted and burned the store. They lingered in the area for a couple of days, then, still following the Santa Fe Trail, headed in a southwesterly direction.

Several Union commanders dispatched troops, but after following the trail for a time they gave up the pursuit and returned to their posts. The U.S. marshal at Leavenworth, James L. McDowell, was more determined: He raised a posse of twenty men and headed west, picking up reinforcements as he went, until he reached the Santa Fe crossing on the Cottonwood River, northwest of Emporia, where he clashed with the Yeager band. McDowell captured twelve and forced the rest to flee, then sent an express rider to Emporia with a warning that guerrillas were in the area. Thirty residents set up an ambush, but the raiders went north around them, broke into small squads, and scattered, making a beeline east for the border, some one hundred miles away.

Marshal McDowell turned his prisoners over to Captain John E. Stewart, the jayhawker with whom Quantrill had ridden before the war, for transportation to Fort Riley. "On the way," according to T. Dwight Thacher, editor of the *Journal of Commerce,* "the bushwhackers attempted to escape . . . the guards fired upon them and the whole number were killed. A good riddance."

On the afternoon of May 8, Yeager and thirteen followers rode up to the Rock Springs stage depot, where they found George N. Sabin, a soldier on furlough, and shot him twelve times. A few hours later they reached Willow Springs, southeast of Lawrence, and stopped at a building that served as a small store, post office, and stage stand. The store owner, David Hubbard, had just sat down to supper when there was a banging on the door. "I was seized, searched, and questioned as to my politics and the state I came from," recalled Hubbard many years later.

The answers not being satisfactory to them, Yeager gave the order to shoot. Three of them obeyed the order. One bullet went through my lungs, the other two missed—they being less than ten feet away. After going through the house and taking what they wanted and taking a horse from the stable, they left following the trail east. Among other things, they took Mr. Waters's pocket-book. Mrs. Waters asked the privilege of taking out some valuable papers, and they allowed her to select some of the most important ones.

At Black Jack they met the stage, relieving the passengers of their money and watches and taking the stage line's most valuable horses. Arriving at Gardner after midnight, they stole money from the express agent and robbed hotel guests of their clothes when their purses yielded little. They also increased the size of what must by now have been a sizable pony herd. They then crossed into Missouri without further incident and were rejoined by their scattered comrades.

"Several of these parties engaged in this work of robbery and murder were . . . recognized by several individuals as secessionists who lived in Kansas . . . at the outbreak of the war and fled to Missouri when Kansas became too hot for them," commented Dwight Thacher. One of these was a man whose name was not widely known at the time but soon would be—Bill Anderson.

The Yeager raid is of particular interest for two reasons. First, Mrs. Howell was wounded, which was a rare transgression in the border war. Both sides generally adhered to strong prohibitions against physically harming women. This gentlemanly, nineteenth-century restraint is all the more remarkable and singular considering the climate of violence and extreme hatred that permeated the region dating back to 1854.

Quantrill himself was very strict on this point: Just before leading the attack on Lawrence, for example, he paused to remind his followers yet again that women—white or black—were not to be touched. During the next four hours, some of his men became wildly drunk on liquor and, filled with blood lust, slaughtered unarmed male civilians, many of them pleading pitifully for their lives as the bullets struck home; female relatives often sought to intercede, kneeling in the dirt, assuming supplicating postures, while other women boldly stood up to the raiders, putting out the fires they set and otherwise defying them. Just a few days earlier the mangled bodies of bushwhacker wives and sisters had been carried out of the Grand Avenue building in Kansas City, the supposed victims of a Yankee plot, yet no Lawrence woman was raped or injured. After the attack was over and Quantrill had withdrawn his band, there remained behind one of Bloody Bill Anderson's followers, Larkin Skaggs, who was so stupid with liquor that he did not realize he was in danger from the massacre survivors. He ineffectually tried to strike a woman named Riggs with a revolver when she held onto his horse to prevent him from chasing down and killing her husband. Mrs. Riggs and Mrs. Howell, then, seem to be singular exemptions to a code of conduct rather steadfastly adhered to by border combatants in general and Quantrill and his band in particular.*

The second reason the Yeager raid is of interest is that it demonstrated how porous the Federal defenses were and how vulnerable even towns deep in the Kansas interior were to attack: "That an insignificant band of guerrillas should have been able to penetrate 150 or 200 miles into Kansas," noted Thacher, "and make their way out again, robbing and

---

*Dr. Thomas P. Lowry, M.D., in his 1994 book, *The Story the Soldiers Won't Tell*, effectively refuted the common contention of earlier generations of American historians that rape was unheard of during the Civil War.

I do not mean to suggest that no western Missouri or Kansas woman was raped, only that the crime appears to have been rare. After nearly six years of examining contemporary border newspapers, diaries, letters, and memoirs, I have come across only about a dozen specific accusations—none involved members of Quantrill's band. Undoubtedly some victims remained silent because of the stigma, but there were enough propagandists on both sides eager to accuse their foes of the most terrible deeds. Had rape been more common, however, there should have been many more accusations. (Incidentally, newspapers of the period were quite willing to print rape stories: In describing the 1864 invasion of Missouri by Sterling Price in a later chapter, I quote from a newspaper account of several gang rapes that is remarkable in its candor, even to providing the victims' names. Kentucky newspapers for the period of 1865–68 contain numerous reports of rape, including the rape of both male and female children, picked up from newspapers published all over the country.)

I must say that my own cynical view of human nature does not allow me to accept easily the results of my own research on this issue—especially with regard to the mistreatment of female slaves—but so far as I am aware no one has documented evidence of the widespread rape of women in eastern Kansas or western Missouri.

One explanation for the lack of violence toward women may be that so often the aggressor and the would-be victim knew each other. It is one thing to rape a stranger; it

murdering as they went, and the military authorities fully informed that they were in the State and leisurely traveling one of its great highways, is certainly not a very creditable state of facts."

Quantrill arrived back in western Missouri while the Yeager incursion was still in progress, and he did not need an indignant newspaper editor to help him understand its strategic implications. He would shortly begin the preparations for the Lawrence raid, which, from his own perspective, would have to be one of the greatest achievements of his military career.

———————•◆•———————

Quantrill's return from Virginia did not go unnoticed. On May 5, the day after Yeager had his tooth extracted in Council Grove, Lieutenant Colonel Walter King spent an hour with a man he characterized as his "most trusted spy," a man with the nom de guerre "John De Courey." After the interview, King dispatched a report from Lexington, Missouri, to his superiors. "Quantrell is here," he informed them.

> He came from Price to conscript; he came with 40 men; he has joined Reid's, Jarrett's, Todd's, Younger's, and Clifton's gangs to his own, which give him 125 to 150 men; he disbanded his force on Sunday night, with orders to rendezvous on Thursday night on the Big Sni, precise place not definitely learned; has orders from Price to stop bushwhacking and horse stealing. Price is to invade southeast Missouri, and Quantrell is to annoy Kansas and Western Missouri; intends to conscript all of military age; has [passed] secret notice among Southern men to come to his camp and get property taken by mistake; came here to stay, and not to take away any recruits; seems to be rather elevated

---

is quite another to rape a woman whom you know and whose family you know—and who is capable of revealing your identity to vengeful menfolk.

In a 1991 essay published in *The Australasian Journal of American Studies,* historian Michael Fellman offered another explanation: "Men on each side feared that turnabout would mean that their women kin might be raped later on." Speaking of Confederate guerrillas, he added that "more profoundly this omission to rape was one key piece of evidence that to a limited degree at least [they] meant what they said when they proclaimed that they were fighting alien invaders in defense of the South, at the centre of which was family, home, and on the pedestal in the centre, woman. Killing and mutilating enemy men was done in service to a warrior version of these higher embodiments of male honour. Women shared these basic values, which they knew offered them a certain general protection from men, which men did not accord one another."

in his purposes by his six or eight months' experience with the regular forces. . . . He neither will give or expect quarter. . . .

The situation on the border that Quantrill found upon his return was not so much different as worsened. During his absence a number of Federal commanders had adopted extermination policies with regard to Confederate partisans. On April 23, 1863, for example, Major General Curtis, commander of the Department of Missouri, issued General Order No. 30, which stated that "Whoever shall be convicted as a guerrilla . . . shall suffer death, according to the usage of nations, by sentence of a military commission." Privately, Curtis had already given even blunter instructions to his subordinate officers: "They deserve no quarter; no terms of civilized warfare. Pursue, strike, and destroy the reptiles. . . ."

Despite the appeals by some high-ranking officers on both sides that partisans enlist in regular armies, bands of jayhawkers, redlegs, and bushwhackers had been roaming freely throughout the winter and spring. Common criminals found their deprivations convenient cover for sticking up civilians on the highways—or even after dark on the streets of the larger towns—and horse theft had become endemic. "Stealing is carried on to such an extent that a man can scarcely ride out five miles without his horse [being] taken from him, and men who have been known to have money, are gagged and hung until they deliver up or tell where their money is," lamented editor Thacher on March 3, 1863.

Kansans complained bitterly of being held up by redlegs, while in Missouri bushwhackers riddled passing river steamers, demanding that the vessels be turned into the bank so passengers could be robbed and government property appropriated or thrown overboard; some pilots took to lining their cabins with iron sheeting, leaving slits through which they could see to navigate, but many found it prudent to comply.

Bridges were burned, and homes were surrounded at night by parties of "ruffianly thieves," who robbed the occupants and sometimes led the menfolk away to be shot, took all the horses and mules, and too often burned houses and barns.

Wagon trains and stagecoaches, railway depots and even railroad trains were preferred targets. Gangs broke into jails and set horse thieves free, and towns suffered hit-and-run raids. "During the past year," wailed the Olathe, Kansas, *Mirror* in May, "every town in the county has been sacked, and one burned . . . sixty of its citizens have been killed by rebel bandits . . . $100,000 worth of property has been destroyed or carried away, and . . . a reign of terror has prevailed in nearly all parts of the county. . . ."

Many people living on the other side of the line thought there was enough blame to go around. "Tod's and Quantrell's gangs are roaming the country," noted the Kansas City, Missouri, *Journal of Commerce,*

> which is also harassed by a set of thieves and robbers known on the border as "Red-legs." These last are reported to be organized to the number of seven or eight hundred, who make it their chief business to steal and plunder—carrying off the fruits of their pillage into Kansas, where they find a market for it."

Jayhawking had "grown to be an enormous evil," as one Kansas newspaper put it, adding, "no citizen [feels] safe in his property from these marauding bands of men. . . ."

At the same time it must be noted that a number of Kansas newspapers, especially those published in Leavenworth, were carrying advertisements for stock: "Horses with a good title, from $70 to $100, and Jayhawked horses from $25 to $50."

In describing various crimes and raids, editors occasionally fell back on simply attributing them to "some jayhawkers or bushwhackers (it is not known which)" or expediently lumped all possible perpetrators together as "guerrillas, bushwhackers, jayhawkers, red legs, & c."

Since many of these individuals habitually wore civilian clothing just as ordinary highwaymen and thieves did, their ideological allegiances were frequently not discernible. The confusion of identity was increased by the practice of Quantrill's men and other guerrillas of sometimes donning the blue uniforms that had been stripped from Yankee corpses. Furthermore, some militia, motivated by greed or the desire for revenge, committed robberies and murders themselves, and even regular Federal troops seem to have occasionally allied themselves with redlegs. At the beginning of April, for instance, according to a letter published in the St. Louis *Missouri Republican,* "thirty or forty Kansas Red Legs and one hundred and fifty to two hundred of Burris' regular United States soldiers . . . entered the southwest part of [Lafayette] county and burnt at least thirty houses and killed at least fifty men who were unarmed, and had heretofore lived in peace and quiet through all the troubles. . . ."

Militia being permitted to make random seizures of firearms had a convenient excuse to search private homes and, in the process, loot them.

To make matters worse, Federal and Confederate foraging parties routinely hauled away crops and stores of food from hard-pressed farmers.

Most Missouri newspapers were staunchly Unionist and therefore gave the greatest coverage to Southern partisan depredations. Articles were punctuated with howls of outrage and demands that authorities put an end to bushwhacker activities, as well as an occasional lucid insight. Back in the summer of 1862, for instance, the St. Louis *Missouri Democrat,* in an article later approvingly reprinted by border newspapers, made an unusually intelligent suggestion:

> The fact is there can be no success against these bands until the present system is abandoned and something *analagous* [sic] to the system of the enemy is adopted. A band of one hundred guerrillas under proper leadership, will elude a thousand of our troops and keep twenty counties in a state of perpetual fear. . . .
>
> The only true system is to *scour the country.* Let a regiment of mounted troops instead of operating by companies or battalions, operate in squads of twenty or thirty men. A full regiment would make thirty parties of that size. Let them take as many different directions, operate under general orders, and not be too much confined in the letter. Let [those captured] be shot upon the spot. Such bands under skillful and prudent leaders, co-operating with loyal citizens, could clear twenty counties of guerrillas and keep them clear.

On May 23, 1863, editor Dwight Thacher offered a simpler but similarly promising approach.

> These bushwhackers rarely concentrate in large bodies. They prowl and lurk in the bushes to shoot down a passing traveller, or make midnight raids upon defenseless citizens. Their mode of warfare is much like that of the savage Indians. To put them down the troops must be put into the field and kept constantly in motion. [The guerrillas] must be *hunted* from their covers. It is of no use to keep large bodies of troops idle about the towns. Station a sufficient guard to protect the towns, and put the rest in the field and keep them there. Let the pursuit be vigorous and constant.

The frustrated Federal commanders ignored such rare and perceptive ideas, adopting instead a policy of burning the houses not only of bushwhackers' families but also of those suspected of being sympathizers and supporters. One day in late January 1863, for example, a Federal patrol burned thirteen Jackson County "Secesh houses"; a few weeks later another scout burned nine Cass County houses. In mid-February, the village of Lone Jack was partially destroyed. "The work goes bravely on," applauded Dwight Thacher. Even a rural church thought to be a guerrilla rendezvous went up in flames.

Many captured bushwhackers were summarily executed or were shot while supposedly trying to escape, and as the weather warmed, an increasing number of those accused of merely being their abettors died before reaching jail.

The aforementioned Colonel William R. Penick, headquartered in Independence, was a particular menace to Southerners. A Radical Unionist, he maintained that the guerrillas would be driven out of the region "if hemp, fire, and gunpowder" were freely used. Over the winter his troops had been pillaging and burning houses in Jackson County and tormenting Southerners with such fervor that many believed they were worse than Jennison's jayhawkers. They seemed to take special delight in shooting or stringing up elderly men, with the result that many were afraid to leave their homes even in daylight, and their sons went into hiding or joined the partisans.

In late January, Penick had begun arresting the wives and sisters of some of the most notorious bushwhackers in order to stop their acting as spies and to use them as hostages to prevent their menfolk from carrying out threats to execute prisoners. On April 7, Dwight Thacher, noting that the partisans' families provided them with sustenance as well as intelligence, advocated exiling them.

We do not recommend "making war on defenseless women and children," but we do urge the necessity of adopting the plan that is being carried out in the army of the Cumberland and Mississippi, that of placing the families of rebel soldiers, guerrillas, and sympathizers, over the Federal lines, and keep them there until the war is ended. This being carried out, there will be no place for treason in its various shapes to nestle about and seek refuge.

Five weeks later, Thacher made the suggestion again in bolder terms.

Every bushwhacker's family should immediately be sent beyond the lines. Those who aid and abet the bushwhackers, or give them information, or conceal them, or in any way whatever assist them, are as bad as the bushwhackers themselves, and should be ordered out of the country. The necessities of the case demand very stern and active measures.

Exile would not become official policy until General Thomas Ewing issued Order No. 10 on August 18, but in the spring various Federal commanders began rounding up and confining women, intending that they be sent south in the hope that their menfolk would follow them.

Given the fact that the Federal military was unable to subdue the partisans and the criminals, and given the vociferous complaints of newspaper publishers and civilians about the situation, it was inevitable that the Lincoln administration would make a change in command. On May 24, Major General John M. Schofield relieved Major General Curtis as commander of the Department of the Missouri, which included the entire state of Kansas. A New York native and the son of a Baptist minister, Schofield had graduated from West Point, but when the war began, he was on leave, teaching physics at Washington University, in St. Louis. He returned to duty, serving as Lyon's adjutant and seeing action at Wilson's Creek. He had commanded the Missouri Militia and the Army of the Frontier, but at the time of his promotion by Lincoln he was still only thirty-two years old.

"Let your military measures be strong enough to repel the invader and keep the peace, and not so strong as to unnecessarily harass and persecute the people," Lincoln instructed him. "It is a difficult role, and so much greater will be the honor if you perform it well. If both factions, or neither, shall abuse you, you will probably be about right. Beware of being assailed by one, and praised by the other."

A difficult role indeed: While privately opposed to slavery and wishing to see Missouri slaves speedily emancipated, Schofield was no radical, and as a soldier he felt he should not publicly clash with the state's governor, Hamilton R. Gamble, whose caution, conservatism, and opposition to the radicals' schemes for immediate emancipation had earned him the derogatory nickname "Granny." As a consequence, Senator James H. Lane drew a bead on Schofield, going so far after the Lawrence massacre as to travel to Washington to appeal to Lincoln personally for Schofield's removal. Lincoln stood by Schofield on that day, but at the beginning of the new year 1864, some eight months after replacing General Curtis, Schofield himself would be reassigned.

When Schofield took command, Grant was struggling to take Vicksburg, and General Halleck had asked that all commanders send every soldier they could spare to Mississippi. Schofield quickly dispatched half his regular troops—about twenty thousand men. The gesture won him high praise in Washington, but it spread his remaining regular forces dangerously thin, necessitating that he rely almost entirely on militia to protect Kansas and Missouri.

On June 9, 1863, Schofield made another move that would have an even more profound impact on the two states. He divided the District of Kansas into two sections: the "District of the Frontier" and the "District of the Border." Schofield's order creating the District of the Frontier stated that it would consist of "The Indian Territory, the State of Kansas south of the 38th parallel, the western tier of counties in Missouri south of the same parallel, and the western tier of counties of Arkansas." General Blunt, who had been commander of the old District of Kansas, was put in charge of this area and was headquartered at Fort Scott. He was bitterly unhappy with the reduction in his authority.

A Maine native, Blunt had gone to sea when he was fifteen years old. Returning after five years he earned a medical degree and established a practice in New Madison, Ohio. In 1856, this fierce abolitionist moved his family to Greeley, Kansas, where he treated patients and railed against slavery. As a delegate to the Wyandotte convention of 1859, he involved himself in writing the constitution of Kansas. On May 1, 1861, two weeks after the firing on Fort Sumter, he answered Lincoln's call for 75,000 volunteers to suppress the Southern rebellion. He served as a lieutenant-colonel in Lane's Kansas Brigade and became Kansas's first major general. Battle-tested and personally courageous, he was also querulous and a bit paranoid, forever complaining of being stabbed in the back by fellow officers and "my personal and political opponents."

Blunt was a Lane ally, of course, and it would seem that Schofield was trying to protect himself against the senator by reducing Blunt's authority and exiling him to a remote stretch of the country. Blunt would not remain there too long: In five months, disgraced by the slaughter of his men at Baxter Springs, he would be relieved of his command.

The other division, the District of the Border, had its headquarters in Kansas City and included, in Schofield's words, "the State of Kansas north of the 38th parallel, and the two western tiers of counties of Missouri north of the same parallel and south of the Missouri River." The district encompassed more than 57,000 square miles, was 460 miles wide if measured east to west, and, on the Missouri side, included Jackson, Lafayette, Cass, Johnson, Bates, Henry, and parts of Vernon and St. Clair counties. These counties contained many Southerners, of course, and were infested by numerous guerrilla bands.

As commander of this immense hornets' nest of a district, Schofield chose a thirty-three-year-old Ohioan, Brigadier General Thomas Ewing, Jr. Ewing's father had been a U.S. senator and cabinet officer under two presidents. In 1829, Senator Ewing's neighbor, Judge Charles Sherman, died suddenly, and the senator took as a ward one of his sons, William Tecumseh, age nine. Later, Senator Ewing would arrange for Sherman's appointment to West Point, and Sherman would in turn marry the eldest Ewing daughter, thus becoming the brother-in-law of Thomas, Jr., as well as his sometime business and law partner.

General Ewing moved to Leavenworth, Kansas, in 1856, intending to enrich himself by speculating in land and to practice law and enter politics. His investments failed, driving him deeply into debt, but he was elected chief justice of the Kansas supreme court. In August 1862, he acted as a recruiting agent for Lane's 11th Regiment and resigned from the court on September 13 to become the regiment's colonel. (When Lane's sworn enemy, Kansas Governor Charles Robinson, refused to issue Ewing a commission, Lane arranged for President Lincoln himself to do it.) Since Ewing's regiment had been instrumental in the Prairie Grove victory, he was promoted to brigadier general.

Ironically, while Ewing was a Lane protégé, he personally detested the man and his radicalism. Ewing was at best indifferent to slavery as a moral issue—he despised most abolitionists—but because of his overriding ambition to become U.S. senator from Kansas and because he knew Lane's power in the state, he cynically allied himself with the firebrand. By choosing Ewing as commander of District of the Border, Schofield seems to have been trying to create a buffer between himself and Lane.

Like Schofield and Blunt, Ewing would not survive very long in his new post, but his promotion was initially greeted with great enthusiasm and touching optimism. The publisher of the Olathe *Mirror* unabashedly admitted to being "an ardent admirer of the General. . . . He is emphatically *a man of brains,* and is destined eventually to occupy the highest position . . . in the State." The editor of the Emporia *News* was no less enthusiastic: "Gallant Gen. Ewing . . . has adopted the motto of extermination to the bushwhackers that infest our borders. We hope he will succeed. No man could have been appointed to this important trust that would have suited the people better."

Ewing responded by vigorously attempting to end the region's partisan violence and disorder. When in late June a Kansas militia unit made a raid into Missouri and stole forty head of cattle, Ewing had the commanding officer and all the men arrested and the stock returned to the rightful owners. On June 26 he gave a speech at Olathe in which he announced the arrests and assured listeners that "there is little at present to fear on this side of the border from guerrilla bands." He promised to "drive out or exterminate every band of guerrillas now haunting" western Missouri.

I will keep a thousand men in the saddle daily in pursuit of them and will redden with their blood every road and bridle path of the border, until they infest it no more.

I mean, moreover, to stop with a rough hand all forays for plunder from Kansas into Missouri.

He added pointedly that

There are very many men in Kansas who are stealing themselves rich in the name of liberty. These men must find some other mode of giving effect to their patriotic zeal. . . . I now notify them that they will be compelled to quit stealing, or get out of this District, or get me out of it. I shall inflict on all men who go into Missouri to plunder, the severest penalties. . . .

The brave speech was applauded by all the state's newspapers with the single exception of radical Daniel Anthony's Leavenworth *Daily Conservative.*

Soon after the speech, Ewing sent detectives to Leavenworth. The detectives had been instructed to locate and confiscate stolen property, but before they could do anything, Anthony, who had recently been elected mayor, had them arrested on trumped-up vagrancy charges. On July 19, a furious Ewing countered by declaring martial law in Leavenworth County. He indicated privately that he intended to maintain martial law as long as Anthony was the mayor, but in September some of his detectives seized Anthony, threw him into a wagon, and carried him to Kansas City.

Embarrassed by the public revelation of their action and Quantrill's recent raid on Lawrence, Ewing sheepishly revoked martial law. (Jayhawkers went right on using Leavenworth as a center of operations.)

As the summer progressed, Ewing received a crash course in the frustrations of guerrilla warfare. Four or five times he heard of large numbers of jayhawkers coming together here or there, always only twenty or thirty miles east of the line, and threatening Lexington, Independence, Warrensburg, or Harrisonville; he hurriedly sent troops to head them off. Scouts and spies frequently warned him that bushwhackers were about to raid Shawnee, Olathe, Paola, Mound City, and other towns in Kansas near the eastern border. He dutifully placed garrisons in these and a number of other towns and issued arms and rations to volunteer militia companies who guarded them. Whenever he dispatched troops, the enemy dispersed, until, as summer drew to a close, he found his own forces "scattered throughout . . . this district . . . especially the border counties, besetting their haunts and paths."

Little is known of Quantrill's life during the early summer of 1863. He made a few minor raids and set a couple of ambushes shortly after his return from Richmond. It is certain that he spent some time planning the Lawrence raid, and it seems likely that he whiled away many hours romancing a lovely young Jackson County girl, Sarah Catherine King. Nevertheless, his fame or infamy continued to grow, and newspapers had him riding here or there, taking part in one or another raid or skirmish, threatening this town or that military outpost. He was beginning to have a mythic presence, and, fittingly, songs were written about him, which were sung in Missouri parlors and around campfires, and which would be preserved and collected by musicologists fifty or even eighty years later.

> *Arise, my brave boys, the moon is in the west,*
> *And we must be gone ere the dawning of the day;*
> *The hounds of old Pennock will find but the nest,*
> *For the Quantrell he seeks will be far, far away.*
> *Their toils after us shall ever be vain,*
> *Let them scout through the brush and scour the plain;*
> *We'll pass through their midst in the dead of night,*
> *We are lions in combat and eagles in flight.*

And when they are weary and the chase given o'er,
We'll descend like thunderbolts down from the cloud;
We'll ride through their ranks and bathe in their gore,
Smite down the oppressor and humble the proud.
Few shall escape us and few shall be spared,
For keen is our saber, in vengeance 'tis bared;
For none are so strong, so mighty in fight,
As the warrior who battles for our Southern right.

Kansans composed less flattering songs—about "Quantrell the ruf-fian," of course—and it is oddly appropriate that the song quoted above, "Quantrell's Call," was sung to the tune of "The Pirate's Sere-nade." Many of his adversaries and victims routinely used phrases to describe him and his men that evoked the negative aura of buccaneers: "cut-throats," "freebooters," and even "land pirates." It was said they rode "under the black flag," and that Quantrill had a personal Jolly Roger, whose design supposedly consisted of red letters on a plain dark background misspelling his name as "Quantrell." (William Gregg was one of several veteran bushwhackers who would in their later years unequivocally deny that any such flag ever existed, and at the onset of the Lawrence raid a black man would run through the streets shouting a warning: "See those men, they have no flag!") Finally, like Captain Kidd and other fabled pirates, legends persisted that Quantrill had buried a hoard of Lawrence treasure, which was long and eagerly sought: "Every crag and cranny of [Jackson] county . . . and every ravine and cave has been scrutinized over and over again by anxious natives," a Kansas City *Star* correspondent snickered in 1910. "Many a ton of dirt has been spaded up by the fortune hunters, who imagined they had a new clue to Quantrell's gold."

Most bushwhackers grew their hair long and had beards, goatees, or mustaches and long sideburns. They favored round-brimmed hats and tucked their baggy pants into high-topped cavalry boots.

When not wearing a confiscated Yankee uniform, a raider sported over his regular shirt a gray or brown "guerrilla shirt," knitted by his wife, sweetheart, or sister, decoratively embroidered and bearing a num-ber of pockets for ammunition. He had two or four revolvers stuck into his holsters and wide leather belt, often with another four on his horse.

The horse would have been selected from the finest stock available on the border, while the Federals struggled on inferior army plugs.

Bushwhackers preferred revolvers manufactured by Colt, the thirty-six-caliber 1851 Navy Colt and the forty-four-caliber 1860 Army Colt being most commonly used. Like all the era's weapons the Colts fired black powder, which sometimes was slow, or entirely failed, to ignite. Worse, as firearms expert D. Michael Gooch explained in 1994,

> Black powder left a gummy residue when fired quickly jamming weapons and causing severe rust within hours. The sheet of flame and cloud of white smoke produced by firing were guaranteed to reveal the position of the shooter, greatly aiding counter-fire and lessening chances for the shooter's survival.

The revolver could take a cartridge made of black powder and a ball wrapped in combustible paper; otherwise, the shooter had to pour, in Gooch's words, "a specified amount of black powder into each of the pistol's six chambers, followed by placing a ball on top. A hinged rammer under the barrel was used to press fit each load in turn. A firing cap was then placed on a tube screwed into the rear of each chamber. . . ."

Finally, a prudent shooter would cover the loaded chamber with grease to keep out moisture, because black powder would not ignite if it was wet, and Quantrill's band rode in a region veined with rivers and creeks that had to be crossed, and where snow and rain were prevalent and fog not uncommon. If the chambers weren't greased, when one bullet was fired the powder in the other five chambers could ignite, ruining the weapon and mangling the shooter's hand.

Since the quality of caps was as various as that of powder, the revolver might not fire when the hammer struck the cap. "If the cap did explode two further problems could occur," noted Gooch.

> First, the recoil from the shot could blow the cap back, whereupon it dropped into the hammer slot in the frame, blocking the hammer from falling on the next cap. Second the spent cap could loosen, and when the cylinder turned for the next shot, wedge between the cylinder and frame, either binding the cylinder or retarding free travel.

The pistol would then be inoperable.

The Colt's front sight was a brass bead, the rear sight a notch cut in the top of the hammer. This did not make for a very clear sight picture under even the best of circumstances. Colts were generally sighted to be "dead-on" at fifty yards, so shots aimed at closer targets would be high, and those aimed at targets farther downrange would be low. This assumes, as Gooch observed, "that the sights on the pistol being shot were aligned . . . in truth every revolver was different, and could print anywhere, horizontally or vertically. The guerrilla had to know exactly where the particular pistol in his hand printed to achieve any semblance of accuracy."

For all its disadvantages, the pistol was the weapon of choice for bushwhackers because muzzle-loading, single-shot muskets were no more reliable and were nearly impossible to reload on horseback. Having four or even eight revolvers meant that a guerrilla was able to switch weapons quickly if one failed to work and, if he was lucky and all the pistols functioned properly, he might fire as many as forty-eight bullets without having to reload.

Union soldiers were at a distinct disadvantage in a fight with Quantrill's Raiders. Their muzzle-loading, single-shot rifles were no match for Sharps carbines and Navy Colts. When, after years of vociferous complaints by troops in the field about the inadequateness of their long guns, Union military authorities finally issued pistols, some models proved to be so mediocre that the bushwhackers usually disdained to loot them from the slain.

———◆·◆———

Many people, including a few eyewitnesses to their attacks, would later claim that Quantrill's Raiders rode into battle with their reins between their teeth and a revolver in each hand. In 1897, Frank James, speaking to the correspondent for the Columbia *Missouri Herald,* dismissed such tales as "simply dime novel stuff." He added, "There was never any such thing. We always held our horses with one hand and the pistol with the other. It was as important to hold the horse as it was to hold the pistol."

———◆·◆———

The stronghold of Quantrill's Raiders was the Sni-A-Bar country in Jackson County, near the Lafayette County line. This was a region of deep, narrow ravines and high hills with steep, rocky slopes, thickly covered by dense woods and tangled thickets and pocketed with caves. Many of Quantrill's men were natives of Jackson County and knew the

Sni-A-Bar like the backs of their hands—every bridle path and trail. "Federal troops, on the other hand, usually lacked such valuable information and were slow to acquire it," observed Dr. Castel. "As a consequence, the bushwhackers were able to roam at will by little-known routes, while the Union soldiers, sticking to the main-traveled roads, searched for them in vain."

The guerrillas also benefited enormously from the support of the civilian population. It will be recalled that female relatives and sympathizers purchased ammunition and acted as spies and couriers—even children sometimes carried messages or picked up spent lead after skirmishes or target practices.

As a result of the repeated raids by jayhawkers and redlegs and the abuses of the militia, many residents of western Missouri looked upon bushwhackers as their saviors and protectors. They passed along intelligence and provided food, shelter, and horses. Even a man who was a Unionist or tried to remain neutral would find it necessary to assist Quantrill and his men, who, if denied, might beat him up or even kill him, then take what they wanted anyway.

———※◆※———

"On Quantrill's return to the state military operations began in earnest, however, on a different line from the previous year," wrote William Gregg.

> During the year 1862 the men were kept close together and all under the watchful eye of Quantrill. Not so in 1863, there was Todd, Pool, Blunt, Younger, Wilson, and others. Each had companies, often widely separated, and only called together on special occasions, all of whom, however, recognized Quantrill as Commander in Chief with Lieut Gregg as ajutant.

It is an overstatement to call Quantrill a commander in chief, but it is true that by the summer of 1863 Quantrill was the leader of the most fearsome band of guerrillas operating in Missouri and that some of his followers had branched out, forming bands of their own. Other, independent bands were drawn to him by his reputation and made alliances with him. To Gregg's list two notable names should be added: Bill Anderson and Dick Yeager.

Membership in such bands could be fluid: A man might belong to one outfit for awhile and, then, for any number of reasons, shift to another. Frank James, for example, rode first with Quantrill and later Bill Anderson, then rejoined Quantrill again. Leadership could be fluid, too: A captain who lost the confidence of his followers might be driven from camp or simply have his authority given to another by vote.

Although Quantrill was largely quiet during June, July, and August, his lieutenants and the other guerrilla chieftains and their followers took up the slack. "Occurrances were thick and fast during the summer of 1863," Gregg wrote in his memoir.

> Todd would annihilate a party of the Enemy in western Jackson County . . . Blunt another in the eastern portion . . . Anderson somewhere in Kas, or Cass Co., Mo. Pool in Lafayette or Saline . . . Younger on the high Blue. Some one of these commanders were in collision with the enemy almost every day up to about the 1st [of] August, when the enemy ceased their activity from some cause or other, giving [us] much needed rest. . . . The enemy had been more savage, if possible, than ever before. . . .

Gregg was wildly exaggerating the number of clashes and casualties, but the bushwhackers certainly were busy.

One of those who linked up with Quantrill in 1863, trailing his followers behind him—including his own brother Jim, five years his junior—was the aforementioned William T. "Bloody Bill" Anderson, twenty-four years old. His parents, William and Martha, were from Kentucky, and the family—including three sons and three daughters—had settled briefly in Salt Spring Township, Missouri, sometime before 1850, then moved to Agnes City, Lyon County, Kansas, in 1854. "The Andersons were of a rough type," commented Judge L. D. Bailey, "and their reputation as to horse flesh was somewhat unsavory." Indeed, as teenagers Bill and Jim had supplemented their father's meager earnings as a farmer by stealing ponies.

On May 12, 1862, their father was killed by a man named Arthur I. Baker. According to Bailey, who was a newspaper publisher and historian, Baker had led a party of neighbors on the trail of some horse thieves who turned out, when captured, to be Bill and Jim. The boys managed to secure their release from jail and disappear, but their father was furious at Baker; the betrayal was all the more aggravating because Baker had been courting one of the Anderson daughters, then abruptly announced shortly after the boys' arrest that he would marry a young schoolteacher instead.

On the morning of the wedding, the elder Anderson entered Baker's kitchen and moved through the house, carrying a double-barrel shotgun with both hammers cocked. The prospective bridegroom, who was in a second-floor room dressing for the ceremony, heard the frightened exclamations of servants and guests, picked up his own shotgun, ran to the head of the stairs, and cut loose at Anderson as he was climbing toward him. The charge penetrated his chest and angled downward.

The wedding went on as scheduled, but, as Judge Bailey observed, "the bloody nuptials brought a bloody retribution." Baker had a store on the Santa Fe Trail and did a brisk business selling supplies to passing wagon trains; late on the night of July 1, 1862, Bill Anderson rode to the store with his newly formed band. While the rest hid in the bushes, one man unknown to Baker was sent to pound on the door of his darkened house, pretending to be the master of a wagon train camped nearby, in need of groceries. When roused from their beds, Baker and his new, youthful brother-in-law, who was employed as his clerk, opened up the store. Asked for whiskey, the two sleepy men descended into the cellar through the trapdoor, one to draw the whiskey while the other held the light. The Anderson brothers and their minions burst into the store, slammed the trapdoor shut, and piled boxes of goods on top of it. "We've got you at last!" one cried. "We're going to burn you alive in your hole!"

They set the store ablaze and stood in the yard for some time, watching it burn. They then fired Baker's house—the womenfolk had taken to the woods—and rode away.

A neighbor of the Anderson family, O. F. O'Dell, said that the brother-in-law managed to crawl through a small window in the cellar's back wall, but Baker was too large a man to squeeze through the confined opening: "He shot himself through the head to keep from the horrible death of being burned alive." Other of Baker's neighbors agreed that he had committed suicide but told Judge Bailey the brother-in-law had suffered a grimmer fate: There being no window in the cellar, he had tried to escape the burning building by digging through a dirt wall.

This he finally effected, but not until he was fearfully burned. He succeeded in crawling into a clump of tall weeds at the back side of the store near which he made his exit, and lay concealed until the fiends had seen the building fall and left. He then crawled with painful effort to the creek but a few rods distant and found a temporary relief from pain by lying in the cool water. There he was found [the] next morning, but his injuries proved fatal, and he expired in dreadful agony. . . .

Bill Anderson fabricated a story about his father's death, saying he had been tortured and killed by Yankees. As time went by and he became increasingly cruel and violent, he actually seems to have come to believe the lie himself.

———•◦•———

Another man who was drawn to Quantrill in 1863, but who would soon become a member of Anderson's band, was a slim twenty-year-old, Alexander Franklin James. James's father, Robert, was a Baptist minister and farmer from Kentucky, who owned seven slaves. By 1850, he was living on a farm near Kearney, Clay County, Missouri, with his wife, Zerelda Cole, two small sons, and an infant daughter; however, he decided to join the California gold rush in order to minister to the miners. He fell ill and died shortly after reaching the West Coast, and within a year his twenty-six-year-old widow married Benjamin Simms, fifty-two. "The union proved unhappy and in less than a year was terminated by a separation," related the 1885 *History of Clay County.* "The lady alleges that the chief [cause of] trouble arose from the fact that her three little children, Frank, Jesse, and Susie, whom she always humored and indulged, gave their old step-father no end of annoyance." Shortly after the separation Benjamin Simms died. Zerelda's third marriage, to Dr. Reuben Samuel, a physician and farmer, proved happier, presumably because he found a way to placate the rambunctious children.

On May 4, 1861, eighteen-year-old Frank joined a Clay County home guard unit. We know that he fought in the Battle of Wilson's Creek, and, according to the *History of Clay County,* he was also "present at the capture of Lexington and marched with Price's army into Southwest Missouri. At Springfield he was taken with measles" and "was left behind in the hospital" as Price retreated in February. He was taken prisoner and paroled, and he went back to the family farm.

In the spring of 1862, he accepted the amnesty offered by the Federal military. The Liberty *Tribune* of May 2, lists him as one of a small number of men who had recently taken the oath of allegiance and had given a $1,000 bond for future good behavior to Colonel Penick.

There was no separate peace for Frank in Missouri: The *History of Clay County* tells us that Penick twice arrested him on charges of aiding and abetting the Confederate cause in violation of his parole. The second time he was jailed in Liberty but escaped, determined "to go to the brush." For a time he rode with a guerrilla chieftain named Fernando Scott and took part in a raid on Missouri City. Then, hearing Quantrill was back from Richmond, he decided to join him. "I met Bill Gregg, Quantrill's First Lieutenant, in Clay County," Frank once recalled,

and with him rowed across the Missouri River to Jackson County and joined Quantrill on the Webb place on Blackwater ford of the Sni. This was in May 1863. I will never forget the first time I saw Quantrill. He was nearly six feet in height, rather thin, his hair and moustache was sandy and he was full of life and a jolly fellow. He had none of the air of bravado or desperado about him. We all loved him at first sight. . . . He was a demon in battle and did not know how to be afraid.*

Not long after Frank joined Quantrill, the militia visited the James farm. They put a rope around Dr. Samuel's neck and hauled him up a tree limb repeatedly, asking where Quantrill's camp was; then, after he passed out, they left him dangling to look for fifteen-year-old Jesse. (Zerelda cut Samuel down in time to save his life, but his brain had been permanently damaged due to the lack of oxygen.) They found Jesse

---

*Frank was one of several people who in remembering Quantrill exaggerated his height. In 1974, anthropologist Michael Finnegan examined Quantrill's shinbones and used the Trotter and Gleser formulas to determine that he had stood just over five-nine. The passage of so many decades and the tendency to idealize a fallen comrade may explain why people close to him remember him as taller than he was.

Quantrill's hair has been described as being of every shade between platinum and dirty brown; the variation is perhaps attributable to such factors as cleanliness and exposure to the sun. His mother said his hair was auburn, and a lock of it, which had been taken from his grave in 1887 and subsequently donated to the Kansas State Historical Society, was, when I examined it in 1992, a very light brown with a reddish tint; however, ground burial sometimes alters hair coloring.

plowing in a cornfield and beat him with a whip. Robertus Love, a journalist who in later years became close to Frank, asserted that baby-faced Jesse immediately tried to join the Quantrill band but was rejected as being too young. Decades later, after Jesse had become famous, some Lawrence survivors would manufacture tales of having encountered him, wild and cruel, during the raid, but Love was correct: Jesse was tending a tobacco crop that August and did not become a guerrilla until the following summer, when he joined Anderson's band.

Both Zerelda and Reuben were arrested—the date is unknown, though it may have been that very day—and charged with "feeding and harboring bushwhackers." They were confined in the St. Joseph jail; at least one of Zerelda's children was held with her. On June 5, Zerelda obtained her release by signing an "Oath of Allegiance," swearing to "support, protect, and defend the Constitution and Government of the United States against all enemies, whether domestic or foreign. . . ." It is not certain when Dr. Samuel was set free; however, he was still confined on July 6. On that date several of his neighbors wrote a letter to the authorities testifying to his good character and asking that he be discharged. When Zerelda gave birth to her next child, she defiantly named her Fannie Quantrell Samuel.

<hr>

In all likelihood, it was soon after his return from Richmond that Quantrill met and fell madly in love with the aforementioned beautiful, shapely farm girl Sarah "Kate" King. The Robert King place was near Blue Springs, not far from the Morgan Walker farm, and one day Kate returned home from school to find her father standing on the front porch talking to a young man with a scraggly mustache who flashed her a winning smile. She thought him extremely handsome and was struck by his blue eyes.

She had hurriedly put her school books and lunch pail inside the house and returned to stand on the porch beside her father and the stranger, listening to their conversation. Quantrill impressed her as being polished, debonair, and polite. He, in turn, was enchanted, and gallantly complimented her on her looks. "She was a buxom girl, of sturdy build and well developed for her years," related a Kansas City *Star* reporter in 1926.

She was lively and jolly; a disposition which years of turmoil and suffering since have not changed. Old-timers who knew her say she was pretty beyond question. The farm life, spent mostly outdoors and a great deal of time on horseback, had given her health and vigor and rosy cheeks. She could ride a horse like one born to the saddle. Ever since she was old enough to hold a rein her father had provided her with a mount, one that she could call her own.

So far as is known Kate never wrote a memoir, and none of her correspondence has ever come to light. Most of what we know about her is derived from the *Star* article, which was published on May 23, under the title "The Strange Romance of Quantrill's Bride." At the time, Kate was seventy-eight years old and was residing in the Jackson County poorhouse. She was using the name Sarah Head—Walter Head, a fellow resident, had become her fourth husband—and was careful not to reveal her background to other residents because some had been bushwhacker victims. In the unsigned article, the reporter did give her maiden name but otherwise identified her only as "Kate Clarke," which was the name she used during her relationship with Quantrill.

Kate told the reporter that after the first meeting Quantrill quickly became a regular visitor to the farm, stopping by every few days, always at a time he knew she would be at home and always bringing some little gift. Soon they were taking rides around the countryside. An expert horseman himself, he was impressed with her riding skills and a little anxious as well: She loved to ride hard and never hesitated to jump a creek or a fence. Sometimes he held her horse's rein to restrain the animal.

Kate's parents realized that a romance was developing and sought to end it by forbidding their daughter to see Quantrill anymore. "But," noted the *Star* correspondent, "as is so often the case, the parental ban only served to deepen her regard for the young gallant." The rides resumed in secret.

Neighbors who had spotted the couple warned Robert King, and he gave her such a "severe scolding" that she "trembled for days afterwards whenever she thought of her father's wrath. Yet, trembling with fear, she continued to meet the guerrilla far away from possible detection." They stayed off the roads and "rambled" through the woods, often stopping to sit on creek banks and talk. Mostly he told her the truth about himself—his birth in Ohio and years as a schoolteacher, that his was a family of Northern sympathizers, that Mary Quantrill had defied Confederate soldiers by waving a U.S. flag—but he also related the polished lies about the supposed murder of his brother by jayhawkers and his own calculated revenge.

While Quantrill had repeatedly lied to Missouri Southerners—including his own followers—about his background, he was honest with Kate, so why he felt the need to mislead her about his brother is puzzling. She told the reporter that in her youth she had been a zealous rebel and that during their courtship she quickly came to idolize Quantrill. Perhaps his telling her the shopworn fabrications was a natural attempt to impress her and encourage her inclination to put him up on a pedestal.

(Anyway, like almost everyone else in this story, Kate was not above a little fanciful embroidery herself: She told the journalist that arising before dawn on the morning of the Lawrence massacre, anxious about Quantrill's safety, she had left the bushwhacker camp in Missouri and ridden ninety miles in five hours, reaching him, as it turned out, just in time to accompany him on the arduous two-day retreat back across the line! None of the Lawrence survivors recalled seeing a woman join the raiders; none of the pursuers reported seeing a woman among their quarry; and not one of Quantrill's men ever mentioned her being with them.)

One day Quantrill and Kate spent too long conversing by a stream, and she did not get home until after dark. Her father became suspicious. As soon as she could get away again, she went to Quantrill's camp and told him she "feared to meet him anymore." According to Kate, he took her to a country preacher's home, six miles away, and they were married. They slept on the floor of an abandoned cabin that night beneath a borrowed blanket. Thereafter Kate gave her last name as Clarke, which Quantrill suggested in order to hide their relationship from his enemies.

One of the persistent debates among Quantrill aficionados concerns whether Kate was Quantrill's wife or mistress. Those who have varying degrees of admiration or sympathy for Quantrill are naturally inclined to believe Kate was his wife, while those who consider him a villain, psychopath, or monster prefer that his relationship with Kate be, by the standards of that age, an immoral one.

There is no direct evidence to support either argument, and the only people in a position to know—Quantrill, Kate King, and, possibly, a backwoods preacher—obviously have been dead for a long time. It should be noted, however, that those who disbelieve Kate's marriage claim have long seized with delight on the first name of Bill Anderson's love, Bush Smith, suggesting that she was nothing more than a prostitute and his sometime mistress. The latter allegation, at least, is false: Several years ago a Quantrill buff named Mark Dugan actually discovered the Anderson wedding license in the dusty labyrinths of a Texas courthouse. Unfortunately, it is doubtful that such conclusive proof of a Quantrill-King marriage will ever turn up.

The *Star* article contains another historical puzzle, this one having to do with Kate's age and the year she became involved with Quantrill. She was vague about the date, indicating, according to the reporter, that "it was about sixty-five years ago," which points toward the year 1861. Kate said she was thirteen years old at the time, adding, perhaps to keep Quantrill from condemnation for being a cradle robber, that she looked older, at least sixteen. The 1860 census lists her as being twelve years old, so she would have been thirteen the following year; the article further stated that her marriage to Quantrill lasted "three and one-half years," all of which is consistent with her having met Quantrill in 1861. The recollections of Quantrill's men, however, were that he became involved with her in 1863, and Kate herself supplied no memories of life with him for a period of two years between the time of their supposed elopement in the spring or summer of 1861 and the morning of August 21, 1863. (In addition to the fantastic ride to Lawrence that she claimed to have made, she said that after the raid he gave her "seven diamond rings, three pins and four sets of earrings out of the loot." The concrete detail is convincing, the more so because jewelry played a part in her later life: After Quantrill's death, she said, she sold some of her jewels to buy a St. Louis "boarding house" so she could support herself.) It seems likely, then, that Quantrill's veterans were correct when they said he met Kate in 1863 after his return from Richmond. She would have been fifteen years old.

There is yet another Quantrill controversy that involves Kate King. His disparagers have long perpetuated the story that far from courting Kate, he kidnapped her like some feudal land baron, and "it took her some time to become reconciled to the life to which he doomed her, but . . . [eventually] she became infatuated with him, even wearing a man's clothing and riding in the ranks to be near him."

The account Kate gave in the 1926 interview of Quantrill's courtship was refutation of the charge that he had kidnapped her, and she stated categorically that she had never ridden with him "in a fight" or "assumed a man's outfit." To the contrary, she said, she "was always safer dressed as [a] girl."

The most convincing corroboration of her assertions comes from Fletch Taylor. He broke with Quantrill in 1864: Quantrill had him arrested and tried to turn him over to Confederate military authorities for court-martial on robbery and murder charges. Thereafter, Taylor had very little good to say about either Quantrill or Kate King, whom he swore was in later life a whorehouse madam. No one would have taken greater pleasure in charging Quantrill with kidnapping and sexual misconduct, but Taylor made no such allegation; indeed, in a letter to W. W. Scott he said that Quantrill "took Kate King from [her] home in the summer of 1863 and she went willingly . . . he borrowed my Gray mare for her to ride on to a place some five miles from camp." (It will be recalled that Kate said they went to a country preacher's house six miles away.)

"From that time on he never did much fighting," Taylor sneered. To the contrary, over the next two years Quantrill fought in a number of skirmishes and battles; more to the point, in the four or five months that followed the onset of his relationship with Kate King, he led the audacious attack on Lawrence and then routed Blunt's troops at Baxter Springs. As one eminent Civil War historian put it, these were "the only victories won by the Confederacy in the West in 1863."

So love had not drained from him his martial desires, but then, one should not expect an objective appraisal from Fletch Taylor. His remark smacks of revenge and a survivor's smug self-satisfaction: When he wrote those words in 1879, he was the prosperous vice president of a mining company, and Quantrill was moldering in his grave.

At Baxter Springs Quantrill capitalized upon a momentary opportunity when he unexpectedly encountered Blunt's command, but the Lawrence massacre was the result of preparation and extensive scouting. Lawrence lay some forty miles across the line, with many Yankee posts and patrols in between, but it is hardly surprising that, even forgetting his own personal history, Quantrill should find it an enticing target: It will be recalled that Lawrence was the "capital" of the Kansas Free State movement, an important station on the Underground Railroad, and a recruiting center for Union troops. Furthermore, as was noted earlier, the town had been founded and initially settled by abolitionists and was even named after a prominent Boston abolitionist and treasurer of the New England Emigrant Aide Company, Amos Lawrence. Before the war Lawrencians made raids on nearby Southern strongholds.

The town's most impressive building was the Free State Hotel, erected with money from the company to provide comfortable temporary shelter for newly arriving Northern zealots. The town was raided by Missouri border ruffians in 1856, of course, who destroyed the hotel. The hotel's proprietor, Colonel S. W. Eldridge, defiantly erected a new hotel on the ruins of the old, making it even more imposing—four stories and brick—and luxuriously appointed. Quantrill designated it the first and most important target.

Lawrence was also the home of Kansas's first governor, Charles Robinson, a onetime agent of the company and leader of the Free State movement, as well as Jim Lane. (During the spring and summer Lane had built a handsome, two-story brick house for himself and his family.) Lawrence was a headquarters for jayhawkers, of course, and most of the goods stolen from Missouri Southerners had been auctioned there. Indeed, Lane's new house was said to contain two pianos stolen from Jackson County music lovers.

Throughout the summer, Quantrill diligently collected the reports of informants and sent in a number of spies, one of whom had stayed at the Eldridge House, posing as a stock trader and spending stolen money with abandon. Quantrill even reconnoitered the area himself, although because of the likelihood of being recognized he had stayed outside the city limits. He had a local woman draw up a list of males to be targeted for death and houses to be burned.

Lawrence residents seemed to sense Quantrill's malevolent interest, and frequent rumors of an impending attack caused periodic bouts of mass hysteria. Men formed a new home-guard company, and demands were made that Federal authorities supply weapons. A shipment of ancient, rusty muskets finally arrived, but probably because there was an ordinance forbidding the carrying of firearms within city limits, the mayor insisted that they be stacked in an arsenal instead of distributed.

At the end of July "reliable sources" warned General Ewing that Quantrill was assembling his band on the Snibar for a raid on Lawrence in mid-August. The general dispatched an infantry company to reinforce the local garrison under Lieutenant T. J. Hadley and at the same time sent a detachment into the Snibar to deal with the bushwhackers. When Quantrill could not be found and August 15 passed without incident, Ewing withdrew the reinforcements from Lawrence—and then Hadley was ordered to pull out as well. All that remained were two small contingents of white and black recruits, untrained and unarmed. Quantrill soon learned of the town's vulnerability from two spies he had recently sent in, Fletch Taylor and John Noland, a black member of the band.

Ironically, rather than being a cause for increased alarm, the removal of most of the soldiers calmed the populace. Lieutenant Hadley's home was in Lawrence, and he had a brother on Ewing's staff; surely if there were any danger, he would have pulled strings to prevent his troop's withdrawal. "It was evident . . . that the military authorities at Kansas City, who ought to know, did not consider the place in danger," commented Lawrence clergyman Richard Cordley shortly after the massacre. Anyway, for three years there had been rumors of an imminent attack, and the rebels had never arrived. At the present moment Quantrill was thought to be more than fifty miles away—too far to penetrate into "loyal country" without detection. Thus, observed Cordley, "The people never felt more secure, and never were less prepared, than the night before the raid." With the benefit of hindsight some raid survivors would ruefully conclude that the false sense of security was the product of too many alarms, too many rumors. It was a variation, they thought, on the little boy who cried "wolf."

And it was just what Quantrill had been waiting for. When one prisoner taken in the raid asked him why he had not struck Lawrence a few weeks earlier, Quantrill replied: "You were expecting me then—but I have caught you napping now."

CHAPTER 9

"The Most Diabolical Deed
of the Whole Civil War":
The Lawrence Massacre

On August 10, 1863, Quantrill called his officers and the chieftains of allied bands together at his camp near Blue Springs to tell them of his plan to attack Lawrence. Not all his men were as confident of success as he was. The war council dragged on for twenty-four hours. Lawrence was too deep in enemy territory, some argued, and there were too many Yankee troops prowling around; even if they could reach the town with impunity, they would have to fight all the way back to Missouri.

"The undertaking is too hazardous," one lieutenant complained succinctly.

"I know," Quantrill said, "but if you never risk, you will never gain."

The spirited debate went on. He refuted every objection and then called on Fletch Taylor, just back from his spy mission, to report on what he had seen. With Hadley gone, there were only those small contingents of white and black recruits in the area. The citizens were complacent, and the streets were wide and ideal for charging horsemen.

William Gregg let his mind drift back to January 28, 1862, when he had followed in the wake of a Jennison raid into western Missouri. Thirteen houses were still burning, and the redlegs had left only devastation behind. A year later a squad of Penick's men had arrived at the Sanders place. They forced the old woman to cook them supper, then burned the house down. A foot of snow was on the ground and it was bitterly cold, but the womenfolk were not permitted to save even a shawl or coat from the flames. The militia took the old man with them, though his wife begged for his life, and shot him soon after. They also killed Uncle Jephthah Crawford that night and burned his house, too, snatching the lace cap from his wife's gray head and casting it into the flames. How many Missourians had been murdered by Lane and the other Kansans? Age made no difference to jayhawkers or redlegs: Old men were strung up, young boys shot down—Henry Morris was only eleven when he was killed. How many homes had been plundered and burned? Every officer in Quantrill's band could recite a litany of atrocities, had friends or loved ones among the victims.

Quantrill knew what was in their hearts. "Lawrence is the great hotbed of abolitionism in Kansas," he told them. "All the plunder—or the bulk of it—stolen from Missouri will be found stored away in Lawrence, and we can get more revenge and more money there than anywhere else in the state."

The council voted unanimously for the raid.

The officers rejoined their bands and ordered preparations begun. (For security reasons they did not disclose the target, although many believed it was Kansas City.) During the next week the men devoted themselves to cleaning and oiling their pistols, molding bullets, and mending their harnesses. Some of their women went to Kansas City to procure a large quantity of pistol caps and powder.

On August 13, the looming, three-story brick building at 1409 Grand Avenue in Kansas City that General Ewing was using as a prison for some of the Southern girls who had been arrested as spies or were being held until they could be transported out of the state collapsed. The females, none of whom was older than twenty, had been confined on the second floor, and as the building began to shake and walls to split apart from one another, a guard scooped up two girls and carried them outside. Nannie McCorkle leaped out a window. Thirteen-year-old Martha Anderson tried to follow, but, according to the accounts of survivors, she had annoyed the guards earlier that morning and to punish her they had shackled a twelve-pound ball to her ankle. She went down in the wreckage.

Soldiers and civilians rushed to the scene; however, a great cloud of dust prevented the immediate extrication of the victims from the rubble. A few of the girls who were buried near the surface managed to free themselves and stood wailing and cursing the Yankees. As soon as the dust dissipated sufficiently, the bystanders set to work digging through the ruins. Groans and screams could be heard, and one girl—thought to be fifteen-year-old Josephine Anderson—kept begging for someone to take the bricks off her head. After awhile she fell silent. A large crowd gathered and angrily listened to the shrieks and the moans, and watched the removal of the bodies. A messenger was sent for Major Preston B. Plumb, Ewing's chief of staff, and by the time he arrived on the scene the crowd's mood had become so ugly that he called out the headquarters's guard and ordered them to fix bayonets to prevent a riot.

It is no longer possible to determine how many prisoners were being held on the second floor—contemporary estimates range between nine and twenty-seven—but, as the reader will recall, the toll among relatives of Quantrill's Raiders was high. Josephine Anderson died before being freed, and another Anderson sister, Mary, eighteen, was, in a phrase common in that era, "crippled for life"; the third sister, Martha, suffered two broken legs, injured her back, and her face was severely lacerated. Charity McCorkle Kerr, John McCorkle's sister and Cole Younger's cousin, died. Also killed were twin sisters of another member of the band, Mrs. Armenia Crawford Selvey and Mrs. Susan Crawford Vandevere. Nothing is known about the other girl who was fatally injured, and who is identified only as Mrs. Wilson. Nearly all the survivors were badly hurt.

Within a few hours a rumor spread that Ewing had commanded his soldiers "to remove the girders under the structure in order to convert it into a deadfall for the deliberate purpose of murder."

Other, apparently confirming rumors centered around an elderly merchant who, as Connelley put it, "had a store of cheap goods on the first floor—a medley of merchandise, including flashy jewelry, clothing, groceries, and liquors." It was alleged that in the hours before the collapse he frantically had removed all his stock with the help of the guards. It was even claimed that he was in such a hurry he piled his goods in the street—further "proof" that the collapse was engineered.

The Yankees only aggravated hard feelings when they alleged that the girls were themselves responsible for what happened because they had weakened the building's walls by tunneling out of the cellar in an escape attempt.

There is absolutely no evidence that the Southern girls had tried to escape, and, the bushwhackers' heartfelt contention to the contrary, today hardly anyone believes that Ewing had the building's foundation undermined. The building is usually described as being old, cheaply and badly constructed, and "rickety," the result of being poorly maintained. The immediate cause of the collapse is attributed to a windstorm or to a sudden, strong gust of wind that started a chain reaction.

George Caleb Bingham came to a very different conclusion. Beginning only three weeks after the tragedy, Bingham undertook what would prove to be a thirteen-year investigation to establish culpability for the tragedy. Unfortunately the results of Bingham's investigation would be buried in the collections of the National Archives for the better part of a century, escaping the scrutiny of historians.

Although Bingham's credentials as a Unionist were unimpeachable, he had financial and personal motives for trying to lay the blame on Ewing: Bingham's second wife, Eliza, was a daughter of the late Reverend Robert S. Thomas, whose estate owned the building and would be reimbursed for its value if it could be established that the Federal military authorities were somehow responsible for its loss; and, for reasons that will be made clear shortly, Bingham had developed a personal enmity toward the general and was determined to thwart his political ambitions.

To understand what Bingham's investigation uncovered, it is necessary to know that the building in question shared a common wall with one owned by Mrs. Elizabeth Cockerel, which had been taken over by Ewing for use as a guardhouse. Survivors stated that it fell first, triggering the collapse of the Thomas House.

Bingham was able to establish that far from being an ancient, dilapidated structure, the Thomas building was just six years old, and he collected the testimonies of a number of reliable people who had been in the building that summer and who stated that it was sound and in good repair.

On September 10, 1863, Solomon S. Smith, the mason who built the "Thomas House," swore in an affidavit that he had used only the "hardest and best Quality bricks" and that "the foundation walls . . . were eighteen inches thick and the partition walls thirteen inches thick," constructed upon "solid clay Seven feet deep." Smith stated that he had laid the brick for all the buildings on the "entire Block" to the same specifications. He added that the walls of the Thomas House

were Sufficiently thick and Substantial to support Six Stories. . . . Except undermining the Walls in Some way or removing the Supports aforesaid, this affiant further Says that the Rev. R. S. Thomas Building was a good and Substantial Building, that the adjoining Buildings were also good and Substantial Buildings and Could only [have] given way by removing the Columns aforesaid or by cutting the walls or undermining the foundations in Some way.

On the same day that Bingham deposed Smith, Elijah M. McGee, a future mayor of Kansas City, gave Bingham an affidavit in which he swore that when he had visited the place on August 11, he went into the cellar and found that the "Posts or Columns" supporting the adjoining wall between the Cockerel and Thomas houses "had been cut away from the Girders . . . and the Girders had already sunk two or three feet. . . ." Afraid the building might fall at any moment, McGee had hurried outside.

McGee's testimony was corroborated by his son-in-law, Charles H. Vincent:

Soldiers cut away and removed the center-posts or columns and partitions, leaving no support for the roof and joists of the Cockerel building; some time after [the removal] this affiant noticed that the girders in the center of the Cockerel building on which the joists rested had given way, and the building was about to fall.

That these three men would give written testimony against the Federal military during the war, at a time when they were living in Kansas City, where Ewing had his headquarters, gives them a special credence.

Eleven years later, long after Ewing had permanently moved east, Dr. Joshua Thorne finally came forward with an explanation for the removal of the center posts that was as natural as a sudden gust of wind. In 1863, Thorne had held the rank of acting assistant surgeon in the U.S. Army and was in charge of the United States General Hospital in Kansas City. He was responsible, among other things, for the medical care of female prisoners. Dr. Thorne swore that in addition to the Southern girls confined on the second floor, imprisoned in the cellar were women "of bad character and diseased." The guards cut three large holes in the common cellar wall so that they might gain access to the whores. In no time at all, said the somewhat prudish Dr. Thorne, the cellar had become "a house of prostitution" and "the soldiers of the garrison and the guard in charge very frequently were in [there] and together with its inmates in a condition of most beastly intoxication." Venereal disease became rampant.

Thorne had warned his superiors that the "building had become insecure," but nothing was done. On the day before the collapse he had once again "found many of the female prisoners intoxicated—one of the women was cutting with an axe at one of the posts in the basement—which supported a girder and upon which girder the joists of the floor above rested—[and I] reported to the officer on duty the fact of the drunken condition of the women and the danger in cutting away the supports of the building. . . ."

The next morning he had gone directly to Ewing himself, then arrived back on Grand Avenue in time to see the dust cloud rising and hear the screams.

———◆◆◆———

Despite Bingham's efforts the Thomas estate never was reimbursed for the value of the building, which was appraised at $5,000. He submitted the results of his investigation to the U.S. government, but the bureaucrats used technicalities to avoid paying. Two legislative bills that would have required the reimbursement died in Senate committees, and Bingham's affidavits were forwarded to the National Archives by Senate staffers.

———◆◆◆———

In his classic study, *Gray Ghosts of the Confederacy,* Richard S. Brownlee points out that the calamity threw a "shadow over the rest of the Civil War on the border," intensified "the ferocious hatred of the guerrillas for the Union forces," and "tore the last thin covering of mercy from the hearts of Quantrill's boys. More serious, from this moment on, Bill Anderson . . . became insane because of the injury to his sisters, and his attitude toward all men who supported or served the Union was that of a homicidal maniac."

It is sometimes said that the Lawrence raid was in direct retaliation for the supposed intentional murders of the Southern girls. This is not true, but the extraordinary savagery and wholesale destructiveness of the raid may be attributed in part to the bushwhackers' rage and indignation over the tragic event.

On August 18, just four days after the prison's collapse, General Ewing made matters even worse. With General Schofield's approval he issued Order No. 10, thus putting into effect a plan he had been considering for some time:

Officers will arrest and send to the district provost-marshall for punishment, all men (and all women not heads of families) who willfully
aid and encourage guerrillas, with a written statement . . . of the proof
against them. They will discriminate as carefully as possible between
those who were compelled, by threats or fears, to aid the rebels and
those who aid them from disloyal motives. The wives and children of
known guerrillas, and also women who are heads of families and are
willfully engaged in aiding guerrillas, will be notified by such officers to
remove out of this district and out of the State of Missouri forthwith.
They will be permitted to take, unmolested, their stock, provisions, and
household goods. If they fail to remove promptly, they will be sent by
such officers, under escort, to Kansas City for shipment south, with
their clothes and such necessary household furniture and provision as
may be worth saving.

Despite the restraints Ewing built into the order, bushwhackers understood its implications: Their loved ones would be forced from their
homes and banished from the state with very little money and few possessions. Coming so soon after the prison collapse, it was an especially
terrible blow.

On the night Ewing published Order No. 10, Quantrill's 150-man
company broke camp and rode to the site of the prearranged rendezvous, Captain Perdee's farm on the Blackwater River. Anderson
showed up with forty men and Blunt with a hundred more, bringing the
approximate total to three hundred.

The next morning the column swung west toward Lone Jack and proceeded at a cautious pace, slowed by the necessity of sending scouts in
every direction to locate and find ways around Union troops.

It took the better part of a day to travel ten miles, and upon arriving
at the Potter place, Quantrill called a halt to wait for the cover of darkness. The men fed their horses and ate a light supper, then Quantrill
called them all together. He told them the true target was Lawrence.
"Boys," he shouted. "This is a hazardous ride, and there is a chance we
will all be annihilated. Any man who feels he is not equal to the task can
quit, and no one will call him a coward." Only a few men left. The rest
saddled up and rode through the night. Just before dawn they found
themselves at the headwaters of the Grand River, Cass County, four
miles from the Kansas line. Concealed in timber, they rested until 3:30
P.M., and not long after resuming their march they encountered Confed-

erate Colonel John D. Holt and one hundred new recruits from northern Missouri. Holt accepted Quantrill's invitation to come along and "christen" his troops. About the same time the band was reinforced by fifty farmers and townsfolk from Bates and Cass counties, drawn by rumors of an impending raid, eager for plunder, and bringing the approximate total to 450—which was, according to Dr. Castel, "the largest such force ever assembled under one command during the entire Civil War."

Slowly and cautiously the column rode across the rolling prairies toward Lawrence. Ten miles inside the border, at a point two and a half miles south of Squiresville, Quantrill called a halt so the men could feed their horses while it was still light. He consulted the death list compiled by the Kansas woman and sent a squad to the house of a Colonel Sims to murder him. Sims was not at home, and the would-be assassins contented themselves with requiring his wife to fix them supper.

The march was resumed after dark, the band swinging south to Spring Hill, then northwest to Gardner. After following the Santa Fe Trail for a few miles, the column broke to the north toward Lawrence. Quantrill and some of his men knew the area well enough in daylight, but on a moonless night following a faint trail that meandered into woods where even the stars could not be seen and everything was pitch black, it was too easy to get lost. Wandering off in the wrong direction with only a few crucial hours until dawn would be disastrous, so when they stumbled onto a farmhouse they impressed the owner as a guide. Before long someone recognized him as a former Missourian, and he was shot. They progressed from farm to farm, surrounding every house and demanding the man of the family come out. If he was German, he was immediately murdered; otherwise he was commandeered as a guide and shot when he was recognized as an abolitionist or jayhawker or when the next house was in view. Ten men died in an eight-mile stretch. The last of these, Joseph Stone, was unluckier than the rest: He had caused Todd to be arrested in Kansas City at the beginning of the war, so his fate was sealed as soon as Todd saw him. Since Stone resided only twelve miles from Lawrence, Todd clubbed him to death with a Sharps carbine rather than risk a neighbor's hearing a gunshot and racing to town with a warning.

Stone lived beside the Little Wakarusa, and Quantrill saw many familiar landmarks. Just in case, though, a small boy named Jacob Rote who lived on the Stone place was taken along, riding behind a guerrilla. (Jacob was kept with the band through the whole bloody morning; just before the retreat began Quantrill dressed him in a new suit looted from a store, gave him a horse, and sent him home.)

The bushwhackers trotted through Franklin shortly before dawn. Dr. R. L. Williams watched them pass in a column of fours. He had the presence of mind to note that many of them had tied themselves in their saddles to prevent their falling from their horses if they fell asleep. He heard their officers urging them on: "Hurry up! We ought to have been in Lawrence an hour ago!" "Rush on, boys! It will be daylight before we get there!"

Beyond the town limits they broke into a gallop.

Two miles from Lawrence they rode up a ridge overlooking the town. Quantrill sent Gregg and five men to reconnoiter. We are told that while Quantrill waited for the scouts' return he found himself recalling his days in the town, his adventures with the border ruffians, his life with the Delaware Indians, the romance with Anna Walker . . .

Some of the men around him were losing their nerve. They had expected to strike while the citizens were asleep in their beds, but now the sun was rising and the town looked large and formidable.

"Let's give it up," one man said. "It's too much."

"It's madness to go on," a second agreed.

Others murmured assent.

Quantrill wheeled his horse and rode among the ranks. "You can do as you please," he shouted. "I am going to Lawrence!"

He spurred his horse forward, and the others followed to a man, though one cried out, "We are lost!"

The first victim was Reverend S. S. Snyder, who had a farm east of town. A United Brethren Church minister, he had been commissioned as lieutenant of the 2nd Colored Regiment and was its recruiting agent. Snyder was in the barnyard, sitting on a stool milking a cow, when two guerrillas peeled away from the main column, rode through his gate, and shot him to death.

A young couple, John Donnelly and Sallie Young, were out for a morning ride. They saw the column approaching the town but were not alarmed at first because many of the men were wearing Federal uniforms. When they realized the truth, Sallie Young urged Donnelly to run for his life while she dashed for Lawrence to warn the others. Donnelly, who was unarmed, refused until he saw four men break away from the column and head for them. He spurred his horse into a gallop through cornfields, leaping fences and ditches. He got away and did not return to town until the raiders were gone. "My horse saved me," he told John C. Shea twelve years later. "He took the fences and ditches with a mad bound."

Sallie Young was captured and taken along. Throughout the morning she was forced to lead small squads of bushwhackers to houses that belonged to men on the death list.

After the raid was over, she was reunited with Donnelly, and they rode through Lawrence together. Women whose husbands had been killed and whose homes had been burned and who were standing in the street beside the few pitiful possessions they had managed to save from the flames shouted obscenities at her for helping the enemy. This was unjust: She had often tried to intercede for the victims. "For some she pleaded," related Shea in a letter to the Chicago *Times* dated July 12, 1875,

> for others she grew bold enough to order that they might be spared, and again she implored with tears streaming down her face. She never faltered where she thought she could save the lives or property of her friends. She importuned so often for others that she was finally told by Quantrell that she must look out to save herself, as his men were becoming exasperated with her.

Still, feelings ran so high against her that she was arrested on charges of being a spy and was taken to Fort Leavenworth. Shea, who had interviewed a number of massacre survivors, told the *Times* readers that since there was "no shadow of evidence against her she was honorably discharged."

The guerrillas clattered into town, cutting across vacant lots and down empty streets. Near the center of Lawrence, Quantrill called a halt and sent Holt's company to cover the east side of town, Blunt's men to cover the west. He dispatched eleven men to Mount Oread to act as lookouts to watch for the approach of Federal troops, then led the rest of the band toward the river. Gregg appeared and showed the way to a camp occupied by twenty-two white recruits of the 14th Kansas Regiment. The bushwhackers galloped among the tents, knocking them down and trampling the soldiers under their horses' hooves, shooting those who tried to run. Seventeen were killed, five wounded.

The next target was the nearby camp of the 2nd Colored Regiment; however, the unarmed blacks had been alerted by the gunfire and fled. This was not cowardice but hard-won border realism: The certainty of their fate at the hands of Southern guerrillas had stripped black soldiers of the luxury of self-delusion. This realism extended to black civilians; hearing gunfire coming from the camp, white citizens told themselves it resulted from fireworks, target practice, or youthful high jinks, but many blacks wisely assumed the worst and looked for a place to hide.

Quantrill now led most of the men in a wild charge down Massachusetts Street; the rest went down parallel streets. Despite their ferocity, at least one victim could not help admiring their skill and daring.

The horsemanship of the guerrillas was perfect. They rode with that ease and abandon which are acquired only by a life spent in the saddle amid desperate scenes. Their horses scarcely seemed to touch the ground, and the riders sat upon them with bodies erect and arms perfectly free with revolvers on full cock, shooting at every house and man they passed, and yelling like demons at every bound. On each side of this stream of fire . . . were men falling dead and wounded, and women and children, half dressed, running and screaming—some trying to escape from danger and some rushing to the side of their murdered friends.

They dashed along Massachusetts Street, shooting at every straggler on the sidewalk, and into almost every window. They halted in front of the Eldridge House. The firing [now] ceased and all was silence for a few minutes. They evidently expected resistance here, and sat gazing at the rows of windows above them, apparently in fearful suspense.

Suddenly the hotel gong began to ring loudly, frantically. The raiders shouted obscenities and pulled back to the opposite side of the street—but no volley was discharged from the windows. It was only someone trying belatedly to warn the guests.

Captain Alexander R. Banks, the provost marshal of Kansas and a hotel resident, had been awakened by the gunfire and looked out a front window to see rebels in the street. In the hallway, guests were arguing over what should be done. Some nervous souls wanted to do nothing, to let events take their course and see what happened, but many more wanted to surrender the building if their safety were guaranteed. Banks, who knew what the enemy was capable of, pulled a sheet off his bed and waved it out the window, calling for Quantrill.

Quantrill rode forward on a magnificent brown gelding said to have been taken from Buel at the Battle of Independence. On Quantrill's head was a low-crowned, soft black hat with a gold cord for a band. His face was sunburned and weather-beaten, and he had a few days' stubble of beard. He wore a brown woolen guerrilla shirt, which was, noted Connelley, "ornamented with fine needlework and made for him by some devoted daughter of the South." Four revolvers were stuck in his belt, and his gray trousers were stuffed into handsome cavalry boots.

"What is your object in coming to Lawrence?" Banks asked.

"Plunder," he answered.

"We are defenseless and at your mercy," Banks said. "The house is surrendered, but we demand protection for the inmates."

Quantrill agreed; then, wheeling his horse toward his followers, he ordered a few men to stay with him. Dismissing the rest, he rose in his stirrups and screamed, "Kill! Kill and you will make no mistake! Lawrence should be thoroughly cleansed, and the only way to cleanse it is to kill! Kill!"

While his men scattered in every direction, Quantrill secured the hotel. He set guards around the perimeters and ordered that the occupants leave—he meant to burn the place. As male and female guests filed down from the top floors, bushwhackers met them at the bottom of the stairs with drawn revolvers and forced them to "shell out." Other guerrillas scrambled upstairs to ransack the rooms. One chamber door was locked—the two Ohioans inside refused to open it. A bullet fired through the door struck one of the Ohioans in the hip. The door flew open and they rushed out, the wounded man limping badly, blood spreading down his clean white pants.

Judge L. D. Bailey had arrived from Topeka late the night before and had slept soundly in his fourth-floor room. Hearing shouts he got out of bed and looked out the back window; the only man he saw was a black waiter hurrying away. Bailey called out, asking, "What's up?"

"Why, the Quantrell Gang is here," the waiter replied. "And they've killed Addison, and they shot Joe Eldridge twice." He ran across the yard and was gone. (Addison Waugh was a clerk in Griswold's drugstore, situated on the ground floor. Joe Eldridge was the "slow-witted" brother of the hotel owner.)

Bailey threw on his clothes and was slipping his gold watch into his pocket "when it occurred to me that I best put it out of sight." He looked around for a hiding place, and his eye fell on the stove. He slipped the watch and a wallet containing $400 under cold ashes and carpet sweepings, having first thoughtfully taken three small bills out of the wallet and put them into a "porte-monie," which he dropped into his pocket. When it was his turn to be robbed, the thieves might be cross if he had nothing to give them.

Leaving his room he saw that his boots, which he had left outside the door the night before to be polished, were gone, and he went down the stairs in stocking feet. The long, third-floor corridor was jammed with seventy-five or eighty guests and boarders, and the guerrillas passed among them collecting their money, watches, and other valuables. One tapped Bailey on the shoulder with the barrel of a revolver.

"Your money, if you please!" he said quietly, as practiced as a railroad conductor asking for tickets.

Bailey handed over the purse, adding huffily that "There is not much in it, but I shall want a dram by and by, and I guess you had better leave me fifty cents to pay for it."

The robber gave him an amused glance, took the three small bills out of the purse, closed the spring, and handed it back.

Bailey opened it quickly and counted the small shin plasters, which totaled eighty cents. He stiffly thanked the man, who smiled thinly, and went down the corridor to the stairs. He encountered Quantrill standing on the second from the top step, a pistol in one hand. Bailey was unimpressed: Quantrill "was not a man whom I should have been frightened at meeting in a lonely place—in ordinary times." He "did not look more formidable or ferocious than many a man I have met at other times and passed without fear. I should not have known him to be the dreaded Quantrell but for the fact that a youngish man, whose name I think was Spicer, was leaning over the banister talking to him."

Arthur Spicer was trying with a desperate congeniality to remind Quantrill of their former association, how they had been border ruffians together at the north ferry. "We called you Charley Hart then, you know," Spicer said.

Quantrill gave him a cold look. "It makes no difference what they call me."

Spicer hastily withdrew.

Bailey went down to the first floor and was told by a woman that the hotel was to be destroyed. He refused to believe it and went to find Quantrill.

"Yes, it will be burnt," the guerrilla chieftain confirmed quite civilly.

Bailey tried to convince him to rescind the order.

"Yes, it is pretty rough," Quantrill agreed, "but we have had our houses burnt, and we will burn also."

Mrs. F. B. Bancroft required Bailey's help. Her husband, a major assigned to the 8th Kansas Regiment, had fallen ill at the siege of Vicksburg and been furloughed home to recover or die. He was so sick that, sitting slumped in a large upholstered chair, he had not lifted his head once during the morning's excitement. Bailey and the major's brother carried the chair downstairs. (Bailey first stopped at his own room and retrieved his wallet and watch and, assuming rightly that the bushwhackers would pity Mrs. Bancroft because of her husband's invalidism and would not search her, gave them to her to conceal in her voluminous Mother Hubbard.)

As they carried Major Bancroft outside they saw that many buildings had already been set ablaze, including those housing the printing offices of the hated Lawrence *Republican* and the *Kansas Tribune*. Bailey was sure that "the whole town had been fired, and would soon be in ashes."

Men were spurring their horses up and down the street, firing their guns in the air and screaming; the saloons and whiskey shops having been the first places broken into, many of the mounted men were already reeling drunk in their saddles. Some had looted small toy American flags from a store and contemptuously tied them to their horses' tails. A Baptist preacher named Larkin M. Skaggs cut down a huge flag that had been flying from a tall flagstaff nearby and tied it to a long rope attached to his saddle. He raced up and down Massachusetts Street, said Bailey, "putting his horse through various turns, jumps and caricoles to make the old flag jump and roll by turns fifty feet behind his horse in the deep dust." Bancroft's head still hung down, but Skaggs's mount galloped close enough to the chair for the flag to be pulled through the major's line of sight. "There they are, dragging the American flag in the dust! God damn them!" the dying soldier cried, his voice breaking and copious tears rolling down his pale, sunken cheeks.

As the Eldridge House refugees tried to cross the street, wild riders circled around them, hemming them in like sheep in a pen, and shouting obscenities and threats. One started firing shots down into their midst. One man was killed before Quantrill appeared and ordered him to stop.

The man protested that he was only shooting at a redleg.

Quantrill replied that these people were under his protection and that he would kill him if he fired on them again. Quantrill escorted the refugees to Nathan Stone's Whitney House.

"Years ago old man Stone treated me with kindness," he announced, "and I'll be damned to hell if a hair on his head will be injured!"

He ordered the refugees inside and posted sentries around the building. This "was for our protection," Bailey realized, "to keep the drunken and violent members of the gang from molesting us."

Having taken steps to protect Nathan Stone's property and keep his word to Major Banks, Quantrill appropriated a team of white horses and a buggy. He toured the town to see how the raid was progressing and then visited Mount Oread for a view from the heights.

Not everyone fared as well as the guests of the Eldridge House.

The Johnson House was surrounded, and one guerrilla called out, "All we want is for the men to give themselves up, and we will spare them and burn the house."

There were fourteen men inside. A few hid themselves, but the rest surrendered. They were robbed of their valuables and marched into the street; suddenly, the bushwhackers opened fire, killing all but two, who were both wounded—James B. Finley and a man named Hampson.

Finley started running as soon as the firing began. Several villains pursued him, shooting at his back. Although badly wounded, he kept going, sprinting through buildings, dodging across empty lots and down side streets. He burst into a partially completed building on Massachusetts Street and threw himself into a hole being dug for a well. Another civilian raced into the structure right behind him but made the mistake of going out the door on the other side. A guerrilla who happened to be riding by shot him down. Those in pursuit of Finley rode up and asked the guerrilla if he had seen a fugitive. The murderer said he had—he had killed him.

The men went in pursuit of other quarry.

Finley lay in the well too weak from loss of blood to climb back out. Eventually rescued by survivors, he lingered for six weeks before dying of his wound.

When Hampson was shot, he fell to the ground and played dead among the corpses. He lay so close to the fast-burning hotel that when it collapsed he was certain he would be burned alive. However, the enemy was everywhere, and he knew that if he moved, he would be killed. His dilemma was resolved when his wife found him. She convinced a raider to help her carry her husband's "corpse" out of danger. She found a handcart and put him into it, covering him with rags. She wheeled the cart down streets while riders swirled all around her, firing their pistols and committing mayhem.

Dr. Jerome Griswold, who was a newlywed, ran a boardinghouse. He was renting rooms to the Honorable S. M. Thorpe, his wife, and children, as well as two newly married couples—Mr. and Mrs. Josiah F. Trask and Mr. and Mrs. W. H. Baker. Thorpe was a Kansas state senator; Trask was the editor of the Lawrence *State Journal;* and Baker was partner in a grocery business, Ridenour & Baker. (It was Ridenour & Baker's warehouse that in 1860 Quantrill had been charged with burglarizing.)

Trask had just stepped onto the porch to determine the reason for all the noise when five bushwhackers rode through the gate. They leveled their pistols at him and, cursing furiously, demanded that the house be surrendered. Trask said he was willing, so long as the women and children would be protected.

"They will not be harmed," one man assured him. "We have come to burn Lawrence, but we do not want to harm anybody if we can help it. If the citizens make us no trouble, they will receive no harm." He added that Trask and the other men would be taken to a central location and confined with the rest of the male residents, "until we do what we came for, and then you can all go free."

Trask went inside to tell the others. Being "well-armed" and "young and vigorous," as the Reverend Cordley characterized them, "they were disposed to remain in the house and defend themselves," but Trask convinced them to give themselves up. They went outside and were robbed. They were marched single file toward the downtown, a raider on horseback trotting beside each man, cursing him for being slow and urging him to hurry. A pistol shot rang out, and Baker was struck in the neck. As he fell a bullet pierced his wrist. Thorpe dropped with a bullet through the abdomen. Trask, his executioner having missed the first time, ran twenty yards before being cut down. Griswold sprinted back to his house and was climbing over his fence when he was struck several times.

The guerrillas returned to the house and plundered it. The women, who had witnessed the shooting of their husbands from a balcony, were not permitted to go to them. Each time they tried, they were driven back with threats and obscenities. They were robbed of their jewelry—even their wedding rings. Mrs. Trask, who had been married only a few months, begged to be allowed to keep hers.

"You have killed my husband, let me keep his ring," she pleaded.

The ring was yanked from her finger.

A torch had just been applied to the house when the appeals of one of the women touched a bushwhacker; he drove the others out of the building and put out the fire. The men rode away believing they had killed all four victims, but Baker and Thorpe were still alive. Other raiders frequently rode by, but whenever the street was empty the two wounded men talked softly together. "You may live, but I cannot recover," Thorpe told Baker. Once two rebels came by, and one noticed that Baker was still breathing. "Fred," he said to his cohort, "one of them damned nigger-thieving abolitionists ain't dead yet. Go and kill him."

Fred rode up beside Baker and put a bullet through his right lung.

Chastised as well as wounded, Baker instantly improved his ability to feign death. Another man ambled by, looking for money, and he rolled Baker onto his side, slipped his knife blade into his pocket, and ripped an eighteen-inch gash in the trousers. Finding nothing, he rolled Baker over and slashed an eighteen-inch gash in the other pants leg. There was nothing to steal but Baker's hat, which he took, and rode away in disgust.

After the raid the two wounded men were carried back into the boardinghouse. Baker made a slow recovery, but Thorpe, shot through the bowels, lingered in agony until the next day, then died.

It is obvious that many of Quantrill's Raiders meant to kill every man and teenage boy capable of bearing arms against the South, but it would seem that the death list Quantrill had had compiled especially singled out prominent citizens for execution: The Griswold boardinghouse residents included a physician, the editor of an influential newspaper, a prosperous merchant, and a powerful politician. These were not the only important names on the death list: Jim Lane's was at the very top.

At the first sound of gunfire, Lane had leaped out of bed and wrenched the nameplate off his front door. He sprinted through his house and went out the back door, hightailing it across a cornfield barefoot and clad only in his nightshirt. He ran over hills and through fields until he came to a deep ravine, where he hid for a time. He started out again, still heading west, and eventually came to a farmhouse where he borrowed a battered straw hat, a pair of old shoes, and a pair of trousers. The owner was as short and fat as Lane was tall and lean, so the outfit added to the general's comical appearance.

Lane walked on until he came to another farm, where he procured a plow horse and blind bridle—but there was no saddle to be had. He rode off bareback to warn area residents of the attack and to organize a posse.

Quantrill did not need a nameplate to identify Jim Lane's house; he forced Arthur Spicer to point it out. Catching Lane had been a major objective of the raid—Quantrill meant to take him back to Jackson County and hang him—but the only consolation was to burn his magnificent new home. Though her husband was the most hated enemy, Quantrill and his men treated Mrs. Lane with utmost courtesy. Before they torched the house, they let her save many of her possessions and assisted her in carrying canned fruit and preserves out of the cellar. As the flames spread, she wrung her hands over the loss of the piano in the parlor, so they went back inside and cheerfully wrestled with it. It was bulky and heavy, and some of them were terribly drunk, so that, unable to get it through the door, they were finally forced to abandon it as the flames drew near.

"Give Mr. Lane my compliments," Quantrill told his wife with ironic courtesy. "Please say I would be glad to meet him."

"Mr. Lane would be glad to meet you under . . . more favorable circumstances," she coolly replied.

Edward Fitch was a schoolteacher and one of Lawrence's earliest residents. He had been a member of the home-guard company formed that summer to protect the town and so was on the murder list. Inebriated bushwhackers burst into his house and began starting fires. One of them shot Fitch down, emptied his revolver into the corpse, and then, borrowing a comrade's pistol, emptied that one as well.

Mrs. Fitch tried to drag the body outside, but the heartless men would not allow it. She started to take his picture from the wall; however, she was told to leave it to burn. She stood beside her husband's corpse so stupefied with grief that she took no notice of the spreading flames. A guerrilla had to threaten her with a pistol to get her to lead her two small children from the place.

She sat with them on the grass and watched her house burn, while riders crisscrossed in front of her, shouting and firing their pistols in the air. One dismounted and stepped across the threshold, yanked the boots off Fitch's corpse, and pulled them on his own feet, then rode away. Mrs. Fitch continued her sad vigil until her husband's body was consumed, and the house fell in upon the remains.

Twelve days later she wrote a letter from "The City of Sorrow" to her parents-in-law, telling them about their son's death. "Oh, I feel as tho' I was crushed into the dust with the weight of sorrow which has rolled upon me!—oh the <u>utter desolation</u>—the heart breaking despair I have endured. My brain reels!—my reason totters—had it not been for <u>our</u> children—Edward's darlings—that I had to live for, I do not think I <u>could</u> have endured."

Sixty-year-old Otis Longly was a peaceful, churchgoing man who had stayed out of the political controversy on the border. Men rode up to the small farm on the outskirts of town where he lived with his wife. "Be merciful," she begged them. "We are old people and cannot live long at best." They chased the old man around the yard and shot him repeatedly. They set fire to the house, but after they had ridden away, she put it out.

Another elderly man, whose name was Miner, hid himself in a large, fenced-in corn patch that had been planted in the park. "Hearing the racket around Mr. Fisher's house near by," wrote Lawrencian J. S. Boughton, who collected the accounts of massacre survivors in 1884,

he ventured to the edge of the corn to gratify his curiosity. He was seen and immediately shot at. He ran back into the corn, but had not proceeded far before he heard them breaking down the fence. The corn was evidently to be searched. He ran, therefore, through the corn, and lay down among the weeds beyond. The weeds only partially covered him, but it was the best he could do. He had scarcely lain down, when the rebels came dashing through the corn, and stationing a picket at each corner to prevent escape, they searched the field through but found no one. They did not happen to look among the grass almost at their very feet.

Other survivors hid in the same corn patch or made their way to various cornfields on the outskirts of town; still others ran to the river and crossed on the ferry or slipped into the brush that grew along the near bank. The woods to the east of Lawrence were, in Boughton's words, "alive with refugees." Some of those caught near the center of town tried to conceal themselves in tall grass or weeds—or in their own gardens. Mr. Strode, a colored blacksmith, had planted a patch of tomatoes "no more than ten feet square. He took his money and buried himself among the vines." A squad burned his shop a few yards away "but did not discover him."

Levi Gates lived a mile northwest of Lawrence. Hearing gunfire and assuming that the citizenry would make a stand, he grabbed his musket and ran for town. When he arrived, however, he found that the enemy was firmly in control. Still, he drew a bead on a horseman and fired. His shot made his target jump in his saddle but did not kill him. Gates reloaded and fired again. Whether he succeeded in hitting the man a second time is not known; however, the shots attracted the attention of several guerrillas, who rode down on him, killed him, and pounded his head to pulp with their pistol handles and rifle butts. In addition to the man Gates shot, at least two other raiders are known to have been wounded. One was Jim Bledsoe, who had tried to cut the ferry cable. Gathered on the far riverbank were some militia who had camped there the previous night. Bledsoe saw the soldiers take aim with their rifles but thought he was out of range. He took a bullet in the groin. One of Holt's recruits was also wounded by the sharpshooters, and word soon spread that the open country around the ferry was to be avoided.

A few well-armed and stalwart townsfolk barricaded themselves inside brick houses or stone buildings and took potshots from windows. Warnings were passed to stay clear of these places as well.

Captain George W. Bell was the county clerk and an officer in the 14th Kansas Regiment. His house sat on a hill not far from Lawrence. When he spied bushwhackers riding toward town, he seized his musket and cartridge box and hurried after them, hoping to marshal a defense. By the time he arrived the Eldridge House had been surrounded, and he realized that resistance was futile. He started back home but, encountering the enemy, ran into a partially completed house. Another man ran in with him, and they climbed up on the joists. A guerrilla came in and started shooting at them. Bell had glimpsed the man's face and recognized him. He called down to him, identified himself, and convinced him to hold his fire. The man promised to protect Bell—and the other fellow—if they would come down. He led them outside, where a cluster of bushwhackers waited. "Shoot them," someone cried. Both men were cut down in the volley. Bell died, but the other man, though severely wounded, recovered.

Later the man who had deceived Bell led a gang to his home.

"We have killed your husband," he told Bell's wife, who had not known of his death, "and we have come to burn his house."

The torch was applied, but the woman and her six children extinguished it.

George Holt and John L. Crane were partners in a shoe store near the Johnson House. They surrendered to a single raider who promised to protect them. He robbed them and turned them over to another man, saying, "Shoot them—they have been in Missouri killing our people." Before the two civilians could protest, the second man opened fire. Crane died instantly; Holt was badly wounded. Their building was plundered and burned.

Sixty-year-old Dennis Murphy was asked for a drink of water. He went into his house, brought out a cup, and handed it over. "As the fiend took the cup with his left hand he shot his benefactor with his right," related Boughton.

The same thing happened to George Burt, who lived just down the street. He was standing by a fence when a guerrilla rode up and demanded his money. Burt handed up his pocketbook; the man took it in one hand and shot him with a pistol in the other.

One man saved his house and his life by paying $1,000. Another handed the same sum to one rebel and was killed by another.

A physician with a gun at his head led two raiders to the best liquor stores, found money for them, and, following their orders, even set fire to several of his neighbors' houses. He expected to be killed anyway, but they let him go.

August Ehles, a German blacksmith, ran into the corn patch in the park, carrying a small child. Before long the child grew cranky and began to cry. The bushwhackers used the noise to locate the father and killed him. The child lay in its dead father's arms still wailing.

Another German, George Albach, was sick in bed. Raiders ordered the house cleared so they could burn it. Using the mattress as a stretcher, family members carried Albach out into the yard. When the guerrillas had the fire roaring they came outside and shot Albach to death. "These are species of cruelty to which savages have never yet attained," commented a survivor.

One man, running down the road, was shot at and tumbled into the gutter. His wife ran to his body and began to scream and wring her hands in grief. The assailant, assuming from the woman's behavior that the man was dead, did not bother to check and rode on. As soon as he was gone, the husband whispered, "Don't take on so, wife. I don't know as I am hit at all." It turned out he was correct.

Reverend Cordley recounted two instances of men dressing in women's clothing to escape being killed. A man named Winchell burst into the home of the Reverend Charles Reynolds, rector of the Episcopal church. Mrs. Reynolds quickly "arrayed him in female attire, shaved off his mustache with a knife, and set him in a rocking chair with a baby in his arms, and christened him 'Aunt Betsy.' Bushwhackers searched the house but ignored 'Aunt Betsy.' "

An unidentified officer deserted the camp of recruits as soon as the attack commenced. He was pursued by several horsemen who took potshots at him. He dashed into the house of a black family, and "in a twinkling of an eye, slipped on a dress and shaker bonnet, passed out at the back door, and walked deliberately away. The rebels surrounded the house, and then some of them entered and searched, but found no prey."

Guerrillas barged into George H. Sargeant's house on New Hampshire Street. They robbed the family and told everyone to move the furniture into the yard because the house would be burned. A raider assisted in carrying the piano outside before the torch was applied. Sargeant and his wife stood on the grass watching the place go up; a small, forlorn crowd collected around them, including Charley Palmer, a printer named Young, and several women. A squad rode by and opened fire on the men. Palmer was killed, and Sargeant fell seriously wounded. Young was unhurt but dropped to the ground feigning death.

One bushwhacker noticed Sargeant was still alive. He dismounted and coolly reloaded his pistol, saying, "I'll soon finish him." Mrs. Sargeant threw herself across her husband's prostrate body, begging for his life. The rebel leaned over, extending the gun barrel past her shoulder, and sent a bullet crashing into her husband's skull. Sargeant nonetheless survived for eleven days before succumbing. Young was lying so close to the burning house that his skin was scorched by the heat; however, he never moved a muscle. When the women bystanders realized he was alive, they dragged him into the weeds, put him in a line of corpses, and covered them all with sheets to protect him.

"The ladies of Lawrence were brave and plucky," Quantrill commented later, "but the men of Lawrence were a pack of cowards." The first half of the statement is indisputably correct. "The courage and persistence of the women saved a great many houses and a great many lives," noted Cordley.

The ladies were wonderfully brave and efficient that morning. Some of them, by their shrewdness and suavity, turned raiders from their purpose when they came to their houses. Sometimes they outwitted them, and at other times they boldly confronted and resisted them. In scores of cases they put the fires out as soon as those who kindled them left the house. In some cases they defiantly followed the raiders around, and extinguished the flames as they were kindled.

Cordley related the story of one woman who had stationed herself near the concealed entrance to a cellar close to the center of town. She directed every "poor fugitive" who happened by to the entrance, saving ten. Eventually guerrillas, "noticing that their victims always disappeared when they came into this locality, suspected this woman of aiding in their escape." They demanded that she show them the hiding place, but she refused. One of them drew his revolver and pointed it at her head.

"Tell us, or I will shoot you."

"You may shoot me, but you will not find the men," she replied.

When they saw they could not intimidate her, they left.

A dignified lady met squad after squad as they came into her yard and determinedly engaged the men in conversation, certain, as she explained later, that if she got them talking she "could get at what little humanity was left in them." Thus she kept her house from being burned.

Another woman took a more direct approach: She wrote the word "Southern" over her door and saved her house.

A rebel rode up to a house at the south end of Lawrence and asked a woman where her husband was.

She said he had been killed, although he was only at a neighbor's place, tending a wounded man.

He eyed her closely and asked, "Madam, where are your sympathies?"

"I am a Southerner," she quickly lied.

He said he thought he recognized her—they had met in Boonville, Missouri. She readily agreed, though she had never seen the man before nor visited the town. He was so pleased to meet an old acquaintance that he assigned four men to guard her house. Two of the guards later insisted they had seen her in Springfield. She went along, though she had never been there either. As John C. Shea put it, "[she] kept up the conversation about Missouri as best she could, always giving ready answers. Thus her house was protected during the occupancy of the town. When the raiders left, their leader bade her adieu in a kindly manner. This lady had come up the Missouri River on a steamboat, which was all the acquaintance she had with the state."

Judge Bailey told of a girl who was equally quick witted and displayed even greater nerve. She was an orphan who worked as a maid for the family of a German saloonkeeper. He was shot when the bushwhackers made their first charge down Massachusetts Street. She witnessed the murder, and then some of the brutes ordered her to go back inside and "furnish" them with liquor. She managed to slip the contents of the cash drawer into her pocket unobserved, then "with assumed cheerfulness, helped each ruffian to his favorite 'poison' chatting meanwhile, as gaily as circumstances would allow." She was pretty and young, pretended to be helpless and flirtatious, and she was more than willing to serve them liquor, all of which "made a favorable impression."

Once she looked outside and saw bushwhackers about to kill a young man. Although he was a total stranger, she rushed out from behind the bar and plunged through the door, wailing theatrically.

"He is my dear brother," she cried, "my only brother!" She begged piteously for his life. Her pleas were so heartfelt that "their savage hearts relented, and he was spared."

After this remarkable introduction, observed Bailey, "[their] acquaintance ripened into friendship, and the end was marriage."

(This was not the only "love match" that resulted from the raid. A young apprentice who worked at Lee's Photograph Gallery took refuge under a corncrib. A few minutes later a daughter of Captain Bell crawled under the crib, too, and, as Bailey put it, "then and there began an acquaintance ending in marriage.")

The bushwhackers seemed intent on looting and destroying every commercial and government building in town. The county courthouse was burned, resulting in the loss of all the records. The Simpson Brothers' bank went up, and the fire spread to the adjoining building, which housed the Lawrence *Journal*. South of the Eldridge House was a clothing business owned by Colonel Eldridge in conjunction with a man named Ford. Guerrillas pounded on the door and were admitted by the two clerks hiding inside, James Perrine and young Jim Eldridge. The safe was a formidable one, and Eldridge was sent under armed escort to Ford's home to get the key. After the safe was emptied, the villains forced the two young men to fit them with new clothes, then killed them and set the place ablaze.

Henry S. Clarke, a furniture dealer, had risen early that morning and pushed aside the window curtains—and saw a column of cavalrymen galloping four abreast. Coming in the opposite direction was a teenage son of Mayor Collamore, on his way to hunt chickens. The column split, and the boy was enveloped. The bushwhackers cut loose, and young Collamore fell off his horse, severe wounds in his arms and legs. His assailants left him for dead, but he was carried to safety and made a slow recovery.

Clarke went out into the front yard, saw rising smoke in the distance, and realized from its location that his store had been set ablaze. Civilians were being murdered, and clearly there was no chance of escape . . . then Clarke saw a handsome officer riding slowly south, carrying a cigar box in one hand.

"Good morning, Colonel," he called out, "your boys have got us this time."

"Yes, you have made the spoon, and we are making you eat with it today," the officer replied. They bantered cheerfully back and forth, and after awhile the amiable officer introduced himself as Colonel John Holt of Vernon County, Missouri. Holt treated Clarke to a cigar, and Clarke in turn offered Holt breakfast.

"Well, I shall not refuse, as the Feds will give me little rest for two or three days."

Holt remained on his horse, and Clarke brought coffee and cake out to him. As a precaution against being poisoned, Holt required his host to taste everything first, then ate heartily. Holt made the Clarke house his headquarters and remained there until the retreat. Numerous guerrillas came by and were fed by Clarke's sister and wife. The last man to appear at the gate was told all the food was gone, and he begged Mrs. Clarke to give him something. She brought out a few cold potatoes on a plate, and he ravenously devoured them, exclaiming between bites, "Oh, how good they are!"

Clarke's attempts to ingratiate himself with Holt proved efficacious: A swarthy bushwhacker with a beard that hung nearly to his waist happened by, drew his revolver, and pointed it at Clarke's breast. Holt sternly called out, "This man is my prisoner! I am using him!"

The would-be assassin rode on.

———— ◆ ————

A guerrilla entered J. G. Sands's stable, on the corner of Pinckney and Tennessee streets. He stole a carriage horse and a pet pony named Freddie. As he led them into the alley behind the stable, four comrades rode up. "Why in hell aren't these houses burnt?" one asked. The four dismounted and were collecting kindling when Freddie broke away and galloped past. The thief raced after him, shouting for the others to help capture him. They remounted, and the pony led them all on a merry chase before finally being lassoed in another part of town. The five men became caught up in plundering where they found themselves and forgot the intact residences behind the stable. Thus, Boughton concluded, "the providential escape of the pony undoubtedly saved, not only the houses, but also the lives of Dr. Fuller, B. W. Woodward and J. G. Sands," who were hiding in them.

Judge Louis Carpenter, a staunch Unionist who had been married less than a year, lived with his bride in a new brick house on the northwest corner of Berkeley and New Hampshire streets. He had been appointed reporter for the state supreme court but had resigned to enlist in the army. He had risen to the rank of colonel before returning to Lawrence, apparently due to ill health. He had served as the probate judge of Douglas County, and in 1862 had been a candidate for state attorney general.

Several squads stopped by his house throughout the morning, taking whatever suited their fancy, but he was so genial that they did not harm him.

Shortly before the retreat, however, another group rode into his yard and called for him to come outside. Once again he tried making amiable conversation, but these men were drunken and sullen. One asked him where he was from.

"New York," he replied.

A man drew his revolver, saying, "Oh, it's you New York fellers that are doing all the mischief."

Judge Carpenter ran back into the house and upstairs, followed closely by the man, who wounded him repeatedly. Slamming doors behind him as he passed through rooms, his blood spurting onto walls and door frames, Carpenter ran on, going back down the stairs and into the cellar. He was found standing amid large pools of his own blood and driven outside. He was shot again and fell mortally wounded. "His wife ran to him and threw herself on him to shield him from further violence," wrote Reverend Cordley. "The brute deliberately walked around her to find a place to shoot once more. He finally raised her arm, and thrust his revolver under it and fired so that she saw the charge enter her husband's head."

The guerrillas set the house ablaze and rode away. Mrs. Carpenter's sister, who had just arrived from Emporia for a visit the day before, managed to put it out.

William Laurie, a farmer who lived twenty miles away, had come to town the day before to transact some business. He had brought along his wife and baby and his brother John. When the shooting began, the two panic-stricken brothers ran up and down the streets trying to get away. They were chased and shot repeatedly until they fell to the ground. Their pursuers had emptied their revolvers and were standing over them, reloading, when Mrs. Laurie knelt beside them and, cradling her infant in her arms, begged for their lives.

John, seeing no compassion in their faces, pleaded that if they must kill him, at least spare his brother.

But William Laurie had been captured in Quantrill's Shawneetown raid and had escaped. One of the bushwhackers who stood over them suddenly recognized him.

"We are not so particular about you," he told John, "but that fellow, we will put him through."

After both brothers were executed, the guerrilla turned on the distraught Mrs. Laurie.

"We are fiends from hell," he told her. "Get into the house, or, by heavens, we will serve you the same."

J.W.V. Thornton was a carpenter who lived on Winthrop Street with his wife and sister-in-law. When two rebels began kicking at his door, he hid upstairs in a wardrobe room. One peered into the room but did not see him. The man set fire to the bed and a washstand and went downstairs. Mrs. Thornton smothered the flames with a blanket and dragged the mattress downstairs, where she encountered the two guerrillas. They set the mattress afire again and told her if she put it out this time they would lock her and her sister-in-law in the house and burn it down.

Mrs. Thornton told them she was not afraid—they would not dare burn her.

One man offered a compromise: If she had a revolver in the house and would give it to him, no harm would come to her or her sister and the house would be spared.

She refused, and they told her to remove anything she wanted to save—"and do it damned quick." Once the fire had grown too big to be extinguished, they went outside and wandered off.

As the flames spread and smoke filled the house, Thornton left his hiding place and threw all the furniture he could out the second-story windows. He then went downstairs and threw furniture out the first-floor windows. The fire forced him outside, where two bushwhackers sat on their mounts. They had stopped in amusement to watch the furniture flying through the air. Thornton recognized one of them—a small, fair-skinned man named Jones, who used to live in Allen County, Kansas, until he stole some horses and drove them across the border. The other man was tall and dark-haired; he was filthy and wore a black silk shirt.

They ordered Thornton to pick up a piece of furniture they particularly fancied and haul it away for them. As he started to comply, he heard one say, "Shoot him anyhow, damn him."

He ran. A bullet struck him in the hip, but he managed to dodge around the corner of his house. He leaped up onto the porch and threw himself inside as a bullet pierced his leg, shattering a shinbone. His wife hurried in after him.

They could not remain inside for long. They came out, eyes streaming tears from the smoke, Thornton supported and shielded by his wife. In the alley behind the house the two men were waiting. They spurred their horses forward, the tall one wedging Mrs. Thornton away from her husband. Jones rode up beside Thornton, who seized Jones's knee with his left hand to hold himself up while he grabbed for Jones's revolver with his right hand. The gun went off, the ball slicing through Thornton's felt hat, slashing open his left eyebrow and embedding itself in his cheek. Jones fired four more times, but only one bullet wounded Thornton, entering the small of his back at an angle and coming to rest in the right hip. Still Thornton struggled, and Jones pounded on his head with the pistol, striking him seven times.

"Stand back and let me try," the other bushwhacker said impatiently. "He is the hardest man to kill I ever saw."

Thornton, faint from loss of blood, let go of Jones's leg. The dark-haired man blazed away but even at close range was a poor shot: Thornton was struck only once, in the thigh. He sat down on an embankment with his own burning house at his back.

John Shea, who heard the story from Thornton and his wife, wrote that when Thornton sat down Jones "urged his horse forward, and, as he came up to the prostrate man, suddenly pulled his horse back upon his haunches and then threw him forward to trample the life out of the wounded, bleeding man. As luck would have it the forefeet of the animal came down on each side of Thornton's left leg." Jones leveled his revolver, but Mrs. Thornton darted in and grasped the horse's bridle and forced the animal backward, crying, "For God's sake, men, let him alone. He's killed now."

The guerrillas, "abashed at their cowardly conduct, or awed by the presence of the pleading wife, slunk away to the middle of the street" and reloaded their revolvers. After a few moments they rode away, no doubt looking for a more sprightly victim to play with.

Two women assisted Mrs. Thornton in rolling her husband onto a lounge tick and dragging him to an empty lot, where, remaining conscious despite his pain, he watched the progress of the raid. He saw Nathan Stone and J. H. Brown murdered. He witnessed the shooting of a one-armed peddler, the burning of many buildings, and the beginning of the retreat.

He bled profusely and must have been feverish because his wife, at his request, kept pouring cold water over his body.

J.W.V. Thornton's hip had been broken, and a thighbone as well as a shinbone had been shattered. He had been shot repeatedly, although all but two of the bullets passed through his body. One of the remaining two was extracted, the other he carried until the day he died. His scalp and face had been severely lacerated by the repeated pistol blows; these wounds were sutured. He was confined to his bed for eight months, and he never really recovered.

"Mr. Thornton's sufferings have been great," Shea told the *Tribune* readers in 1875. "The broken and shattered bones of his hip and limbs have come away at different times, causing intense suffering and long-confined illness. Today he is a mere wreck, although before the raid he was a healthy, robust man." He was a pitiful sight on the streets of Lawrence, "a cripple who by the aid of a couple of stout sticks slowly hobbles along. Although emaciated and wan, with shriveled and paralyzed limbs, the face of this man, when scrutinized closely, presents lines of brightness and intelligence which one would hardly seek on a frame so feeble."

Thornton was never able to resume the carpenter trade. His wife supported him and their children "with her needle" and by teaching. "This case appeals strongly to the State or National authorities for aid," asserted Shea.

> A pension should be given to such a family as this. Thornton is deserving of the care and attention which the nation gives to her wounded and maimed soldiers. I hope . . . the authorities of Kansas [will] extend an influence to that end that one who has suffered much through the cruelties of civil strife may be placed beyond want in his declining years.

It is highly unlikely that officials paid heed to this eloquent plea. There were repeated efforts to enact legislation both in the U.S. Congress and the Kansas legislature to compensate victims of the raid, but it was not until May 5, 1887, after a bitter struggle, that what came to be known as "The Quantrell Raid Claims Bill" finally passed the Kansas House of Representatives. This bill authorized the issuing of bonds whose proceeds would be used to reimburse property owners for losses not to exceed $1,500 per person.

There is no record that the state or federal government ever compensated any victim for disabling injuries or any widow for the loss of a wage-earning husband or any orphan for the loss of a father. Those made destitute by the raid were left to the mercy of religious and private charities.

———— ·•◆•· ————

A free-state Democrat from Boston, Mayor George W. Collamore had been mocked by some fearless citizens as "our nervous mayor" for his efforts to have troops stationed in the town. When guerrillas, shouting for him to come out, surrounded his house, he slipped into an attached building in which there was a well. He and his hired hand, Patrick Keith, lowered themselves into the well. Cursing raiders searched the house from top to bottom but found nothing. They carried their plunder outside and applied the torch.

Mrs. Collamore softly called into the well, asking her husband if he was all right; he replied that he was, and she went outside confident that he would be safe.

The house was completely consumed. After the ashes cooled, Mrs. Collamore cleared the debris from around the well and called to her husband again. This time there was no answer: It was believed that poisonous gas generated by the fire had killed both men.

Captain Joseph G. Lowe, the mayor's close friend, went down into the well, supported by a thin rope. A residue of gas—or perhaps smoke—suffocated Lowe, and the rope broke as an attempt was made to bring him back up. Eventually, the three bodies were hauled out of the cold water together.

A gang ordered Mrs. Gurdon Grovenor to draw water for themselves and their horses. One young man jumped from his horse and offered to help her. He told her he was sickened by what was happening. He must have been one of the Missouri farmers along for the ride because he claimed that "They told me they were only coming up to recover some stolen horses. I have not killed a man nor burnt a house yet, and I do not mean to."

Many of Holt's green recruits and even some bushwhackers were equally appalled. They showed civilians their unfired weapons and apologized for the slaughter. A few even intervened to stop murders from being committed: Cole Younger is credited with saving a dozen people. (A number of residents were Free Masons, as were some of Quantrill's followers; thus some Lawrencians were able to save themselves by the quick employment of secret hand signals and other signs.)

The Speer family suffered greatly that day. The patriarch, John Speer, Sr., was the collector of internal revenue for Kansas and a pioneering editor and publisher of the *Kansas Tribune*. Quantrill's men set fire to his tax office, destroying all the records, but by the time a squad reached his home on the eastern outskirts of town, he was hidden with his younger children in some undergrowth. His house was set ablaze; however, his wife managed to put it out.

Speer's eldest three sons had worked at the paper until such a late hour the previous evening that they had bunked with friends and apprentices rather than make the long journey home. When the firing started, William "Billy" Speer, fifteen, and his friend Charles Prentice stayed hidden in the back of the liquor store where Prentice was a clerk and where they had spent the night. Hearing bushwhackers battering down the front door, they went out the back door and crawled under the building. It was set ablaze. As whiskey from broken bottles dripped onto them through the floor, Billy told Charlie that being shot was better than being roasted. They slipped into the street and became separated. A guerrilla demanded to know Billy's name. Thinking fast, the boy replied, "William Smith." The dim-witted fellow consulted the death list and let him go.

Billy made himself useful offering to hold the horses of various looters and thus saved his life.

Unfortunately, his two brothers were not so lucky. Seventeen-year-old Robert and an apprentice had slept in the building that housed the *Republican* office. The building burned, and nothing that could be recognized as human remains was found in the ashes. Survivors believed that the fire was so hot, both corpses were entirely consumed, and thus, noted Connelley,

> no trace of the body of either was ever found. In indescribable sorrow and the undying hope of a mother, Mrs. Speer placed the dish and chair at his place at the table every meal she ever spread in her home until her death in the vain expectation that he might, through the providence of God, be still alive and come back to her before the meal was finished.

John Speer, Jr., nineteen, had spent the night in the *Tribune* office with a printer, M. M. Murdock. As soon as the alarm was raised Murdock climbed into a well and so escaped harm.

John was determined to get home to protect it from the raiders. He had gone only one block when he met Larkin Skaggs, the "hard-shell" Baptist preacher who had earlier dragged the large U.S. flag behind his horse. A native Kentuckian, Skaggs came from a respectable family. He moved to Cass County, Missouri, as a young man and got caught up in the struggle over slavery: "But for the awful conditions existing on the border," observed Connelley, who had gotten to know the man's family while growing up in Kentucky, "Larkin M. Skaggs would have died in his own bed and in his church, a respected and useful member of society." He had participated in the first Lawrence raid and the sackings of Osawatomie and bragged that he had taken part in many other raids into Kansas during the territorial period.

Skaggs demanded Speer's money. The boy handed over his pocketbook, saying there was very little money inside, but it was all he had. Skaggs immediately shot him and rode away, leaving him for dead. Speer had not died, although he was so badly wounded that he was unable to move. He lay quite close to a house that was set ablaze by three bushwhackers. When the heat became unbearable, he begged them to move him and not let him burn alive. In response one of them shot him to death.

The men casually rode away, and, ironically, the fire went out.

Judge Samuel A. Riggs—who in 1860 had been the district attorney responsible for indicting Quantrill for burglary, larceny, arson, and kidnapping—also had the misfortune of making the acquaintance of Larkin Skaggs. Riggs was fleeing his house when the preacher rode into the yard and began questioning him in a loud, angry voice. Hearing the confrontation, Mrs. Riggs hurried outside to be beside her husband. Skaggs must have been dissatisfied with the answers because he suddenly drew a revolver. Judge Riggs knocked the weapon aside and ran. Skaggs attempted to pursue him, but Mrs. Riggs seized his horse's bridle rein. She held on though she was dragged around the house, over a woodpile, and through the yard to the street again. During the whole ordeal Skaggs was swearing and striking at her with his pistol and threatening to kill her, but she did not let go until her husband was well out of sight.

Perhaps the most remarkable adventures of the day were experienced by the Reverend H. D. Fisher and his family. Fisher was a prominent abolitionist before the war and had been, it will be recalled, a chaplain in Jim Lane's Kansas Brigade. He had served in the Union army during the war but was on sick furlough from his regiment. Earlier in the month he had accompanied one hundred sick and wounded soldiers to a hospital in St. Louis, then gone to Leavenworth on a military errand. His resistance lowered by fatigue, he came down with chronic tonsillitis, or, as he told the readers of his turn-of-the-century memoir,

> I [became] ill, having been seized with quinsy, to which I had long been subject, [and] repaired to my family at Lawrence, a very sick man, reaching home about the middle of August. It thus happened that I was there, an invalid, at the time of the most fearful and barbarous occurrence of the War of the Rebellion. . . .

Hearing shooting and gunfire in the street outside his door, he dressed quickly and hurried to turn out his blooded horse and pony, believing "they would be less likely to be stolen if loose upon the prairie than if tied in the stable." With his two eldest sons, ages twelve and ten, he started for Mount Oread to hide in the bushes that lay to the west. His illness had drained all his energy and he struggled to run, but as he approached the hill he saw pickets stationed on the slope and knew he would never get past without detection. "The boys were smaller and could dart through the hazel and sumach bushes skirting the hill, and they ran on while I decided to go back to the house."

The boys soon became separated. Willie, the eldest, fell in with a school friend, Bobbie Martin, who was fourteen years old and big for his age. Unfortunately Bobbie was wearing the pants of his father's old Federal uniform, and one of the pickets, seeing the color, gave chase and opened fire. A bullet slammed into the back of Bobbie's head, splattering blood and brains into Willie's face. Willie was so horrified that, remarked his father nearly a half-century later, "he has never fully recovered his nervous vigor."

The younger Fisher boy, Edmund, caught up with Freddie Lopez, eleven years old. They managed to elude the pickets, though, Edmund would recall many years later, "we [were] shot at a number of times, the whine of the bullets speeding us more swiftly, the guerrillas probably mistaking us for men as we flew through the sumach and hazel bush." After running for miles, "we attained the seclusion of an old graveyard . . . where we lay between the graves, frightened all but to death. . . ." They spent a dry, solemn day watching the smoke rise from the burning town, too fearful to leave the cemetery even to find a drink of water.

When Reverend Fisher arrived back at his house, he slipped into the partially dug cellar. Hearing him, his wife called down a warning to stay hidden.

A moment later four bushwhackers barged into the house and demanded to know where her husband was.

"Do you think," she replied, "that he would be fool enough to stay about the house and you killing everybody you can? No, sir, he left with our little boys when you first came to town."

One cursed her, suggesting she was lying.

"It is not very gentlemanly to doubt the word of a lady," she said. She held an infant in her arms, and Josie, a seven-year-old, clung to her skirt. "Besides, I don't want you to swear in the presence of my children."

They decided to search the cellar and demanded a candle. Mrs. Fisher had none but, hoping to disarm them with cooperation as well as boldness, she gave the leader a lamp. He clumsily turned down the wick into the bowl, so that it could not be lighted. Mrs. Fisher handed her infant to another man and went upstairs for another lamp. While he walked the floor, cooing to keep the baby content, the others set to ransacking the house. When the lamp arrived, three raiders went into the cellar.

Fisher had worked his way on top of a bank of dirt under the entrance to the kitchen and had heard the exchanges between the intruders and his wife. As the three came down the stairs, he lost heart and was prepared to surrender—until he heard them cock their revolvers. The ceiling was low, and the leader was forced to keep ducking to avoid striking his head, while at the same time holding the lamp to one side to keep from singeing the skin on his face. The resulting body contortions and shifting of the lamp cast huge shadows, which luckily fell across the dirt bank and hid Fisher, whose left foot was shaking so violently that he was forced to press his right foot on it to keep it still. In any case, the search was a cursory one: Mrs. Fisher's attitude had convinced the bushwhackers that her husband was gone.

She stood cradling the baby in one arm while pressing her free hand against her ear to deaden the noise of the expected gunshots. Instead she heard the clump of the intruders' boots as they came upstairs. Climbing to the second story, they quickly set some fires and, leaving one man behind to see that she did not put them out, rode away.

She went upstairs, followed by the man who had remained. "Madam," he said, "if there is anything you wish to save, I'll help you save it." He had held her baby, and she thought the gesture had touched his heart.

"Turn in and help me put the fire out," she replied as she stamped on the flames and tried to smother them with a cloth.

"It would cost me my life to do that, but I can help you save your stuff if you want me to."

"If you can't help me put out the fire," she answered, "just get on your horse and ride off. Tell them that it was burning when you left, and I'll soon put it out myself."

"I'll do so," he agreed, "but it will do you no good. This is one of the marked houses and is bound to go." He cautioned her again to save what she could because the house would surely be burned, then left.

She carried buckets of water from the well and extinguished the flames. She went into the cellar and told her husband that she expected other brutes would come by and reignite the house. She advised him to pray and promised to do all she could to save him. Fisher lay in the dirt listening to the thunder of horses' hoofbeats, the crackling of the flames of burning buildings, the crashes when they fell, "the shouts of the human demons and the screams of the dying." He tried to shut out the sounds by reciting Bible verses: "The shadow of the Almighty was all over me. . . ." After awhile the sound of his wife's voice penetrated his consciousness; he realized she was standing right above him, loudly talking to the children so he could hear her voice and be comforted.

A few moments later there came the heavy thudding of boots on the floor—three more guerrillas had entered the house.

One asked for her husband, and she said he was gone.

"I'm damned glad of it," the guerrilla replied, which surprised her—but then, he and his friends were obviously very inebriated.

When they saw the charring and realized she had put out the fire, they raged and swore. They tore off window shutters, broke up chairs and a bookcase, and set them ablaze. Then two left, the third staying behind to watch her.

"I'll kill you if you try to put the fire out," he warned, flourishing his revolver.

After placing her children outside in a safe place, she marched purposefully to the well, filling pans, tubs, and buckets. The kitchen roof was ablaze, and she climbed onto the stove and threw water on the ceiling, wetting the boards, then dragged a table outside and used it to climb onto the roof and put out the flames. The roof of the main house was on fire, too, and she returned to the well, soaked her dress with water, and climbed back on the roof, throwing water and stamping out flames. Her heroism only delayed the inevitable: She was forced to return to the ground as the whole second story became engulfed and quickly collapsed onto the first floor.

Fisher, still lying just under the door between the kitchen and the main house, heard the crash. "I expected to be cremated alive, when suddenly I saw a little stream of water trickling through a knothole in the floor." His wife was casting buckets of water across the boards above where he lay. She continued to soak the small patch of floor until the heat was unbearable.

"You must come out or burn alive," she called. "I can't keep the fire back any longer."

He crawled out of the cellar entranceway, and she rolled him in a carpet and dragged it across the yard and tucked it against a large bush. She piled chairs on top of the carpet, while four guerrillas lounged thirty yards away, idly watching her save a few pathetic possessions.

After the raid was over, Reverend Fisher crawled out of the carpet to see the ashes of his home. His son Willie returned, dazed and covered with blood, to report the death of his friend. Mrs. Fisher left her small children with a neighbor woman and, fearing Edmund had been killed or was lying on the prairie bleeding to death, went searching for him, carrying a sheet to wrap his corpse in.

Edmund and Freddie Lopez had remained hidden in the distant cemetery until twilight brought the unhappy prospect of spending the night among ghosts, and so they were at last willing to forsake their refuge. As dusk fell, Mrs. Fisher encountered her son on the crest of Mount Oread, filthy and parched and filled with dread. Throwing aside the sheet, she ran to embrace him, crying with joy.

The Fishers' stable had not been burned, and they lived in the hayloft until they could rebuild their home with money sent from his former pastorate in Leavenworth.

<hr/>

The bright August morning was already becoming quite hot; however, the air was mercifully still. The slightest breeze would have spread burning ashes and greatly increased the destruction. Enormous columns of black smoke rose high in the sky, acting as beacons to signal Federal troops. Shortly after 9:00 A.M. the Mount Oread pickets sent a message to Quantrill that the dust of a small cavalry force had been spotted in the far distance. He quickly spread the word to rally at the south end of town.

As Colonel Holt was preparing to leave, he turned to Mrs. Clarke. Referring to stragglers, he said, "If they attempt to burn your house, say that Colonel Holt made his headquarters here and he left orders for the house to be spared."

Holt had three wounded men—two recruits and bushwhacker Jim Bledsoe—put into a carriage and rode away.

George Todd rode by the Clarke house on a newly acquired horse and wearing a splendid new uniform, which had been in the wardrobe of Captain Banks, the state provost marshal. Other guerrillas were heard to argue jovially, as they passed, over who had killed the most men.

Larkin Skaggs appeared, asking where a black preacher named Dudley Lee lived. "That damned nigger belongs to me," he said, "and I am going to find him."

Clarke replied truthfully that he did not know Lee.

Skaggs did not believe him: "I think I can refresh your memory," he said, drawing his revolver and leveling it.

The prospect of instant death turned Clarke into a convincing liar. He pointed to Turner Hall and said that Lee preached there, and then he gestured toward some small tenement shacks in the distance and swore one was Lee's residence.

Skaggs spurred his horse toward the tenements. "I knew I could refresh your memory," he laughed as he rode away.

A few minutes later several riders stopped and advised Clarke to remove whatever the family wanted from the house—they were going to burn it. Clarke said the house was not his; he rented it from a "widow lady." (In fact, it belonged to a bachelor named Watts.)

"We don't want to injure widows, as the Union men did with us," one replied, and they went on their way.

Two more men followed on their heels, demanding to know where Clarke was from. Clarke hesitated—revealing he was a native New Yorker would surely have unhappy consequences. His sister stepped forward: "We are Canadians."

The interrogator shrugged. "All right, we are not meddling with British subjects."

Unfortunately, portly William Faxon chose that moment to walk out of a house across the street.

"He's a Dutchman," one bushwhacker exclaimed to the other. "There must be sauerkraut in that paunch!" They raced over to him and tried to shoot him, but their pistols were out of ammunition. They knocked him down and savagely beat him, then left him for dead. They set fire to his house, then joined the retreat. (Mrs. Faxon put the fire out; her husband made a complete recovery.)

After Clarke witnessed Faxon's being beaten, he allowed his wife and sister to persuade him to hide. As soon as he was out of sight a couple of stragglers dashed up and announced the house would be burned. Mrs. Clarke told them what Colonel Holt had said, and they left.

Another raider demanded to see the man of the house. Told by Mrs. Clarke that he was not at home, the man insisted that he had seen him in the yard a few minutes ago, but when she persisted, he gave up, saying he would be satisfied with money. She said she had none.

"I must have some specie," he told her. "All the ladies have specie."

She gave him her porte-monie, which contained a few pieces, and he went on his way.

———•◦•———

Quantrill had ordered William Gregg to round up stragglers. At the foot of Mount Oread he found one drunkard clumsily trying to set a small house on fire. Three times Gregg dragged him out of the yard, but he always struggled free and staggered back to the house, greenbacks falling out of his overstuffed pockets. He finally passed out on the porch. By now there was money strewn all over the grass, and Gregg, disgusted with the fool, picked up a roll of bills and rode away. The next day he counted the bills, which were the only plunder he had taken, and found he had $192. He was astonished: There might have been $1,000 in the yard and the inebriate's pockets.

A mob of drunken stragglers committed the day's single cruelest atrocity. As they were leaving Lawrence, they passed Daniel W. Palmer's gunsmith shop. Palmer and an employee were standing in the doorway, having just come out of hiding because they believed all the raiders were gone. The two men were shot at and wounded. "The building was fired, the hands of the two wounded men tied together, and both flung into the burning building," wrote Hovey E. Lowman in 1864. The men rose and struggled through the flames to the door, but "the fiends . . . filling the air with their horrible shoutings of joy and exultation," pushed them back inside with their rifles. The flames burned away the ropes that bound them.

> Mr. Palmer arose the last time. His hands were . . . raised above his head, the red, fierce flames wrapped him in a sheet of unutterable agony. One cry to the All Merciful—"O God save us!"—pierced the roar of the fire and the tumult without, and he sank into the embers as upon a bed. The hideous shout of triumph set up by the fiends as they passed on [reverberated].

Larkin Skaggs was the last straggler in town. He had given up looking for his escaped slave and went back downtown to the Whitney House to settle a grudge with Lydia Stone. Early in the raid Skaggs had robbed her of a diamond ring, which Quantrill himself had long ago given her in gratitude for her having nursed him through a near-fatal illness in 1860. Lydia immediately went to Quantrill with a complaint about the theft and a description of the thief. He sent for Skaggs and forced him to return the ring, at the same time publicly dressing him down for disobeying his orders to leave the Stone family alone. Skaggs gave Lydia the ring, muttering as he did so that she would be "damned sorry for it."

Now with Quantrill having withdrawn, Skaggs was determined to exact revenge. Lydia was not at the Whitney House, however, so he could do nothing but torch the place. When her father, Nathan Stone, protested, Skaggs shot him dead.

Skaggs meandered through the streets, so drunk that he was reeling in his saddle. He stopped at the home of Fred W. Read and dismounted.

"I have come to pay a call," he told Mrs. Read solemnly as he entered the house.

"I am not receiving calls," she replied fearlessly. When the raid began, her husband had taken refuge on the second floor of his house. While he stayed hidden, the indomitable Mrs. Read dealt with successive visitations by guerrilla squads—seven in all. Repeatedly the house was set ablaze, and each time she extinguished the flames. One drunkard noticed the fire damage resulting from earlier attempts and had a comrade hold her wrists while he piled bedding and curtains on top of a lounge beside a second-story window. When the smoke drove them from the house, they dragged her out after them.

"Damn you, put it out if you can!" They laughed as they rode away.

She wrapped herself in a wet blanket and used pillows to push the burning debris out the window.

Since most bushwhackers stole only what they could carry on their horses, her house was looted piecemeal. The first who stopped got the money. Others took the jewelry, cutlery, and even her husband's "biled" shirts; the horses were led from the stable. One man, who arrived too late to find anything of monetary value, pulled the fancy new cover right off the piano. He used it as a saddle blanket.

She had no compunction about boldly talking back to the plunderers, scolding them for their crimes and refusing to be cowed. Only once did she plead: A man found a pair of coral armlets belonging to a recently deceased little daughter.

"Oh please let me keep these to remember her by," she begged as tears fell. She called them "little souvenirs of a buried treasure."

"Damn your dead baby!" came the heartless reply. "She'll never need them again!"

At last a squad happened by whose leader was sober and kindly. She pointed out the looted house and the charred ruins of the stable and out-buildings, then gestured toward the column of smoke on Massachusetts Street that indicated her husband's store was ablaze.

"You seem to be an officer," she said. "Look at this house and at that burning store and say if you have not punished us enough."

The officer told his men to leave the place alone. He remained on the porch for half an hour, shooing away all who approached.

But the officer had withdrawn with the rest, and Skaggs now stood in her parlor demanding matches. She refused to give him any; however, he found some himself and struck one after another against the piano. Each time one flared she blew it out.

"You are the queerest woman I ever saw!" he finally declared in exasperation.

At this moment James Faxon appeared at the door.

"Run for your life!" Mrs. Read cried.

Faxon took off with Skaggs stumbling behind him, revolver in hand. Skaggs returned a few moments later, furious that Faxon had gotten away and announcing he would now kill her. For some reason the thought suddenly penetrated his besotted brain that because his comrades had retreated, he had been left to the unlikely mercy of the survivors and so was in grave peril.

He hastily remounted his horse. "I have staid here so long I fear I shall be killed!" he cried and spurred his horse in a southeasterly direction. A party of men who were in pursuit of Quantrill spotted him and gave chase, turning him so that he raced northeast toward Eudora. His horse was very strong and fast and, cutting across fields and brakes and jumping fences, gradually pulled away from the pursuers. Skaggs might have gotten away except that he ran into a second party of men in a lane in front of him. He was disarmed, knocked from his horse, and herded back toward town.

Billy Speer had made his way home, picking up a discarded musket in the yard, and had sat down on the front porch. A passing rider shouted, "We have one of them!" Speer stepped out into the street and started toward the crowd just as Skaggs managed to break free and run toward him. Billy drew a bead on the drunken preacher, who was only ten feet away and closing, and hit him in the shoulder, dropping him.

White Turkey, one of a party of Delaware Indians who were passing through town in pursuit of the raiders, put an arrow into Skaggs's chest and then scalped him. Other men then cut loose with their firearms.

His body was hung from a tree, and vengeful survivors pelted it with stones and riddled it with lead. The next day some blacks cut it down and dragged it behind a horse—just as he had dragged the U.S. flag behind his horse—while a mob ran behind, throwing rocks at it. When all the clothes and skin had been worn off, the blacks threw what was left of the corpse into a ravine and set it on fire. The bones were left for scavengers. Sometime during the following winter small boys visited the ravine and broke off the finger bones to retrieve Skaggs's rings.

Once Quantrill was gone, the Reverend Richard Cordley, who had managed to get out of town early in the raid, hurriedly returned. "I [was] anxious to know how great the disaster was. The first man I met was John Speer. . . . He was covered with ashes and soot as if he had been through the fire." He "eagerly" seized Cordley's hand.

"I want you to help me find my boy," he said. "They have killed one, and the other I cannot find. He slept in the printing office, and I expect he was burned with the building." The two men raked among the embers in the cellar with poles "but could find no signs of his boy, and no signs of him were ever found."

Cordley resumed his walk. He saw the wounded being tended, and "I went from one stricken group to another, helping as I could. Every one had a tale of horror or of marvelous escapes, and to tell all I heard and saw that day would . . . equal the story of any Indian massacre ever written."

His own house had been burned. "All that remained was a bed of embers and ashes. Not a book or sermon, not a letter or paper, not a relic of childhood or memento of friend was saved." He stood surveying the damage with his wife and his good friend, the Reverend Louis Bodwell. Mrs. Cordley wept quietly until Bodwell turned to her and gently said, "Don't cry, Mary. You have got all you asked for. We are all here."

She dried her eyes. As Cordley himself put it, "So many all about us were carrying heavier sorrows, that we could but be thankful at our own escape."

Three Kansas jayhawkers *(clockwise from top)*: James H. Lane, an unprincipled U.S. senator and general who had no moral qualms about slavery but freed slaves while raiding throughout Missouri because he believed it weakened the South; famed horse thief Colonel Charles R. "Doc" Jennison, an abolitionist who made no distinction between Missouri Unionists and Southerners when stealing their livestock and other property; and preacher and schoolteacher Captain James Montgomery.

This ambrotype has been passed down through the collateral descendants of Quantrill's sister-in-law, Caroline A. Quantrill. According to family tradition the subject is William Clarke Quantrill as a teenager.

All known copies of this photographic image of William Clarke Quantrill have been altered: A mustache has been added and the hair thickened to depict him as Missourians remembered him.

GEORGE HART

This *carte de visite* was found hidden in the backing of another picture by workmen who were demolishing an old Kansas City, Missouri, building in the early 1950s. Quantrill scholars and aficionados have identified the subject as William Clarke Quantrill.

THE KANSAS STATE HISTORICAL SOCIETY

Abraham "Bullet Hole" Ellis, who was shot in the forehead by Quantrill. The embedded bullet and skull fragments were subsequently removed by an army surgeon.

George Todd, a Quantrill lieutenant who deposed him at gunpoint in 1864 and drove him from the band.

A dapper young Frank James.

THE DENVER PUBLIC LIBRARY, WESTERN HISTORY DEPARTMENT

Bushwhacker Jesse James, age sixteen or seventeen, armed with three revolvers and wearing a "guerrilla shirt" with deep pockets to hold ammunition.

THE JACKSON COUNTY, MISSOURI, HISTORICAL SOCIETY ARCHIVES

Sarah "Kate" King Clarke, who was either Quantrill's wife or mistress. In later years she claimed they were married, but several of his former followers said otherwise.

The renderings of two nineteenth-century artists, who tried to depict the horrors of the Lawrence massacre.

Famed artist George Caleb Bingham's 1870 painting *Order No. 11,* depicting the suffering caused by General Thomas Ewing's depopulation of four western Missouri counties.

George W. Maddox, the only Raider ever tried for the Lawrence massacre. The jury, which was probably bribed, took just ten minutes to acquit him.

Physician and general James G. Blunt, whose men were routed and slaughtered by Quantrill and his Raiders in the Baxter Springs massacre. Blunt later became insane and died while a patient at St. Elizabeth's Asylum, Washington, D.C.

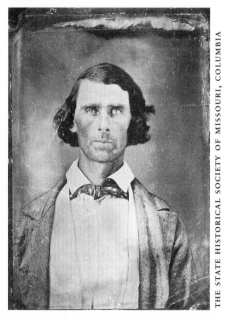

A clean-shaven Dave Pool.

Three of Quantrill's followers. *Left to right:* "Little Archie" Clement, Dave Pool, and Bill Hendricks.

A rakish
"Bloody Bill"
Anderson in life,
and in death.

Marcellus Jerome Clark, alias Sue Mundy, the "wild woman guerrilla" of Kentucky, with whom Quantrill rode in 1865.

General John M. Palmer, who hired "decoy guerrilla" Edwin Terrell to hunt down Quantrill.

Edwin Terrell, who became an outlaw after the war.

Death registry records for Louisville, 1865–70, were believed lost or destroyed for half a century until the author found them in 1992. Terrell's death is listed in Book 2, page 137, entry 98.

Quantrill's elderly, grieving,
bad-tempered mother,
Caroline Clarke Quantrill.

William Walter Scott,
Quantrill's boyhood friend,
who stole his bones and
tried to sell his skull.

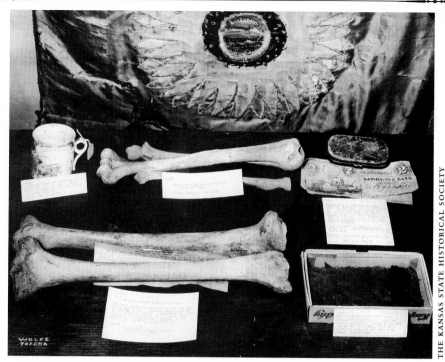

Quantrill's bones in a Kansas State Historical Society display case, along with some relics of the massacre: a chipped china mug and a charred New Testament, which were dug out of some ruins, and the pocketbook of murdered John Speer, Jr., found on the body of his killer, Larkin Skaggs.

ANOTHER NATURE FAKER,
But Uncle George Martin is the man who can arise to emergencies.

After press reports in 1907 that Quantrill was living in Canada under the alias John Sharp, the Topeka *Farmers Mail and Breeze* published a cartoon suggesting what the Society's secretary should do with Quantrill's bones.

Dignified, aging
reformed outlaws
Cole Younger *(top)*
and Frank James.

Elderly veterans at a Quantrill reunion. William Gregg *(front row, third from right)* sometimes gave interviews to the press, bragging about the Lawrence massacre, which outraged massacre survivors.

Father Mark Carter reads the interment service for "our brother William," October 30, 1992.

Two Dover maintenance workers (Michael Bott, *left,* and Larry Pruni) lower a fiberglass infant's coffin containing Quantrill's skull into his grave.

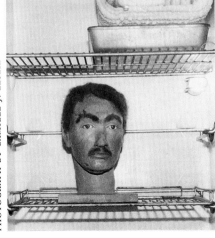

The wax head of William Clarke Quantrill in the Dover Historical Society's refrigerator.

His gratitude did not keep him from assessing the great destruction that had been visited on Lawrence.

The buildings on Massachusetts street were all burned except one, and that had been ransacked and robbed, and two boys lay dead upon the floor. The fires were still glowing in the cellars. The brick and stone walls were still standing bare and blackened. The cellars between looked like great caverns with furnaces glowing in the depths. The dead lay all along the street, some of them so charred that they could not be recognized, and could scarcely be taken up. Here and there among the embers could be seen the bones of those who had perished in the buildings and been consumed where they fell. . . . As [I] passed along the street, the sickening odor of burning flesh was oppressive. . . . Around one corner lay seventeen bodies. Back of a livery stable on Henry street lay five bodies piled in a heap. The undermost man of these was alive, and had lain under the dead for four hours, and so saved himself from a fatal shot. He was severely wounded but recovered. Going over the town [I] saw the dead everywhere, on the sidewalks, in the streets, among the weeds in the gardens, and in the few remaining homes. The women were going about carrying water to the wounded, and covering the dead with sheets. To protect the wounded from the burning sun, they sometimes spread an umbrella over them, and sometimes made a canopy with a sheet or a shawl. Now and then [I] came across a group, a mother and her children watching their dead beside the ashes of their home. A little later there could be seen a woman sitting among the ashes of a building holding in her hands a blackened skull, fondling it and kissing it, and crying piteously over it. It was the skull of her husband, who was burned with the building. But there was not much weeping and not much wailing. It was too deep and serious for tears or lamentations. All addressed themselves to the sad work that had to be done.

No one realized the extent of the disaster until it was over. Every man was so isolated by the presence of the raiders in every part of the town, that each knew only what he saw. . . . Besides the buildings on the business street, about one hundred houses had been burned, and probably as many more had been set on fire and saved by the heroic exertions of the women. Most of the houses not burned were robbed. . . . So many had been killed that every man we met on the street seemed to come from the dead. The first salutation was: "Why, are you alive?" The embers were still red, the fires were still burning, as we began to gather the dead and wounded from among the ruins.

The corpses were brought from all over town to the Methodist Church, which functioned as a makeshift morgue. Soon the entire floor was covered with bodies. Those that were identifiable were numbered and marked with the names of the deceased. Gurdon Grovenor, who came to the church to find his brother-in-law's remains, would remember the scene all his life: "Mothers and wives were coming in and as they recognized the lifeless bodies of their sons and husbands, they gave way to their grief, and their sighing and moans were most pitiful and brought tears of sympathy from the most careless."

By the end of the day, many corpses had been collected, the wounded located and tended to, and homeless survivors had crammed into the parlors and spare rooms of the still-standing houses, whole families in a single room, sleeping on floors in borrowed bedclothes.

On Saturday a man named Tom Corlew was accused by furious residents of being a Quantrill spy. A jury was impaneled, and three judges were chosen to hear the case. He was even allowed to have a lawyer to defend him. Witnesses alleged that he sent his family out of town the day before the raid. "He represented that he had come from Illinois," remembered William Speer decades later, but "quite a number of negroes testified that they had seen him in Missouri, and that he was a rabid rebel. Although the jury went out to consider the verdict, they returned desiring the crowd to take responsibility, and by a vote [the crowd] decided to hang him."

John Speer, Sr., who brought out an edition of his newspaper, the *Kansas Tribune,* six days after the raid, using a Topeka printing press, told his readers that Corlew had "exhibited a great deal of trepidation during the trial, his eyes rolling wildly; but when his time came, he seemed more composed, merely feeling his throat, but making no outcry." A rope was thrown over a barn joist and tied around his neck. He was made to stand on a dry-goods box, which was pulled out from under him. While he thrashed and twisted, bystanders took out pistols and shot holes in him.

Fifteen-year-old Billy Speer, perched on a rafter, saw it all.

As the sun climbed higher and the temperature rose it was clear that the burial of the victims, as Judge Bailey delicately put it, "could not be neglected on account of the intensity of the heat." There were no coffins available, and, according to Reverend Cordley,

Many carpenters were killed, and most of the living had lost their tools. But they rallied nobly, and worked night and day, making pine and walnut boxes, fastening them together with the burnt nails gathered from the ruins of the stores. It sounded harsh to the ears of friends to have the lid nailed over the bodies of their loved ones; but it was the best that could be done.

Many men were away at war and so many others had been killed in the raid that relatively few able-bodied males were left in town to heft shovelfuls of dirt. Here again, however, the people of Lawrence came together, and after three days a total of 122 bodies had been buried in the Oread Cemetery—fifty-three of them laid side by side in a long trench—and many others in their own yards. Brief services were sometimes held in homes, beside the graves, or even in the street.*

---

*The accepted figure for the number of slain is 150. So far as I can determine Cordley was the first to use it. In *A History of Lawrence, Kansas,* published in 1895, Cordley also provided what he characterized as "a partial list of names" of the dead, totaling 126. Connelley examined the list and rounded it off to "about" 150, adding that since "many bodies were consumed in the flames the exact number can never be known." The problem with the list is that owing to the rapid decomposition of the corpses in the summer's heat, many were buried without ever being identified. The bodies of at least twenty-two blacks were found, for instance, but only three made Cordley's list. Some of the German immigrants were unknown to the Lawrencians in the burial parties, and there were strangers in town that day, including workers who were building a windmill and a bridge. It later came to light that seven laborers and a foreman died. Thirteen of those who went into the mass grave were not identified. An attempt was made by those in the organized burial parties to number every corpse they put into the ground, but some individuals were buried by families, friends, or neighbors.

On the afternoon of August 26 three men on the scene sent a dispatch to the St. Louis *Missouri Democrat,* stating that "Up to this morning 183 bodies were buried in Lawrence. The remains of 7 more bodies are found." Cordley wrote that "it was at least a week before all the dead were found," which means that this figure is low, too. James Finley and George Sargeant both died of their wounds after that date, and Robert Speer's body was never found, bringing the total to 193. Thus the final total, if it ever could be known, would be around two hundred, not 150.

Incidentally, Dr. Richard Sheridan, professor emeritus of the University of Kansas at Lawrence, who has been researching the massacre for a number of years, thinks my figure is conservative.

Other raid statistics are not in dispute. Fewer than thirty people who had been wounded survived, and there were at least eighty-five widows and 250 orphans. One hundred and eighty-two buildings had been destroyed, including about one hundred residences. Cordley thought that "A very conservative estimate [would place] the entire loss at $1,500,000." Other responsible estimates ranged as high as $2.5 million—in Civil War–era dollars.

The digging was stopped on Sunday long enough for a brief devotional service to be held at the Congregational church. Many present were wearing the only outfits they had saved from the flames. "It deepened the impressiveness of the scene," Cordley thought, "to remember that a large portion of the women and children were newly made widows and orphans." The visiting minister who conducted the service did not give a sermon, but the Scriptural lesson he chose was from the Seventy-ninth Psalm:

> O God, the heathen are come into thine inheritance.
> The dead bodies of thy servants
> they have given to be meat unto the fowls of heaven,
> the flesh of thy saints unto the beasts of the earth.
> Their blood have they shed like water around Jerusalem;
> and there was none to bury them.

The recitation did little to calm the populace. That very night mass hysteria seized Lawrence. Rumors had been spreading that before withdrawing various bushwhackers had warned some of the womenfolk to "desert the town," saying they would be back and would "kill every man, woman, and child who dared to remain." The rumors, thought one survivor, created a general "uneasiness, so the people were in a frame of mind that required very little to create a panic."

Suddenly a man galloped into town from the south, shouting at the top of his lungs, "They are coming again! They are coming again! Run for your lives! Run for your lives!" People streamed from their houses and raced through the night. Some shrieked; others bellowed warnings:

"Run for your life! Run for your life! They are on us again!"

"Run for your life! Quantrell is coming back!"

"The bushwhackers are here!"

A large mob of men, women, and children flew toward the river. A few compassionate adults followed more slowly behind, lugging the wounded, using mattresses as stretchers, but others, terrified and unencumbered, fled mindlessly in all directions. Some hitched up spooked, wild-eyed, bridleless horses to carriages, then scurried madly about, frantically looking for harnesses. Others sprinted to the ferry and crossed the river or hid themselves in the bushes along the near bank or dove into cornfields on the outskirts of town. A few men donned dresses and bonnets, but many more rallied at the arsenal, determined to make a stand this time. They passed out the ancient muskets, broke open the only two kegs of powder that remained, chopped lead bars into slugs: "We were prepared to give the enemy some rough shot," recalled Peter Ridenour. Several men who had horses rode south to identify the exact position of the guerrillas, but returned an hour later having found no sign of them.

Eventually it was learned that a farmer had burned a haystack, and another man, seeing the fire in the distance, "imagined he saw an army," as Ridenour put it. "As soon as we received this information . . . our little military company broke ranks, and each went to his home."

The panicked citizens who had gone into hiding had no way of knowing that the alarm was false, of course, and despite the fact that the temperature was unusually chilly and a series of thunderstorms struck, "they spent the whole night hiding in cornfields and in the bushes drenched with rain and trembling with fear as to what developments daylight would bring," remembered Ridenour.

Families were separated in the stampede; mothers carrying the smallest children in their arms were separated from the larger children, and husbands and fathers, who remained when families ran away, spent the night in hunting their dear ones. The terror and suffering of hundreds that night cannot be described or realized. Many of them did not return until noon the next day; they were afraid to leave their hiding places until they were found and assured that the bushwhackers had not come.

Monday turned out to be a lovely day. The heavy rains had doused most of the still-smoldering fires, although the bright sunshine, thought Ridenour, made the ruins look even more "black and desolate." Some despondent souls, feeling, as Cordley phrased it, "that there could be no security for life or property after this, and it was madness to attempt to rebuild," took whatever worldly goods they had left and departed, but most "made it a matter of conscience" that "Lawrence must be rebuilt at all hazards and rebuilt at once."

Less than two days' worth of food remained, but as word of the atrocity spread, area farmers drove wagons loaded with vegetables to Lawrence. Survivors' friends and acquaintances who lived elsewhere sent whatever could be spared—clothing, knives, forks, chairs, and cookstoves.

In the days and weeks following the raid, a "Civilian And Military Ball" was held in Kansas City, the proceeds going to "Lawrence sufferers," and the cities of Leavenworth, Wyandotte, and Topeka sent large shipments of provisions and clothing. St. Louis contributed $10,000 with the stipulation that the money "be loaned without interest to parties desiring to rebuild."

A few lucky Lawrencians had hidden their money and jewelry and so had something to spend to revitalize the economy. Furthermore, at the onset of the attack, railroad agent James E. Watson had hidden a tin box containing $13,000 in cash and valuables in a ravine; over the next few panic-stricken days, because there was no lockable safe left in town, he continued to shift the box's hiding place until he managed to distribute all its contents to the rightful owners.

The Simpson brothers had lost their homes as well as their bank building, but the robbers could not open the safe; heat from the fire had not destroyed its contents. The brothers had a cheap, temporary wooden building hastily constructed inside the foundation walls and resumed business. They soon erected a brick building around the temporary one and, when it was completed, had the wooden one dismantled and carted away.

Peter Ridenour discovered the fire that had consumed his store had been so intense that nails in stacks of kegs had melted and run "together in[to] a solid mat of iron." The safe, which was not fireproof, had sat beside the kegs and fallen through the burning floor. The key having disappeared, he chopped a hole in the door with an ax.

I found the paper in our ledger and journal not burned, although the leather binding was burned so that it crumbled off. The paper was quite yellow, but the writing was legible. There was in the safe six hundred and ten dollars in drafts and currency which was not injured so much but it could be used. I put ten dollars in my pocket and sent six hundred dollars to our creditors. The contents of the safe, the damaged stock of iron and steel, an empty corn-crib next to the alley, and our lot were the only property we had left. We owed a few thousand dollars for goods that we had bought just long enough before for them to [arrive] and be burned. I sat down and figured up what we owed and made an estimate of what property we had, including what we might collect on accounts due us; this was not very much, as we had not been doing much credit business. . . . We had insurance on our goods, but there was a clause in the policies that excepted losses caused by "riot, invading enemies, or overpowering thieves"; so we never received one dollar of insurance.

The earnings of several years' hard labor in business, together with the little capital we put in at the start, had all been swept away in an hour by the devouring flames . . . [To make matters worse, my partner] Mr. Baker's life was still hanging in the balance. [But] I studied the situation over for an hour or two, and came to the conclusion that we must start again, and did not know of any place more favorable to start than right where we were. We were among people who knew us well; the surrounding country was prosperous; so there was a demand for a trading-point. Why should Lawrence not be rebuilt, and why should not we share in the burden and in the profits?

Ridenour came upon a group of black laborers standing in the street, hired them to clean out the cellar, and told them to find shovels wherever they could. He emptied out the corncrib and rolled into it two barrels of salt that had survived the fire. A wagon arrived containing goods ordered before the raid, and these were put into the corncrib, too. He hoisted the Stars and Stripes "to attract attention to the fact that we had a store [in] the alley." He was back in business.

Bricklayers and carpenters were drawn to the flag and applied for work. Customers showed up and made purchases. Other people expressed astonishment that Ridenour was starting over; however, a number of fellow merchants quickly followed suit, making arrangements for credit from lumber mills in neighboring communities. "In a few hours the sound of hammers could be heard in several places on Massachusetts Street, nailing up temporary buildings, and it was not many days before the stone-hammers and mason's trowel could be heard erecting many of the permanent buildings which still stand fronting on Massachusetts Street."

Ridenour sent orders to Leavenworth's wholesale grocers. In making sales, he accepted only cash, "and when one lot of goods was sold out, we had the [money] to pay for them, less what we used in paying for labor and material in rebuilding the store. Our sales were reasonably large and profits good, so that the profits each week very nearly paid for the building as it went along."

* * *

The people of Lawrence recognized the need to defend what they were so diligently rebuilding—there were several more mass panics before winter set in—so the men formed a new home-guard unit, known simply as the "Rifle Company." The members drilled frequently and chipped in to buy Smith & Wesson rifles and revolvers, which they carried at all times. Three block houses with gunport holes were constructed in strategic locations. Eight men were detailed for each block house every night, and all persons approaching after dark were challenged. In his memoir Ridenour wrote,

> This guard-duty was . . . quite a tax on the strength of the citizens, as they were all engaged in some kind of business or labor during the day. When one's time came to do guard-duty after a hard day's work, he would dread the task of having to patrol the streets for half the night and to remain in the block-house during the other half, so it was not an uncommon thing for some members to shirk their duty; they would remain at home and go to bed, in place of obeying the order to appear for duty; but there was a sufficient number in the company who were determined to keep up the guard and enforce discipline. It frequently happened that the officer of the night had to send a squad to men's houses and make them get out of bed and come on duty.

Finally military authorities stationed two companies of regular troops in Lawrence, and the Rifle Company was disbanded. The soldiers threw up earthworks on a hill overlooking the town and placed several pieces of artillery. "No child was ever more delighted to 'see the soldiers' than were the people of Lawrence when these troops came in," observed Richard Cordley.

———◆———

On November 18, 1863, the Douglas County grand jury issued indictments against Quantrill, George Todd, Colonel Holt, George W. Maddox, and other raiders who had been recognized.

By the following spring, seventeen large brick stores were finished and filled with merchandise. Two newspapers had been reestablished, and telegraph wires had been brought into town. The bridge across the Kansas River was completed—the only one for a great distance—which lured many travelers.

Late in the summer of 1864, the commander of the military district at Indianapolis telegraphed the Lawrence mayor, informing him that a man calling himself Charley Hart and fitting Quantrill's description had been taken into custody. A town meeting was held at which a delegation of three men who knew Quantrill was selected, and the hat was passed for the money to send them to Indiana to identify him and, hopefully, bring him back for trial. Peter Ridenour volunteered to go along at his own expense. The delegates, armed with extradition papers and two revolvers apiece, traveled by stage, boat, and rail. After forty-eight hours without sleep they viewed the prisoner in his cell—and saw that he was not Quantrill. Military authorities, who were intent on executing him after the formality of the identification, were almost as disappointed as the Lawrencians.

The rebuilding effort was halted during the summer and fall of 1864, first by fears of guerrilla attacks, then by Sterling Price's raid. After Price was defeated, progress resumed. The Eldridge House was rebuilt, and several new churches were constructed as were a steam-driven flour mill and a huge windmill to power a plow factory. Streets were graded, and there were new sidewalks and culverts, schools and a cemetery.

At the end of 1865, Reverend Cordley proudly noted that

"the burnt district" is now almost a solid block of brick and stone stores. Dwellings have not only risen from the ashes of those destroyed, but half a dozen have appeared where none was before. The completing of the railroad to the opposite bank of the river has given a new impulse to trade. . . . Thus has Lawrence risen from her ashes and more than eclipsed her former glory.

Being a survivor of the massacre became a badge of honor. For many years a harness shop ran advertisements bragging, "Established in 1855; stood the drought in 1860; totally destroyed in 1863; defies all competition in 18——!" In 1890, an Atchison newspaperman named Ed Howe observed, "In Lawrence the aristocratic families of the place are those whose fathers hid in a well, or otherwise escaped the Quantrill devils, or whose mothers witnessed the awful scene."

On February 8, 1866, George W. Maddox was brought to the Lawrence jail and locked in a cell. There was disagreement about how he came to be confined. The *Missouri Republican* alleged he had been kidnapped across the border and illegally brought to Lawrence; however, the *Kansas Tribune* reported that he had been arrested near Pleasant Hill, Missouri, charged with the murder of a Unionist, and "delivered up to the sheriff of Douglas County on a requisition from the Governor of Kansas." Either way, the militia was called out to guard the jail since it was feared his friends would try to break him out. The still grieving Mr. and Mrs. Speer visited him in his cell, seeking information about their missing boy. Granted a change of venue, Maddox was put on trial in Ottawa. The jury took just ten minutes to acquit him, which is either a stirring testament to the essential fairness of the American system of jurisprudence or an indication of the wholesale bribery of the jurors.

Many Lawrencians had attended the trial confident that Maddox would be found guilty and hanged. Pandemonium must have erupted in the courtroom immediately after the announcement of the verdict because Maddox was able to slip out the back door of the courthouse unnoticed. His wife was waiting in the alley with two swift horses. By the time the spectators realized what had happened and rushed outside, Maddox and his wife had too much of a head start to be overtaken.

Perhaps Maddox's acquittal discouraged other would-be kidnappers and Kansas legal authorities alike: Although for many years after the war Lawrence survivors occasionally proposed extraditing and prosecuting ex-bushwhackers, Maddox is the only one ever known to have been tried on charges stemming from the atrocity.

CHAPTER 10

"We Prayed That Night or Succor Might Come": The Pursuit of Quantrill and the Issuing of Order No. 11

Quantrill's audacious strike against Lawrence had caught the Yankees napping, but though off balance, confused, and alarmed, they scrambled to recover.

Shortly after 7:00 P.M. on the night of August 20, 1863, a farmer galloped into the Federal camp at Aubry, just west of the Kansas border. His farm was seven miles south of town, and he breathlessly told of having been held prisoner in his own yard by scouts claiming to be Union soldiers. His disinterested guards had casually allowed him to watch as a company of men rode by, heading southwest in the direction of Paola; he counted two hundred "troopers" before they realized what he was doing and hustled him out of sight behind the house. He was certain there were a total of four companies—eight hundred men.

The Aubry commander, Captain J. A. Pike, hurriedly sent dispatches to other military outposts and to Ewing's headquarters at Kansas City, warning of the incursion and correctly surmising that Quantrill was its leader. Unfortunately, he made no attempt to alert any of the towns that might have been potential raid targets, and neither did he give chase: He had one hundred soldiers at his disposal, but in defending himself many years later he would claim that only twenty-one able-bodied men were on duty and therefore he considered it "suicide" to "attack the eight hundred reported by the farmer."

Military bureaucracies habitually look for a scapegoat to blame for any disaster, and in writing his report ten days after the massacre, General Thomas Ewing, who was no fool, anxiously pointed an accusing finger at Pike: "By Captain Pike's error in judgment in failing to follow promptly and closely, the surest means of arresting the terrible blow was thrown away, for Quantrell would never have gone as far as Lawrence, or attacked it, with 100 men close on his rear." Ewing proved as adept at bureaucratic infighting as he was at the bloodier sort of combat: Pike was so overwhelmed by condemnation from both army and civilian sources that he withdrew into wounded silence for half a century.

Hobbled by a lack of accurate intelligence and ignorant of the enemy's actual position, true strength, and destination, other Federal officers nonetheless responded to Pike's alarm aggressively. They sent dispatches of their own, relaying the warning to other commands, then set out with what men were available, searching for the invaders' trail or heading directly for which town they deemed to be the most likely target—Paola, Osawatomie, or Olathe.

Captain Charles F. Coleman, stationed at Little Santa Fe, which was just across the border in Missouri, raced southwest to Aubry with eighty men. He assumed command of Pike's Company K, 9th Kansas Volunteer Cavalry, and Company D, 11th Kansas Volunteer Cavalry, and resumed his march. He struck the enemy's trail five miles south of town, followed it for three miles, and lost it again in the darkness. He blundered around for two hours before he found the trail again, then followed it to Gardner.

"I learned that they had passed through six hours before," Coleman wrote in his report on August 30. "I sent runners south and west to notify the inhabitants that Quantrill had gone north with a large force." He resumed the pursuit, and in the hot, bright morning the bushwhackers' target was revealed: "I soon could see the smoke from the burning of Lawrence and pressed on as fast as our jaded horses would permit."

Six miles southeast of town, Coleman was overtaken by Major Preston B. Plumb. When Pike's message had reached Kansas City, Ewing was at Fort Leavenworth, so Plumb, his young chief of staff, took the only troops available—thirty infantrymen—mounted them on heavy horses, and, shortly after 1:00 A.M., set off southwest on the Santa Fe Trail. He galloped into Olathe at dawn, having ridden thirty miles in four hours. Waiting on the public square was Lieutenant Cyrus Leland, Jr., who had arrived the previous day from Black Jack, in Douglas County, Kansas, and spent a sleepless night trying to figure out the enemy's destination. As Plumb and Leland conferred, a great column of black smoke arose in the western sky. "Quantrell is in Lawrence!" Plumb said, and, accompanied by Leland, struck out northwest across the prairie, the most direct route to the town.

Passing over a road south of Captain's Creek Crossing, he saw the tracks of many horses and followed them until he encountered Coleman. Combining Coleman's force with his own, Plumb again struck out across the prairie until he spied clouds of dust and plumes of smoke to the west: The bushwhackers were burning farmhouses and settlements as they withdrew. Plumb led a hard gallop in an attempt to cut off their line of retreat.

Meanwhile, Jim Lane had ridden into Lawrence on the borrowed plow horse, still without a saddle. His nightshirt was tucked into the borrowed pair of trousers, and he was armed with only a small pistol. He brought with him a dozen farmers he had rounded up, and he called for volunteers among the massacre survivors. A dozen men mounted horses that had been abandoned by the raiders. As Lane followed Quantrill's trail, more farmers joined him, men whose houses and barns were still smoldering.

The survivors quickly found that the horses the guerrillas had left behind were played out, but many other members of the ragtag outfit were no better mounted: They rode mules or old brood mares with colts following; some had saddles, but others rode bareback. They were armed with squirrel guns or ancient muskets, shotguns or pepper-box pistols; a few had nothing more lethal than corn knives. But when they came to the torched little village of Brooklyn and found a lingering party of bushwhackers setting fire to a house, they charged, putting their startled adversaries to panicked flight.

Quantrill led his band southeast down the Lawrence–Fort Scott Road, harried and annoyed by Lane's civilian volunteers. Then, Major Plumb's force converged with Lane's and the chase began in earnest. An occasional raider fell from his horse, wounded or dead, but fatigue prevented more substantial vengeance: Most of the Federal troops had ridden fifty or even seventy miles without food or rest, and their mounts were exhausted. The guerrillas had stolen so many fresh horses at Lawrence that each time a man's mount faltered, he shot it and threw his saddle on the back of another.

Still, the Yankees kept so close that the bushwhackers felt compelled to lighten the load on their mounts and pack horses by discarding much of their plunder—including women's dresses, hats, bolts of cloth, children's toys, and furniture.

Shortly before noon, they arrived at Josiah Fletcher's place. The Fort Scott Road detoured around the property, but they took a shortcut—a lane that bisected the farm. This proved to be a mistake, because at one point the lane narrowed as it passed between cornfields, forming a bottleneck, which caused them to pause and bunch up as they waited to pass through.

Plumb's cavalry advance had time to close the distance. As they bore down, George Todd, thinking fast, rallied twenty stragglers and countercharged. The bushwhackers emptied their revolvers at close range into the Yankees' front ranks, wounding or killing many horses. As the animals went down, the horses of the following ranks stumbled over them or shied and fell. Some civilians had dismounted beside the road and, standing in a cornfield, directed a harmless, undisciplined volley at Todd's men. They returned the fire, panicking the civilians, and sending them fleeing down the lane into the next rank of troops.

Taking advantage of the enemy's confusion, Todd's men galloped for the bottleneck. Todd's own mount had been shot out from under him, and he brought up the rear at a dead run. Afraid that his comrades would mistake him for a foe, he tore off the Federal uniform coat he had looted from Captain Banks. Only later did he remember that several large wads of U.S. greenbacks were in the pockets.

Once clear of the bottleneck the raiders spurred their horses down the lane and back onto the Fort Scott Road, but after going only a few miles they came to East Ottawa Creek. It took time for hundreds of men to ford the stream, time enough for the Federal advance to regroup and come on. Quantrill himself formed a skirmish line, then led the countercharge. The Yankees were driven all the way back to Fletcher's farm.

Returning to the creek, Quantrill ordered Gregg to cut out sixty men and hold the rear until the main command had finished fording. Gregg called for volunteers and braced for the Federals to strike again, but when, after a long, tense wait, they failed to appear, he gave up and took his men through the water. Quantrill was waiting in the woods on the other side. "Form your sixty men in a skirmish line and hold the rear," he told Gregg. "Fall back on me whenever it may be necessary, but whatever you do, don't let them break your line."

It was clear to Major Plumb that his men would never be able to overtake Quantrill due to the exhaustion of their horses. A number had collapsed and died along the way; the remainder were now absolutely jaded. Their riders were hardly better off: cotton-mouthed, gasping, ravenous, soaking wet with sweat, asleep in their saddles.

Still, Plumb was a valiant, determined officer, and he was unwilling to give up the chase. Fortunately there was an alternative. Throughout the morning, as word of the massacre spread along the Kansas border, more than 150 farmers and residents of small towns had made their way to his column. These men and their horses were still relatively fresh, and Plumb assigned Lieutenant Leland to lead them. Dividing them into three companies, Leland raced after the guerrillas, who had left the Fort Scott Road on the far side of East Ottawa Creek and were making a beeline for Paola.

Some of the civilians' horses were fleeter than others, of course, and they had different gaits. Furthermore, neither the men nor the horses had any cavalry training, so that during the afternoon's pursuit, Leland's command was often strung out over two or three miles, all the way back to the lagging troopers. At the first skirmish, two-thirds of the civilians broke ranks, some pressing forward to fight, while the rest hurried to the rear. Leland quickly found that only "20 to 50 of [them] could fight very well," but that was enough: He pressed Quantrill all the way to Paola.

Whenever the civilian advance came into view, Gregg would dismount his men and form them into two lines several hundred yards apart, facing the enemy. The men on the forward line would cut loose with their revolvers and hold their position as long as possible, then fall back through the second line and form a new line. This fight-and-retreat, fight-and-retreat maneuver would continue until the Union cavalry finally caught up, at which time the guerrillas mounted their horses and dashed after their comrades.

The civilians took casualties, but they managed to kill a number of bushwhackers, including stragglers and, in their frustration and fury, the wounded.

Once, after an extended skirmish, Gregg's rear guard was driven into the back of the main column. Quantrill turned the whole band and forced the enemy to retire.

Up until this moment there had been no desertions. Beset and pursued, the guerrillas believed their only hope of getting safely to Missouri was to stick together, but seeing the enemy pressing so close, Joab Perry suddenly lost his nerve. He broke from the ranks and set off in a northeasterly direction, riding a magnificent horse, with six Colt pistols stuck in his belt, and, as Gregg put it, "his long hair standing out in the Kansas breeze." Watching him go, Gregg was furious at the betrayal and wanted to kill him, but John Jarrett restrained him. "No, let him go. He will get it soon enough."

As it happened, Jarrett was wrong. Gregg commented in his memoir that Perry "made it through to Missouri, unscathed as far as bullets were concerned, however he was horseless, bootless, coatless, and with only one revolver out of the six, the remainder of his clothing torn to shreds, his flesh terribly mutilated by brush and briar." One man who saw him remarked with satisfaction that "He was the most woe-begone object I have ever beheld."

By 4:00 P.M. Gregg was exhausted and so hoarse from shouting that he could barely whisper. He asked to be relieved, and Quantrill assigned Todd to take his place.

———◆·◆———

Just before sunset the guerrillas approached Paola. They intended to cross Bull Creek, which was on the west side of Paola, at a ford, but riding to the crest of a hill they saw arrayed on the far side of the ford, which was about a mile away, a mixed force of cavalry, militia, and armed residents. Although there were fewer than one hundred men, they were strategically positioned, so that if Quantrill was to continue his course to the border, he would have to cross the stream and engage them even as the Yankees' much larger force was closing in from behind. Nevertheless, Quantrill led his band down the hill and formed a battle line. Before he could give the command to charge, however, Leland struck Todd's rear guard, driving them right into the back of the battle line. Once again Quantrill turned the band and charged up the slope. Leland was forced to retreat all the way back to Plumb's column.

Quantrill took his men back over the hill, swung north, and escaped into the heavy timber.

Major Plumb had now been in the saddle for nineteen hours, as had most of his men. Many of their horses had broken down on the march; more than half of those still alive would die over the next two days as a result of their exertions. Plumb went wearily into Paola, turning over command of the pursuit to Lieutenant Colonel Charles S. Clark.

Clark had himself arrived in Paola only a few hours earlier, having made a meandering, fifty-five-mile march from Coldwater Grove, Missouri, with thirty men, seeking the bushwhackers' whereabouts—just in time to learn that they were heading right for him. He hurriedly arrayed his own men, along with garrison cavalry troopers and citizens, for battle at the ford, but night fell before the enemy arrived. Clark did not see Quantrill turn north to avoid the ford.

Clark sent out scouts and waited. They returned at 11:00 P.M. Still Clark lingered. . . . "At 2 o'clock the following morning, having received satisfactory information as to the direction of the enemy, I got the command together and gave chase at daylight. . . ." He never explained the long delay between when his scouts reported and when he started out, a delay made all the more puzzling by the enlargement of his force: One hundred and ten militia reinforcements arrived prior to 2:00 A.M. Even so, he would have been badly outnumbered and would have been chasing in the dark a heavily armed band containing many tough fighters and expert horsemen with a motley assortment of cavalry, militia, and civilians. By waiting until morning he gave Major Plumb's troopers a much needed night's rest and thus doubled the size of his command. In the process, however, he also gave Quantrill a twelve-hour lead.

Quantrill, with Gregg by his side, led the column through Bull Creek Valley. After awhile they came to a pond, and the two men rode their horses in flank-deep. Neither had had any water since morning, so they dipped their hats in and drank gratefully. Beyond the pond was a house and a man and two women drawing water from their well, giving at least a pint to every guerrilla.

Once during the night Quantrill called an hour's halt. The men had been without sleep for more than twenty-four hours and were exhausted by the excitement of the raid and retreat. When it came time to wake them after such a brief and tantalizing respite, "all were stiff and stupid," as Connelley phrased it, and some had to be kicked into getting to their feet. They wound their slow, weary way through the darkness, once more heading east, crossing the border only a few miles from where they had entered Kansas some thirty-six hours earlier.

As the sun came up they found themselves at the headwaters of the Grand River in Cass County. Quantrill sent a few men to obtain food from nearby farmers. Everyone else unsaddled his horse and tried to stretch painfully cramped limbs. This respite proved hardly longer than the one the night before: No sooner had the food details returned than

Quantrill, looking west through a spyglass, spotted troops pouring across the state line, and an armed local sympathizer rode up to whisper a warning that twelve hundred Federals were amassed on the other side of a divide four miles to the east.

Quantrill mounted his horse and rode among his men, ordering them to "Saddle up" and warning that Kansans were approaching. Some of the men wanted to fight rather than run any farther—until they were told of the fresh Missouri troops just over the divide.

It was evident, however, even as cinches were being tightened, that many of the horses would not be able to endure another running fight: Some stood with their ears drooping and their tongues hanging out, totally exhausted, while others had become sick from drinking too much water. He decided to begin dispersing some of the band now: Those men whose mounts were in the worst shape should abandon them and take to the bush or chance hiding with them through the long day, then, after dark when they were rested, strike out for home. Approximately one hundred slipped away.

The carriage containing Bledsoe and the two wounded soldiers from Holt's company had been hauled all this way, but it would clearly be a hindrance in the desperate hours ahead. The team was unhitched and led off; the conveyance, with the three casualties still on board, was hidden in the woods.

The local's estimate of the strength of the Missouri militia proved a gross exaggeration, as Quantrill may have suspected: His men clashed with no more than 150, put them to flight, and then took off in all directions.

A short time later Colonel Clark reached the campsite. It was his hodgepodge army Quantrill had spotted through the spyglass—not only cavalrymen, militia, and Paola residents, but also some Lawrence survivors and other enraged Kansas civilians. A night's rest and a brisk morning's ride had not affected Clark's conservatism: "Finding my command, both men and horses, very much exhausted, and feeling further pursuit that day useless, I halted and spent the time picking up scattered ones that had stopped in the brush on Grand River."

The members of Clark's force were thoroughly riled and often disinclined to "pick up" a hapless guerrilla—except as one picks up a corpse to toss it into a wagon—or an open grave.

The carriage was easily discovered. The two youthful, green soldiers commenced to beg piteously for their lives. Bledsoe, probably no older than they but already a grizzled veteran of border warfare, silenced them: "Stop it! We are not entitled to mercy! We spare none and do not expect to be spared!"

He turned to the enemy. "Just take us out of this trap and put us on our knees facing you and shoot us," he said. "We are not able to stand on our feet. Let us see you. Do not shoot us from behind."

One of the executioners was White Turkey, the Delaware Indian who had entered Lawrence immediately after the raid and had been hunting Quantrill ever since. He lifted the scalps of all three and took their ears, too. (Coming upon the bodies a few hours later, Andy Blunt studied the mutilations for a moment, then said to his companions, "We had something to learn yet, boys, and we have learned it. Scalp for scalp hereafter!")

Over the next few days other raiders died cursing their murderers or praying or pleading or were as silent as stones. Some fought to the death, and a few were allowed to surrender, though their fate was too often the same as those who resisted.

Some Union officers maintained a deliberate policy of refusing to take prisoners or quickly executed those who surrendered. "I yesterday had one publicly shot," Colonel Bazel F. Lazear bragged to his wife in a letter dated September 10.

He was a prisoner we took the evening after we had the fight with Quantrell and was in the Lawrence raid. He is the second prisoner I have had shot and I will have every one of them shot I can get hold of, as such inhuman wretches deserve no mercy and should be shot down like dogs where ever found. There is more excitement in this section of the country than I have ever seen before I believe. Quantrell is in here yet with some three hundred men but they are so scattered that it is hard to find them. I shall stop writing for I have so much to do that I cannot think of nothing to write about. . . .

Kansas redlegs were not inclined to be more compassionate. Three captured guerrillas were turned over to a guard detailed by Captain George H. Hoyt. Hoyt, a redleg who in civilian life was a lawyer and had defended John Brown at Charleston, Virginia, ordered the prisoners to empty their pockets. The first man disgorged a few measly, pathetic trinkets he had taken as plunder—small toys, marbles, mouth organs, shoestrings, and buttons. Seeing the cheapness of the plunder, Hoyt was astonished. He drew his pistol.

"I will kill you for being a damned fool," he roared and shot the man dead, then dispatched the other two prisoners as well.

Chasing and fighting a 450-man guerrilla band was dangerous work, but tracking down the scattered remnants was blood sport. For a week the hunt went on. Home-guard units, redleg gangs, and civilian posses as well as cavalry troops and militia all converged on Cass and Jackson counties and fanned out, riding down roads, through fields and woods, following streambeds. They watched creek crossings and searched barns and farmhouses.

If they found a man in his own home wearing a brand-new set of clothes, they "encouraged" him to confess he had been at Lawrence, then hanged him from the rafters. Two men sitting at a kitchen table were suspect; if they reached for their guns when the door was kicked in, trying to defend hearth and home, they were shot down. Several men riding together were no less suspicious; if they could not convincingly and instantly establish their loyalty to the Union, they ended up swinging from tree branches. (Cyrus Leland hanged three so high that their feet could not be touched by a man riding beneath them. Leland nailed an order to the trunk: "Don't cut them down!") If six men were discovered lounging around a campfire or eating breakfast in a farmer's yard, they were instantly fired on; only the fleet and the lucky survived.

There is no way of determining how many of the vengefully killed Missourians had actually taken part in the raid. Some of those dispatched east of the border might have been more or less deserving of their fate—outlaws, men who had been at Lawrence, or bushwhackers who belonged to other bands. Undoubtedly, however, there were also innocent souls among the victims who happened to be in the wrong place at the wrong time . . . who had just splurged on a new suit, sat down in their own kitchens for a repast, or set out for town with a brother or a friend . . . and looked up, startled, at the sound of fast-approaching hoofbeats . . . who died of lead poisoning or a hempen necktie by dreadful mistake.

On August 27, Ewing reported to Schofield that a total of about eighty had been killed. "I think it will largely exceed 100 before any considerable part of our troops withdraw from the pursuit. No prisoners have been taken, and none will be. All houses in which Lawrence goods have been found have been destroyed, as well as the houses of known guerrillas, wherever our troops have gone."

Ewing did not explain how Lawrence plunder could be distinguished from legally purchased clothing and household goods.

In a guerrilla war, attack breeds vengeance, reprisal triggers reprisal. Those caught in the middle bear the brunt, regardless of their sympathies. When the furious bloodletting begins, few pause to ask those closest at hand which side they are on, or even if they have a side. Kansans and Missourians alike suffered in the raid and its aftermath. People died, houses and shops were burned, and a little wealth was redistributed. Some Missouri bushwhackers returned home, pockets stuffed with cash and baubles. Kansans who lived along the line of retreat came out of their houses after all the riders had passed and the dust had settled and picked up discarded plunder, emptied the pockets of bodies left lying beside the road, took the reins of the blood-splattered horses that stood nearby, cropping grass, and led them back to their own corrals.

Two bloody weeks had changed nothing. The war went on just as before.

On August 28, spies reported that Quantrill was safely in Johnson County and that Cole Younger was "on the waters of the Big Blue." Over the next few days, military units gradually broke off the hunt, one by one, as ammunition ran out or officers became discouraged. Official military reports were written, some containing proud boasts of enemy casualties, others concluding with some variation on a standard, frustrated border litany: "Finding my command, both men and horses, very much exhausted, and feeling further pursuit useless, I halted . . . and returned to camp." (No one felt more mournful and luckless than Major L. K. Thacher: "I scoured the country and woods for three days, dividing my command into small parties, and at night secreting men along the paths and roads I supposed they would pass. For two days I also searched the guerrilla haunts on the Little Blue, running into a party of two of them near Fristoe's place, capturing a revolver and horse of one of them, but to my chagrin, killed neither of them. I returned to-day, after [being] out six days and nights, having traveled over many a long and difficult mile, and having failed to accomplish what I had hoped to.")

Given the disorganized nature of the pursuit, it is not surprising that the total number of raider casualties remains a mystery. William Gregg claimed that only one man was killed during the retreat, and that just five more died after the band dispersed. These figures are absurdly low; it is obvious that Gregg was sentimentally rewriting history. Old bushwhackers, remembering the violent engagements of their youth, seem always to have been afflicted with a need to attenuate their own losses—or more often, deny they lost anyone at all—and to greatly inflate the number of enemy killed. It was a way of mystically affirming the justness of their cause, as if the righteous would always go through battle unharmed and the wicked would be slain in vast numbers.

Journal editor Dwight Thacher gleefully estimated on September 1 "that not less than from one hundred to one hundred and fifty of these outlaws have been killed since the raid on Lawrence." This number is at least closer to the truth. Eight Federal officers reported having killed a total of ninety-seven guerrillas. A ninth obstinately refused to make a distinction between the recently defunct and the merely traumatized: "We killed and wounded about 30 of them."

Still, caution is advisable. There is a natural tendency among frontline soldiers to inflate enemy casualties as a way of impressing superiors. At the same time, we do not have a count from any of the redleg bands or civilian vigilantes. Some of these would have left corpses in their wake. So the final count might be one hundred or more. After all these years there is no way of making an accurate tally; however, the low end of Thacher's range seems at least plausible.

Had Quantrill lost one hundred men, his band would have been devastated. This was not the case: In the spring, Todd, who had deposed him, resumed guerrilla operations as though nothing had happened. Undoubtedly some of Quantrill's men had been killed—especially those who volunteered for the rear guard, which took the brunt of the charges from Leland's civilians. Some of the fallen, however, might have belonged to Blunt's or Anderson's band or would have come from the ranks of Holt's green recruits. Still others would have been farmers or Missouri civilians who followed Quantrill into Kansas for plunder, only to find during the rapid retreat that their horses were too slow or their own horsemanship inadequate to keep them out of range. And, of course, many of those killed after the band scattered in Missouri may not have participated in the raid at all.

As it happened, Quantrill had no need to worry about finding replacements for whatever men he had lost. Thomas Ewing was about to become his best recruiting agent. Ewing had a conventional military mind and, like more than a few conventional soldiers who have found themselves mired in an unconventional war, thwarted and frustrated by an elusive and wily foe, he struck out at the civilian population. Like other conventional soldiers who tried such strategies, he failed to choke off support for the enemy, succeeding only in bringing disrepute on the cause he served and making himself thoroughly despised.

———————

Ewing must have known he was in trouble from the moment he received word of the incursion. It will be recalled that he had spent the night of August 20 at Fort Leavenworth, and, because the telegraph office was closed from 11:00 P.M. to 8:00 A.M., he did not receive the warning dispatches until 10:45 A.M. on the twenty-first. There was no cavalry stationed at the fort, and the available militia companies, being in transit to Fort Laramie, were unarmed. Ewing had arms and horse equipment issued at once and started out at 1:00 P.M. with three hundred men, heading south through eastern Kansas. His force marched to Leavenworth City and then to the Kansas River; it took five hours to find enough boats to carry his men across the river, and then he pushed on through De Soto to Lanesfield. By now it was near daybreak, and the men were exhausted—four had died of sunstroke that day, one lieutenant keeling over dead as he dismounted to rest. Ewing, feeling he could travel faster alone, left the command and hurried on. He reached Quantrill's Grand River camp after dark, more than twelve hours since the band had dispersed.

There was nothing more Ewing could do that night—except rendezvous with Jim Lane. The two men faced off in a log cabin. Lane was furious, absolutely wild. He blamed the Lawrence massacre on Ewing's "milk-and-water administration." He swore to go to Washington and have Ewing removed.

Ewing was not timid or cowardly, but he suffered from an equally lamentable personality trait: overweening ambition. Aspiring to have a political career in Kansas after the war and knowing Lane's power in the state and his connections in Washington and how badly, therefore, Lane could damage him, Ewing composed a lengthy decree on the spot. (It seems likely that Ewing had been contemplating such an order for some time. It was in keeping with the thinking of Schofield and some other Union generals and was a logical successor to Order No. 10.) As Lane read it, he was mollified. Beneath all the lawyerly exactitude and tortuous wording, Ewing was requiring nothing less than the depopulation of nearly three thousand square miles of western Missouri. Ewing and Lane left the cabin together. In the yard, with his aides and supporters as witnesses, Lane felt compelled to threaten Ewing one more time.

"You are a dead dog, if you fail to issue that order," he told him, then rode away.

Three days later, on August 25, newspapers published Ewing's General Order No. 11:

I. All persons living in Jackson, Cass and Bates Counties, Missouri, and in that part of Vernon included in this District, except those living within one mile of the limits of Independence, Hickman's Mills, Pleasant Hill and Harrisonville, and except those in that part of Kaw Township, Jackson County, north of Brush Creek and west of the Big Blue, are hereby ordered to remove from their present places of residence within fifteen days from the date hereof.

Those who, within that time establish their loyalty to the satisfaction of the commanding officer of the military station nearest their present places of residence, will receive from him certificates stating the fact of their loyalty and the names of witnesses by whom it can be shown. All who receive such certificates will be permitted to remove to any military station in this district, or to any part of the state of Kansas except the Counties on the eastern border of the state. All others shall remove out of this District. Officers commanding companies and detachments serving in the counties named, will see that this paragraph is promptly obeyed.

II. All grain and hay in the field or under shelter, in the district from which the inhabitants are required to remove, within reach of military stations, will be taken to such stations, and turned over to the proper officers there; and report of the amount so turned over made to District Head-Quarters specifying the names of all loyal owners and the amount of such produce taken from them. All grain and hay found in such District after the 9th day of September next, not convenient to such stations, will be destroyed. . . .

In the months ahead Lane would campaign to have General Schofield replaced and would give speeches on the border waving the bloody shirt, calling for reprisals against Missourians, but he kept what in effect was his part of the bargain: He rarely criticized General Thomas Ewing.

Many other people had no such compunction. Ewing was accused of "Copperheadism" and inefficiency, of being a "do nothing" and a "let alone," and of showing a damnable leniency toward the traitors that permitted the Lawrence massacre. A mendacious rumor spread—and was eagerly picked up by the St. Louis *Missouri Democrat*—that the general's own soldiers were so angered by his milksop policies that they stoned his headquarters. As for Order No. 11, hardly had it been issued than the editor of the St. Louis *Missouri Republican* thunderously pronounced it "inhuman, unmanly, barbarous. There may be guilty persons in the counties named, but to issue such a mandate is to depopulate all that section of country. This order ought never to have been issued, and we hope it has been rescinded."

Ewing, of course, had no intention of rescinding it, and his supporters rushed to his defense. On September 2, the officers and men of Company G, 11th Kansas Volunteers, wrote to the editor of the Leavenworth *Daily Conservative*, castigating him for his "efforts to traduce and malign one of the most efficient officers in the Department of the Missouri." They intimated none too subtly that Ewing's critics were giving "aid and comfort to the enemy by counteracting the efforts of the commander to suppress the outlaws and guerrillas that have infested the border of our State since the commencement of this rebellion." The letter bore fifty-two signatures.

Two days later the "Union men of Kansas City, Mo., and Loyal Refugees from the counties of Jackson, Cass, Bates and Vernon" held a meeting and passed a series of resolutions praising Ewing as "eminently just, vigilant and correct" and affirming the propriety of the controversial order: "the only true policy for this section [of the state] . . . no loyal man has been injured by it."

General Frank Blair, home on leave from Sherman's army, joined the raging debate. He told a St. Louis crowd that Ewing was responsible for failing to thwart "that hellish and diabolical scheme of Quantrell to destroy the people of Lawrence." Ewing had become so "excited and unmanned" by his mistake that he sought to cover it up by condemning "one entire slice of the State of Missouri, thirty-five miles deep, to devastation, rapine and plunder. It is the subterfuge of an imbecile."

Blair and the St. Louis editors were a long way from western Missouri, but the publisher of the Lexington *Union* lived in Lafayette County. The proximity to the border had evidently made him paranoid. He held that Ewing was "only the tool of Lane." The senator was "leagued with his old acquaintance, Quantrell, to rob the people of Missouri and kill off his enemies in Kansas; [he] has, at the same time, killed Gen. Ewing."

Ewing was far from dead. His greatest supporter was T. Dwight Thacher. The editor was unequivocally certain that Order No. 11 was an absolute necessity. Its enforcement, he predicted on September 1, "will soon leave the guerrillas no places of rendezvous—no recruiting places—no resident spies. They must depend solely upon themselves and the brush, and if an active campaign is kept up against them, they must soon be driven out or exterminated."

———◆◆◆———

Cass County had ten thousand residents on the day Ewing's order took effect. Fifteen days later fewer than six hundred remained. Altogether, more than twenty thousand people were displaced from the western Missouri counties.

Most of the good horses had been requisitioned by Union troops or stolen by redlegs, jayhawkers, or bushwhackers, so deportees mounted bony nags, mules, or oxen. Others, wrote historian Lew Larkin,

> traveled in oxcarts and rickety wagons, improvised conveyances of two off-sized wheels on either side of large, reinforced crates, and in other contraptions that defied description.
>
> The moving vehicles contained clothing and a few other possessions, or whatever they could hastily get together, and babies and old people who could not walk. Youngsters of six years and older, men and women able to walk, stumbled alongside the vehicular oddities.

Sometimes a family would set out alone, but often neighbors banded together to form wagon trains and welcomed strangers to join their ranks. They headed north, east, or south for Missouri counties unaffected by the proclamation. Prosperous Unionists went back to their former homes in the eastern states, but the poorer ones were forced to live squalidly in shanties near military posts. Southerners drifted toward

Kentucky, Tennessee, or Texas. Some desperate souls gambled on Kansas and crossed the line.

None of this conveys the misery and sorrow of the exile.

"I can affirm, from painful personal observation, that the sufferings of the unfortunate victims were in many instances such as should have elicited sympathy even from hearts of stones," wrote George Caleb Bingham in 1877.

As soon as he had read Ewing's order, Bingham left his state treasurer's office in Jefferson City and traveled west by buggy and river steamer to the general's Kansas City headquarters, where he tried to convince him to rescind the edict. Ewing refused and got into a loud argument with Bingham. Ewing finally shouted for Bingham to get out of his office. "If you persist in executing this order, I will make you infamous by my pen and brush as far as I am able," Bingham told the general before he left.

Instead of promptly returning to Jefferson City, he headed south to witness firsthand the terrible suffering and devastation. For the rest of his life he would bitterly remember what he saw.

Bare-footed and bare-headed women and children, stripped of every article of clothing except a scant covering for their bodies, were exposed to the heat of an August sun and compelled to struggle through the dust on foot. All their means of transportation had been seized by their spoilers, except an occasional dilapidated cart, or an old and superannuated horse, which were necessarily appropriated to the use of the aged and infirm.

It is well-known that men were shot down in the very act of obeying the order, and their wagons and effects seized by their murderers. Large trains of wagons, extending over the prairies for miles in length, and moving Kansasward, were freighted with every description of household furniture and wearing apparel belonging to the exiled inhabitants. Dense clouds of smoke arising in every direction marked the conflagrations of dwellings. . . . The banished inhabitants . . . crowded by hundreds upon the banks of the Missouri River, and were indebted to the charity of benevolent steamboat conductors for transportation to places of safety. . . .

Even tough-minded Colonel Bazel Lazear, who had unhesitatingly shot captured bushwhackers, was appalled. "It is heartsickening to see what I have seen," he wrote his wife. "A desolated country and women and children, some of them all most naked. Some on foot and some in old wagons. Oh God."

Enforcement was assigned to militia units; their ranks held many Kansans and Missouri Unionists whose families had been victims of bushwhackers or had lived for years in fear. These men went about their business with unbridled enthusiasm. Redleg bands and Kansas civilians quickly joined in, looting and burning with undisguised glee.

They swooped down on farmhouses, stealing money, jewelry, and livestock from the occupants, then ignited the buildings. If the place had already been abandoned, they hurriedly set fire to it and raced to the next house, hoping to catch the hapless residents before they could get their possessions together and flee. The enforcers did not practice economic discrimination: "With systematic destruction," observed Larkin, "the torch was applied to the one-room cabin, the clapboard house, the porticoed mansion and to the barn, the smokehouse, and all outbuildings." Fires spread across open fields and through dry woods, blackening vast stretches of landscape. The air grew hazy with smoke. This bleak terrain would be referred to for decades as the "Burnt District."

Since many of the young men were away serving in the Union or Confederate army or had joined guerrilla bands, those who were shot down tended to be harmless old men or mature upright citizens, valued members of their communities: physicians, judges, merchants, ministers, and missionaries.

Redlegs struck the John Cave farm, which was near Lone Jack. Cave and some other menfolk were loading wagons, intending to leave the area in the morning. Cave's daughter, Matilda Ann, watched the men being led away: In addition to Cave there were two of her uncles, William and David Hunter; a cousin, Andy Owsley; and two neighbors, Cal Tate and Ben Potter. The redlegs marched them only a short distance, then shot them.

The Hunter brothers' ancient father dug a wide shallow grave. He placed the six corpses side by side, covered them with quilts, put a pillow beneath each head, and said a brief prayer. The heartsick survivors then set out on their sad journey.

Frances Twyman and her family joined a column heading west. Forty-seven years later she still remembered the many children who piteously cried for bread or to "be taken back to their homes." One woman had stowed her children in an ox-drawn wagon. When the wagon neared a bridge over a stream, the oxen, sensing water, started running, and the woman lost control of the team. "It looked like the wagon would turn a somersault over the oxen," recalled Mrs. Twyman. "We all thought the children would be killed, but Providence watched over them." After the near tragedy, the mother stood alone and helpless, weeping and wringing her hands, and cursing the Federals.

Another woman had two cows hitched to a wagon; a little boy was leading them. There were some boughs on the wagon, an old-time coverlid stretched over them. Inside the wagon was a very sick child. The wagon halted, the mother got out with her sick babe in her arms and seated herself under the friendly shade of a tree. It was apparent to all that the child was dying. There sat the mother with her child dying in her lap; her husband had been killed, she was forced to leave her home, driven out into the cold world with her children. O, the anguish of that broken hearted mother as she sat there, with tears streaming down her pale cheeks, knowing she was powerless to save her child. Some kind-hearted people of the neighborhood came to her assistance. The crowd surged on, women and children dragging their weary limbs through the dust and heat.

Gradually the caravan split up, some people going to Lafayette and Saline counties, while others, like the Twymans, went to Howard County. By November all the Twymans were terribly homesick and decided to move to Missouri City, Clay County, "just across the river from our home." Three adults—including Frances's feeble seventy-two-year-old mother—and six children piled into a two-horse buggy and traveled northwest through Saline, Carroll, and Ray counties. The weather was bad—near-constant snow and sleet—and no one would give them shelter at night; they tried to rent rooms, even outbuildings, and were turned away. They managed to reach Missouri City, but then the eldest daughter, Julia, sixteen years old, sickened and died. "The hardships we had to endure under Order No. 11 were too much for one of her delicate nature," Mrs. Frances Twyman wrote in 1913. "She was my only daughter. She was too pure for this earth."

Twenty-five-year-old Laura Harris, who lived near Westport, had a husband in the Confederate army. After his discharge, he was persecuted by Unionists until he slipped away and joined Quantrill.

"Into my wagon I loaded one hoarded feather bed, two pairs of pillows and an old trunk, a prized object brought from Virginia by my parents," Mrs. Laura Harris Bridges told a Kansas City *Star* reporter in 1929. Mrs. Bridges, who was two days shy of her ninety-first birthday, said the trunk contained "a few bare necessities in the way of cooking utensils, etc." She put her own small son in the wagon, along with two neighbors, eighty-four-year-old Buckner Muir and his blind son, Sam, who was fifty-six. She hitched up a team of horses and joined a column of sixty-one women and children headed for Texas. Mrs. James Cabness, who as a little girl had been in the same column, remembered that "Everyday or two Yankee soldiers would unload our wagons in search of something to steal. They said they were hunting firearms." Still, the refugees trudged south, subsisting on sweet potatoes and cornbread.

Not far from Clinton, Missouri, which was southwest of Sedalia, they encountered three hundred redlegs. Despite the fact that they were now in Henry County and were therefore outside the area affected by Order No. 11, the Kansans stole all the stock but a single team of horses. They also scattered on the ground whatever food they decided they did not want.

"We were in sorry circumstances and began to look around for some means of locomotion," said Mrs. Bridges.

I started out with several others on foot. About a mile away, to my joy, I ran across my old crippled, blind mare, which the robbers had taken, but left along the road. I suppose because she was blind and maimed. Some of the party found a farmer who had a team of oxen.

We traded what few belongings we had left for the team and several other teams until we had enough to hook our wagons. Try as we would we could not drive the oxen. Since the lead oxen were hitched to my wagon, I was compelled to lead them every step [of the way].

This pitiful little group made five miles a day all the way to Van Buren, Arkansas, where they stopped for a brief rest. Kindly local people replenished their stock of provisions. They resumed their meandering trek, frequently wandering off course and being forced to retrace their steps. Having passed through the Cherokee Nation "into the arid country to the south," they were horrified to find their water supply exhausted.

The third day out, when all of us were about famished and I was the only one who had a drop of water in my keg, the oxen began to bawl and run. We knew this meant there was water close at hand. God must have been with us for we had gone scarcely a mile when we stumbled on a large shallow hole in the earth filled with water. Millions of flies and mosquitoes were hovering over the water, which had a green scum over it, but at that, nothing has ever looked so good to me.

The greatest misfortune of all happened soon after continuing our journey. Thomas Walton, 3 years old, a member of the party, became ill with membranous croup. His condition grew worse, and though we chanced to meet an Indian doctor, who treated him, he soon died. He was a favorite of us all and we could not bear to bury him in that wasteland. One of the women offered the sideboards of her wagon, another a sheet, and with these crude materials we fashioned a coffin and placed the little body in it and the coffin in my wagon.

They went on to Boggy Depot, where they encountered a Confederate detachment. The soldiers provided a metal casket and buried the child "with full military honors in respect to his father, a lieutenant colonel in the Confederate army."

One night shortly thereafter everyone was awakened by a rebel yell. Mrs. Bridges's husband and Dick Yeager—who had a wife among the company—rode into camp. The next day the column reached Salt Springs, Texas, where her husband procured a mule so she could ride. She took her son to a farm near Dallas, where they remained until the war's end. Even there she was not safe from tragedy: "My husband was killed June 29, 1865." She returned to Jackson County, accompanying her sister and brother-in-law. "My sole possessions were a wagon or two and some loose stock." As the result of the postwar chaos, "the trip back was made under even worse conditions than the trip out."

───── ◆ ─────

Ewing's political enemies plotted against him, but to no immediate effect: Two months after he issued Order No. 11 the whole of Kansas was added to his district. Dwight Thacher asserted increased authority was "a handsome recognition of that officer's able and successful administration of affairs on the border, and [it] shows just how much weight the partisans' clamor raised against him had with the President." Thacher went on to assess enthusiastically the general's accomplishments.

If we contrast the condition of the border now, with what it was when General Ewing came here, we can see at a glance how successful he has been. At the time of his advent, not only the border, but the entire State of Kansas was overrun with organized bands of horse-thieves, who were having things pretty much their own way. The farmers of Kansas could hardly keep stock enough to till their farms. General Ewing suppressed this with a strong hand. He dispersed the bands, restored the property which they had taken, and broke up their places of rendezvous. Now, although there are occasional instances of theft, as there always are, and more numerous in times of war, still the great public evil of open, notorious, barefaced stealing, has been broken up.

Again, the bushwhacking troubles were at their height when General Ewing came among us. Quantrell, Todd, Parker and the various gangs, had obtained a firm foothold, and were carrying terror all over the border. The dense summer foliage hid them from pursuit, and their operations of murder and robbery had grown into a perfect system. General Ewing at once commenced an active campaign against them, and in three months time he has driven them from the border.

Thacher was being overly optimistic about the bushwhackers, of course, but during his tenure Ewing did reduce horse thievery and gave the guerrillas some frantic moments. These accomplishments would have ensured him little lasting renown after the war ended, but Order No. 11 would make his name despised in western Missouri for generations.

There was yet another bureaucratic reshuffling on January 1, 1864, this one to Ewing's detriment: Secretary of War Edwin M. Stanton announced the creation of the Department of Kansas, which was also to include Colorado, Nebraska, and the Indian Territory; General Samuel R. Curtis was placed in command. Ewing was left in charge of only the Missouri portion of his District of the Border, but even this was quickly taken from him: On January 8, Schofield incorporated the Missouri remnant into the District of Central Missouri and ordered Ewing to report to General Curtis for reassignment.

On January 14, Brigadier General Egbert Brown, who had been given command of the border counties affected by Order No. 11 and who disapproved of it, issued an order permitting all persons not actively "disloyal or unworthy" to return to their homes. Nearly all of those who had been driven from Bates, Vernon, and Cass counties remained in exile until the end of the war, but some Jackson County residents came back, including a number of Southerners.

At the end of the month, Lincoln replaced Schofield with General William S. Rosecrans. Schofield may have been relieved; he had been agitating for a field command. He remarked in his memoir that "I had always longed for purely military service in the field, free from political complications." He was sent to join Sherman in Tennessee. "I left [Missouri] without regret and with buoyant hopes of a more satisfactory service in a purely military field." Unfortunately, Sherman's generals were given to bickering, quarreling, back-stabbing, infighting, and glory-hunting. Despite these distractions, Schofield managed to distinguish himself, as one historian put it, "by his efficient handling of the Army of Ohio and by his important victory over Hood at Franklin."

On February 28, 1864, Curtis assigned Ewing to the command of the Colorado Territory, a move clearly calculated to exile him from Kansas politics. Ewing appealed to friends in high places, and twenty-one days later the War Department ordered him to report to General Rosecrans, who placed him in command of the District of St. Louis.

By May, Colonel Ford, commander of Union forces in Jackson County, complained that it "is full of bushwhackers, and they have friends all through the country who furnish them with food. . . . I am satisfied that there are many families that are feeding them that have proved their loyalty. . . ."

Thus, ironically, despite all the suffering and economic dislocation Order No. 11 caused, it was negated less than six months after being issued and thus never fulfilled its purpose: to drive the guerrillas permanently from western Missouri.

"No greater act of imbecility was committed in Missouri during the whole Civil War than the issuing and executing of (Order No. 11)," argued historian Eugene Morrow Violette in 1918. Forty-five years later Dr. Castel, in an essay published by the *Missouri Historical Review,* observed that

> Order No. 11 was the most drastic and repressive military measure directed against civilians by the Union Army during the Civil War. In fact, with the exception of the hysteria-motivated herding of Japanese-Americans into concentration camps during World War II, it stands as the harshest treatment ever imposed on United States citizens under the plea of military necessity in our nation's history.

CHAPTER 11

"Brave Men and True Were Scattered and Strewn over the Ground": The Baxter Springs Massacre

Order No. 11 had rendered the fall an inauspicious season for bush-whacking. While it had not reduced the bushwhackers to starvation—released livestock roamed the landscape and hams and bacon hung in unburned smokehouses—it had deprived them of something nearly as crucial as food to guerrilla fighters: civilian support. There was no one to nurse or conceal them or to resupply them with blankets, clothing, and ammunition; lacking the intelligence reports of informants, they were dangerously ignorant of Federal troop movements. With the civilian population gone, any man abroad could safely be assumed to be a rebel and dealt with accordingly.

The burning of so many cornfields and woods meant that vast stretches of country had been denuded, greatly reducing hiding places and locations for secluded ambush. The Yankees, still furious over the Lawrence massacre and their failure to run down the raiders during the retreat, seized the advantage and aggressively hunted their quarry. They constantly patrolled the roads, followed streams and creeks looking for camps, and scouted the hills. Most guerrillas still managed to elude them, but now and then the Federals' diligence was rewarded and they succeeded in wounding and capturing a man or killing one outright. More often they surprised a small cluster of bushwhackers sitting around a fire, putting them to instant, ignominious flight and forcing them to abandon cooking utensils, food, precious ammunition, and—perhaps just as valuable with winter nigh—clothing and blankets.

"So the villains are being picked off daily, one by one, and sometimes in large numbers," Dwight Thacher noted cheerily. "They cannot run far now-a-days without meeting a squad of soldiers." He was exaggerating the frequency and number of deaths, but no man was safe on the open road and no camp was secure for very long. Quantrill was as harried and vulnerable as the rest.

On September 15, Captain C. F. Coleman, on a sweep through the Snibar Hills, picked up a trail of horses' hoofprints and followed it to Quantrill's own camp. In a report written that very evening, Coleman's superior, Colonel William Weer, stated that Coleman "promptly attacked" the camp, "killed two of the guerrillas, captured some forty horses, destroyed all their substance stores, including some flour recently stolen from a citizen, all their bedding, clothing, ammunition, and some arms. The enemy fired but one volley, and at once disappeared in the thick underwood, where pursuit was impossible."

Weer was ecstatic: "The effect of this surprise is most damaging to the designs of Quantrell in making another raid upon Kansas."

Widespread rumors to the contrary, Quantrill was too busy trying to stay out of enemy clutches to contemplate another foray across the line. He frequently moved his camp, always under the cover of darkness. While temporarily ensconced near Wellington he felt safe enough to send for Kate King. One day shortly after she arrived a Federal patrol rode right by the camp without noticing it. Quantrill hurriedly assembled forty men and started out to surprise the foe. However, he soon had second thoughts and turned back: An attack would only reveal his presence in the area and intensify the hunt.

He soon established a new camp at the Stanley farm, but the Federals quickly picked up the trail again. He and Kate were in a one-room log cabin socializing with Todd and his latest mistress when pickets spotted cavalry in the distance and sounded the alarm. The two women were quickly put on fleet horses and sent on their way. The guerrillas then saddled up and took off before the camp was struck.

Quantrill next tried a site on the east fork of the Little Blue, then bivouacked at Joe Dillingham's farm. It proved an admirable hideout because it could be approached only by one route and so was easily guarded. The men sent out at night for provisions and forage were careful to cover their tracks, and for the brief time that Quantrill lingered in the camp, the Yankees did not discover it.

Under other circumstances Quantrill might have tarried on the border for another four or five weeks, collecting loot and creating havoc, but rather than remain like a badger in a burrow, he passed the word that his men should rendezvous on September 30 at Captain Perdee's farm, which was situated on the Blackwater River in Johnson County.

Four hundred to five hundred men answered Quantrill's call—bushwhackers and embittered male civilians set adrift by the enforcement of Order No. 11, Confederate deserters, and newly mustered-out Confederate veterans. Colonel Holt also arrived with his recruits, having been unable to get out of Missouri because of stepped-up Federal patrols.

"Quantrill then bore a commission as colonel from some Confederate authority, perhaps General Sterling Price, possibly Thomas C. Reynolds, Confederate governor of Missouri," wrote Connelley. "At the rendezvous was organized the First Regiment, First Brigade, Army of the South, and Quantrill as colonel was put in command." Connelley's willingness to believe Quantrill had a colonelcy is an extremely rare act of generosity toward his subject. In fact, as will be seen shortly, neither Price nor Reynolds gave Quantrill a colonelcy, and there is recently uncovered evidence casting serious doubt on Quantrill's ever having been commissioned a colonel by any military or governmental authority. It is true, however, that the men at the rendezvous organized the "First Regiment, First Brigade, Army of the South" and that "Colonel" Quantrill was in command. On the morning of October 2, shortly before dawn, he started the column south. Near Carthage he swung west and entered Kansas, then went south by rapid marches on the Fort Scott-Fort Gibson Road.

Four days later, on the morning of October 6, an advance under Dave Pool captured two Federals who were driving a mule-drawn wagon loaded with lumber. They told Pool they were assigned to the military post at Baxter Springs. This was surprising news—neither Pool nor Quantrill nor, apparently, anyone else in the 1st Regiment knew of the fort. Pool had the teamsters killed, dispatched a picket to alert Quantrill, and set out to investigate.

Actually, Fort Blair, such as it was, had been built only the previous July. It sat on the north slope of a hollow through which ran a creek, and it had originally consisted of nothing more than a square-shaped dirt-

and-log embankment, each wall being four feet high and one hundred feet long. Lieutenant James B. Pond had arrived on October 4 with reinforcements. On the morning of October 6, the entrenchment being too small to house the additional troops, Pond had the west wall taken down so that the north and south walls could be elongated. He inadvertently further increased the post's vulnerability by sending out a foraging party—eight wagons and sixty cavalry troops, which was all the men with serviceable mounts he had. The remaining garrison consisted of only forty-five dismounted white troopers and fifty black infantrymen. Twenty of the whites were on sick call that morning, felled by "intermittent fever" or the prospect of hard work. They lay in tents inside the stockade. Never was malingering more fortunate: When the attack came they were within easy reach of their weapons.

After the picket relayed Pool's message, Quantrill sent Gregg and his company to support Pool, and then, intending to attack the fort from the north, led the main column off the road and into the woods, where, lacking a guide, he quickly became lost. While he was trying to get his bearings, Pool was making his approach to Fort Blair through the timber to the east; Gregg joined him, taking the right flank. A more perfect setup for a surprise attack could hardly be imagined. The foraging party had been ordered to scout the area, and since no warning had been sent back to Pond, it was assumed that there was no danger. The men were casually eating lunch, most of them clustered around the kitchen tent on the creek bank, the rest scattered in small groups around the clearing, their rifles stacked in neat rows in the center of the fortification. Lieutenant Pond was dining alone in his tent two hundred yards west of the fort. The only piece of artillery was a twelve-pound mountain howitzer, which sat outside the north wall. Pond had brought it with him from Fort Scott, but neither he nor anyone else presently in camp had received instructions in its operation.

It was high noon. One moment there were only the sounds of soft laughter and the hum of pleasant conversation; an instant later, the air was filled with gunfire, hoofbeats, and hoarse cries. Pond burst out of his tent, saw the guerrillas charging, and sprinted for the fort, shouting for his men to rally there. The enemy closed the distance so fast that Pond and some of the others had to run between their horses. Pond had the farthest to go; when he reached the stockade, he found many of his men already inside—but just as many bushwhackers had galloped in, too. Bullets whizzed in every direction, thumping against the logs. The soldiers acted courageously, firing their rifles, refusing to panic. The blacks in particular "fought like devils," Pond noted proudly. "Thirteen of them were wounded [in] the first round, and not one but fought the thing through." The guerrillas were quickly driven out.

When Pond saw some of them forming a battle line for another charge, he dashed for the howitzer, calling over his shoulder for men to follow him. "Whether the men heard me or not I am unable to say, as the volleys of musketry and the yells of the enemy nearly drowned every other noise," Pond wrote in his report, "but none came to my assistance." He worked the howitzer alone and managed to fire three salvos, which landed in the foes' ranks, throwing them into confusion and breaking their line. They hastily retreated up the slope. Gregg, who had become separated from the rest, chasing down some Yankees who had run away from the fight, rode off to find Quantrill, leaving Pool to deal with the fort.

Artillery—even a lone, light field howitzer—is a formidable psychological weapon against cavalry, and, with the Federals in the entrenchment putting up a withering fire, Pool was disinclined to make another charge. He had his men keep up a desultory firefight with the soldiers and waited for Quantrill to arrive.

Quantrill was otherwise occupied. At this moment he was, in fact, busily engaged in slaughtering the cavalry escort of General James G. Blunt.

On October 4, Blunt, who, it will be recalled, was commander of the District of the Frontier, received dispatches at Fort Scott informing him that a superior Confederate force was threatening to lay siege to Fort Smith, Arkansas, some 150 miles to the south. "I immediately left for that post, accompanied by a part of my staff, and taking with me the records, papers, and property belonging to the headquarters of the district," he wrote in his official report, dated October 19. "My escort consisted of Company I, Third Wisconsin Cavalry, and Company A, Fourteenth Kansas, about 100 men (all the available mounted men that could be spared from this post)." The entourage also included the brigade band, which rode in a specially constructed wagon, and several civilians, notably James O'Neal, artist-correspondent for *Leslie's Weekly,* and Lydia Stevens Thomas, wife of Captain Chester Thomas, quartermaster of Fort Gibson. Mrs. Thomas, who rode in her own top buggy pulled by a fine pair of dapple gray mares, had hurriedly left her home in Topeka and was frantically trying to reach her gravely ill husband.

At noon Blunt's column arrived at a point some four hundred yards north of Fort Blair. Knowing that he was close to the fort but unaware that it was under siege at that very moment—because the fight was being waged in a hollow and there were heavy woods between the fort and his position, the sounds of gunfire were muffled—he called a halt so that the train could close up. He ordered the bandwagon to be brought to the head of the column; he had only recently secured the band and a new flag, and presumably he wanted to make a showy entrance into the camp with colors flying to the blaring accompaniment of martial music.

After fifteen minutes, everything was ready: The bandwagon was in place; the musicians had their instruments and their music out. Blunt had just given the forward command when Quantrill, who was still disoriented, wandered out of the woods east of Blunt's position.

By one account Blunt was dressed in civilian attire and had been riding "in a carriage behind a pair of beautiful dun horses with docked tails, and beside him on the seat of the carriage was a five gallon demijohn of brandy, with which to treat his friends." When he saw Quantrill's force, it is said, he had to hastily call for a horse. In his official report set down thirteen days after the massacre and in his memoir, written in 1866, he made no mention of such potentially embarrassing details, but in the latter document he did note that he had been quite ill during the summer and fall and "confined to my bed" for an unspecified period ending September 12, on which date he was still so weak he was only "able to ride in a carriage."

In any case, since the bushwhackers were wearing Federal uniforms, some of Blunt's officers thought they were a welcoming party sent out from Fort Blair. The general himself "supposed them to be Lt. Pond's cavalry on drill," but as he watched they formed a ragged line and advanced at a walk. He estimated that they were one hundred strong. Closing to three hundred yards they halted, "and my first suspicion of their being an enemy was aroused by seeing several men, supposed to be officers, riding hurriedly up and down their line, and apparent confusion among the men." A Union cavalry troop would have been better trained, far more disciplined, and, hopefully, more competently led.

Blunt ordered the escort to form a line facing east—Company A of the 14th Kansas on the right, and Company I of the 3rd Wisconsin on the left. He also "sent the wagons, with the band, clerks, orderlies, cooks, and other non-combatants to the rear" and rode forward himself to "reconnoiter and endeavor to ascertain to a certainty what the approaching force was." Fifty yards in front of his own line he heard for the first time "a brisk firing of musketry" coming from the south and understood that Pond was under attack.

More mounted men came out of the woods and formed a second line. He thought there might be two hundred in the second line—that made three hundred on the prairie before him. He had only sixty-five green recruits in the line behind him, the remaining thirty-five making up the rear guard. As he watched, the first line of guerrillas resumed their advance, still at a walk.

At two hundred yards they commenced firing.

Two Kansans from Company A wheeled their horses and started to run. Major Henry Z. Curtis and the other officers drove them back into line, but before the officers could return to their places the two turned and ran again—along with eight others.

Quantrill, seeing the line beginning to break, shouted, "Charge!" His men loosed a high-pitched rebel yell and spurred their horses.

The rest of the Kansans took flight. For a few wild heartbeats longer, Company I held the line, twenty-five facing three hundred, then they tore after the rest.

Blunt turned in his saddle to order his men to fire . . . and saw "with shame and humiliation" that "the whole line [was] broken, and all of them in full gallop over the prairie, completely panic-stricken."

Blunt, on a fleet horse, raced back and joined Curtis in trying to halt and rally the troops. It was no use.

The bushwhackers, as always mounted on superior horses, quickly closed the distance and selected individual targets, riding down on them and shooting them at close range. They were like long-taloned, piercing-eyed falcons swooping down on fat pigeons.

Thirty Federals tumbled out of the saddle in the first few minutes alone. Eighty-two went down, dead or wounded, in a quarter hour. "They killed our men as fast as they caught them, sparing none," Lieutenant Colonel Charles W. Blair complained bitterly. A headquarters clerk was more succinct: "It was simply a Butchery."

The first line had swept past Curtis and Blunt. The second line neared.

"My God, what shall we do?" Curtis cried.

"Sell out the best you can," a lad near him advised, "but don't be taken prisoner."

Curtis galloped west on a parallel course with General Blunt. They soon came to a wide, deep gully. The general's horse made the leap, but the rebound threw Blunt out of the saddle. He rode for a mile clinging desperately to the animal's neck before righting himself.

Curtis was not so lucky. His horse was tensing to spring over the gully when it was shot in the hip. The wound was superficial, but the animal was knocked off balance, threw his rider over his head, and fell into the gully. The horse then managed to clamber back out of the gully and ran frantically over the plain.

A bushwhacker had pursued Curtis across the prairie because, as one eyewitness explained, "the major was dressed in a very fine Staff Officers Uniform & rode a large Grey horse making quite a conspicuous figure in the mix up. . . ." Curtis handed over his revolver as a gesture of surrender, as if that would save him. The guerrilla fired the revolver, putting a bullet into the major's temple.

"I've killed Blunt! I've killed the old son of a bitch!" the murderer shouted, assuming the glorious uniform connoted command.

The cry was taken up by others nearby and spread across the field of carnage. "We've killed Blunt!" "The son of a bitch is dead!"

Sergeant Jack Splane also tried to surrender. As soon as he handed over his arms, his captors fired a fusillade, striking him five times. As Splane lay with bullets in his head, chest, bowels, an arm, and a leg, he heard one assailant say, "Tell old God that the last man you saw on earth was Quantrell." He passed out but survived.

Private Jesse Smith, shot several times, lay facedown, feigning death. The act was utterly convincing: His attacker danced a jig on his "corpse," shouting curses.

Lieutenant A. W. Farr was riding in a carriage at the time of the attack. Unarmed, he jumped out of the conveyance and tried to escape on foot. His body was found riddled with bullets and buckshot.

Trooper Frank Arnold had been shot five times in the face. He lay all day hardly daring to breathe. After dark he stumbled into the fort, his countenance so disfigured that the post surgeon, Dr. W. H. Warner, would say it "could not be recognized as belonging to a human being."

———◆———

As the men of the 14th Kansas streamed past, the drivers of the supply wagons and ambulances wheeled their teams and lashed them westward. The bandwagon driver, however, chose a southwesterly course. One of Quantrill's men, William Bledsoe, who was fat and jovial, rode up beside the wagon and demanded its surrender. He was shot out of the saddle. Todd, Gregg, and twenty others gave chase. After only fifty yards the left front wheel ran off the axle, tipping over the wagon and spilling everyone out.

The musicians—some of whom were German—were wearing "elegant uniforms with fancy swords and revolvers," said Dr. Warner. However, he stressed that the side arms were "made not for fighting, but for show," and the musicians were "nonbelligerents." As the bushwhackers rode up, the musicians all waved their handkerchiefs as token of surrender. The delicate gesture was futile. Bledsoe had been extremely popular and was deeply loved by everybody. Just before his friends opened fire, Todd raged at the musicians, demanding to know why they had not waved their kerchiefs at Bledsoe.

In addition to the fourteen musicians, the wagon had also contained correspondent O'Neal, a teamster, a twelve-year-old drummer boy, and the band leader, a German named George Pellage. They all were killed except the drummer boy, who was severely wounded and passed out. O'Neal's fine civilian clothes were removed, and the other bodies were searched and thrown into the wagon or under it. Then matches were applied.

The little drummer boy came to in the midst of flames. He "crawled a distance of 30 yards," reported Major Benjamin S. Henning, "marking the course by bits of burning clothes and scorched grass, and was found dead with all his clothes burned off except the portion between his back and the ground as he lay upon his back."

———— ◆ ————

When Trooper Charles H. Davis, who was Mrs. Thomas's driver, saw the rout begin, he had turned the carriage to the west and whipped the horses.

"What are we going to do?" Mrs. Thomas cried.

"Get away from here if we can," he told her, and added that she should lay down on the floor. She complied, slipping under the seat with her head next to the dashboard. A reporter who interviewed Davis years later wrote that "[he] got on his knees and leaned far over the dashboard, with his head down as low as he could get it, arms extended, his left hand grasping the reins, his right plying the whip, and the horses running at full speed."

Several bushwhackers gave chase. The buggy's top was up, so they could not see that a woman was inside; they riddled it with bullets, but neither Mrs. Thomas nor Trooper Davis were hit. The buggy gradually pulled away, but after three miles the horses were exhausted. Davis halted the carriage in a hollow and got out. He saw two riderless horses trotting in his general direction and managed to stop them as they came up. They had McClellan saddles on their backs. Mrs. Thomas hurriedly mounted one animal, which had been wounded, and Davis mounted the other. They set off at a gallop.

After going about half a mile, they stopped, weary and uncertain what they should do. Looking to their left they saw a little group of mounted men, standing still, about three quarters of a mile away. The men wore Federal uniforms, but since many of the guerrillas had been dressed in blue earlier that day, there was no telling which side these men were on. Davis and Mrs. Thomas, having decided to approach them cautiously, started their horses toward the men at a walk. One man detached himself from the group and came in their direction. Davis told Mrs. Thomas to stay where she was and rode forward alone.

When he got within hailing distance, he learned that the cluster of men was a pathetic remnant of Blunt's command. He called to Mrs. Thomas, and they rode forward together. There were ten men, including General Blunt himself. He had managed to rally fifteen but had sent the rest with an officer back to Fort Scott for reinforcements. Now he delegated one to escort the lady to safety.

"You go with Mrs. Thomas to Fort Scott," he ordered the trooper. "Go in a northwest direction across the prairie, keeping away from the road."

Davis remained with Blunt and never saw Mrs. Thomas again.

She and her new escort traveled until nightfall, then halted in a grove of cottonwood trees beside a stream. She was assisted from her saddle, her clothes stiff with blood from her horse's wound. Several other survivors of the skirmish found the grove in the darkness. "The soldiers watched while I slept the sleep of exhaustion with the sod for a pillow," Mrs. Thomas remembered later.

Shortly before dusk the next day, they made Fort Scott.

Mrs. Thomas was confined to her bed for more than a week. As soon as she was sufficiently recovered she returned to Topeka. She was a beautiful young woman, only twenty-one years old, but she never recovered her health. On December 3, 1864, she died; a reporter wrote that "her end [was] no doubt hastened by the terrible ordeal through which she had passed."

Charlie Davis survived the war and returned to Wisconsin. He lived to be an old man, and in his later years often ruminated over an odd trick of fate. He had not been Mrs. Thomas's original driver; Trooper John C. Pratt had been given the detail. The day before the massacre, Pratt had been kicked in the leg by a horse while unhitching the team, and Davis took his place. "I confidently believe that I owe my life to the kick of a horse," he always maintained.

<hr />

Many of Blunt's troops carried canteens filled with whiskey, and more liquor was found in the supply train wagons. The guerrillas sat in groups on the bloody field with corpses all around them and drank copiously and feasted on Yankee rations. Quantrill himself got drunk—the first time Gregg had ever seen him inebriated—and swaggered across the prairie joking with his men and crowing, "By God, Shelby could not whip Blunt. Neither could Marmaduke. But I whipped him!"

At age fifteen, Riley Crawford was the youngest of the guerrillas, but his thirst and appetite were not adversely effected by either the slaughter or the proximity of dead bodies. He filled his belly and got roaring drunk. It will be recalled that eight months earlier a squad of Penick's troops had visited his parents' house and burned it down. They also killed Riley's father. Mrs. Crawford had personally brought her sons to Quantrill and asked him to make soldiers of them, so that they might avenge their father.

When Riley finished eating, he staggered over to a fallen Yankee and playfully struck him with the broad side of a cavalry sabre, shouting, "Get up, you Federal son of a bitch!" To his amazement, the man leaped to his feet. He had been feigning death and mistakenly believed Riley had seen through his desperate ruse. Riley drew his revolver and brought the final curtain down on the poor fellow's play-acting.

Anderson and Todd wanted to try to capture the fort again, but Quantrill refused. "No, there is nothing to be gained by it; besides, we would probably lose fifteen or twenty men, and I would not give the life of one of my men for the whole business."

He did send Todd to the fort—but alone and under a flag of truce. Todd demanded the surrender of the garrison in the name of "Colonel" Quantrill. When Pond refused, Todd asked for an exchange of prisoners. Several of Dave Pool's men were missing, and Quantrill assumed that they had been captured.

In making his report the following day Pond stated,

I answered that I had taken no prisoners; that I had wounded several of his men, whom I had seen fall from their horses, and would see that they were cared for, provided he would do the same by our men. He said he had 12 privates and the adjutant-general (Major Curtis) prisoners, and that I had killed about 50 of his men, and if I would promise to take care of his wounded, and see that they were paroled after they were able to leave, he would promise me that no harm should befall Curtis or our men. This, I think, was intended for a blind to find out what I had done, as they had already murdered Major Curtis and all the prisoners.

At 4:00 P.M., some two hours after Todd parleyed with Lieutenant Pond, Quantrill once more started the column south for Texas. William Bledsoe's body and three wounded men were carried in an appropriated ambulance. Two prisoners were also in tow—black civilians who were well known to many of the Missourians: a Kansas City barber named Zack, who had a good reputation and would be put to work cutting hair in Texas during the coming winter; and Jack Mann, who had committed so many crimes in Jackson County that he had become notorious and been forced to flee.

Blunt, having returned to Baxter Springs with his little squad, shadowed Quantrill's column as it started south. The route lay across what he called "the field that was strewn with our dead." Nearly every corpse bore a head wound, showing, he thought, that "all who fell wounded or were taken prisoner were inhumanely murdered." He continued to trail the raiders for a time, then returned to Baxter Springs after dark. He sent messengers north to Fort Scott and south to Fort Gibson in the Indian Territory, instructing the commanders to intercept the column, if possible, at the Arkansas River. In the meantime, "I kept scouting parties on their trail to watch their movements until I could procure troops to pursue them."

The guerrillas rode fifteen miles, and then, having crossed the Kansas border into the Cherokee Nation, they camped for the night.

Some of them must have felt some satisfaction at the day's events. Eleven of their comrades had been lost; however, in their wake lay many putrefying Yankee corpses. They had had their pick of plunder from the cargoes of nine fully loaded six-mule team wagons and had captured many rifles, but the sweetest spoils were Blunt's personal possessions: his clothing, sword, firearms, saddle, buggy, and two commissions (brigadier general and major general), as well as all his official papers, correspondence, letters, various "headquarters equipage," and two stands of colors, including a flag—the finest Gregg had ever seen— inscribed, "Presented to Maj. Gen. James G. Blunt by the ladies of Leavenworth, Oct. 2nd 1863."

———————◆·◆·◆———————

Neither Blunt nor any of the officers at Fort Blair ever made a complete list of casualties; the following accounting comes from the various official reports and eyewitness statements. Six white soldiers and one black soldier had been killed at the fort; ten whites and thirteen blacks were wounded. Lieutenant Ralph E. Cook, commander of the 2nd Kansas Colored, was dead, as was Johnny Fry, a Pony Express rider. A woman and child who were in camp were also both wounded. Blunt lost eighty-two dead, eight wounded, and, initially, five missing. (During the night following the fight these men staggered into the fort, having played dead throughout the long day. The other four, like Trooper Arnold, were, observed Dr. Warner, "so badly disfigured and covered with blood as not to be recognizable.") Five of the wounded later died, bringing the total dead to ninety-eight, including Fry, O'Neal, and Jack Mann, who was subsequently murdered by the bushwhackers.

———————◆·◆·◆———————

On the morning of October 7, the guerrillas resumed their march to Texas, Blunt's scouts still following at a safe distance. As the day progressed, the wounded complained that Bledsoe's body was beginning to smell. Coming to an abandoned house with a freshly plowed field, Quantrill called a halt. Jack Mann was told to dig two graves. Since there was no shovel, Mann used a board from the house siding to push aside the soft, newly turned earth. Bledsoe's corpse was wrapped in blankets and put in one of the shallow graves. Mann was then shot, and his body tumbled into the other.

(In the spring, some bushwhackers returning from Texas stopped by the field to visit their beloved friend's grave. They found that four-footed "varmits" had dug up both corpses and devoured all the flesh, gnawed on the bones, and scattered them.)

Quantrill and his men rode west until they crossed the Verdigris River, then turned south, crossing the Arkansas on the morning of October 10, at a point eighteen miles west of Fort Gibson. Here they encountered a unit belonging to the 1st Indian Home Guard. In his report to General Price, Quantrill would grandly claim that the unit consisted of "about 150 Federal Indians and negroes . . . gathering ponies." General Blunt's scouts gave him a slightly smaller estimate—twelve Creeks. There is no dispute about their fate. "We brought none of them through," Quantrill said simply.

On the night of October 11, the guerrillas camped on the north fork of the Canadian River, forty-five miles south of the Arkansas, deep in the Indian Territory. Blunt's scouts decided they had come far enough and started the journey back to Kansas. The next day, Quantrill arrived at Confederate General Douglas H. Cooper's camp on the Canadian. Quantrill penned a report to General Price on October 13 in which he understated his own losses, claiming only three killed and three wounded. However, he also underestimated Blunt's casualties, saying that he left "about forty of them alive."

Quantrill concluded by promising to send Price on "some future day . . . a complete report of my summer's campaign on the Missouri River." Beneath his signature he affixed his rank as "Colonel." Despite his promise to write a further report, none has ever been found, and in all probability Quantrill never got around to writing one.

—·◆·—

Six days after Quantrill wrote his report, on October 19, General Schofield relieved Blunt of the command of the District of the Frontier and ordered him to Leavenworth. Blunt traveled to Fort Smith instead and appealed to the secretary of war. Stanton assigned him to recruit and organize the 11th Regiment, U.S. Colored troops. He subsequently resumed command of the District of the Frontier, commanded the District of the Upper Arkansas, fought Arapahoes and Cheyennes, and served against Price in 1864.*

On November 2, Sterling Price instructed his assistant adjutant-general, Major Lauchlan Maclean, to reply to Quantrill. After extending Price's congratulations to him and his "gallant command" on their march from the Missouri River to the Canadian, Maclean informed him that

> General Price is very anxious that you prepare the report of your sum-
> mer campaign, alluded to by you, at as early a date as practicable, and
> forward it without delay, more particularly so as he is desirous that
> your acts should appear in their true light before the world. In it he
> wishes you to incorporate particularly the treatment which the prison-
> ers belonging to your command received from the Federal authorities;
> also the orders issued by General Blunt or other Federal officers regard-
> ing the disposition to be made of you and your men if taken or van-
> quished. He has been informed that [the] most inhumane [orders] were
> issued. . . . [He] wants to have all the facts clearly portrayed, so that
> the Confederacy and the world may learn the murderous and uncivi-
> lized warfare which they themselves inaugurated, and thus be able to
> appreciate their cowardly shrieks and howls when with a just retalia-
> tion the same "measure is meted out to them." He desires me to con-
> vey to you, and through you to your command, his high appreciation
> of the hardships you have so nobly endured and the gallant struggle

---

*Thirty-five years after the Baxter Springs massacre, on March 30, 1898, James B. Pond received the Medal of Honor for his actions on that day. The citation contained no reference to Pond's foolishly having made Fort Blair vulnerable by taking down a wall, failing to put out pickets, and sending all his able-bodied cavalry away, although it rightly credited Pond's heroism in rallying his troops and beating back the attack: "While in command of two companies of cavalry was surprised and attacked by several times his own number of guerrillas, but gallantly rallied his men, and after a severe struggle drove the enemy outside the fortifications. First Lieutenant Pond then went outside the works and alone and unaided [fired?] a howitzer three times, throwing the enemy into confusion and causing him to retire." Pond's younger brother, George, was also awarded the medal, in his case for heroism at the Battle of Drywood, Kansas, May 15, 1864.

you have made against despotism and the oppression of our state, with the confident hope that success will soon crown our efforts. . . .

Northerners had indeed been shrieking and howling over the Lawrence massacre, and accounts of the Baxter Springs massacre served only to increase the noise level. "Take it all in all," remarked Major B. S. Henning, "there has not been a more horrible affair (except the massacre at Lawrence, in Kansas) happened during the war, and brands the perpetrators as cowards and brutes." Major Henning had fought at Baxter Springs and had helped bury the mutilated dead, but Northern sympathizers everywhere were horrified by the two massacres as word of them spread. As the result, a kind of dormant demonology was awakened: Beginning in late August 1863, and continuing even after the war's conclusion, one finds startlingly frequent references in letters, diaries, and newspaper articles written by loyal civilians and even in cold Federal military reports to the bushwhackers as "demons," "devils from hell," and "fiends incarnate." In the midst of the Lawrence raid one brute had brushed aside the pleas of a woman, saying, "We are fiends from hell," and many accepted the assertion as almost literal, doctrinal truth.

CHAPTER 12

"The History of Every Guerilla Chief Has Been the Same": The Usurpation of Quantrill

After remaining a few days at General Cooper's camp, Quantrill took his band into Texas, settling on Mineral Creek, fifteen miles northwest of Sherman. The men built shacks, fished, and killed deer for meat.

Quantrill sold the six-mule team and ambulance in which the wounded had been carried from Baxter Springs and used the money to buy four 100-pound sacks of green coffee. This was a rare treat, but it did not last long: Men kept stealing beans to use as barter with farmers. Sherman storekeepers suddenly noticed items disappearing off their shelves. Even heavy sacks of dry goods vanished as if by a magician's wand.

When not hunting or pilfering, the bushwhackers drank moonshine whiskey or rode to Sherman, where they raced their horses. Quantrill often won—he was an excellent rider, and his latest mount, Old Charley, was fleet. The horse was exceedingly tame and obedient with Quantrill on his back, but if anyone else tried to ride him, he would paw the earth, buck, and bite.

The other regular race winner was Dick Maddox. He was an exceptional horseman and an expert at rope tricks, too. Liquor did not diminish his skills: He got drunk every time he had the chance, which was frequently, and then would put on amazing displays of bronco busting and lariat twirling.

While the guerrillas indulged in loutish entertainments, Confederate military authorities continued an ongoing debate about their worth. Major

General J. Bankhead Magruder, commander of the District of Texas, lustily cheered the victory at Baxter Springs, believing it brightened "our prospects," and Brigadier General Henry E. McCulloch, the brother of Benjamin McCulloch, had been mightily impressed when he first heard the erroneous report of Blunt's death. After learning that Blunt had survived and hearing sickening details of the massacre, however, McCulloch was considerably sobered. As commander of the Northern Subdistrict, he was Quantrill's immediate superior—and thus responsible for his behavior— while he wintered in Texas. "I do not know what his military status is," McCulloch complained to General Edmund Kirby Smith.

> I do not know as much about his mode of warfare as others seem to know; but, from all I can learn, it is but little, if at all, removed from that of the wildest savage; so much so, that I do not for a moment believe that our Government can sanction it in one of her officers. Hence, it seems to me if he be an officer of our army, his conduct should be officially noticed, and if he be not an officer of our army, his acts should be disavowed by our Government, and as far as practicable, he be made to understand that we would greatly prefer his remaining away from our army or its vicinity.
>
> I appreciate his services, and am anxious to have them; but certainly we cannot, as a Christian people, sanction a savage, inhuman warfare, in which men are to be shot down like dogs, after throwing down their arms and holding up their hands supplicating for mercy.

General Smith did not share McCulloch's negativism. He thought the bushwhackers would be particularly effective against either marauding Indians or invading Yankees. McCulloch was not convinced: "I have but little confidence in men who fight for booty, and whose mode of warfare is but little, if any, above the uncivilized Indian, and who now say they are afraid to enter our army regularly for fear of being captured."*

McCulloch was concerned that they might even have a negative effect on the morale of regular troops and civilian Texans, too.

---

*A number of Confederate officers and officials, including General Sterling Price, tried repeatedly to convince the Missourians to join the regular army, but they steadfastly refused. Some were Confederate deserters who feared what might happen if they again came under the authority of their former commander. Furthermore, all guerrillas knew their fate if captured. As Price put it, "They have been outlawed by the Federal authorities, and expect no mercy or clemency at their hands, not even the chances of prisoners of

Public sentiment had changed greatly, and our cause was being strength-ened according to the security felt by the masses, and the people and the troops began to feel that they had some hope of protection in this army, and all had determined to make the fight outside of Texas. Now the people will lapse back into their former apathy; our friends feel weak-ened; our opposers strengthened, and our cause morally, deeply injured.

General Smith was still not converted. In fact, he saw a marvelous opportunity to show McCulloch the Missourians' usefulness. With the war going badly, quite a few conscripts had failed to report for duty and the desertion rate had become alarmingly high; some of the conscripts and deserters had Union sympathies and formed jayhawker bands. They hid in swamps and forests, emerging only to rob and kill civilians. It demoralized regular troops to hunt down neighbors, friends, and com-rades; thus, Smith enthusiastically explained to McCulloch,

no better force could be employed than that of Quantrill's Missourians. Their not being from the state will make them more effective. They are bold, fearless men, and moreover, from all representations, are under very fair discipline. They are composed, I understand, in a measure of the very best class of Missourians. They have suffered every outrage in their person and families at the hands of the Federals, and, being out-lawed and their lives forfeited, have waged a war of no quarter when-ever they have come in contact with the enemy. Colonel Quantrill, I understand, will perform that duty, provided rations and forage are issued to his men and horses; this you are authorized to order. . . .

McCulloch firmly instructed Quantrill that he was not to kill any deserters or conscripts but was to bring them before him for regimental assignment. Quantrill asserted the right to shoot any who fired on his men. The general and the guerrilla chieftain salvoed back and forth, nei-ther willing to concede the point. In the end, McCulloch reluctantly loosed Quantrill.

---

war; and they think that if used only as scouts and rangers to ascertain and watch the movements of an enemy, they would be able to protect themselves against any surrender of our forces, should such a calamity overtake us." In other words, as long as they remained independent partisans, they would be free to slip away if an army surrendered. Even Price had to admit "their objections are not without foundation."

Quantrill struck a small jayhawker band camped in Jernigan's Swamp, killing a few, capturing the rest.

The only tangible result of the raid was that the breach between him and McCulloch widened. The general was unhappy about the deaths, and Quantrill decided he would not undertake any further such missions. There was no use bringing in Unionists: When spring arrived, they would simply take the arms and ammunition that they had been issued, desert, and head for Federal lines.

Indian renegades were another matter. When a Comanche raiding party swooped down on Gainesville, McCulloch ordered the bushwhackers to go after them, and Quantrill immediately obeyed. Historian Lloyd D. Lewis has posited that "Quantrill, if viewed objectively, was a great cavalryman, probably as skillful as General Nathan Bedford Forrest." Perhaps, but this time he was in pursuit not of Federal cavalry or militia or jayhawkers but Comanche. These Indians, according to Denis McLoughlin, "were probably the finest horsemen the world has ever seen." For a week the increasingly disheartened guerrillas kept up their futile pursuit without ever closing the gap.

Upon their return, McCulloch ordered them to "destroy all the whiskey stills in the Red River Valley," because the Indians in General Cooper's army were getting "drunk so often that they were worse than useless." The assignment was not a happy one for Quantrill's men—they were dedicated customers of the very same stills themselves. In the end, they chose to carry out the order only selectively, smashing just one still and killing the three operators. They carried all the stock back to their camp.

The other, presumably chastened distillers continued to do a land-office business with the Missourians.

Drunk, they rode through the streets of Sherman, yelling and discharging their pistols in every direction. They shot church steeples full of holes, blasted locks off doors, knocked the hats off men's heads, and generally terrorized decent folk.

The Christmas Eve shenanigans were particularly memorable. Dick Maddox and some cronies stopped by a friend's house and guzzled down all his eggnog. Then Maddox sniffed out a barrel of whiskey that was stored in the cellar. The barrel was quickly emptied. By now, according to the recollection of W. L. Potter, they "were like all other men on a christmas spree." Potter's notion of typical holiday behavior is remarkable. Reeling in their saddles, they galloped to the town's only hotel, which happened to be owned by Ben Christian, a good friend of Quantrill. Nevertheless, they rode onto the porch and into the lobby, taking potshots at gaslights and door knobs. Their horses' hooves broke through the floorboards and kicked the furniture into kindling.

Next, still "wild & full of Reckless fun," they decided to have their pictures taken. After the photographer was finished, they broke his cameras and wrecked his studio.

They might have turned the entire town into a shambles if Ben Christian had not sent a frantic message to Quantrill. Considering his wayward followers' advanced state of inebriation, he thoughtfully brought along George Todd and every man still in camp. The celebrants were rounded up and led away. The next day Quantrill sent them back to town, hangdogged and hungover, to apologize and pay for the damages.

On New Year's Eve, a number of bushwhackers held a dance in their own honor at Jim Crow Chiles's house. They had not deigned to invite the entire outfit, and so some of those who had been left out felt insulted. These aggrieved fellows went to town to break up the party, and a small riot ensued. Once again, Quantrill had to be called to restore order.

No one was seriously injured in either of these rowdy incidents, but they were emblematic of the band's growing dissipation and hooliganism. Many of Quantrill's "old men"—who had been with him since the early days—were dismayed by the breakdown in discipline and the escalating violence. As the long winter wore on and their patience wore thin, they said their good-byes and slipped away singly or in bunches. . . . Some went back home to Missouri and resumed bushwhacking, while others joined the regular army.

One of those who left Quantrill was William Gregg, which is an indication of just how bad things had gotten because the two men had been through a lot together and had once been close. Gregg's disillusionment had begun at Lawrence. He had been appalled at the indiscriminate slaughter, and he blamed Quantrill, even allowing for the fact that the chief "could not have his eye on every man, for the men were scattered promiscuously over the town." There was no excusing the way he divided the stolen money, though: Before the raid Quantrill promised to give much of the loot to the suffering people of Jackson County and to distribute the remainder equitably; however, the abused citizenry received nothing, and he had arranged for Todd and his men to have the lion's share. Charley Higbee, a Todd lieutenant, ended up with "the largest sum," and immediately disappeared. "It was reported afterwards that he went to Canada," Gregg remarked in his memoir. "Soon after the close of the war, we heard of Higbee at Ft. Worth, Texas, in the banking business. In the eyes of the survivors of Quantrill's band and the people of Missouri a traitor."

Gregg went to Quantrill to tell him he was leaving. Quantrill praised him for being a "good soldier and a good officer and an honest man," yet he did not try to dissuade him.

"I have no fault to find with you, but I think it best that you should go away," Quantrill said. He added pointedly, "You have some enemies in camp."

Gregg had righteously and publicly denounced two of Todd's men, Fletch Taylor and Jim Little, for thievery. Not only were Taylor and Little watching for an opportunity to shoot him in the back, Todd was, too. Quantrill's authority over the band was so diminished that he could not even prevent the assassination of his old friend.

In his memoir, Gregg said he enlisted with Jo Shelby and was soon appointed captain of Company H. In the fall of 1864, Shelby sent Gregg back to northwestern Missouri to enlist new recruits. After completing his mission, Gregg lingered long enough to marry. His dark-eyed, raven-haired bride, Miss Elizabeth Hook, to whom he had been engaged for two years, had an ideal Confederate pedigree. Over the past few years, Federals had jailed her father, freed the family's slaves, stolen every horse and slaughtered every pig, and taken all the money and jewelry—and even the homespun blankets. Lizzie's mother was not broken or defeated; she continued to feed and clothe passing Confederate soldiers, and hide and nurse those who were wounded.

When a young reb was killed in a barnyard, Lizzie and four other Southern girls, fearing the corpse would be devoured by hogs, carried it to the Hook residence. They placed it on a board, washed it, and combed the hair. "We kept vigil over the body until morning," Lizzie recalled many years later. "The only sound through the night was the continual drip, drip of the blood from his wounds. Next morning . . . we summoned the old men of the neighborhood, who nailed together a rough box for a coffin." The corpse was buried in the woods. After the war, the boy's father disinterred the remains and reburied them in his family plot.

On November 3, 1864, Lizzie and Bill Gregg were married. It was a real bushwhacker ceremony. Gregg wore a new uniform with four shiny Navy revolvers tucked in his belt. A dozen long-haired guerrillas, pistols and spurs gleaming, were witnesses. After a late supper, the twelve stood guard outside the house, protecting the bride and groom on their wedding night.

Four days later the newlyweds started for Texas with a column that included Mr. and Mrs. James A. Hendricks—Gregg's sister and brother-in-law—Dick Maddox and his wife, and fifty men. The women rode sidesaddle, their trousseaus loaded in an ambulance along with the provisions. They pushed forward as long as they could each day, then slept on beds of grass, and were moving again at dawn. When their ambulance broke down, the men located a Federal column with a small train of wagons. They charged, scattering the militia. "Selecting the best one of the wagons," Lizzie remembered, "we put our team to it, loading in our valises, trunks, provisions, etc., and resumed our march." They crossed into the Cherokee Nation, skirmished with Federal cavalry, black militia, and Indians. They passed dead horses and mules, flanks sawed away by hungry "Johnnies." They subsisted on apples and hastily butchered cattle and ate Indian dog as a last resort. (The women gamely pronounced it tasty.)

After crossing the Red River, the column disbanded. The other two women settled in Sherman, while Mrs. Gregg went to live with an aunt in Waxahachie. Captain Gregg returned to his command and served until the war was over, then took his wife home to Missouri.

Another of those who left Quantrill in the winter of 1863–64 was Cole Younger, although the exact date is not known. In his autobiography Cole claimed that he subsequently served as a lieutenant in Captain John Jarrett's company, then assumed command when Jarrett "went north." He saw service under generals Henry McCulloch, Kirby Smith, and Marmaduke . . . fought cavalry, Comanche, and "pestiferous" Apaches in Texas . . . cotton thieves in Louisiana, and mounted infantry in Arkansas . . . cut telegraph wires and captured wagons in Colorado. Near the end of the war, he said, he was one of five men "disguised as Mexican miners" who took a boat from Guaymas, Mexico, to San Francisco, "then traveled by stage to Puget Sound, sailing for Victoria, [B.C.]." He was vague about the mission, other than saying that he and the others were to escort "a secret service officer named Kennedy" who was evidently to take charge of "two vessels of the Alabama type, built in British waters, [which] were to be delivered at Victoria." Presumably Cole meant that the warships were to be sailed into Southern waters to fight. In any case, the trip—if it occurred—was for naught: "On our arrival at Victoria . . . we found that Lee had surrendered, and the war was at an end."

Were even half of these claims true, Cole would have had an extraordinary wartime record. However, nothing can be verified.

When he wrote his autobiography, in 1903, Cole was fifty-nine, and, as noted earlier, he seems to have become one of those old men who spin yarns. By 1915, Cole's tendency to fabricate had become so pronounced that in applying to the Missouri government for what was known as a "Pension for Ex-Confederate Soldiers," he swore under oath that he had enlisted in 1861 and served not only as a lieutenant of "Co. F., [commanded by] Capt. Jarrett," Hays's cavalry regiment, and in Colonel Ben Elliot's 9th Missouri Cavalry, but to have seen action in "Nearly all battles fought in Missouri and Arkansas," 1861–65. He further swore that he "Was not discharged or captured. Went to Old Mexico with General Shelby."

Cole's pension application was forwarded to the U.S. War Department's adjutant general for verification. He was not amused.

There are no records on file in this office of Colonel Upton Hay's [sic] Command, Confederate States Army or Missouri State Guard, and no record has been found of the service, capture or parole of a man named Cole Younger as a member of this organization.

The name Cole Younger has not been found on the rolls, on file in this office, of any company of the 9th Missouri Cavalry (under command of Colonel Benjamin Elliott), Confederate States Army, and no record has been found of the capture or parole of a man of this name and organization.

The name Cole Younger appears on a list of Captain William E. [sic] Quantrill's Company (in which Captain Jarrett also served). List is undated and period covered is not stated. No further record has been found.

Missouri ex-Confederate pensions were restricted to those who served for at least six months in the Confederate army. Application denied.

Cole's whereabouts and activities during the sixteen or eighteen months after he left Quantrill may always remain a mystery. One Missouri newspaper reported in 1864 that Cole Younger was in New Mexico. Whether or not Cole was actually there, it is generally accepted that he was in California at war's end, staying with an uncle, and did not return to Jackson County until the fall of 1865.

As the winter of 1863–64 wore on, Confederate military authorities in Texas became at least as dismayed over the bushwhackers' behavior as Quantrill's "old men." They were still steadfastly refusing to enlist, and while some officials had acknowledged the validity of their arguments in October or November, by January little sympathy remained. Hundreds of deserters roamed free, and Quantrill continued to refuse to arrest them. Robbery and murder had become ever more common, and since some recent culprits wore Federal uniforms, suspicion naturally fell on the Missourians. The citizenry "believe that they have committed all the robberies that have been committed about here for some time," observed McCulloch, "and every man that has any money about his house is scared to death, nearly, and several moneyed men have taken their money and gone where they feel more secure."

Something had to be done. On January 11, 1864, McCulloch ordered Quantrill to "proceed as rapidly as possible to the headquarters of Major-General Magruder" at Bonham, Texas, "where you will immediately be placed in the face of the enemy."

Quantrill remained on Mineral Creek.

"So much mischief is charged to [Quantrill's] command here that I have determined to disarm, arrest, and send his entire command to you or General Smith," an exasperated McCulloch informed Magruder on February 3. "This is the only chance to get them out of this section of country, which they have nearly ruined, and I have never yet got them to do any service. Whenever orders have gone to them they have some excuse, but are certain not to go." After describing the latest murder attributed to them, he added that "nothing can be proved on them, because the people are afraid to swear against them. They regard the life of a man less than you would that of a sheep-killing dog. I regard them as but one shade better than highwaymen."

For some reason McCulloch thought better of his plan to disarm and arrest the Missourians. He decided instead to send them as far away from him as he could. On February 9, he ordered Quantrill to Corpus Christi—the city was five hundred miles away, a measure, perhaps, of the general's rage. In an attempt to head off any objections the guerrillas' new commander, Brigadier General H. P. Bee, might have to the move, McCulloch wrote him a dissembling note.

> There is no doubt about their being true Southern men, and, no odds what happens, will fight only on our side. They have been bad behaved in some instances, but have not been guilty of a fourth of what has been charged against them. They are in a country filled with the very worst character of men, numbers of whom are hid in the brush and come out at night and rob and steal; and there are plenty of enemies to the country who would have been glad to get up a conflict by telling bad tales upon them besides those that were true, and I really think the people are to a great extent unnecessarily uneasy about them. If these men are not kept on partisan service they will disband and scatter through the country, where, if bad men, they will do us great harm; if kept together under Quantrill they can be controlled, and if they do not act properly, then disarm and put the last man of them to work on fortifications. Take hold of them yourself and use them for our country's best interest. They are superbly armed and well mounted, and there is no reason that they should not do good service. They have not been paid for months; this should be done immediately, and let them see that they are to be treated properly and required to behave so themselves.

McCulloch might have saved himself the trouble: Quantrill had no desire to ride to Corpus Christi.

With the Confederate hierarchy determined to enlist him or get rid of him, and his control lessening on his own men, Quantrill tried to extricate himself from the situation.

On February 24, he wrote an appeal to Governor Reynolds, asking to be allowed to join in "any forward movements in Mo. this spring." He added an inducement: "I could raise at least 400 men Missourians (young men) who will not go into the service under any other circumstances. They all have good arms and horses. They are composed of good families of Mo. and there is no doubt they would make good soldiers. If you can assist me any let me know at this place [Sherman] as early as convenient."

Beneath his signature, Quantrill stated his rank: "Cap Comg Partisans."*

Fifteen days later, Reynolds replied, gently urging Quantrill to accept the inevitable.

A man of your ability should look forward to a higher future. You must see that guerilla warfare, as an honorable pursuit, is pretty nearly "played out," and if you wish to rise, you should acquire the confidence of the regular authorities by conforming to the policy they adopt. . . . Strive to organize a regular command and enter the regular Confederate

---

*The question of whether or not Quantrill was ever commissioned a colonel is one of the thorniest and most controversial concerning his life.

John N. Edwards wrote that Quantrill did not receive a colonel's commission in Richmond during the winter of 1862–63, but in the latter part of the nineteenth century several of Quantrill's followers would insist that he had.

Connelley, in a rare burst of generosity toward his subject, flatly stated that Quantrill "bore a commission as colonel from some Confederate authority, perhaps General Sterling Price, possibly Thomas C. Reynolds, Confederate governor of Missouri." To the contrary, Reynolds's letter books show that early in the winter of 1863–64, he and Price consulted with each other, trying to figure out who had promoted Quantrill.

The facts are as follows:

It was the custom both in the Union and Confederate armies in the early stages of the war for soldiers to elect their officers. However, by the summer of 1863, the custom had largely died out in the regular armies of both sides.

As noted earlier, Quantrill's service record contains pay vouchers, reimbursement receipts, and other forms from the government in Richmond or the Confederate military in which Quantrill is addressed as "captain," leaving no doubt as to his formal recognition under the Partisan Ranger Act. The last of these documents extant is dated April 3, 1863.

Six months later, Quantrill called his band together for a march from Missouri to Texas. Four hundred men showed up, including bushwhackers, male civilians, mustered-out Confederate veterans, and Colonel John D. Holt and his recruits. Connelley wrote that "At the rendezvous was organized The First Regiment, First Brigade, Army of the South. . . ."

On October 6, after slaughtering Blunt's troops at Baxter Springs, Quantrill sent Todd under a flag of truce to Fort Blair, demanding its surrender in the name of "Colonel" Quantrill. A week later, on October 13, while still en route to Texas, he wrote a report to General Price, which he signed as "Colonel." However, in the February 24, 1864, letter to Governor Reynolds, Quantrill gave his rank as "Cap Comg Partisans"—captain commanding partisans.

Thus, the available hard evidence shows that Quantrill claimed the rank of colonel only for a brief period that coincided with his leading the "First Regiment" to Texas.

Service. All authority over undisciplined bands is short-lived. The history of every guerilla chief has been the same. He either becomes the slave of his men, or if he attempts to control them, some officer or some private rises up, disputes his authority, gains the men, and puts him down. My opinion of you is that you deserve a better fate, and should rise higher than you now stand. You see I am frank even to bluntness, but I trust you will carefully consider what I write. If you have time to see me before leaving I hope you will come to Marshall.

You told me that the "no quarter" system was forced on you in self-defense; let me urge you to embrace the earliest opportunity to abandon it, and establish the relations of ordinary warfare between your command and the enemy.

Reynolds was prophetic: In less than four months Quantrill would be overthrown by Todd. The trouble began with a couple of dastardly crimes. The body of a Confederate major named Butts was found beside the Red River. He had been shot, and his watch and pocketbook were missing. His horse, still saddled, was hitched to a nearby tree nearly starved to death. Then, four men rode onto a Colonel Alexander's place, killed him, and took his money.

My theory explaining this enigma is based upon the fact that the bushwhackers continued the practice of electing officers long after the Union and Confederate armies abandoned it: According to John McCorkle, they were holding elections at least as late as the end of October 1864. I therefore theorize that when the 1st Regiment was formed, the men elected Quantrill colonel—the more appropriate rank for regimental command, and otherwise, Colonel Holt, as the highest-ranking officer on the scene, would have been in charge. A majority of the men present would have been members of Quantrill's band or other guerrilla bands and would not have wanted a regular army outsider like Holt to have authority over them.

Upon reaching Texas, the 1st Regiment broke up, and Quantrill was once more in charge just of his own band. He may have automatically resumed his former rank, viewing the colonelcy as a brevet rank, but another explanation is equally possible. We know that General Henry McCulloch had had at least one face-to-face meeting with Quantrill in Texas, and there is a suggestion in Reynolds's correspondence that he met with Quantrill, too. McCulloch was as curious about Quantrill's colonelcy as Reynolds was, and it is not hard to imagine either the general or the governor asking Quantrill who commissioned him a colonel and, learning the truth, informing him that he was a *captain*.

In any case, Quantrill never again called himself colonel; in Kentucky newspapers of 1865 and in the recollections of those who knew him, his rank is always that of captain.

At first the culprits' identity was a mystery. In fact, it was assumed that Butts had been assassinated by a disgruntled civilian because he had been so vociferously critical of rich men who arranged for themselves or their sons to serve, as W. L. Potter put it, "either in the Quartermasters Department, the Commissaries Department, the Transportation Department, or some other department . . . simply to keep them out of the bullet department." Eventually, however, a bushwhacker went to Quantrill and whispered that Fletch Taylor had killed both men. He implicated three others in the robbery and murder of Alexander.

This was too much for Quantrill. These victims were Confederate officers—and Major Butts was Ben Christian's father-in-law. Quantrill had Taylor seized and sent a message to General McCulloch, asking that Taylor be court-martialed. He also arrested the three other men. Before they could be sent to McCulloch, however, sympathetic guards let them saddle their horses and escape in the night.

Quantrill called all the men together. According to Potter, he

told them that if there was a Man in his Command that had been guilty of Robbing any Person While in Texas, that if they would come out and acknowledge their guilt & Promise that they Would Never again repeat it & that they were sorry for it, that they could remain in the command the same as ever & He would not Permit them to be punished for it. He also told them that if one of his Men was Guilty of committing any depredations on the Property of citizens of Texas & they did not acknowledge it then & there & if it was afterwards Proved against one of them that they were Guilty of Violating the Law, that he would not shelter them but Would have them punished to the full extent of the Law & he would also Expel them from his command. Not one of them admitted their guilt. at the same time he told them that if there was any Man or Men in his Command that did not like his style of commanding them, or if any of them wished to withdraw from his command, they could take their Horses & Weapons and they were Welcome to leave and go where they pleased.

Bill Anderson stepped forward. "I won't belong to any such a damned outfit," he said. He rode out of camp with twenty men and went to McCulloch's headquarters at Bonham. Fletch Taylor was already there. Taylor had admitted to McCulloch that he had killed Major Butts; however, he swore that Quantrill had ordered the deed. Anderson gave McCulloch an "earful," claiming that Quantrill and his men were guilty of a vast array of felonies.

McCulloch sent Quantrill a message, informing him he had Taylor in custody and intended to try him. Quantrill should report to headquarters, bringing all his witnesses with him. It was not difficult for Quantrill to imagine what sorts of accusations Anderson and Taylor were whispering in the general's ear. He left George Todd with a dozen men to guard the camp and took the remainder of the band—approximately sixty men—to Bonham.

McCulloch had his headquarters on the second floor of the City Hotel. Quantrill rode up to the building just at noon, climbed down, and hitched his horse to the rail. He told the others to stay mounted and to be alert for trouble.

As he walked into McCulloch's office, the general got up from his desk. "Quantrill," he said, "you're under arrest. Remove your side arms and throw them on the bed."

"What's the meaning of this?" Quantrill asked as he stepped over to the bed, which was in the corner of the room. He unbuckled his belt and laid down his two Navy revolvers. He had been disarmed by a constable at John Bennings's cabin after the Morgan Walker affair. Someone had wanted to hang him then, too.

McCulloch told him about Taylor's charges, and said that he should consider himself a prisoner. McCulloch added that he would accept Quantrill's parole and see that he was treated fairly, then he softened a bit.

"Well, it's dinner time. Come and go down and have dinner with me."

"No, sir, I will not!" Quantrill flared. "I consider this a strange way of doing business, General McCulloch. I have preferred a criminal charge against one of my officers. I placed him under guard. He made his escape from my camp, and now you place me under arrest on his word. No, sir! I will not go to dinner. By God, I do not care a god damn if I never eat another mouthful in Texas!"

McCulloch left Quantrill sitting in his office, guarded by two privates. They stood by the door, cradling their rifles. After awhile Quantrill rose from his seat, saying he wished to get a drink of water. He filled a cup from the water cooler, which stood near the bed. He lifted the cup to his lips, then, dashing it to the floor, he sprang to the bed. He seized his revolvers and trained them on the fumbling, amazed guards. He made them lay down their arms and move away from the door. Buckling on his gunbelt and taking the key from the door, he stepped outside and locked it. He ran down the stairs and bumped into two more soldiers. They found themselves staring down his revolver barrels. Reluctantly, they laid down their arms and backed into the street.

Quantrill's men, disregarding his orders, had dismounted. They were shaking hands and talking with some members of Anderson's band who had happened by.

"Boys, the outfit is under arrest!" Quantrill shouted. "Get on your horses, and let's get out of here!"

Instantly they broke off their conversations with Bloody Bill's followers and hauled themselves into their saddles. They waited while Quantrill unhitched Old Charley and mounted. Together they spurred their horses and, whooping and yelling, raced out of town.

McCulloch sent Colonel J. Martin's regiment of Texas militia after Quantrill, with orders to bring him back dead or alive. Martin was joined by Anderson and his band. Anderson's men, who formed the advance, occasionally got close enough to their former comrades to exchange shots, but no one on either side was hurt.

Quantrill dispatched a messenger on a racehorse to the Mineral Creek camp. He meant to cross the Red River at Colbert's Ferry. Todd was to bring his men and all the ammunition they could carry and rendezvous on the Sherman-Bonham Road.

Before Quantrill and Todd could meet, however, Quantrill's pursuers closed in and drove him from the road. He swung north toward the ferry. Todd, still traveling east, forded Bodark Creek and spotted mounted men in the heavy timber beside the road—Anderson and twenty others who had broken off the chase. Todd took his men into the woods on the opposite side of the road.

The two bands blasted away, but little harm was done: Each side had only one man slightly wounded.

"If you are not a damned set of cowards," Anderson called, "come out into the open and fight like men!"

"You have the most men," Todd replied. "If you are not a set of God damn cowards, come in here and take us!"

The firing resumed. Some tree trunks were splintered, but no one else was wounded. In the end, Todd gingerly eased his band away and followed the sound of distant gunfire until he found Quantrill.

On the north bank of the Red River Quantrill ordered his men to form a line—Colonel Martin was approaching the river from the south. Instead of leading a charge, however, Martin rode into the water alone, bearing a white flag. Quantrill met him in the middle.

"I do not want to fight Confederate soldiers," Quantrill told Martin, "and I will not unless I am compelled to. But if you and your command follow me any further, I will fight you as long as I have one man alive with a cartridge to burst and the strength to pull the trigger."

The prospect of trying to cross the river with sharpshooting bushwhackers lined up on the other side was not a pleasing one to Colonel Martin.

"I have no jurisdiction in the Indian Territory, neither does McCulloch," he replied, "and I have no authority to follow you any further."

He returned to Bonham to make his report to General McCulloch. Quantrill established a camp in the Choctaw Nation and paid his respects to General Cooper.

Later that night, a few of Anderson's more audacious souls slipped into the camp and kidnapped Andy Walker. They also tried to steal Old Charley—insult of insults; however, the horse reared and kicked and whinnied so loudly that they were forced to give up and sprint away.

W. L. Potter claimed in a letter to W. W. Scott that Quantrill and his men subsequently "made an attack on Ft. Smith. They did not succeed in capturing it." Nothing else is known of this engagement.

Sometime in early April, Quantrill started back to Missouri with Todd and sixty-four men. It was an unusually rainy spring, and they slogged through mud the whole way. Nearly all the rivers and streams were swollen and had to be forded by swimming the horses. Quantrill and Todd crossed the Osage first and built fires on the far bank to guide the rest. The Grand River was a raging torrent and could not be forded; they followed along its southern bank until they eventually found a rickety bridge. On the other side of the bridge, hammered by rain, they stumbled on a cluster of small log cabins. The weather was too inclement even for hogs: They had taken refuge inside. The bushwhackers joyfully butchered all of them, cooked the meat on spits, and, bellies full, slept contentedly in the fouled, stinking cabins.

They cautiously made their way through southwestern Cass County, capturing an occasional Federal, taking him along for a short distance and pumping him for information before killing him. They slipped into Johnson County and stopped at a farm near Chapel Hill. The women of the house cooked biscuits and bacon, and the guerrillas ate like ravenous wolves. The journey had been hard on them: They were gaunt, exhausted, and bedraggled. Many were on foot, their horses having died along the way, and the surviving mounts were worn out. After the meal, Quantrill ordered his followers to split into groups of three or four, scatter, and forage for horses, saddles, firearms, and food. He and Todd would scout Jackson County.

It was soon clear that conditions there were "plenty squally." General Egbert Brown, the commander of the District of Central Missouri, was determined to stamp out bushwhacking and had his troops "on the alert for Quantrell's return." Colonel James H. Ford's 2nd Colorado Cavalry regiment had been sent into Jackson County itself for the express purpose of whipping out the notorious band. Ever since their arrival, the twelve hundred Coloradans had been warmly welcomed and extravagantly complimented by Unionists, and now they were eager to tangle with Quantrill's Raiders.

Quantrill and Todd passed the word for their followers to rendezvous in Lafayette County. They established a camp—and promptly had a falling out. The ostensible cause was a card game—Quantrill accused Todd of cheating—but the conflict had been building for a long time. When the band had originally been formed, in 1862, Todd had wanted to be elected first lieutenant, but Quantrill had supported William Haller, who was one of his very earliest disciples. Haller had won, and though Todd had been elected second lieutenant, he was resentful and petulantly quarreled with Quantrill.

"Take your horse and outfit and leave this camp," Quantrill told him.

Todd left, accompanied by a few admirers. They fought independently for a short time until a reconciliation could be effected.

Todd was elected captain of the "First Regiment" in the fall of 1863; however, like a sullen child, he nursed every real or imagined slight. Even receiving the lion's share of the Lawrence money had not placated him. He had long been waiting for his chance to supplant Quantrill, and his behavior was increasingly inconsistent and erratic: He willingly assisted in arresting drunken bushwhackers on the streets of Sherman, but he plotted against Gregg; yet he came to Quantrill's aid after the escape from McCulloch's headquarters. In the Mineral Creek camp, he sometimes resorted to the liquor bottle and was rowdy and uncontrollable when drunk. Despite his personality flaws (or perhaps because of them), the younger, wilder members of the band were drawn to him and away from Quantrill.

One winter's day he was bragging about his prowess and enormous courage. "I'm not afraid of any man on this planet!" he asserted.

"How about me?" Quantrill asked pleasantly.

Todd was not ready for a final showdown.

"Oh, well," he shrugged, "you were the only damned man that I ever was afraid of."

Five months later, playing seven-up for hundred-dollar pots in the Lafayette camp, Todd saw his chance to repay Quantrill for shaming him and at the same time steal his crown.

Bystanders agreed with Quantrill that Todd was cheating, but Todd drew his revolver first, getting the drop on him. Glowering and making threats on Quantrill's life, Todd forced him to back down.

No leader of a violent gang could be humiliated and expect to remain in control. Quantrill saddled Old Charley and rode out of camp with eight or ten of his faithful "old men."

Early in June he went to Bone Hill and picked up Kate King. He took her into Howard County, where they were joined by those who had sided with him.

———◆———

Anderson and Todd were very active in the summer of 1864, raiding through western and central Missouri. Where was Quantrill while they were stealing all that loot, spilling all that blood?

There is a long-standing tradition, still current in Dover today, that Quantrill came home to see family and friends. However, Caroline Quantrill always insisted that she never saw her son again after he went West in 1857. W. W. Scott, Quantrill's old friend, believed her, which means he did not see him in Dover in 1864, nor did he ever hear from reliable people of such a visit. Finally, there is Kentuckian James Wakefield's assertion that in the spring of 1865, Quantrill told him of his intention to send money to his mother and sister. His sister had died in 1863, which he would have known had he returned to his family in 1864. Therefore, the long-standing tradition cannot be true.

After Price invaded Missouri near the end of the summer, several Federal informants claimed to have seen Quantrill with one of the columns, being carried in a sling, and the *Kansas Tribune* picked up the rumor, exulting that "Quantrell has consumption." During Price's retreat, the newspaper reported, prisoners from a Topeka regiment "frequently" saw him carried along in an ambulance and were certain he was "sick beyond hope of recovery." Quantrill's father having died of tuberculosis, it has been suggested that Quantrill may indeed have been suffering the ravages of the disease. Riding through Kentucky in 1865, however, he was healthy and vigorous, so if he had consumption in 1864, he experienced a miraculous remission.

Statements made by Kate King and Fletch Taylor as well as oral traditions passed down by residents of Howard County indicate that she and Quantrill remained in the county during the summer and much of the fall. An anthropologist who examined Quantrill's skull in 1982 concluded that Quantrill had had two molars extracted about a year before his death; thus Kate may have been his nurse for a time as well as his lover.

In 1926, Kate said nothing about Quantrill having troublesome teeth, but she lovingly recalled that after they went into Howard County, he put up a tent and added on a kitchen. It was as near to a "permanent home" as they ever had, she said. He taught her how to smoke, and they "whiled away many hours beside the stove, planning the future," while he puffed on a cigar, she on a pipe.

CHAPTER 13

"A Carnival of Blood": Anderson and Todd During the Summer and Fall of 1864

An outbreak of hydrophobia struck Kansas City in the early months of 1864. There were unheeded calls for the muzzling of all dogs, and strays were routinely shot. Family pets that had been bitten by suspect animals were also killed or, if particularly beloved, tied to trees until the passage of time revealed whether or not they developed the disease. People who had been bitten applied madstones to wounds and hoped that the claims of their curative powers were true. " 'Death to dogs' is a sentiment which is growing in popularity everyday," snickered Dwight Thacher.

> The *crack* of a revolver, followed by a significant yelping, may be heard most any hour of the night. Fire away, we don't own a pup, but bury the victims from sight. A live dog may be dangerous, but a dead one is certainly a nuisance if lying on the streets or vacant lots of the city.

Many border residents would soon harbor similar notions about guerrillas: *Death to dogs*.

In the warm spring weather the grass and leaves grew, providing forage and cover for partisans, and those who had gone south for the winter drifted back, mostly in small groups. Few seem to have camped in Bates, Vernon, or Cass County, which remained largely depopulated, but drifted farther north or east. Some determined Southerners—who had furnished false evidence of their loyalty—having returned to Jackson County,

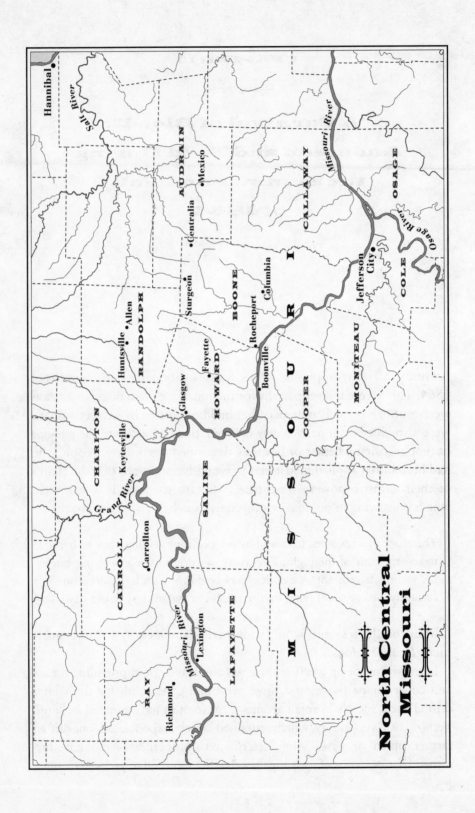

North Central Missouri

Quantrill's followers found haven there or, more often, in Lafayette County, where many Jackson County Southerners had taken up residence after being driven out of their homes by Order No. 11. So the location of the strife shifted, but its character remained largely unchanged.

Guerrillas raided towns, robbed wagon and railroad trains, cut telegraph wire, and demanded the surrender of steamboats. They held up travelers and stagecoaches, looted stores and houses, shot furloughed or discharged Federal soldiers, and burned bridges. As always, they scoured for prized boots, overcoats, and blankets. (With Ewing gone, common rustlers once more used the partisan strife as a convenient cover, and horse theft again became epidemic.)

The Federal military authorities remained incapable of stemming the violence, although not for lack of trying.

Throughout the spring and summer Colonel Ford's Coloradans continued their aggressive scouts and had some success, as did other unit commanders, and the military tried some new measures. For instance, orders were issued formally requiring that the pilot's houses and engine rooms of all steamers be lined with boiler iron, but so many pilots still surrendered their vessels that some masters found it necessary to offer $1,000 to any pilot who could take a "boat safely through" from St. Louis to Leavenworth.

Since many of Quantrill's former band and other guerrillas had Federal uniforms and thus were able to ride right up to an enemy patrol and cut loose on the unsuspecting troopers, district commanders tried various systems of identification. For a brief time these proved efficacious, but the bushwhackers soon figured out what was happening and made it their business to discover the current signs and countersigns. Their efficiency is indicated by the exasperated elaborateness of the order issued by General Egbert Brown to his command:

The following signals and pass words for July, 1864, will be transmitted by sub-district commanders to the commanding officers of each scout, detachment, or escort detailed from their respective commands, every precaution being taken to prevent their being known to unauthorized persons: During the daytime the commanding officer of a scout, detachment, or escort, upon observing the approach of a party or body of men, will ride a few paces in advance of his command and raising his hat or cap, with arm extended full height, will lower it slowly and place it upon his head. The commanding officer of the party thus challenged will immediately answer the same by raising the hat or cap from the head and extending the arm at full length horizontally, bringing the arm back slowly and replacing the hat or cap upon the head. The signal to be given and answered, where the nature of the ground will permit, before the parties have approached nearer than 300 to 350 yards.

At night the party who first discovers the approach of another, when within challenging distance, will cry out loud and distinctly, "Halt!" and the party thus challenged will immediately answer, "Lyon," to be followed by a counter challenge of "Who comes there?" to which the party last challenged will answer "Reno." The failure of either party to answer promptly and correctly will be the signal to commence firing. The badges to be worn during the month of July will be as follows: On the odd days, as the 1st, 3rd, 5th, 7th, &c., a red strip of cloth fastened around the hat or cap, and on the even days of the month, as the 2nd, 4th, 6th, 8th, &c., a white strip will be worn in the same manner, the colors alternating each day.

Special care will be taken to avoid mishaps through negligence or the failure on the part of the men to change badges as herein directed.

Six days after the order took effect George Todd concealed his men in the brush along the Independence-Glasgow road, hoping to ambush a patrol. They waited most of the day, succeeding only in stopping and robbing the stage. They held the driver and the only passenger in a nearby house so the Yankees would not be alerted to their trap. At five o'clock, Todd gave up and, accompanied by Lee McMurty, rode to the house to release the prisoners. While Todd and McMurty were gone, a twenty-six-man detachment of the 2nd Colorado under Captain Seymour W. Wagner came down the road. The concealed bushwhackers cut loose, and Wagner was killed. His men tried to put up a fight; however, they were armed with inferior Savage pistols, which frequently misfired. Seven troopers died before the rest fled.

Todd put the only one of his men who had been wounded in the stage with the bags of mail and went back to the Sni Hills. Frank Smith remarked in his memoir that this was the first encounter Quantrill's Raiders had had with the 2nd Colorado. They were impressed with the Coloradans' "sand" and good horses.

The following day Lexington newspapers received four letters from Bill Anderson, addressed variously to the "citizens and the community at large," as well as to several named Federal officers. Responding to editorials that civilians arm themselves and resist the bushwhackers, Anderson warned,

> Listen to me, fellow citizens . . . do not take up arms [against us] if you value your lives and property. It is not in my power to save your lives if you do. If you proclaim to be in arms against the guerrillas I will kill you. I will hunt you down like wolves and murder you. You cannot escape. It will not be Federals after you. Your arms will be no protection to you. . . . I will kill you for being fools. Beware, men, before you make this fearful leap.

Having railed against the Yankees for what they had done to his sisters—and, supposedly, his father—he bragged,

> I have fully glutted my vengeance. I have killed many. I am a guerrilla. I have never belonged to the Confederate Army, nor do my men. A good many of them are from Kansas. I have tried to war with the Federals honorably, but for retaliation I have done things, and am fearful will have to do what I would shrink from if possible to avoid.

In the other letters, literate though sometimes incoherent, Anderson was by turns playful, humorous, and malevolent. Having heard that General Egbert Brown had incarcerated a number of Southern women and had convened a military commission that sentenced Miss Anna Fickle of Warrensburg to three years in prison for attempting to aid a Confederate prisoner's escape, he gave Brown a chilling warning.

> I do not like the idea of warring with women and children, but if you do not release all the women you have arrested in La Fayette County, I will hold the Union ladies in the county as hostages for them. I will tie them by the neck in the brush and starve them until they are released, if you do not release them. The ladies of Warrensburg must have Miss Fickle released. I hold them responsible for her speedy and safe return. General, do not think I am jesting with you. I will resort to abusing your ladies if you do not quit imprisoning ours.

Anderson never carried out his threat, but his willingness to make it is evidence of his viciousness or, perhaps, dementia. Either way, he put down his pen and went back to glutting his vengeance.

Other partisan leaders were busy, too. Indeed, by now it was clear that Missouri was suffering its worst summer of bushwhacking. Reports of deprivations were published daily in the newspapers. Numerous large gangs roamed, particularly north of the Missouri River. Their leaders included "Coon" Thornton, John Thrailkill, Silas Gordon, Clifton Holtzclaw, Caleb Perkins, and a Baptist preacher, the Reverend Captain Tom Todd.

Sterling Price was busy planning an incursion into Missouri at summer's end, of course, and he had spies and emissaries roaming the state. Undoubtedly he passed word that he wanted the Yankees distracted and softened up.

General Egbert Brown intensified his anti-guerrilla campaign, sending out patrols day and night. In a period of twenty days beginning July 1, for example, he dispatched a hundred patrols, which killed two hundred of the enemy, while he lost forty-two. His cavalry marched ten thousand miles and took no prisoners. Yet, if anything, the number of rebel outrages only increased.

On July 10, Coon Thornton captured Platte City without firing a shot. Fletch Taylor, who had accompanied Thornton, gave a fiery speech in which he called for death to all Radical Unionists, as he flourished a bloody knife that he claimed was "fresh from the bosom" of a radical. (Colonel Ford crossed into northern Missouri with most of the 2nd Colorado and gave chase. On July 14, he caught up with Thornton near Camden Point, defeated him, and scattered his band.)

Just one day after Thornton took Platte City, Anderson and his followers left Saline County, heading north. They forded the Missouri in a single skiff, making repeated trips and swimming their horses behind the boat. For the next three and a half months Anderson would range back and forth through the counties of central Missouri on the northern side of the Missouri River until he was killed.

Having crossed the river Anderson and his followers made their way east through southern Carroll County. Since this area was a hotbed of Unionism, they killed farmers in their fields and riders they encountered on the roads, five in just the first hour, including an old man named Hiram Griffith, who had been working behind a plow until Arch Clement threw him to the ground and cut his throat from ear to ear with a bowie knife, leaving him writhing in a pool of his own blood. Nearing the Chariton County line they met eighteen-year-old Solomon Baum, a Confederate sympathizer.

Anderson asked if he was a Union man.

Since everyone in the band was wearing a blue uniform, Baum assumed his interrogator was, as the 1881 *History of Carroll County* put it, "a ruffianly federal who would mistreat him if his answer was not favorable."

"I am," he replied.

As a rope was thrown over a tree limb, Baum realized his mistake and begged for his life, swearing he loved the South.

Anderson grew bored with his entreaties.

"Oh, string him up," he ordered. "God damn his little soul, he's a Dutchman anyway."

They left his body swinging in the warm summer breeze.

Before long they came upon Cyrus Lyons, who with the help of two neighbors was digging a well in his yard. Lyons had three children and a wife who was seriously ill. Anderson called him over to the fence and asked, "Why ain't you in the service?"

Lyons, like Baum, assumed he was talking with a Yankee. "I do belong to the militia," he replied.

"Well, why in hell ain't you out trying to drive out the bushwhackers? Didn't you know they were in the country?"

Lyons said he had not been informed that he was needed and that while in the service, he always had tried to do his duty and was ready to do so again.

"Well," roared Anderson, "I guess you have done enough. I am Bill Anderson, by God!" He shot Lyons dead.

Three other guerrillas jumped their horses over the fence and killed the neighbors. As they rifled their victims' pockets they joked and laughed about the "sly trick" they had played on the "three damned milish."

Mrs. Lyons, having heard the gunfire, got out of bed and crawled on her hands and knees across the floor, trying to reach her husband. She collapsed in the doorway.

When word of the incursion reached Carrollton, a captain named Calvert, the commander of the militia company to which Lyons belonged, set out on the malefactors' trail; however, after following it to the Chariton County line, Calvert broke off the chase, because, as the anonymous author of the *History of Carroll County* noted, he had "gone quite as far as was desirable or prudent."

"The Devil is loose in Chariton and Carroll counties with scarcely three feet of chain to his neck," warned the Columbia *Missouri Statesman*.

He roamed into Randolph County, too. On July 15, Anderson led his followers into Huntsville, where he had once lived. They killed one man, robbed stores, and held up both Unionists and Southerners. They rode away with a reported $40,000 taken from banks' and merchants' safes, but ten miles down the pike they encountered a Captain Smith and his company of 9th Cavalry Missouri State Militia. There was a running fight for four miles before the bushwhackers' superior mounts pulled away. "The road on which the chase occurred was strewn with ribbons, silks, and other items of their plunder," noted a Federal officer.

The next stop was Rocheport, in western Boone County, where many Southern sympathizers resided. After riding into town at dawn on July 18, the guerrillas let it be known that they did not intend to rob the place since, as the *Missouri Statesman* paraphrased their remarks, "from appearances [it] had been pretty well cleaned out before their arrival." They added that they "didn't want to rob anymore no how as they had as much as they wanted, exhibiting purses crammed with greenbacks taken at Huntsville."

They were looking for small boats in which to cross the river, but, finding none, they fired into the steamer *War Eagle,* intending to use it as a ferry. However, General Rosecrans had recently decreed that all boats sailing above Jefferson City must have armed crews. The *War Eagle* returned the fire and chugged on. The next boat coming up the river did turn to shore south of town—in order to land some cavalry. Unfortunately, the Anderson gang was gone, and the troopers only briefly and unsuccessfully pursued the band.

Two days later, George Todd rode east into Saline County and attacked Arrow Rock, fourteen miles southeast of Marshall. Twenty militia were driven from the town. The bushwhackers set fire to a house used as the Federals' headquarters and captured forty horses and $20,000 worth of goods, but the raid was not without its price: Dick Yeager received a head wound. Todd carried him away in an ambulance and hid him at a supporter's house, then returned to the Sni Hills.

A few weeks later a Federal patrol found Yeager and killed him. He was the first of Quantrill's former officers and allies to die that summer. There soon would be others.

Perhaps Yeager's death made George Todd more cautious: Until Price entered Missouri in September, he spent most of the time in hiding, emerging only occasionally to hold up a stagecoach, cut some telegraph wires, or rob the workers on the Missouri Pacific Railroad, which was under construction from Warrensburg to Kansas City.

Anderson took up the slack as he continued raiding through the counties north of the Missouri River in the central part of the state. His activities had drawn young, hotheaded recruits. He entered Renick, Randolph County, on July 23 at the head of a sixty-five-man column. They tore down telegraph wires, set fire to the depot, and, of course, looted stores and houses.

Two local men joined the column, which marched seven miles to Allen. The guerrillas intended to rob the north Missouri train, but a woman whose house they passed en route went to the tracks, flagged down the train, and warned the conductor; the train returned to Sturgeon for a guard. Thirty militia had stopped in Allen and, learning of the enemy's approach, sent a message to Macon City, asking for help, then took refuge in the depot and, as the *Missouri Statesman*'s correspondent put it,

erected a barricade, made of barrels of salt and bales of hay, to hold off the enemy. The latter amused themselves during the "siege" by shooting the horses [of] the militia . . . of which animals they killed nine. In good time a train arrived from Macon City with troops, when the bushwhackers immediately scattered to the brush.

They left the corpses of two comrades in the street. Three more were killed in the pursuit, including the two new recruits from Renick.

The Federal military authorities saw a rare chance to destroy the Anderson band; since many of its members were from the far western counties, they were unfamiliar with local landmarks and place names in the central part of the state and therefore could not easily scatter and find their way to the next rendezvous. Those telegraph lines that were still strung buzzed with orders identical in spirit to the one issued by Brigadier General Clinton B. Fisk: "Follow Anderson's gang day and night until the villain is exterminated."

On July 24 the advance of a fifty-five-man mixed party of militia and armed civilians stumbled on the foe on the Fayette Road. The advance immediately fell back on the main column, and the guerrillas charged. The ranking Union officer, a lieutenant named Kapp, ordered his men to dismount and form a line. As they complied, the bushwhackers fired a volley. All the Federal horses being green, they bucked, reared, or broke away. In the confusion most of the soldiers and civilians high-tailed it into the woods, though a few stalwart types held their ground long enough to fire several rounds into the ranks of the enemy, killing one and wounding Anderson himself. Two militiamen, John W. Daniels and John Nichols, were also slain.

While the raiders busied themselves catching and shooting every one of the green horses they could find—twenty-one in all—Anderson carried his dead comrade to a house and left $35 for "a decent interment." He subsequently permitted a burial party of Huntsville residents under a flag of truce to retrieve the bodies of Daniels and Nichols. Both had been oddly scalped. According to the *Missouri Statesman,* "From the forehead of Daniels a round portion of skin had been cut about the size of a Mexican dollar, and from that of Nichols a longer piece was taken from the center of the forehead to the region of the left temple." A note had been pinned to Daniels's coat collar:

> You come to hunt bushwhackers. Now
> you ar skelpt. Clenyent skept you.
>
> Wm Anderson.

Clearly the author of this note was not the same man who wrote the July 7 letters. Historian Richard S. Brownlee argued that Anderson composed the letters, which means some other, semiliterate brute, who was unable even to misspell "scalped" consistently, painstakingly scratched the note, affixing Anderson's name to it.

The band went north into Shelby County, burning the 150-foot-long Salt River bridge, as well as depots and water tanks belonging to the Hannibal and St. Joseph Railroad.

For unknown reasons, Anderson then split his force in two, sending most of the men southwest back into Randolph County under the command of his brother, Jim, while he rode south and farther west, returning to Carroll County with ten men to rendezvous with Fletch Taylor.

On July 31, Bill's contingent stopped at Mary Mitchell's farm in Hurricane township and demanded supper. Two local men, William Darr and Isaac Dugan, were in tow, impressed as guides, and besides the widow Mitchell, fifty-four years old, there were three ladies in the house: Mrs. Stephen Mitchell, Miss Susan Mitchell, and Mrs. Jabez Calvert, who cradled her newborn infant. "After dinner," commented the anonymous author of the 1881 *History of Carroll County*, "some of the men amused themselves by playing on the violin; others, by chafing and talking to the ladies, and still others, tired out from their hard ride, were lying in the yard asleep, for a guerrilla could fall asleep in a minute, and awaken in an instant at the command, 'saddle up.' "

This night they were awakened by gunfire. A dozen citizens had started after the band, hoping to free Dugan and Darr, but, not anticipating the enemy would stop for a meal and a nap, they expected they were already far away. Approaching the Mitchell place, the posse spied horses in the yard. It suddenly occurred to the civilians that they were, as the *History of Carroll County* phrased it, "indifferently armed" and were about to engage famously well-armed raiders. "Consequently the citizens were in some trepidation as they reached the fence, within twenty steps of the house"; nevertheless, at a signal they cut loose a volley directed at the lighted windows.

China shattered, and chairs and other furniture were splintered. One man was nicked, and Susan Mitchell was shot in the hand. Mrs. Calvert was slightly wounded in the breast, and her infant, who was being dandled by a bushwhacker, was struck on the chin and arm. For a moment there was pandemonium in the house. Taking advantage of the confusion, Dugan and Darr burst outside; Dugan was shot by one of his own friends, who did not recognize him in the excitement. Darr was luckier and escaped into the darkness. Anderson saw Mrs. Stephen Mitchell trying to escape, too, and drew a bead on her back, commanding her to stop. When she kept running, he shot her in the shoulder.

At the same time, the bushwhackers rallied, drew their revolvers, knocked out some of the chinking of a wall, and, using the openings as portholes, returned the civilians' fire.

Alarmed at the firing, some of the horses of the citizens broke away, and the citizens themselves, seeing what a miserable failure their attack had proved, retreated. It was but the work of a few moments for Anderson and his men to mount and pursue, and once in the saddle they were home.

A number of civilians were wounded in the flight, but only one, John Kirker, was killed. He was thrown to the ground when his horse stumbled. A guerrilla named John Maupin shot him and, jumping from his horse, scalped him with a bowie knife . . . then sawed off his head.

The several recent instances of the sportive, unnecessary killing of horses, the beheading of Kirker's corpse, and the intentional shooting of Mrs. Mitchell were all further indications of the continuing sharp decline of the band into brutality. Even some of Anderson's own men reproached him about shooting a woman. "Well, it has got to come to that before long anyhow," he told them philosophically.

Fletch Taylor may have been a bit appalled by Anderson's attitude and the cruelty of his boys. While they continued meandering through Carroll County, robbing and burning houses and playing sly identity tricks on Unionists and militiamen, Taylor rode southwest, linking up with John Thrailkill. On the night of August 8, Thrailkill's band bumped into a militia company four miles from Independence, had a brief fight, and escaped—but not before Taylor had received a load of buckshot in his right arm. A physician named Murphy was kidnapped and amputated the limb below the shoulder. When the Federals heard rumors of the operation, they hunted Murphy down and arrested him. They assumed he was a Southern sympathizer and had operated on the notorious Taylor voluntarily, and so would have treated the good doctor badly, but it turned out that as soon as the guerrillas released him, he had had the foresight to notify a Union officer of his kidnapping and forced surgery. He was allowed to go home, and Yankee scouts diligently hunted the invalid Taylor but found only the camp where the amputation had been performed, which contained some discarded bloody bandages and the pillow he had rested on.

Subsequently loyalist newspapers giddily reported the rumor that "mortification" had set into Taylor's stump, making his death inevitable. To the contrary, he recovered, and for a short time resumed bushwhacking. During a skirmish he was accidentally shot in his remaining arm by one of his own men. That was enough for Taylor: He personally started a new rumor of his own death to throw the enemy off his trail, slipped out of the region, and did not return until the war was over.

The Anderson band attacked a militia company at Fredericksburg, in western Ray County, on August 12, killing its captain and four men. Once again telegraph lines hummed, and units converged from all over.

"Anderson is the worst of all, and he must be killed, or he will cause the death of every Union man he can find," General Fisk wired a subordinate. The general certainly had Anderson's ambition correct. Throughout the rest of the month he continued to operate in Ray, Randolph, Carroll, and

Chariton counties, recruiting and alternately raiding and being chased. (The band had a particularly savage fight with 150 militia near Wakenda, in southeastern Carroll County, on August 15, in which Jesse James received a pistol ball in the chest; he was nursed back to health by a Confederate soldier's family but bore a scar all his life from the wound.)

Federal commanders responded to Anderson's depredations and the feverish activities of the many other guerrilla chieftains by pressing civilians into the militia, assessing "disloyal citizens" huge fines to compensate for soldiers killed, and once again exiling families from the state.

Nothing discouraged the bushwhackers. "The very air seems charged with blood and death," wrote Dwight Thacher. "East of us, west of us, north of us, south of us, comes the same harrowing story. Pandemonium itself seems to have broken loose, and robbery, murder and rapine, and death run riot over the country."

———————

At the end of August, Sterling Price commenced his invasion of Missouri. He wanted to liberate the state, and he arrogantly seems to have expected that his advance into it from Arkansas would cause a general uprising. Knowing him as they did, his superiors had more modest expectations, contenting themselves with the hope that he would be able to attract many recruits—"our great want is men," Kirby Smith had reminded him in a letter dated August 4, "and your object should be, if you cannot maintain yourself in that country, to bring as large an accession as possible to our force." Smith also meant for him to aid the war effort by collecting animals and matériel: "Should you be compelled to withdraw from the State, make your retreat through Kansas and the Indian Territory, sweeping that country of its mules, horses, cattle, and military supplies of all kinds." Price succeeded in carrying out both of these instructions but utterly failed with regard to a third: "You will scrupulously avoid all wanton acts of destruction and devastation, restrain your men, and impress upon them that their aim should be to secure success in a just and holy cause and not to gratify personal feeling and revenge."

On September 8, while Price was still moving through northern Arkansas, one of his agents, John Chestnut, contacted Todd at Bone Hill, specifically asking him to do everything he could to disorganize the Union defenses, paying special attention to cutting telegraph wires and interfering with the railroads by burning bridges and tearing up track.

Todd called his men together and rode east, linking up with Thrailkill's band and then going into Ray, Carroll, and Chariton counties, murdering hapless militiamen along the way. On September 20, Todd and Thrailkill entered Keytesville, in central Chariton County, and had their men surround the courthouse, forcing the timid garrison commander to surrender by threatening to kill every trooper and burn the entire town if he did not.

The previous day Price had crossed the Arkansas line with twelve thousand cavalry troops in three divisions under Shelby, Marmaduke, and James Fagan. His plan was to proceed north through eastern Missouri and capture St. Louis. Unfortunately, Price was the wrong general for such an ambitious undertaking, lacking the organizational and tactical skills, and his force was far less impressive than it seemed on paper. In his biography of Price, Albert Castel wrote that

> Many of the men were ill-clad and in poor health. Four thousand of them . . . had no weapons. The train contained an inordinate number of "wheezy, rickety wagons," and although indispensable for carrying the food and forage required in a barren country, was a serious encumbrance. Approximately half of the armed troops were untrained to fight on foot and the other half were mounted infantry equipped with long-barreled muskets and so practically useless on horseback. About a thousand men lacked mounts, which meant the army could not move with the rapidity associated with cavalry. All of the fourteen cannons were of small caliber, only a few were rifled, and several were crude "home-made" pieces. Most of Shelby's recruits were conscripts and deserters whose overriding desire was to return home . . . and who were in the opinion of one of Price's officers "almost worthless as soldiers." Discipline was extremely slack, especially among the recruits and unarmed men, a situation largely caused and certainly compounded by the utter inefficiency of the majority of the line officers.

John N. Edwards, who, it will be recalled, was Shelby's adjutant, would later comment that it was "the stupidest, wildest, wantonest, wickedest march ever made by a general who had a voice like a lion and a spring like a guinea pig."

While Price's Army of Missouri inched its way toward St. Louis, the bushwhackers dutifully escalated their activities in the state's central counties.

On the evening of September 23, Anderson's band attacked a train of eighteen wagons fourteen miles from Rocheport. The militia escort was put to flight, and the wagons were plundered and burned. The guerrillas rode away leaving twelve soldiers and three black teamsters dead on the ground. "All the soldiers were shot in the head, showing that they had been murdered after being captured," Brigadier General J. B. Douglass bitterly complained. For once pursuing Federal cavalry actually caught up with the band, killing five and scalping the corpses.

That same night Dave Pool and his gang rode into the camp of Todd and Thrailkill, which was near Fayette, in central Howard County. Quantrill also arrived with six or seven men, ready to put aside his grudges and grievances to aid Price's incursion. In the morning Anderson and his followers showed up, some with scalps dangling from their bridles. Jesse James was with them, having made a rapid recovery from being shot five weeks earlier.

Todd and Anderson proposed attacking Fayette, but Quantrill opposed the idea, saying the town was too heavily garrisoned, that nothing would be gained and many lives lost. Anderson and Todd replied that they were going to Fayette, and if he wanted to come along he was welcome; otherwise, he could hide in the woods with the rest of the *cowards*. Heated words were exchanged; still, in the end Quantrill went on the raid.

The band rode quietly into town at 10:30 A.M. with Anderson's men in the lead. At first the citizenry was not alarmed, believing they were Federals on a scout, but then one began shooting at a black man, wearing a Federal uniform, who was standing on the sidewalk. Men, women, and children ran screaming in every direction, and the bushwhackers spurred their horses, galloping to the north end of Fayette, where the garrison was. Fifty soldiers had taken refuge in a log blockhouse built on a ridge.

Anderson led the first charge across an open field. Forty-nine years later, Hamp B. Watts, who, at age sixteen, had been the youngest of the band on that day, would still shake his head at the folly of assaulting such an impregnable position: "Not one of the enemy could be seen, but the muzzles of muskets protruded from every port-hole, belching fire and lead. . . . Horses went down as grain before the reaper." Guerrillas tumbled out of their saddles dead or mortally wounded.

George Todd led the second charge. Men dropped all around him, but his luck held: He was not even scratched. Driven back, he led a third charge, which was also repulsed. The Yankees lost only one man—who had been caught out in the open—and had two wounded, but thirteen raiders had been killed outright, and another thirty wounded, some of whom died that night.

The "demons . . . were properly welcomed by the small force in garrison and most handsomely whipped," cheered General Fisk.

Writing his memoir in 1913, Hamp Watts was no less scornful of what Anderson and Todd had done:

> Leading men, armed only with revolvers, charging an invisible enemy in [a] block-house, to simply imbed bullets in logs, with no possible chance to either kill or inflict injury on the foe, was both stupid and reckless. The defeat of the guerrillas therefore was signal and humiliating. Had the Federals been more deliberate and better marksmen, at least two-thirds of the guerrilla band engaged in the battle would have been killed.

Quantrill had witnessed the debacle at a distance. "Seeing at first view of the stronghold . . . the hopelessness of victory," Watts said, he "had refused to take any part in the assaults." Twenty-three months earlier he had attacked the fortified courthouse at Lamar and seen the dismal results. Now having watched Anderson and Todd repeatedly hurl themselves and their followers across the open ground, he must have realized he could not coexist with these stubborn maniacs. Jim Little had lost a finger, been wounded in the right arm, and shot through both hips. "Boys, I will take Jimmie to cover," Quantrill called. "He is all shot to hell."

He promptly disappeared. When Todd realized that he was not coming back, he flew into a wild rage and blamed Quantrill for the Fayette fiasco. He ordered his men to find him and bring him back so he could kill him. They refused, saying Quantrill was not to blame, that he had always treated them well, and that they would leave the outfit before they would have any part in his murder. Todd then swore he would go after Quantrill himself, but they gathered around him, restraining him and telling him that he would probably be killed and, finally, calming him down.

The band retreated north on the Glasgow Road, camping that night about ten miles from Fayette. The next day, still riding north, the bushwhackers crossed into Randolph County. Late in the afternoon, they passed Huntsville, and Anderson sent a farmer into town with a message demanding its surrender in the name of "the Southern Confederacy."

Lieutenant Colonel A. F. Denny replied, "Tell them if they want us to come in and get us."

After Fayette even Anderson had had enough of charging fortified positions. The column doubled back toward Renick, tearing down miles of telegraph wires and fighting several small skirmishes with Union patrols, whose officers bragged that they "summarily mustered out" every straggler who fell into their hands.

On September 26, the guerrillas crossed into Monroe County. They menaced the town of Paris, but upon learning it contained a large militia force, they turned south into Boone County. As darkness fell, they camped three miles northwest of Centralia, a little village of twenty-five houses and a station on the North Missouri Railroad line.

Earlier that same day, some 130 miles to the southeast, Sterling Price approached Pilot Knob, where Thomas Ewing, who had been dispatched from St. Louis to make a reconnaissance in force, was waiting in Fort Davidson with one thousand infantry and civilian volunteers. Price might have given the fort a wide berth and proceeded toward St. Louis, but, disastrously, he decided to attack, apparently in order to obtain the garrison's arms for his unarmed troopers and to secure an easy victory as a morale booster.

Although the garrison was vastly outnumbered, Ewing held the fort against Price's massive assault. In two days' fighting he lost seventy-eight men, but Price suffered fifteen hundred casualties.

Knowing his command was ultimately facing certain annihilation, Ewing spiked his artillery pieces, ignited a slow fuse in the powder magazine, and withdrew under the cover of darkness. He marched sixty-six miles in thirty-nine hours, fighting a rear guard action much of the way against pursuing Confederate cavalry under Marmaduke. Upon reaching Harrison Station (present-day Leasburg), he had his weary men throw up breastworks of rails and ties. After much discussion with Shelby, Marmaduke decided an attack would be pointless and withdrew his troops. Ewing's brilliant defensive maneuvers had bloodied Price, blunted the "fighting edge" of his army, and, perhaps most crucially, delayed his advance on St. Louis, while the city's defenses were greatly strengthened.

———•◦•———

At 10:00 A.M. on the morning of September 27, Bill Anderson took his band into Centralia, trying to get news of Price's whereabouts. According to several reliable sources, George Todd and his men remained in camp, which relieves them of responsibility for the terrible events of that morning.

The bushwhackers robbed the town's two small stores of all their stock, including goods for which they had no use—bolts of calico and muslin cloth, women's shoes, and even baby slippers. They were no more discriminating at the freight house, where they broke open all the crates. To their vast delight they found four cases of boots and a huge barrel of whiskey. In his 1882 *History of Boone County,* J. Thomas Fyfer calculates that in

> five seconds the head was broken in and "anti-prohibition" flowed down the throats of the guerrillas like water after a long and sultry ride.
>
> News of the discovery of the whiskey spread rapidly, and very soon nearly all of the guerrillas, and Anderson himself, had sampled it, as experts of the border alone can accomplish such a convivial feat of that character. Then the question arose as to the method of carrying a portion of it to camp, that their "comrades in arms" might share with them its exhilarating influence, and it was soon decided that some of the new boots should serve as demijohns, and they were filled to the leg tops, and carried to the camp miles away.

The Columbia stage pulled in at eleven o'clock and was instantly surrounded. The bushwhackers yanked open the doors and demanded to know if any of the men inside were Federal soldiers. None were, but as it happened, a number were prominent Unionists on their way to the Democratic Congressional Convention at Mexico, Missouri, where they were to be delegates. Three were in special danger: Boone County Sheriff James H. Waugh, former sheriff John M. Samuel, and U.S. Representative James S. Rollins.

"Out with your pocket-books!" the guerrillas cried. As each passenger disembarked, a pistol barrel was pressed against his chest, and he was relieved of his money.

One disingenuously complained, "We are Southern men and Confederate sympathizers. You ought not rob us."

"What do we care?" came the retort. "Hell's full of all such Southern men. Why ain't you fighting?"

As the dignitaries were subjected to rapid-fire questioning, they realized that if their true identities were known they would be killed or held for ransom, so they hurriedly made up names—Rollins said he was the Reverend Mr. Johnson, a "minister of the Methodist Church, South."

There was an anxious moment when the bushwhackers started searching the passengers' clothing: Sheriff Waugh had papers and letters in his pockets that would reveal his true identity and office; Rollins did, too, and his name was written in indelible ink in his outer garments. Before their turn came, however, a cry went up: "The train! The train! Yonder comes the train!" The thieves broke off their probing for small change and raced to the depot 250 yards away, seeking greater loot.

The railroad train, with three coaches, an express car, and a baggage car, was on its regular run, bound northwest from St. Louis to St. Joseph, carrying mail and passengers. As it approached Centralia, engineer James Clark had observed a body of riders on horseback but was lulled by their blue uniforms. Nearing the depot, however, he saw men piling ties on the tracks ahead and understood what was happening. "I pulled the throttle wide open and dropped down on the deck," he recalled in 1896. "I intended to go through if the obstruction did not stop us, or throw the engine off the track." Showers of bullets swept engine and cars, shattering all the windows and killing two male passengers. The brakemen took refuge inside the coaches, leaving, said Clark,

> the brakes all set tight, causing the train to stop in front of the depot. The throttle was [still] wide open, slipping the wheels of the engine on the tracks, and so long as the men saw the wheels turning they continued to fire. Seeing they had me foul, I raised up and shut off the throttle and dropped on the deck again.

Six raiders climbed into the cab and relieved Clark and his fireman of money and watches. In the excitement the fireman was shot in the chest; the wound was superficial but bled profusely. "For God's sake, don't kill us," he begged.

"We don't want to hurt any of you," he was told, "but consider yourselves prisoners and under orders."

Such benevolence was not directed at all the passengers—twenty-three were unarmed soldiers in uniform. They were on furlough fresh from the Atlanta campaign, having served under Sherman, and had never fought in the border war. As if that would matter to the bushwhackers who burst into their car. "Surrender quietly," they were told, "and you shall be treated as prisoners of war."

They had no choice. They were held up and driven outside with kicks and shoves. Carried along with them was a German who spoke little English and had the bad luck to be wearing a blue shirt.

Guerrillas moved through the other cars, brandishing their pistols and shouting obscenities and threats while robbing terrified men, women, and even children of money, jewelry, and trinkets. Many of the women and children sobbed, cried, or moaned. An occasional shot was fired into the roof to encourage those reluctant to part with precious personal mementos. Afterward, the civilians were ordered to leave the train; most clustered in small groups near the tracks, "clinging to each other, and not daring to leave without permission," related historian Fyfer. "A few, seemingly stupefied or paralyzed with horror, remained in the cars, some of them crouching beneath the seats."

Anderson and Frank James led a squad into the express car and forced the messenger to "deliver up" the keys to the safe. Inside was $3,000. The next stop was the baggage car, where every valise and trunk was broken open, their contents dumped on the dirty floor. A large cache of greenbacks, said to total $10,000, was discovered.

A newly prosperous Bill Anderson walked outside and climbed upon his horse. The soldiers had been lined up a little distance to the south and forced to strip off their uniforms. They stood in their underwear, many trembling with fear. Opposite them, twenty paces away, had congregated a large mob of inebriated, filthy, long-haired bushwhackers.

As Anderson came up Arch Clement asked, "What are you going to do with them fellows?"

"*Parole* them, of course," Anderson answered sardonically.

"I thought so." Clement laughed. "You might pick out two or three, though, and exchange them for Cave, if you can." Cave Wyatt, the sergeant of the band, had been wounded in a recent engagement and had fallen into Federal hands.

"Oh, one will be enough for that, Arch," Anderson replied. "You take charge of the firing party, and when I give the word pour hell into them."

Then he called out pleasantly, "Boys, have you a sergeant in your ranks?" There were several, but apprehensive that Anderson meant to torture or murder them, none replied. Anderson shouted the question a second time, adding, "If there be one let him step aside!"

Sergeant Thomas Goodman hesitantly came forward. Anderson assigned two men to escort him to safety.

At the signal the drunken firing squad cut loose.

"A dozen of the prisoners, shot through the brain or the heart, fell dead at the first volley," wrote J. Thomas Fyfer.

Others screamed and staggered about with a hand pressed to their wounds until, shot again and again, they tumbled lifeless to the ground. One man, Sergeant [Valentine] Peters . . . a man of herculean stature, stripped to his shirt and drawers, was shot five times through the body, and yet knocked the guerrillas right and left, broke through the line, and, with blood spouting from his wounds, succeeded in reaching the depot and crawling under the platform, which was raised some feet above the ground.

Others wandered about, stunned and bleeding, and in their agony staggered against the very muzzles of the revolvers of the guerrillas. One or two started for the railroad and fell dead with in a few feet of it. Some cried, "O, God, have mercy!" but most of them merely groaned and moaned in the most agonizing manner. The poor German whined pitifully as he expired.

One man lay flat on his back with his hands clenched tightly in the short grass. Another lay with one bullet-hole over the eye, another in his face, a third in his breast. He was unconscious, his eyes were closed, he did not moan, but, with a sort of spasmodic motion, he dragged his right heel on the ground, back and forth, back and forth. "He's marking time," said Arch Clement, jocosely.

The depot was set ablaze, and when the heat drove Sergeant Peters out, he was killed. The raiders hammered the bodies with carbine stocks and pistol butts and hacked at them with sabers. They threw some of the corpses on the tracks and forced the engineer to run the engine over them.

Through the carnage most of the passengers and townsfolk were silent and still, struck dumb with horror. A smattering of the women wept or prayed, and a few of the men stumbled about aimlessly in a daze.

The train crew was compelled to pull the ties off the track and set fire to the cars and the rolling stock in the yard. As the flames climbed higher a Centralian named Thomas S. Sneed moved through the coaches, shooing outside the cowering souls who had remained behind. Engineer Clark was then made to start the engine rolling and jump off. It ran three and a half miles before running out of steam.

A gravel train chugged into town, which was halted by throwing a corpse across the tracks. The crew was robbed, and its cars were burned.

The bushwhackers put Sergeant Goodman, still in his underwear, on a mule and tied more whiskey-filled boots in pairs, yoking them over their horses' necks. They rode out of town cheering.

Back in camp many drank themselves into sleep.

At 3:00 P.M. Major A. V. E. Johnston rode into Centralia at the head of a detachment of 39th Missouri Infantry Volunteers. This newly organized regiment had been in service only two weeks and was armed with muzzle-loading Enfield rifles and bayonets but, of course, no pistols. To make matters worse, Johnston had secured mounts for his men by "pressing" stock from "disloyal" citizens of the area; by the late summer of 1864, pickings were pretty slim: "These animals were of an inferior grade," noted Fyfer, "most of them being old brood-mares and plow horses, with some indifferent mules."

The Volunteers had fought just one skirmish, although they had actually managed to wound three or four of the foe. They had been hunting Anderson and Todd for nearly twenty-four hours. Major Johnston surveyed the smoking ruins of the depot and the cars and the bloody corpses of the butchered soldiers and was determined to have revenge. He interrogated townsfolk about the size of the rebel force and the direction of its withdrawal, then climbed to the attic of the hotel with its proprietor, Dr. A. F. Sneed. Johnston peered out the window toward the enemy camp and saw some men ride out of a small stand of timber a mile and a half away. "There they are now," he cried and raced downstairs. Sneed trailed closely behind, trying to talk him out of attacking. "They largely outnumber you," he argued, "and they are much better armed and mounted, having four good revolvers each and splendid horses." In the morning's excitement he had failed to take note of their Sharps carbines.

The townsfolk had told Johnston that the band numbered no more than eighty, but Sneed believed there were many more in camp—a total of perhaps four hundred. Johnston was rightly incredulous at the number, which was too large by half, but, in any case, he was not going to be deterred.

"And they are armed only with revolvers?" he asked. "Well, they may have the advantage of me in numbers, but I will have the advantage of them in arms. My guns are of long range, and I can fight them successfully at a distance."

When Sneed continued to wring his hands over the size of the rebel force, Johnston brushed him off. "I will fight them anyhow!"

Leaving the wagons, teamsters, two officers, and thirty-five men from Company H in Centralia, Johnston set out with a 120-man column. He soon spotted and chased Dave Pool and ten guerrillas—suspecting that Federals were in the area, Todd had sent Pool on a scout. Pool lured Johnston forward for a mile or two and then gave him the slip, returning to camp with the news. He interrupted Todd and Anderson in the midst of a heated argument. Todd, having heard about the butchery of the soldiers, was furious and scolding, and Anderson was about to break with him, but the prospect of battle caused the two men to put aside their differences.

They came over the crest of a hill and found the Yankees on the next hill, half a mile away. Their plan was to split their force in three: Todd would take about sixty-five men and swing to the left, while Thrailkill and a similar number swung to the right. Their role was simply to distract and confuse the enemy as Anderson made a frontal assault.

Still determined to use his long guns to their best advantage, Johnston ordered ninety of his men to dismount, form a line, and fix bayonets. The other thirty withdrew to the rear to hold the horses, as was common practice with cavalry and mounted infantry when fighting on foot. The horse holders were known as "fourth men."

Seeing the bluecoats dismount, John Koger jocularly called out, "Why the fools are going to fight us on foot!" Then he added soberly, "God help 'em!"

Anderson's men dismounted and tightened their cinches, then climbed back in the saddle and formed a line. They moved slowly down the slope and through a stand of timber, then Anderson shouted "Charge!" They dug in their spurs, laid low on their horses' backs, and pounded up the hill. The Federals fired a single volley. Nearly all the shots were high, though three men were hit. Two of the men, Frank Sheperd and Richard Kinney, were riding on either side of Frank James; Sheperd was struck in the head, and as he fell his brains and blood splashed on James's pant leg. Kinney was not killed outright and clung to his horse, hoping the wound was not fatal. His optimism was unfounded, and he soon died.

The third man, Hank Williams, contracted lockjaw from his leg wound and succumbed four days later.

"Kinney was my closest friend," Frank James remarked solemnly in the fall of 1897. Frank had returned to Centralia because he had been hired to start the horse races at the town fair. He stopped by the battle site, accompanied by various local dignitaries and a Columbia *Missouri Herald* correspondent. Standing in what was now a farmer's hay field, Frank explained,

> We had ridden together from Texas, fought side by side, slept together, and it hurt me when I heard him say, "Frank, I'm shot." But we couldn't stop in that terrible charge for anything. Up the hill we went yelling like wild Indians. Almost in the twinkling of an eye we were on the Yankees' line. They seemed terrorized. Hypnotized might be a better word, though I reckon nobody knew about hypnotism then. . . . Some of the Yankees were at "fix bayonets," some were biting off their cartridges, preparing to reload. Yelling, shooting our pistols upon them we went. Not a single man of the line escaped. Every one was shot through the head. . . . My brother, Jesse James . . . killed the commander of the Federal troops, Major Johnson [*sic*].

Frank and some of the others plunged through the line and headed for the "fourth men." Some of these were so paralyzed by fear that they neither fired their muskets nor tried to escape, instead sitting motionless on their horses until shot out of the saddle. Others fired one round and, with no time to reload, galloped for Centralia. Only a few got very far: As Fyfer observed, "the old sickle-hammed brood-mares and plow horses and the sore-backed mules were no matches in speed for the fine horses, the best in Missouri, ridden by the guerrillas."

The chase went across an open prairie. With their single-shot rifles empty, the soldiers were totally defenseless. The bushwhackers killed them one at a time.

Being an officer, Lieutenant Jaynes was better mounted and actually managed to reach town. "Get out of here! Get out of here!" he shouted to the Volunteers who had been left behind. "Every one of you will be killed if you don't!"

Some disregarded Jaynes, hiding themselves in outhouses or under invalids' beds, where they were discovered and killed. Others ran for

Paris or Sturgeon. In 1897, Frank told of chasing a quarry all the way to the latter, only to have him take refuge in a blockhouse.

As some of Quantrill's veterans grew old they tended to soften the details of wartime deeds or deny their involvement in them, so it is hardly surprising that Frank was more than a little disingenuous in his interview with the *Missouri Herald*. He claimed that he had remained in camp with Todd on the morning of the massacre, although he was a member of Anderson's band and eyewitnesses would later swear to having seen him on the train. In describing the afternoon's battle, he found it easier to leave out the gory and terrible details and to imply that all the enemy had died fighting. What really happened was that as Anderson's boys closed in and circled, they shouted for the Federals to surrender. Some refused, using their rifles as clubs or thrusting with bayonets, but most complied. "They surrendered as we did at Centralia," Sergeant Goodman wrote. His guards had taken him along in the attack, just behind Anderson's line. Watching the guerrillas disarm the soldiers, he closed his eyes "to prevent the tears from welling forth, in token of my sympathizing fears. . . ."

As soon as all weapons had been turned over, the butchery commenced. Frank was right about the nature of the wounds: All the prisoners were shot in the head. "Hell was suddenly transferred to earth, and all the fiends of darkness summoned to join a carnival of blood," Goodman bitterly recalled. "Centralia, with all its horrors, was eclipsed here in the enormity and infamous conduct of the bloody demons!" At least one wounded man was castrated, and his genitals stuffed into his mouth. "Men's heads were severed from their lifeless bodies," Goodman wrote, "exchanged as to bodies, labeled with rough and obscene epitaphs . . . stuck on their carbine points, tied to their saddle bows, or sat grinning at each other from the tops of fence stakes and stumps around the scene."

No wonder Frank wanted it known he was riding hard for Sturgeon.

Afterward Anderson required Dr. Sneed to treat his wounded—several of whom had been bayoneted—and made a local carpenter build coffins for those he had lost. They were buried in a nearby cemetery. His men drifted into town, located more liquor, and once again became, as Goodman put it, "brutally intoxicated. . . . At last the order was given to return, and the drunken cavalcade made night hideous as they straggled, without order or discipline, back to their camp." Todd took his band and established a camp several miles away, which suggests the rift between him and Anderson over the treatment of prisoners was growing wider.

Anderson let his bunch sleep a few hours and then led them south toward the Missouri River, Sergeant Goodman in tow.

The next day, military authorities removed the corpses of the twenty-three soldiers who had been on the train. They required the townsfolk to retrieve the dead from the battlefield. The bodies had been searched for valuables, papers scattered across the ground, and some had been stripped. Major Johnston's nose had been smashed, and all the officers scalped. One man had been pinned to the earth with his own bayonet, but another rose up at the approach of the civilians. He had lain all night with a head wound, afraid to move. He was carried to Mexico for treatment but died that night. A number of the Enfield rifles were found to be loaded but had not been fired at all—like many of the "fourth men," not a few of the green Volunteers in the line had been so terrified by the sight of the bushwhackers' charge they had been unable to shoot.

Four corpses were sent to families for burial in private plots; the rest were laid in a long trench near the railroad tracks east of town.

Because some troopers were never accounted for—bodies never found or men who had had enough of war and run all the way home—the exact number of slain will never be known, but the best estimate seems to be that 123 of the 39th Missouri Infantry had been killed, in addition to the three civilians and the twenty-three soldiers from the train, a total of 149.

Goodman remained a prisoner while the guerrillas undertook a series of night marches, to avoid detection, generally meandering in a south-westerly direction. While he was roughly treated at first, his captors soon developed a more benign attitude toward him, even furnishing him with an ancient coat and a ragged shirt and pants. After a few days they came to an old camp and found Todd and his band. He and Anderson patched things up enough to get drunk together. Everyone except Goodman joined in. "God help me, I never witnessed so much profanity in the same space of time before, nor since; and it is my earnest desire, I never may again. They whooped, ran, jumped and yelled like so many savages. Once, Anderson, leaping on a horse, rode wildly through the crowd; firing his revolvers indiscriminately, and yelling like one possessed."

The next morning a hungover council of war was held, and it was decided to disband. Goodman went with Anderson and some others.

They were now able to travel in daylight. One evening they camped near Rocheport, which was being burned by Federal troops in retaliation for Centralia. They lingered in the area briefly, and then, on the night of October 6, crossed the Missouri near Boonville. They had only one skiff and so were required to make three trips. Goodman had been a prisoner now for ten days and his guards had been increasingly casual about watching him. Some of the horses were restive about going into the water and reared and kicked. In the confusion, Goodman slipped into a thicket near the riverbank and simply walked away.

He covered the twenty-eight miles to Fayette on foot, traveling at night to avoid his former captors.

———◆◆◆———

Two days after the Centralia massacre, on September 29, General Price led the Army of Missouri away from Pilot Knob. He sent some of Shelby's cavalry on a feign toward St. Louis, but capturing it was no longer a serious possibility, and Price now meant to take the state capital, Jefferson City. Governor Reynolds was along in the expedition's train, and the installation of a Confederate government in the capital, even if only temporary, would be a great propaganda victory.

Price's troops encountered little resistance and were able to tear up long sections of the Pacific Railroad and burn bridges. They also stole whatever rare, good horseflesh they came across and—despite Kirby Smith's explicit order to the contrary—they engaged in wholesale looting. Governor Reynolds was thoroughly disgusted.

It would take a volume to describe the acts of outrage; neither station, age, nor sex was any protection. Southern men and women were as little spared as Unionists; the elegant mansion of General Robert E. Lee's accomplished niece and the cabin of the negro were alike ransacked; John Deane, the first civilian ever made a State prisoner by Mr. Lincoln's Government, had his watch and money robbed from him in broad day, as unceremoniously as the German merchant at Frederickstown [*sic*] was forced, a pistol at his ear, to surrender his concealed greenbacks . . . the clothes of a poor man's infant were as attractive spoil as the merchant's silk and calico or curtain taken from the rich man's parlor; ribbons and trumpery gee-gaws were stolen from milliners, and jeweled rings forced from the fingers of delicate maidens whose brothers were fighting in Georgia in Cockrell's Confederate Missouri brigade.

Price made a sincere effort to stop the pillaging; however, many of the line officers who were responsible for enforcing discipline were indifferent, incompetent, or were themselves guilty of theft.

Looting was far from the worst crime Confederates committed. They murdered white and black men, never bothering to bury the bodies, but leaving them beside the road or in fields to be eaten by wild hogs and other animals. According to a dispatch published in the October 13 St. Louis *Missouri Democrat,* some of Price's men had become so degenerate that they brutalized women.

> Mrs. H. Mouse, a German woman, who lived about two miles from this place [Union, Franklin County], was treated most shamefully and basely. After having robbed her house, the rebels put a handkerchief around her neck and strangled her with it, threatening to put her to death if she did not tell them where she had concealed some whiskey, which they alleged she had. She denied having any and offered them the cider she had in the cellar; but they continued their indignities until convinced that she was telling them the truth.

After stating he had permission from the victims to identify them, the dispatch's author, who used the pseudonym "Waldo," gave a rare and remarkably frank description of sexual attacks on several other German women:

> Mrs. Charles Schmidt, living two miles north of this place, whose husband is in the 26th Missouri regiment (being color sergeant of the regiment), was ravished and her person violated by a number of the fiendish ghouls. This was done while Price had his headquarters in this town. Mrs. S. is now nearly dead.
>
> Mrs. Schmich, living in this place, and sister-in-law of Mr. Greifeld, whom Frank Barns killed, was assaulted in her house, not [more than] a square from Price's headquarters, by some of Shelby's men, who took improper liberties with her, and attempted to ravish her, but her cries excited the sympathies of some rebel soldiers less brutal than their fellows, who rescued the poor woman from their clutches. The cries of this woman must have reached the ears of Sterling Price, but no guard was sent to arrest the brutes. The provost guard were too busy pillaging Union people to attend to poor humanity in distress.

Mrs. Frank Schryvor, living about six miles from here, west, whose husband died in the army, was another lady upon whom an outrage was attempted. Being a woman of great spirit and agility, she succeeded, by flight, in escaping from the fiends, and hid from them in the woods.

––––––•◆•––––––

Price's columns slowly advanced across the rolling prairies at an average of only fifteen miles a day. "This pace," observed Dr. Castel, "which would have done little credit to infantry, much less cavalry, was mainly attributable to poor management in marching and to the cumbersome wagon train." Had Price been capable of quickening the pace, his forces might have reached the capital while it was extremely vulnerable, but the Federals had plenty of time to strengthen Jefferson City's defenses, rush all available units there, and arm civilian volunteers. They used this time very well indeed: As late as October 6, one day before the Army of Missouri approached the capital, an additional 2,400 cavalry and eight cannons had arrived from Rolla.

At noon on October 7, Price's troops occupied the hills south of Jefferson City. Below they saw five forts and long lines of heavily manned rifle pits, which were protected by palisades. That night a spy erroneously told Price that the enemy had fifteen thousand men—more than twice the actual amount—but had Price known the truth, it would not have mattered: The Yankees were just too strong and his troops were too demoralized by Pilot Knob and fearful of another debacle.

Early the next morning he ordered a march on Boonville, some forty-five miles to the northwest. Reaching the town on October 10, the Army of Missouri immediately set about looting it. In an unpublished memoir, Brigadier General M. Jeff Thompson stated,

What was done and not done there I do not propose to relate as I had only to try to control my own Brigade, to save their reputation from the demoralization which was seizing the army. The plunder of Boonville nearly completed this demoralization for many officers and men loaded themselves, their horses and wagons with "their rights" and now wanted to turn Southward and save what they had.

Governor Reynolds was no less appalled by the breakdown in discipline: "The hotel occupied as General Price's own headquarters was the scene of public drunken revelry by night."

His own troops' degeneration not withstanding, when Bill Anderson and his boys rode into Boonville on October 11, Price was shocked and revolted by the scalps dangling from their bridles and ordered that they be thrown away. Only then did he allow Anderson to present him with a pair of silver mounted revolvers, whereupon he declared that if he had fifty thousand such men he could hold Missouri indefinitely. (If he had had fifty thousand such men, the entire state would have been engulfed in blood.)

Probably wanting to hamper the Federal military authorities' movement of reinforcements and supplies by rail, Price issued a "special order":

> Headquarters Army of Missouri
> Boonville, October 11, 1864
>
> Captain Anderson with his command will at once proceed to the north side of the Missouri River and permanently destroy the North Missouri Railroad, going as far east as practicable. He will report his operations at least every two days.
>
> By order of Major-General Price:
McClean
Lieutenant-Colonel and
Assistant Adjutant General

Apparently Price did not know Quantrill had been usurped and no longer had a band as such, because he sent him an order to wreck the Hannibal and St. Joseph Railroad. Quantrill never received it.

On October 13, Price marched west toward Kansas City. He was harassed from the rear by a large cavalry force under the command of Major General Alfred Pleasonton, and General Samuel R. Curtis moved his fifteen-thousand-man "Army of the Border" out from Kansas City to intercept him. Curtis had two divisions, one commanded by General Blunt and the other by General George W. Deitzler.

Meanwhile, Anderson was obeying his orders indifferently well. He followed Shelby to Glasgow, Howard County, but sent most of his men about seventy miles farther east into Montgomery County, where they sacked Danville on October 15, killing five former soldiers and torching the business district and several houses. A thirty-five-man contingent then circled through Florence and High Hill, burning the depots there.

That same day, on the outskirts of Glasgow, Shelby bombarded the steamer *Western Wind,* which was lying at the town's wharf and was occupied by Union soldiers, then turned his six-piece battery upon the city hall, which functioned as the Federal commissary depot. The building caught fire, and a strong breeze spread the blaze to a dozen nearby houses, which were entirely consumed. The encircled garrison troops huddled in their rifle pits and held out until 1:30 P.M. In surrendering they extracted a pledge that they would be taken under military escort to Boonville, not left to the tender mercies of the bushwhackers.

According to the *History of Howard and Chariton Counties,* published in 1883, Quantrill came into town with a few followers after the fight and dragged W. F. Dunnica, a prosperous banker, out of his home, forcing him to go to the bank and open the safe. Twenty-one thousand dollars was inside, which must have greatly cheered Quantrill because he personally escorted Dunnica home, so that he would not be harmed by the other raiders milling around the streets.

After Shelby withdrew from Glasgow, Anderson and some of his band visited the house of wealthy, fifty-year-old Benjamin W. Lewis, who, though he was a strong Unionist, was related by marriage to Sterling Price himself. The guerrillas knocked him to the floor in front of his family and beat him with heavy pistol butts. They slashed open his clothing and pricked him with knifes and discharged their revolvers inches from his face so that his skin was powder-burned. They also fired bullets between his legs, blowing holes in his pants and scorching the fabric. They thrust their pistol barrels into his mouth, making obscene suggestions and threatening to blow his brains out.

A correspondent to the St. Louis *Missouri Democrat* alleged that while Lewis was being tormented and tortured, Anderson, who had been drinking copious amounts of wine fortified with whiskey, raped a black female servant.

Lewis gave his tormentors all the money he had on hand, which was $1,000, but Anderson insisted on five times that amount. Lewis was sent into the street under armed guard so that he could borrow money from his neighbors. Eventually he was able to come up with the requisite sum, and he was let go. He and his wife fled the area the very next morning.

After they had gotten away, the *Missouri Democrat* correspondent claimed, a squad of Anderson's men came to the house. They forced two black female servants to cook them breakfast, then gang-raped them.

Anderson did not follow the Army of Missouri's western line of march but continued to range through Carroll and adjacent counties.

Price crossed into Lafayette County on October 18, where he was joined by Todd's band. The next day the Army of Missouri engaged Blunt east of Lexington. From this point on, the fighting would be constant. At noon on the twenty-first, Price forced Blunt to withdraw to the west side of Independence.

The following day General Curtis wrote a letter to his wife. It will be recalled that the Curtis's disarmed son had been killed at Baxter Springs, and because he was wearing a fancy new uniform, he'd been mistaken for General Blunt. Thereafter General Curtis kept track of Quantrill and his followers with a special diligence, railed against them with a special vehemence. Now, in a single sentence, tangled perhaps by the powerful emotions he felt, he informed his wife that "It is certain that among the rebels killed yesterday the notorious Todd, one of the murderers of our son, was among many who were killed."

There are two different versions of how Todd died.

According to the first, Todd, whose band had been acting as Shelby's advance, was cut down in a 2nd Colorado volley. A Spencer rifle ball entered his neck near the base of the throat and exited out the back, just missing the spinal column. He was carried to a Mrs. Burns's house in Independence, where, it is said, he lingered for two hours, sometimes delirious. In moments of clarity, he tried to give those at his bedside a number of messages for various comrades and friends, but because of the neck wound very little of what he said could be understood.

Todd may well have been shot in the throat by a 2nd Colorado trooper, but it is extremely unlikely that a man with such a wound could live for several hours. If this version is correct, then given the circumstances of Todd's being shot and the nature of his wound, it would seem that the deathbed scene is an embroidery.

The second version has Todd leading a small squad on a scout two miles northeast of Independence when he came to a place where the road snaked past a ridge. He rode to the crest alone and rose in his stirrups, surveying the countryside. In the grassy glade below him, an unseen sniper took aim. The ball entered the base of Todd's throat and, passing through, shattered his spine. He pitched forward out of the saddle and tumbled off the precipice, landing in the road below. By the time his men reached him, he was dead. One man galloped off to find a conveyance and returned with an ambulance, in which Todd's body was carried to Independence for burial in Woodlawn Cemetery.

He had been through numerous skirmishes and fights, always in the thick of things, and for a long time he had led a charmed life. He died an anonymous figure in a line of riders or alone in a quiet moment on a splendid horse silhouetted against the sky. Either way, we are told that his men wept bitterly at the side of his grave.

Dave Pool, who also was with Price, merged Todd's band with his own.

• ◆ •

Intending to make a stand, General Curtis had dug in on the western bank of the Big Blue, several miles east of Kansas City; however, on October 22, Price, personally directing a dismounted portion of Shelby's "Iron Brigade," easily breached the line at Byram's Ford. The colonel in charge of the routed troops was "Doc" Jennison. During the fighting Todd's former followers murdered some captured Kansans. Learning of the butchery, Price ordered them to leave the army. Some did; the rest melded into Shelby's force.

That same day Pleasonton attacked Price's rear, mauling Brigadier General William L. Cabell's brigade, capturing four hundred prisoners and two cannons and occupying Independence. In the evening, Price learned from captured Union dispatches that there were strong enemy units concentrating to the south; with Curtis's army to the north at Westport and Pleasonton pressing from the east, the Army of Missouri was in grave danger of being trapped and destroyed. Price wisely if belatedly ordered his train to proceed southward in the morning on the Fort Scott Road.

He covered the movement of the train by sending Shelby, supported by two of Fagan's brigades, to attack the foe at Westport. At the same time Blunt moved forward; for several hours the two forces engaged in a series of charges and countercharges, resulting in heavy casualties on both sides. Then Pleasonton launched an attack against Byram's Ford, which was being held by Marmaduke's troops. The Confederates beat back charge after charge until their ammunition was exhausted, then they fled across the plain, the Yankee cavalry in close pursuit. "The collapse of Marmaduke's division at the Big Blue exposed the flank and rear of Shelby and Fagan to Pleasonton," wrote Dr. Castel. "At the same time Blunt, reinforced by thousands of militia, launched a massive counter attack." Fagan's brigades, which were on Shelby's right, repulsed repeated Federal waves but in the end gave way and retreated south. Shelby and the Iron Brigade were compelled to retreat, too, with Blunt's columns close behind. The Confederates ran all the way to Little Santa Fe, where Blunt broke off the pursuit.

Albert Castel observed that

> From the standpoint of numbers Westport was the greatest battle of the Civil War in the West, with approximately forty-five thousand Northern and Southern troops being either directly or indirectly involved. Strategically Price achieved his main objective of saving his train and escaping south, but tactically he took another licking. Persons who toured the fields about Westport after the fighting ended described it as being strewn with dead horses, saddles, blankets, rifles, cannon balls, and bodies. Many of the Confederate slain, they noted, were boys sixteen or seventeen years old. In all Price probably suffered about a thousand casualties, and the already low morale of his army was further reduced.

The Confederates continued to make their way south on the Fort Scott Road. All were hungry, having been on short rations for some time, and many were ill-clad for the cold weather and were sick with a variety of ailments. General Curtis pursued them with the cavalry troops of Blunt and Pleasonton. He had no trouble following their trail, which, wrote Castel

> was marked by broken wagons and caissons, discarded rifles and . . . bits of harness and debris, and by sick, wounded, and exhausted Confederates lying by the roadside waiting to be captured. In addition, up ahead the Union troops saw long columns of smoke twisting into the air. For the Army of Missouri was now in Kansas—the only regular Southern force ever to enter the state—and Shelby's troopers were taking advantage of the fact to extract revenge for jayhawker deprivations against their friends and relatives.

They burned houses, barns, haystacks, crops, and farm implements, and they murdered some of the male civilians who crossed their path. In turn the Yankee pursuers mistreated and killed rebel prisoners.

On October 25, two of Pleasonton's brigades slammed into Price's rear at Mine Creek, south of the Marais des Cygnes, killing and wounding three hundred and taking nine hundred prisoners, including Marmaduke and Cabell. Only a stand made by Shelby's Iron Brigade prevented a complete route. The starving, dispirited Army of Missouri continued to stumble south, now hardly more than a mob.

That same day Anderson made his last raid through Carroll County, riding east to west on his way to Ray County. In Miami Township he killed one Unionist and impressed another as a guide, an elderly man named Eisenhour or Isenhour. The poor old fellow was tricked into admitting where his sympathies lay, and when he was no longer useful, Anderson directed Clement and three others to "take the guide to the rear and parole him." Eisenhour was led into the brush beside the road, thrown to the ground, and decapitated. The murderers folded the corpse's arms across its chest and tucked the still-bleeding head between them. Then they rifled the dead man's pockets, and rode away.

On the morning of October 26, Samuel P. Cox learned through an informant that the Anderson band was in Albany, southwestern Ray County. Cox was a veteran of the Mexican war and the Sioux Indian uprising of 1847, and he had served as a major in the Federal militia cavalry early in the war. However, in 1862 a bout of typhoid fever had forced him to resign and return home to convalesce. On this late October morning he was serving without commission at the request of Brigadier General James Craig because, as Craig subsequently and laconically explained, "I believed he would find and whip Anderson."

Thus when Cox learned Anderson was in Albany, he took elements of the 33rd and 51st Enrolled Missouri Militia and made a forced march. He encountered pickets a mile west of Albany and drove them through town and into the woods beyond. He ordered most of his men to dismount and form lines across the road and on either side of the road in the trees, while sending the rest forward as an advance. The advance soon found the band, skirmished briefly, then fell back. It was the sort of maneuver the bushwhackers had sometimes used, drawing the enemy into a trap, but Anderson fell for it. When he came in sight of the dismounted militia armed only with muzzle-loading rifles, he must have thought of Centralia. This time, though, his men were not charging spread out across open ground, but down a narrow lane with dense woods on either side, forcing them to bunch close together . . . and these troopers were far more disciplined and competently led than Major Johnston's green Volunteers. . . .

The guerrillas spurred their horses and, firing their pistols and whooping like Indians, thundered down the road. The militia opened fire. Horses went down, screaming and kicking. Only four bushwhackers were killed outright, but many more were wounded. The rest, seeing that the militia lines did not waver, reined up, except two—Anderson and a man named Rains. On they came, bullets whizzing past them, until they reached the enemy lines and passed through, miraculously unharmed. For a few seconds it seemed they would get clean away, but then, fifty paces to the rear, Anderson threw his arms in the air and fell backward off his horse. He was dead with two bullets in his head. Rains escaped alone.

Cox's cavalry chased the band for several miles back down the road, which was covered with the blood of the wounded. Six militia had been wounded in the fracas, one of whom died a few days later.

Anderson's body was searched and the following items were found: "likenesses" of himself and his wife; a lock of her hair; letters she had sent him from Texas; orders from General Price; $600 in gold and greenbacks; six revolvers; a gold watch; a silver watch; and a Confederate flag, a gift from a Southern lady, bearing the inscription, "Presented to W. T. Anderson by his friend, F. M. R. Let it not be contaminated by Federal hands!"

Legends persist that also found on the corpse was a buckskin pouch containing a silken cord with fifty-three knots in it—Bloody Bill's way of keeping score of the men he had killed in vengeance for his sisters. Military reports describing his death make no mention of such a cord, but since its purpose would not have been immediately understood, it may have been ignored in the inventory of his effects.

Anderson's horse was corralled, and human scalps were found affixed to either side of the bridle band.

His body was hauled in a wagon to Richmond, where it was tied in a chair and a revolver placed in the right hand. A bystander held the head at an angle so Dr. Robert B. Kice, a local dentist and "photographist," could take a picture.

Souvenir locks were cut from the hair, and the corpse was placed on display at the courthouse. We are told that people came from all over the surrounding countryside to stare at it.

Later, according to an Anderson family tradition, Yankee troopers cut off the head and genitals. The head was placed atop a telegraph pole, while the body was dragged through the streets behind a horse to the hearty cheers of onlookers.

The next day remains were placed in what one of Cox's men characterized as a "decent coffin," explaining that this was "a respect due not to him but to ourselves and to humanity," and buried in an unmarked plot. In the evening militia were seen spitting and urinating on the grave.

On October 30, Brigadier General Craig presented Cox with two of Anderson's revolvers, as well as his flag, saddle, bridle, and mare, "as a reward for the distinguished service [Cox] has lately rendered his country." Anderson's gold watch went to Cox's second in command, Major John Grimes, and the silver watch and the four other pistols were given to other officers "to be retained as honorable trophies." Craig ordered that the $600 was to be distributed "in just proportion" to those who had been wounded and "to the families of such as were killed in the affair."

Cox was also belatedly commissioned a lieutenant-colonel so he could go on hunting rebels, and in addition, Craig, through his adjutant, ordered that the following expression of gratitude be read to every garrison within the state:

> The General tenders to Colonel Cox, and to the officers and men of his command engaged in this praiseworthy act, his heartfelt thanks and congratulations in ridding the country of such a blood-thirsty villain as Anderson, who has been for months past a terror to the loyal people of Missouri; and he feels satisfied that every well-wisher of [the United States] will join in this congratulations, and that the blessings and prayers of many a disconsolate widow and orphan will ascend to Heaven for the future welfare of Colonel Cox and his brave band.

On October 28, Blunt, at the head of a thousand cavalry, caught up with Price, who had crossed back into Missouri and was at Newtonia, in the southwest corner of the state. Had Blunt held back until other Union brigades caught up, the Army of Missouri would have been destroyed, but perhaps wishing to seize an opportunity to repair his reputation, which had been so badly damaged at Baxter Springs, Blunt rashly attacked. Price, believing he had been struck by Curtis's entire army, ordered an immediate retreat. At the same time he ordered Shelby to hold the Yankees at bay; Shelby counterattacked and drove Blunt back.

This would prove to be the last engagement of the Price incursion. His wretched column staggered into Cane Hill, Arkansas, on November 1. Price called a halt, and rations of corn and salt were distributed—the first many of his men had had for themselves and their animals since leaving Independence. The Army of Missouri suffered wholesale desertions. Although Price would continue on to Texas, in effect his great raid was over. Other than attracting several thousand young recruits, he had accomplished little, and the course of the war was not appreciably affected. What has been described as the "last military effort of the South in the West" was just a bloody, brutal failure.

On November 6, the editor of the St. Louis *Missouri Republican* ruminated over one of Dr. Kice's souvenir ambrotypes

of the celebrated murderer and robber, Bill Anderson, taken while he lay, cold and stark, in the arms of his only master, Death. [Anderson's] mouth is partially open, disclosing his front teeth, and imparting to the expression a half sardonic, hideous grin; while the eyes—those scorching orbs, which have often sent terror to innocent hearts—are partly open, with that wo[e]ful and expressionless appearance belonging to the optics of the dead, induce a peculiar and contradictory estimate of the general contour. Thinking of his demoniac life, and looking upon him lying helpless and forever powerless to murder and pillage, a strange feeling is excited—a contention between a desire to spurn the hideous body of a serpent, dead, and that natural emotion of pity which ever arises on view of the remains of a human being. But the memory of his crimes soon drives away the last vestige of the latter feeling, if any should arise.

It is gratifying in looking upon the picture, to know that there is one devil less in the world.

CHAPTER 14

"Here's a Sigh to Those
Who Love Me":
The Death of Quantrill

The defeat of Price foretold the end of the border war, and Quantrill decided to go east.

In 1909, various elderly ex-bushwhackers gave Connelley conflicting explanations for his decision. Luther Wayman claimed that Quantrill's intention was to "go to Washington and assassinate President Lincoln"; however, Wayman lied to Connelley on several matters, and others found this particular notion to be absurd. Morgan T. Mattox asserted simply that Quantrill "did not believe his men would be permitted to surrender" in Missouri and "he wanted to get them away from where they were known." Connelley himself doubted this explanation: If that were Quantrill's "object, he would have gone to Mexico with Price and Shelby."

Sylvester Akers, who actually left Missouri with Quantrill, said that he was headed for Virginia because he was certain General Robert E. Lee would soon surrender, and he hoped to surrender with Lee's army, presumably so that no notice would be taken of him and his men. Akers appears to have been correct: Several of Quantrill's men who were taken prisoner shortly after the band entered Kentucky told their captors they were on the way to Virginia.

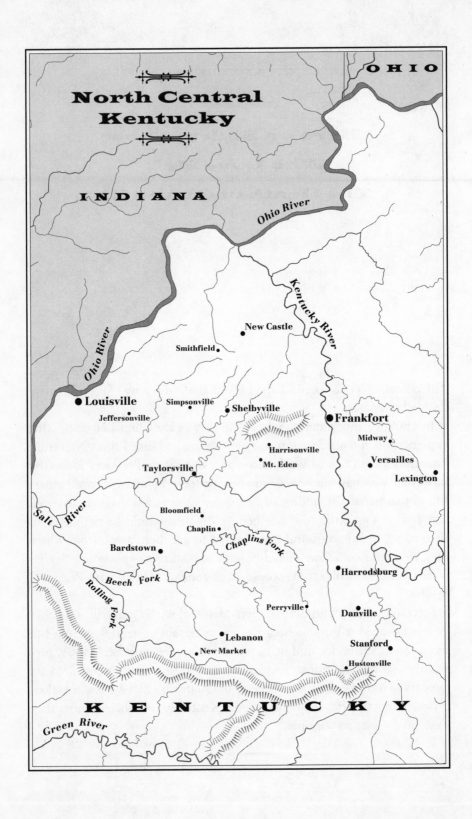

North Central Kentucky

OHIO

INDIANA

Ohio River

Kentucky River

Ohio River

New Castle

Smithfield

Louisville
Jeffersonville

Simpsonville

Shelbyville

Frankfort

Midway

Harrisonville

Versailles

Mt. Eden

Lexington

Taylorsville

Salt   River

Bloomfield

Chaplin

Chaplins Fork

Bardstown

Beech   Fork

Rolling   Fork

Harrodsburg

Perryville

Danville

Lebanon
New Market

Stanford

Hustonville

K E N T U C K Y

Green River

Once he made up his mind to leave Missouri, Quantrill sent Kate King to St. Louis and passed the word for a rendezvous at the Dupee farm in Lafayette County.

A year earlier nearly three hundred had responded to a similar call; this time only thirty-three drifted in. Still, this scant remnant included a number of "old men": John McCorkle, Jim Little, John Koger, "Ol" Shepherd, Dick Burns, Bill Bassham, "Babe" Hudspeth, Allen Parmer, and Frank James. There was also at least one man who might have been unfamiliar to Quantrill—Jesse James.

One day in mid-December they donned Yankee uniforms and rode east into Saline County. Winter had arrived early and hard, so the cold and the ice-clogged rivers and streams slowed them down as they meandered on a southeasterly course. They committed small, discreet robberies when opportunities presented themselves, though none so dramatic or audacious as to arouse Federal military authorities.

Arriving at Tuscumbia, some thirty miles southwest of Jefferson City, they found that Federal militia were comfortably ensconced in a large hotel. Quantrill flourished a commission he had earlier taken from a Colorado officer and introduced himself as Captain William Clarke of the 4th Missouri Cavalry. He asked to see the post commander and was directed to a house on a hill. He and "Babe" Hudspeth made the climb. Quantrill pumped the captain for information concerning the size and location of Union forces in the area, then produced a pistol. The chagrined Federal officer was taken to the hotel and forced to order his men to surrender. After the garrison was disarmed, the guerrillas ate a leisurely breakfast and fed their horses. They picked through a newly arrived shipment of blankets and clothing, loaded the ferry with all the captured arms and ammunition, and required some militiamen to repeatedly operate the rope pulley, ferrying them and their horses across the Osage. Before Quantrill made the last trip himself, he paroled all the prisoners, except one, who was taken along as a guide. The excess arms and ammunition were thrown overboard in the middle of the river, and, on the far side, holes were cut in the bottom of the boat, sinking it. The guide was later allowed to escape.

"We never fired a shot nor hurt a man," John McCorkle remembered. This raid was unremarkable except that it was bloodless, and it was the last Quantrill ever made in Missouri.

They continued riding southeast until they struck the Current River and followed it into Arkansas. Near Pocahontas, which was only fifteen or twenty miles below the border, Joe Hall came down with smallpox. His brother Ike stayed behind to nurse him. A short time later "Ol" Shepherd announced he had decided to head for Texas and join the Confederate army; five other men went along, including John Koger, "Babe" and Rufus Hudspeth, and Jesse James. (There was nearly five years' age difference between the two James brothers, and Frank had been away from home for the past several years, so he and Jesse may not have been close at this time in their lives; anyway, Jesse had been taken under Shepherd's wing.)

When they struck the Mississippi, Quantrill and the remaining Missourians located a leaky yawl and repaired it with fence lumber. They spent the night of January 1, 1865, ferrying themselves across the wide, frigid river, drawing their horses behind the boat. The weary men built fires on the eastern bank so they could dry and warm the animals.

On January 2, Colonel L. B. Fairleigh, commander of the Louisville, Kentucky, garrison hired several civilians to hunt down guerrillas. Among the hirelings was Edwin Terrell, a twenty-year-old scoundrel. Terrell was not long in showing his true colors: He and another man were arrested in Springfield on January 6 by Captain James Nolan on the suspicion that they were Confederate partisans. Since they were operating under Fairleigh's orders, Nolan was compelled to turn them loose. "From what I have heard of these young men since they left Lebanon," Nolan wrote to Fairleigh's adjutant, "I am sorry that I did release them, and I believe their story of killing rebels, capturing horses, etc., to be all fiction and when in [Manton?] they fraternized with the Guerillas and were not troubled by them. I would respectfully request that Col. Fairleigh withdraw his protection passes from them."

It is not known how long Terrell continued to be employed and protected by Fairleigh, but for the next four months he alternately hunted Confederate guerrillas and robbed civilians. Nevertheless, on April 1, the military commander of Kentucky, General John M. Palmer, would put Terrell on his "Secret Service" payroll. Although no written orders have ever been found, subsequent events make it clear that Terrell's assignment was to kill or capture one man: William Clarke Quantrill. Palmer was an ambitious man who was willing to overlook Terrell's misdeeds to achieve an important goal—and not incidentally advance his military career and his prospects in postwar politics—but John Langford, who was in Terrell's band when Quantrill was captured, later commented that "Terrell was a bad man. Perhaps as bad as the man he was hunting down."*

———◆◆◆———

Quantrill and his followers continued to ride on a northeasterly course through western Tennessee for a time. They skirted the larger towns like Brownsville and Paris and stopped at small Federal posts to obtain food and forage under the guise of being 4th Missouri troopers.

Quantrill had intended to traverse the entire state, but something about the military situation there caused him to change his mind. He led his men into the southwest corner of Kentucky, near the little town of Canton, then swung northeast to Cadiz, where they changed course, heading straight east for about twenty miles. Near Hopkinsville they picked up tracks of thirty or forty horses and, in need of fresh mounts, followed with alacrity. As it turned out, the Union cavalry troopers had too much of a head start to be overtaken.

*Almost nothing is certain about Terrell's childhood except that he lived with his parents in Shelby County, near Harrisonville. Federal military records show that on October 7, 1863, at the age of eighteen, he had enrolled in Company D, 37th Kentucky Union Volunteer Mounted Infantry. Seven weeks later he was arrested—the charge is no longer known—and was held in the Bowling Green stockade until March 1864, when he was returned to duty. He was mustered out on December 29, 1864, in Louisville.

There are several curious or intriguing stories about young Terrell that cannot be confirmed. After his death a man came forward who claimed to be his brother and said that before the war Terrell had joined the Dan Rice Circus. E. D. Shinnick, in *Some Old Time History of Shelbyville and Shelby County,* stated that while traveling with the circus, Terrell killed a saloon keeper in Baltimore, Maryland, was tried, and acquitted. There was a circus by that name, but no list of performers and employees exists from the pre–Civil War time period. For reasons that will be set forth later, the "brother" may have been a fraud. I have been unable to find any other source for the murder allegation.

Some who knew Terrell when he was a teenager would say that at the onset of the war he had joined the Dixie Home Guards, which was mustered into the 1st Kentucky Confederate Regiment, and that he later deserted. In 1865, Terrell himself told a number of people that he had served under Confederate General John Hunt Morgan.

The roster of the 1st Kentucky, which fought in Virginia, does not contain the name Terrell or any variant spelling; neither does the roster of Morgan's 2nd Kentucky Cavalry. There is no Confederate military record for Edwin Terrell or any variant spelling.

At dusk the Missourians happened upon a farmhouse. As they approached it, a voice rang out from inside, asking for the current countersign. When there was no reply, six Yankees, who had stopped for supper, opened fire. A bullet struck Jim Little in the thigh, shattering the femur. He fell from his horse, called to his comrades for help, and was dragged to safety. The others took cover, and Quantrill asked for volunteers to set fire to the house. Peyton Long and Frank James crept forward, effectively covered by the rest.

"We will surrender if you will treat us as prisoners," a Federal shouted as flames began to spread.

Quantrill accepted their surrender and paroled them. The fire was extinguished, and Little, too seriously wounded to travel, was carried inside the house. His friends filed in to tell him good-bye. He was left in the care of the soldiers but, after lingering several days, died of his wound.

His death was an evil omen: He and Quantrill had been close friends, and he was one of the early members of the band.

The somber Missourians rode northeast to Hartford, arriving on January 22. At the post Quantrill once more introduced himself as Captain Clarke of the 4th Missouri Cavalry. The commanding officer, Colonel Q. C. Shanks, and a civilian named C. J. Lawton, with whom Quantrill spoke, saw no reason to doubt him. His "troopers" were equally convincing: "Their uniform[s] and good behavior whilst in this place and the conversation we had with said Clarke sufficiently satisfied us that he and his company were Federal," Lawton later sheepishly admitted. "[Clarke] wishing a guide to conduct him to the Ohio River, where the guerrillas most abound, we recommended Lieutenant Barnett."

Barnett knew the region well, and blissfully ignorant of the Missourians' true identity, he readily agreed to act as their guide. Then W. B. Lawton approached "Clarke" privately and asked to go along, too. An enlisted man who had been on leave visiting his family, he needed to return to his regiment at Evansville but had been deterred by the presence of so many partisan gangs in the area. A discharged cavalry trooper named Lownsley, who also sought safety in numbers, joined the column on the edge of town.

Three miles down the road Lownsley was led into a stand of timber and hung; his body was discovered a week later. Lawton was allowed to ride nine more miles before he was shot. Quantrill really did need a guide—Barnett's frozen corpse was found face up, eyes open, with a bullet hole in the forehead, fully sixteen miles from Hartford.

Quantrill took the band east on a serpentine route over hills and railroad tracks, around lakes and through creeks. In a week they traveled some 120 miles as the crow flies, much more than that on horseback.

The long ride had brought them into central Kentucky, an area of high rolling hills, good grazing grass, and fast racehorses. Many inhabitants were Confederate sympathizers, and, as with western Missouri, there were numerous guerrilla bands, some of them led by veterans who had served under the dashing cavalry officer John Hunt Morgan. Quantrill would soon and very briefly align himself with several of these guerrilla chieftains, and undertake a few raids and skirmishes, before he went into hiding as the Federal military turned the tide. He would never leave the state alive.

One of the chieftains with whom Quantrill rode was the notorious Sue Mundy, "the wild outlaw woman," "the girl guerrilla." Sue had been marauding through north-central Kentucky for the previous three and a half months and had become the most feared, hunted, and famous guerrilla in the entire state.

While Sue's exploits were reported by newspapers all over Kentucky, her chief propagandist and the most zealous promoter of her legend was George D. Prentice, the elderly, embittered editor of the Louisville *Journal,* which was the most influential and popular newspaper in Kentucky.

Before the war Prentice hoped that a compromise could be worked out that would keep the Union intact without war, but after Lincoln was elected president, Prentice accepted the inevitable and became a strong supporter. Over the next four years, however, he became disillusioned with the Lincoln administration's policies, as well as those of Kentucky's Federal military commander. Prentice's disillusionment reached its zenith during the summer of 1864, coinciding with a sharp upsurge in guerrilla activity. In response, Lincoln suspended the writ of habeas corpus and declared martial law in Kentucky; Brevet Major General Stephen G. Burbridge, the Federal commander, ruthlessly suppressed newspapers and even books. Prentice, in turn, played up the reports of partisan depredations.

Repeatedly stung by Prentice and other editors and besieged by civilian complaints, Burbridge, who was only thirty-two years old and had been a farmer just three years earlier, adopted a horrifying policy of retaliation: "Wherever an unarmed Union citizen is murdered, four guerrillas will be selected from the prisoners in the hands of the military authorities, and publicly shot to death in the most convenient place near the scene of the outrage." The retaliation policy was quickly expanded to include the murder of Federal soldiers as well as civilians.

Although Burbridge meant that only partisans were to draw lots, inevitably regular Confederate soldiers died. "In county after county," noted Kentuckian L. L. Valentine, "Confederate prisoners, innocent of [murder] or any other crime were shot like hogs at a hog-killing."

In the fall, Prentice championed Lincoln's election opponent, George B. McClellan, and seized on Sue Mundy to embarrass the Federal military. His was the equivalent of a school-yard taunt: *You're so incompetent you can't even catch a girl!*

Burbridge upped the ante, too, by issuing Order No. 8: "Hereafter, no guerrillas will be received as prisoners; and any officer who may capture such, and extend to them the courtesies due to prisoners of war, will be held accountable for disobedience of orders."

Sue was first mentioned in the pages of the *Journal* on October 11, 1864. Four days earlier Samuel Oscar "One Armed" Berry and some other men had robbed a stage outside of Harrodsburg, in Mercer County. After they picketed the road and held up travelers, they rode into town and attempted to rob the bank. A Unionist home-guard company clattered into town. Berry's horse was shot out from under him, so he shot one of the guardsmen, mounted the dead man's horse, and escaped with his comrades.

Prentice headlined his story: GUERRILLA DESPERADOS IN MERCER; FEMALE GUERRILLA

"One of the peculiarities of this band of cutthroats," Prentice wrote,

is the officer second in command, [was] recognized by men as Lieutenant Flowers. The officer in question is a young woman, and her right name is Sue Munday [*sic*]. She dresses in male attire, generally sporting a full Confederate uniform. She is possessed of a comely form, is a bold rider and a dashing leader.

Lieutenant Flowers, or Sue Munday, is a practiced robber, and many ladies, who have been so unfortunate as to meet her on the highway, can testify with what *sangfroid* she presents a pistol and commands "stand and deliver." Her name is becoming widely known, and to the ladies associated with horror. On Friday evening she robbed a young lady of Harrodsburg of her watch and chain. She is a dangerous character and for the sake of the fair ladies of Kentucky . . . we sincerely hope she may soon be captured.

Of course, Sue had not had time to earn the reputation Prentice attributed to her, and by alleging she robbed women, Prentice was cynically appealing to the chivalrousness of male Kentuckians. It is also possible that although Prentice had remarkably reliable sources in central and western Kentucky, he did not know, on October 11, that Sue Mundy was actually a man named Marcellus Jerome Clark. However, within a few weeks he did know about Clark. The knowledge did not cause him to break off his wicked propaganda campaign.

Clark, an artilleryman, had had a rather impressive military career—among other things he had been imprisoned in Indiana after the surrender of Fort Donelson, imprisoned at Camp Morton, in Indiana, escaped, and made his way south. He subsequently joined John Hunt Morgan and participated in what turned out to be Morgan's last raid into Kentucky, in June 1864. Clark was wounded in the Battle of Cynthiana, in the eastern part of the state, and left behind during Morgan's retreat back to Virginia. After Morgan was murdered by his captors, Clark took up with fellow Morgan veteran "One Armed" Berry. (Berry's right hand and forearm had been amputated after they were mangled in a machine in a Lexington factory before the war. Despite the disability he had been allowed to enlist in Morgan's cavalry regiment as a private and rose to the rank of color sergeant.) The men who rode with Berry became the nucleus of the Sue Mundy band.

Various snickering explanations were offered by Clark's mocking enemies as to how he came to be nicknamed "Sue Mundy." The most imaginative was that his fellow soldiers had playfully dressed him in women's attire on May Day and crowned him Queen of the May; they gave him the name "on account of his smooth girlish looking face and long black wavy hair, which he permitted to grow down to his shoulders." It was even said that his prankish comrades introduced him to Morgan himself as Sue Mundy, and the general believed he was a woman. Shortly before his execution Clark hotly denied this story; he cryptically explained that a girl by that name had once stolen a horse and blamed it on him. The incident probably occurred before the war, because eyewitnesses to his guerrilla activities who had known him for many years alternately referred to him without self-consciousness in court-martial testimony as Sue Mundy and Jerome Clark.

Prentice's usual style was to report the facts of a particular Mundy band depredation with some embellishment and searing rhetoric, but on January 27, 1865, he surpassed himself. Fifteen of Sue Mundy's band had recently surprised and slaughtered thirty-five black soldiers who were guarding a herd of U.S. government cattle. The band had been led by Berry and Henry Magruder because Clark was nursing a hand wound, but that did not matter to Prentice. After he gave his readers some details of the atrocity, he once again needled the Federal military:

> Sue Mundy, at the head of a small band of guerillas, has been going to and fro through a few counties of the State for several months, committing outrages and atrocities of the worst [kind]. The theatre of her operations has not been a wide one; she has confined herself within a rather narrow circle. How very strange that she isn't caught. She has no reputation, and probably deserves none, for military sagacity or tact or any other kind of sagacity or tact. Nevertheless she goes where she pleases, and does what she pleases, and none of our military leaders seem to have the ability, if they have the disposition, to lay their hands upon her. We can't imagine what the matter is; surely they are not afraid of her. To permit this she-devil to pursue her horrid work successfully much longer, will be, even if the past is not, a military scandal and shame.
>
> Sue has now been ramping full nine months. Surely, it is high time that she should be confined, if she is ever going to be.

Sue had been "ramping" for only three months, as Prentice knew perfectly well. In the very next paragraph, he removed his stern mask and slipped on a playful one.

> Some say Sue Mundy is a man, and some say a woman. We don't suppose the sexes will quarrel for the distinction of owning her. If she were captured and it should become important to ascertain to which sex she belongs, should the committee consist of women or men?
>
> We have this moment received a communication, assuring us that it has been settled that Sue is a compromise between a man and a woman—a hermaphrodite. Sue, whether of the masculine, feminine, or neuter gender—whether he, she, or it—is certainly a grammatical puzzle. Which of our grammar schools can parse Sue Mundy?

After this bit of whimsy, Prentice returned to depicting Sue strictly as a female until March 14, when he informed his readers that Sue had been captured and brought to Louisville in chains: "Sue Mundy, or Jerome Clark, is a rosy-cheeked boy, with dark eyes and scowling brow."

On January 28, one day after Prentice struggled over the parsing of Sue Mundy, nineteen men rode through Nelson County, in north-central Kentucky. They accosted travelers on the road and took their money and watches, went into general stores and stole clothing. The robbers were actually nominally Unionist Spencer County home guards under the command of Edwin Terrell, but they wore Confederate uniforms and pretended to be members of the Mundy band.

As they entered Bloomfield, they met a genuine Confederate guerrilla named Ike Dudley, took him prisoner, and subsequently killed him. They robbed the post office and stores, called the citizens out in the street, and made them form a line and shell out.

Suddenly, the real Mundy band, led by Jerome Clark, dashed into town and started shooting. The surprised home guards scrambled for their horses and fled, heading east. The guerrillas followed in hot pursuit as the townsfolk cheered. Five miles down the Chaplin Road the home guards came to a farm and took refuge in the barn. The guerrillas charged and were repulsed. They splintered the side of the barn with bullets before withdrawing.

The home guards stayed in the barn until darkness fell, then scampered back to Mount Eden, their home base.

Seventeen home guards had been killed. Exactly how many dead and wounded the guerrillas sustained is not known, since they carried all away. Dick Colter, shot four times, was left in the care of neighbors. He lingered two days before he died.

Referring to the home-guard robberies, Prentice fumed that "Such conduct on the part of men claiming to be Union troops is cowardly, villainous, and disgraceful, and the offenders should be brought to punishment."

The Federal authorities did nothing about Terrell.

At dawn on Sunday morning, January 29, Quantrill and his men rode into Hustonville. After six weeks' hard travel, fresh horses were more precious than money or jewels, and they immediately searched all the stables. The citizens were not alarmed at first: The Missourians wore their Federal uniforms and told everyone they needed the horses for a scout. They found a dozen splendid animals, which belonged to a Colonel Weatherford and some of the town's other rich men. Carefully maintaining their pose, the raiders harmed no one, not even Union officers on leave . . . until Lieutenant G. F. Cunningham sought to interfere.

When Cunningham had heard about the search, he hurried to the Weatherford stable, where he boarded his favorite gray mare. As he entered the structure, Cunningham saw what he took to be a Federal trooper—Allen Parmer—sitting astride his horse. Cunningham, who was only twenty years old and had recently been mustered out of the 13th Kentucky Union Cavalry, seized the bridle and told Parmer to dismount. "I have been a soldier for two years," Cunningham said, "and you shall not take my horse."

When Parmer remained in the saddle, Cunningham, still under the impression that he was dealing with a fellow Yankee, added, "If this horse leaves this stable, it will be over my dead body."

"That is a damned easy job." Parmer sneered and shot him point-blank in the face. The bullet passed downward through his head and broke his neck, killing him instantly.

Parmer turned his pistol on two eyewitnesses, who happened to be relatives of the dead man, and opened fire. They managed to escape the stable with nothing more serious than bullet holes in their clothing.

The Missourians' ruse revealed, they spurred their mounts out of town, heading north toward Danville. As soon as they were gone, Colonel Weatherford raced to Stanford, which was northeast of Hustonville, where he alerted the garrison commander, Captain James H. Bridgewater. He also sent a telegram to Danville that warned of the "approach of the thieves."

He was too late: The raiders had already struck. They stole more horses, robbed citizens, looted a boot store, and wrecked the telegraph office. They then rode west on the Perryville Pike.

Bridgewater clattered into town three hours later at the head of a forty-five-man column. He took up the band's trail and followed it the rest of the day.

As darkness fell, the Missourians were five miles west of Harrodsburg. They divided themselves into three groups and stopped at farmhouses to get supper.

Bridgewater found the house where John Barker and eleven other guerrillas were filling their bellies. He ordered his men to surround it. The Missourians burst out of the house and tried to break through the circle. Four were killed, and the rest—including three wounded—surrendered. Chad Renick, who was at a nearby house when he heard the gunfire, unwisely rode over to investigate and was shot out of his saddle.

The eight survivors were carried to Lexington and imprisoned. On three occasions their jailers sought to torment them by leading them into the yard as if they were to be hung, but each time they came out they cheered for Jeff Davis and dared their captors to execute them, promising their deaths would be avenged.

In April, seven of the prisoners were transported to a Louisville prison. Southern sympathizers soon facilitated their escape. The eighth man, Tom Evans, who had been kept at Lexington because the military authorities believed he had murdered Lieutenant Cunningham, remained confined until the war was over and John McCorkle made out an affidavit that identified Allen Parmer as the killer.

Quantrill had lost a third of his force in the Harrodsburg dust up—and he had walked into a hornet's nest. Union military officers, having fought John Hunt Morgan and a host of indigenous partisans, were far better organized than their counterparts in Missouri had been in 1862 or 1863. Hardly had Quantrill left Danville when half a dozen dispatches were sent from Lexington, Lebanon, and Camp Nelson alerting various garrisons to his presence in the area, correctly identifying the direction of his flight, and ordering his interception. The Kentucky Federals had a better intelligence network, too: On January 30, just one day after his first skirmish, they knew that "the desperate outlaw and blood-thirsty scoundrel Quantrell, of Kansas notoriety," was in the vicinity.

The next day, January 31, George Prentice published an article in which he urged "all three year veterans of Kentucky regiments [to] enter State service or join the Independent Kentucky Scouts, and swear not to cease chasing the guerrillas until the last one of them is driven from or *into* the soil of Kentucky." He noted approvingly that "Captain Terrell of the Independent Scouts is after them with untiring energy." Prentice also mistakenly announced that "the fiend one-armed Berry" had been shot to death and wished "a like fate" to "all the gang, Davis, Marion, Clark, and Magruder."

It is not known exactly when Quantrill met Jerome Clark, but on February 2, they led thirty men into Midway, only twenty miles from Frankfort, the state capital. According to the Lexington *Observer & Reporter,*

> they took possession of the railroad depot building, a large brick edifice, in which there is always a considerable quantity of produce and other articles awaiting transportation, and in which also is the telegraph station; and after robbing the safe of what money it contained and the attaches of the building of their private funds, set fire to [it] and completely destroyed it. They then commenced an indiscriminate robbery of private individuals in town, taking from them their pocketbooks, watches and other articles of value; [and] stole such horses as answered their purposes. . . .

Several guerrillas remarked to their victims that Quantrill was with the gang, and when one citizen was told to shell out and boldly asked to whom he had the *honor* of delivering his money, the reply was "Sue Mundy, alias Captain Clark."

The guerrillas chopped down a few telegraph poles, then rode south. "It was believed that they intended visiting the farm of Mr. R. A. Alexander, for the purpose of supplying themselves from his extensive and superior stock of blood-horses with such as they wanted," commented the editor of the *Observer & Reporter.*

> Fast horses are what they want, as they never stand to fight with anything like a force equal to their own. If they did go to Mr. Alexander's, they doubtless met with a reception very different from what they expected, as that gentleman has made arrangements to meet and successfully repel a much larger force than this should they attempt to interfere with him or his. We hope, therefore, they did not alter their resolution about going to the . . . farm.

As it turned out, the marauders did indeed raid the Alexander place. After they entered the yard, they split into two squads. One surrounded the house, while the other went after the horses. Alexander's careful "arrangements" proved hopelessly inadequate: He lost fifteen horses. The guerrillas then went to the adjoining property and kidnapped Frank P. Kinkead. They forced him to guide them to the Kentucky River and released him unharmed.

The Midway raid was particularly audacious because it was so near the state capital and about the same distance from Lexington. "Can no means be devised of ridding the State of these outlaws?" the *Observer & Reporter* asked. "They should be hunted down with never-ending vigilance, until they are . . . driven from the State."

The Yankees were trying. As soon as authorities learned of the attack on Midway, they telegraphed alarms and dispatched troops. The marauders, however, got away.

On February 8, Quantrill and his band struck a wagon train near New Market, capturing four guards and killing three others. They shot the mules, burned seven wagons, and rode away with the prisoners. Once more there was a furious flurry of messages, and troops were dispatched from Lebanon, Crab Orchard, Campbellsville, Columbia, Danville, Stanford, and Lawrenceburg. This time, however, some pursuing Federals actually caught up with the quarry. There was a running battle across open country all the way to Bradfordsville, where the guerrillas made a stand. The Yankees, most of whom were amputees or had other serious physical disabilities and were from what was commonly known as the Invalid Corps,* dismounted, and the partisans charged. The soldiers, as their commander, Major Thomas Mahoney, remarked, "could not master their horses and load their long guns." A number of animals broke away and ran toward the enemy. In the confusion the Yankees hastily withdrew. The guerrillas shot their four prisoners and went on to Hustonville, where they camped for the night on the Little South Fork.

At 2:00 A.M., Captain Bridgewater hit Quantrill's camp, killing four. Seven managed to mount their horses and gallop away; the other thirty-five fled into the woods. Most of them were barefoot—and there was snow on the ground. The Federals followed the footprints and hunted

---

*The "Invalid Corps" was officially known as the "Veteran Reserve Corps" and, according to General Order No. 76, was made up of enlisted men whose "physical infirmities" incapacitated them "for field service" but would not "disqualify" them for less arduous duties. These infirmities included: epilepsy; "paralysis, if confined to one upper extremity"; "loss of arm, forearm, or hand"; complete loss of sight in either eye or "partial loss of sight in both eyes"; myopia; "loss or complete atrophy of both testicles"; "impeded respiration following injuries of the chest, pneumonia, or pleurisy"; "incipient consumption"; "chronic disorder of the kidneys or bladder"; "chronic diarrhea which has long resisted treatment"; "chronic rheumatism"; "deafness, if in degree sufficient to prevent hearing words of command as usually given"; "loss of a sufficient number of teeth to prevent proper mastication of food."

down four more men. One was shot while attempting to escape—the usual litany—and the fate of the other three is not known but may be surmised.

The Yankees claimed to have information that Quantrill was one of those who fled through the snow barefoot, but three months later he was still riding Old Charley. Either he stole the animal back from the Federals, which seems too mythic a feat even for him, or, more likely, he was one of the lucky seven who escaped on horseback from the Little South Fork.

The day after Bridgewater attacked Quantrill's camp, editor Prentice announced that "Major-General Palmer has been appointed to command in Kentucky. Thank God and Mr. Lincoln."

John M. Palmer, a Radical Republican and abolitionist, was a native Kentuckian who had been active before the war in Illinois politics. He was forty-seven years old, had been mustered into the service as a colonel on May 25, 1861, and had fought in the battles of Stones River and Chickamauga. During the Atlanta campaign, he commanded the Army of the Cumberland's XIV Corps; however, he had jealously clashed with General John Schofield and run afoul of Sherman, who thought little of his military abilities. "I would prefer to move a rock, than to move that man's corps," Sherman commented and forced Palmer's resignation. He had arrived back in Illinois on August 10, just twenty-two days before the Union triumph over Atlanta. He spent the next five months recuperating from a war wound and practicing law. In early February 1864, he traveled to Washington, DC, and met with Lincoln, whom he had supported at the 1860 Republican convention. The president offered him the command of the Department of Kentucky.

"I have commanded troops in the field during my military service," Palmer replied. "I don't want to go to Kentucky and spend my time quarreling with politicians."

"Go to Kentucky, keep your temper, do as you please, and I will sustain you," the president told him.

Palmer was an ambitious man who had held various elective offices in Illinois and, shortly before the war began, had been defeated in a race for a U.S. congressional seat. If he succeeded in Kentucky, which meant suppressing the guerrillas, he would greatly enhance his postwar political prospects. He accepted the assignment without further, disingenuous protests.

Meanwhile, Quantrill went into hiding in Spencer County. He frequently moved from place to place, staying often in Taylorsville or other towns where there were many Southern sympathizers.

We know little of his activities during this period. Between February 10 and May 13, there is only one reference to him in the Louisville papers: On February 14, he "was on the Green River, a few miles east of the Ohio River, in company with several other guerrilla chiefs, among whom was the notorious Davidson." They ransacked a house and searched its occupants "but failed to find any booty of consequence."

On February 17, the Confederate legislature quietly repealed the Partisan Ranger Act of 1862. For nearly three years Southern guerrillas had been fighting under the act's cloak of legitimacy—and now, suddenly, it was gone. (The legislators seem to have been motivated not by any desire to end the destructiveness of guerrilla warfare but by the need to fill up the depleted ranks in regular army units.)

The next day General Palmer assumed command of the Department of Kentucky, and he quickly reassigned the hated Burbridge to Tennessee. Palmer made conciliatory speeches in which he promised to "give protection to all citizens who obey the law" and suppress "the desperadoes and marauders whose object is spoliation and plunder." In his autobiography, *The Story of an Earnest Life,* Palmer commented that "General Burbridge . . . had attempted to terrify the guerrillas by hanging their friends. I chose to pursue a different course, and make war upon the guerrillas personally." He set up his own "Secret Service" and put informants and "guerrilla chasers" on the payroll at very generous monthly salaries.

Five days after Palmer assumed command of Kentucky, Confederate Colonel Robert J. Breckinridge, Jr., was captured near Versailles, about fifteen miles west of Lexington. He had been sent into the state by the South's new secretary of war, General John C. Breckinridge, and his orders, which were found on him, were directed at partisans:

All officers and men now in Kentucky upon military service under authority other than that of the Secretary of War are required to report to Colonel Robert J. Breckinridge, whose orders they are commanded to obey. All who have authority from the Secretary of War, prior to April 4, 1864 . . . whose time has expired, will report to their respective commands or these headquarters. All who fail to obey this order promptly will be at once reported to the existing authorities in Kentucky as not recognized by the Confederate Government as prisoners of war, if captured.

"The guerrillas have had their day in Kentucky," Prentice crowed.

Well, not exactly: Either ignorant of the act's repeal and Breckinridge's orders or choosing to ignore them, many guerrilla bands continued to raid towns and commit highway robberies and murders. Just before Colonel Breckinridge was captured, however, he had sent word to Jerome Clark that he was to report to Paris, Tennessee. Late in February, Clark left the Bloomfield area with Henry Magruder and another guerrilla, Sam Jones. They slowly, cautiously made their way west. At Brandenburg they were joined by yet another guerrilla, Henry Metcalf. The four men struck out on a southwesterly course that would take them to Paris.

On February 26, 1865, Quantrill was staying at Jim Dawson's place, near Taylorsville. Dawson's daughter, Nannie, asked him to write something in her autograph album. He had looted a great many things during his military career and now, to please a girl, he filched some lines from Lord Byron and mixed in a few of his own:

> My horse is at the door,
> And the enemy I soon may see
> But before I go Miss Nannie
> Here's a double health to thee.
>
> Here's a sigh to those who love me
> And a smile to those who hate
> And whatever sky's above me
> Here's a heart for every fate.
>
> Though the cannon's roar around me
> Yet it shall still bear me on
> Though dark clouds are above me
> It hath springs which may be won.
>
> In this verse as with the wine
> The libation I would pour

Should be peace with thine and mine
And a health to thee and all *in door*.

Very respectfully your friend
W. C. Q.

As far as is known, they were the last words Quantrill ever wrote. Nannie Dawson saved the page from her autograph book for twenty-three years, then gave it to Quantrill's querulous, still grieving mother when she visited Kentucky.

It is odd to think of this strange, contradictory man—border ruffian, Confederate soldier, blanket thief, partisan ranger, loving son, cold-eyed killer, schoolteacher, and teamster—spouting English poetry, but the fatalism underlying the verses surely reflected his own mood. He was an inveterate newspaper reader, and as winter drew to a close, headlines tolled the South's impending doom like mallet blows against a sonorous, mournful gong. There was starvation in Richmond while "extortionate butchers" charged $6 a pound for beef . . . Sherman's "entire army" was "in motion in Tennessee . . ." There was fighting near Charleston, and the Confederate cabinet had "fallen to pieces . . ." Lee refused the post of commander in chief. Sherman captured Savannah, and Hood's army was defeated.

***

Riding through Hancock County on March 3, Clark and his three comrades were ambushed by eight home guards. Sam Jones was killed. The other three got away, though Magruder had been shot in the chest. He begged Clark to take him back to Meade County, where he knew a doctor who would treat him. Magruder was so seriously wounded he seemed certain to die, but Jerome Clark's sense of honor would not allow him to abandon the man or to refuse to take him back to Meade County.

The three men took up residence in a mud-chinked tobacco barn on the Cox place, near Webster, about forty miles southwest of Louisville, where General Palmer had his headquarters. Clark and Metcalf fetched Dr. J. P. Lewis, who lived close by. Lewis found that the bullet had passed through Magruder's left lung and gave instructions for his care. Clark and Metcalf built their patient a crude bed, nursed him as best they could, and waited for him to expire.

General Palmer learned through an informer of the whereabouts of the three guerrillas. He dispatched a retired infantry major named Cyrus

J. Wilson and fifty soldiers of Company B, 30th Wisconsin Infantry to Webster. At dawn on Sunday, March 12, the soldiers surrounded the barn and, hearing no sounds coming from inside, heaved a rock against the door, shattering it. Jerome Clark blazed away with a revolver and wounded four before the rest withdrew to a more respectful distance.

Wilson approached the barn under a flag of truce and tried to convince Clark to surrender. Clark knew he would be executed if taken back to Louisville and was inclined to die fighting. Wilson pointed out that surrendering "will give you a few more days to live." Magruder, lying on his bed, pleaded with Clark to surrender, and Wilson continued to urge the same course; finally he suggested that "there might be a chance in a thousand or ten thousand of escape."

After Clark handed over his weapons, Wilson ordered that the prisoners' arms be tied behind their backs and the three be roped together. "Mundy, this is rather hard treatment for a prisoner of war," Wilson explained, "but we are determined that you are not to get loose."

The guerrillas were brought to Louisville by river steamer, arriving on March 13. Clark and Metcalf were put on horses and taken to the military prison. Magruder was placed in an ambulance and carried to the prison infirmary. "Magruder is in a weak condition, and suffering greatly from the effect of his wound," the Lexington *Observer & Reporter* informed its readers. "It is thought he will yield up the ghost before morning dawn."

Sometime that very day—March 13—General Palmer ordered Judge Advocate William H. Coyl to "bring Jerome Clark to trial immediately." Coyl drew up General Court-Martial Order No. 3, which charged Clark with being a guerrilla and with firing on "a detachment of the 30th Regiment Wisconsin," wounding "four privates." Coyl wrote that Clark had been arraigned on March 13 and pled "not guilty." Finally, Coyl noted that the "Court after mature deliberation finds the accused Jerome Clark 'alias Sue Mundy' guilty . . . and sentence[s] him . . . to be hanged by the neck until he is dead."

Palmer affixed his signature, adding, "The proceedings and findings are hereby approved, and the sentence confirmed. Jerome Clark, 'alias Sue Mundy' will be hanged by the neck until he is dead on Wednesday the 15th day of March 1865, at 4 o'clock p.m., at Louisville, Ky."

Clark was not actually court-martialed and found guilty until the next day, so Palmer's advance approval of the verdict and sentence shows that Clark's trial was not the fairest in the history of American jurisprudence.

Although Clark's execution had not been publicly announced, a large crowd had gathered, drawn by the sounds of carpenters' hammers as the gallows was built.

"I am a regular Confederate soldier and have served in the Confederate Army four years," Clark told the crowd. "I have taken many Federal soldiers prisoner and have always treated them kindly. . . . I hope in and die for the Confederate cause."

They were his last words.

The prop was pulled from under the trap, but the drop was only three feet—not enough to break Clark's neck. He slowly strangled to death. "We have seen a great many persons hung," Prentice observed, "but never before did we witness such hard struggles and convulsions. It was feared for a time that he would break the lashings."

After twenty minutes the body was cut down. People pressed in, trying to cut a button from his jacket and snatching at the hangman's rope for a memento. A rumor suddenly spread that there was a fortune in greenbacks sewn into the lining of his jacket, and so after the corpse was placed in a crude wooden coffin, dozens of hands shredded the garment. Two men fought over his black cap and were arrested.

The crowd slowly dispersed.

Sixteen days after Clark's execution, on April 1, General Palmer put Terrell and his thirty-man gang on the Secret Service payroll. Terrell was to receive $50 a month; his first lieutenant, John H. Thompson, got $35; and Second Lieutenant Horace Allen $30. The other twenty-eight men were paid $20 each. The officially sanctioned band of "scouts" donned red attire—Kentucky guerrillas sometimes wore red jackets or even red suits, the color being a symbol of no quarter—and took up the hunt.

(High-ranking Union military officers knew of Terrell's reputation and activities well enough to take a dim view of him; they believed his employment was at best a necessary evil. When, for example, a witness testified at the court-martial of Sam Berry that "Captain Terrell" was "understood to belong to the Federal Army," Judge Advocate Coyl hastily countered that "Terrill [sic] was simply a guerrilla catcher hired by us to catch [guerrillas]. . . . He was a discharged soldier and had not been in the army for a year previous to his going after guerrillas. . . .")

Sometime in early April, guerrilla chieftain Billy Marion captured a military surgeon and sent word to General Palmer that he would kill him if Metcalf and Magruder were not released. He instructed Palmer that "an answer be returned through the newspapers."

"When I got this notice from Marion," Palmer wrote in *The Story of an Earnest Life*, "I immediately proceeded by rail to Eminence, Kentucky, found Terrell there, having sent word to meet me there." Palmer ordered Terrell to capture or kill Marion, then placed notices in newspapers that Magruder and Metcalf would be tried and, if found guilty, executed. He added that if the surgeon were harmed, both men would be immediately hung. The lucky surgeon managed to escape before Marion read Palmer's reply.

Guerrillas led by Quantrill and Marion tangled with Yankees near Bloomfield on April 13. Each side lost two men. Several Federal detachments converged and took up the chase, joined by Edwin Terrell and a couple of his boys. On the morning of April 15, Captain G. W. Penn's company of Casey County state guards "routed" the town of Manton and found Marion and four guerrillas at a "still house." Marion was shot out of the saddle; the others fled through the woods in different directions. While Penn chased the fugitives, Terrell came along and stole Marion's body, loaded it on a Bardstown railroad car, and took it to Louisville, all the while loudly claiming credit for the death of "one of the most bloodthirsty and desperate outlaw leaders operating in the State."

An aid reported to Palmer that Terrell was in front of the headquarters building with Marion's corpse. Palmer went to have a look at it, and Terrell told him that not only had he killed Marion but he had also rescued the surgeon. Palmer believed Terrell on both counts; however, he had no illusions about the man's character. In his autobiography, Palmer concluded his account of Marion's death with this comment: "Terrell was an exceedingly dangerous man; I never let him enter my quarters without keeping a revolver at hand."

(After Marion's death, no other guerrilla tried to make a prisoner exchange with Palmer for Magruder and Metcalf. On September 15, Magruder was carried into a military courtroom lying on a cot, so emaciated that his bones showed through his skin and witnesses who had known him all his life did not recognize him. His trial lasted thirty days, and he was hanged in the prison yard on October 29. Metcalf was also convicted, but he must have had influential friends who whispered in Palmer's ear, since the general, citing mitigating circumstances, commuted his death sentence and gave him five years instead.)

———•·•———

Sometime on the very day that Marion was killed, word reached Palmer by telegraph that Lincoln had been assassinated. The general announced the news in General Order No. 23:

> The purest man of the age has fallen, and the whole nation which was rejoicing over the prospects of a speedy peace is mourning.
>
> Let the people of Kentucky disappoint the miscreants who would involve them in bloodshed and strife, by conducting themselves with calmness and moderation. Avoid all heated conversations and imprudent expressions. Let all unite in every means for preserving order.
>
> The wicked need not rejoice nor the patriotic despond. The Government will still go on, and as great as the calamity is, the country will accomplish its high destiny.

The desultory partisan war went on, too. Guerrillas continued to burn railroad cars, rob, kidnap, and murder, though with gradually decreasing frequency as their numbers were thinned by rapacious soldiers and home guardsmen.

On April 27, Edwin Terrell and his boys rode to the Montgomery place, about ten miles from Louisville. They found Hercules Walker, Montgomery's son-in-law, plowing a field. "After parleying a few moments, the soldiers compelled him to take his mules from the plough and go with them to the house," George Prentice informed his readers. "Here they demanded Walker's pistol, which his wife at first refused to deliver, but finally procured at Mr. Walker's own request. Walker was then requested to step outside toward the barn." As he went across the yard a "scout" who walked behind him shot him point-blank in the back of the head. Terrell and the others then took the dead man's watch and all the men's clothing they could find, then rode away with the two plow mules and a horse.

Threatened with an investigation by a coroner's jury, Terrell lamely alleged that Walker had been furnishing supplies and ammunition to outlaws.

Perhaps a week after Terrell killed Walker, a bushwhacker named Jack Graham was trying to reshoe Old Charley, who, of course, did not like anyone but Quantrill near him. While Graham was paring one hoof with a buttress, the horse suddenly jerked his leg and was hamstrung. The animal had carried Quantrill through skirmish after skirmish, raid after raid. His hide bore numerous white bullet scars. More than once Quantrill's life had been saved by Old Charley's speed and stamina. Quantrill loved this horse and fatalistically saw his crippling as an omen. "That means my work is done," he said deliberately. "My career is run. Death is coming, and my end is near."

The pronouncement quickly proved prophetic.

Quantrill borrowed a horse belonging to Miss Betty Russell, which was a mistake: The animal "had not been in battle and knew not the odor of powder," commented Connelley, "had not heard the rush and roar of clashing arms."

James H. Wakefield owned a farm five miles south of Taylorsville. He made a public show of neutrality, though secretly he aided the Southern partisans. Quantrill began occasionally staying at the place in March. At first he introduced himself as Captain Clarke of the 4th Missouri *Confederate* Cavalry; only later, after he had come to trust Wakefield, did he reveal his true identity.

On the morning of May 10, 1865, Quantrill turned down the lane that led to the Wakefield farm. There were twenty-one men with him, some of them newly recruited former members of Billy Marion's gang. (Frank James and several other "old men" were away on a scout.) As they hitched their horses in the barnyard, a hard rain began to fall, and they took refuge in the barn and an adjacent shed.

At about the same time, Terrell and his scouts came upon horse tracks leading north on the Bloomfield-Taylorsville Road. They spurred their mounts in pursuit and, just before noon, stopped at the shop of a blacksmith, asking if he had seen any riders that morning. The blacksmith pointed south to the great gate of the Wakefield farm and said a body of horsemen had gone in there. A high hill rose just beyond the gate, so that only the top of the barn could be seen from the road.

Quantrill and most of the band had climbed into the hayloft and gone to sleep. A few others played cards or just talked, and several horsed around, throwing corncobs at each other. Wakefield himself stood under the edge of the shed roof in conversation with Dick Glasscock. Suddenly another guerrilla, Clark Hockensmith, looked up the slope and saw riders bearing down, unslinging their carbines as they came.

"Here they come!" Hockensmith cried as the rifles began to crack.

Quantrill's men scrambled for their horses, cutting loose with their pistols at the same time. Most managed to mount and ride down the bridle path to the south; they jumped a gate and fled through an orchard. However, some of the horses shied and broke away when their owners tried to mount; the men dashed across the lot behind the barn, dove into a pond, and stayed low in the water until the pursuit swept past, then scampered through shrubs and between fence rails for the trees to the west.

Quantrill's horse reared and bucked so wildly that, expert rider though he was, he could not pull himself into the saddle. He, too, gave up and sprinted down the bridle path, calling for help. Glasscock and Hockensmith reined in their horses and waited, firing back to check the pursuit. As Quantrill tried to climb up behind Glasscock on his mare, the animal was shot in the hip and became unmanageable. Quantrill turned and fired at the approaching scouts, then ran alongside Hockensmith, desperately trying to mount. A bullet struck him in the back at the left shoulder blade, ranged down, and lodged against his spine, paralyzing him below the shoulders. He fell face down in the mud.

One of the scouts who galloped past in pursuit of the others fired at Quantrill's prostrate form and with freakish good luck shot off his right index finger—his trigger finger. Glasscock and Hockensmith were quickly overtaken and killed. If they had not tried to save Quantrill, both men surely would have gotten away.

The scouts came back for the man lying in the mud. They yanked off his boots, stole his pistols, and searched his pockets, finding a picture of a young woman. They then rolled him onto a blanket, carried him into Wakefield's house, and laid him on a lounge. The scouts began to ransack the house, but Wakefield slipped Terrell $20 and Thompson $10 and threw in a jug of whiskey. The looting immediately ceased.

Interrogated by Terrell, Quantrill insisted he was Captain Clarke of the 4th Missouri Confederate Cavalry. He asked to be allowed to stay on the farm to die. Terrell at first denied the request, but, because the prisoner was paralyzed, he finally relented. However, he warned that he was going off on a scout and would hold Wakefield accountable if "Clarke" was missing when he came back. "I promised to stand good for him," Wakefield remembered many years later, "as he had pledged me his word and honor that he would not let anyone take him away."

Terrell rode off and resumed the hunt—for Quantrill.

Wakefield sent for a physician, Dr. Isaac McClaskey, who examined the wound and pronounced it fatal.

Quantrill told Wakefield that he had left a sum of money in safekeeping with a Missouri woman, Mrs. Olivia D. Cooper, and wanted to arrange for it to be delivered to his mother and sister in Dover.

After dark some of his men, including Frank James, came to visit him.

"Frank," Quantrill said, "I have run a long time, but they have got me at last."

James proposed taking him to what he later described as a "rough and broken section of country near Samuels Depot," where the Yankees would never be able to find him.

"No, I will die, and it is no use," Quantrill told him.

When others continued to urge him to let them carry him away and hide him, he still refused, explaining that he had given his word to stay and that if he broke it, the house would be burned and Wakefield punished. Besides, he said again, he knew he was going to die and did not want to be "dragged around." Terrell had promised not to move him if he did not try to get away.

The next night more of his men appeared, once more pressing him to let them spirit him away, but he would not change his mind.

The next morning, Friday, May 12, Terrell and his gang reappeared, bringing an old Conestoga wagon drawn by two mules. Terrell had learned through an informant the real identity of his stricken prisoner. Straw from the Wakefield barn was thrown into the back of the wagon and Quantrill placed on top of it, propped up by pillows. (Before setting out, Quantrill had managed to whisper to Wakefield that he would get a message to him from Louisville about the money for his family.) Then Terrell and his men formed themselves into a column enveloping the wagon and set off for Louisville.

Progress was slow—Terrell did not want his vaunted prisoner to die en route. Stopping in Jeffersonville for the night, Terrell sent for two physicians to care for him. They confirmed his paralysis and concluded that his back was broken. Quantrill thought he recognized one of the physicians as someone who had treated him not long ago in Shelby County.

"I am the man," Dr. Samuel N. Marshall replied. "I have moved here."

"So have I," Quantrill joked.

Somewhere along the way, two young women gave him a beautiful bouquet with a card attached that read, "Compliments of Miss Maggie Frederick and Sallie Lovell to Mr. Quantrell."

The flowers were still fresh when he got to Louisville. "This [bouquet] was presented to the distinguished bandit, we suppose, as a testimonial of his valor," the *Daily Union Press* editor commented dryly. "A strange way some people have of showing their loyalty."

At eleven o'clock on the morning of May 13, Terrell reported to General Palmer's headquarters in Louisville, wagon in tow. Quantrill was then carried to the military prison's infirmary.

Terrell was promptly paid off and sent on his way. The quickness of his termination suggests once again that the military authorities found employing such a disreputable fellow left a bad taste in their mouths. It also clearly indicates what assignment Terrell had been given on April 1: As soon as he handed over Quantrill, Terrell was dismissed from Palmer's Secret Service.

On May 14, editor Prentice happily announced Quantrill's arrival in the city and the expectation that he would die. "All the honor for his capture is due to Captain Terrill [*sic*] and his company of 'decoy guerillas.' The news of his capture will cause great joy throughout the Union. The inhuman outrages that he committed years ago, such as burning the town of Lawrence, &c, are still fresh in the memory of our people."

That same day, however, the Louisville *Daily Democrat* regretfully announced that Terrell had gotten the wrong man, an imposter, adding, "We have been assured that [the real Quantrill] was at last accounts a colonel in the rebel army under Price."

Twenty-four hours later Prentice felt compelled to agree with his rival:

> It is said that Quantrell, so-called, who was shot through the body by Terrell's men and brought to this city, isn't Quantrell, the fiend-like ruffian who murdered the population of Lawrence, Kansas, but only a fellow that has assumed his name. Yet he deserved his fate. A fellow that would take the name of such a devilish miscreant as the Kansas murderer should have a bullet through each separate bone and bowel in his body.

Although in later decades, as Quantrill's postmortem fame grew, there would be many men who swore to have seen him alive after the war or even to be the notorious bushwhacker himself, there is no doubt Terrell had gotten the right man.

On the evening of May 19, according to the *Journal,* Terrell and his "fantastically arrayed followers" walked into Louisville's United States Saloon. A large crowd quickly gathered outside "to get a glimpse at these independent warriors." Terrell ordered drinks "all around." The bartender hesitated, but these customers were heavily armed, so he was "soon persuaded to deal out. After the parties had swallowed their stimulants they unanimously smashed the glasses and left the room, forgetting to remunerate."

The following night these raffish men made amends for their bad behavior: In a clash with a guerrilla band led by a man named Froman, they captured seven, including the leader himself. Among their other prisoners was a man who a few weeks earlier had participated in the gang rape of a woman in the vicinity of Bardstown.

As he lay dying in the infirmary, Quantrill was ministered to by a Catholic priest, Father Michael Power. The priest converted him to Catholicism and administered the last rites. Quantrill gave Power "an order" to Olivia Cooper that instructed her to hand over some of the money she was keeping for him, so that Power could buy him a cemetery plot and a headstone. Quantrill wanted the rest of the money given to Kate King.

There is a legend that he was visited by a beautiful woman who wept copious tears as she left the infirmary, and there are several women who later claimed the honor of having been with Quantrill at the last: the aforementioned Mrs. Cooper, who had been exiled from Missouri for the duration of the war; Mrs. Neville Ross, whose son rode with the band in Kentucky; and Kate King. In her 1926 interview with the Kansas City *Star* reporter, Kate said that a priest had stopped by the St. Louis boardinghouse where she resided to pass on a message that her husband "had been wounded in a scuffle on a farm and was not expected to live." She hastily packed and arrived at his bedside three days "before the end" and was with him "as he breathed his last." This seems fanciful, although it is possible. The trip by rail from St. Louis would not have been a difficult one. If we are to believe Wakefield that Quantrill originally meant to leave his ill-gotten gains to his mother and sister, then something changed his mind—after all, he instructed Mrs. Cooper to give the bulk of the money to Kate King. A visit from her might have caused his change of heart. (Curiously, she denied that she ever received any bequest from him.)

It is said that Quantrill remained quite cheerful to the end. He maintained his odd silence toward his family, making no effort to contact his mother, to tell her he was dying, to ask her to come to his side.

William Clarke Quantrill died at approximately 4:00 P.M. on June 6, 1865, twenty-seven days after he was wounded and captured. He was twenty-seven years old.

Probably as a result of the confusion over his identity, Kentucky newspapers hardly noticed the famous guerrilla's passing. In a brief announcement on June 7, the editor of the *Daily Democrat* felt compelled to remind his readers of the wounding and capture of "a guerrilla calling himself William Clark, Captain in the Fourth Missouri rebel cavalry, but generally supposed to be the infamous monster 'Quantrell,' " in order to laconically inform them that "He died of his wounds yesterday afternoon about 4 o'clock."

George Prentice was no less succinct: "William Clark, alias Quantrell, captain Fourth Missouri cavalry, who was wounded and captured as a guerrilla, near Taylorsville, Ky., May 10, died in the military prison hospital in this city, yesterday evening about 4 o'clock. . . ."

Quantrill was buried under a tree in the cottage yard of the St. Mary's Catholic Cemetery. Father Power feared that the body would be stolen, so he instructed the sexton that no mound was to be formed over the grave, the earth was to be kept level. The priest disregarded Quantrill's request for a headstone and told the sexton and his wife that they should throw their kitchen slops and night soil over the grave to obscure it.

CHAPTER 15

"The Outlaw Is a Deformity on the Face of Nature": The Postwar Years

Major General Grenville M. Dodge had been given command of the Department of the Missouri on December 9, 1864. In a report written seven months later he remarked that he had found the state had only just begun

> to recover from the effects of Price's raid. The cavalry was mostly dismounted and the troops generally in bad discipline and condition. The greater portion of the State was in a state of confusion approaching anarchy, continually fermented by marauders, guerrilla bands, and roving Confederates, who were murdering, robbing, plundering and committing all the outrages known to crime or barbarous warfare.

Like his ambitious predecessors, he was determined to stamp out bushwhacking. He ordered that the troops in his command be "immediately equipped, mounted, and fitted for active service." He sent them out of the comfort and relative luxury of towns into the snowy "brush" with orders to "hunt down and exterminate all bands of guerrillas and marauders." He also stationed thirty-one militia companies in the most infested and troubled counties.

Dodge aggressively applied the policy of banishing Southerners—Bill Anderson's sisters were exiled in late January 1865, for example, and in early February, twenty-six families were given twenty days to vacate Clay County. The Federals let it be known that this was "only the first installment." Indeed, a short time later the Reuben Samuel family was one of six forced out of Clay County. The James boys' mother and step-father found a home in Rulo, Nebraska. (This policy would remain in effect until the end of the war. On April 27, more than two weeks after Lee's surrender at Appomattox Courthouse, General Dodge's superior canceled it. He explained that there was a "sufficient number of disloyal men and lawless vagrants" in the Southern states and that Missouri would have to "deal with" its own "malefactors.")

Although most bushwhacker bands had gone south before the snow fell, a few still remained in the Sni Hills or elsewhere in western Missouri. They now and again emerged from their lairs to cross frozen rivers and, avoiding the cavalry patrols, commit as much mayhem as opportunity and weather permitted. They cut telegraph lines and robbed stores, mail carriers, and stagecoaches. They plundered river steamers run aground on sandbars and tried to board the railroad train that ran between Warrensburg and St. Louis. Here and there a Union man would be called out into his yard and murdered in front of his wife. Coats and jewelry were forcibly taken from houses, horses from barns. Black freed-men were occasionally targeted to be hung from tree limbs or gate posts; notes were affixed to their clothing that warned other former slaves to return to their masters or leave the area.

Newspaper reports of these various outrages were punctuated by the familiar howls of editors who demanded that the Federal authorities put an end to the partisans.

The cavalry troopers were trying. They scouted a lot more than they skirmished, of course, but their diligence sometimes paid off. One day in late February the Boone County cave in which four "bush-fiends" had taken up residence was located. They put up a fierce fight, though their fate was never in doubt. Dink Robinson was, reported the *Weekly Journal of Commerce,* "perforated with rifle and pistol balls." Jim Carter was also gunned down; his killers subsequently used his "ghastly corpse" for target practice, then pounded it "to jelly" with their rifle butts. One-armed Harvey Rucker was mortally wounded in the abdomen but managed to get away and die in agony somewhere else. The fourth man fled into the undergrowth but got only three hundred yards before he was struck in the back by no fewer than five bullets.

This little engagement seems to have been one of the greatest Federal victories of the late winter as measured by the number of enemy slain. More often, the cavalry raced to the scene of the most recent malefaction and followed the outlaws' horse tracks, but only now and then did they get close enough to wound one of the fast-fleeing culprits.

As the weather began to warm, bushwhacker bands set out for Missouri from Texas and Arkansas. One of the first arrivals crossed into southeast Lafayette County sometime around March 23. They were fired on by blacks and returned the fire, killing three. "Why is this state of things suffered?" railed the editor of the Lexington *Union*.

> Have the people become lost to all sense of shame, have they lost all self-respect, have [they] bid an everlasting farewell to every feeling and impulse of their manhood? Why do they not rise en masse and drive those murderers from the land? It is not possible to have peace and quiet with cut throats roaming at large over the country. Then why not apply the remedy now while you have the power to do so?

A few days later the Columbia *Missouri Statesman* put it more succinctly: "Let the sight of a guerrilla be a signal to shoot him. If he comes to your home shoot him. If you meet him on the road shoot him down." Since they had suffered the deprivations of war for eleven years, many Missourians were inclined not only to agree but to act.

On March 30, some Clay County citizens had a fight with bushwhackers and killed two. These civilians "say they desire to harm no one," commented the Liberty *Tribune* approvingly, "but that they are not going to have their territory destroyed and themselves ruined by a few desperadoes who have no interest in the country beyond what they steal."

A week later two guerrillas rode into Smithville to get their horses shod. As the word of their arrival spread, townsfolk armed themselves, arrested them, and turned them over to soldiers. "Bushwhackers will find it to their interest to stay out of Clay County," the *Tribune* smugly observed. The question was, where could they safely go? Two brothers named Bledsoe were arrested by citizens near Neosho, in the southwest corner of the state. The civilians proposed to try them, but the brothers convinced a justice of the peace to grant a change of venue. As they were being transported, they were overtaken by vigilantes and hung. Two other brothers, James and Rucker Matlock, were arrested in Clark County, in the northeast corner of the state, and, while they were being carried to Macon, they were killed "attempting to escape."

Colonel Chester Harding, Jr., who now commanded the District of Central Missouri, was pleased. "I take it to be a good sign of returning peace that the citizens are taking this kind of bushwhacking into their own hands." Militia and volunteer cavalry troopers were heartened as well. They scouted, remarked another officer, "every day and night."

Lee surrendered on April 9, and Lincoln was assassinated five days later, on April 14, but on the border guerrillas continued to be a problem: In late April and early May alone dozens were killed in minor skirmishes and clashes.

Not all the news was good from a Federal perspective. Many militia units were still poorly armed, and the numbers of cavalry troops were wholly inadequate to deal with the swelling partisan population.

By May 8, the Yankee intelligence network had identified at least five large bands in western Missouri, which ranged in size from one hundred to three hundred men. There were also numerous gangs of ten, twenty, forty, or even seventy men, and reports came in daily of the arrival of more. Several towns were sacked, and individuals, caught on the open road, were robbed and sometimes murdered.

Union officers felt the pressure building. Some responded with bravado, promising to "exterminate" every guerrilla, even if the odds were "5 to 1" against their soldiers. Colonel Harding took a more realistic approach. On May 1, he pointed out to General Dodge that the "worst elements . . . have friends, wives, mistresses, fathers, mothers, &c., living with us. My men will certainly kill them if they come through the brush," he asserted bravely, but added, "I respectfully suggest that some general plan be made known by which repentant rebels may have at least the benefit of becoming prisoners of war."

General Dodge thought he had a good idea. "In reference to your letter relative to bushwhackers who desire to give themselves up," he replied on May 7,

> you can say to all such who lay down their arms and surrender and obey the laws that the military laws will not take any further action against them, but we cannot protect them against the civil law should it . . . take cognizance of their cases. It is useless for them to continue the contest, and sooner or later they will be caught, and no terms will be granted them.

Word of the new Federal surrender policy was slow to circulate in the bush, and while some individuals and guerrilla bands came in, others roamed free, disruptive and evasive, through May and June. Officers who reported the results of scouts sometimes listed a few enemy slain; more often they employed such dismal sentence fragments as "Found no enemy" and "Did not find anything."

———◆◆◆———

Meanwhile, some of Quantrill's old band who were still in Texas decided to go to Mexico with Shelby to fight for the Emperor Maximilian; their dream was to establish a new Confederate state south of the border. The rest—about one hundred men—chose to go back to Missouri. Dave Pool was their leader, and their ranks included Fletch Taylor, Jim Anderson, "Ol" Shepherd, Arch Clement, and Jesse James. They progressed slowly through the Indian Territory and southern Kansas, occasionally skirmishing with Federal units, then crossed into Missouri in early May.

The band entered Johnson County on the night of May 6 and split in two. One squad rode to Kingsville and murdered four railroad teamsters; the other men struck Holden, where they cut the telegraph line, looted stores, and killed a militiaman and known thief named Duncan.

Colonel Harding's troopers took off in hot pursuit and actually managed to get close enough to slay three raiders. The rest rendezvoused near Lexington, having murdered another fifteen men along the way. They told farmers they did not believe that Lee had surrendered; it was "a damned Yankee lie." The band split again. Half the men rode into the Sni Hills with Dave Pool, then scattered and burrowed deep into hiding places; the other half—mostly Anderson men—put themselves under the command of "Little Archie" Clement.

On the morning of May 9, Clement sent a letter to Major B. K. Davis, commander of the Lexington post, in which he threatened retaliation if any of his friends were hurt and promised to "treat all men who reported for militia duty as public enemies." This was hardly news, but two days later Clement fired a second salvo.

Six Miles Out The Field, May 11, 1865

Major Davis, *Lexington, Mo.:*

Sir: This is to notify you that I will give you until Friday morning, 10 a.m., May 12, 1865, to surrender the town of Lexington. If you surrender we will treat you and all taken as prisoners of war. If we have to take it by storm we will burn the town and kill the soldiers. We have the force, and are determined to have it.

I am, sir, your obedient servant,
A. Clement,
OPERATOR.

Nothing came of this audacious bluff, and Clement and Jim Anderson soon joined forces and roamed around Howard County.

———•◆•———

On May 16, Brigadier General I. V. Pratt, Missouri State Militia, breathlessly informed General Dodge that Quantrill and Dave Pool were in the vicinity of Macon with their bands and were "anxious" to surrender. This was just the latest in a grab bag full of wildly contradictory rumors about the "author of the Lawrence massacre." During the winter informants had him hiding in Missouri and planning various imminent, horrifying raids. Beginning in March he was said repeatedly to be returning from Texas to resume the war. By May he was alternately roaming the Sni Hills or the banks of the Blue or approaching Missouri's southern border intent on giving himself up. His death was reported at a time when he still lived, and he was seen alive in Washington, DC, six months after he died. (Many border newspapers did not publish authentic accounts of his death until late July.)

———•◆•———

Two weeks of hiding out in the Sni Hills afforded Dave Pool ample opportunity to appraise the prospects for guerrillas in peacetime Missouri. He collected as many of his followers as he could find and, on May 21, led them to a point a mile and a half outside of Lexington. The Liberty *Tribune* subsequently announced that at 1:00 P.M. Pool sent a messenger into town under a flag of truce to offer

the surrender of his band. Col. Harding and his staff went out to meet them. . . . Pool had forty-eight men. They marched into town military style, and halted in front of the Provost Marshal's office. They were ordered to dismount and advance two paces and lay down their arms, ammunition, &c.

The oath was then administered, and all were permitted to return to their homes. Pool is to assist the military in bringing in the balance of the bushwhackers.

Twenty-four hours after Pool surrendered, Harding had wired General Dodge, "Bushwhacking is stopped." The announcement was premature. A few days later, for example, Jim Anderson and his followers murdered five men near Haynesville, Clinton County. Nevertheless things were winding down. By the end of May more than two hundred guerrillas had surrendered at Lexington alone.

———— ◦ ✦ ◦ ————

"Ol" Shepherd wrote to Captain John Younger on May 25 that he and his "little band" wished to "quit fighting and obey the laws of the country." He offered to hand over stolen pistols and horses and promised to leave the country, but

> we must keep our side arms—for you know we have personal enemies that would kill us at the first opportunity. . . . I have a horse that I rode from Texas, that there is no use in a man talking about me giving up.
>
> Now, Capt. Younger, these words I write in earnest; there will be no use in talking about myself and band coming to Liberty if you don't allow us our side arms, and give us an honorable parole. We are willing to blot out the past and begin, anew. If I come to Liberty I will let you know distinctly that I and my men intend to behave ourselves and not throw out any insinuations nor insults to soldiers nor citizens, nor [do] we intend to take any from them. Understand me we blot all out and begin anew.

Shepherd was informed that his surrender "must be upon the same terms that others of your 'Profession' are being accepted." He and his men came in anyway. After they surrendered, they were allowed to go their way. (Two months later Shepherd was arrested, charged with robbery by a Unionist. The alleged crime had been committed several months earlier, while Shepherd was still in the bush.)

On May 31, Colonel Harding reported to his superiors that Dave Pool had spent a week scouring the countryside in order to turn up forty men. They

> were lying by twos and threes in the brush from the Sni Hills to the mouth of La Mine. . . . Pool has been out with Lieutenant Saltzman . . . and has showed him some of the tricks of the bushwhackers, among others is that of spreading their blankets across the road and

marching their horses on the blankets to prevent a trail being made. Pool is doing good work. The Governor promised him full pardon if he keeps on as he has now started.

Most of the men who rode with Clement and Jim Anderson surrendered on June 10, but the two leaders continued to demand special terms. After four days the impatient Federals broke off negotiations and orders were given that "If they are found, kill them at once. Hold no further parley with them . . . but destroy them wherever found." Clement and Anderson hastily rode to Texas.

<hr />

So far as is known, the last guerrillas to surrender were some of those who followed Quantrill to Kentucky. Among the sixteen men who rode to Samuels Depot, in Nelson County, on July 26, 1865, were Frank James, John Harris, Allen Parmer, R. M. Venable, Payne Jones, and Andy McGuire. They were paroled on the orders of General Palmer and allowed to go home.

Apparently Jesse James never took the oath or got his papers. There is a tradition, generally believed to be true, that he was on his way to Lexington, Missouri, with some others to surrender when, despite their white flag, they were ambushed by Union soldiers. Jesse was struck in the chest but managed to flee into the woods. He shot the horse of one pursuer, and another wisely gave up. "That night Jesse lay in the bed of a creek to soothe his fever," wrote William A. Settle, Jr., in *Jesse James Was His Name*. "The next day he dragged himself to a field, where he was found by a plowman. When he had recovered strength enough to travel," friends carried him to Reuben Samuel's home in Nebraska. In later times he would sometimes display the two closely placed bullet scars on his chest—the one from 1864, the other from 1865.

<hr />

"We cannot now resist the conviction that the future status of our country will be strictly peaceful and quiet," the editor of the *Tribune* had exulted on June 2,

and we earnestly exhort all our citizens to set themselves diligently about the restoration of their former property. The farmers may now plant in security and gather in safety. The merchant will not need a convoy. Everything promises well. Let us hope that a few years will remove all traces of war, and so soothe and soften its memories, that we may feel once more the happiness of former times.

Throughout the summer other editors wrote equally hopeful editorials. Undoubtedly the vast majority of Missourians agreed with them, wanting only to resume their former lives and ponder the reports of Jeff Davis in his spare prison cell, the prosecution of the Lincoln conspirators, and the controversy over the loyalty oath. In lighter moments there were also the debates about the length of women's skirts and the impropriety of female ice skaters donning what newspapers referred to as "artificial or false calves" to make their legs appear more shapely.

Unfortunately, peace did not come quickly to the state in general nor to the troubled border region in particular. Robberies were regularly committed as well as the occasional murder, and these crimes were usually blamed on ex-bushwhackers. Sometimes suspects were lynched rather than turned over to authorities; even when they were jailed, impatient mobs or vigilante gangs would now and then remove them from their cells and hang them from trees.

As the families driven out by Order No. 11 returned, they found a bleak, barren landscape where once lush farms had been: vast empty stretches of charred fields and woodland broken by the occasional blackened chimney, which marked the place where a house had stood. (Since Jennison was alleged to have raided through the four affected counties during the evacuation in the fall of 1863, these chimneys soon came to be called "Jennison's Monuments" or "Jennison's Tombstones," and the devastated area would be known for half a century as the "Burnt District.") Reading the recollections of the dispossessed, one thinks of nothing so much as a nuclear strike zone. Nevertheless, many stalwart farm families set to work rebuilding, depending on the rich Missouri soil to recover. "I can forgive, but never forget," Lizzie Gregg wrote in 1913. Many others could do neither: Even into the 1930s, Democratic politicians in western Missouri, who sought to gain advantage over Republican rivals, would invoke the pain caused by Order No. 11.

There was much else to be bitter about. Returning guerrillas and soldiers from both sides had old scores to settle—with fists, guns, or even lawsuits; a Southern man had little chance of a fair hearing in court. Radical Republicans seized control of the state government and adopted a constitution that disenfranchised all who had sided with the Confederacy; it also forbade them to serve as a juror, hold political office, or be a practicing attorney, college professor, teacher, bishop, priest, minister, deacon, church elder, or the director or manager of a corporation. Amnesty was given to Union soldiers for acts committed after January 1, 1861, but Confederates were held responsible for their acts committed either as civilians or while in the service.

Radicals took over local government, too, either by cowing already elected officials or electing their own kind by intimidating voters. It would be many years before moderate forces became an important factor in Missouri politics.

With the rapid postwar demobilization of the Union army and the abandonment of small garrisons, Southerners had to rely on militia for protection, and too often these were highwaymen themselves or, in the words of one regular army officer, "the most condemned set of ruffians I ever saw." Radical Unionists killed ministers whose sermons they found objectionable and formed "strong arm bands" with such evocative names as "Vigilance Committee," "Regulators," and "Avengers." These bands lynched criminal suspects but also terrified and murdered innocent civilians.

Some former Confederates and Southern sympathizers gave up and moved away. Others, like the Younger brothers, rode the outlaw trail; they attributed their criminality to continued harassment by Unionist neighbors. Most hunkered down, stayed home, and hoped that things would improve.

Gradually they did. Easterners, who had not suffered and been embittered by the brutality of border warfare, flooded the state, moving to the towns and cities or buying up tracts of land sold for back taxes. Railroad lines were built, farms mechanized, and cities became industrialized. By 1870, Missouri was the "fifth largest industrial state" in the nation as measured by value of product, and St. Louis was the "third largest city in terms of number of plants and value of product, behind New York City and Philadelphia." As Missouri prospered, the Radical Unionists lost favor. The state government became interested in fostering the economic boom, not in the persecution of old enemies.

In those areas of eastern Kansas and western Missouri that made up the border region, hard feelings remained, but old adversaries at least coexisted. Except for the ongoing outlaw problem, a new, peaceful normalcy was measuredly attained. After such a long period of conflict, violence, and misery, people were at least able to get on with their lives.

———◆·◆———

Fletch Taylor, who prospered as the vice president and general superintendent of the Joplin Mining and Smelting Co., delighted in telling everyone that **Kate King** used the money Quantrill had left her to open a fancy "bagnio" in St. Louis. It will be recalled that Quantrill had had Taylor arrested in Texas, with the intention that he be court-martialed, and thereafter Taylor disparaged his former leader whenever he could. To plant as true a fabricated story that the love of Quantrill's life became a whorehouse madam would be the ultimate, snickering put-down. Kate herself would later insist that she never received Quantrill's bequest but had hocked jewels he gave her—loot from raids—to establish a boardinghouse. She married a rich man named J. R. Claiborne. Four years after the end of the war, she visited her family and found them living in a shack thrown together after their home was burned by Kansans. She built them a new house and, after she returned to St. Louis, periodically sent them money.

She married three more times, the last while she and her betrothed were "inmates" of Jackson County Home for the Aged—also known as the poor farm. They ran away to be married when she was seventy-four. Even married couples were not permitted to live together in the home, so she resided alone in a room, often sitting in bed, propped up against pillows, reading. In 1926, as we know, she granted an interview to a Kansas City *Star* reporter, during which she repeated Quantrill's old lies about his birthplace and the murder of his brother by jayhawkers. She had heard by then that these were falsehoods but continued to believe them because her one true love had told them to her. In the home, she called herself Sarah Head and did not reveal her real identity to fellow inmates because some of them had been bushwhacker victims and still harbored resentments. During her final years she kept to herself, rarely speaking, content to dream of her life long ago with her "guerrilla warrior."

Quantrill's "girl bride" died on January 9, 1930. She was eighty-two. Her body remained for a month at the funeral home before relatives could be located and persuaded to pay for the burial. On February 7, she was finally interred in the Maple Hill Cemetery, Kansas City, Kansas. Only a few friends attended.

In her interview, Kate never mentioned that she had children, but today, if you spend much time in Jackson County researching the Quantrill story, one elderly man or another will offer to arrange a meeting between you and the granddaughter of Kate's eldest child, whom, they say, was fathered by William Clarke Quantrill. (The great-granddaughter of Quantrill and Kate King!) Somehow these meetings never quite take place.

The reputation of **Jim Lane** had been severely damaged by the Lawrence raid. Critics charged him with cowardice because he had failed to catch up with and destroy the retreating Quantrill band. Even supporters suspected him of holding back. He ran for reelection to the Senate in 1864, dogged by charges of corruption and ineptitude. A young woman even horsewhipped him on a Washington street because he had propositioned her. He seemed likely to be defeated, until Price's army neared Kansas City and he took part in the series of engagements that won the day. After his reelection and his benefactor Lincoln's assassination, Lane tried to curry favor with President Johnson, which earned him the enmity of Radical Republican Kansans, who had once been his closest supporters.

His career ruined, his mind began to deteriorate. He tried to jump from a St. Louis hotel room window. A doctor took him to a Leavenworth-area farm, where he could be watched over by family and friends. At 5:00 P.M. on Wednesday, July 5, 1866, Lane was riding in a wagon with his brother-in-law and another relative. When the wagon was halted so that one of the others could open a gate, Lane got out, stepped to the back of the wagon, and produced a secreted derringer. "Good-bye, gentlemen!" he called, then put the muzzle into his mouth and pulled the trigger. The barrel had been angled upward, so the small-caliber bullet exited out the top of his skull. He lingered in agony for ten days.

In reporting on his suicide, the Liberty *Tribune* suggested he had been haunted "day and night" by the "dozens" of men he had murdered and by the recollected screams of women and children as they ran from their burning Osceola homes. "Lane closed his career properly for a life like his," Kansan Samuel Smith wrote to ex-governor Charles Robinson. "No one can blame a person for wishing to hurry away from such a life as his [was]. Not a paper here has spoken well of him that I have seen. The sentiment seems to be that the world is purer + better that he is gone. His suicide is his own verdict on his life + actions in that he had neither peace of mind nor peace of conscience."

His grave is in Lawrence's Oak Hill Cemetery. The Lane family obelisk is just up the slope from the monument to the Lawrence massacre dead.

Shortly before the surrender at Appomattox, **George Caleb Bingham** resigned the office of Missouri state treasurer and resumed painting. In his studio, which was a log cabin at the end of Osage Street in Independence, he glued pieces of walnut board together, planed the surface, and began a painting that depicted the cruelty of Order No. 11. When the boards started to crack, he glued canvas over them, but further cracking caused the canvas to wrinkle. He began a second painting on linen cloth stretched in a frame. After a few months, during which he worked on other paintings, the canvas on the walnut boards stopped wrinkling, and so he painted alternately on the canvas and the linen. He was delayed and distracted by political events in Missouri—particularly the loyalty oath, which he opposed—and his efforts to raise money for Confederate widows and orphans.

Meanwhile **Thomas Ewing** left the army and moved to Washington, DC, where he opened a law office. His first big case was an extremely unpopular one: He defended three of the Lincoln conspirators—Samuel Arnold, Edward Spangler, and Dr. Samuel Mudd. Given the evidence and the climate of vengeful hysteria, acquittal was impossible; however, Ewing managed to save all three clients from the gallows. Andrew Johnson offered him the cabinet post of secretary of war, but he declined because he believed that association with the embattled president might hurt his own political prospects.

In December 1868, Bingham finished the painting on linen cloth. Lew Larkin, in a 1955 biography of Bingham, described it this way:

The prairie, spreading out until it touches the sky, is stabbed by rising columns of smoke from the burning homes and fields. The wretched victims blend into the horizon, stumbling along, bent and miserable, with their scanty possessions tied in bundles, while others pull carts, wagons, and strange-looking vehicles.

In the central foreground and to the left there is the front part of the house that is being looted. Raiders toss articles from a balcony to a wagon below. Furniture is being moved out.

The white-haired master of the house stands grim, straight and defiant, one hand clenched at his side, the other raised forbiddingly towards two menacing Redlegs.

One ruffian in the foreground is in the act of drawing his pistol. He wears red Moroccan leggings and the blue coat of a federal soldier.

A daughter of the master, her arms around her father's neck, begs him not to resist the Redlegs. Another daughter is on her knees beseeching the menacing Redleg not to pull his gun.

The master's son has been shot, his hat on the ground nearby, a thin stream of blood oozing from his head, the wife prostate over his body. The master's wife has fainted and is being held by a Negro mammy, while a grandson wildly clutches the old master's leg.

On a horse, coldly oblivious to the tragic scene, sits a Union soldier staring straight out of the painting, the likeness of Thomas Ewing, and on another horse over to his left is the likeness of Jim Lane.

Many people had visited Bingham's studio while he was at work on the painting, and word of it had spread through the state. The editor of the *Missouri Statesman* commented that "Bingham's 'Order No. 11,' almost before it has received the finishing stroke of the artist's brush, is achieving a celebrity which significantly foreshadows the high rank which it will, in the future, take as a work of genius."

Not everyone was enthusiastic. Some Missourians wanted only to forget the war and feared the painting would keep old animosities alive. Others suggested Bingham was really a Confederate sympathizer or he would not have executed such a painting. Bingham scoffed at his critics and took "Order No. 11" on tour through Missouri cities and towns. Huge crowds flocked to see the picture and to listen to his discourses.

Such was the acclamation that Bingham quickly completed the second painting so that he could send the first one to Sartain of Philadelphia and have an engraving made. Bingham expected to do a brisk business in print sales, but money was not his only motivation: Ewing had moved back to Ohio, had switched from the Republican to the Democratic party, and was obviously preparing for a political career. The prints would be devastating propaganda against him.

Ewing tried twice to be the Democratic party's nominee for governor. Each time Bingham sent vitriolic letters, pamphlets, and reproductions of his painting to Ewing's political foes in Ohio, and each time Ewing was passed over.

It is difficult to judge from this distance how much credit Bingham deserved for Ewing's defeats. Larkin believed the painter's efforts were pivotal, but David G. Taylor, a scholar who studied Ewing's political career, gave Bingham short shrift. Taylor cited a variety of factors, including not only the collapse of the Grand Avenue building and suffering caused by Order No. 11, but also Ewing's controversial business dealings, his maneuvers within the Ohio Democratic party, his stands on some of the issues of the day, and so on.

Party leaders did nominate Ewing to be his district's congressional candidate. It was a smart move: Ewing's father had been a U.S. senator, had held several cabinet posts, and was venerated in southern Ohio, so Ewing, capitalizing on the family name, was elected in the fall of 1876. He was reelected in 1878 and positioned himself to run for governor in 1879.

Bingham, who was in poor health, rallied to battle his old enemy one more time. In the midst of composing the latest withering indictment of Ewing, Bingham was stricken with cholera morbus. He lingered for two days, feverish and comatose, before he died on the morning of July 7, 1879.

Many of those attending his funeral came from the "Burnt District," which had been devastated by Kansans after Order No. 11 had been issued. "They regarded Bingham as their champion, defender and friend," Larkin observed, "someone who believed with them that an injustice to humanity is unpardonable and must be mirrored to succeeding generations to prevent recurrences."

Near the end of July, James Rollins Bingham, the artist's eighteen-year-old son, released to the press his father's last, unfinished letter. Widely reprinted under the title "A Voice from the Tomb," it was more than just a recapitulation of old charges. Bingham had documented previously unknown instances of brutality, some of them committed "within a stone's throw of [Ewing's] headquarters." The effect was to make Ewing seem even more heartless and culpable. "These facts," Bingham had argued, "clearly show that Ewing was in intimate association with the basest criminals whose robberies and murders were perpetrated almost in his presence, and which, if he did not approve, he at least permitted."

Out of 668,666 votes cast, Thomas Ewing lost by 17,029, or less than 3 percent. Here again, it is impossible to know the impact of Bingham's propaganda, but controversy is rarely thought desirable by politicians. If

Bingham's efforts and last letter caused a shift of 1.5 percent of the electorate, then he had ended the general's political career.

Ewing moved to Yonkers, New York, where he established a successful law practice.

Sometime in the late 1880s, Curtis B. Rollins, the son of Bingham's great friend James S. Rollins, visited Ewing in his law office. The talk turned to Bingham. Ewing expressed no bitterness toward the artist, praising him as a man of high ideals but with "so little understanding of military necessity that before he would commandeer a mule or a load of corn from a farmer in the line of his march, he would first have to consult the constitution to see that he was within the law."

On January 20, 1896, Thomas Ewing was crossing a downtown Yonkers street when he was struck by a cable car. He was carried to his home and died the next day.

Arch Clement returned to Lafayette County from Texas in the summer of 1866. Although he had a price on his head, he made no effort to hide; on the contrary, he was often to be found in some Lexington saloon, drinking with Dave Pool.

At 11:00 A.M. on the morning of December 13, Clement rode into town at the head of twenty-six heavily armed men. Dave Pool brought up the rear. They stopped at the City Hotel, repaired to the bar, and drank their fill. Then, in obedience to a recent order that required all men over eighteen to register for possible muster into the state militia, they proceeded to the militia office at the courthouse. Major Bacon Montgomery, who had been notorious for his brutality and cruelty during the war, enrolled them and then told them to leave town.

All obeyed, but three hours later "Little Archie" returned and resumed his place at the City Hotel bar. Major Montgomery sent a three-man squad to arrest him. When they entered the bar, "Little Archie" drew a revolver and cut loose, then fled through the side door. He vaulted onto his horse and raced down Franklin Street. As he passed the courthouse, sharpshooters opened fire from the windows. Clement was riddled with bullets. His horse slowed to a walk, and his body fell facedown in the dirt.

No doubt many Missourians and Kansans breathed a sigh of relief when they heard the news.

His corpse was washed, dressed, and put on display. The inevitable photograph was taken. There is disagreement today over where he is buried: Graves in two different western Missouri cemeteries are said to contain his remains.

After the war, **General James G. Blunt,** whose men had been massacred at Baxter Springs, settled in Leavenworth and resumed his medical practice; however, a few years later he moved to Washington, DC, where he solicited claims before various federal agencies. On April 9, 1873, he was one of several men charged with "conspiracy to defraud the government and a body of Cherokee Indians in North Carolina." The case dragged on for two years before it was dismissed. He continued to solicit claims for most of the decade. On February 12, 1879, he was admitted as a patient to St. Elizabeth's Insane Asylum, diagnosed as having a "softening of the brain." He suffered partial paralysis and convulsions and died in confinement on July 25, 1881.

His body was transported to the Anthony Buchly undertaking establishment on Pennsylvania Avenue and placed on ice. After a two-hour viewing on July 28, the corpse was put into a metal casket, which was taken to the Baltimore and Potomac train depot, escorted by a contingent of the Kit Carson Post, Grand Army of the Republic. The casket was shipped express to Blunt's son-in-law in Leavenworth.

Despite having been routed at Byram's Ford by the Iron Brigade, **Colonel Charles "Doc" Jennison** and his Kansas cavalry troopers fought Price's army with such ferocity and tenacity that they won high praise from General Blunt, their commanding officer. Before long, however, Jennison's temper got him in trouble again: He wrote a blistering letter of complaint and accusation to Blunt's adjutant, and Blunt had him arrested and court-martialed. He was found guilty of one count of "conduct prejudicial to good order and military discipline" but was given only a slap on the wrist. Blunt next investigated rumors that during the Price campaign Jennison and his men had plundered and burned the homes of defenseless women, summarily hung "bushwhackers" who sometimes turned out to be loyal citizens, and stolen cattle. Jennison's second court-martial in five months concluded on May 20, 1865. He was convicted of three principle charges and dishonorably discharged from the service.

He returned to Leavenworth and promptly got into a gunfight with Daniel Anthony. Jennison was wounded in the leg and brought to trial but was acquitted.

Unlike Blunt, "Doc" Jennison did not resume his medical practice. He prospered as a saloon keeper, gambling-house operator, farmer, and breeder of racehorses and cattle. He was elected president of the Leavenworth city council, served two terms in the Kansas House of Representatives, and one term in the state senate. Oddly, given his abolitionist background, he consistently opposed Negro suffrage and regularly denounced "Republican corruption."

As he grew into middle age, he was afflicted with ill health, especially a severe pain in his side and a persistent cough. He died on June 21, 1884, at the age of fifty. He was buried in Leavenworth's Greenwood Cemetery.

For many years after the war, Kansas auctioneers and horse breeders had found it profitable to brag with a wink that their animals were "out of Missouri by Jennison." In 1867, one Kansas City paper commented approvingly that "Jennison has done more to develop Kansas as a stock growing State, than any other man. He imported more good horses from Missouri in his time, than all the dealers combined. The stereotyped pedigree of most of our blooded horses is 'out of Missouri by Jennison.' "

However, the passing decades saw such a decline in his reputation that in 1903, his wife, who had kept thick scrapbooks of newspaper clippings that reported his prewar and wartime deeds, found it politic to insist she knew almost nothing about that period in his life.

William H. Gregg and his wife settled first in Jackson County and then in Kansas City, Missouri. They had ten children; tragically, one boy died in infancy and fifteen-year-old twin daughters succumbed to typhoid fever on the same day. Gregg worked as a carpenter, handyman, and teamster. In later years he came to be plagued by rheumatism, Catholicism, Republican politicians, and big-city high rents. As his arthritis worsened, he tried to find a less physically arduous way to make a living. He was a deputy sheriff and police station turnkey, but these were precarious political appointments: A change in administration meant he was thrown out of work once more.

He became the unofficial historian of the Quantrill band and attended all the reunions. He was befriended by William Connelley, who had begun writing his Quantrill biography and used him to smooth the way with other, suspicious ex-bushwhackers. In the cases of those who resolutely refused to trust a Kansan, Connelley would feed his questions through Gregg. Connelley prevailed upon Gregg to write his memoir and some shorter autobiographical essays, which are today essential sources for anyone researching Quantrill. When Connelley's ferociously negative book was published, there seems to have been a long silence between the two men, but eventually their relationship resumed. They genuinely liked and respected each other, and Gregg, ill and often impoverished, needed Connelley to help him find work. (The staunch Yankee sympathizer once wrote a reference letter to the governor of Missouri, recommending Gregg for the post of superintendent of a Confederate home!)

William Gregg died at age seventy-eight on April 22, 1916, of "senile atrophy of the heart." He also had cancer, and he was heartbroken: He knew that Lizzie, his beloved wife of fifty-one years, was fatally ill with cancer, too. She followed him ten days later, on May 2, 1916.

Edwin Terrell continued his violent ways after the war, which in peacetime made him an outlaw, not a decoy guerrilla. He came to be charged with murdering four men in four different counties.

One victim was an Illinois stock trader named William R. Johnson. On Sunday morning, August 27, 1865, Tommie Fox, an Irishman who preferred fishing to attending church, hooked Johnson's corpse and pulled it to the surface of Clear Creek, a mile and a half south of Shelbyville. Johnson had been shot in the back of the head and relieved of $1,600. Rocks had been stuffed into the pockets of his coat and pants before his corpse was thrown into the water. Since he was last seen two days earlier in the company of Terrell and his former lieutenant, John H. Thompson, both men were arrested and confined in the Shelbyville jail.

On the night of Tuesday, September 19, Terrell and Thompson tried to escape. They made a rope from torn pieces of shirts and underwear with which to lower themselves to the ground. Terrell used a case knife to cut mortar away from the bricks around the window of their cell, while Thompson covered the noise by playing a banjo. Terrell was loosening the last few bricks when a passerby noticed what was happening and gave the alarm. The two men were confined in separate cells.

Their ten-day trial, which began on March 12, 1866, ended in a hung jury. Authorities heard rumors that they would be lynched or were about to be broken out of jail by their gang and therefore sent them to the Louisville jail for safekeeping.

Terrell and another prisoner, John L. Wethers, were transferred to the Taylorsville jail on Monday, April 9, so they could be tried for the murder of Enuis Wooten, a blacksmith. "The jail at Taylorsville is a new one, and is considered very secure," *Journal* editor George Prentice assured his readers, "being constructed of stone in every part except the ceiling and roof." Nevertheless, when strangers were observed loitering in the town, the judge called for volunteers to guard the prisoners. There were no takers.

At 2:00 A.M. on Friday morning, April 13, seven heavily armed men with soot-blackened faces visited the jailer's house. They forced him to go to the jail and unlock their comrades' cell. Ironically, Terrell and Wethers were nearly finished cutting a hole in the oaken ceiling with a smuggled auger; in a few more minutes they would have escaped without assistance.

Six weeks later, on Saturday, May 26, Terrell made the mistake of going to Shelbyville, accompanied by his uncle, John Baker, and Wethers. The Louisville *Journal* reported that the three men

> were all armed to the teeth. This blood-seeking party dashed into town and began to abuse and threaten the citizens, drinking and carousing and disputing the power of any man or set of men to arrest them. For a while they had complete charge of the town, and the intimidation of the people appeared to favor their devilish intentions and warrant the impunity of their hectoring, defiant conduct.

However, a judge ordered their arrest, and the marshal, taking no chances, formed a posse of thirty-five men. Wethers eluded capture and got clean away. Terrell and Baker were cornered, managed to break through the posse, and were pursued. "The pursuing party then commenced a simultaneous and deadly firing, several balls taking effect on Terrell," George Prentice told his readers.

> One shot entered his back, near the spinal column, and, ranging through the body, came out at the breast near the collar bone, inflicting, it is believed, a mortal wound. The other shots penetrated various parts of his body. Baker received nine balls, one of them going directly through his heart. . . . [He] fell into the road and died in a few seconds. . . . Baker had in his breast pocket a new memorandum-book, which was perforated with three large balls, showing the firing of the citizens to have been very accurate.

Two of the posse were slightly wounded.

Terrell was carried to Louisville, where he was confined in the city jail. The jailhouse physician, Dr. T. W. Knight, extracted five buckshot and one bullet from his back, but one of his legs remained paralyzed. His other wounds were so severe that the doctor was certain he would die. "The state is thus well rid of a notorious outlaw," crowed the Franklin *Commonwealth*.

The newspaper was a bit premature: At the end of the month, Dr. Knight announced that his patient's "naturally vigorous constitution" was enabling him to rally and that he would recover. Four months later Terrell was deemed well enough to survive being transported back to Shelbyville for trial, along with John Thompson. (Thompson soon made his escape with two other prisoners: They tore planks from their cell's floor, cut a hole in a brick wall, and, using a rope made from a blanket and a sheet, lowered themselves ten feet to the ground. A fourth prisoner tried to follow but was too fat: He became wedged fast in the hole until freed by the jailer.)

Terrell was never tried for the murder of William Johnson. In chronic and terrible pain, severely constipated and emaciated, he was eventually released, giving his own bond. He went to live with his brother-in-law in Mount Eden.

Terrell quietly returned to Louisville on November 4, 1868. He was admitted to the City Hospital, formerly the Marine Hospital, because, as a contemporary city directory explained, it had been "originally established for the benefit of disabled boatmen" and was now used "as a clinique by the medical schools" in the region. Terrell hoped that a surgeon would be able to locate and extract more buckshot and bullets from his back and thus give him a measure of relief. A friend visited him shortly after his admission.

I found him in a pitiable condition—his leg paralyzed, his bowels almost at a deadlock, and his arms not much thicker than willow-wands. Indeed, his entire system seemed exhausted. His mind alone was unimpaired. About every ten or fifteen minutes he had what he called a shock of nerves in his spine. During these paroxysms he would be rolled together like a ball, and moan piteously with pain. He often expressed to me his desire that death would come quickly to relieve him from such agonizing torture.

When the surgery was performed, no bullets or pellets were located. Thereafter Terrell went into a swift decline. He sent for clergymen, although it is not clear that he "made his peace with God." An obituary published in the Louisville *Courier Journal* stated that during his last days he

> seemed often to have a disposition to talk, and frequently recounted to his nurse the scenes of blood and strife through which he had passed. He prized very highly a clipping from a newspaper which had given the details of his bold dash into Shelbyville at the time he received his wounds. His last request was that his revolver and the heavy gold ring he had taken from the finger of the dead guerrilla Marion might be given to his brother.

Even as he lay dying Terrell could not resist prevarication and deception. He told the hospital staff the same lies he had told General Palmer and other officers in 1865: that he had served under John Hunt Morgan, had been court-martialed for having killed an officer, and was released from prison by Yankee soldiers the night before his scheduled execution.

When he awoke on the morning of December 13, Terrell asked for whiskey. The hospital staff realized the end was near and sent for his spiritual advisers. Before they arrived, at approximately 10:30 A.M., Edwin Terrell died. He was twenty-three years old.

He was buried in a pauper's grave in the cemetery of the workhouse. This was not an entirely fitting last resting place, since the institution was for those who committed only minor offenses and misdemeanors.

In less than two weeks a man appeared who said he was Terrell's brother, John, from Missouri. He had the body disinterred and "temporarily" reburied in a private cemetery. He let it be known that he planned to have his brother's corpse shipped to Missouri for burial in "his native soil," and then he disappeared.

Fragmentary records in the hands of Terrell's collateral descendants indicate Edwin Terrell had a brother or cousin named Johnny; however, the Terrell family was from Kentucky, not Missouri. If the man who had Terrell's corpse exhumed really was a relative, then by lying about where the Terrells lived, he may have been trying to protect them from persecution. On the other hand, it is possible he was not related to Terrell: He may have been a friend or a member of Terrell's gang who wanted to get the body out of a pauper's grave; or he may have had no connection to Terrell at all and was simply after the revolver and ring.

In Nebraska during the summer of 1865, **Jesse James** made a very slow recovery from his chest wound. At one point, afraid that he would die, he begged his mother to take him back to Missouri so that he would not breathe his last breath in a "Northern" state. They traveled by boat to Harlem (now North Kansas City) and stopped at the boardinghouse of his uncle, John Mimms. There Jesse was nursed by his cousin Zerelda "Zee" Mimms. They became engaged but did not marry for nine years. In the fall, Jesse was taken by wagon to the family farm in Clay County. In all probability, **Frank James** was already in residence.

The James brothers seem not to have been a special target of persecution. They had not been guerrilla leaders and were virtually unknown: I have been unable to find a single mention of Jesse's name in Civil War–era newspapers, and some of the few passing references to Frank identify him only as "James of Clay Co." For four years the boys cultivated the farm and stayed out of trouble. Jesse even joined the Baptist Church in Kearney and was baptized.

Cole Younger, on the other hand, was well known to Unionists in west-central Missouri. After he came back from California in the autumn of 1865, his enemies would give him no rest. He later insisted that he had been the victim of two assassination attempts. He was indicted for murdering a man at Paola. When Cole heard rumors that the vigilantes were after him, he went into hiding. In his autobiography, he said that he first sought refuge with an uncle in Howard County, then went to Louisiana.

While Cole was supposedly secreted in Howard County, the first in a series of daylight bank robberies occurred in western Missouri that would later be blamed on the Youngers and the Jameses.

On the afternoon of February 13, 1866, a dozen men rode into Liberty. Some of them posted themselves at strategic locations about the town, while two others, dressed in blue soldiers' overcoats, entered the Clay County Savings Bank. They drew pistols and filled a cotton wheat sack with paper currency, government bonds, and gold and silver coins. As the bandits started to make their getaway, they opened fire on two bystanders, killing one, a young college student named George Wymore. The gang escaped a hastily organized posse in a blinding snowstorm and got away with $60,000.

Although newspapers did not connect the Jameses and Youngers with the crime, of the nine identified suspects, six were Quantrill followers: "Ol" Shepherd, Bud Pence, Donny Pence, Frank Gregg, James Wilkerson, and Joab Perry.

Eight months later, at noon on October 30, four men barged into a Lexington bank and took $2,011.50 from the cash drawer. The posse, which was led by Dave and John Pool, came close enough to the fleeing robbers to catch sight of them; however, they got away. Dave Pool attributed the inability to overtake them to the fleetness of their horses, but it was suggested that he and his brother did not really want to capture old bushwhacker comrades.

The next robbery was foiled when, on March 2, 1867, the owner of a private Savannah, Missouri, banking house refused to hand over the keys to the vault. One of the six would-be bandits shot him, though not fatally.

Three residents of Richmond, Missouri, were not so lucky. On May 22, a dozen men converged on the town, meeting in front of the Hughes and Wasson Bank. Four dismounted, entered, and soon emerged with $4,000. However, several citizens realized that a robbery was in progress and tried to intervene. Mayor John B. Shaw drew his pistol and ran toward the bank; he was gunned down. Young Frank Griffin took a position behind a tree and cut loose with a cavalry rifle; a bullet struck him in the forehead, killing him instantly. B. G. Griffin saw his son fall and, maddened by grief, raced over to the bank door; he was shot in the head at point-blank range. His murderer put a second bullet in him as he lay on the ground. A posse overtook the bandits at sundown, but after a short fight, they escaped into the woods.

Two nights later a habitual criminal named Felix Bradley was taken from the Richmond jail and hanged on the outskirts of town. Since he had been incarcerated at the time of the robbery, he had an airtight alibi. However, he had told fellow inmates the bank would be held up a few hours before it actually was.

Thomas Little, a Quantrill guerrilla, was arrested in late May, charged with the robbery, and lodged in the Warrensburg jail. Although he had collected affidavits from Lafayette County residents who swore that he was in Dover on the day in question, he was given a mock trial by a mob, then executed.

Warrants were issued for five men, including at least three other Quantrill veterans: Allen Parmer, Payne Jones, and Andy McGuire. Parmer's employer corroborated his assertion that he was in St. Louis on May 22, so he was not arrested or harmed. When a posse found Payne Jones at the family homestead near Independence, he put up a fight and got away. Unfortunately, during the shootout he killed a member of the posse and a little girl who got in the line of fire. Jones himself was murdered a short time later, as was another Richmond suspect, Dick Burns.

Late in the year Andy McGuire was arrested in St. Louis, where he had been honeymooning under the alias James Cloud. On February 25, 1868, James M. Devers was arrested in that state and charged with the crime. Both men were confined in the Richmond jail, awaiting trial. Near midnight on March 17, a fifteen-man "vigilance committee" entered the jail and locked up the deputy sheriffs who were acting as guards. Then, noted the Richmond *Conservator,* the vigilantes "walked off with the prisoners who were found, hanging, next morning, *dead,* in a hollow east of the negro school house." It is said that when Devers realized he was about to die, he confessed to the crime.

In reporting the lynching three days later, the editor of the *Conservator* was genuinely outraged: "We but repeat the verdict of everyone in denouncing this whole affair as dastardly in its every sense and as injurious to our community, which has hitherto had the reputation of a quiet lawabiding place." It would seem that not *everyone* thought vigilante justice was so reprehensible or injurious to the community. Indeed, certain facts of the case suggest that the sheriff or some person or persons in authority may have wanted to deter other would-be bank robbers: The vigilance committee had used a set of keys to enter the jail; the deputies put up no resistance; and the bodies of the accused were left hanging until noon.

Perhaps it was the vehement reaction of Missourians to the Richmond robbery that caused the gang to make a change in venue. Three days after McGuire and Devers were lynched, six bandits struck the N. Long & Co. bank in Russellville, southwestern Kentucky. They got away with an estimated $12,000 in a wheat sack.

D. G. Bligh, a Louisville detective who investigated the Russellville holdup, concluded that two of the culprits were "Ol" and George Shepherd. (Both were Quantrill guerrillas, of course, and suspects in other robberies. It will be recalled that Jesse had gone to Texas in 1864 with "Ol.") When Jackson County law enforcement officers located "Ol" at his father's home, he resisted arrest and was killed. George was arrested in Kentucky, found guilty, and sentenced to three years in prison.

Bligh eventually came to the conclusion that Cole Younger, John Jarrett, and Frank and Jesse James had also taken part in the robbery, although none was ever formally charged.

The James boys finally came to public attention as the result of the robbery of the Daviess County Savings Bank, Gallatin, northwestern Missouri, on December 7, 1869. One man entered the building and asked the principal owner, Captain John W. Sheets, to change a $100 bill. While the banker was turned toward the vault, a second man entered and, according to a contemporary newspaper article, said to Sheets, "If you will write out a receipt, I will pay you that bill." After the banker had compliantly sat down and begun writing, the second man suddenly drew a revolver and shot him through the heart and head. The two bandits then opened fire on bank clerk William A. McDowell, who fled the building shouting that Captain Sheets had been murdered. McDowell received a flesh wound in one arm.

As the robbers emerged from the bank, they were fired on by enraged townsfolk. The man who killed Sheets was unable to mount his frightened mare. He was dragged forty feet before he could free his foot from the stirrup. He then climbed up behind his comrade, and they galloped out of town. They stole a farmer's horse and after dark forced another local to guide them out of the area.

It was known that they escaped into Clay County, and the horse that had been abandoned was quickly identified as belonging to Jesse James. A three-man posse led by Deputy Sheriff John S. Thomason rode to the James farm. Thomason placed two men in the woods behind the house, then he and his son dismounted and walked into the yard. As they approached the house, the stable door was suddenly thrown open, and two horses raced out ridden by Frank and Jesse, holding pistols in their hands. The horses jumped the barn-lot fence as the brothers and the posse exchanged shots. Only Sheriff Thomason's horse could take the fence, so he pursued the fugitives alone. Historian Settle wrote that

> A short distance down the road Thomason reined up, dismounted, took deliberate aim, fired, and missed. His frightened horse broke loose and dashed on, caught up with the fugitives, and ran even with their mounts for a distance; then one of the brothers reached out with a pistol and shot the animal dead.

Thomason had to borrow a horse from Mrs. Samuel to ride back to Gallatin.

That Jesse was one of the Gallatin culprits is not disputed today, but the second man is thought to have been Jim Anderson: The cashier overheard him make a remark to the effect that Sheets had been one of those responsible for the death of his brother Bill and that he was bound to have revenge. (Sheets resembled Major Samuel P. Cox, who also lived in Gallatin and who had led the company that killed Bloody Bill.)

The James brothers stayed out of sight for eighteen months. Then, on June 3, 1871, four men stole $6,000 from the Ocobock Brothers' Bank at Corydon, in south-central Iowa just across the Missouri border. The culprits bore strong physical resemblances to Frank, Jesse, Cole, and Clell Miller. Their trail led back to the James farm.

The fame of these outlaws grew quickly, and soon it seemed that every victim of a stick-up in a four-state area claimed to have been robbed by them—especially by Jesse James. They were blamed for robberies committed hundreds of miles apart on the same day, and though they often protested their innocence of particular crimes and furnished alibis, they were not believed. The American public embraced the legend, manufactured by dime novelists and fabricating "biographers," that Jesse James was a romantic figure, a kind of Missouri Robin Hood.

Whenever things grew too hot for the Jameses in their home state, they took up residence with their families under assumed names in Kentucky or Tennessee. Jesse and Zee had four children, all born in the latter state: a set of male twins, who soon sickened and died; a daughter, Mary; and a son, Jesse Edwards, who throughout his life was constantly and mistakenly referred to in newspapers as "Jesse James, Jr." Frank married Annie Ralston in 1874, not long after his brother's wedding. They had only one child, Robert Franklin, who was also born in hiding in Tennessee.

(Cole's romantic entanglements have been the subject of much snide speculation. In his autobiography, he stated that he married his "dear sweetheart" after returning from Texas but coyly declined to identify the lady. Interviewed by a reporter while incarcerated in Minnesota, he flatly denied having ever wed. He was at pains to refute the widespread rumor that he had had an affair with Myra Belle Shirley, better known as Belle Star, "the Bandit Queen," "the Female Jesse James." And, of course, he also insisted that contrary to popular belief he was not the father of her daughter, Pearl. He repeated these denials in his book, and this may have been one of those increasingly rare occasions when the practiced prevaricator was actually telling the truth.)

Pinkerton agents and other detectives prowled through Missouri during the outlaws' heyday, determined to bring them to bay. At least three agents were murdered by members of the Younger clan, and Cole's brother, John, was in turn killed by a Pinkerton in 1874. A few months later, on the night of January 26, 1875, Pinkertons threw a small incendiary device—an iron ball that contained a flammable liquid—through the Samuels' kitchen window. The detectives' intention was to burn the house and drive out Frank and Jesse James, whom they believed were staying there. Dr. and Mrs. Samuel, who had been asleep and were awakened by a noise outside the house, used a poker and shovel to move the ball into the fireplace. A second ball was lobbed through the window. This one exploded just as the Samuels were maneuvering it onto the hearth. A large metal fragment tore a hole in the side of nine-year-old Archie Peyton Samuel. He lived an hour. Mrs. Samuel's right hand was so badly mangled that it had to be amputated.

The accidental killing of the James boys' small, retarded brother and the crippling of their mother won them wide sympathy and added poignancy to their legend.

It used to be commonly believed that the Pinkertons had not meant to burn the house, only to smoke out Frank and Jesse, but a letter written by Allan Pinkerton after the incident has recently come to light:

> About half past twelve . . . we commenced firing the building. Our men battered in the window, then flung the fireballs into the house. Wild cries of dismay were heard from inside and soon the residents ran from the house which was lit up bright as day.
>
> Mrs. Samuel was bitter . . . and used anything but polite language. I had given positive order that no harm was to be done to the woman or Dr. Samuel.
>
> The men we were in search of must have left. . . .

The Jesse James gang, as it came to be known—much to the disgust of Cole, who did not get along with Jesse—was famous for its smooth, practiced holdup techniques. The Northfield, Minnesota, robbery attempt was a disastrous exception. On Thursday, September 7, 1876, five strangers took up positions around the town, while three others went into the First National Bank with the inevitable wheat sack. They were stalled by the cashier, who pretended that the vault had a time lock. He was pistol-whipped, and his throat was slashed before he was shot to death. A teller was wounded as he fled. The delay had allowed citizens to get their rifles and shotguns. Those who had no firearms picked up rocks.

As the outlaws tried to make a getaway, one ordered Nicholas Gustavson, a Swede who understood little English, to get indoors. He was gunned down when he failed to comply. The townsfolk loosed a hailstorm of bullets, shotgun pellets, and stones. Bandit William Stiles was shot through the heart. Clell Miller took a load of bird shot in the face and neck, then was killed by a rifle bullet. Samuel Wells, alias Charlie Pitts, was seriously wounded. Bob Younger's right elbow was shattered, and his horse was killed. Cole pulled him up on his own horse, and they galloped out of town.

Jesse James had been recognized, and Minnesotans, furious over the murder of two innocent men, were determined to catch the culprits. As telegraph wires spread the word, men formed posses to scour the countryside or took up positions guarding bridges, fords, trails, and roads. Robertus Love, a turn-of-the-century St. Louis newspaper correspondent, who knew Frank James and other members of the gang, wrote that

> The scattered army of chasers included the chiefs of police from Minneapolis and St. Paul, private and police detectives from those cities, Pinkerton operatives, mayors, sheriffs, deputies and many unofficial recruits. Some were on horseback, others afoot; some carried antiquated weapons, others were armed with the latest models of shotguns, rifles and sixshooters.

Forced to avoid roads and open prairies, the outlaws cautiously crept in a southwesterly direction, through a region of lakes, dense forests, and swamps. They hid during the daylight hours and traveled at night, and they soon became lost. Hard, cold rain fell day after day, making them miserable. They had all received multiple wounds, which ached and were constantly reopened by rough travel.

When they broke camp on Saturday, they left their horses tied and set out on foot. It was a desperate ruse: Their hunters were looking for six *mounted* men. On Monday, they came upon an abandoned farmhouse in a wood three miles from Mankato, and they huddled inside. For two nights and a day they rested, tended their wounds, and listened to their empty bellies growl. In five days, they had gotten less than fifty miles from Northfield.

About this time, Jesse and Frank separated from the others. They wandered for awhile, eventually stole horses, and got clean away. There is a tradition, generally believed to be true, that the separation came about because Jim Younger was so badly wounded that he was slowing down the escape, and the Jameses proposed that he be abandoned—or killed—for the sake of everyone else. Cole would not agree, to put it mildly, and the other three sided with him.

As the four remaining fugitives limped on, they were occasionally sighted, and they were finally tracked to a thicket near Lake Hanska. Several posses converged on the spot. Captain W. W. Murphy formed a battle line of seven volunteers who ran toward the thicket, exchanging volleys with the trapped men. At the same time, other Minnesotans, who had gathered on a bluff overlooking the thicket, cut loose. Every time a bandit showed himself long enough to take a shot, a dozen rifle barrels swung in his direction. Finally Bob Younger rose and called out, "I surrender! They're all down but me!"

There were five bullets in Sam Wells's corpse. Jim Younger's upper jaw had been shattered, and he had four other fresh wounds in addition to those received at Northfield. Cole Younger was wounded a total of eleven times in the two fights. Bob Younger had received a chest wound besides the shattered elbow.

Faced with charges of murder and complicity in murder, the Youngers pled guilty in order to avoid the hangman's noose. They were given life sentences and sent to the penitentiary at Stillwater, northeast of St. Paul. They were immediately barbered and their heads were examined by an expert phrenologist, to determine their moral capacities.

In his cell, Cole, otherwise known as prisoner 699, read the law, Shakespeare, the Bible, and theology books. He also whiled away the decades by avidly following through the newspapers the shenanigans of the country's politicians. Since he believed that the Northfield raid had been botched because the three gang members who went into the bank were drunk, he became a fierce temperance advocate.

In 1881, Missouri Governor Thomas T. Crittenden offered a $10,000 reward for each of the James boys. It is often inaccurately said that this was a "dead or alive" reward; to the contrary, the money was to be paid only upon arrest and conviction. Nevertheless, on April 3, 1882, Robert Ford put a bullet in the back of Jesse's head. While it is certain that Bob and his brother, Charlie, did not receive $10,000, evidence suggests they were given a small portion of the reward, probably a few hundred dollars. Frank, perhaps reflecting on the fact that there was still a reward on his head and that the money had actually been put up by railroad and express company executives, who would have liked nothing better than to see him dead, too, decided to turn himself in.

The statute of limitations had run out on many of the Missouri crimes of which he had been accused. In other cases, witnesses had died or disappeared or were too frightened to testify. In the end, Frank was tried only for the murder of Frank McMillan, a passenger who had been killed during the robbery of a train near Winston, Daviess County, Missouri, on the night of July 11, 1881.

The trial, which was held in Gallatin, commenced on August 21, 1883. So many people wanted to attend that it was held in an opera house. Frank was defended by seven lawyers, including a former lieutenant governor, a former congressman, and two veterans of the Union army. (The chief prosecutor, William H. Wallace, let it be known that he and his family had suffered under Order No. 11.) General Jo Shelby was a character witness for the defendant, but unfortunately he was almost literally blind drunk when he testified. It did not matter: The jury voted to acquit. Years later prosecutor Wallace would complain that one of Frank's lawyers had managed to pack the jury with those sympathetic to his client.

Frank was subsequently arrested and removed to Huntsville, Alabama, where he was tried "for complicity in the robbery of the paymaster at Muscle Shoals in March, 1881." He was again acquitted but was arrested once more as soon as the verdict was read and transported back to Missouri, accused of taking part in an 1876 train robbery. The charge was dismissed just two days before the trial was to begin, owing to the death of the principal witness.

No longer a target of prosecutors, Frank found work as, among other things, a shoe salesman and a doorman in a burlesque house. He eventually bought an Oklahoma farm and, as we know, sometimes made a bit of money putting his prowess with a pistol to good use as a starter for horse races.

Frank steadfastly refused lucrative offers to appear in lurid melodramas that depicted his and his brother's exploits—and sued theatrical producers who put on these wildly fanciful shows—but he consented to play minor parts in such traveling stock-company plays as *The Fatal Scar* and *Across the Desert*.

Bob Younger died of tuberculosis in the prison infirmary, but Cole and Jim were paroled in the summer of 1901. One of the conditions of their parole was that they remain in Minnesota. They were hired as tombstone salesmen. An injury forced Jim to give up the trade, and he briefly became an insurance salesman, until it was discovered that policies written by convicted felons were invalid. He fell madly in love with a St. Paul newspaperwoman; however, when she learned that parolees were not permitted to marry, she left him. Depressed and jobless, he remarked that "I reckon a fellow might as well cut his throat and be done with it." Instead, he went back to his St. Paul hotel room and put a bullet in his brain.

Cole was the beneficiary of the sympathy Jim's suicide engendered: Less than a year later, on February 4, 1903, he was granted a full pardon and returned to Missouri.

He and Frank formed the "Cole Younger and Frank James Historical Wild West Show." As the terms of Cole's pardon forbade him to "exhibit himself in public in any way," he sat in the audience and talked with spectators and held receptions afterward. However, Frank was a passenger on the stagecoach that was robbed and rode in the grand finale. The two righteous old bank robbers were furious when they discovered that a gang of confidence men had been following along behind the show and had set up shop wherever it had engagements and fleeced the customers with rigged games of chance.

After Frank had had enough of show business, Cole merged the show with the "Greater Lew Nichols Show." On Sunday, June 7, 1908, this odd, hybrid enterprise—really, a traveling street carnival—arrived by train in Richmond, Missouri, for a six-day engagement. Tents were pitched around the town square; they housed what a newspaper advertisement described as "11 High Class, Moral, Refined Shows." Two "Big Brass Bands" deafened music lovers who ventured too close. Fifteen "up-to-date" concessions sold food and baubles. Admission was charged for entrance to each tent, and those willing to pay the price had their choice of seeing, among others, "The Old Plantation, The Live Octopus, The Den of Horrors, The Japanese Vermeltes, The Girl from Dixie, [or] The Mysterious Edna." For those who wanted more lively fare, there was "General" Cole Younger's "Big Roman Coliseum."

Free entertainment was also offered. Twice a day "dare devil" trapeze artists and acrobats performed. Each evening at five o'clock a hot-air balloon ascended into the clouds, and a young woman "aeronautess" leaped out of the basket, plunging down headfirst as the crowd gasped, then opened a parachute and floated safely to earth. At ten-thirty the

"Great Colton" jumped off an eighty-five-foot ladder and landed in a small net.

During his stay in Richmond, Cole was dismayed to learn his old comrade, "Bloody Bill" Anderson, had been buried "without benefit of clergy." He enlisted the help of prominent local men to conduct a service. On Monday afternoon, June 8, a procession formed on the public square that included area dignitaries and carnival employees. Led by a drum major, they marched to the cemetery as carnival musicians solemnly played the "Funeral March." They tramped down high weeds and formed a square around the potter's field grave, which was simply an indentation in the earth recently strewn with flowers. Cole praised Anderson as a "fearless man, standing back for nothing in the performance of his duty." Cole added pointedly, however, that he personally knew "nothing of his work in 1864 north of the river." A minister read from the Scripture, and a renowned lawyer delivered a stirring eulogy that would be remembered for years to come.

Frank James lived the last years of his life on the Clay County farm. He charged the curious fifty cents a head to tour the place. He died there on February 18, 1915. Since he was afraid that his corpse would be stolen from a grave, he had left instructions for cremation. Until his wife died, his ashes were stored in, of all places, a bank vault. After her death on July 6, 1944, his ashes and hers were interred together in an Independence cemetery.

In early March 1916, a Minneapolis *Journal* correspondent made his way to the Lee's Summit house where Cole lived with his niece, Nora Hall. He found Cole seated in a chair, stroking the hair of a two-year-old grandnephew. The old bushwhacker was heavy and bent with years, his voice tremulous. He had planned to go to the San Francisco World's Fair but declining health had forced him to cancel. He was deeply depressed over the recent death of his friend Frank James. He spoke with bitterness about the murder of his father and complained yet again that the Northfield raid had gone awry because the gang members who went into the bank had been drinking whiskey. Astonishingly, he also claimed that six hundred Federal troops and militia had been waiting in Lawrence on the day of the raid, and thus Quantrill's band had won a great victory against overwhelming odds! Perhaps, knowing that his own time was short, he could not bear to recall all those innocent, unarmed victims. Anyway, he said he had joined the Christian Church two years earlier on the anniversary of the massacre.

Shortly after Cole gave the interview, his condition worsened, and he was confined to his room. He died of uremia on March 21, 1916. He was buried in the family plot, beside his mother and his two brothers. "I have been shot twenty-eight times," he once wrote, "and am now carrying in my body fourteen bullets that physicians have been unable to extract. Twelve of these wounds I have received while wearing the gray, and I have ever been proud of them, and it has been one of my keenest regrets that I did not receive the rest of them during the war with Spain."

Quantrill's fame grew enormously in the 1870s, largely as the result of the vastly increasing notoriety of his disciples. Biographers and dime novelists who chronicled the lives and crimes of the Youngers and the Jameses, wildly inaccurate though they were, stimulated interest in their wartime leader. Before long, Quantrill was himself the main character in abysmal fiction and the subject of biographies of widely varying degrees of reliability and fairness. So great became his celebrity that American popular culture bestowed upon him the rarest of accolades, reserved only for the likes of John Wilkes Booth, Jesse James, Butch Cassidy, the Grand Duchess Anastasia, Amelia Earhart, Adolf Hitler, John F. Kennedy, and Elvis Presley: He was widely reported to be alive long after his death.

It was usually said that he had survived the Wakefield fight though badly wounded, was found by an admirer, and nursed back to health. Or that he recovered while confined in the Louisville infirmary and escaped, leaving the corpse of another patient in his bed and dressed in the dead man's clothes. He hid out in Chile. He went to Mexico and raised cattle. He became an Arizona schoolteacher or a rancher in Brownsville, Texas. He was a logger in Oregon. He bought a plantation near Augusta, Georgia. He owned a cotton farm in Arkansas. He took up residence in Los Angeles or New York (although it is odd to think of him on teeming city streets). He was a trapper in British Columbia, a justice of the peace in Walla Walla, Washington. He moved to the Hawaiian Islands, married a native girl, fathered a slew of children, and grew rich investing in real estate on the island of Maui. He became a Methodist minister in Huntsville, Alabama, wore a brace of six-guns under his frock coat, and astonished his flock with marksmanship feats at church picnics. When Frank James was confined in the city, awaiting trial, Quantrill went to visit him in his jail cell. As Quantrill stepped through the barred door,

Frank exclaimed, "Hell, Bill, they told me you was dead!" It was even alleged that he sometimes returned to Missouri to visit old comrades or was spotted riding near Lawrence.

John Dean, who had survived the Morgan Walker ambush, retreated to Connecticut after the war, where he fearfully issued dire warnings that Quantrill and Jesse James were prowling together in Colorado many years after Terrell got paid off and Robert Ford was handed his thirty pieces of silver. Lawrence survivor Fred W. Read received a letter from a man who wanted $5,000 to reveal Quantrill's current whereabouts; Read counteroffered $2,500, but before a deal could be struck, the man inconveniently died.

Repeatedly and with growing exasperation Frank James and Quantrill's relatives stepped forward to refute the latest electrifying rumor, but it did no good: Quantrill's name boosted circulation, and newspapers all over the country picked up these stories, in the process further spreading his fame. Only infrequently was a healthy skepticism exhibited. In 1882, a Nashville journalist telegraphed the St. Louis *Post Dispatch,* "Quantrell, the guerilla, not dead. Living in Tennessee. Want the particulars?" An editor replied, "We happen to know that Q is curled up in a cemetery in Louisville, Ky., and the man who killed him is sleeping nearby." That same year the Cleveland *Leader* introduced an article by sourly warning readers that it contained "The Semi-Annual Statement That the Great Guerilla Still Lives."

The most credible and unfortunate sighting of Quantrill occurred in 1907. During the summer, American businessman J. E. Duffy, who claimed to have known Quantrill in 1860 and, as a Union cavalry officer, to have chased him through Missouri and Kansas during the war, visited Coal Harbour, Vancouver Island, British Columbia. He bumped into a beachcomber who called himself John Sharp and bore a resemblance to the infamous bushwhacker, even, as it turned out, to having a scar on his back at the shoulder. (He also possessed two Colt pistols carved with the initials *WCQ.*) At first Sharp denied he was Quantrill; however, as Duffy persisted in urging him to admit his true identity, he gave in. The two men talked for hours, and, according to Duffy, Sharp displayed an encyclopedic knowledge of Quantrill's partisan career. He wept copious tears as Duffy filled him in on the deaths of some of his former comrades. He said he had escaped the military infirmary in Louisville, after a surgeon pronounced him fatally wounded, and rode seventy miles on a stolen horse to make good his getaway.

"When John's sober, his name is Sharp," one local wag commented, "but when he's drunk he's the cruel Quantrell."

Duffy failed to heed the jibe, and after he left Coal Harbour, he gave an interview to a Canadian newspaper about his remarkable find. The story spread east and south like wildfire. Even Los Angeles and New York City newspapers reprinted it. More to the point, the startling announcement appeared in the August 9 edition of the Lawrence *Daily Journal*.

On October 1, two Americans arrived in Coal Harbour. It would later be charged that they came from Lawrence. They made their way to Sharp's shack on Quatsino Sound. They beat him with a two-foot long iron fireplace poker and the butt of a shotgun and left him for dead. Found covered with blood and welts, he refused to identify his attackers and called for whiskey. Alcohol proved to have no medicinal powers: He died the next day. Arrest warrants were issued for his murderers, but they were never apprehended.

After Sharp's death, the number of sightings declined, although as late as 1910, Frank James felt compelled to assert one more time that he knew for a fact Quantrill died in Kentucky in 1865.

Quantrill's fame went through a precipitous decline following World War II. Depression-era folks still know who he was, but few born after 1945 recognize his name. Hollywood has not helped: Only two films were made about him—one in 1940, the other a B-grade flop in 1958; both were truly dreadful, and in each case the slim young guerrilla was played by a paunchy middle-aged man. ("Bloody Bill" Anderson appears as a minor character in Clint Eastwood's *The Outlaw Josey Wales;* he is shown in a sympathetic light and is played by a sixtyish former television star.) The last novel about Quantrill published in this country came out in 1938; the last major biography was written by a Kansan in 1962.

Cole Younger's fame has declined, too, though not as drastically. Ironically, his association with Jesse James, whom he neither liked nor trusted, has seen to that. Jesse's star remains bright. Novels are still written about him, and he has been played on the screen by the likes of Tyrone Power and Robert Duvall. But these days most people express surprise upon learning that the Youngers and the James boys fought in the Civil War. To the American public they are not actual men with worries, frailties, families, and day-to-day lives, but silver-screen heroes—utterly unreal, larger than life, two-dimensional entertainment to be consumed right along with the boxes of Raisinets and Goobers and the buckets of popcorn topped with buttery flavoring.

"What Would His Skull Be Worth to Your Society?": The Bizarre History of Quantrill's Remains

If in her youth Caroline Clarke Quantrill had been shy and brooding, she had become in later years positively querulous, manipulative, and quarrelsome, quick to take offense, to turn on relatives and friends, and to attack her newly perceived adversaries with vitriolic rhetoric. It may be that the hard life she had led soured her. In any case, it is impossible not to feel sympathy for her.

She had lost her own parents in an epidemic while still a child, and she had little education and no trade. Thus, when her husband succumbed in 1854, she was left destitute and was forced to take in boarders and do other people's laundry to support herself and her brood. The four children she lost early all died in infancy, not childbirth: One survived for just five months, the others seven, eight, and thirteen months. They lived, in other words, long enough for her to nurse them and cradle them in her arms and, as we would say, bond with them; then one by one they died. A fifth child, Mary, suffered from curvature of the spine, and died at age twenty-five in 1863; and a sixth, Franklin, was apparently arthritic, because one turn-of-the-century source stated that he was afflicted with a "white swelling in one of his knees which made him a cripple for life." When Franklin died in 1881, he left behind a widow and four daughters, with whom Mrs. Quantrill quickly fell out. Her eldest son, William, who suffered a lingering death in 1865, although she did not know it at the time, was reviled by her neighbors and many of her fellow countrymen as a blood-drinking monster. Her last surviving child, Thomas, proved unambitious and irresponsible, to say the least, unable to provide much support for her. Thus for most of her adult life, Caroline Clarke Quantrill was beset by successive familial tragedies and dire, grinding poverty.

In 1869 or 1870, wanting to find out what had become of her eldest son, she sent Thomas to Paola, Kansas, where he looked up some of the transplanted Doverites with whom his brother had lived in 1857. Thomas was hospitably treated, and he repaid the kindness by "borrowing" a pistol from Judge W. R. Wagstaff's hired man and a fine pony, saddle, and bridle from Wagstaff's daughter, then disappearing.

We do not know what Thomas may have discovered about his brother's life during the war and his death, but sometime after Thomas returned home, W. W. Scott decided to learn what he could, probably at Caroline Quantrill's urging. He wrote letters to the former Dover residents and later made contact with some of Quantrill's "old men" in Missouri, and he slowly pieced the story together. Scott, who happened to be a Union army veteran as well as a newspaper publisher, eventually decided to write his friend's biography but found it necessary to delay the project until Mrs. Quantrill died: As he explained to an acquaintance, "She knows me so well as to be certain it would not be anything short of 'the truth, the whole truth, and nothing but the truth;' and that she does not want."

In the spring of 1879, Thomas showed up in western Missouri, still trading on his brother's memory; indeed, he was now spelling his last name "Quantrell," which was how Quantrill's Missouri admirers and friends believed it should be spelled. "His roving brother took dinner with me, he was dead broke," Fletch Taylor wrote to W. W. Scott. "He had eyes like Q. and some of his movements remind me of Q. . . ." Since he was among veteran bushwhackers with a history of violence, Thomas seems wisely to have behaved himself: There are no reports of thievery.

Scott visited Louisville in the spring of 1884—his notes on the trip do not reveal the exact date—and made his way to the old St. Mary's Cemetery, now known as the St. John's Catholic Cemetery. He found the sexton, Patrick Shelly, confined to his bed, seriously ill, but his wife, Bridget, showed him where Quantrill was buried. The couple had conscientiously followed Father Power's instructions: As Scott put it, "there were no signs of a grave."

Scott returned to Dover and then, in early December 1887, came back to Louisville escorting Mrs. Quantrill. On December 7, they went to the cemetery and learned that Patrick Shelly was dead and Bridget had been formally appointed sexton. Mrs. Quantrill convinced Bridget to allow the grave to be opened so the bones could be placed in a zinc-lined box and reburied. (Mrs. Quantrill had originally wanted to take the bones back to Dover, but Bridget, an Irish immigrant, was fearful of the wrath of the authorities if proper legal procedures were not followed and would not hear of it.) It was agreed that the grave would be opened the following afternoon.

The weather turned unpleasant overnight. The sky was overcast, and it was cold and drizzling. So while Mrs. Quantrill remained in her hotel room, Scott went alone to the cemetery. At 3:00 P.M. he stood in the sexton's yard, watching the gravedigger, Louis Wertz, scratch at the ground with a spade. Wertz was unenthusiastic, complaining about the chill and the damp. Scott slipped him a dollar and paid Mrs. Shelly $2.50. The bones were uncovered in an hour. "Every vestige of coffin had disappeared except a rotten piece [of board the] size of a man's hand," Scott wrote in his notes. "His hair had slipped off in a half circle around the skull and was of a bleached yellow color." Also in the grave were a fragment of a Union army sock and some shirt buttons.

Scott wrapped the skull in newspaper. The ribs and part of the backbone crumbled when touched; however, everything else went temporarily into a small box, which was not zinc-lined. The grave was filled in, and the box buried near the surface.

Scott carried the skull back to the hotel and the next morning showed it to Mrs. Quantrill, who was, he observed, "much affected." She identified it by means of a chipped molar in the lower right jaw. She refused to let him take the skull back to Mrs. Shelly; she insisted it must be buried beside Quantrill's father and brothers. She would "manage in some way to get the other parts of the body."

Scott and Mrs. Quantrill then took the train to Samuels Depot, leaving the skull behind in the hotel checkroom, once more wrapped in newspaper and nestled in a basket. They went to see Donny Pence and his wife. The two women hit it off immediately, and the Pences invited Mrs. Quantrill to stay the winter. She pressed Scott to return to Louisville, get the bones under the pretext of having them put into a zinc-lined box, take them and the skull back to Dover, and bury them. Scott protested against the scheme, but Mrs. Quantrill persisted: She would *not* go home without her son's remains and "on account of forms and proofs and red tape" she "might not be able to get them at all . . . or at least not without much trouble." She promised to visit Bridget Shelly and "smooth the matter over."

"I did not approve of the deception," Scott wrote in his notes, but "I . . . secured them and brought them home and placed them where agreed upon." The last statement is a bit misleading: He did not bury them in the family plot; he stored them in his newspaper office in a box. Mrs. Quantrill did subsequently call on Mrs. Shelly to arrange for the sale of her son's now empty plot; however, her idea of smoothing things over was to blame Scott for the theft of the bones and deny she had anything to do with it.

On December 17, Scott wrote Major Franklin G. Adams, secretary of the Kansas State Historical Society, enclosing a lock of Quantrill's hair. "What would his skull be worth to your Society?" he asked.

> I am not speculating in dead men's bones, but if I could get a part of the money I have spent, I see no reason why the skull might not as well be preserved in your cabinet, as to crumble in the ground.
>
> Please consider this letter strictly confidential, and mark your answer "Personal." Destroy [this] letter when read, and I will do the same with yours. No one in the world knows I can get the head, but I can.

Adams disregarded his instruction to burn the letter, which is today on file at the historical society. He offered to raise $25 or $30 to purchase the skull, but Scott was afraid the newspapers might get hold of the story. "The mother is now old, and I would not for any money have her feelings hurt. In a short time she will pass away, and then publicity would not matter."

Why did Scott try to sell the skull? His research had given him a decidedly negative view of his old school chum that allowed him to traffic in his bones with a clear conscience, and money was clearly the main issue: Over the course of his life Scott tried his hand at several different business enterprises, which suggests that he was far from being financially secure. Furthermore, he had made several trips on Mrs. Quantrill's behalf and had paid her travel expenses, and his stated purpose in trying to sell the skull was to recoup some of the money he had spent.

Over the course of the winter, Mrs. Quantrill visited many of her son's Kentucky friends and former comrades. She went to the Wakefield farm, looked over the terrain, and heard Wakefield describe the ambush and her son's time as an invalid in his house. She gradually wore out her welcome with the Pences. Her personality was grating, and to people who were, to say the least, not wealthy themselves, her poverty was burdensome. Her son Franklin had died six years earlier, and her only surviving child, Thomas, rather than settle down and support his mother, moved to Tucson, Arizona, where he got a succession of low-paying jobs. He was astonished to find himself among so many Mexicans and Indians. He wrote letters to his mother in which he promised to send money, though there is no evidence that he ever did. She in turn urged him—and appealed to Scott to press him—to move to Texas, where she presumably thought there would be fewer Hispanics and Native Americans and where the climate and economic prospects might be better. Thomas relented and settled in Burnet, Texas, but he did not send for his mother.

As spring blossomed in Kentucky, Mrs. Quantrill wished to make a pilgrimage to Missouri and convinced Scott to accompany her. They rendezvoused in St. Louis on May 8, 1888, and proceeded to Independence. Scott left Mrs. Quantrill there and went alone to Blue Springs to meet with some of Quantrill's "old men." He then went to Lawrence, where at his request he met with officials from the Kansas State Historical Society at the home of massacre survivor Fred W. Read. Scott seems next to have gone to the society's headquarters in Topeka, before he headed to Abilene to interview some bushwhacker veterans or others who had known Quantrill, then returned to Dover.

Scott's motivation in meeting with the historical society officials is not entirely clear. His correspondence indicates he wanted to show them the material he had collected on Quantrill; since he planned to publish a biography after Mrs. Quantrill's death, he may have been trying to enlist their help. Undoubtedly he was still anxious to sell the skull: He had lugged it all the way from Dover, but there was still no sale despite his having given the seemingly irresistible inducement of Quantrill's two shinbones.* He stipulated that their existence be kept secret until Mrs. Quantrill's death.

Mrs. Quantrill remained in Missouri throughout the summer and fall. She briefly visited Zerelda Samuel at her Kearney farm, and she went to various other places, sought out the friends of her "Dear lost Boy," as she referred to him in letters sent to W. W. Scott, and desperately scoured for photographs of him. She heard the stories of the persecution of Missouri's Confederate sympathizers and quickly adopted their point of view, railing in letters against "low-lifed Black Republicans" and "dirty, low-lifed Union Men." She claimed proudly though disingenuously that because her husband was a native of Hagerstown, Maryland, her son was a Southerner by heritage. She complained bitterly that her daughter-in-law—Franklin's widow—was opening her mail and cursed the gossips of Dover: a "dredful low class of people . . . who delight in Slandering + telling Lies. I think if God ever makes another Hell, he aught to make it there, Sink it in to a bottomless Pit." She even turned against Scott himself. A woman reporter had nosed around Dover and gathered scurrilous stories about the Quantrill clan; Scott gave her Quantrill family photographs in return for a promise that nothing bad would be printed about Mrs. Quantrill. When Mrs. Quantrill found out about the pictures, she was furious. After Scott tried to calm her, she sent him a blistering letter in which she contemptuously called him a

---

*In 1974, Kansas State University forensic anthropologist Dr. Michael Finnegan, Ph.D., was given two shinbones by the staff of the Kansas State Historical Society and asked to examine them. The shinbones were supposedly Quantrill's, but Dr. Finnegan concluded that they were from two different individuals, one of whom was only seventeen when he died. Finnegan theorized that two bodies might have been buried in the same grave; however, Kansas State Historical Society archaeologist Randall M. Thies recently discovered that in 1903 two different groups of bones had been given the same accession number by mistake. Mr. Thies established that the historical society had indeed received from W. W. Scott a right and left tibia. In 1992, these bones were examined by Dr. Roy R. Peterson, Ph.D., a retired professor of anatomy at Washington University School of Medicine, St. Louis. Dr. Peterson found the bones were "consistent in texture, maturity and stature."

Scott also had three arm bones that he believed all came from Quantrill's right arm. Connelley, who bought the bones from Scott's widow, perpetuated this misconception in his book, and during the years the bones were on display at the historical society, they were mislabeled as such. In fact, according to Dr. Finnegan, they were the right ulna and humerus (from the right forearm and upper arm) and the left radius (from the left forearm).

"Yankey Man" and "a Professed friend who was not true," and branded him untrustworthy.

> Now I will Tell You some Thing of your Self. The foalks in These parts didnot have any confidence in you, from The fact of you being a Yankey Man. They could not depend on Your word. They did not know but you were a Son of Some Old Yankey, hunting up something to make money out off.
>
> I cannot understand what you mean By saying You were such a great friend to me in my dark days when I nieded one, and always took my Part and defended me. I don't know of any dark days I ever had onely when I lost my Husband and Children. They were dark days that is true, But I could not help it. You talk as if I had done Something dredful, and you were trying to save me.
>
> You may as well Give up writing [the] History of my Dear lost Boy, for You never will get any Thing correct. no one but His Men + friends + My Self could get up a correct History of him. His Men never will Enlighten The Yankeys on The Subject. So what They gather up will be mostly Lies.

Some ex-bushwhackers, notably Frank James, believed Mrs. Quantrill to be a charlatan. Quantrill had falsely claimed that he was born in Hagerstown and had had a brother killed by jayhawkers, and thus when his mother told a very different story, she was suspect. (To this day there are Quantrill buffs who argue that the woman who visited Missouri in 1888 was an imposter. The letters she wrote to Scott during this period have been preserved in the Kansas Collection of the University of Kansas at Lawrence and are beyond question authentic.)

Most of her son's admirers and former comrades, however, accepted her. Several of those who lived in the Jackson County area chipped in and sent her a train ticket to Blue Springs, so that they might hold a reception in her honor. She arrived wearing a cheap calico dress with only one petticoat and a worn calico sunbonnet—obvious indications of her poverty. Town gossips whispered at the shabbiness of her attire until the old guerrillas passed around a purse, filling it with money, and chose a delegation of wives to escort her back to Independence and buy her a new outfit. The women ultimately selected what a newspaper correspondent would describe as a "dark dress, of fashionable cut and material and the necessary undergarments, including particularly a sufficiency of petticoats.

There was also a hat, a triumph of the milliner's art, to replace the old bonnet."

The "ice cream social" was held on May 11 at the City Hotel. Tables laden with food and drink had been set outside on the lawn. Fourteen ex-bushwhackers attended, including William Gregg, Andy Walker, John Koger, and Hi George. Ten women were also present—wives and sisters. Mrs. Quantrill, sixty-eight years old and slim, sat "stiffly upright in her chair." Her gray hair was tightly drawn back into a bun, and her "dark eyes were bright and quick." While the other women debated in hushed tones over whether she was really Quantrill's mother, the men quietly reminisced among themselves about their wartime exploits. A correspondent for the Kansas City *Journal* was impressed with their gentle demeanor: "They were an intelligent and well behaved lot of men, and did not seem possessed of any of the bloodthirsty characteristics ascribed to them. If they ever had, the refining influence of twenty-three years of peace and civilization have evidently transformed them into good law abiding citizens."

One by one they stopped by Mrs. Quantrill's chair and "talked with her about her son, and told her of the parts in the great internecine strife that they had enacted while with him."

When she left Blue Springs "practically the entire population was at the station to see her off. The last they saw of her was the flutter of a handkerchief at a window as the train swept around the bend."

In mid-October, she looked up Olivia D. Cooper, with whom her son had left the $800. Mrs. Cooper admitted she had once had the money but claimed to have given it all to Kate King, "except what the priest got." The two women did not get along, to put it mildly. "She is the hardest case I ever meet," Mrs. Quantrill thought. "If I hat gone alone, no doubte My life would have been in danger. She gave me a dredful Cat-tialing, Says I am not Quantrill's Mother."

Mrs. Quantrill returned to Dover sometime in the spring of 1889. The town fathers at first resisted the idea of burying the remains of so infamous a native son in the Fourth Street cemetery, but they were eventually won over, agreeing only so long as the ceremony was private and the plot unmarked. Just five people attended the funeral: Scott, Mrs. Quantrill, her minister, a distant relative, and a family friend. How many bones went into the ground is uncertain—in addition to the shinbones already donated to the Kansas State Historical Society, Scott secretly retained at least three arm bones and the skull. (He had already divided Quantrill's hair with "the mother." He occasionally gave away little sprigs of the hair to someone he wanted to impress or from whom he sought a favor. He even gave a lock to Mrs. John Dean, widow of Quantrill's bitter enemy and chief defamer of his name.)

On February 17, 1890, Thomas wrote to his mother for the last time.

Dear Mother

i Take The Pleasure of Droping you a fiew Lines To Let you know That i am Well and hope you are Well also i Think of you day and night and Will Send for you in The Spring I have Left that Part of The Country i Was in and am goying To The Capital i Think i Can Catch on to Something There The Peopel is Verry kind to me We have PLenty of firends out here Every Body is Shaking hant With me i have to Do Something Before Spring Did You Receive my Last Letter Dont Worry aBout me i Will Try and have Money By Spring Texas is my State to Live in it is a fine CLimate Would You Like to Live on The Cost [coast] The Peopel say i look Brave Like William most all of The Young Ladies fall in Love With me i Was at a Big Geathering Lately and We had a Big time They Preachiate [appreciate] us highly and Would Like verry much to see you i have Something in View i may make it if so i Will have Plenty of money if i Win i Will Clise for the Preasant Right soon and tell me all of The News i Will Right more the Next time give my RespeCts to The friends if There is eny

Yours as Ever an affectinate Son
Thomas Quantrell

Long after friends and neighbors presumed him dead, his aged mother pathetically insisted that Thomas was alive and would someday return to her.

No one knows his fate. He was a thief, a moocher, and a double-dealer; it may be that his clever money-making scheme involved fraud and that it went awry, getting somebody—a would-be victim, an exposed partner—mad enough to kill him. On the other hand, his resemblance to his brother was often remarked upon, and he was not shy about using his appearance and last name to his advantage. It has been theorized that he encountered a Texas hard case who bore an old grudge against a certain dead guerrilla chieftain. . . .

Mrs. Quantrill had some sort of accident, fracturing an arm and a shoulder. She grandly announced she had been accepted by the Lexington, Kentucky, Confederate Home. Scott worked quietly behind the scenes to raise money for her travel and living expenses in the home, and she actually took up residence there; however, she soon left, explaining enigmatically that her "benefactor" had "lost his fortune." This may be a reference to Scott: It will be noted that he *raised* money to send her to Lexington rather than give it to her himself, so perhaps he had fallen on hard times.

Mrs. Quantrill took refuge in another Lexington institution, the St. Joseph's Hospital, which was run by the Sisters of Nazareth. This is further evidence of her indigence: The hospital was known locally as the Home of the Friendless.

After a time she tired of the place and returned to Dover. She was forced to stay in the Tuscarawas County Poorhouse, while Scott fought to get her admitted to the Odd Fellows Home for Women in Springfield, Ohio. Officers of the group were reluctant to accept the mother of the notorious guerrilla, but since her husband had been a member in good standing, Scott eventually prevailed.

On April 29, 1901, Mrs. Quantrill wrote a letter to a Dover friend, her last known correspondence. All the old hurts had healed, the old controversies were forgotten; now she was just an impoverished elderly woman. "I have a room all to My Self," she related proudly, "with [a] Nice dreser + five drawers + looking glass + heater + good Bed all right. But that dont ease a Lonely Heart. No doubt You may think That With all these surroundings I would be happy. But not so. I am miserable as the day is long, Get so dreadful homesick To see You all and go To Philla [New Philadelphia] + Dover To see all The friends There." She hoped to get back in the spring. In the meantime, "Will have To Try and be contented."

Despite his clandestine shenanigans with Quantrill's bones, Scott had been her true friend and benefactor for thirty years. He had remained loyal to her even when she raged against him and had always willingly given her money. "He is A good friend of mine," she wrote, "and Tryes To encourage Me all He can. But he don't Know it all, only Sees the bright side of iT. Somethings are verry unpleasant."

On November 6, 1902, William Walter Scott died of a heart attack. He had delayed writing his long-planned Quantrill biography until "the mother" was gone, and she had outlived him. Scott's widow wrote a letter to the secretary of the Kansas State Historical Society in which she pleaded that her husband's attempts to sell the skull be kept a secret. She did not want his good name besmirched. She then sold all his files to one of the society's officers, William E. Connelley—along with the three Quantrill arm bones. When she sent the files to Connelley, she somehow neglected to include the bones. He was so frantic over the omission that she felt it necessary to ship them express.

Connelley later tried to swap the bones and a lock of Quantrill's hair to a westerniana collector for Jesse James's gun; he also attempted to trade for "Wild Bill" Hickok's revolver, holster, and gun belt. When both deals fell through, he donated the bones to the historical society. After Connelley's death, the voluminous files that first Scott and then he had so painstakingly compiled were broken up and sold to collectors. In recent years some have been donated to various historical societies and libraries, but many others have been lost or are still in private hands.

Mrs. Caroline Cornelia Clarke Quantrill died in the Odd Fellows Home on November 23, 1903. She was eighty-three years old. Her obituary quoted her loving, sentimental, sometimes disingenuous defense of her long dead son: "Clark was always a good boy. He was very, very good to me. He never forgot his old mother. Why, he sent me money all the time he was away from home, even when he was a Confederate soldier. He always divided his pay with me. He was kind and noble."

Just three days after Mrs. Quantrill's death, on November 26, the Kansas State Historical Society's current secretary, George W. Martin, announced that the society had a lock of Quantrill's hair and what he mistakenly thought were Quantrill's thighbones and would be putting them on display.

The uproar was immediate and intense. "The public shuddered with a disgusted surprise when it learned" of the proposed exhibit, according to one Topeka newspaper. The announcement had prompted "a great deal of talk in Kansas," Martin himself observed. "Some of it being just general interest, but a great deal of it very severe criticism."

On November 29, the Reverend J. T. McFarland, standing in the pulpit of Topeka's First Methodist Church, opined that

> The bones of a good man should be permitted to sleep unmolested, the bones of a wicked man should be left to rot with his memory.
>
> My motion is, and I would like to have a rising vote of the people of Kansas in its support, that the bones of William C. Quantrell, cattle

thief, horse thief, bandit and cutthroat, be thrown into the Kaw River, and that the space be preserved in our Historical Society rooms for mementoes of things honorable and of good repute.

Other ministers followed McFarland's lead and thundered from their pulpits against granting Quantrill even the dubious distinction of having his body parts displayed. Newspaper editors waded in, fuming. For example, the December 3 edition of the Kansas City *Journal* contained an editorial that reminded readers of Quantrill's guerrilla exploits and then, referring to the bones and lock of hair, stated that

Such grewsome [*sic*], loathsome relics should not be numbered among the possessions of the society. These souvenirs can teach no lesson, point no moral, nor satisfy any reasonable curiosity. Their presence is contaminating and revolting and suggests reflections derogatory to the refinement and good judgment of the gentlemen in charge of the affairs of the society.

Officers of the Kansas division of the Grand Army of the Republic, the national society of Union Civil War veterans, went further: They told Secretary Martin that the bones must go or they would see that he did.

Martin was not cowed. After all, he pointed out in a letter to Mrs. Scott, "The National Museum in Washington, [DC,] has a portion of the bones of J. Wilkes Booth, and I know somewhere the government has the skeleton of [Charles J.] Guiteau," assassin of President Garfield. As for Quantrill, Martin thought that "no historical museum would refuse such things as the bones of such a devil so closely identified with their immediate history."

Quantrill's shinbones went on display in a glass case, along with the three arm bones, which had been donated by Connelley, and some relics of the Lawrence raid: a chipped china mug and the charred fragments of a New Testament, dug out of the ashes of burned buildings, and the pocketbook of young John Speer, found on the body of Larkin Skaggs.

The controversy eventually died down—that is until August 9, 1907, when the Topeka papers carried stories about John Sharp. Many Kansans therefore believed that Quantrill was alive and demanded in letters to newspapers that the "fraudulent bones" be discarded. The August 17 Topeka *Farmers Mail and Breeze* published a long, wicked satire in the form of a letter. "After a lapse of 42 years I find that it is useless to longer attempt to keep the secret of my existence from the public," wrote "Bill Quantrell."

> I was shot in the fight in Kentucky. . . . Several bullets passed through me at the time of the shooting, one passed directly through both lungs, another tore its way through my brain, and a third passed exactly through the center of my heart. I immediately felt myself growing weaker and after riding half a mile fell from my horse.
>
> I was captured by the enemy. . . . After letting me lie on a cot for a couple of days the Yanks buried me, under the impression I was dead. Their mistake was natural and I have never felt hard toward them on account of my interment. As a matter of fact my condition would have led almost anyone to the same conclusion. I had for instance, stopped breathing some twenty-four hours before I was buried. My heart had also ceased to pulsate at the same time that my breathing apparatus ceased to do business. The evidence was so convincing that for more than two weeks after my burial I myself labored under the impression that I was dead.

"Bill" claimed it took two days for him to cut his way out of the grave with a pocketknife.

> I see from the papers that your Historical society has what purports to be a few of my bones and a lock of my hair. I have been wondering for many years what had become of those bones and that hair. Having been bald for several years I have ceased to worry about the hair but I have several times felt the need of the thigh bone and the upper arm bone and also the shoulder blade. I suppose that in gathering myself together preparatory to leaving the grave, I must have overlooked these parts of my anatomy.

Just in case Secretary Martin missed the point, on the opposite page was a large cartoon that depicted him with a newspaper under his arm, the headline reading, QUANTRELL IS ALIVE AND WELL IN CANADA, in the act of kicking Quantrill's skeleton out the society's door.

Martin was convinced that Sharp was a "rank fraud" and that the bones and hair truly were Quantrill relics. By 1910, however, the doubters and complainers had won the day: The bones were consigned to a vault. So many visitors continued to ask to see them that the clerks were soon sick of retrieving them from the vault. "The clerks do not handle the bones as tenderly as Secretary Martin does," commented a reporter in the January 24, 1910, Kansas City *Journal*. "They yank them around, shake them together, hoping no doubt they will fall to pieces."

The bones eventually came to be stored in the archaeology laboratory. For many years those who wished to see them were led up three flights of dark stairs, past a heavily screened door, and through a narrow corridor dimly lit by tired fluorescent lights and crowded by rows of metal shelves. The bones were in a compartment flanked by collections of fading war ribbons and peeling leather equipment. Since the shinbones had been mislabeled as thighbones, many who examined them remarked on how small a man Quantrill must have been.

When I examined them in 1992, the arm bones had a reddish tint and were flaking badly, the result, it is thought, of exposure to sunlight in the glass case. The shinbones had a greenish, almost greasy-looking cast, and the bulbous ends appeared swollen and rough. Although Quantrill was only five-nine, to the layman the shinbones seemed outsized and blunt, like weapons a Neanderthal might wield.

Secret lodges and fraternal orders flourished in America during the late-nineteenth and early-twentieth centuries. In 1905, several Dover boys formed the D.J.S. Club. (The meaning of the initials is no longer recalled.) In 1910, the club became the Zeta Chapter of the Alpha Pi fraternity; members ranged in age from thirteen to sixteen. Someone obtained a skull from W. W. Scott's son, Walter. It was shellacked and nicknamed "Jake," but Walter privately told several of his friends it was Quantrill's skull.

"Jake" came to be used in Zeta's initiation ritual. The initiate would enter a darkened room to see sitting on a table a triangle of three candles with the skull in the center. Red lights, wired into the eye sockets, glowed disconcertingly. Behind the table stood four boys in black robes; monks' cowls obscured their faces. Beside the table a cauldron of "molten lead" hung on a tripod over a fire. (The molten lead was actually hot water covered with a layer of aluminum powder paint; the fire was just more red lights.)

In an article published in the Summer 1981 issue of *Old West*, Samuel C. Ream, a Doverite who had been a member of the fraternity, wrote that the initiate

> approached the table and was told to place his right hand on the skull. He then swore an oath of loyalty and secrecy to the fraternity. Finally he was commanded to dip his hand into the pot of boiling lead to prove himself trustworthy. After this was done he was declared to be a member of the Alpha Pi Fraternity.

A total of 243 boys were initiated into the Zeta Chapter during its thirty-two-year existence. Zeta disbanded in 1942, a victim of declining membership due to the Great Depression and the Second World War. Nelson McMillan, a fraternity trustee, bought the skull and kept it in a box in his cellar until 1960, when it was displayed at the Zeta Chapter's fiftieth anniversary banquet. At the end of the evening "Jake" was returned to the basement box. In 1972, McMillan handed the skull over to the Dover Historical Society, and the trustees had the wax head made, then consigned it to a 1929 General Electric refrigerator with a canister top. The skull was put in a glass display case in the society's Reeves Museum. (The skull remained in the case almost constantly for the next twenty years; on the day I first visited the museum it had been removed to be photographed.)

———•◦•———

Even before the Civil War ended, there was agitation in Lawrence for the establishment of a new cemetery, where the bones of the "Raid martyrs" might be suitably interred: Indignant relatives complained that in the Oread Cemetery cattle browsed "the herbage" above the trench and "careless teamsters" irreverently drove their wagons over it. The campaign for a new cemetery picked up steam after Appomattox, led by several massacre survivors, notably *Kansas Tribune* publisher John Speer, whose two sons had been victims. The creation of a new cemetery was seen as a way of honoring those who were butchered in 1863, and, at the same time, it was judged to be an emblem of prosperity, a way for the city to keep up with arch-rival Topeka. After a forty-acre site east of town was surveyed in the summer of 1865, Speer gushed that

When completed, this cemetery will be a most beautiful resort—will be a source of just pride to every citizen of the town and cannot fail to add greatly to the attractions of the city in the estimation of all intelligent and refined people visiting or settling among us. It is a project well worthy of a liberal patronage of every one, and we trust that patronage will not be employed with a sparing hand.

The Oak Hill Cemetery was not formally opened until May 30, 1870, which was Decoration Day. Nineteen months later the trench and many of the massacre victims' graves in the Oread Cemetery were opened and the bones were moved to a plot on the southern slope of a hill near the center of the Oak Hill Cemetery. It became the custom of loved ones and survivors to place flowers on the mass grave on each anniversary of the atrocity.

A public outdoor meeting of survivors was announced for the evening of August 21, 1891. However, rain forced a postponement until the next night, when the gathering in South Park witnessed a twenty-one-gun salute, was serenaded by a regimental band, prayed over by a minister, and endured windy speeches by several of their own. Then they got down to the solemn business of forming an association to organize annual reunions and the election of officers.

In 1894, survivors began collecting donations to build a monument to the slain. The following year, on Decoration Day, the $1,500 Vermont gray granite monolith was unveiled. On the western face of the six-foot-by-eight-foot rectangle, the inscription reads:

DEDICATED TO THE MEMORY OF
THE ONE HUNDRED AND FIFTY CITIZENS
WHO DEFENSELESS FELL
VICTIMS OF THE INHUMAN FEROCITY OF BORDER
GUERILLAS LED BY THE INFAMOUS QUANTRELL
IN HIS RAID UPON LAWRENCE
AUGUST 21ST. 1863

———

ERECTED MAY 30TH 1895.

Some had intended that the names of all the victims would be chiseled into the monument, but that would have required an even larger stone and consequently greater expense. The eastern face therefore testifies to bleak pecuniary reality:

THE ROLL OF THEIR NAMES MAY BE FOUND
IN THE CITY CLERK'S OFFICE, LAWRENCE
AND ON THE RECORDS OF THE
STATE HISTORICAL SOCIETY, TOPEKA.

Ex-bushwhackers were for a long time disinclined to follow the example of Union and Confederate veterans, who rushed to organize and attend reunions. "At first it was not safe for them to gather in a group," observed Richard S. Brownlee, "and later a great many of their number, for various reasons, were in hiding and on the run." It was not until Saturday, September 10, 1898, that the first annual reunion of the "Quantrell Band Survivors" was held at Blue Springs. Five hundred people attended, including thirty-five former guerrillas.

J. Frank Gregg had his old comrades line up against a fence and began calling the roll, but he was suddenly interrupted by repeated, alarmed shouts of "Blue Coats! Blue Coats!" We are told that the startled, aging warriors were for a moment transported back to 1863, "when that cry was a warning of life and death." This time it was only Hi George playing a prank.

Frank James was the center of attention, of course. This was during the period when he worked as a burlesque house doorkeeper and was also, as a newspaper correspondent put it, "engaged in the business of race horse starting at county fairs." His clothes reflected his affluence: He "wore neat checked trousers, black coat and vest, red necktie and patent leather shoes."

The crowd shouted for him to make a speech, but he declined, allowing as how, while he had done many foolish things in his life, he had never done anything that dumb. He and his fellow veterans swapped reminiscences, showed each other their scars, bragged about their prosperous farms. The deaths of valued comrades were solemnly recalled. A band played at intervals. After a picnic lunch, various senators and congressmen, unwilling to follow Frank's wise precedent, speechified, but even their bluster and drivel could not dampen the occasion, nor cause the guests to entertain second thoughts about meeting again in twelve months.

Over the next few years the reunions were held at different places on a variety of dates in August, September, or October, usually coinciding with a county fair or street carnival, where the once fearsome bushwhackers were a greater attraction than merry-go-rounds, chuck-a-luck games, and livestock and farm implements exhibits. Before long, however, it became the custom to meet on a weekend in late August at the Blue Summit farm of an elderly spinster, Miss Lizzie Wallace. During the war, Colonel Penick had arrested Miss Wallace's father, John, charged him with furnishing supplies to Confederates, jailed him, and scheduled his execution. The night before he was to die, Quantrill and his band surrounded the jail, freed Wallace, and whisked him out of the county. He did not see his family again until 1865. After Order No. 11 was issued, Yankees came to the Wallace house, cut the rugs into saddle blankets, and then applied the torch. Mrs. Wallace and her children fled in an oxcart. Thus for "Miss Lizzie," hosting the reunions was an inadequate way to express her gratitude, "a bit of pure idealism in a hastening and often unlovely world," as one poetic newspaper correspondent put it. Even in later years, when her income declined and she was beset by misfortune, she clung "to this last luxury—the reunion of Quantrell's band."

The reunions became two-day affairs. The old bushwhackers brought their families. A long table was set up in a grove of trees, where once these men in their younger incarnations hid in ambush for Federal troops who patroled the Independence-Kansas City Road, or if the weather was inclement, in the dining room of the brown-shuttered, high-gabled mansion that John Wallace built after the war; above the mantel hung a painted portrait of Quantrill, his hair darkened and wonderfully thickened and sculpted, his face expressionless, eerily cold. Attendees gnawed fried chicken, pimento cheese sandwiches, and homemade pickles, spooned potato salad, and selected from a vast variety of pies and cakes. Orphaned children sang sentimental ballads. "Colored" orchestras serenaded. The daughters of veterans gave speeches in which they extolled Quantrill's virtues, recounted the brave deeds of his band, and excoriated Order No. 11 and myriad other Yankee cruelties. The ex-guerrillas meandered about wearing bloodred cloth badges emblazoned with a legend that announced which number of reunion this was and inevitably misspelling the hallowed leader's name. They joked harmlessly with one another, told increasingly tall tales, diagrammed battles in the dirt with their canes, and worried over crop prices. Association officers were elected for the coming year, and in the evening, when the old folks retreated upstairs, the young rolled up the rugs and do-si-doed to the fiddler's sawing, while a child plunked the parlor piano's ivory keys.

Like the proverbial jungle waterhole, every sort of beast seems to have come to the Wallace farm at one time or another. Politicians, especially for some odd reason prosecutors up for reelection, glad-handed and orated, favorably comparing Quantrill's Raiders with Teddy Roosevelt's Rough Riders of San Juan Hill fame. Journalists arrived from all over and hovered, asked foolish or condescending questions, and then dutifully took down the preposterous answers. Freed from the constraints of parole, Cole Younger began attending in 1905, burly and thick with decades of greasy prison food and, nearly six feet tall, towering above the rest. Hoards of the idly curious came to gawk at the assembled veterans or pester Frank and Cole for autographs; teenage boys futilely tried to engage them in discussions about banditry. Outsiders were sometimes sent advance invitations to join in the fun, notably Cyrus Leland, who had vengefully chased Quantrill from Lawrence into Missouri; Lieutenant Reuben A. Randlett, who long ago had been an affectionately treated prisoner; and even Kansan William E. Connelley—before his book was published—shoe-horned in by William Gregg. Jesse James, "Junior," was always welcome and frequently attended. Of special interest was John Noland, a black veteran of the band, who tried never to miss a reunion and was intensely proud of his Confederate service. He loved to relate how Federal military officers had offered him $10,000 (!) to betray the band and had received only scorn in reply. Another black veteran, Henry Wilson, who had taken up residence in Lawrence after the war, attended less frequently, though when he did he bragged about his abilities as a spy and would recall how he had run for miles to escape Union troops, who were setting Negroes free, in order to join Quantrill's band.

In the early years, while the old men's stomachs were still healthy and settled, whiskey bottles and flasks were passed around. As Cole might have predicted, drink caused a certain amount of trouble. After Missouri Democratic legislators reneged on a promise to elect Frank James a House doorkeeper, he drunkenly announced at the 1904 reunion that he would support Republican Teddy Roosevelt for president in the upcoming election. He nearly started a riot, and it was said that had a less beloved man made the endorsement, he would have been killed. Even so, the next year an attempt was made to remove him from the position of lieutenant of the organization, but Cole, briefly detaching himself from

the mob of admiring females who clustered close around him, successfully counseled forgiveness. "Whiskey makes the best of men act like
fools," he declared. The crowd was lucky he did not launch into one of
his long-winded, patented tirades against demon rum.

That same year a presumably besotted ex-bushwhacker remarked to a
journalist that the only thing he regretted about the Lawrence massacre
was that he and his comrades had not "wiped out the whole damned
town." The fact that the Quantrill reunions were often held on the same
weekends as those of Lawrence survivors had caused considerable indignation west of the border, which was amplified by William Gregg's
unfortunate tendency to grant lengthy interviews to reporters detailing
his recollections of the raid, which were always promptly, furiously
rebutted by survivors in letters to newspapers. However, this comment
was too much. Howls of rage and grief pierced the Lawrence air, and
Judge Samuel A. Riggs, a former county prosecutor and massacre survivor himself, announced his intention to dust off the forty-three indictments that a grand jury had handed down in the fall of 1863 and
proceed with prosecution. An appeal was made to the governor of
Kansas that he demand of his Missouri counterpart the extradition of
the palsied, milky-eyed malefactors. Apparently neither politician saw
anything to be gained by entering the fray because they each maintained
a cautious, levelheaded posture rare for any of their ilk. The controversy
slowly cooled like banked fireplace embers.

Then, on October 17, 1906, the Kansas City *Journal* published a piece
by an Oak Grove correspondent, which alleged that Frank Gregg
planned to hold the next Quantrill reunion in Lawrence itself. The article said that the ex-bushwhackers would ride from Independence to
Lawrence, "following as nearly as possible the route followed forty-four
years ago," and that "George W. Martin, secretary of the Kansas Historical Society, will be asked for the loan of the Quantrell thigh
bones. . . . These will be borne at the head of the procession." Newspapers around the state immediately seized on the story, and once more
roars and lamentations, threats of prosecution and even lynching were
heard in Lawrence before Hi George managed to point out that Frank
Gregg had been dead for two months, which made his giving an interview on any subject somewhat out of the ordinary. The article turned
out to have been a political dirty trick designed to embarrass a Kansas
gubernatorial candidate who was a Confederate veteran.

At the 1907 reunion, Jim Cummins and David Edwards got into a heated argument. Both were residents of the Higginsville Confederate Home, and Edwards accused Cummins of having stolen his pet raccoon. Edwards so loved the beast and was so aggrieved at his loss that he drew a pistol and fired at Cummins. He missed, but the shoes of two by-standers were struck by the ricocheting bullet. Cummins stepped forward and grabbed his hand. As the two men grappled, a deputy marshal joined in, and all three fell down and rolled around on the ground until Edwards, seventy-eight, was subdued. After he spent the night in the local jail, he was returned to the Confederate Home. Cummins, fifty-six, laughed the whole thing off. "I won't prosecute Edwards," he said. "I'll let it pass. I'm not afraid of him. He was standing less than three feet from me when he pointed the revolver at my head and fired, and all he did was to hit two other men on the feet. He'll never have a better chance to kill me again, and if he couldn't succeed this time he can't do it later."

The attempted murder had not been allowed to interrupt the merry-making. "Oh, it was nothing!" one woman remarked. "I turned around to see who was fighting and then went about my business."

The reunions were quieter after that. The numbers of ex-bushwhackers in attendance declined precipitously as death thinned the ranks. Many of the remnant came on crutches or in wheelchairs. Women scolded them when, reminiscing, they became too agitated—or they dared to light cigars. Time and the nearness of the Grim Reaper began to have a mel-lowing effect. In 1913, for instance, Frank James urged his comrades to adopt a new spirit of humility. "I believe," he said, "that if we expect to be forgiven, we must forgive. They did some very bad things on the other side, but we did, too." It would not have been possible to make such an admission at the gathering just a few years earlier.

In 1917, one newspaper carried an advance notice of "What May Be the Last Reunion." The announcement was premature: The gatherings continued until 1929, which was the thirty-second annual reunion. Only five ex-guerrillas attended: Frank Smith, George N. Noland, Henry Wilson, and two brothers, William F. and D. C. Hopkins. Exhausted by the close of the second day's festivities, they voted to limit future reunions to a single day.

They need not have bothered.

The 1930 reunion was canceled at the last minute due to a death in the Wallace family.

The next summer, Miss Lizzie's brother, Jefferson Davis Wallace, sent out invitations to the remaining survivors, and only Frank Smith replied. Thus, on August 19, 1931, Wallace regretfully informed newspapers that the reunions were at an end.

On March 3, 1932, which happened to be his eighty-sixth birthday, Frank Smith died. For the next twenty years, men would step forward swearing to have ridden with "Cap'n Quantr'll"—or their descendants would make the claim on their behalf in obituaries—but Frank Smith was the last authentic bushwhacker whose death we can verify.

After the war he had settled down on his father's farm near Blue Springs, and in time he became a deacon in the Baptist Church and a pillar of the community. He married and had eleven children. His obituary noted that in later years, "tall, weary, his body parts worn out by age and steady work," he left the farm to one of his sons and moved to a neat frame house in Blue Springs, where he kept a cow and tended a little garden. At the reunions, he was "the most reticent of the assembled veterans. Others talked boldly of their part in the controversial [Lawrence] raid, but Frank Smith usually spent his words only on comradely inquiries, or talk about the weather and crops." The son of a transplanted North Carolina slave owner, Frank had become "firmly convinced," in the words of his son Hubert, "that slavery was wrong, and that the Union view was the right one."

———◆———

Eight years after Frank Smith's death, Lawrence suffered its third invasion in a century. This time the culprits were Hollywood celebrities; the occasion was the premier of a dreadful movie, *The Dark Command,* a totally inaccurate cinematic depiction of Quantrill's guerrilla career. Among the myriad historical howlers: John Wayne, playing a fictional town marshal, learns of Quantrill's planned raid at the last moment, sends the women and children to hide in the courthouse, rallies the menfolk, has barricades thrown up, and directs the slaughter of bushwhackers as they ride down the main street. The town is burned, but only one or two male residents are killed. Wayne chases down the fleeing Quantrill and kills him.

At 10:15 A.M. on Thursday, April 4, 1940, a five-car special train pulled into the Santa Fe station, and, as the high school band struck up a tune, the stars disembarked: Walter Pidgeon—the paunchy, forty-two-

year-old Canadian who played the slim, youthful guerrilla chieftain—
John Wayne, Gabby Hayes, and Roy Rogers. Gene Autry also stepped
from the train, on hand to promote his unrelated upcoming release, *El
Rancho Grande,* along with costar June Storey and two lovely actresses
who had no discernible purpose for being there other than to increase
the aura of glamour: Wendy Barrie and Ona Munson, who had played
Belle Watling in *Gone With the Wind.* Five planes circled and dropped
flowers, as the celebrities strutted on the platform before a screaming,
welcoming crowd. Pidgeon was "the favorite with the feminine set," a
local reporter observed, but John Wayne was besieged by autograph-
seekers; he signed scraps of paper, hats, algebra books (school classes
were dismissed for the momentous occasion, of course), and even baby
shoes, plucked from tiny feet by hysterical mothers. Fifteen thousand
yahooing fans lined the route to the Eldridge House Hotel to glimpse
the stars.

The highlight of the afternoon was a sixty-unit, two-mile-long parade,
which commenced at 2:15 P.M., led by grand marshal Autry in fancy
cowboy duds. Lawrence dignitaries rode on horseback, bands blared,
and Indians performed tribal dances. Antique wagons and carriages
were interspersed with open cars in which the celebrities rode perched
on the backs of seats, waving to the throng of eighty thousand.

In the evening, the "Burning of Lawrence" was staged in South Park.
Twenty-five National Guardsmen, who portrayed bushwhackers, reen-
acted the slaughter of the white recruits—another twenty-five guardsmen—then robbed townsfolk in period theatrical costumes. A Republic
Studios special effects technician burned the specially constructed repli-
cas of the Eldridge House Hotel and two other buildings. The heat of the
flames caused some of the dead to rise and move to a cooler locale.
Afterward, two thousand lucky patrons repaired to the flood-lit Dickin-
son and Granada Theatres and paid 75 cents per ticket to see the film.
(A last-minute wildcat ushers' strike was hurriedly settled so that the
show could go on.) They cheered as John Wayne foiled the raid, slaughtered the guerrillas, and gunned down Quantrill.

Still living in Lawrence on that day were twenty-one massacre survivors. Most had been children at the time of the raid and so would have
remembered little of what had transpired, but one, Maria Elizabeth
Tyson, had been sixteen. What she, or any of the others who grew up
hearing stories of the atrocity, thought of the fantastic film plot or the

reenactment is not known. Contemporary newspaper articles noted, however, that even after the stars departed, Quantrill was still widely hated in Lawrence; merely mentioning his name was like "waving a red flag in front of a bull."

If his memory was less reviled in his hometown, he nevertheless remained a black sheep. His last known surviving blood kin were two spinster nieces, Franklin's daughters. Both of these pious, upright women lived to a ripe old age, and they steadfastly refused all their lives to talk about their infamous uncle. One day they hired a neighbor boy to lug all Quantrill's possessions down from the attic and into the yard and burn them. One sister tended the fire while the other went back and forth with the boy, watching him closely to see that he did not secretly save anything from the flames.

In early March 1982, Mark Dugan, an aspiring writer and a native of Jackson County, Missouri, applied to the Dover City Council for permission to place a marker over Quantrill's grave. The politicians reacted with much levity and promised to study the matter, a sure way to bury it. Dugan, who had spent decades researching Quantrill's life, would not be denied. Seven months later, on October 18, fifty people gathered at the cemetery for a short ceremony dedicating the U. S. government–issue tombstone. The mayor delivered a few equivocal remarks, and a Roman Catholic priest blessed the grave. (Because the town's only priest refused to have anything to do with a service for a man he reportedly referred to as "that bastard," a visiting priest from a neighboring village who possessed conveniently little knowledge of Civil War history had been recruited.) Dugan read a speech in which he defended the dead man, as American and Confederate flags gently waved behind him. Then Dugan furled the flags and took down the temporary flagpoles, and everyone went home.

One day in 1987—the exact date is no longer recalled—Robert L. Hawkins III had a casual conversation with Gaylord Patrick O'Connor, a lineal descendant of a bushwhacker, and was shocked to hear that the Kansas State Historical Society had five of Quantrill's bones and that his skull was on display in the Reeves Museum. Bob Hawkins is a burly, forty-five-year-old attorney and an eighth-generation Missourian with a profound interest in Civil War history. He is also eloquent, shrewd, absolutely dogged, and enormously charming, which combined gifts make him a formidable proponent of any cause he champions.

While Hawkins, who at the time was the commander in chief of the Missouri Division of the Sons of Confederate Veterans,* was no great admirer of Quantrill, he immediately decided that his bones should be properly buried. As Hawkins expressed his sentiments to me in a 1992 interview, "It would be inappropriate to leave the remains of any American soldier in a box in a museum. That would be true no matter which side he fought on in this war or any other war." Hawkins wrote a letter to the Kansas State Historical Society in which he inquired about the bones and was told that by law, relics donated to the society for preservation could not be deaccessioned and turned over to an outside party.

In 1989, the Kansas legislature passed the Unmarked Burial Sites Preservation Act, which prohibited "unauthorized disturbance of any unmarked burial sites" and provided "procedures for the proper care and protection of unmarked burial sites and human skeletal remains found in the state." The act created an Unmarked Burial Sites Preservation Board "attached to the state historical society." While the politically correct act was meant to protect Indian burial sites and facilitate the deaccessioning of Indian bones from Kansas museums and provide for their proper interment, the anthropologists at the Kansas State Historical Society seized on the opportunity to rid their collections of the vast quantity of human bones of all races that had accumulated over the years.

Quantrill's bones were taken out of the third-floor archaeology laboratory and stored in a small pine box resembling a miniature coffin, which was labeled and put on a shelf in a cavernous fourth-floor room of the Center for Historical Research at 120 West Tenth Street, Topeka, along with wooden boxes that contained the remains of a hundred or

---

*The national organization, whose members are lineal or collateral descendants of Confederate soldiers, was founded in 1896 in Richmond, Virginia, at a meeting of the United Confederate Veterans, whose aging members wanted to protect the memory of their military service in perpetuity. The first national commander in chief of the Sons was Jeb Stuart, Jr. Today there are approximately 23,000 members scattered in fifty states and some foreign countries. The chapters of the organization are called "camps," and the Missouri Division, which was founded in 1900, has nine camps with a total of approximately five hundred members.

In the summer of 1992 Bob Hawkins was elected commander in chief of the national organization.

more human beings. A six-foot-high barrier and gate constructed of two-by-fours and chicken wire kept out even the janitors. Only anthropologists, other scientists, and professionals with proper credentials and a legitimate purpose were allowed into the enclosure, and then only after their applications had been approved by the UBSP Board. For eighty-five years Quantrill's bones had been routinely, even casually handled, but I was the only one given permission to examine them once the Unmarked Burial Sites Preservation Act went into effect.

Since the act removed the legal impediments to Hawkins's plan it was a godsend. (Indeed, as soon as he learned that it was under consideration by the legislature, he had vigorously lobbied Kansas legislators he knew on behalf of its passage.) He enlisted the aid of the Missouri Sons in plotting a strategy to wrest the bones and skull from the historical societies and find a cemetery where they could be buried. It was soon decided that the most appropriate location would be the Confederate Cemetery at Higginsville, Missouri, which, of course, is the former site of the Confederate Home, where some of Quantrill's men lived out their last years, and where at least six of them are buried.

Hawkins now turned his attention to the Missouri Department of Natural Resources, which has responsibility for public cemeteries in the state, seeking permission to bury the Quantrill remains at Higginsville. The director, G. Tracy Mehan, was sympathetic, but middle-level bureaucrats thought the bones would more properly be buried in Dover and raised objection after objection. Hawkins answered them all, and Mehan gave his approval.

In the late summer of 1992, just as everything seemed to fall into place, however, Mehan resigned as director of the MDNR in a dispute with the Missouri legislature, and his subordinate was fired. Hawkins took a ten-day vacation, and the middle-level bureaucrats tried a flanking maneuver: They sent a fax to Tuscarawas County common pleas court Judge Roger Lile, asking if there were any interest in burying the Quantrill bones in Dover. Judge Lile turned the fax over to Earl P. Olmstead, who then approached the board of trustees of the Dover Historical Society and quickly won agreement to bury the skull and bones in Quantrill's grave. The board stipulated, however, that the ceremony was to be conducted with no publicity and a minimum of fanfare. "We don't want a huge crowd or a circus," Chairman Les Williams explained. "Quantrill deserves a little bit of dignity."

"I returned from my vacation," Bob Hawkins told me, "and set to work mending fences and putting out fires." In other words, he lobbied Ron Kucera, the new acting director of the MDNR, and quickly won his approval, but the members of the UBSP board were a harder sell. Some thought Dover was the appropriate burial site, and others objected to Hawkins's funeral plans. One groaned that "The Sons just want to put on a big show." But the Sons were unembarrassed. As one commented to me, "Those people in Dover practically want to bury Quantrill's remains at midnight."

In the end Bob Hawkins won the day. During a conference call convened at 9:30 A.M. on September 28, 1992, the UBSP board voted unanimously to approve Hawkins's application to bury the bones at Higginsville with full military honors.

James Keown, a pharmacist by trade and a talented avocational carpenter, set to work building a casket of an authentic nineteenth-century design. He purchased unfinished one-inch-thick oak slabs from an Amish colony in Audrain County and hammered them together with square nails ordered from the Tremont Nail Company in Massachusetts, the oldest manufacturer of such ironmongery left in the United States. The completed casket measured six and a half feet long by two and a half feet wide and was sixteen inches deep.

Hawkins had originally scheduled the funeral for 11:00 A.M. on October 31, which was Missouri Confederate Secession Day, but hearing too many jokes made about Halloween, he rescheduled it for 10:00 A.M., October 24.

At 8:00 A.M. on that morning he rendezvoused at a Higginsville-area Best Western Motel with Dr. Michael Finnegan, Randy Thies, and Thies's two assistants, Bruce Zimmerman and Susan Zuber. Hawkins brought along his thirteen-year-old-son, Benjamin, and Jim Keown. After a leisurely breakfast in the motel's Camelot Restaurant, everyone repaired to the rear of the building, and Randy Thies produced a cardboard museum box. In the box were the bones and a small glass vial containing a lock of hair, which had long ago been donated to the historical society by Mrs. John Dean. To keep the bones and the vial from knocking against each other, Thies had swathed each in acid-free, museum-grade plastic wrap. Hawkins asked that the bones and hair be unwrapped and placed on the ground. "This is symbolic," he explained. "This man's bones will be touching the soil in Missouri for the first time in 127 years." The bones and the vial of hair were laid in the grass.

Hawkins had expended much effort attempting to find a zinc-lined box, but, there being none available, the bones and vial of hair, once more individually swathed in plastic wrap, were placed inside a red plastic Igloo-brand beverage cooler. Keown also placed inside the cooler a bottle he had brought along that contained a piece of acid-free paper on which he had printed a statement that identified the bones and gave a brief history of Quantrill's life. The cooler's lid was then glued down with epoxy. The casket was taken out of the back of Keown's pickup truck and placed on the ground. The cooler was wedged inside, and the oak lid was nailed down. Most of the members of the party took turns hammering in the nails, using Keown's hammers. (He had brought along four hammers: one belonging to his young son, his own hammer, and two that had belonged to his father and his Confederate ancestor. "So he was in full flower with the symbolism," Hawkins thought.) Hawkins himself did not feel the need to participate in the nailing down of the lid, but his boy did, "so he'll be able to tell his children about it."

There were enough extracted bent nails for everyone to take one as a souvenir, and Keown distributed wood shavings and chips left over from his handiwork.

The casket was put back in the bed of Keown's pickup truck, and the procession made its way to the cemetery.

Six hundred people attended the ceremony, some in period costumes. Inside the white clapboard chapel, where the elderly residents of the Confederate Home used to worship, the casket, covered with a Confederate flag, sat on an iron bier. Seated in the second row of the chapel was a five-man squad in dress uniforms from a nearby military academy, including one teenage African-American, the only one of his race in the entire crowd. I found myself wondering how much of the Quantrill story this black teenager knew and what his thoughts were. However, as the squad was under the command of an adult "officer," I chose not to put the young man on the spot by questioning him.

An honor guard of reenactors in full Confederate regalia—the 5th Missouri Infantry, C.S.A.—posted the colors on either side of the casket as dozens and dozens of cameras flashed and video cameras whirred. It seemed I was the only one in the room without a piece of recording equipment.

In the Scriptural reading Father Hugh Behan quoted the words of Jesus from John 5:24–9. One sentence was especially fitting since Quantrill embraced Catholicism only on his deathbed—"Anyone who hears my word and believes Him who sent me has eternal life, and does not come under judgment, but has passed from death to life."

Chris Edwards, the descendant of a Confederate soldier, sang "Hallowed Ground" in a lovely tenor voice, accompanying himself on the guitar, and at the conclusion of the song, he placed the flat of one hand on the casket lid in a comforting gesture, a sorrowful expression on his face.

Some people had criticized the idea of burying an "evil" man in the cemetery, and in his homily, Father Behan, a self-described pacifist and an Irish immigrant with a profound interest in American history, evoked the recent controversy over the celebration of the five-hundredth anniversary of Columbus's voyage and warned against judging historical figures outside the context of their times and retroactively applying "our understanding of morality and ethics, of rightness and wrongness, back into another century."

He spoke against the new tyranny of those extremists on the left and right, who seek to enforce their own standard of political correctness on the majority. As Father Behan summarized his view in a subsequent interview with me, "I was honored to do [the service] because I was delighted to be part of something that would slap down some of the politically correct people today. This man was a human being and deserves a decent burial regardless of what he may have done, and it wasn't my judgment to decide if he was going to heaven or to hell—that was God's judgment to make. And so I will refuse as a priest to be part of funerals if the criterion is, 'Was this man politically correct or not?' " Father Behan added with a laugh, "I'm going to say: If he was a human being, let's give him a decent burial!"

In his eulogy Bob Hawkins answered those who thought Quantrill's bones should have gone to Dover:

> We do not wish him buried where people are ashamed of him, where no one remembers or cares to recall the brutality of a partisan warfare that created men like Captain Quantrill and those who rode with him, where he would be laid to rest with a sense of relief that a difficult task had finally been done, with no military honors and no remembrance of the suffering and sacrifice of days gone by. He belongs here—here, with those who were truly his people.

Referring to the Confederate flag draped over the casket, Hawkins remarked that we haven't done a very good job of protecting the memory of the Confederate soldier. His suffering and sacrifice are a legacy for all Americans, even those unconnected by blood to the events of the 1860s, but we live in an age in which history is colored by present-day political orthodoxy, and it is very difficult to overcome the wrenching away of our flag by the media who give it over to use of hate groups who have no right to it, and whose use of it would cause many of these men buried in this cemetery outside to roll in their graves. Let several hundred of us meet for a memorial service and we are lucky if there is a mention in local newspapers, but let five persons don sheets and hoods and dare to use this flag, and their image with the flag prominently displayed will be on the front page of newspapers from coast to coast.

As the pallbearers, all but one of whom were genealogically certified descendants of Quantrill's Raiders, wheeled the casket outside and the procession to the grave began, the assembly sang "What a Friend We Have in Jesus," which was Jesse James's favorite hymn.

At the graveside Father Behan read the Roman Catholic funeral liturgy for a committal service and spontaneously prayed for an end to hatred, bigotry, and divisiveness and for a healing within America and the world.

At the end of the half-hour ceremony, a twenty-one-man squad of the 5th Missouri Infantry fired three volleys, and the casket was lowered into the grave. Some reenactors had proposed that they spur their horses out of the nearby woods at this moment, firing pistols, and deposit a single, reverential rose on the casket, but Commander in Chief Hawkins had nixed the idea. He had also forbidden the presence of an artillery unit. As he explained to me later, "We don't claim to be press experts, but our experience is that when you have cannons show up all the pictures are of the cannons. And we wanted the focus to be on the grave, not on people charging up on horseback from the brush, not on cannons." But he had not counted on a woman in period costume plunging forward as the casket disappeared below the surface to place a black flag on its lid. (The woman was Mrs. Kathleen Yoder, a Methodist minister and the great-great-niece of Dave Pool, and the gesture reflected her belief that Quantrill's band actually used a black flag as a standard.) Hawkins invited "anyone who cares to honor this man or any of the men who rode with him to pass by the grave and cast a bit of soil upon the casket."

Present at the graveside was a pleasant, obviously sincere young man who claimed to be Quantrill's great-great-grandson. There are at least fifteen families scattered around the United States—and even a family in Australia—that claim they are linearly descended from Quantrill. However, there is not even a hint in the memoirs and letters of Quantrill's men that he sired any children, and like the other claimants this fellow had no evidence at all; in his case he had only recently learned of the supposed lineage from the ramblings of a dying, elderly relative. Yet he was instantly accepted by the Missouri Sons and had been chosen as one of the pallbearers. After the service several women in period costumes fluttered around him, giddy and gushing, as if he were a Hollywood celebrity. Jim Keown ceremoniously presented him with a chip of casket wood and a bent nail.

Many people had their pictures taken in front of the grave, standing at its head, sometimes shaking hands with the claimant. After the crowd departed, bags of cement were opened and dumped over the casket—so that seeping rainwater would form a solid crust over it to deter would-be grave robbers—and the grave was filled in.

Six days later, at 2:00 P.M. on October 30, Quantrill's skull, nestled in a thirty-by-twenty-two-inch white fiberglass child's coffin, was buried in Dover's Fourth Street cemetery. Only twenty-two people were in attendance, among them two men and three children who lived on the borders of the cemetery and, drawn by the crowd, had wandered up.

Father Mark Carter led the singing of the first verse of "Amazing Grace"—"that saved a wretch like me"—then read the standard Catholic funeral for "our brother William" and squirted a jet of holy water over the coffin from a transparent plastic squeeze bottle.

A hole had been dug three feet down in the Quantrill grave—it was feared that going deeper might uncover the bones buried in 1889 and thus potentially trigger lawsuits from Quantrill family descendants. The grave diggers slowly shoveled the dirt back in the hole, stopping occasionally to step into it and jump up and down and back and forth in a kind of cheery dance that tamped the earth down. No one thought to empty bags of cement into the grave, and my half-joking suggestion that a cement truck be backed up to the hole after the ceremony had been ignored, so those who remained to watch the grave diggers expressed the fear that the skull would be dug up as a Halloween prank.

The grave diggers placed sod on top of the plot and vigorously raked it until it blended in with the surrounding grass, then threw their shovels and rakes into the back of a truck and slowly drove away. A disk jockey from the Dover radio station WJER recorded brief interviews with Father Carter, Les Williams, and Bob Hawkins, who had flown in for the ceremony.

The drizzle that had fallen throughout the service turned to a cold, hard rain, and the crowd slowly dispersed, leaving me alone beside Quantrill's grave.

A Calvary cross in a circle is at the top of the slate gray granite marker's face. Below is a simple inscription:

> WILLIAM CLARK QUANTRILL
> CAPT MO CAV
> CONFEDERATE STATES ARMY
> JUL 31 1837   JUN 6 1865

Some three hundred miles to the southwest of Dover, the Louisville neighborhood that grew out around the St. John's Catholic Cemetery is decaying, and the graveyard itself is untended and dilapidated. Fragments of shattered whiskey and beer bottles are sprinkled in the long, matted, uncut grass. Many headstones have been tipped over, broken, or spray-painted with graffiti. Deep ruts are gouged in the ground, the tire tracks of racing motorcycles. There is no indication that a famous man's bones were once interred here.

Six hundred miles farther west, the old Oread graveyard, now known as the Pioneer Cemetery, shows signs of vandalism, too. Many of the headstones have been broken, and their shards have been puzzled together and cemented into the ground. One warns:

> Remember friends as you pass by
> as you are so once was I
> As I am so you must be
> prepare for death and follow me.

Another, whose name and birth and death dates are completely gone, is more sentimental than severe:

Oh cruel death Oh greedy grave
To steal and hide away
The Idol of a lover's heart
As your own lawful prey.

A crease cuts across the cemetery ground, ugly and disconcerting as a facial scar, the vestige of the trench that once held the raid martyrs' bones. At least three individual graves of massacre victims remain.

Samuel, "son of Evan & Elizabeth Jones," is buried between two tall, thick bushes that stand like brawny sentinels. His epitaph asserts his grieving parents' belief that "he shall rise again in the resurrection at the last day." They must have been quite elderly and fragile when he died— he was forty-eight years old. In the fashion of the time, his age is finely calculated: "48 Ys. 10 MS 9 D."

Chester Hay's marker is shaped like an open book. A crack splits "Aug 21" from "1863." He had lived just twenty-eight years, one month, and eight days. His only epitaph is a single brutal fact: "Killed in the Lawrence massacre."

The third grave is in the southeast corner of the cemetery, near one of the newly installed streetlights and a section of wooden-railed fence.

George W Coat
Killed in the mas-
sacre at Lawrence
Aug 21, 1863
Aged 28 years
2 M's 7 D's

The first line of the epitaph is missing, lost to a vandal's sneering fun.

It breaks not friendship's chain
Farewell, the faithful hearted
Shall live and love again.

There are no signs of vandalism at the Oak Hill Cemetery across town. It is well cared for by busy, watchful city employees. A green moss or fungus grows on the white marble of the ten-foot-high Lane family obelisk. The birth and death dates of the general's wife and children are given, but only his name and rank appear, as if derangement and suicide obliterate all other pertinent details.

Down the slope is the similarly imposing Speer family obelisk. Like an increasingly sorrowful dirge, the chiseled letters on the four sides bear solemn testimony to the tragedies visited on that afflicted family.

JOHN SPEER
BORN IN
KITTANNING, PA.
DEC 27, 1817
DIED IN DENVER
DEC. 15, 1906

ELIZABETH D. SPEER,
WIFE OF
JOHN SPEER
DIED
APRIL 9, 1876
AGED 56 YRS.

JOHN M.
AGED
13 yrs. 10 ms. 21 ds.
———

ROBERT
aged 18 yrs.

*These boys were killed
in the Lawrence Mas-
sacre Aug. 21, 1863—
the elder found mur-
dered in the streets;
the younger supposed
to have been burned in
ruins. His body never
found.*

OUR LITTLE JOE
aged

6 yrs. 10. ms. 26 ds.
Accidentally shot
Aug 4, 1865

ROSE SPEER
BORN FEB 29, 1864
DIED IN DENVER
APR. 25, 1889

EDWARD NEFF
Accidentally killed
October 22, 1876.
Aged 26 yrs. 5 ms.

MARY E.
His Wife
Born Oct. 7, 1850
Died Dec 6, 1886

Someone has pushed a small white wooden cross into the ground before the face of the obelisk that memorializes the two sons killed at Lawrence. A cluster of red plastic flowers and green leaves are fixed to the center of the cross with a bow made from ribbon patterned on the American flag: red and white stripes below, a field of blue above, tiny white stars in the bright, endless, and indifferent firmament.

———◆———

The wax head remains in the Dover Historical Society's refrigerator. Not long ago someone slammed the door on it and mashed the bulbous end of the nose. It has been more or less pushed back into place. A number of long, wide cracks have appeared in the wax, like ugly, bloodless wounds. At the society's annual Christmas party the head is always festooned in seasonal red and green ribbons, and last year someone who perhaps had partaken of too much holiday cheer suggested sticking a wick in the top of the head and using it as a giant candle. The head is brought out now and then to adorn some festive occasion, and it is increasingly deemed to be hilarious, a local joke. Alive, Quantrill terrified tens of thousands, but the passage of time has taken away much of his stature and diminished his reputation to the point where he is a source of levity to the descendants of his boyhood friends and neighbors.

Notes

ABBREVIATIONS

BSM—Baxter Springs Museum, Baxter Springs, Kansas

CHS—Chicago Historical Society, Chicago, Illinois

CMH—Columbia, *Missouri Herald*

CMS—Columbia, *Missouri Statesman*

Denver #—William E. Connelley papers, the Denver Public Library Western History Collection. (The papers are organized into numbered envelopes.)

DCHS—Douglas County Historical Society (headquarters in the WCM)

DJC—Kansas City Daily *Journal of Commerce*

DMD—St. Louis, Missouri, Daily *Missouri Democrat*

DMR—St. Louis, Missouri, Daily *Missouri Republican*

DWJC—Kansas City Daily *Western Journal of Commerce*

JCHS—Jackson County Historical Society Archives, Independence, Missouri

KCJ—Kansas City, Missouri, *Journal*

KCS—Kansas City, Missouri, *Star*

KCT—Kansas City, Missouri, *Times*

KC-UKL—Kansas Collection, University of Kansas Libraries, University of Kansas at Lawrence

KSHS—Kansas State Historical Society, Topeka, Kansas

LC-J—Louisville, Kentucky, *Courier-Journal*

LDC—Leavenworth, Kansas, Daily *Conservative*

LJ-W—Lawrence, Kansas, *Journal-World*

LKDD—Louisville, Kentucky, Daily *Democrat*

LKDJ—Louisville, Kentucky, Daily *Journal*

LKT—Lawrence, *Kansas Tribune*

LO&R—Lexington, Kentucky, *Observer & Reporter*

LPL—Lawrence Public Library, Lawrence, Kansas

LT—Liberty, Missouri, *Tribune*

NA—National Archives, Washington, DC
Perkins—Perkins Library, Duke University, Durham, NC
QSB—Quantrill Scrapbooks, formally designated as William Clarke
      Quantrill, 1837–1865, Clippings (B QU2, Clippings), KSHS
SHSM-C—State Historical Society of Missouri, Columbia
SLG-D—St. Louis *Globe-Democrat*
UBSPB—Kansas Unmarked Burial Sites Preservation Board
WCM—Watkins Community Museum of History, Lawrence, Kansas
WHMC-C—Western Historical Manuscript Collection, Columbia, Missouri
WJC—Kansas City, Missouri, Weekly *Journal of Commerce*
WWJC—Kansas City, Missouri, Weekly *Western Journal of Commerce*

INTRODUCTION

In *Reminiscences of Dover,* published in 1879, W. W. Scott spelled
Quantrill's middle name, which was also his mother's maiden name, Clark.
In *Quantrill and the Border Wars,* Connelley spelled the name Clarke, triggering a debate among Quantrill buffs that has continued to the present
time. A convoluted sentence in Homer Croy's introduction to the 1956
reprint of the Connelley book has led some people to believe that the proper
spelling is Clark, but that Connelley changed the spelling to honor his own
mother, whose maiden name was Clarke. In fact, Connelley's research into
the family genealogy in the collections of the Denver Public Library and a
"Necrology" on file at the Kansas State Historical Society show that his
mother's maiden name was McCarty.

The truth is that Quantrill's mother spelled Clark without an *e,* while her
husband spelled it with an *e.* (See her letter to W. L. Potter, November 23,
1897, in the Kansas Collection, University of Kansas Libraries, and
"Quantrill the Terror," LC-J, May 13, 1888.) The parents disagreed over
the spelling of the Christian name of their youngest surviving son: respectively Thomson or Thompson.

I have spelled the name Clarke for three reasons: (1) Mrs. Quantrill was
a truly terrible speller who could not even spell *cat* correctly; (2) Kate King
spelled the name Clarke (KCS, May 23, 1926), and since Quantrill told her
to use the name as an alias, it seems likely he spelled it that way; (3) nearly
everyone who has written about Quantrill since 1910 has used Connelley's
spelling, which makes it conventional wisdom.

In spelling other individuals' names, I have given the most credence to the
following types of sources: military service records; court-martial tran-

scripts; signed documents and letters; the Quantrill band roster in his service record (NA). In instances where these records are unavailable, I have fallen back on census records and city directories, which I have found occasionally to be less reliable.

Thus, for example, those who have written about Jerome Clark or his ancestors have usually spelled the name with an *e,* but his service record and court-martial transcript both spell the name Clark. Dick Yeager's name is sometimes spelled Yager, but the Quantrill band roster spells it Yeager. The 1860 Federal Census for Nelson County, Kentucky, lists Dr. Isaac McClasky, but the court-martial transcript for Sam Berry spells the name McClaskey (*U.S.* v. *Samuel Oscar Berry,* 405). At the beginning of his testimony, the doctor would have been asked to spell his name, so there is less likely to be a mistake.

CHAPTER 1: THE WAR OVER KANSAS TERRITORY 1854–1861

The chapter begins with six paragraphs of general observations based on my research.

Wide and diverse opinions, the election of 1860, and the conditional Unionists: Michael Fellman, *Inside War,* 5; William E. Parish, *Turbulent Partnership: Missouri and the Union,* 1–6; Richard S. Brownlee, *Gray Ghosts of the Confederacy,* 10–11; Cole Younger, *The Story of Cole Younger by Himself,* 16.

The trouble began with the Kansas-Nebraska Bill, its worrisome implications, and the number of slave owners: John H. Gihon, M.D., *Geary and Kansas,* 27–28; Fellman, *Inside,* 6–7 (text and table 1.1); Floyd C. Shoemaker, "Missouri's Proslavery Fight for Kansas, 1854–55," 222; Randall M. Miller and John David Smith, *Dictionary of Afro-American Slavery,* 497.

Fellman's observation about Missourians in the 1850s, Missouri was not a Deep South state, and it was a rural state: Fellman, *Inside,* 5–8; E. D. Kargau, "Missouri's German Immigration," 33–34.

Southern senators assume Kansas will be a slave state, and Thayer's intention to destroy slavery: Gihon, 27–28. Eli Thayer, *A History of the Kansas Crusade,* 31.

Six of Thayer's companies set out, "The Kansas Emigrants," and other emigrants are drawn to the territory, too: Louise Barry, "The Emigrant Aid Company Parties of 1854," 115–16; John Greenleaf Whittier, *The Poetical Works of John Greenleaf Whittier,* 176–77; Daniel W. Wilder, *The Annals of Kansas,* 50–51; Albert Castel, *A Frontier State at War,* 3; Jay Monaghan, *Civil War on the Western Border, 1854–1865,* 7–8.

The first party disembarks and sets off: A. T. Andreas, *History of the State of Kansas,* 312–13; Castel, *Frontier,* 11, 213; Monaghan, 9–10.

The pilgrims settle on a townsite that becomes Lawrence: Barry, 121–22; Andreas, 312; Leverett Wilson Spring, *Kansas: The Prelude to the War for the Union,* 35; Monaghan, 6, 10–11; Richard Cordley, *A History of Lawrence, Kansas,* 6, 10, 12; Charles Robinson, *The Kansas Conflict,* 70. There is disagreement among sources as to whether Robinson or Charles H. Branscomb chose the site; see, for example: Barry, 121; Spring, 35; Andreas, 312. It is possible that Robinson first took notice of the place when he passed through the area on the way to California in 1849; see Robinson's *Kansas Conflict,* 31–37. (Hereafter this work will be cited simply as C. Robinson.)

Note: Historians these days argue that the Emigrant-Aid societies had relatively little impact on the developments in the Kansas Territory. I have written about Thayer's companies because of the important part their members played in the founding of Lawrence and in the town's prewar history. Further, I believe that the talented propagandists who were members of the aid societies contributed significantly to the heightened emotional climate that characterized the prewar period on the border. Finally, as Richard S. Brownlee observed, "If the emigrant societies were not actually supplying Kansas with many people, those they did send were giving the area a shrill and vital anti-slavery leadership." (Brownlee, 8.)

The election of November 29, 1854, Nebraska ballot stuffing, and the majority of Kansas voters are proslavery: Wilder, 52–53; Monaghan, 14; Spring, 43; Lloyd Lewis, "Propaganda and the Kansas-Missouri War," 8; Brownlee, 8; Shoemaker, 234–35; James C. Malin, "The Proslavery Background of the Kansas Struggle," 295–97.

Emigrants pour into Kansas in the spring of 1855: Brownlee, 7–8; Wilder, 70; Monaghan, 17–19; Lewis, 9–10; Malin, 296–97; Spring, 39.

The election of March 30, 1855: Monaghan, 18–20; Wilder, 59, 63.

Robinson predicts war, asks for weapons, which are sent, and the new legislature meets: Cordley, *Lawrence,* 37–38, 59; Monaghan, 20–21, 29; Shalor Winchell Eldridge, *Recollections of Early Days in Kansas,* 22; Sara T. D. Robinson, *Kansas: Its Interior and Exterior Life,* 143.

Sections 1–7 of the Act are reproduced in Wilder, 73–74.

Lawrence grows, the Eldridge House is built, newspaper correspondents arrive, and William Phillips describes a border ruffian: Monaghan, 21; Eldridge, 24; William Phillips, *The Conquest of Kansas by Missouri and Her Allies,* 29; Gihon, 107, has a similar description. Some sources have Eastern newspaper editor Horace Greeley coining the phrase "border ruffian," but Monaghan, 23, credits James Redpath of the Chicago *Press and Tribune.*

By the summer of 1855, the Kansas population had doubled, and John Brown: Monaghan 24; Stephen B. Oates, *To Purge This Land With Blood*, 24, 33, 36–37, 42, 49, 61–64.

James Lane and his enormous gift for intrigue: Albert Castel, "Jim Lane of Kansas," 23; Wendell Holmes Stephenson, *The Political Career of General James H. Lane*, 20–24, 30, 38–39, 42–43, 45; Monaghan, 31.

Lane the subject of rumors, he switches sides, frees slaves, but advocates "Black Laws," and is appointed a general: Stephenson, 45–46, 106–7; Spring, 71.

Lincoln is indebted to Lane because of the protection Lane offered: Stephenson, 98, 104; John I. Speer, *Life of General James H. Lane*, 233–36; James M. McPherson, *Battle Cry of Freedom*, 277–79, 285–86; John G. Nicolay and John Hay, *Abraham Lincoln: A History*, 4, 90–93; Edgar Langsdorf, "Jim Lane and the Frontier Guard," 13.

The Nicolay and Hay quotation: 106–7.

The Guard disbands: Stephenson, 105. Stephenson, *Ibid.*, and Speer (*Lane*, 236) held that Lincoln and Lane were intimate friends, but Langsdorf ("Jim Lane," 25), disagreed. For more on the Lincoln-Lane relationship through 1864: Speer, *Lane*, 236; Stephenson, 141; Spring, 274.

The murder of Charles Dow and the aftermath, including the rescue of Branson: *Report of the Special Committee Appointed to Investigate the Troubles in Kansas*, 1040–60, especially 1042, 1046, 1051, 1059, 1063. See also, G. Douglas Brewerton, *The War In Kansas*, 150–58. Secondary sources: Phillips, 153–63, 176, 231; Cordley, *Lawrence*, 46–52; Spring, 86–90; Gihon, 50–53; Sara T. D. Robinson, 104–9. Branson was told by the sheriff that there were several peace warrants outstanding against him (*Report,* 1063).

Sheriff Jones retreats to Franklin, organizes a posse, and marches on Lawrence, and Lawrence is defended: *Report,* 1066–92; Phillips, 203–7, 295; Cordley, *Lawrence,* 52–58; T. H. Gladstone, *The Englishman in Kansas,* 22–23; Speer, *Lane,* 51–52; Stephenson, 54–56; Andreas, 117–18, 319; Wilder, 87–88; Monaghan, 38–39; Alice Nichols, *Bleeding Kansas,* 57–59, 64, 70, 75; Sara T. D. Robinson, 129, 132, 142.

On December 3: Albert Castel, *William Clarke Quantrill,* 6–7. See also: Phillips, 211–15; Oates, 108–110; Cordley, *Lawrence,* 54–56; Nichols, 58.

The governor brings the "war" to an end: *Report,* 1069–72, 1081–82; Brewerton, 191–94; Andreas, 118–19; Speer, *Lane,* 62–65; Spring, 100; Nichols, 70, 75; Phillips, 220–27.

The January election: Wilder, 107–8, 113–14; Monaghan, 46.

A murder after the election: Spring, 72–73; Hildegarde R. Herklotz, "Jayhawkers in Missouri, 1858–1863," pt. 1, 267; Monaghan, 46; Wilder, 108.

In "How Bloody Was Bleeding Kansas?," Dale E. Watts has challenged conventional wisdom by arguing that only "157 violent deaths" occurred "during the territorial period" and that just fifty-six were politically motivated. In another twenty-five cases "politics or slavery" may have been "a significant contributing factor." More often "people found themselves caught up in violence stemming from land disputes, thievery, personal feuds, the spasmodic functioning of frontier justice, and perhaps limitless other causes besides the slavery issue." Whatever the exact number of politically motivated murders, they—and what the propagandists made of them—greatly aggravated the tension in the border region.

Sheriff Jones goes to Lawrence: Phillips says there was one assassin, "a young man, almost a boy," 255–56. See also Wilder, 116; Cordley, *Lawrence*, 87–88; Andreas, 126; Speer, *Life*, 77–79; Sara T. D. Robinson, 199–208.

The Douglas County grand jury meeting at Lecompton issues indictments, and Lawrence is sacked: Cordley, *Lawrence*, 91–92, 99–102; C. Robinson, 235, 252–53; Sara T. D. Robinson, 218–19; Spring, 111–12, 118; Phillips, 289–98, 300–1; Andreas, 130; Gladstone, 34–37.

Gladstone's observations on the border ruffians: 40–41.

Gangs fan out for revenge, and John Brown and his followers kill five: Oates, 130, 132–39; Spring, 141–54; Phillips, 332–33.

Missourians cross the line looking for Brown, and two of his sons are captured: Oates, 143, 145; Phillips, 332–33.

Henry Clay Pate is captured by Brown: Oates, 152–54; Phillips, 337–42; Spring, 152–56.

Starr's observation, Southerners board steamboats, and the Castel quotation: Stephen Z. Starr, *Jennison's Jayhawkers*, 10; Monaghan, 65; Castel, *Quantrill*, 12–13.

In August Lane initiates a campaign, forts are captured, and Clarke leads an army into Kansas: Castel, "Lane," 24; Spring, 179–86, 239; Stephenson, 76–77. Lane was not present during the capture of one of the "forts"—which were more like blockhouses or even fortified log cabins.

Montgomery routs Clarke and takes revenge by posing as a schoolmaster: Andreas, 302; Spring, iii, 238, 241; Monaghan, 81.

The attack on Osawatomie, Lane's army clashes with the raiders, newspapers appeal to readers, and wagon trains cross into the territory: Oates, 64–65, 76, 168–72; Andreas, 145, 876–77; Spring, 190–94; Speer, *Lane*, 117–22; Monaghan 78–79, 91.

Governor Geary, 100,000 arrive, and two elections: Oates, 176; Gihon, 109; Monaghan, 93; Andreas, 162–63, 170–71; Oates, 217, 256; Wilder, 192–94, 238–40. See also, McPherson, 162–69.

The Marais des Cygnes massacre: Andreas, 1104–6; Monaghan, 103; Spring, 246–47; William P. Tomlinson, *Kansas in Eighteen Fifty-Eight,* 63–75; Whittier, 185; Andreas, 1105.

Lane's problems, as winter settles in, and John Brown's raid of December 19: Castel, "Lane," 25; Stephenson, 96–98; Monaghan, 109; Herklotz, pt. 1, 276–77; Oates, 288, 349–51.

Eli Snyder's raid, and authorities attempt to stamp out bushwhacking: Herklotz, pt. 1, 279–82; Letter of Captain James E. Mooney in Jonas Viles, ed., "Documents Illustrating the Troubles on the Border, 1858," pt. 2, 296.

In 1860, Montgomery and Jennison are active: Monaghan, 118, 120–21.

The August election, Germans and others form companies, and Montgomery's announcement: Parish, 1–2, 4–6; William H. Lyon, "Claiborne Fox Jackson and the Secession Crisis," 423, 426, 428; Arthur Roy Kirkpatrick, "Missouri on the Eve of the Civil War," 99–100; Herklotz, pt. 2, 505; Monaghan, 118–19, 124.

Jennison tries and hangs Hinds and Scott, kills Moore, the governor offers a reward for Jennison, meetings are held, and residents flee: Andreas, 1106; Starr, 33–35; Herklotz, pt. 2, 505–7; Letter of G. A. Parsons in Viles, pt. 3, 73–74.

The Lincoln administration reorganizes the command structure: Castel, *Frontier,* 51, 56–57, 77, 81–82, 89.

Jennison, the recollection of Mrs. Harris, the attack on Morristown, which shocked an enlistee: Herklotz, pt. 3, 69–71; Henry E. Palmer, "The Black-Flag Character of the War on the Border," 456, 460; Starr, 33; N. M. Harris, "Atrocities Upon the Missouri Border," in Missouri Division, United Daughters of the Confederacy, comp., *Reminiscences of the Women of Missouri During the Sixties,* 216–17.

The Harrisonville and Independence raids, and Bingham on the latter: Starr, 42; Herklotz, pt. 3, 70–72; Brownlee, 46; Bingham's letter, February 12, 1862, in C. B. Rollins (ed.), "Letters of George Caleb Bingham to James S. Rollins," pt. 5, 53–57; Lew Larkin, *Bingham: Fighting Artist,* 133–37.

The good effects of hanging or executing Jennison—according to Bingham—Palmer describes Jennison's men returning, General Hunter orders Jennison to West Point, and Halleck's letter and his order to Pope: Bingham's letters of January 22 and February 12, 1862, Rollins, 46, 49; Henry E. Palmer, 460; clearly Palmer is indulging in hyperbole—see Starr, 62; Herklotz, pt. 3, 73–74; *The War of the Rebellion: A Compilation of the Official Records of the Union and Confederate Armies,* series 1, vol. 8, 448–49, 507. (Hereafter this source will be cited as OR, and all citations will be to volumes in series 1 unless otherwise specified.)

The military bureaucracy deals with Montgomery and Jennison: DJC, April 15, 1863; WJC, July 25, 1863; P. J. Staudenraus, "Occupied Beaufort, 1863," 142, 144; Brownlee, 49; Starr 132–38, 140–43, 145, 147, 151, 161–62.

Union commanders are unable to suppress the bushwhackers, and Mrs. Adcock's first recollection of the war: Brownlee, 51; J.A.B. Adcock, "Personal Reminiscences of the Civil War," in Missouri Division, 91.

High-ranking Federal officers are hampered, Halleck's statement, secessionists forbidden to have guns, and Brownlee's observation on arson and the murdering Federal troops: OR, vol. 8, 439; Brownlee, 32, 142–43, 170–71.

Redlegs: Starr, 201, 214–15; Castel, *Frontier,* 112–13, 214–15; Ed Blair, *History of Johnson County Kansas,* 203–5; George W. Martin, "Memorial Monuments and Tablets in Kansas," 279–81.

C. M. Chase's observations on redlegs, jayhawkers, and bushwhackers: letter of August 10, 1863, in Lea Barnes, ed., "An Editor Looks at Early-Day Kansas," 121–22.

Fremont's martial-law decree, loyalty oaths, imprisonments, fines, disloyal men are forbidden from raising crops or operating a business: Brownlee, 145, 150, 157–59, 161–67, 169, 173–74.

Schofield orders every able-bodied man to enlist, and the suppression of newspapers: OR, vol. 13, 10–11, 506–7; Brownlee, 83–84, 176–77.

Description of Quantrill: Henry S. Clarke, "W. C. Quantrill in 1858," 218; Holland Wheeler, "Quantrill a Suspicious Loafer," 225; Sidney S. Herd, "Always Under an Alias, and Without Visible Means of Support," 227.

Edwards, Connelley, and Gregg quotations: John N. Edwards, *Noted Guerrillas,* 31; Connelley, *Quantrill,* 41; William H. Gregg, *A Little Dab of History,* 5–6, 8.

CHAPTER 2: QUANTRILL'S FAMILY BACKGROUND AND EARLY YEARS

The chapter title is adapted from a sentence in Connelley, *Quantrill,* 41.

The story of the murdered brother: Edwards, *Noted,* 32–43. The memoirs and autobiographies of ex-bushwhackers repeat the story: Gregg, *Little,* 2–4; O. S. Barton, *Three Years with Quantrill: A True Story Told by His Scout John McCorkle,* 25–26; Younger, *Story,* 14.

Quantrill's, birth and his parents' background: Connelley, *Quantrill,* 23, 29–31, 33, n. 16. See also LC-J, May 13, 1888. Unfortunately after Connelley's death his Quantrill files were broken up and sold by his heirs. Some today are in the collections of the KSHS, KC-UKL, Perkins, Denver, and CHS. However, many files are still in private hands or have become lost.

Luckily, Connelley reproduced entire documents in his footnotes, which makes his book invaluable for any Quantrill biographer.

Quantrill's uncles, grandfather, and father: Connelley, *Quantrill,* 17–18 (text and n. 2), 28 and 33.

Jesse Duncan: Connelley, *Quantrill,* 18–21, text and notes.

See below note on Mary A. Quantrill: Connelley, *Quantrill,* 22–24, text and notes; Whittier, 245–48.

Those wishing to know more about the history of Dover should consult the following: William W. Scott, *Reminiscences of Dover;* James W. Eaton, *A Very Dear Place;* J. B. Mansfield, *A History of Tuscarawas County;* Federal Writers' Project of Ohio, *Guide to Tuscarawas County.* There has long been confusion over where Quantrill was born, because for a time in the nineteenth century, Dover was known as "Canal Dover." There is an oral tradition in Dover that the name change came about because three other towns were founded in Ohio and named Dover, and so to lessen the confusion the U.S. Postal Service assigned the name "Canal Dover" to Dover, Tuscarawas County. After the other three towns died out, underwent name changes, or were incorporated into other towns, Doverites resumed using the original name of their town. I have found no documentation for this oral tradition, but I have never run across any other explanation for the name changes, either in writing or oral tradition.

Quantrill's early life: LC-J, May 13, 1888; Connelley, *Quantrill,* 42–44, text and notes. Denver #4, 5, 43 contain clippings giving a very different portrait of Quantrill than the one painted by Beeson. Some of these clippings have Connelley's handwritten notes on them, so there is no doubt he read them.

Scott's quote: Joplin *Morning Herald,* April 29, 1881, Denver #43.

Quantrill at age 16 and his mother: Connelley, *Quantrill,* 32–34, 44.

Quantrill described his first trip out west in a series of letters that are in the KC-UKL: to his mother, August 8, 1855; September 18, 1855. To Edward Kellam, October 2, 1855. To his mother, November 17, 1855; February 21, 1856; July 14, 1856. See also Connelley, *Quantrill,* 44–52, text and notes.

For the rumors about Quantrill's murdering a man, Connelley, *Quantrill,* 51–52, text and notes. Castel, *Quantrill,* briefly covered Quantrill's early years, 23–26.

CHAPTER 3: QUANTRILL'S WESTERN TRAVELS

The chapter title is adapted from a sentence Quantrill wrote to his mother in a letter dated July 30, 1859.

Quantrill's traveling to Kansas: Connelley, *Quantrill,* 54–58, 62–63, text and notes; Quantrill's letter to his mother, March 8, 1857.

The claim in Franklin County and life on Torrey's farm: Andreas, 877; Connelley, *Quantrill,* 62–63, text and notes; Quantrill's letter to his mother, May 16, 1857.

The claim dispute, Quantrill's thievery, and the resolution: Andreas, 877; Connelley, *Quantrill,* 66–67, text and n. 4 and 5; Beeson's letter, Connelley, *Quantrill,* 68, n. 6; "The records in the United States Land Office," Denver #30; letter of Joe Hobson to Connelley, October 22, 1907, Denver #50. See also Castel, *Quantrill,* 27.

The Torrey family's continued defense of Quantrill: Connelley, *Quantrill,* 69, n. 7.

Beeson's return to Ohio and the establishment of Tuscarora Lake camp: Connelley, *Quantrill,* 71–72, text and notes.

The quotations on the swindles, Jim Lane, the Democrats, and "the girls" come from a letter Quantrill wrote to W. W. Scott, January 22, 1858.

Connelley alleged that Quantrill stole from his friends: *Quantrill,* 74.

Connelley heard about Quantrill's being hired to drive cattle from a man named J. B. Forbis: *Quantrill,* 84–85; see also Forbis's letter to Connelley, December 13, 1910, Denver #70.

The tough teamsters hired for the Utah expedition: Norman F. Furniss, *The Mormon Conflict 1850–1859,* 121–22; Connelley, *Quantrill,* 79.

For the causes of the Mormon War see Furniss, Chapters 1–4, especially: 12, 29, 31, 33–34, 38–41, 68, 77, 79, 82, 84, 87–88.

Buchanan declares Utah to be in a state of rebellion: Furniss, 95; Philip Shriver Klein, *President James Buchanan,* 315–17.

The expedition to Utah: Furniss, 100–1, 105, 109, 113, 115–18, 123, 126, 144, 148–52, 156, 184–87, 203, 205–6. The best source on what became known as the "move south" is Richard D. Poll, "The Move South," 65–88.

Quantrill wrote to his mother about the blizzard in the South Pass, October 15, 1858.

R. M. Peck's letter was published in *The National Tribune,* September 22, 1904, and reprinted in Connelley, *Quantrill,* 75–76, n. 13. See also: Peck's letter to Connelley, November 6, 1907, Connelley papers, KSHS.

In his October 15 letter Quantrill told his mother about the Colville gold mines, praised the Mormons' industriousness, and said she "need not expect me home till you see me there."

In his next letter, which was also addressed to his mother and dated December 1, 1858, he wrote of his illness and being hired by the U.S.

Army. He wrote to her again on January 9, 1859, to say he had lost the job.

Quantrill's July 30, 1859, letter to his mother tells the story of his journey to Pike's Peak, the Indian attack on his friend, and his own weather-beaten appearance.

Quantrill also related his experiences traveling to Pike's Peak in a letter to his sister dated March 23, 1860, and one to his mother dated January 26, 1860. The January 26 letter also reveals the shift in his political views.

Quantrill meets and joins the border ruffians: Herd, 226–27.

Quantrill often expressed homesickness in his letters and a longing to return to Dover. See, for example, his letters to his mother dated February 8, 1860, and March 25, 1860.

In his last letter home, June 23, 1860, Quantrill offered to send his mother the money to put a new roof on her house and also promised to send her $50. He added, "I have money in my pocket for you and will sent it as soon as you write and probably sooner. . . ." A few months of riding with border ruffians had clearly changed his financial condition.

CHAPTER 4: THE MORGAN WALKER RAID

The chapter title is adapted from a sentence in an undated clipping from the Lawrence *Kansas Tribune* in Connelley, *Quantrill,* 121.

For Quantrill's life in Lawrence before the war, see the following essays, which were published in vol. 7 of the *Transactions:* W. A. Johnson, "Early Life of Quantrill in Kansas," 212–14; Clarke, "Quantrill," 218–23; Samuel A. Riggs, "An Outlaw When He Took to the Bush," 223–24; Wheeler, 224–26; Sidney S. Herd, "Always Under an Alias, and Without Visible Means of Support," 226–28. See also: Connelley's interview with Herd, entitled "Yesterday, Monday, November 4, 1907," 1–3, KSHS.

Quantrill and the north ferry border ruffians: Herd, 226–28; Castel, *Quantrill,* 30; Connelley, *Quantrill,* 104–5, 109.

Connelly's observations on the McGees and Jake Herd, *Quantrill,* 105. See also: Connelley, "Yesterday," 3–4.

The party of abolitionists and blacks captured by Jake Herd: John Doy, *The Narrative of John Doy,* 22–49.

Doy was tried twice and was eventually broken out of jail by a party of Kansans led by John Brown. See Doy, 76–115; *History of Buchanan County, Missouri,* 280–82; Theodore Gardner, "An Episode in Kansas History," 851–55.

Ike Gaines: Connelley, *Quantrill,* 114–17, text and notes. Connelley collected material on Doy and Gaines, which is in Denver #21. See also: Connelley, "Yesterday," 4–5.

The racehorse White Stockings: Herd, 227. See also: Connelley, *Quantrill,* 116–17, and "Yesterday," 5.

Captain John Stewart: Clarke, "Quantrill," 220; Herd, 227; Castel, *Quantrill,* 32; Connelley, *Quantrill,* 117–18, text and notes.

The theft of the Kickapoo cattle: Sam Walker's letter in Connelley, *Quantrill,* 118–20, n. 6.

The attack on Stewart's fort: Connelley, *Quantrill,* 119–21, and "Yesterday," 5–6.

The attempted kidnapping of Allen Pinks: Wheeler, 225; Doy, 53–54, 61, 65–72; Connelley, *Quantrill,* 134–37, and "Yesterday," 6–9.

The autumn raid into Cass County: Herd, 227–28; Connelley, 122–23.

The runaway slave hidden in a barn, the indictment of Quantrill, and his escape from the sheriff: Samuel Riggs, 224; untitled KCJ article in Connelley, *Quantrill,* 138–39, n. 4. Dean's letter to John Savage, June 8, 1879 (John Dean correspondence, KSHS).

The Morgan Walker raid: Independence *Democrat* in the *Jefferson Inquirer,* December 22, 1860; letters from Andy Walker to W. W. Scott, dated February 3 and February 22, 1883, in Connelley, *Quantrill,* 159–60, n. 6; the interview with Walker published in the May 12, 1888, KCJ; Dean's letter to Samuel Walker, July 31, 1879, in Connelley, *Quantrill,* 161, n. 6; Dean's statement to W. W. Scott in Connelley, *Quantrill,* 161–62, n. 6. Seven letters from Dean to Savage written during 1879, in KSHS; August 15, 1863, letter of Charles Monroe Chase to the *True Republican and Sentinel,* republished by Lela Barnes, 130. See also Connelley, *Quantrill,* 139 (n. 4), and 140–65, text and notes, and 174–180, text and notes; Clarke, "Quantrill," 221.

The aftermath of the raid: Connelley, *Quantrill,* 178–81.

See below note on Dean and Southwick's military service: John J. Lutz, "Quantrill and the Morgan Walker Tragedy," 327, 329–30; Connelley, *Quantrill,* 153, n. 4.

Anna Walker: Connelley, *Quantrill,* 197–98.

Claiborne Jackson is inaugurated, and Kansas is admitted to the Union: Parish, 5–7; Wilder, 310–12; Stephenson, 101–3; Thomas L. Snead, *The Fight for Missouri,* 17–25.

Quantrill is arrested, transported to Stanton, and released: Connelley, *Quantrill,* 181–95, text and notes; Castel, *Quantrill,* 44; letters of W. L. Potter to W. W. Scott, January 20, 22, 1896, Connelley papers, KSHS. Copies of the legal documents are also in the Connelley papers, KSHS.

CHAPTER 5: QUANTRILL BECOMES A GUERRILLA

The chapter title is adapted from a sentence in a letter from Abraham Ellis to W. W. Scott, January 5, 1879, in Connelley, *Quantrill,* 228–29, n. 4.

Lincoln's call and Jackson's reply: Monaghan, 129; William F. Switzler, *Switzler's Illustrated History of Missouri,* 346–47.

Quantrill goes to Texas and meets Joel Mayes: LeRoy H. Fischer and Lary C. Rampp, "Quantrill's Civil War Operations in Indian Territory," 158–60; Connelley, *Quantrill,* 198.

The proslavery militia musters at Lindell Grove, Lyon captures the arsenal, and the Camp Jackson Massacre: Monaghan, 129–32; Parish, 23–24; Switzler, 348–56.

Lyon had drawn a line in the sand, and the state legislature reacts: Albert Castel, *General Sterling Price,* 14–15.

See below note on why Missourians fought: Connelley's "Interview With Morgan T. Mattox," 15 and 25 (Denver #65); Hale and Eakin, *Branded as Rebels,* 326.

It seems likely that Mattox was exaggerating to some degree when he said that fifty-four of Quantrill's earliest recruits were *all* motivated by revenge, that *all* came from the "best families" of Missouri, and that to qualify for Quantrill's band every man had to be "moved by injury" to himself or his family.

Jackson travels to St. Louis and meets with Lyon: Snead, 198–200, 203–4; Switzler, 360–61. William Lyon, "Claiborne Fox Jackson and the Secession Crisis," 439. William Lyon believed that Jackson and Price were sincere, but Castel (*Price,* 17, n. 39) offered a strong counterargument. See also Arthur Roy Kirkpatrick, "Missouri in the Early Months of the Civil War," 238, 242–44.

General Lyon dramatically ends the negotiations: Snead, 199–200.

Jackson and the others return to Jefferson City: Switzler, 361–62; Monaghan, 135.

Lyon brings his army to Jefferson City: Switzler, 362–63; Castel, *Price,* 4–5, 26. OR, vol. 3, 11–14.

Jackson and the legislators flee south, Lyon camps at Springfield, Price links up with McCulloch, and the Battle of Wilson's Creek: OR, vol. 3, 57–69, 98–100, 466–68; Castel, *Price,* 26–28, 31, 33–34, 39–43, 45, 47–50; Switzler,

374–75, 378–92; Snead, 268–92; CMH, September 24, 1897; Daniel O'Flaherty, *General Jo Shelby*, 86–87.

Julia Lovejoy: "Letters of Julia Lovejoy, 1856–1864," 181–82.

Price captures Springfield, McCulloch departs for Arkansas, and Quantrill stays with Price: Castel, *Price*, 48–50; Connelley, *Quantrill*, 198.

Fremont's declaration of martial law, Price skirmishes with Lane's Kansas Brigade, Lane's pursuit of Price: Andrew Rolle, *John Charles Fremont*, 205–6; Switzler, 390–92; Castel, *Price*, 49–50, and *Frontier*, 52–54; Monaghan, 195; Spring, 275; Herklotz, "Jayhawkers in Missouri," pt. 3, 67; OR, vol. 3, 162–64, 485, 490.

The siege of Lexington: Castel, *Price*, 50–9; Colonel James A. Mulligan, "The Siege of Lexington," in Robert U. Johnson and C. C. Buel, eds., *Battles and Leaders of the Civil War*, vol. 1, 307–12; O'Flaherty, 88–93; Edwards, *Noted*, 51; OR, vol. 3, 171–93; Switzler, 396.

Osceola: Spring, 276; John Speer, "The Burning of Osceola," 306–7, 309; Stephenson, 111; Wiley Britton, *The Civil War on the Border*, vol. 1, 148 (hereafter cited as Britton, *CW*); Henry E. Palmer, 457. In his official report Lane claimed the town burned because he shelled it (OR, vol. 3, 196). See also: OR, vol. 3, 516–17; Herklotz, pt. 3, 68–69; Castel, *Frontier*, 54.

Lane continues to march north: Monaghan, 196–97; Spring, 277.

Fremont leaves Jefferson City: Switzler, 397–99; Castel, *Price*, 57–59.

Lane returns to Kansas City: Monaghan, 207; H. D. Fisher, *The Gun and the Gospel*, 166–68.

Quantrill left Price: Connelley, *Quantrill*, 200; Castel, *Price*, 56–57.

Jayhawkers in Blue Springs area: Connelley, *Quantrill*, 200–4, including n. 4; Castel, *Quantrill* 65–66; KCJ, May 12, 1888.

Missouri legislature passes an ordinance of secession: Brownlee, 18.

See below note on Halleck and Price: Castel, *Price*, 67–70, 73–79, 82.

The Andrew Walker band and Castel's observation on Quantrill's becoming the leader: KCJ, May 12, 1888; Castel, *Quantrill*, 66.

The nucleus of Quantrill's Raiders and the hanging of Searcy: Edwards, *Noted*, 53; Castel, *Quantrill*, 67; Connelley, *Quantrill*, 201–2, text and notes.

Manasseth Gap: Castel, *Quantrill*, 67.

The Riley ball: Castel, *Quantrill*, 67–69.

Cole joins the band: Younger, *Story*, 17; W. C. Bronaugh, *The Youngers' Fight for Freedom*, 33–34.

In his autobiography, Cole gave a family history that Marley Brant has shown in part to be inaccurate: Younger, *Story*, 7–8, 16; Brant, *The Outlaw Youngers*, 5–14; Edwards, *Noted*, 55.

The confrontation with Walley, the murder of Colonel Younger, and the persecution of the Younger relatives: Younger, *Story,* 8–11, 15–17; Barton, 120–23. For sources on the collapse of the Grand Avenue building, see annotations for Chapter 9.

Elkins and Foster: Younger, *Story,* 12; Bronaugh, 34–36; "Saved by Cole Younger," the Chanute Daily *Tribune,* April 30, 1909, Denver #24.

Captain Oliver's report: OR, vol. 8, 57.

Raid on Independence: Gregg, *Little,* 10–11; Connelley, *Quantrill,* 223–24; Younger, *Story,* 17–18.

Aubry raid and "Bullet Hole" Ellis: OR, vol. 8, 506; letters of Ellis to Scott, January 5, 18, 1879, in Connelley, *Quantrill,* 227–30, n. 4, and text, 224–27; L. B. Rozar, "Bullet Hole Ellis," 12–15.

Randlett, a prisoner of the Quantrill band: Gregg, *Little,* 28–29; Connelley, *Quantrill,* 199 (n. 2), 232 (n. 5), 237 (n. 2), and text, 225–35. See also material on Randlett in KC-UKL, RHMSP131.

CHAPTER 6: AMBUSHES AND REPRISALS

Chapter title is adapted from a sentence in Gregg, *Little,* 16.

Halleck's order and the Liberty raid: OR, vol. 8, 611–12; LT, March 21, 1862; Castel, *Quantrill,* 72–73; DMR, March 14, 1862; Gregg, *Little,* 5, 9–10; Connelley, *Quantrill,* 236–38.

Quantrill draws a line and first blood and the Tate farm ambush: Gregg, *Little,* 11–12; OR, vol. 8, 346–47, 359; Younger, *Story,* 18–19; Castel, *Quantrill,* 73–75; Connelley, *Quantrill,* 238–41, 248.

The fight with Peabody and the Lowe farm ambush: OR, vol. 8, 358–61, and vol. 13, 57–58; LT, April 25, 1862; Castel, *Quantrill,* 77–79; Connelley, *Quantrill,* 249–51. Gregg included a supplement to *Little,* which has material on this ambush: section 2, 1–10.

Gregg on the series of surprises: *Little,* 12.

Partisan Ranger Act and Order No. 47: "An Act to Organize bands of Partisan Rangers," *Public Laws of the Confederate States of America,* 48; OR, ser. 2, vol. 3, 468.

Quote of Captain John B. Kaiser: OR, vol. 8, 360.

The trip to buy ammunition: Edwards, *Noted,* 72–75; Connelley, *Quantrill,* 254; Castel, *Quantrill,* 80–81; Younger, *Story,* 22–23.

The apple woman yarn: Younger, *Story,* 23–24.

Quantrill resumes operations: Castel, *Quantrill,* 80–81.

Quantrill's men rob the mails: OR, vol. 13, 120–22.

Upton Hays, the expedition south, Major Bredett's search, and the failure of commanders to locate the guerrillas: OR, vol. 13, 120, 131–32; Gregg, *Little,* 14; Brownlee, 71; Castel, *Quantrill,* 81; Connelley, *Quantrill,* 255.

Major Gower attempts to destroy Quantrill: OR, vol. 13, 154–59; Gregg, *Little,* 16–21; CMS, July 25, 1862; Brownlee, 72–75; Castel, *Quantrill,* 81–84; Connelley, *Quantrill,* 257–58.

The Castel quote: *Quantrill,* 83–84.

CHAPTER 7: THE RAID ON INDEPENDENCE

Chapter title is adapted from a sentence in W. L. Webb, *Battles and Biographies of Missourians,* 141.

Quantrill hid out on the Little Blue, and the ambush of Todd and the others: Connelley, *Quantrill,* 260; Castel, *Quantrill,* 85–86.

Upton Hays's recruiting and Schofield's orders: OR, vol. 13, 402–3, 506; Webb, 137–38; Castel, *Quantrill,* 87; Connelley, *Quantrill,* 261.

Hughes enters the county, decides to attack Independence, Mattox scouts the town, and Hughes's battle plan: Connelley, "Interview With Mattox," 11, and *Quantrill,* 259–63, text and notes; Webb, 139; Brownlee, 92–94; Castel, *Quantrill,* 88.

Mrs. Wilson and Buel's lack of preparedness: Britton, CW I, 316–17; Webb, 139–40; Connelley, *Quantrill,* 261.

The fight in the town: OR, vol. 13, 226–27; LT, August 15, 1862; Britton, CW I, 318–23; Barton, 58–62; Webb, 140–46; Connelley, *Quantrill,* 262–267, text and notes; Castel, *Quantrill,* 92; Connelley's "Interview with Mattox," 11–12.

The fight in the field and the later stages of the fight in the field: OR, vol. 13, 227–29; Barton, 61; Britton, CW I, 319, 321–24; Webb, 140–46, 342–45, 353–56; Connelley, *Quantrill,* 264–67; Castel, *Quantrill,* 90–92; Brownlee, 95; Younger, *Story,* 23–24.

Quantrill returns to Anna Walker, the men are mustered into the service, and the band's organization: Barton, 62–64; Gregg, *Little,* 23–24. See also: Younger, *Story,* 24, 26; Brownlee, 99; Connelley, *Quantrill,* 269; Castel, *Quantrill,* 92–93.

Aftermath of the Independence fight: Brownlee, 97; Britton, CW I, 324–25; Connelley, *Quantrill,* 267.

Schofield's and Totten's actions: OR, vol. 13, 15.

Lone Jack: OR, vol. 13, 237–39; LT, August 29, 1862; Barton, 63–66; Gregg, 24–25; Britton, CW I, 329–35; Brownlee, 98–99; Connelley, *Quantrill,* 270; Castel, *Quantrill,* 93; Webb, 147–67.

Younger's actions during and after the fight: Younger, *Story,* 24, 26–30; Bronaugh, 35–37.

The retreat and the fight with Burris: OR, vol. 13, 253–6.

Levi Copeland: Gregg, *Little,* 25–28; Barton, 64.

The raid in revenge for Hoy and the raid on Olathe: OR, vol. 13, 803; Gregg, *Little,* 29–32; letter of E. W. Robinson to Scott, May 9, 1881, KC-UKL; Connelley, *Quantrill,* 271–73.

Burris's pursuit of Quantrill: OR, vol. 13, 267–68; Gregg, *Little,* 31–33; Barton, 65–66.

David's pursuit of Quantrill: OR, vol. 13, 312–14; Gregg, *Little,* 34–46; Connelley, 273–74.

Shawneetown raid: Gregg, *Little,* 36–38; Brownlee, 103; Connelley, *Quantrill,* 274–75.

The Palmyra massacre: Joseph A. Mudd, *With Porter in North Missouri,* 299–307; OR, vol. 13, 719; Switzler, 416–21; Brownlee, 89–90. Younger devoted Chapter 13 of his autobiography to the massacre, 41–44.

Robbery of the mail coach and Little's Pursuit: OR, vol. 13, 339.

The march to Arkansas and Catherwood's pursuit: OR, vol. 13, 347–48, 781–82; Gregg, *Little,* 38–41; Brownlee, 105; Connelley, *Quantrill,* 275.

Colonel Lewis and Lamar: Gregg, *Little,* 41–42; Barton, 74–75; OR, vol. 13, 352–54; Connelley, *Quantrill,* 276; Castel, *Quantrill,* 100.

For an example of the civilian reaction: OR, vol. 13, 440.

Reports of Generals Brown and Loan: OR, vol. 13, 796–97, 806–7.

CHAPTER 8: PRELUDE TO THE LAWRENCE MASSACRE

Chapter title adapted from a sentence in Quantrill's speech in Edwards, *Noted,* 158.

Marmaduke and Shelby: O'Flaherty, 64, 141.

The trip to Richmond: Edwards, *Noted,* 156–58; KCJ, March 24, 1881; Gregg, *Little,* 42. See also: Castel, *Quantrill,* 103; Connelley, *Quantrill,* 278–79, 281. Connelley suggested that Price may have given Quantrill a colonel's commission, but the Thomas C. Reynolds letter to Price, October 30, 1863, shows clearly that neither Price, McCulloch, Kirby Smith, nor Reynolds gave Quantrill a commission: Colonel Quantrill "is not known to the officials here as a Confederate officer." Reynolds letter book #4463, 171–72. The original letter books are part of the Reynolds Manuscript Collection, Library of Congress. The WHMC-C has a microfilm copy.

Todd goes back to Jackson County, and the battles of Cane Hill and Prairie Grove: Gregg, *Little,* 42–43; Edwards, *Shelby and His Men,* 94–104,

125–27; O'Flaherty, 137–44, 157–69; Connelley, *Quantrill*, 280; Castel, *Quantrill*, 103.

McCorkle goes home, and McDowell betrays Cole: Barton, 80–88; Younger, *Story*, 36–37; Edwards, *Noted*, 135.

The experiences of the bushwhackers with Shelby: O'Flaherty, 166–68.

The Yeager Raid: WWJC, May 10, 1863; DWJC, May 16, 1863; *Council Grove Press*, May 11, 1863; D. Hubbard, "Reminiscences of the Yeager Raid," 168–71; George Pierson Morehouse, "Diamond Springs," 799–801; Ethylene Ballard Thruston, "Captain Dick Yeager," 3–4. See also: Castel, *Quantrill*, 104–6.

Note: T. Dwight Thacher purchased the *Western Journal of Commerce* from D. K. Abeel in mid-April, 1863. His first edition was published on April 15. Some forty days later he changed the name of the newspaper by dropping the word *Western*. The first edition of the daily newspaper that carried the new name was published on Tuesday, May 26, 1863. For the announcement of the sale and change of proprietor, see the daily *Western Journal of Commerce,* April 14, 1863. In the first mention in my text I have referred to the newspaper simply as the *Journal of Commerce* to avoid confusion.

See below note on rape and the treatment of women: Charles Chase's August 8, 1863, letter to the *True Republican* in Barnes, 118; Thomas P. Lowry, *The Story the Soldiers Wouldn't Tell*, 123–31; Michael Fellman, "Inside Wars," 1–9; SLG-D, September 20, 1898.

Thacher on the Yeager raid and Quantrill returned from Virginia: WWJC, May 10, 1863; OR, vol. 22, pt. 1, 320.

The border situation: I have used articles from border newspapers, especially the LT, DWJC, DJC, and CMS. Quotations and specific details were taken from the following: OR, vol. 8, 688–89; Leavenworth *Evening Bulletin* in LT, Nov. 28, 1862; DWJC, January 24, 31, February 11, 19, March 3, April 7, and May 14, 19, 1863; WWJC, April 25 and May 23, 1863; *Missouri Republican* in LT, April 17, 1863; Olathe *Mirror* in DWJC, May 16, 1866; *Missouri Democrat* in LT, August 1, 1862; WWJC, May 14, 23, 1863.

John Schofield: Schofield, *Forty-six Years in the Army,* 1, 14, 69, 71, 74; DWJC, March 24, 1863.

Schofield divided the District of Kansas and General Blunt: OR, vol. 22, pt. 2, 315; OR, vol. 22, pt. 1, 15; Blunt, "General Blunt's Account," 211–14, 219, 242–43; Connelley, *The Life of Preston B. Plumb,* 136.

Ewing: *Dictionary of American Biography,* 237–38; *Biographical Cyclopaedia and Portrait Gallery,* 1131–132; Castel, *Frontier,* 25–26; David G.

Taylor, *The Business and Political Career,* 4–6, 10–11, 156–57, 159; Emporia *News* in DJC, July 3, 1863; Olathe *Mirror* in WJC, July 4, 1863.

Ewing and Anthony: Schofield, 84; Andreas, 437; Taylor, 163–66; Castel, *Frontier,* 112–13, 149; OR, vol. 22, pt. 2, 388–92.

Ewing's efforts to stop raids: OR, vol. 22, pt. 1, 579.

"Quantrill's Call": "Quantrell's Call," *Confederate Veteran,* vol. 13 (November 1905), 518; *Ballads and Folksongs,* 353–54, 374–75. For other Quantrill songs: Thomas D. Isern and Mark D. Weeks, " 'Quantrill's Raid on Lawrence,' " 1–11; John Avery Lomax, *Cowboy Songs and Other Frontier Ballads,* 142–46; Vance Randolph, *Ozark Folksongs,* 356–58.

Cathy Barton and Dave Para have collected a number of folksongs—and composed others—about the Civil War in western Missouri, including several about Quantrill's life and military career; they have performed them on two excellent recordings from Big Canoe Records: *Johnny Whistletrigger* and *Rebel in the Woods* (the latter with Bob Dyer).

No black flag: SLG-D, September 20, 1898; Sophia L. Bissell, " 'See those men!' " 25.

Captain Kidd's gold: "Hunting Quantrell's Gold," KCS, November 27, 1910, Denver #69.

Appearance and apparel: period photographs; CMH, September 24, 1897; Connelley, *Quantrill,* 317–22; Castel, *Quantrill,* 114–15.

Weaponry: D. Michael Gooch allowed me to quote from his essay, originally published in *The No Quarterly.*

Frank James's remark, the raiders' stronghold, and civilian support: CMH, September 24, 1897; my own observations while touring the Sni-A-Bar country; Castel, *Quantrill,* 111–15.

Two Gregg quotes: *Little,* 44–46.

The Anderson family, the death of the father, and the retribution: William Anderson family entries, 1850 Federal Census for Randolph County, Missouri, and 1860 Federal Census for Agnes City Township, Kansas; *The Emporia News,* May 17 and July 12, 1862; L. D. Bailey, "Bill Anderson's Gang," in Charles R. Green's *Early Days,* vol. 1, 45–47; O. F. O'Dell, "And the Parts Respectively Played," in Green, vol. 1, 48–50; Jacob Van Natta, "Narrative of Jacob Van Natta," in Green, vol. 2, 54 and 57; William Michael Shimeall, *Arthur Ingraham Baker,* 216–27, 229–30.

Frank James's family background and military experience: CMH, September 24, 1897; *History of Clay and Platte Counties, Missouri,* 234–35, 266; William Settle, *Jesse James Was His Name,* 6–8, 14, 20.

See below note on Quantrill's height: Dr. Finnegan's unpublished laboratory notes, a copy of which Randy Thies provided to me.

The torture of Dr. Samuel: Robertus Love, *The Rise and Fall of Jesse James*, 45–46; *History of Clay*, 266. The James Family Farm Museum, Kearney, Missouri, has in its collections the oath Zerelda Samuel signed and the letter written by her husband's neighbors.

Quantrill's relationship with Kate King: Robert King family entry, 1860 Federal Census for Jackson County, Missouri; KCS, May 23, 1926; KCJ, March 24, 1881; Connelley, *Quantrill*, 282–83, 451. Over the years several Missouri writers have argued that Kate was Quantrill's wife, but there is no proof one way or the other: no marriage registry record or marriage license; so far as I am aware, not even an entry in a family Bible.

Reasons for the Lawrence massacre: Gregg interview in SLG-D, September 20, 1898; Gregg, *Little*, 48–53; Gregg, "The Lawrence Raid," 1, 3–4. Additional reasons for the raid are set forth in my first chapter. See also: Connelley, *Quantrill*, 284–97.

Rumors of an impending raid, Lawrencians' responses, Lieutenant Hadley, and Quantrill's reply: Reverend Richard Cordley, "The Lawrence Massacre," 1–3; H. E. Lowman, *Narrative of the Lawrence Massacre*, 33–38, 95. See also: Connelley, *Quantrill*, 309–10.

CHAPTER 9: THE LAWRENCE MASSACRE

Quantrill's council of war: SLG-D, September 20, 1898; Gregg, *Little*, 48–53; Barton, 124; Connelley, *Quantrill*, 310–12.

Collapse of the Grand Avenue building: Although Quantrill's men were convinced that the collapse had been engineered at Ewing's order, today, with one notable exception, no scholar or writer of whom I am aware holds that position. The exception is Thomas Goodrich, who used a quotation from Connelley's *The Life of Preston B. Plumb*, 149, to argue in a conversation with me that Ewing was, in fact, responsible. (Mrs. Sue Womack, a survivor, stated that she knew the soldiers engineered the collapse "because I saw the soldiers going into the Jew's store as thick as bees all day.") Immediately after quoting the remark, Connelley dismissed it as absurd but offered no other explanation; in *Quantrill*, 301, he followed the Federal military's explanation: the Southern girls "dug under the foundation wall" in an escape attempt, weakening it so the building collapsed in a "wind-storm."

Cole Younger (*Story*, 9) and McCorkle (Barton, 120–23) always believed the collapse was engineered, but the explanation that the building was dilapidated has become widely accepted: See Brownlee, 118; Castel, *Quantrill*, 119–20.

There are approximately 100 pages in the Grand Avenue file, a copy of which is in the Native Sons Archives, but unfortunately they are not consecutively numbered. The statements and affidavits of the following individuals are particularly relevant: Charles H. Vincent, Solomon S. Smith, Elijah M. McGee, Joshua Thorne, and George Caleb Bingham. The file also contains typescripts of three valuable newspaper articles: Kansas City *Post,* May 29, 1912, and February 27, 1916; KCT, December 15, 1938.

Other sources for the collapse: DJC, August 14, 15, 1863; Connelley, *Plumb,* 145–50, and *Quantrill,* 300–1; Brownlee, 118–20; Fred Barton, "Bill Anderson and Not Charlie Quantrell . . . ," unidentified newspaper clipping, Denver #63.

McCorkle himself said that the murder of the Southern girls was "the direct cause of the famous raid on Lawrence," Barton, 122. See also Gregg, "Lawrence," 3–4.

In later years there was much confusion as to the names and ages of the Anderson girls. To clear the matter up, I have used Anderson family entries in the following Federal censuses: 1850 Randolph County, Missouri, and 1860 Agnes City Township, Kansas.

Order No. 10: OR, vol. 22, pt. 2, 450–51. For Ewing's state of mind on the subject of deportation, see *Ibid.,* 428.

The ride to Lawrence: Gregg, *Little,* 52–57, and "Lawrence," 2–3; Cordley, *A History of Lawrence, Kansas,* 200–2; Barton, 124; Lowman, *Narrative,* 39, 41–43, 45–48; Connelley, *Quantrill,* 310–16, 323–27.

Note: Reverend Cordley wrote three different accounts of the massacre: "The Lawrence Massacre," published in *The Congregational Record* in September and October, 1863, and republished as "Pastor Richard Cordley's Account of Quantrill's Raid," with an Introduction and Postscript by Richard B. Sheridan; chapters 15–17 of *A History of Lawrence, Kansas;* and chapters 11–13 of *Pioneer Days in Kansas.* Each of these accounts contains information that the other two do not have. As a result, I often cite more than one of these accounts for a single subject.

While I have collected articles from a number of newspapers, I have based my description of the raid primarily on the accounts of eyewitnesses—survivors and participants.

The murder of Reverend Snyder: Lowman, 49; J. S. Boughton, *The Lawrence Raid,* 5; Cordley, *Lawrence,* 201–2.

Sally Young and John Donnelly: John C. Shea, *Reminiscences of Quantrell's Raid,* 3–4, 22; L. D. Bailey, *Quantrell's Raid on Lawrence,* 19–20.

Quantrill disposed his troops and the attack on the recruits: SLG-D, September 20, 1898; Gregg, *Little*, 57–58; Lowman, 51–53; Castel, *Quantrill*, 126; Cordley, "Massacre," 4–5, 8–9, and *Lawrence*, 203; Boughton, 6.

The realism of blacks: Boughton, 10; R. G. Elliott, "The Quantrill Raid as Seen from the Eldridge House," in Eldridge, 184–85; Cordley, "Massacre," 8, 19.

The horsemanship quote is from Cordley, "Massacre," 5; for the sake of clarity I have inserted a phrase ("upon them with bodies erect and arms") and replaced the word "main" with "Massachusetts" from a similar description in *Lawrence*, 203–4.

Surrender of the Eldridge House: Chase letter, August 22, 1863, in Barnes, 146; Bailey, *Lawrence*, 6–12; Lowman, 53–55; Cordley, "Massacre," 6, and *Pioneer*, 188; Shea, 20.

In a letter dated August 23, 1863, which is in the collections of the Attica, New York, Historical Society, survivor Robert Stevens described the raid and claimed to have been the one who convinced Quantrill to spare the hotel guests and to have sent for Quantrill when the bushwhackers fired into the crowd. Lowman made no mention of Stevens, but Bailey, *Lawrence*, 8–9, credited both Stevens and Banks with negotiating the surrender of the hotel.

Quantrill's kill order and the sacking of the Eldridge House: Gregg, *Little*, 59; Bailey, *Lawrence*, 6–14; Lowman, 55–57; Castel, *Quantrill*, 129. For more on Arthur Spicer, see Lowman, 80–82.

The Johnson House: Boughton, 8–9, 24; Lowman, 59; Cordley, "Massacre," 7, 20, and *Lawrence*, 210–12; Connelley, *Quantrill*, 349–50.

The Griswold boardinghouse: Lowman, 60–65; Shea, 9–10; Boughton, 15–16; Cordley, "Massacre," 13, and *Pioneer*, 193–94.

Jim Lane: Bailey, *Lawrence*, 31–32; Boughton, 30; Lowman, 67–68; Cordley, *Pioneer*, 204.

Edward Fitch: Letter of Mrs. Fitch, September 2, 1863. The original letter is in the possession of Roger Fitch, but he donated a copy to the WCM. See also: Boughton, 17; Cordley, "Massacre," 14, and *Lawrence*, 214–15.

Otis Longly, Miner, and the survivors' hiding places: Boughton, 23–24, 26–27; Cordley, "Massacre," 11, 18–19, 22, and *Lawrence*, 217–18, 221.

Mr. Strode, Levi Gates, and Bledsoe: Lowman, 71–72; Boughton, 11, 24; Cordley, *Pioneer*, 190–91, 199–200; Connelley, *Quantrill*, 378.

George Bell, George Holt, and John Crane: Lowman, 86–88; Boughton, 11; Cordley, "Massacre," 9–10, and *Lawrence*, 208–9; Bailey, *Lawrence*, 18; Connelley, *Quantrill*, 354–55.

Dennis Murphy, George Burt, and the two men who paid $1,000: Boughton, 18; Cordley, "Massacre," 15–16; Chase's letter, August 22, 1863, in Barnes, 147.

August Ehles and George Albach: Cordley, "Massacre," 16; Boughton, 18–19.

The man who told his wife not to "take on so": Cordley, "Massacre," 24, and *Lawrence,* 225.

The men who dressed as women: Cordley, "Massacre," 23, and *Lawrence,* 224–25. Cordley's remark about the officer is from *Pioneer,* 202.

George Sargeant: Boughton, 19–20; Cordley, "Massacre," 15, and *Lawrence,* 218.

The courage of women: Cordley, *Pioneer,* 201–2, 206–7.

Other examples of courageous women: Boughton, 9, 20; Cordley, "Massacre," 11; Shea, 10.

Lawrence massacre marriages: Bailey, *Lawrence,* 34–35; Shea, 24.

James Perrine and Jim Eldridge: Bailey, *Lawrence,* 18, 28; Boughton 18; Cordley, "Massacre," 15, and *Lawrence,* 215.

Henry Clarke: Henry S. Clarke, *Incidents of Quantrell's Raid on Lawrence,* 2–3, 6–9. See also Shea, 4–6.

The Sands stable and Judge Carpenter: Clarke, *Incidents,* 5; Boughton, 16, 19; Cordley, "Massacre," 14, and *Lawrence,* 213–14.

The Laurie brothers: Connelley, *Quantrill,* 275, 348–49.

J.W.V. Thornton: Shea, 17–19; Cordley, "Massacre," 17, and *Lawrence,* 217.

Quantrell raid claims: Lawrence *Evening Tribune,* March 5, 1887; Olathe *Mirror,* June 16, 1887; QSB, vol. 2, 147b, 149b–150; State of Kansas, *Session Laws of 1887,* Ch. 180, 269–72; Topeka *Journal,* February 21, 1899; G.W.E. Griffith, *My 96 Years in the Great West,* 159–61; *Sixth Biennial Report of the Auditor of the State* of Kansas for the years ending June 30, 1887, and June 30, 1888, iii, 484–90; *Seventh Biennial Report* for years ending June 30, 1889, and June 30, 1890, 517; *Eighth Biennial Report* for June 30, 1891, and June 30, 1892, 552.

The bill called for the state to pay off the certificate holders in annual payments stretched over ten years, beginning in 1890. However, the state failed to make the February 1899 payment, probably because most survivors had long since sold their bonds to New York City institutional investors. The state's credit rating was jeopardized, which seems to have induced the politicians to make the payment. See the Topeka *Capital,* April 20, April 29, and May 6, 1899.

Mayor Collamore: Lowman, 65–67; Boughton, 14; Bailey, *Lawrence*, 20; Cordley, "Massacre," 12, and *Lawrence*, 211–12.

Mrs. Grovenor: Boughton, 29.

Unfired weapons, Cole Younger, and Free Masons: Clarke, *Incidents*, 10; Cordley, *Pioneer*, 208–9; Edwards, *Noted*, 196–97.

The Speer family: "Hon. John Speer," *The United States Biographical Dictionary*, 326–28; John Speer, Sr., "Quantrell and His Men," SLG-D, October 8, 1898; Connelley, *Quantrill*, 355–57, 381–82, n. 1 and text.

There was disagreement and confusion among survivors and historians over the ages of the murdered Speer sons and the circumstances of their deaths—see, for example, Lowman, 92; Bailey, *Lawrence*, 8; H. D. Fisher, 183. Even the information about the boys on the Speer family obelisk, which is in Lawrence's Oak Hill Cemetery, is erroneous. I have used the following three sources to resolve these matters: John Speer family entry, 1860 Federal Census for Douglas County, Kansas; the account of his sons' fates by John Speer, Sr., which was published in LKT, August 27, 1863; "Wm." Speer, "My Story of the Quantrell Massacre," Manuscript Department, KSHS. See also: John Speer, Sr., "Quantrell and His Men," SLG-D, October 8, 1898, and Shea, 13.

Judge Riggs: "Personal Experiences of Samuel A. Riggs," in Henry Earle Riggs, *Our Pioneer Ancestors*, 207–9. See also: Boughton, 26; Cordley, "Massacre," 22, and *Lawrence*, 223.

Reverend Fisher: DJC, September 27, 1863; H. D. Fisher, 160, 166–67, 170–71, 175, 184–99. See also: Charles E. Fisher, M.D., "A Boy in Quantrill's Raid," an undated LJ-W clipping in the vertical file, "Lawrence History: Quantrill Raid," LPL.

Preparations for the retreat, Skaggs, William Faxon, and Clarke's experiences: Clarke, *Incidents*, 10–15; Cordley, *Lawrence*, 210; Connelley, *Quantrill*, 378–79. See also: Shea, 6–8.

Gregg and the stragglers: Gregg, *Little*, 60; Connelley, *Quantrill*, 380.

Palmer's gunshop: Lowman, 93; Cordley, "Massacre," 16–17, and *Lawrence*, 216.

Skaggs, the Stone family, and Mrs. Read: Bailey, *Lawrence*, 17–18; Boughton, 20–23; Cordley, *Lawrence*, 231–32; Connelley, *Quantrill*, 367, 380, 382.

There are many contradictory accounts of how Skaggs died—for example, "Statement of George W. White" (typescript, WCM); "Account of Eye Witness J. M. Henry" (typescript, WCM); "Another Eye Witness Tells of the Killing of Skaggs" (typescript, WCM); Samuel Riggs in *Ancestors*, 208. I have used what I consider to be the most reliable sources: John Speer in LKT, August 27, 1863; "Wm." Speer, "My Story," 5. Other useful sources: the manuscript of Andrew Williams, which has been given the title *Narrative of Former Slave*, 7–9 (KC-UKL); R. G. Elliott, "The Quantrill Raid as Seen from the Eldridge House," in Eldridge, 191–93. In 1898, while indignantly refuting comments made to SLG-D by William Gregg, John Speer added an embellishment to the death of Skaggs: that Mrs. Speer pointed Skaggs out to Billy and said, "There is one of them—go shoot him." As if on cue, Skaggs broke free, and Billy obeyed his mother's call for revenge (SLG-D, October 8, 1898).

The mistreatment of Skaggs's corpse: Chase, letter of August 22, 1863, in Barnes, 145; Andrew Williams, 8; Elliott, 193; Connelley, *Quantrill*, 382, n. 1. In 1912, a worker digging a sewer ditch in Lawrence's Central Park accidentally exhumed bones believed to be those of Skaggs—LJ-W, September 10, 1912.

Some Missouri Quantrill buffs today disparage the notion that many raiders got drunk. However, I am particularly struck by the fact that three of the earliest accounts of the massacre mention drunkenness: Chase, whose letter was written just six days after the massacre (in Barnes, 147); John Speer, whose account was published six days after the raid (LKT, August 27, 1863); Lowman, 77, whose memoir was published in 1864.

Cordley's walk and encounter with Speer: *Pioneer*, 183–85, 218–19; *Lawrence*, 238–40. (The long quote is put together from similar passages in both sources.)

The Methodist church, Gurdon Grovenor, and the survivors' temporary housing: Connelley, *Quantrill*, 365, n. 6; Cordley, *Pioneer*, 219, and *Lawrence*, 239–40; Elliott, 195.

The execution of Tom Corlew: LKT, August 27, 1863; William Speer, 5–6; Andrew Williams, 8–9; LDC, August 27, 1863. See also: Burton J. Williams, "Quantrill's Raid on Lawrence: A Question of Complicity," 145–49.

Burial of the dead and the church service: Cordley, "Massacre," 24–25, and *Pioneer*, 219–21, and *Lawrence*, 240–42; Bailey, *Lawrence*, 30.

See below note on the Lawrence casualties: Cordley, *Lawrence*, 242–46, 256, and "Massacre," 25–26; LDC, August 26, 1863; Connelley, *Quantrill*, 385–88, n. 2 and 3; Andreas, 323. The *Missouri Democrat* dispatch dated August 26, 1863, was reproduced in the OR, vol. 22, pt. 2, 487–88. Of all the survivors who wrote accounts of the massacre, Cordley's estimate of the number of dead was the most conservative. For example, Bailey, (*Lawrence*, 30) said that 180 graves were dug and actually asserted that there were "nearly 200 dead" (23).

The panic: LDC, August 25, 1863; Peter D. Ridenour, *Autobiography of Peter D. Ridenour*, 173–75; Cordley, *Lawrence*, 248–49, and *Pioneer*, 222–23; Shea, 13; H. D. Fisher, 202–4.

Monday and the relief of Lawrence: Ridenour, 175–76; Cordley, *Pioneer,* 226–28, 230, and *Lawrence,* 251; LDC, August 23, 1863; DJC, August 26 and September 2, 1863.

James Watson and the Simpson brothers: Shea, 10–13; Cordley, *Pioneer,* 231–32.

Ridenour revives his business and the rifle company: Ridenour, 176–83, 185–86; See also: Cordley, *Lawrence,* 251–52, and *Pioneer,* 231–33.

The indictments and the progress of the rebuilding effort by the spring of 1864: Quantrill's Confederate service record (NA) includes the indictment for the Lawrence massacre; Richard B. Sheridan's postscript to Cordley's "Massacre," 27–28.

The wrong Charley Hart: Ridenour, 190–96. Quantrill's service record includes the telegram sent by the commander of the military district at Indianapolis as well as a "Requisition for [a] Fugitive from Justice," addressed to the governor of Indiana from the governor of Kansas. This document was in the possession of Ridenour and the other delegates who traveled to Indianapolis and who hoped it would enable them to take custody of Quantrill and bring him to Lawrence for trial.

The rebuilding of Lawrence in 1864, Cordley's observation about "the burnt district," and the badge of honor: Sheridan's Postscript to "Massacre," 27–28; Cordley, *Lawrence,* 250, 256.

Ed Howe's remark quoted in the Lawrence *Journal,* February 26, 1890.

George W. Maddox is jailed and tried: LKT, February 9 and November, 23, 1866, and March 29 and April 4, 5, and 12, 1867; DMR, April 7, 1867; KCS, April 16, 1933. LT, April 12, 1867, also alleged that Maddox was kidnapped. The WCM has Maddox's appeal for a change of venue.

CHAPTER 10: THE PURSUIT OF QUANTRILL AND
THE ISSUING OF ORDER NO. 11

Chapter title is adapted from a sentence in Gregg, *Little,* 67.

Captain Pike and Ewings's criticism: J. A. Pike, "Captain Pike's Statement," 313–14; OR, vol. 22, pt. 1, 580–83, 585, 587, 589.

Captain Coleman: OR, vol. 22, pt. 1, 589–90.

Major Plumb, Lieutenant Leland, Captain Coleman, and the beginning of the pursuit: OR, vol. 22, pt. 1, 580, 589–92; Connelley, *Quantrill,* 397–98.

Jim Lane: Connelley, *Quantrill,* 398–41; Castel, *Quantrill,* 136–37.

The DJC, August 27, 1863, has a detailed article on the retreat based on the account of Samuel Boles, who was taken along as a prisoner. Private

Hervey Johnson, whose unit engaged in the pursuit of the raiders, wrote two interesting letters about his experiences which, along with a third letter, have been compiled and edited by William E. Unrau, "In Pursuit of Quantrill: An Enlisted Man's View," 386–91.

The retreat on the Lawrence-Ft. Scott Road, the condition of the horses, and the discarded plunder: OR, vol. 22, pt. 1, 590; OR, vol. 22, pt. 2, 479–80; Connelley, *Quantrill,* 399–401, and *Plumb,* 641.

The Fletcher farm: Castel, *Quantrill,* 137–38; Connelley, *Quantrill,* 401–3; Gregg, *Little,* 64.

Gregg and sixty men: Gregg, *Little,* 65–66. See also Connelley's note on the Ft. Scott Road, *History of Kansas,* vol. 2, 642, n. 9.

Among the references to the exhaustion of horses and men: OR, vol. 22, pt. 1, 583, 590, 592.

Captain Leland and his civilian "militia": OR, vol. 22, pt. 1, 592; Leland's letter to his mother, September 2, 1863, Cyrus Leland, Jr., Collection, Manuscripts Department, KSHS. See also Robert S. LaForte, "Cyrus Leland, Jr., and the Lawrence Massacre," 177–78. Leland's report, which does not always appear to be written in chronological order, seems to indicate that Plumb gave him command of the civilians before the Fletcher farm fight, but Connelley, who interviewed Leland, wrote that it was after the fight (*Quantrill,* 404). See also: Connelley's "Interview with Cyrus Leland, Jr.," Denver #56.

Gregg's tactics, the civilians murder stragglers and the wounded, and Gregg's men driven into the back of the main column: Gregg, *Little,* 66; Connelley, *Quantrill,* 404–5; OR, vol. 22, pt. 1, 592–93; Castel, *Quantrill,* 138.

Joab Perry and Gregg's exhaustion: Gregg, *Little,* 67, 69–70; Connelley, *Quantrill,* 406.

Paola: OR, vol. 22, pt. 1, 581, 585–86, 592; Gregg, *Little,* 67–69; Connelley, *Quantrill,* 406–7, 410–11, and *History of Kansas,* vol. 2, 643–44.

Quantrill moves through Bull Creek Valley, allows his men to briefly rest, calls a halt at the Grand River, and orders his men to saddle up: Gregg, *Little,* 70–73; Barton, 128; Connelley, *Quantrill,* 409–10, 413–14; Castel, *Quantrill,* 140.

The dispersal begins, the guerrillas skirmish with the militia, and Clark reaches the campsite: OR, vol. 22, pt. 1, 586; Gregg, *Little,* 73; Barton, 129–32; Connelley, *Quantrill,* 414–15.

The execution of Bledsoe: Connelley, *Quantrill,* 415–16; Gregg, *Little,* 72; Edwards, *Noted,* 207.

The killing of bushwhackers in Missouri: Lazear's letter to his wife, September 10, 1863, in Vivian K. McLarty, ed., "The Civil War Letters of Colonel Bazel Lazear," 390–91; OR, vol. 22, pt. 1, 588–89, 591; Connelley, *Quantrill,* 412–13, 418–19; DJC August 26, 27, 28, September 17, 1863; WJC, September 5, 1863; The Richmond *Examiner* in WJC, September 26, 1863.

Ewing's August 27 report: OR, vol. 22, pt. 2, 479–80.

The search is broken off: OR, vol. 22, pt. 1, 588–89, 593; OR, vol. 22, pt. 2, 525. The Yankees aggressively scouted for Quantrill for some time—especially because of rumors that he intended to make another raid into Kansas—but it appears that J. T. Ross may have written the last report of any officer trying to hunt down Quantrill in the immediate aftermath of Lawrence—September 4, 1863 (OR, vol. 22, pt. 2, 511).

Bushwhacker casualties: SLG-D, September 20, 1898; Gregg, *Little,* 69–70, 73, and "Lawrence," 5; OR, vol. 22, pt. 1, 582, 584, 586, 588, 590–91, 593; OR, vol. 22, pt. 2, 479–80, 511, 537; DJC, September 1, 1863.

Ewing's activities on August 20–21, his meeting with Lane, the issuing of Order No. 11, and the criticism/defense of Ewing: OR, vol. 22, pt. 2, 473; Connelley, *Quantrill,* 417–18; Taylor, 167–68; LDC, August 25, 1863; DJC, September 1, 3, 5, and October 1, 1863; letter to *Conservative* editor published in WJC, September 19, 1863; WJC, September 12, 26, 1863.

Depopulation of Cass County and other counties: *History and Directory of Cass County* (1908), 128; *The Old Settlers' History of Bates County,* 42–43; W. O. Atkeson, *History of Bates County, Missouri,* 317–18; Ann Davis Niepman, "General Orders No. 11 and Border Warfare During the Civil War," 198, 204–6.

Deportees rode nags, traveled in oxcarts: William H. Wallace, *Speeches and Writings,* 256; Barton, 132–33; Lew Larkin, *Bingham: Fighting Artist,* 210–12. The Larkin quote is from 210.

Martin Rice wrote a powerful description of the plight of the "fugitives" and of the refugee columns in *Rural Rhymes and Talks of Olden Times,* 113.

Bingham quote: February 22, 1877, letter of George Caleb Bingham in DMR, February 26, 1877.

Bingham argues with Ewing: C. B. Rollins, "Some Recollections of George Caleb Bingham," 480–81; interview with Curtis B. Rollins in KCS, November 13, 1932; Larkin, 201–6.

Bingham quote: DMR, February 26, 1877.

Lazear's reaction: Lazear letter of September 10, 1863, in McLarty, 390.

The enforcement: Eugene Morrow Violette, *History of Missouri,* 384; Larkin, 216–17; *History of Cass County,* 129.

Matilda Ann Cave's experience: KCS, March 6, 1939. See also: Rice, 113–16.

Frances Twyman: "Reminiscences of the War," in Missouri Division, 263–67.

Laura Harris Bridges: KCS, May 12, 1929; KCT, August 3, 1931.

Other pertinent documents on Order No. 11: *The Henry County Democrat,* August 25, 1938; "Emily Steele's Letters Tell of Pillage And Northeast Jackson County Tragedies," *Jackson County Historical Society Journal,* 6–7, 11; Kansas City *Journal-Post,* August 8, 1937; Charles R. Mink, "General Orders No. 11," 132–36; Switzler, 426–27; Mary Gentry Shaw, "My Most Unforgettable Character," 5, 15.

Ewing's political enemies plot against him, Kansas is added to his district, and Thacher assesses his accomplishments: OR, vol. 22, pt. 2, 472, 477, 693; Taylor, 169; DJC, November 7, 1863.

The January 1 reshuffling, General Brown's order of January 14, and the return of Jackson County residents: OR, vol. 34, pt. 2, 7, 49, 79–80, 464, 682, 757. Castel, *Frontier,* 163–64; Taylor, 169.

Schofield is replaced, Ewing is reassigned, and Ford's complaint: Schofield, *Forty-six Years,* 106–112; OR, vol. 34, pt. 2, 7, 757; Castel, *Frontier,* 163.

Violette and Castel quotations: Violette, 384–85; Albert Castel, "Order No. 11 and the Civil War on the Border," 357.

Chapter 11: The Baxter Springs Massacre

Chapter title is adapted from a statement made by Major Benjamin S. Henning, OR, vol. 22, pt. 1, 697.

Examples of descriptions of the destruction caused by Order No. 11: *Old Settlers' History,* 43; Atkeson, 318.

The hunt for guerrillas: OR, vol. 22, pt. 2, 524–25, 534, 537; OR, vol. 22, pt. 1, 619–20. DJC, October 29 and December 29, 1863; WJC, September 26 and October 9, 1863. Thacher quote: WJC, September 26, 1863.

Colonel Weer's report: OR, 22, pt. 1, 619.

Quantrill's supposedly planning another Kansas raid: OR, vol. 22, pt. 2, 520–21, 524, 532, 538.

Quantrill busy avoiding the enemy: Castel, *Quantrill,* 148–9.

The rendezvous and formation of the First Regiment: Gregg, *Little,* 78; Barton, 133–35; Connelley, *Quantrill,* 421.

Dave Pool captures the pickets: Gregg, *Little,* 79; Barton, 135–36; OR, vol. 22, pt. 1, 700; Connelley, *Quantrill,* 424.

Ft. Blair: OR, vol. 22, pt. 1, 695, 698–701; Wiley Britton, *The Union Indian Brigade,* 309–10, and *The Civil War on the Border,* vol. 2, 212–13; Barton, 136; Connelley, *Quantrill,* 422. Dr. W. H. Warner, "The Battle at Baxter Springs," in Andreas, 1152–153.

Quantrill sends Gregg to Pool, gets lost, and the attack on Ft. Blair: Gregg, *Little,* 79–81; Warner, in Andreas, 1152–153; an untitled, handwritten account of the massacre by an anonymous clerk assigned to Blunt's headquarters, 1, in BSM; Britton, *Union,* 318–20, and CW 2, 213, 222–24; OR, vol. 22, pt. 1, 691–92, 695, 698–701.

Blunt marches to a point near Ft. Blair and is routed by Quantrill: OR, vol. 22, pt. 1, 688–89, 691–701; Barton, 136–37, 140; Gregg, *Little,* 81–83; Britton, CW 2, 216–20, and *Union,* 313–16; James G. Blunt, "General Blunt's Account of His Civil War Experiences," 247–48; J. J. Jones's letter to the editor, *National Tribune,* March 6, 1884, Denver #35; headquarters clerk's account, 1–5; Connelley, *Quantrill,* 425–27. In putting together the account of Quantrill approaching Blunt's force and the beginning of the rout, I have used not only Blunt's two accounts but also the reports of Colonel Blair and Major Henning.

Jack Splane and the others who were shot: OR, vol. 22, pt. 1, 697; Warner in Andreas, 1152–153; headquarters clerk's account, 6; Jones's letter, Denver #35.

The murder of Bledsoe and the band musicians: Warner, in Andreas, 1153; Gregg, *Little,* 83–85; Barton, 139; OR, 22, pt. 1, 695–96; Connelley, *Quantrill,* 429–30.

Trooper Davis and Mrs. Thomas: "Lydia Stevens Thomas," *The Club Member,* 4–5; "In Memory of a Quantrell Massacre," KCS, August 30, 1908; QSB, vol. 3, 84–87. See also: headquarters clerk's account, 5–6; Connelley's "Interview with John Koger," 18.

Quantrill and his followers get drunk, Riley Crawford, and Anderson and Todd want to try again to capture Ft. Blair: Connelley, *Quantrill,* 430–31; Gregg, *Little,* 50–52, 85–86; OR, vol. 22, pt. 1, 700–701. See also: Connelley's interview with Gregg, entitled "Quantrill at Baxter Springs," 2–4 (Connelley papers, KSHS).

Quantrill sends Todd to the fort, then leads the band south with Blunt following and camps for the night: Connelley's "Interview with John Koger," 16; Gregg, *Little,* 86; OR, vol. 22, pt. 1, 689–90, 692–93, 696, 699–701; Barton, 141–42; Blunt, 248; Connelley, *Quantrill,* 432–33, n. 6; Castel, *Quantrill,* 152–53.

The guerrillas' casualties and plunder and the Yankee casualties: OR, vol. 22, pt. 1, 693, 695, 697–701; Warner, in Andreas, 1153; Jones's letter, Denver #35; Blunt, 248; Gregg, *Little,* 85; Barton, 143. Major B. S. Henning did include in his report (OR, *Ibid.,* 698) a list of the dead and wounded, but it is incomplete.

The October 17, 1863, WJC reprints a letter written by Blunt on the evening of the seventh, giving an account of the massacre. The DJC, October 11, 1863, has a long and useful article on the massacre.

The march resumes, Bledsoe is buried, Mann is murdered, and an Indian Home Guard company is slaughtered: Connelley's "Interview with John Koger," 16–67; Barton, 141–42; OR, vol. 22, pt. 1, 689, 700–1; Castel, *Quantrill,* 153; Connelley, *Quantrill,* 432–34, text and n. 6 and 7; Barton, 146; WJC, October 17, 1863.

Blunt is relieved of command and later military career: Blunt, 248–63; Castel, *Frontier,* 161–65.

Major MacLean's letter to Quantrill: OR, vol. 53, 908.

See below note on Lieutenant Pond and his brother: this information was provided by Edward F. Murphy of the Medal of Honor Historical Society, Mesa, Arizona. See also the obituary for James Pond, "Major Pond Dead," KCS, June 21, 1903, in Denver #52.

Examples of the northern press reaction to Lawrence reprinted in: LDC, August 27, 29, 1863.

Major Henning's observation on Lawrence and Baxter Springs and the "fiends from hell" quotation: OR, vol. 22, pt. 1, 697; Connelley, *Quantrill,* 349.

CHAPTER 12: THE USURPATION OF QUANTRILL

Chapter title is adapted from a sentence in a letter Governor Thomas Reynolds wrote to Quantrill, March 10, 1864, Reynolds letter book #4464, 120.

Quantrill goes to Texas, establishes a camp on Mineral Creek, and his followers steal and entertain themselves: Gregg, *Little,* 86–87; Connelley, *Quantrill,* 435–56; Castel, *Quantrill,* 155, 157, 160–1.

The ongoing debate among Generals Magruder, McCulloch, and Smith: OR, vol. 26, pt. 2, 339–40, 348, 379, 383.

See below note: OR, vol. 53, 907–8; see also, McCulloch's observations in OR, vol. 34, pt. 2, 942.

Quantrill and McCulloch debate over deserters and the attack on Jernigan's Swamp: OR, vol. 26, pt. 2, 430–31; OR, vol. 34, pt. 2, 945; Connelley's interview with Sylvester Akers in *Quantrill,* 439, n. 2.

Fighting Comanches: OR, vol. 26, pt. 2, 526, 531–32; Lewis, 11; Denis McLoughlin, *Wild and Woolly, an Encyclopedia of the Old West,* 108–9; Castel, *Quantrill,* 159–60.

LeRoy H. Fischer and Lary C. Rampp have established that during December 1863, Quantrill and his band participated in two expeditions into Arkansas as part of a combined force under the command of Colonel Stand Watie. Quantrill was in at least one brief skirmish, but little else is known about his actions during these expeditions, which is why I have not mentioned them in the text. (See Fischer, 168–70.)

The destruction of the still, the bad behavior of drunks, the Christmas Eve shenanigans, New Year's Eve, and the "old men" leave: letter of W. L. Potter to W. W. Scott, March 11, 1896, in Connelley papers, KSHS; Gregg, *Little,* 75–77, 87; OR, vol. 34, pt. 2, 942; Castel, *Quantrill,* 161.

In writing of the band's growing dissipation I was thinking of a comment Gregg made in *Little,* 86: "It was [in Sherman] that the disintegration of Quantrill['s] command began." Morgan Mattox told Connelley that "From the first six to the sixty men who went to Quantrill, all were of the best families in Jackson, Cass, and Lafayette counties." But "as the war progressed men of bad principle, thieves and robbers got into the band to rob, murder and plunder."—Connelley's "Interview with Mattox," 15.

Gregg leaves Quantrill: Gregg, *Little,* 75–77; Connelley, *Quantrill,* 445–47. See also: Connelley's summary of an interview with Gregg, entitled "Additional to Disintegration of Quantrill's Band," 2–3 (Connelley papers, KSHS).

Gregg's later military career, Elizabeth Hook, the corpse of the Confederate soldier, and the marriage: Gregg, *Little,* 87, 93–94; Mrs. W. H. Gregg, "Can Forgive, but Never Forget," in Missouri Division, 27–29; Barton, 179–80. William H. Gregg's name appears on the roster for Company M, 1st Regiment Infantry, 8th Division, Missouri State Guard and also on the roster of the 12th Missouri Cavalry.

The trip to Texas: Mrs. Gregg in Missouri Division, 29–30; Gregg, *Little,* 94–99; Connelley's "Interview with Mattox," 39–40. Both Mr. and Mrs. Gregg spell Dick Maddox's last name Mattox, but no one named Richard Mattox was associated with the Quantrill band. Connelley, who tried to be careful about the spelling of names, was certain the man in question was Dick Maddox ("Interview with Mattox," 39). See also Hale and Eakin, 279.

Cole Younger's military service after the fall of 1863: Younger, *Story,* 48–52; Gregg confirms that Cole left the band, *Little,* 87; in an interview published in KCJ, May 12, 1888, Andy Walker stated that Cole went to

Mexico after leaving the band; LKDJ, April 30, 1865, reported that Cole "is now in old Mexico." The paperwork on Cole's pension application is on file at WHMC-C. Some ex-guerrillas seem to have found ways around clause #2 on the pension application—the requirement that they had served "for not less than six months in the army," but at my request Ms. Mary Beck searched the files of the Missouri State Archives, Jefferson City, and was unable to find any record of payment to Cole, which means he never got a pension.

The ongoing problems with Quantrill's Raiders and McCulloch's attempts to get them under control: OR, vol. 34, pt. 2, 853, 941–45, 957–58; *Ibid.*, pt. 3, 742–43; *Ibid.*, 53, 963.

Quantrill writes to Reynolds and the governor's reply: Quantrill's letter, February 24, 1864 (CHS); Reynolds's letter, March 10, 1864, Reynolds letter book #4464, 120.

See below note on Quantrill's rank: Edwards, *Noted,* 158; Connelley, *Quantrill,* 281, 421; "Receipt for Articles Purchased," April 3, 1863, Quantrill Confederate Service Record, NA; the reports of Pond and Quantrill in the OR, vol. 22, pt. 1, 699, 701; Reynolds's letter to Price, October 30, 1863, Reynolds letter book #4463, 171–72; Barton, 175–76. In his letter to Quantrill of March 10, Reynolds wrote, "You told me that the no quarter system was forced on you. . . ." Yet Quantrill's letter of February 24 makes no such claim, which suggests the two men may have had a face-to-face conversation.

The murder of Major Butts and Colonel Alexander, the arrest of Quantrill, his escape and pursuit by Colonel Martin and renegade bushwhackers, and the establishment of a camp in the Choctaw Nation: letter of W. L. Potter to W. W. Scott, February 29, 1896, in Connelley papers, KSHS. In addition to the Potter letter, Connelley used other sources, therefore his account is valuable, too: *Ibid.*, 439–48; See also: Castel, *Quantrill,* 164–68.

Fischer and Rampp have documented some of Quantrill's activities and fights after he escaped from Texas: 175–81.

The return to Missouri: Barton, 145–49; OR, vol. 34, pt. 3, 109, 121–22, 272, 312–13, 328, 447, 499; Castel, *Quantrill,* 168; Edwards, *Quantrill,* 226–28; Fischer and Rampp, 178.

Military conditions: OR, vol. 22, pt. 2, 693–94, 702–3; *Ibid.*, 34, pt. 2, 79–81, 89; Barton, 152.

Todd and Quantrill split: Potter's letters to Scott, January 22 and March 11, 1896, in Connelley papers, KSHS; Connelley, *Quantrill,* 436, 442, 447, 449–50.

Quantrill goes into Howard County with Kate, was rumored to have TB: KCS, May 23, 1926; Fletch Taylor's May 4, 1879, letter to Scott, KC-UKL; the *Kansas Tribune* in the Wyandott, Kansas, *Commercial Gazette,* December 10, 1864.

CHAPTER 13: ANDERSON AND TODD DURING
THE SUMMER AND FALL OF 1864

The chapter title is adapted from a sentence in Thomas M. Goodman, *Sergeant Thomas M. Goodman's Thrilling Record,* 24.

The outbreak of hydrophobia, and the citizens want guerrillas killed: DJC, January 27, March 27, April 1, 1864; OR, vol. 34, pt. 4, 363–64.

Guerrillas return, mostly in small groups, and commit depredations: OR, vol. 34, pt. 3, 420–23, 552; *Ibid.,* pt. 4, 51, 54, 363–64. CMS, April 1, 29, and June 17, 1864. DJC, May 3, 27, 29, and June 3, 12, 14, 1864; LT, May 27 and June 10, 1864.

Colonel Ford's Coloradans, the military tries other measures, and General Brown's elaborate signs and countersigns: OR, vol. 34, pt. 3, 420, 423, 550; *Ibid.,* pt. 1, 996; *Ibid.,* vol. 41, pt. 2, 128, 390; DJC, June 14, 21, 28, 29, 1864; LT, July 1, 1864.

George Todd ambushes Captain Wagner: OR, vol. 41, pt. 1, 49–52; *Ibid.,* pt. 2, 73–74; DJC, July 8, 10, 12, 1864; Barton, 152–54; Castel, *Quantrill,* 176.

Anderson letters: reprinted in OR, vol. 41, pt. 2, 75–77; CMS, July 22, 1864, has a brief article about Anna Fickle.

Brown's July campaign: OR, vol. 34, pt. 1, 996.

Thornton captures Platte City and is defeated: OR, vol. 41, pt. 2, 128–29, 160, 185. LT, July 15, 29, 1864; DJC, July 15, 1864; DMD, July 18, 1864; St. Joseph *Herald* in DMD, July 21, 1864; Castel, *Quantrill,* 178.

Anderson raids into Carroll County; Hiram Griffith, Cyrus Lyons, and others are killed: *History of Carroll County, Missouri,* 343–46; CMS, July 22, 1864; OR, vol. 41, pt. 2, 427; DJC, July 24, 1864.

Anderson crosses the river, raids Huntsville and Rocheport and fires on the *War Eagle:* CMS, July 22, 29, 1864; LT, July 22 and August 5, 1864; DMD, November 11, 1864; OR, vol. 41, pt. 1, 230–31; *Ibid.,* pt. 2, 209, 216.

Todd attacks Arrow Rock, Yeager is wounded and killed, and Todd goes into hiding: OR, vol. 41, pt. 2, 267–69, 290, 309–11, 336–37, 339, 347, 359–60, 388–89, 391; *Ibid.,* pt. 1, 50–51; CMS, July 29, 1864; DMD, July 26, 1864.

Anderson raids Renick and Allen: OR, vol. 41, pt. 2, 367, 394, 490; DJC, July 28, 1864; CMS, July 29, 1864.

The Federal military authorities see a rare chance to destroy Anderson: OR, vol. 41, pt. 2, 411–12, 441, 479.

The fight with Lieutenant Kapp, the killing of the horses, the scalping of the two dead men, and the poorly spelled note: OR, vol. 41, pt. 2, 367; *Ibid.*, pt. 1, 125; CMS, August 5, 1864; Brownlee, 199–200.

Anderson burns bridge and other railroad property: OR, vol. 41, pt. 2, 422–23.

Anderson splits force in two: OR, vol. 41, pt. 1, 230–31; CMS, August 19, 1864.

The July 31st visit to Mrs. Mitchell's house: *History of Carroll County*, 348–51; CMS, August 19, 1864; listings for Mitchell and Calvert families, 1860 and 1870 Federal Censuses for Carroll County, Missouri.

Fletch Taylor and Thrailkill: OR, vol. 41, pt. 1, 258–59; *Ibid.*, pt. 2, 572–73, 622–23; LT, August 12, 1864; DJC, August 19, 1864; Taylor's letter to W. W. Scott, May 4, 1879 (KC-UKL).

Anderson attacks militia near Fredericksburg, the Fisk telegram and other telegrams, Anderson's raids through the rest of the month: *History of Ray County, Missouri*, 302; *History of Carroll County*, 351–54; CMS, August 12 and September 2, 1864; Caldwell County *Banner* in DMD, August 22, 26, 1864; OR, vol. 41, pt. 2, 689–90, 718; *Ibid.*, pt. 1, 249–50, 253, 299–300, 740; CMS, August 26, 1864; Settle, 27.

The Federals respond and Thacher's observation: OR, vol. 41, pt. 1, 251; *Ibid.*, pt. 2, 748, 762, 795, 858–59; WJC, July 30, August 6, 13, 1864.

The Price invasion begins; Kirby Smith's instructions: Castel, *Price*, 196–204; OR, vol. 41, pt. 2, 1040–41; *Ibid.*, pt. 1, 624–26.

John Chestnut contacts Todd, and Todd rides west: Edwards, *Noted*, 282–89; Castel, *Quantrill*, 183; OR, vol. 41, pt. 1, 424–29; *Ibid.*, pt. 3, 254–55, 277, 394; *History of Carroll County*, 356–58.

Price enters Missouri, the wrong general for the undertaking, his army unimpressive, and Edwards's comment: OR, vol. 41, pt. 1, 627; *Ibid.*, pt. 2, 1020. Castel, *Price*, 202, 204, 207; Jennie Edwards, comp., *John N. Edwards*, 232.

Anderson's raid into the Rocheport area, Quantrill links with Todd and Pool, the plan to attack Fayette, and the attack is made: OR, vol. 41, pt. 3, 348–49, 351, 416, 440; *Ibid.*, pt. 1, 415, 432–33, 440–41, 740; DJC, September 29, 1864; Hamp B. Watts, *The Babe of the Company*, 17–21; Barton, 159–62; Edwards, *Noted*, 291; Castel, *Quantrill*, 185–87; J. Thomas Fyfer, *History of Boone County, Missouri*, 437–39.

The band retreats north, Anderson demands the surrender of Huntsville, the band rides toward Renick and menaces Paris, and camps near Centralia: Watts, 22–23; Fyfer, 439; OR, vol. 41, pt. 3, 397. By the way, Anderson captured and tortured Denny's father, CMS, August 12, 1864.

Price, Ewing, and Pilot Knob: Edwards, *Shelby,* 386–90; Castel, *Price,* 209–11, 214–18, 221; OR, vol. 41, pt. 1, 308–9, 445–52, 628–29. DMD, October 6, 1864.

The band enters Centralia, robs the stores and the freight house and the stagecoach: Fyfer, 443–45.

The capture of the train, the passengers are robbed, and the soldiers surrender and are taken outside: Clark gave two very similar accounts of his experiences that were published in newspapers and have been collected in a scrapbook, "The Centralia Massacre 1864," 6–14 (SHSM-C); Fyfer, 445–48; Goodman, 13–14, 17, 19, 20–24. See also the "Statement of the Conductor of the Train," DMD, October 10, 1864.

Anderson calls for a sergeant, Goodman comes forward, and the soldiers are executed: Fyfer, 447–49; Goodman, 23–25, 27–31; Clark in "Centralia," 8.

The train crew clears the tracks, a gravel train chugs into town, and the bushwhackers return to camp with Goodman: Barton, 163; Fyfer, 450; Clark in "Centralia," 8; Goodman, 27–28.

Note: In an interview with a correspondent for the CMH, September 24, 1897, Frank James was careful to say that he had not been in Centralia that morning and knew "nothing" of what had transpired "save from hearsay," but he belonged to Anderson's band and did not explain why he remained behind. Fyfer, whom I find to be a very good source, wrote that Frank James was with Anderson (446).

Major Johnston rides into town in command of his newly organized regiment, which had fought only one skirmish: Fyfer, 452–53.

Johnston surveys the scene, interrogates the townsfolk, sees men in the distance, argues with Sneed, and is determined to fight: Fyfer, 453–54.

Leaving some men and wagons behind, Johnston sets out chasing Dave Pool, and the guerrillas' battle plan: Barton, 163–64; Fyfer, 455–57; CMH, September 24, 1897; Goodman, 30–32.

Major Johnston deploys his troops, John Koger's comment, Anderson's charge, and the guerrillas who were killed: CMH, September 24, 1897; Fyfer, 457–58; Goodman, 31–32; Barton, 164–65.

The massacre and its aftermath: Goodman, 32–34; CMH, September 24, 1897; Fyfer, 458–62; Barton, 165–66; OR, vol. 41, pt. 1, 443; *Ibid.,* pt. 3, 440–41, 488, 491, 521–22.

In writing of Centralia—occurrences both in the morning and afternoon—I have also used the following: "The Centralia Massacre 1864," 1–2; Edgar Rodemyre, *History of Centralia, Missouri,* 24–40; CMS, September 30, 1864; DMR, September 30, 1864; DMD, September 29, 30 and October 4, 1864; LT, September 27, 1864; OR, vol. 41, pt. 1, 309, 417, 440.

Goodman's experiences until his escape: Goodman, 35–57 and 60–61.

Price leaves Pilot Knob, Reynolds is disgusted, the soldiers loot and murder: Castel, *Price,* 221–22, 225; Reynolds's letter "To the Public," December 17, 1864, reproduced in Edwards, *Shelby,* 471; OR, vol. 41, pt. 1, 631–32. In April 1865, several witnesses testified before a Federal military court of inquiry concerning the lack of discipline in Price's army, *Ibid.,* 716–17, 719–20.

Women are raped: DMD, October 13, 1864.

Price moves slowly, occupies the hills south of Jefferson City, and his soldiers plunder Boonville: Castel, *Price,* 223–27; OR, vol. 41, pt. 1, 418–20, 631; Reynolds's letter in Edwards, *Shelby,* 471. See also Thompson's report, OR, vol. 41, pt. 1, 663–65, and DMR, October 20, 22, 1864.

Anderson and Price: DJC in LT, November 4, 1864; OR, vol. 41, pt. 1, 632, 718, 888; *Ibid.,* pt. 3, 839; *Ibid.,* pt. 4, 354; Castel, *Quantrill,* 196–99.

Price moves west: Castel, *Price,* 223, 227; OR, vol. 41, pt. 1, 632–33.

Anderson follows Shelby to Glasgow, his men raid Danville, and some circle through Florence: *History of Saint Charles, Montgomery, and Warren Counties,* 646–55; OR, vol. 41, pt. 1, 888; *Ibid.,* pt. 3, 893; DMD, October 20, 21, 22, 1864.

Most sources state that Danville was captured on the fourteenth, but I believe the best source is OR, vol. 41, pt. 1, 893, which reports that the raid occurred on the fifteenth.

Shelby and Quantrill at Glasgow: *History of Howard and Chariton Counties, Missouri,* 288–89; OR, vol. 41, pt. 1, 422, 437–39; DMD, October 21, 24, 1864.

The torture of Benjamin Lewis and the rape of his female servants: DMD, November 12, 1864; Switzler, 435, n. 1.

Price crosses into Lafayette County, is joined by Todd, and engages Blunt: Castel, *Quantrill,* 197; OR, vol. 41, pt. 1, 633.

General Curtis announces Todd's death: OR, vol. 41, pt. 4, 190. See also: CMS, November 11, 1864.

First version of Todd's death: Edwards, *Noted,* 321, and Shelby, 421; Barton, 174–76; LT, November 4, 1864.

Second version: Connelley's "Interview With Mattox," 5–6, 34, and *Quantrill*, 454–55. See also: Gregg, *Little*, 89–90.

For more on Todd's death, see Virginia Hays Asbury, "An Anomaly of Written History," 138.

Curtis makes a stand, Pleasonton attacks Price's rear, Price covers the movement of the train, and the collapse of Marmaduke's division: Castel, *Price*, 230–35; OR, vol. 41, pt. 1, 633–34; *Ibid.*, pt. 4, 194, 206, and 274.

Castel's observations on the Battle of Westport, the retreat, and the action at Mine Creek: Castel, *Price*, 235–45; OR, vol. 41, pt. 1, 636–38; *Ibid.*, pt. 4, 334.

Anderson's last raid, Samuel Cox skirmishes with and kills Anderson, and the aftermath: *History of Carroll County*, 362–64; OR, vol. 41, pt. 1, 317, 422–24, 434, 442; *Ibid.*, pt. 4, 316–18, 334, 354, 726–27; CMS, November 11, 1864; *St. Joseph News* in the LT, November 11, 1864; DMD, November 3, 4, 1864; KCS, August 25, 1912; *Ibid.*, August 16, 1913; the Columbia, Missouri, Daily *Tribune*, August 21, 1913, clipping in the SHSM-C. See also Donald R. Hale, *They Called Him Bloody Bill*, 75–82; KCS, October 14, 1906, Denver #44. The last name of the dentist who took the death ambrotype is sometimes rendered Rice, but the 1880 Federal Census for Ray County, Missouri, and the *History of Ray County, Missouri*, 557–58, show the correct spelling to be Kice.

Wiley Britton wrote a detailed account of Anderson's death, which he said came from Cox's "own lips." It is at odds with the official reports on some details—for example, that one of the Yankee militiamen died immediately rather than dying of his wound, or wounds, later on, and that Anderson had on his person a "commission as colonel, signed by Jefferson Davis, President of the Southern Confederacy." Britton's book was published in 1899, some thirty-five years after the events, so Cox's memory—or Britton's—may have been playing some minor tricks. In most respects the account is consistent with established facts and is quite valuable (CW II, 540–46).

The end of Price's raid: Castel, *Price*, 246–55; OR, vol. 41, pt. 1, 638–40; *Ibid.*, pt. 4, 1069.

The quotation on Anderson is from the DMR, November 6, 1864. In 1967, Lee's Summit historian Donald R. Hale located Anderson's grave, which had been obscured by the passage of time and the re-landscaping of the cemetery. He applied for a federal government tombstone to mark the grave—a free tombstone is available for any American who served in the military, including Confederates—and he cemented it into place without ceremony one warm, sunny April Sunday afternoon.

CHAPTER 14: THE DEATH OF QUANTRILL

Chapter title is adapted from a line in a poem Quantrill wrote in Nannie Dawson's scrapbook. The line is actually "borrowed" and adapted from George Gordon, Lord Byron's "My Boat Is on the Shore," *The Complete Poetical Works of Byron,* 230–31.

Quantrill's reason for leaving Missouri: Connelley, *Quantrill,* 456–58, n. 2 and 5; Barton, 180, 190. See also: Connelley's "Interview with Mattox," 26; OR, vol. 49, pt. 1, 616.

Quantrill sends Kate King to St. Louis, calls for a rendezvous, and only thirty-three respond: Connelley, *Quantrill,* 456–57.

The men don Yankee uniforms, stop at Tuscumbia, and cross the Mississippi: Barton, 180–83, 186; Edwards, *Noted,* 384–85; Connelley, *Quantrill,* 458–59; *Ibid.,* 479, n. 6.

There are reports of Quantrill's journey in the OR, vol. 41, pt. 4, 715, 782, 945, 960.

Colonel Fairleigh hires civilians, including Terrell: Terrell's letter to Fairleigh, January 6, 1865, and the correspondence between Captain Charles Bauer and Captain James Noland, in Terrell's Confederate service record (NA); John Langford's letter to W. W. Scott, September, 8, 1888, Filson Club Historical Society.

See below note on Terrell's background: his letter to Fairleigh and company muster roll records in his service record; LC-J, December 14, 15, 23, 26, 1868; Ed D. Shinnick, *Some Old Time History of Shelbyville and Shelby County,* 73–74. The December 26, 1868, LC-J reported that Terrell had worked for the Dan Rice Circus; records for the Dan Rice Circus are in the Circus World Museum Library, Baraboo, Wisconsin, but do not include personnel records for this period.

In an odd coincidence, an Edward L. Terrell served a one-year term of enlistment in Company G, 1st Kentucky Infantry. He subsequently enlisted in Company K, 7th Kentucky Cavalry, which was a Morgan regiment, but deserted. Finally, he enlisted in Company B, 9th Kentucky Infantry; he was captured on April 21, 1863, and paroled six days later. However, his signature on the parole in his Confederate service record (Kentucky State Archives, Frankfort) does not match Edwin Terrell's signature and handwriting in his letter to Fairleigh.

Quantrill and the band move through Tennessee, swing north into Kentucky, and have a fight at a farmhouse: Barton, 190–91; Edwards, *Noted,* 389–92. McCorkle said that Old Charley was hamstrung by a blacksmith in

Canton, and Edwards, 390, made a similar claim. If that had been true, however, Quantrill would have had plenty of time to accustom another horse to gunfire, which was not the case. Connelley is undoubtedly correct in stating that the crippling occurred much later—see *Quantrill,* 466–67, 471, and "Interview with Mattox," 9, 36–37.

The Missourians reach Hartford and leave with three Yankees, who are killed: OR, vol. 49, pt. 1, 657–58; Edwards, *Noted,* 392–95; Barton, 190–91.

Quantrill takes the band east: Barton, 191–93; Edwards, *Noted,* 396.

George Prentice and General Burbridge: Dumas Malone, ed., *Dictionary of American Biography,* vol. 15, 186–87; John James Piatt, ed., *The Poems of George D. Prentice,* vii, xi–xiii, xvii–xviii, xxv, xxxvii–xli. Betty Carolyn Congleton, "George D. Prentice: Nineteenth Century Editor," 99, 108, 111, 116–17; L. L. Valentine, "Sue Mundy of Kentucky," pt. 1, 180, 185–86; Lewis Collins and Richard H. Collins, *History of Kentucky,* 133, 135–36; LKDJ, October 21, 28 and November 3, 1864; Allen Johnson, vol. 3, 270.

The first mention of Sue: LKDJ, October 11, 1864. See also: *Ibid.,* November 9, 1864.

Clark's background: the muster rolls of his military service record (NA); Clark's statement on the gallows in LKDJ March 16, 1865; LKDD, March 16, 1865; Exhibit A, "Statement of Jerome Clark, alias Sue Mundy," *United States* v. *Jerome Clark* (NA); L. F. Johnson, *Famous Kentucky Tragedies and Trials,* 187–88.

The Mundy nickname and Prentice surpasses himself with the hermaphrodite joke: Young E. Allison, "Sue Mundy," 300, 305; Robert Emmett McDowell, *City of Conflict,* 188; testimony of Cyrus J. Wilson and Lewis O. Marshall in *United States* v. *Clark,* 10–11; LKDJ, January 27, 1865.

Terrell raids through Nelson County and fights with the Mundy band: LKDJ, January 31 and February 1, 1865; LKDD, January 31 and February 1, 1865; Collins, 153.

The Quantrill band raids into Hustonville: LKDJ, February 10, 1865; Barton, 193.

Danville, the pursuit by and fight with Bridgewater: OR, vol. 49, pt. 1, 16–18, 612–13, 616; Barton, 193–96, 210–11; LKDJ, February 2 and 10, 1865; LKDD, January 31, 1865.

Quantrill is known to be in Kentucky, and George Prentice urges all veterans to fight the guerrillas: LKDJ, January 31, 1865; OR, vol. 49, pt. 1, 18, 612, 625.

Midway: LO&R, February 4, 1865; LKDJ, February 4, 5, 10, 1865; LKDD, February 4, 1865; OR, vol. 49, pt. 1, 634–35.

The wagon train near New Market: OR, vol. 49, pt. 1, 35–36 and 673–77; Henry C. Magruder, *Three Years in the Saddle,* 116; LKDD, February 10, 1865. See also the Frankfort *Commonwealth,* February 10, 1865.

See below note on the "Invalid Corps": OR, series 3, vol. 4, 1275–280.

Bridgewater hits Quantrill's camp: OR, vol. 49, pt. 1, 684, 694, 698.

Prentice thanks God for Palmer's appointment and Palmer's background: LKDJ, February 10, 1865; John M. Palmer, *The Story of an Earnest Life,* 1, 3, 42–43, 56, 78, 92–93, 144–47, 169–87, 197–98, 202–21, 224–26; Greg Foster, "Sherman's Feuding Generals," 41–45, 70–75.

The repeal of the Partisan Ranger Act: *Public Laws of the Confederate States of America,* 202.

Palmer assumes command, and Breckinridge is captured: Palmer, 226–32, 267; LKDJ, February 13, 25, 1865; LO&R, February 22, 1865; LKDD, February 25, 1865; OR, vol. 49, pt. 1, 764, 770; Collins, 155.

Guerrilla bands continue their activities: see, for example, LKDJ, March 19, 22, 1865; Collins, 157.

Clark starts to leave the state: Magruder, 120–22; Valentine, pt. 1, 204–5.

Quantrill writes in Nannie Dawson's scrapbook: the original page is in KC-UKL; Byron, 230–31. See also: Connelley, *Quantrill,* 464–65.

The headlines come from various Kentucky newspapers of the period.

Clark and his comrades are ambushed, they take up residence in a barn, Palmer hears of them and dispatches Wilson: testimony of Cyrus Wilson, *United States* v. *Clark,* 6–7; Magruder, 122–23; Palmer, 272; LKDJ, March 4, 14, 1865; LKDD, March 14, 1865; Valentine, pt. 2, 279, 281; L. F. Johnson, 182.

Wilson negotiates, Clark surrenders, is tied up, and the guerrillas arrive in Louisville: Wilson testimony, *United States* v. *Clark,* 8–9; LKDJ, March 14, 1865; LKDD, March 14, 1865; Valentine, pt. 2, 283–84, 286.

Palmer orders Clark's trial and approves the sentence: Most of the pages of the Clark court-martial transcript have been consecutively numbered; however, Palmer's March 13, 1865, approval of the sentence does not have a page number. It is in packet #2. See also Valentine, pt. 2, 285–86.

Clark's execution: LKDD, March 16, 1865; LKDJ, March 16, 17, 1865; Valentine, pt. 2, 286.

Terrell is hired but not admired by high-ranking Federal military officers: Office of the Quartermaster General 1815–1905, *Reports of Persons and Articles Hired 1865,* April and May reports (NA); Palmer, 268; *United States*

v. *Samuel Oscar Berry,* 439–40 (NA); letter of J. M. Ridlon to the *National Tribune,* April 14, 1904. Ridlon enclosed a copy of the May report, which the editor commented upon. In the past, writers have assumed that Terrell was hired on May 1. In fact, both the April and May rosters show he was hired on April 1.

Marion captures a surgeon, Palmer reacts, Quantrill and Marion tangle with Yankees, and Terrell steals a corpse: Palmer, 267–68; OR, vol. 49, pt. 1, 512; letter of G. W. Penn in LKDJ, May 2, 1865. See also: LKDJ, April 12, 17, 1865; Frankfort *Commonwealth,* April 14, 1865.

The court-martials of Magruder and Metcalf: Valentine, pt. 2, 304–6; LKDJ, June 3 and October 20, 21, 1865. The original Magruder court-martial transcript is in the NA.

Lincoln's assassination and Terrell's band kills Walker: General Order No. 23 in Frankfort *Commonwealth,* April 18, 1865; LKDJ, April 27, 28, and May 1, 1865; LC-J, December 14, 15, 1868; LKDD, December 14, 1868.

Old Charley is hamstrung: Connelley's "Interview With Mattox," 9, 36–37, and *Quantrill,* 466–67, 471.

James H. Wakefield, the visit of the Quantrill band, the last skirmish: letter of Wakefield to Scott, June 13, 1888, in Connelley, *Quantrill,* 475–77, n. 3: See also: Connelley's text, *Ibid.,* 471–74; Connelley's "Interview with Mattox," 30–31; Barton, 206; LKDD, May 13, 1865; LKDJ, May 14, 1865; Castel, *Quantrill,* 209.

Quantrill is interrogated, is left behind by Terrell, is visited by his men, is carried to Louisville: Barton, 206–7; Connelley's "Interview with Mattox," 30–31; letter of Mrs. Samuel N. Marshall to Scott, January 22, 1883, KC-UKL; the Wakefield letter, Connelley, *Quantrill,* 476–77, n. 3 and text, 477–80; Daily *Union Press* in *Ibid.,* 481, n. 2; "Quantrell's Death Verified," *Confederate Veteran,* 285; KCT, September 30, 1941 (JCHS); LKDJ, May 14, 1865.

There has been some confusion in the past over when Terrell was discharged. But the May 1865 *Reports of Persons . . . Hired* shows that Terrell was discharged on May 10. Ridlon's letter to the *National Tribune* is inaccurate as to the date Terrell brought Quantrill to Louisville but accurate as to the date of Terrell's discharge.

The newspapers' confusion over the identity of Quantrill: LKDJ, May 14, 15, 1865; LKDD, May 13, 14, 1865, in Connelley, *Quantrill,* 482, n. 2.

Terrell and his followers cause a stir in the United States Saloon and clash with Froman's band: LKDJ, May 20, 22, 1865.

Scott's notes (Connelley, *Quantrill,* 35, n. 19) indicate he was told Quantrill was converted by a Father Powers. Louisville city directories for

1866–67 and 1868–69 and Louisville archdiocese records show that the man's name was Michael Power. The notes also show Scott had learned about the money Quantrill left to the priest. See also: Barton, 207.

Scott and Mrs. Quantrill both thought the sexton's last name was Scalley. Louisville city directories for 1866–85 and the 1870 and 1880 federal census for Jefferson County, Kentucky, show it to be Shelly or Shelley. He was buried in the St. John's Cemetery, and the cemetery records give the last name as Shelly.

The women who claim to have visited Quantrill as he lay dying: "Quantrill and His Famous Command," *Confederate Veteran*, 279; KCS, May 23, 1926; Connelley, *Quantrill*, 481–82; Edwards, *Noted*, 437. A remark that Mrs. Cooper made to Mrs. Quantrill indicates that she visited her son after he left Wakefield's farm—Mrs. Quantrill to W. W. Scott, October 17, 1888 (KC-UKL). According to LC-J, May 13, 1888, a woman named Mrs. Brady also claimed she was with Quantrill when he died; his bedside must have been very crowded.

Quantrill's last days, death, and burial: LKDD, June 7, 1865; LKDJ, June 7, 1865; Scott's notes, Connelley, *Quantrill*, 35, n. 19.

Chapter 15: The Postwar Years

Chapter title is adapted from a statement Cole Younger made in his lecture, "What My Life Has Taught Me," 6. The original typescript—with Cole's handwritten corrections—is in the WHMC-C.

General Grenville Dodge is given command, finds the state has only begun to recover, and attempts to stamp out bushwhacking: OR, vol. 48, pt. 1, 329–330.

Southerners are banished: WJC, January 28 and February 11, 1865; LT, February 10, 1865; OR, vol. 48, pt. 2, 224; Settle, 30. The James Family Farm Museum, Kearney, Missouri, has in its collection the banishment order, dated January 29, 1865.

Examples of the depredations of bushwhackers: LT, January 6, 27, and March 3, 10, 1865; WJC, January 7 and March 4, 8, 1865.

The Yankees fight "bush-fiends" and the military's attempts to suppress the guerrillas: WJC, February 25, 1865; OR, vol. 48, pt. 1, 34, 643–45.

The guerrilla bands return, the CMS reacts, the *Tribune* approves: Lexington *Union* in LT, March 31, 1865; LT, April 7, 1865.

Two guerrillas ride into Smithville, the Bledsoe brothers, the Matlock brothers: LT, April 7, 28, 1865; WJC, April 29, 1865.

Colonel Harding is pleased, dozens of guerrillas killed in skirmishes and clashes, and the intelligence network identifies five large bands: OR, vol. 48, pt. 2, 286–87, 342–43, and 354–55.

Union officers feel the pressure building, Harding makes a suggestion, which General Dodge likes, but word of the new policy is slow to circulate: OR, vol. 48, pt. 2, 286–87, 337, 341–43, 352, 355–56, 371, 784, 838; *Ibid.*, pt. 1, 290–91, 293.

The guerrillas return from Texas under Dave Pool: OR, vol. 48, pt. 2, 337, 342, 352, 370–71; WJC, May 13, 1865. See also: Brownlee, 235; Castel, *Quantrill,* 217–18.

Clement's two dispatches: OR, vol. 48, pt. 2, 370, 408–9, 545, 599, 614.

Examples of rumors about Quantrill: OR, vol. 48, pt. 1, 1077, 1126; *Ibid.*, pt. 2, 337, 472; LT, May 26 and December 8, 1865.

Dave Pool surrenders: LT, May 26, 1865; OR, vol. 48, pt. 2, 470, 545, 599, 705.

Ol Sheperd demands special terms, then surrenders, and is arrested: LT, June 9 and July 28, 1865.

Dave Pool turns up forty men, Clement and Anderson: OR, vol. 48, pt. 2, 705–6, 785, 837–38, 848, 872; Brownlee, 240.

Frank James and the others surrender, but Jesse is ambushed: Settle, 29–31; Connelley, *Quantrill,* 478–79. The James Family Farm Museum has a page from the "Roll of Confederate Soldiers Tak[ing] Amnesty," which lists private Jesse James (#86) as having surrendered at Lexington on May 21, 1865. However, James might not have been present; his name may have been on a list prepared in advance of those who would be surrendering.

The quotation on the future is from the LT, June 2, 1865.

Issues for the citizens to ponder: LT, June 2, 1865; LT, March 16, 23, 1866; Lexington Weekly *Missouri Valley Register,* October 25, 1866.

Examples of crimes and lynchings: LT, May 26 and June 9, 16, 23, and September 1 and November 17, 1865; LT, February 16 and July 27, 1866.

There was much to be bitter about, Radicals seize all levels of government, demobilization of the army, Unionists form strong armed bands, and some Confederates give up or ride the outlaw trail: Fellman, *Inside War,* 231–42; Lexington, Missouri, *Express* in LT, October 13, 1865; Lizzie Gregg in Missouri Division, 27–30.

Order No. 11 evacuees return, the Drake Constitution and the persecution of Southerners: Younger, *Story,* 53–56; Lexington, Kentucky, *Gazette,* July 28, 1865; Thomas S. Barclay, "The Test Oath for the Clergy in Missouri," 345–380; Howard L. Conard, *Encyclopedia of the History of Missouri,* vol. 2, 313, 315; *Ibid.*, vol. 5, 1–2; *Journal of the Missouri State Convention,*

20–24, 258–62; *The Old Settlers' History of Bates County, Missouri,* 43; Atkeson, 318–19; *History and Directory of Cass County,* 128–29.

Conditions gradually improve: Fellman, 242–47.

Kate King: Kansas City *Journal,* March 24, 1881; KCS, May 23, 1926; KCT, February 5, 6, 7, 1930; Topeka *Capital,* February 5, 1930; Fletch Taylor's letter to W. W. Scott, May 4, 1879 (KC-UKL); Adrienne Tinker Christopher, "Kate King Clarke—Quantrill's Forgotten Girl Bride," 21–22.

Jim Lane: Connelley, *James Henry Lane,* 122–24; Albert Castel, "Jim Lane of Kansas," 28; Letter of Samuel C. Smith to Charles Robinson, August 5, 1866 (Robinson Collection, KSHS); LT, July 6, 1866; Louisville *Courier* in Lexington, Kentucky, *Gazette,* July 14, 1866; Speer, *Lane,* 313–16; Stephenson, 159.

Bingham and Ewing: Larkin, 233–38, 241–42, 244–63, 276, 287–89, 292–93, 299–300, 307–11, 314–29; Taylor, 190, 193–96, 288, 293–95, 310, 323–25, 333; C. B. Rollins, "Some Recollections of George Caleb Bingham," 480–81; DMR, February 21, 26, 1877; CMS, January 1, 1869. See also a pamphlet titled, "An Address by George Caleb Bingham," 11–14, SHSM-C.

Arch Clement: Weekly Lexington *Missouri Valley Register,* December 20, 1866; LT, December 21, 1866. There are two eyewitness accounts of the ambush in the Denver Public Library: G. N. Moses, "The Killing of Archie B. Clements," 1–8, #85; "Statement of Captain J. M. Turley," 1–9, #41. See also: Brownlee, 242–43. There is a reference to Dave Pool's public carousing in the *Register,* December 27, 1866.

General Blunt: biographical note to James G. Blunt's "General Blunt's Account," 211, n. 1; obituaries in the following Washington, DC, newspapers: *Evening Star,* July 28, 1881, and *The Washington Post,* July 28, 1881. Since Blunt was a physician, it sometimes has been claimed that he was a resident on the staff of the asylum, not a patient. However, in addition to the two obituaries cited above, which state he was confined in St. Elizabeth's, the asylum's patient and personnel records are in the collections of the NA; they show (1) that he was never on the staff and (2) that he was admitted as a patient and died in confinement.

Charles Jennison: Starr, 333–36, 358–62, 364–69, 377, 380–81, 384–85; *Journal of Commerce* in LT, November 8, 1867; Connelley's "Jennison" (an interview with Jennison's widow, Mary Hopkins Jennison), 1–5 (KC-UKL). The C. R. Jennison Scrapbooks, two volumes, are in the KSHS.

William H. Gregg: I have put together the story of his later years from typescripts of the following letters he wrote to Connelley: September 3 and December 8, 1903; February 18 and December 2, 1904; April 30 and May 13, 1906; June 28, 30, and August 14, 1909; July 14, 1916. (These letters are in the KC-UKL.) I also used B. James George, Sr., *Captain William Henry Gregg,* and the biographical note attached to Gregg's *Little* (WHMC-C).

Edwin Terrell: When I began researching this book, little was known about Terrell's life after the war, and his death was a much speculated upon mystery. Therefore, I will depart from the way in which I have annotated material on the later lives of people who were connected to the Quantrill story and identify sources for each incident in Terrell's last years.

Terrell charged with murdering four men, and one victim was William Johnson: LKDJ, September 21, 1865, and May 2, 1866; Shinnick, 71–73; LC-J, December 14, 1868; LKDD, December 14, 1868.

Terrell and Thompson nearly escape and are tried: LKDJ, September 21, 1865; Shinnick, 72.

Terrell and Wethers transferred to the Taylorsville jail, are broken out: LKDJ, April 16, 1866.

Note: Once freed, Terrell and Wethers let it be known they would hunt down the jurors who voted to convict them, and Terrell later visited Mt. Eden, where he bragged that he could not be captured—LKDJ, April 23 and May 2, 1866. See also LKDJ, May 7, 1866.

The Shelbyville fight, Terrell is taken to Louisville, operated on, and believed dying: LKDJ, May 28, 1866; *Gazette,* September 1, 1866; LO&R, June 2, 1866; Franklin *Commonwealth,* May 29, 1866.

Dr. Knight announces that Terrell will recover: LKDJ, May 29, 1866. Incidentally, Wethers was captured on May 29 near Shelbyville—LKDJ, May 31, 1866.

Terrell and Thompson are returned to Shelbyville, and Thompson escapes: LKDJ, September 26, October 25, and November 2, 1866.

Terrell is never tried and is released: Shinnick, 73.

Terrell returns to Louisville, is visited by a friend, operated upon, and dies: LC-J, December 14, 15, 1868; LKDD, December 14, 1868; Louisville death registry records, book 2, 137, entry #98.

Terrell is buried, his "brother" appears, and Terrell family records: Louisville death registry records, *Ibid.;* LC-J, December 23, 26, 1868; Terrell family records were supplied to me by Cathy Barton Para. References in Terrell's letter to Fairleigh, January 6, 1865, and the LC-J, December 14, 1868, all clearly show the family resided in Kentucky, not Missouri.

Jesse James makes a slow recovery in Nebraska, returns to Missouri, is nursed by his cousin Zee, and he and Frank are not a special target of persecution: Settle, 31–32.

Cole Younger returns to Missouri, is persecuted, and goes into hiding: Younger, *Story,* 53–57.

Liberty Bank robbery: LT, February 16, 23, and March 2, 1866; Settle, 33–34, 36; Younger, *Story,* 56.

The Lexington and Savannah banks: the Lexington *Caucasian* in DMR, November 3, 1866; LT, March 8, 1867; Settle, 34.

Hughes and Wasson Bank: Richmond, Missouri, *Conservator,* May 24, 1867; Settle, 35–37.

The lynching of Felix Bradley: Richmond, Missouri, *Conservator,* June 1, 1867.

Lynching of Thomas Little: Warrensburg, Missouri, Weekly *Journal,* June 5, 19, 1867.

The lynching of McGuire and Devers: Tri-weekly *Missouri Republican,* March 20, 1868; Richmond, Missouri, *Conservator,* March 21, 1868; Tri-Weekly *Missouri Democrat,* March 23, 1868.

N. Long and Company Bank: DMR, March 23, 26, 1868.

Detective Bligh: Settle, 37–38.

The Gallatin bank robbery: Settle, 38–40.

The Ocobock Brothers: Settle, 43.

The James brothers hide out under assumed names, and their personal lives: Settle, 69–70, 91–92, 129, 132, 165.

Cole's romantic entanglements: Younger, *Story,* 55, 72–73; Glenn Shirley, *Belle Starr,* 66–73; Burton Rascoe, *Belle Starr,* "The Bandit Queen," 119.

Pinkerton agents: Settle, 59–61, 76–77, 85–86; the Pinkerton letter is in the collection of the James Family Farm Museum.

The Northfield robbery and the pursuit and capture: Settle, 92–94. Robertus Love, *The Rise and Fall of Jesse James,* 196, 199, 202–3, 205, 208–10, 212–13, 218–21, 226–27, 234–37; Younger, *Story,* 87, 89.

Cole, otherwise known as prisoner 699: Younger, *Story,* 112–14; W. C. Heilbron, *Convict Life at the Minnesota State Prison,* 7–8, 12–19. Heilbron includes as a supplement an essay by Cole Younger, "Real Facts About the Northfield, Minnesota, Bank Robbery," which contains some information about his confinement, 125, 147.

The reward, the assassination, Frank surrenders and is tried in Missouri: Settle, 110, 117, 119, 131, 134–35, 137–39, 140, 142–44.

Frank James's arrest and trial in Alabama and the aborted attempt to prosecute him again in Missouri: Settle, 149–50, 152–53, 157.

Frank's employment and theatrical career: Settle, 163–64; Love, 424.

Bob Younger dies, Cole and Jim are paroled, are employed, Jim commits suicide, and Cole is pardoned: Younger, *Story,* 99–105; Love, 415–16; Settle, 162–64; Bronaugh, 291–99.

The James-Younger Wild West Show: Younger, 105–6; Bronaugh, 299–305; Love, 423–24; Settle, 164.

The Greater Lew Nichols and Cole Younger Shows and Anderson's funeral: articles and an advertisement in the *Richmond Missourian,* June 4, 11, 1908; E. L. Pigg, "Belated Funeral of 'Bloody Bill' Anderson," 48–49.

Last years and death of Frank James: Settle, 164–65. There still exists a picture postcard that was sold by Frank to tourists in which he is shown posed at the farm's front gate; a sign giving the cost of a tour is quite legible.

Cole's last years and death: Minneapolis, Minnesota, *Journal,* March 19, 1916; Topeka *State Journal,* March 22, 1916. I have also used an unidentified obituary in the JCHS. Cole's remark about the bullets is from his essay in Heilbron, 146–47.

I have my own collection of newspaper and magazine articles reporting the various claims that Quantrill did not die in 1865. The QSB comprise the best single source for such newspaper clippings, particularly volume 1.

John Sharp: Jon McDermott, "Mystery Man of Quatsino Sound," 14–16, 63; Lawrence Daily *Journal,* August 9, 10, 12, 13, 1907; KCJ, August 17, 1907. See also T. W. Paterson, "Quantrill Is Not Dead," 10–11, 54–56.

EPILOGUE: THE BIZARRE HISTORY OF QUANTRILL'S REMAINS

Chapter title is adapted from sentence in a letter W. W. Scott wrote to Major Franklin Adams, December 17, 1887 (KSHS).

Caroline Quantrill: LC-J, May 13, 1888; KCJ, May 12, 1888; Scott's notes on Mrs. Quantrill and the letter of Frances Thompson, Connelley, *Quantrill,* 33–34, n. 15–17 and text, 30.

Thomas goes to Kansas and western Missouri, and W. W. Scott does research for a book: letters to W. W. Scott from Fletch Taylor, May 4, 1879, and John S. Beeson, November 27, 1878 (KC-UKL); KCT, November 2, 1881, in Connelley, *Ibid.,* 30, n. 10–11; Scott's letter to Major Adams, September 1, 1888 (KSHS).

Scott's trips to Louisville: his notes in Connelley, 35–36, n. 19.

The travels and activities of Mrs. Quantrill, Thomas, and Scott during the years 1887–90 can be traced through their correspondence in the KSHS. Mrs. Quantrill to Scott: January 7, February 19, March 18, 29, April 11, 16, 22, 27, May 20, June 5, July 1, September 20, October 17, 1888; February 3, 22, March 5, 1889. Thomas to his mother: February 18, 1888. Thomas to Scott: March 24 and April 23, 1888. Scott to Mrs. Quantrill: September 22, 1888; January 29 and February 6, 1889.

Scott's attempts to sell the skull: his letters to Adams, December 17 and (n.d.) 1887, and May 8 and September 1, 1888; letter from James B. Abbott to Adams, May 10, 1888. George A. Root, "In Re Quantrill's Bones," August 28, 1912, a one-page typescript. The QSB (vol. 2, 71–76) has newspaper articles describing Scott's visit to Kansas. All the above letters and documents are in KSHS.

See below note on the bones in KSHS: photocopies of Dr. Finnegan's laboratory notes, dated December 18, 1974; September 7, 1992, letter of Roy R. Peterson to Thomas A. Witty, Jr. (UBSPB papers, KSHS); Randall M. Thies, "Skeletons in the Closet: Human Remains Accessioned by the Kansas State Historical Society," 3–4.

Mrs. Quantrill remains in Missouri, adopts a Southern point of view, and rails against her daughter-in-law, Scott, and the gossips of Dover: see her letters to Scott dated July 1 and October 17, 1888, and February 3, 22, and March 5, 1889.

Mrs. Quantrill visits Blue Springs, and a reception is held in her honor: KCJ, May 12, 1888; Paul I. Wellman, "She Remembers When Quantrill's Mother Came to Blue Springs," KCS, August 30, 1942, in QSB, vol. 4, 14–16.

Mrs. Quantrill visits Mrs. Cooper: Mrs. Quantrill's letter to Scott, October 17, 1888.

Mrs. Quantrill returns to Dover: Samuel C. Ream, "Treatise on the Skull of William Clarke Quantrill," 14.

Thomas Quantrill's last letter is in the KC-UKL.

Mrs. Quantrill's injury and final decline into poverty: *National Tribune,* December 10, 1903; Lexington, Kentucky, *Morning Herald,* March 27, 1898; "The ODD Fellows," an otherwise unidentified *Missouri Democrat* clipping in Denver #42; Connelley, *Quantrill,* 39–40; the DHS has an undated letter Mrs. Quantrill wrote in the hospital to Mr. C. C. [Perakirk?].

Mrs. Quantrill's last letter, the death of W. W. Scott, the letter of his widow, and the deal she made with Connelley: Mrs. Quantrill's letter of April 29, 1901 (there is no salutation), KC-UKL; Mrs. Scott's letter of December 10, 1903, to George Martin (KSHS); "Tribute to W. W. Scott," *Iron Valley Reporter,* November 20, 1902, Connelley papers, KSHS; Carl Breihan, "Quantrill's Bones Are Moving," 64; Root, "In Re."

Connelley tries to swap the bones, and Mrs. Quantrill dies: George Hart, "The Quest for Quantrill's Bones," 26; *National Tribune,* December 10, 1903; KCJ, November 24, 1903.

George W. Martin's announcement, the uproar that follows, Martin is not cowed, the bones go on display: KCS, November 26, 30, 1903; KCJ,

December 3, 1903; George W. Martin, "Secretary's Report to the Annual Meeting," 124; Edgar Langsdorf, "The First Hundred Years of the Kansas State Historical Society," 323–24; two letters Martin wrote to W. W. Scott, November 8, 14, 1901; Martin's letter to Mrs. Scott, December 4, 1903; Scott's letter to Martin, November 11, 1901; Mrs. Scott's letter to Martin, December 10, 1903. All the letters are in KSHS.

The bones in the display case, the wicked satire, the clerks are sick of the bones, and the bones are stored in the laboratory: a photograph of the display case is in KSHS, #FK2.7 Hi.Mu * 77; *Farmers Mail and Breeze,* August 17, 1907; KCJ, January 24, 1910; Edward Knowles, "The Bartered Bones of William Quantrill," 20.

The D.J.S Club and the fraternity ritual: Samuel C. Ream and Marian E. Karpisek, "Quantrill's Skull," 38; Ream, "Treatise," 19–22. In 1972, Ream, a trustee and past president of the DHS, took a series of sworn affidavits from former members of the fraternity and others who had knowledge of it and of the story of the skull; these are on file at the DHS.

The Oak Hill Cemetery: Cathy Ambler, "Oak Hill Cemetery and the Rural Cemetery Movement," 46–53, 55–57, 62–70; LKT, November 16, 1865.

Decoration Day, 1870: Lawrence *Republican Daily Journal,* May 29 and June 1, 1870; LKT, May 29 and June 1, 2, 1870. No date for a formal dedication of the cemetery has ever been identified. One might pick various dates for the "opening" of the cemetery—the day the land was bought or the cemetery plotted, or the first body buried—but it is obvious from newspaper articles that there was great effort made on the part of Lawrencians to make the ceremonies for Decoration Day, 1870, (which was the first time the holiday had been celebrated in Lawrence) very special, and the June 1st *Republican* compares the ceremonies to the "opening" or "consecration" of various other named cemeteries.

The first annual meeting of survivors: Topeka Daily *Capital,* August 23, 25, 1891; Lawrence Daily *Journal,* August 21, 24, 1891.

The Douglas County Historical Society collection, RHMS 84:2:16, contains documents on the efforts to raise money and to design the raid martyrs' monument (KC-UKL).

The ex-bushwhackers at first don't have reunions, first annual reunion: Brownlee, 245; Kansas City *World,* September 11, 1898; KCS, September 11, 1898; the Oak Grove, Missouri, *Banner,* October 9, 1959.

Donald Hale has a collection of articles about the reunions, which he shared with me. I have collected additional articles from the Quantrill scrapbooks (KSHS), the JCHS, and microfilm rolls of western Missouri newspapers. Space limitations preclude my documenting every detail, but the most important aspects of the reunion story come from the following:

Lizzie Wallace: KCT, September 20, 1967; KCS, September 17, 1967, and "She Opens Her Home Each Year for Reunion of Quantrell's Famous Band to Pay Old Debt of Gratitude," unidentified clipping, JCHS.

Frank James supports Roosevelt, and the ex-guerrilla who regretted not burning the whole town: KCJ, August 21, 1904, in Denver #53; KCS, August 26, 30, 1905; Topeka *Capital,* August 31 and September 1, 1905. See also three partially identified clippings in JCHS: "To Locate Survivors," August 31, 1905; "And Proud of Quantrell," August 25, 1905; "Forgiving Guerrillas," August 27, 1905.

Campaign hoax: KCJ, October 17, 18, 1906; KCS, October 17, 1906.

The 1907 reunion: KCJ, August 23, 1907; Oak Grove *Banner,* August 30, 1907.

The 1929 reunion, and the 1930 reunion is canceled: KCS, August 29 and September 1, 1929; Independence *Examiner,* August 21, 1930.

Frank Smith: KCS, March 4, 1932.

Dark Command premier: Lawrence Daily *Journal World,* April 3, 4, 5, 6, 1940; KCS, March 29 and April 5, 1940. The staff of the Lawrence Public Library supplied me with copies of other clippings from the library's vertical file.

Franklin's daughters, and Mark Dugan places a marker: I interviewed a number of Doverites who knew them; the Dover–New Philadelphia *Times Reporter,* March 2 and October 19, 1982.

Information concerning the struggle over the burying of the bones and skull, the two funerals, the cemeteries, and the current status of the wax head comes from my own observations and my interviews with: Robert L. Hawkins, III; Randy Thies; James Keown; Father Hugh Behan; Chris Edwards; Cris Nixon; and Linda Harper. In addition, Randy Thies, in his role as case investigator for the UBSPB, has established and maintains thick files of correspondence, clippings, and documents related to the bones and the bones story, UBS cases #1991-20 and 1992-2; he kindly allowed me access to this material.

Select Bibliography

Allison, Young E. "Sue Mundy." *Register of the Kentucky Historical Society,* 57 (October 1959): 295–316.

Ambler, Cathy. "The Oak Hill Cemetery and the Rural Cemetery Movement." Typescript. Bound. 140 pages. 1990. Kansas Collection, University of Kansas Libraries, University of Kansas at Lawrence.

"An Act to Organize Bands of Partisan Rangers." *Public Laws of the Confederate States of America,* First Congress of 1862. Richmond, Va.: R. M. Smith, 1862.

Andreas, A. T. *History of the State of Kansas.* Chicago: A. T. Andreas, 1883.

Asbury, Virginia Hays. "An Anomaly of Written History." *Confederate Veteran,* vol. 22 (March 1914): 138.

Atkeson, W. O. *History of Bates County, Missouri.* Topeka, Kans.: Historical Publishing Company, 1918.

Bailey, L. D., et al. *Quantrell's Raid on Lawrence.* Lyndon, Kans.: C. R. Green, 1899.

Ballads and Folksongs Collected by the Missouri Folk-Lore Society. Columbia: University of Missouri, 1940.

Barclay, Thomas S. "The Test Oath for the Clergy in Missouri." *Missouri Historical Review,* 18 (April 1924): 345–80.

Barnes, Lela, ed. "An Editor Looks at Early-Day Kansas: the Letters of Charles Monroe Chase." *Kansas Historical Quarterly,* 26 (Summer 1960): 113–151.

Barry, Louise. "The Emigrant Aid Company Parties of 1854." *Kansas Historical Quarterly,* 12 (May 1943): 115–55.

Barton, O. S. *Three Years With Quantrill: A True Story Told by His Scout John McCorkle* (1914). Norman, Okla.: University of Oklahoma Press, 1992.

Biennial Report of the Auditor of the State and Register of State Land Office. The sixth, seventh, and eighth reports. Topeka, Kans.: Kansas Publishing House, 1888, 1890–91.

Biographical Cyclopaedia and Portrait Gallery, Ohio volume. Cincinnati, Oh.: Western Biographical Publisher, 1883–95.

Bissell, Sophia L. " 'See those men! They have no flag!' " *American Heritage,* 11 (October 1960): 25.

Blair, Ed. *History of Johnson County, Kansas.* Lawrence, Kans.: Standard Publishing Co., 1915.

Blunt, General James G. "General Blunt's Account of His Civil War Experiences." *Kansas Historical Quarterly,* 1 (May 1932): 211–65.

Boughton, J. S. *The Lawrence Massacre.* Lawrence, Kans.: J. S. Boughton, 1884.

Brant, Marley. *The Outlaw Youngers: A Confederate Brotherhood.* Lanham, Md.: Madison Books, 1972.

Breihan, Carl. "Quantrill's Bones Are Moving." *Westerner,* 5 (January–February, 1973): 40–41, 62, 64.

Brewerton, G. Douglas. *The War in Kansas* (1856). Freeport, N.Y.: Books for Libraries Press, 1971.

Britton, Wiley. *The Civil War on the Border* (2 vols). New York: G. P. Putnam's Sons, 1899.

———. *The Union Indian Brigade.* Kansas City, Mo.: Franklin Hudson Publishing Company, 1922.

Bronaugh, W. C. *The Youngers' Fight for Freedom.* Columbia, Mo.: E. W. Stephens Publishing Company, 1906.

Brown, A. Theodore. *Frontier Community: Kansas to 1870.* Columbia, Mo.: University of Missouri Press, 1963.

Brown, Dee Alexander. *The Bold Cavaliers: Morgan's 2nd Kentucky Cavalry Raiders.* Philadelphia: J. B. Lippincott, 1959.

Brownlee, Richard S. *Gray Ghosts of the Confederacy: Guerrilla Warfare in the West, 1861–1865.* Baton Rouge, La.: Louisiana State University Press, 1958.

Byron, George Gordon. *The Complete Poetical Works of Byron.* Boston: Houghton Mifflin Company, 1905.

Castel, Albert. *A Frontier State at War: Kansas 1861–1865* (1958). Lawrence, Kans.: Kansas Heritage Press, 1958.

———. *General Sterling Price.* Baton Rouge, La.: Louisiana State University Press, 1992.

———. "Jim Lane of Kansas." *Civil War Times,* 12 (April 1973): 22–28.

———. "Order No. 11 and the Civil War on the Border." *Missouri Historical Review,* vol. 57 (1963): 357–68.

———. "Quantrill's Bushwhackers: A Case Study in Partisan Warfare." *Civil War History,* 13 (March 1967): 40–50.

————. *William Clarke Quantrill: His Life and Times.* New York: Frederick Fell, Inc., 1962.

Christopher, Adrienne Tinker. "Kate King Clarke—Quantrill's Forgotten Girl Bride." *Westport Historical Quarterly,* 4 (June 1968): 21–22.

Clark, Thomas D. *A History of Kentucky.* Lexington, Ky.: The John Bradford Press, 1954.

Clarke, Henry S. *Incidents of Quantrell's Raid on Lawrence, August 21, 1863.* An interview by S. W. Brewster. Lawrence, Kans.: Jeffersonian Printer, 1898.

————. "W. C. Quantrill in 1858." *Transactions of the Kansas State Historical Society,* 7 (1901–2): 218–23.

Collins, Lewis and Richard H. Collins. *History of Kentucky* (1874) (2 vols.) Frankfort, Ky.: Kentucky Historical Society, 1966.

Conard, Howard L. *Encyclopedia of the History of Missouri,* vols. 2 and 5. St. Louis, Mo.: Southern History Company, 1901.

Congleton, Betty Carolyn. "George D. Prentice: Nineteenth Century Editor." *Register of the Kentucky Historical Society,* 65 (1967): 94–119.

Connelley, William E. "Additional to Disintegration of Quantrill's Band." Typescript. Three pages. Connelley papers, Kansas State Historical Society.

————. *History of Kentucky,* vols. 2 and 4. Chicago: The American Historical Society, 1922.

————. "Interview with Cyrus Leland, Jr." Typescript. Four pages. Denver, Colo.: Denver Public Library Western History Collection.

————. "Interview with John Koger." Typescript. 22 pages. Denver, Colo.: Denver Public Library Western History Collection.

————. "Interview with Morgan T. Mattox." Typescript. 40 pages. Denver, Colo.: Denver Public Library Western History Collection.

————. *James Henry Lane.* Topeka, Kans.: Crane & Company, 1899.

————. *The Life of Preston B. Plumb.* Chicago: Browne & Howell Company, 1913.

————. *Quantrill and the Border Wars* (1910). New York: Pageant Book Co., 1956.

————. "Quantrill at Baxter Springs." An interview with William H. Gregg. Typescript. Six pages. Connelley papers, Kansas State Historical Society.

————. "Yesterday, Monday, November 4, 1907. . . ." An interview with S. S. Herd. Typescript. 12 pages. Connelley papers, Kansas State Historical Society.

Cordley, Richard. *A History of Lawrence, Kansas.* Lawrence, Kans.: Lawrence Journal Press, 1895.

——. "The Lawrence Massacre." *The Congregational Record,* 5 (September and October 1863): 98–115. Reproduced under the title *Pastor Richard Cordley's Account of Quantrill's Raid* with an Introduction and Postscript by Richard B. Sheridan. Typescript. 27 pages.

——. *Pioneer Days in Kansas.* New York: The Pilgrim Press, 1903.

Davis, William C. *The Orphan Brigade: The Kentucky Confederates Who Couldn't Go Home.* Baton Rouge, La.: Louisiana State University Press, 1980.

Dictionary of American Biography, vol. 3. New York: Scribner's, 1964.

Dobak, William A. "Civil War on the Kansas-Missouri Border: The Narrative of Former Slave Andrew Williams," in Napier, Rita, *History of the Peoples of Kansas.*

Doy, John. *The Narrative of John Doy of Lawrence.* New York: N.p., 1860.

Duke, Basil W. *A History of Morgan's Cavalry.* Bloomington: Indiana University Press, 1960.

Eaton, James W. *A Very Dear Place: The History of Dover, Ohio, 1807–1982.* Typescript. 24 pages. Dover, Oh.: Dover Historical Society.

Edwards, Jennie, comp. *John N. Edwards Biography, Memoirs, Reminiscences and Recollections.* Kansas City, Mo.: Jennie Edwards, 1889.

Edwards, John N. *Noted Guerrillas, or The Warfare of the Border* (1877). Dayton, Oh.: Morningside Bookshop, 1976.

——. *Shelby and His Men.* Cincinnati, Oh.: Miami Printing Company, 1867.

Eldridge, Shalor Winchell. *Recollections of Early Days in Kansas.* Topeka, Kans.: Kansas State Historical Society, 1920.

Elliot, R. G. "The Quantrill Raid as Seen from the Eldridge House," in Eldridge, Shalor Winchell, *Recollections of Early Days in Kansas.*

"Emily Steele's Letter Tells of Pillage." *Jackson County Historical Society Journal* (Fall 1980): 6–7, 11.

Federal Writers' Project of Kentucky, Work Projects Administration. *Military History of Kentucky.* Frankfort, Ky.: The State Journal, 1939.

Federal Writers' Project of Ohio, Work Projects Administration. *Guide to Tuscarawas County.* New Philadelphia, Oh.: New Philadelphia Chamber of Commerce, 1939.

Fellman, Michael. *Inside War: The Guerrilla Conflict in Missouri During the American Civil War.* New York: Oxford University Press, 1989.

———. "Inside Wars: the Cultural Crisis of Warfare and the Values of Ordinary People." *The Australasian Journal of American Studies,* 10 (December, 1991): 1–9.

———. "Rehearsal for the Civil War: Antislavery and Proslavery at the Fighting Point in Kansas, 1854–56," in Perry, Lewis and Michael Fellman, eds., *Antislavery Reconsidered.*

Fischer, LeRoy H. and Lary C. Rampp. "Quantrill's Civil War Operations in Indian Territory." *The Chronicles of Oklahoma,* 41 (Summer 1968): 155–82.

Fisher, H. D. *The Gun and the Gospel.* Chicago: Medical Century Co., 1899.

Forster, Greg. "Sherman's Feuding Generals." *Civil War Times Illustrated,* 34 (March/April 1995): 40–45, 70–75.

Furniss, Norman F. *The Mormon Conflict 1850–1859.* New Haven, Conn.: Yale University Press, 1960.

Fyfer, J. Thomas. *History of Boone County, Missouri.* St. Louis: Western Historical Company, 1882.

Gardner, Theodore. "An Episode in Kansas History: The Doy Rescue." *Kansas Historical Collections,* 17 (1926–28): 851–55.

Garwood, Darrell. *Crossroads of America: The Story of Kansas City.* New York: W. W. Norton, 1948.

George, B. James. *Captain William Henry Gregg, Confederate and Quantrillian.* N.p.: B. James George, 1973.

Gihon, John H. *Geary and Kansas.* Philadelphia: Charles C. Rhodes, 1857.

Gladstone, T. H. *The Englishman in Kansas* (1857). Lincoln, Nebr.: University of Nebraska Press, 1971.

Goodman, Thomas M. *Sergeant Thomas M. Goodman's Thrilling Record* (1868). Maryville, Mo.: Rush Printing Company, 1960.

Green, Charles R. *Early Days in Kansas* (2 vols.). Olathe, Kans.: Charles R. Green, 1912.

Gregg, William H. "The Lawrence Raid." Typescript. 5 pages. Topeka, Kans.: Kansas State Historical Society.

———. *A Little Dab of History Without Embelishment* [*sic*]. Handwritten. 126 pages. Columbia, Mo.: Western Historical Manuscript Collection—Columbia.

Griffith, G.W.E. *My 96 Years in the Great West.* Los Angeles, California: N.p. 1929.

Hale, Donald R. *They Called Him Bloody Bill.* Clinton, Mo.: The Printery, 1975.

———. *We Rode with Quantrill.* N.p.: Donald R. Hale, 1982.

—— and Joanne C. Eakin, comp. *Branded as Rebels*. Independence, Mo.: Wee Print, 1993.

Harrison, Lowell H. *The Civil War in Kentucky*. Lexington, Ky.: The University Press of Kentucky, 1975.

Hart, George. "The Quest for Quantrill's Bones." *Real West*, 15 (May 1972): 24–26.

Heilbron, W. C. *Convict Life at the Minnesota State Prison*. St. Paul, Minn.: W. C. Heilbron, 1909.

Herd, Sidney S. "Always Under an Alias, and Without Visible Means of Support." *Transactions of the Kansas State Historical Society*, 7 (1901–2): 226–28.

Herklotz, Hildegarde R. "Jayhawkers in Missouri, 1858–1863," pt. 1. *Missouri Historical Review*, 17 (April 1923): 266–84.

——. "Jayhawkers in Missouri, 1858–1863," pt. 2. *Missouri Historical Review*, 17 (July 1923): 505–13.

——. "Jayhawkers in Missouri, 1858–1863," pt. 3. *Missouri Historical Review*, 18 (October 1923): 64–101.

Hickman, W. Z. *History of Jackson County, Missouri*. Topeka, Kans.: Historical Publishing Company, 1920.

History and Directory of Cass County, Missouri. Harrisonville, Mo.: Cass County *Leader*, 1908.

History of Buchanan County, Missouri. St. Joseph, Mo.: St. Joseph Steam Printing Company, 1881.

History of Carroll County, Missouri. St. Louis: Missouri Historical Company, 1881.

History of Clay and Platte Counties, Missouri. St. Louis, Mo.: National Historical Company, 1885.

History of Howard and Chariton Counties, Missouri. St. Louis, Mo.: National Historical Companies, 1883.

History of Jackson County, Missouri (1881). Cape Girardeau, Mo.: Ramfire Press, 1966.

History of Lafayette County, Missouri. St. Louis, Mo.: Missouri Historical Company, 1881.

History of Ray County, Missouri. St. Louis, Mo.: Missouri Historical Company, 1881.

History of Saint Charles, Montgomery, and Warren Counties, Missouri. St. Louis, Mo.: National Historical Company, 1883.

Horn, Stanley F. *The Army of Tennessee*. Norman, Okla.: University of Oklahoma Press, 1941.

Hubbard, D. "Reminiscences of the Yeager Raid, on the Santa Fe Trail, in 1863." *Transactions of the Kansas State Historical Society,* 8 (1903–4): 168–71.

Isern, Thomas D. and Mark D. Weeks. " 'Quantrill's Raid on Lawrence.' " *Mid-America Folklore,* 14 (Fall 1986): 1–11.

Johnson, Allen, ed. *Dictionary of American Biography.* New York: Charles Scribner's Sons, 1929.

Johnson, L. F. *Famous Kentucky Tragedies and Trials.* Lexington, Ky.: Henry Clay Press, 1972.

Johnson, Robert U. and C. C. Buel, eds. *Battles and Leaders of the Civil War* (4 vols.). New York: The Century Company, 1884–88.

Johnson, W. A. "Early Life of Quantrill in Kansas." *Transactions of the Kansas State Historical Society,* 7 (1901–2): 212–14.

Journal of the Missouri State Convention, January–April 1865. St. Louis, Mo.: *Missouri Democrat,* 1865.

Kargau, E. D. "Missouri's German Immigration." *Missouri Historical Society Collections,* 2 (January 1900): 23–34.

Kirkpatrick, Arthur Roy. "Missouri in the Early Months of the Civil War." *Missouri Historical Review,* 55 (April 1961): 235–66.

Klein, Philip Shriver. *President James Buchanan.* University Park, Pa.: Pennsylvania State University Press, 1962.

Knowles, Edward. "The Bartered Bones of William Quantrill." *True West,* 15 (September–October 1967): 20–21, 48.

Langsdorf, Edgar. "The First Hundred Years of the Kansas State Historical Society." *Kansas Historical Collections,* 41 (Autumn 1975): 265–425.

———. "Jim Lane and the Frontier Guard." *Kansas Historical Quarterly* (February 1940): 13–25.

Larkin, Lew. *Bingham: Fighting Artist.* St. Louis, Mo.: State Publishing Co., 1955.

Lewis, Lloyd. "Propaganda and the Kansas-Missouri War." *Missouri Historical Review,* 34 (October 1939): 3–17.

Lomax, John Avery. *Cowboy Songs and Other Frontier Ballads.* New York: The Macmillan Company, 1938.

Love, Robertus. *The Rise and Fall of Jesse James.* New York: G. P. Putnam's Sons, 1926.

Lowman, H. E. *Narrative of the Lawrence Massacre.* Lawrence, Kans.: Journal Press, 1864.

Lowry, Thomas P. *The Story the Soldiers Wouldn't Tell: Sex in the Civil War.* Mechanicsburg, Pa.: Stackpole Books, 1994.

Lutz, John J. "Quantrill and the Morgan Walker Tragedy." *Kansas Historical Collections,* 8 (1904): 324–31.

"Lydia Stevens Thomas." *The Club Member,* 5 (May 1907): 4–5.

Lyon, William H. "Claiborne Fox Jackson and the Secession Crisis." *Missouri Historical Review,* 58 (July 1964): 422–41.

McDermott, Jon. "Mystery Man of Quatsino Sound." *American West,* 10 (March 1973): 13–16, 63.

McDowell, Robert Emmett. *City of Conflict.* Louisville, Ky.: Louisville Civil War Round Table Publishers, 1962.

McLarty, Vivian K., ed. "The Civil War Letters of Colonel Bazel Lazear," pt. 2. *Missouri Historical Review,* 45 (July 1950): 387–401.

McLoughlin, Denis. *Wild and Woolly: An Encyclopedia of the Old West.* Garden City, N.Y.: Doubleday & Co., 1975.

McPherson, James M. *Battle Cry of Freedom.* New York: Oxford University Press, 1988.

———. *What They Fought For 1861–1865.* Baton Rouge, La.: Louisiana State University Press, 1994.

Magruder, Henry C. *Three Years in the Saddle.* Louisville, Ky.: Major Cyrus J. Wilson, 1865.

Malin, James C. *John Brown and the Legend of Fifty-six.* Philadelphia: The American Philosophical Society, 1942.

———. "The Proslavery Background of the Kansas Struggle." *Mississippi Valley Historical Review,* 10 (June 1923–March 1924): 285–305.

Malone, Dumas, ed. *Dictionary of American Biography,* vol. 15. New York: Charles Scribner's Sons, 1935.

Mansfield, J. B. *A History of Tuscarawas County.* Strasburg, Oh.: Gordon Publishing, 1975.

Martin, George W. "Memorial Monuments and Tablets in Kansas." *Kansas Historical Collections,* 11 (1909–10): 279–81.

———. "Secretary's Report to the Annual Meeting for Fiscal Year 1903." *Kansas Historical Collections,* 8 (1904): 118–26.

Miller, Randall M. and John David Smith. *Dictionary of Afro-American Slavery.* New York: Greenwood Press, 1988.

Mink, Charles R. "General Orders, No. 11: The Forced Evacuation of Civilians During the Civil War." *Military Affairs* (December 1970): 132–36.

Missouri Division, United Daughters of the Confederacy, comp. *Reminiscences of the Women of Missouri During the Sixties.* Jefferson City, Mo.: The Hugh Stephens Printing Co., (1913?).

Monaghan, Jay. *Civil War on the Western Border, 1854–1865.* Lincoln, Nebr.: University of Nebraska Press, 1984.

Morehouse, George Pierson. "Diamond Springs, 'The Diamond of the Plains.' " *Collections of the Kansas State Historical Society,* 14 (1915–18): 794–804.

Mudd, Joseph A. *With Porter in North Missouri* (1909). Iowa City, Ia.: Press of the Camp Pope Bookshop, 1992.

Napier, Rita. *History of the Peoples of Kansas: An Anthology.* Lawrence, Kans.: The University of Kansas, 1985.

Nichols, Alice. *Bleeding Kansas.* New York: Oxford University Press, 1954.

Nicolay, John G. and John Hay. *Abraham Lincoln: A History,* vol. 4. New York: The Century Co., 1909.

Niepman, Ann Davis. "General Orders No. 11 and Border Warfare During the Civil War." *Missouri Historical Review,* 66 (1971–72): 185–210.

Oates, Stephen B. *To Purge This Land with Blood: A Biography of John Brown.* Amherst: University of Massachusetts Press, 1984.

Office of the Quartermaster General 1815–1905. Reports of Persons & Articles Hired 1865, April and May reports, in the National Archives.

O'Flaherty, Daniel. *General Jo Shelby: Undefeated Rebel.* Chapel Hill: University of North Carolina Press, 1953.

The Old Settlers' History of Bates County, Missouri. Amsterdam, Mo.: Tathwell & Maxey, 1897.

Palmer, Henry E. "The Black-Flag Character of the War on the Border." *Transactions of the Kansas State Historical Society,* 9 (1905–6): 455–66.

Palmer, John M. *The Story of an Earnest Life.* Cincinnati, Oh.: The Robert Clarke Company, 1901.

Parish, William E. *Turbulent Partnership: Missouri and the Union.* Columbia, Mo.: University of Missouri Press, 1963.

Paterson, T. W. " 'Quantrill Is Not Dead; I Can Prove It' by John Sharp as reported by T. W. Paterson." *Real West,* 9 (July 1966): 10–11, 54–56.

Perry, Lewis and Michael Fellman, eds. *Antislavery Reconsidered: New Perspectives on the Abolitionists.* Baton Rouge, La.: Louisiana State University Press, 1979.

Phillips, William. *The Conquest of Kansas by Missouri and Her Allies.* Boston: Sampson & Co., 1856.

Piatt, John James. *The Poems of George D. Prentice Edited with a Bio-graphical Sketch by John James Piatt.* Cincinnati, Oh.: Robert Clarke & Co., 1876.

Pigg, E. L. "Belated Funeral of 'Bloody Bill' Anderson." *Frontier Times,* 30 (January 1953): 48–49.

Poll, Richard D. "The Move South." *Brigham Young Studies,* 29 (Fall 1989): 65–88.

Public Laws of the Confederate States of America. Fourth session of the First Congress, 1863–64. Richmond, Va.: R. M. Smith, 1864.

"Quantrell's Call." *Confederate Veteran,* 11 (April 1903): 158.

"Quantrell's Call." *Confederate Veteran,* 13 (November 1905): 518.

"Quantrell's Death Verified." *Confederate Veteran,* 19 (June 1911): 285.

"Quantrill and His Famous Command." *Confederate Veteran,* 18 (June 1910): 279.

Randolph, Vance, ed. *Ozark Folksongs,* vol. 4. Columbia, Mo.: University of Missouri Press, 1980.

Rascoe, Burton. *Belle Star, "The Bandit Queen."* New York: Random House, 1941.

Ream, Samuel C. "Treatise on the Skull of William Clarke Quantrill." Typescript. 25 pages. Dover, Oh.: Dover Historical Society.

—— and Marian E. Karpisek. "Quantrill's Skull." *Old West,* 17 (Summer 1981): 36–38.

Report of the Special Committee Appointed to Investigate the Troubles in Kansas. Washington (DC?): Cornelius Wendell, 1856.

Rice, Martin. *Rural Rhymes and Tales of Olden Times.* Kansas City, N.p.: Ramsey, Millett and Hudson, 1882.

Ridenour, Peter D. *The Autobiography of Peter D. Ridenour.* Kansas City, N.p.: Hudson Press, 1908.

Riggs, Henry Earle. *Our Pioneer Ancestors.* Ann Arbor, Mich.: Henry Earle Riggs, 1942.

Riggs, Samuel A. "An Outlaw When He Took to the Bush." *Transactions of the Kansas State Historical Society,* 7 (1901–2): 223–24.

Robinson, Charles. *The Kansas Conflict.* Lawrence, Kans.: Journal Publishing Co., 1898.

Robinson, Sara T. D. *Kansas: Its Interior and Exterior Life.* Lawrence, Kans.: Journal Publishing Co., 1899.

Rodemyre, Edgar T. *History of Centralia, Missouri.* Centralia, Mo.: Press of the Fireside Guard, 1936.

Rolle, Andrew. *John Charles Fremont.* Norman, Okla.: University of Oklahoma Press, 1919.

Rollins, C. B., ed. "Letters of George Caleb Bingham to James S. Rollins," pt. 5. *Missouri Historical Review,* 23 (October 1938): 45–78.

———. "Some Recollections of George Caleb Bingham." *Missouri Historical Review,* 20 (July 1926): 463–84.

Rosar, L. B. "Bullet Hole Ellis." *Westport Historical Quarterly,* 4 (June 1968): 12–15.

Schofield, John M. *Forty-Six Years in the Army.* New York: The Century Co., 1897.

Scott, William W., comp. *Reminiscences of Dover.* Canal Dover, Oh.: *Valley Reporter* newspaper, 1879.

Settle, William A. *Jesse James Was His Name.* Lincoln, Nebr.: University of Nebraska Press, 1966.

Shaw, Mary Gentry. "My Most Unforgettable Character." *Jackson County Historical Society Journal* (July 1965): 5, 15–16.

Shea, John C., ed. *Reminiscences of Quantrell's Raid.* Kansas City, Mo.: Isaac P. Moore, 1897.

Shimeall, William Michael. "Arthur Ingraham Baker: Frontier Kansan." Master's thesis. Emporia, Kans.: Emporia State University, May 1978.

Shinnick, Ed. *Some Old Time History of Shelbyville and Shelby County.* Frankfort, Ky.: Blue Grass Press, 1974.

Shirley, Glenn. *Belle Star and Her Times.* Norman, Okla.: University of Oklahoma Press, 1982.

Shoemaker, Floyd C. "Missouri's Proslavery Fight for Kansas, 1854–55." *Missouri Historical Review,* 48 (April 1954): 221–36.

Snead, Thomas L. *The Fight for Missouri.* New York: Charles Scribner's Sons, 1886.

Speer, John. "Accuracy in History." *Transactions of the Kansas State Historical Society,* 6 (1897–1900): 60–69.

———. "The Burning of Osceola, Missouri, by Lane, and the Quantrill Massacre Contrasted." *Kansas Historical Collections,* 6 (1897–1900): 305–12.

———. *Life of General James H. Lane.* Garden City, N.Y.: John Speer, 1897.

Speer, "Wm." "My Story of the Quantrell Massacre." Typescript. 6 pages. Topeka, Kans.: Manuscript Department, Kansas State Historical Society.

Spring, Leverett Wilson. *Kansas: The Prelude to the War for the Union.* Boston: Houghton Mifflin and Company, 1896.

Starr, Stephen Z. *Jennison's Jayhawkers*. Baton Rouge, La.: Louisiana State University Press, 1973.

State of Kansas. *Session Laws of 1887*. Topeka, Kans.: Kansas Publishing House, 1887.

Staudenraus, P. J. "Occupied Beaufort, 1863: A War Correspondent's View." *The South Carolina Historical Magazine*, 64 (1963): 136–44.

Stephenson, Wendell Holmes. *The Political Career of General James H. Lane*. Topeka, Kans.: Kansas State Historical Society, 1930.

Switzler, William F. *Switzler's Illustrated History of Missouri from 1541 to 1877* (1879). New York: Arno Press, 1975.

Taylor, David G. "The Business and Political Career of Thomas Ewing, Jr: A Study of Frustrated Ambition." Ph.D. dissertation. University of Kansas, 1970.

Thayer, Eli. *A History of the Kansas Crusade*. New York: Harper & Brothers, 1889.

Thies, Randall M. "Skeletons in the Closet: Human Remains Accessioned by the Kansas State Historical Society." An unpublished paper presented at the 14th Annual Flint Hills Conference, Manhattan, Kans., March 20, 1992. Typescript. 4 pages. Topeka, Kans.: Kansas State Historical Society.

Thomas, Edison H. *John Hunt Morgan and His Raiders*. Lexington, Ky.: The University Press of Kentucky, 1985.

Thruston, Ethylene Ballard. "Captain Dick Yeager—Quantrill Man." *Westport Historical Quarterly*, 4 (June 1968): 3–4.

Tomlinson, William P. *Kansas in Eighteen Fifty-eight*. Indianapolis: H. Dayton, 1859.

Townsend, William H. *Lincoln and the Bluegrass: Slavery and Civil War in Kentucky*. Louisville, Ky.: University of Kentucky Press, 1955.

The United States Biographical Dictionary, Kansas volume. Chicago: S. Lewis & Co., 1879.

United States v. *Jerome Clark*. Records of the office of the Judge Advocate General (Army). MM1731–MM1733. Handwritten manuscript. 55 pages. Washington, DC: National Archives.

United States v. *Samuel Oscar Berry*. Records of the office of the Judge Advocate General (Army). MM3528. Handwritten manuscript. 528 pages. Washington, DC: National Archives.

Unrau, William E., ed. "In Pursuit of Quantrill: An Enlisted Man's Response." *Kansas Historical Quarterly*, 39 (Autumn 1973): 379–91.

Valentine, L. L. "Sue Mundy of Kentucky," pt. 1. *Register of the Kentucky Historical Society*, 62 (July 1964): 175–205.

———. "Sue Mundy of Kentucky," pt. 2. *Register of the Kentucky Historical Society,* 62 (October 1964): 278–306.

Viles, Jonas, ed. "Documents Illustrating the Troubles on the Border, 1859," pt. 2. *Missouri Historical Review,* 1 (July 1907): 293–306.

———. "Documents Illustrating the Troubles on the Border, 1860," pt. 3. *Missouri Historical Review,* 2 (October 1907): 61–77.

Villard, Oswald Garrison. *John Brown, 1800–1859: A Biography Fifty Years After.* Boston: Houghton Mifflin Company, 1911.

Violette, Eugene Morrow. *History of Missouri.* Boston: D. C. Heath & Co., 1918.

Wallace, William H. *Speeches and Writings of William H. Wallace with Autobiography.* Kansas City, Mo.: Western Baptist Publishing Company, 1914.

War of the Rebellion: Official Record of the Union and Confederate Armies (128 volumes). Harrisburg, Pa.: The National Historical Society, 1971.

Watts, Dale E. "How Bloody Was Bleeding Kansas?" *Kansas History,* 18 (Summer 1995): 116–29.

Watts, Hamp B. *The Babe of the Company.* Fayette, Mo.: *Democrat-Leader Press,* 1913.

Webb, W. L. *Battles and Biographies of Missourians.* Kansas City, Mo.: Hudson-Kimberly Publishing Company, 1900.

Wheeler, Holland. "Quantrill a Suspicious Loafer." *Transactions of the Kansas State Historical Society,* 7 (1901–2): 226–28.

Whittier, John Greenleaf. *The Poetical Works of John Greenleaf Whittier,* vol. 3. Boston: Houghton, Mifflin and Company, 1892.

Wilder, Daniel W. *The Annals of Kansas.* Topeka, Kans.: George W. Martin, 1875.

Williams, Andrew. *Narrative of Former Slave Andrew Williams.* Handwritten manuscript. 11 pages. Lawrence, Kans.: Kansas Collection—University of Kansas Libraries, University of Kansas at Lawrence.

Williams, Burton J. "Quantrill's Raid on Lawrence: A Question of Complicity." *Kansas Historical Quarterly,* 34 (Summer 1968): 143–49.

Woodson, W. H. *History of Clay County, Missouri.* Topeka, Kans.: Historical Publishing Company, 1920.

Younger, Thomas Coleman. *The Story of Cole Younger by Himself* (1903). Provo, Utah: Triton Press, 1988.

———. "What My Life Has Taught Me." Typescript with author's handwritten corrections. 20 pages. Columbia, Mo.: Western Historical Manuscript Collection—Columbia.

Index

ABOUT THE AUTHOR

EDWARD E. LESLIE is a professional writer who was born in Baltimore, Maryland, and raised in nearby Towson. So far as he knows, none of his ancestors fought in the Civil War.

He is the author of *Desperate Journeys, Abandoned Souls: True Stories of Castaways and Other Survivors*.

ABOUT THE TYPE

This book was set in Sabon, a typeface designed by the well-known German typographer Jan Tschichold (1902–74). Sabon's design is based upon the original letter forms of Claude Garamond and was created specifically to be used for three sources: foundry type for hand composition, Linotype, and Monotype. Tschichold named his typeface for the famous Frankfurt typefounder Jacques Sabon, who died in 1580.